LAW for the BUSINESS ENTERPRISE

SECOND EDITON

Samuel D. Hodge, Jr.
Temple University

Learning Solutions

Boston   Burr Ridge, IL   Dubuque, IA   New York   San Francisco   St. Louis
Bangkok Bogotá Caracas Lisbon London Madrid
Mexico City   Milan   New Delhi   Seoul   Singapore   Sydney   Taipei   Toronto

Law for the Business Enterprise, Second Edition

1 2 3 4 5 6 7 8 9 0 QDB QDB 13 12 11

ISBN-13: 978-0-07-804733-6
ISBN-10: 0-07-804733-1

Learning Solutions Manager: Dave Fleming
Production Editor: Jessica Portz
Cover Design: Alexa Voluck
Printer/Binder: Quad/Graphics

DEDICATION

*"It is an exciting time where the only limits you have
are the size of your ideas and the degree of your dedication."*

—author unknown

This book is dedicated to Moshe Porat, Rajan Chandran, and Diana Breslin-Kundson for their extraordinary vision, ideas and leadership. I would also be derelict if I did not thank them for their support and confidence over the years that has allowed me to experiment and grow in the classroom.

—Samuel D. Hodge, Jr.

ACKNOWLEDGMENTS

"Tell everyone what you want to do
and someone will want to help you do it."

—W. Clement Stone

This book is the product of a number of unselfish people who helped take an idea for a new course and turn it into a reality. This acknowledgment is a small token of my appreciation for that assistance and guidance. Therefore, many thanks are extended for the contributions by S. Jay Sklar, Barbara Schneller, Michael Valenza, Joseph Beller, Avi Cohen and Terry Halbert, as well as the editorial and research assistance provided by Kajal Ariana Alemo.

A special acknowledgment is also extended to Jakarta M. Eckhart of NiteOwl Creations for her more than 20 years of assistance and advice with the layout and design of this and other texts by the author.

TABLE OF CONTENTS

CHAPTER 1   LAW IN BUSINESS, AN OVERVIEW **1**

1.1   Introduction... 1
1.2   The Study of Law 2
1.3   The Courtroom... 2
1.4   The Evolution of the Jury Trial........................... 4
1.5   The Players 7
1.6   Case Analysis... 9
          Case: Champion v. Dunfee.............................. 10
          *Case: State of Washington v.
                   Sean Tyler Glas*.................................. 12
1.7   Elements of a Judicial Opinion........................... 14
1.8   Briefing of a Case 16
          Case: Klein v. Raysinger 17
          Case: Congini v. Portersville Valve Co. 18
          Case: Currie v. Phillips 21
1.9   Status and Process.. 22
          *Case: PNC Bank Corporation v. Workers'
                   Compensation Appeal Board*.................. 24
1.10   Christopher v. Roberts 25
          Case: Larry Swalberg v. Todd Hannegan 27
1.11   Precedent: The Backbone of American
          Jurisprudence... 30
          Case: State of Washington v. Boyd................... 31
1.12   Problem One—A.. 32
          Case: Alumni Ass'n. v. Sullivan 33
          Case: Koller v. Rose 37
1.13   Legal Research.. 38
1.14   Problem One—B.. 47
1.15   Review Cases... 51

CHAPTER 2   CLASSIFICATIONS OF LAW **55**

2.1   Public Law v. Private Law.................................... 55
2.2   Criminal Law 55
          Case: Gary v. Dormire 57
2.3   Constitutional Law... 58
          Case: Katzenbach v. McClung 61
2.4   Problem Two—A 66
          Case: Gonzales v. Raich.................................. 67

2.5   Administrative Law 73
     Case: United States v. Martha Stewart 76
2.6   Contract Law.. 77
     Case: Green v. Morris 79
2.7   Tort Law.. 80
     Case: Marvin Katko v. Edward Briney 82
2.8   Problem Two—B 84
     Case: Raith v. Blanchard............................... 85
2.9   Property Law.. 91
     Case: Kent v. Sexton 92
2.10   Family Law 93
     Case: Patricia Cochran v. Johnnie Cochran, Jr. 94
2.11   Violations of Public and Private Law 96
     Case: Tual v. Blake 97
2.12   Review Cases 99
2.13   Internet References 100

CHAPTER 3   **CONTRACTS** **103**
3.1   Introduction.. 103
3.2   Kinds of Contracts 103
     Case: Sattler v. Sattler................................. 105
     Case: In re Estate of Wiley 107
     Case: Sokaitis v. Bakaysa.............................. 109
3.3   The Elements of a Contract 110
     Case: John Leonard v. Pepsico, Inc. 110
3.4   Offer.. 112
3.5   Acceptance.. 112
     Case: Kimrey v. American Bankers Life Assurance Company of Florida.................. 113
     Case: Trinity Homes, L.L.C. v. Fang............ 117
3.6   Consideration 118
     Case: Jo Laverne Alden v. The Estate of Elvis A. Presley....................................... 120
3.7   Problem Three—A 121
     Case: Roger Lindh v. Janis Surman 122
3.8   Capacity 127
     Case: Darko Milicic v. Basketball Marketing Co., Inc..................................... 128
3.9   Legality 129
     Case: Farrell v. Whiteman 129
3.10   Problem Three—B 131
     Case: Randi Giunto v. Florida Panthers Hockey Club, Ltd. 132

3.11	Statute of Frauds	135
	Case: *Arya Group, Inc. v. Cher*	136
3.12	Problem Three—C	137
3.13	Uniform Commercial Code	143
	Case: *Wilson v. Brawn of California, Inc.*	146
3.14	Agency	148
	Case: *Gaines v. Kelly*	150
3.15	Problem Cases	152
3.16	Internet References	154

CHAPTER 4   **TORTS**   **157**

4.1	The Law of Torts	157
4.2	Negligence	157
4.3	Duty of Care	158
	Case: *Norton v. Hawkinson*	159
	Case: *Ford v. Applegate*	160
	Case: *Atcovitz v. Gulph Mills Tennis Club, Inc.*	162
4.4	Problem Four—A	165
4.5	Breach of Duty	169
	Case: *Michaelene Gon v. Dick Clark's American Bandstand*	169
4.6	Proximate Cause	170
	Case: *Pellman v. McDonald's Corporation*	171
4.7	Damages	172
4.8	Defenses to a Negligence Action	173
	Case: *Rekun v. Pelaez*	173
	Case: *Mitchell Telega v. Security Bureau, Inc.*	176
4.9	Imputed Negligence	177
	Case: *James DeFulio v. Spectaguard, Inc.*	177
4.10	Problem Four—B	179
	Case: *John Lowe v. California Professional Baseball*	180
	Case: *Garcia v. Grepling*	185
4.11	Intentional Torts	186
4.12	Infliction of Emotional Distress	186
	Case: *Coca-Cola Bottling Co. v. Hagan*	187
4.13	Assault and Battery	188
	Case: *Margaret Andrews v. Richard Peters*	189
	Case: *Laura Vetter v. Chad Morgan*	190

4.14   Invasion of Privacy 191
        Case: Nancy Garrity v. John Hancock
        Mutual Life Insurance Company 192
        Case: Toffoloni v. LFP Publishing
        Group, LLC 194
4.15   Defamation.. 196
        Case: Kevorkian v. Glass 197
        Case: Texas Beef Group v.
        Oprah Winfrey 199
4.16   False Imprisonment....................................... 200
        Case: Christopher Vincent v.
        Charles Barkley 201
4.17   Tortuous Interference with a Contract 202
        Case: Vigoda v. DCA Productions
        Plus Inc. 202
4.18   Products Liability.. 203
        Case: Virginia Brumley v. Pfizer, Inc. 204
4.19   Review Cases 206
4.20   Internet References 208

CHAPTER 5   **PROPERTY LAW BY: BARBARA SCHNELLER, ESQ. AND**
             SAMUEL D. HODGE, JR., ESQ. **211**
        5.1   Introduction.. 211
        5.2   Ownership.. 211
                Case: University of Montana v.
                Mark D. Coe 213
        5.3   Problem Five.. 214
        5.4   Personal Property 220
        5.5   Acquiring Title to Personal Property 221
        5.6   Bailments 223
                Case: Mark Hadfield v. Sam Gilchrist 225
        5.7   Real Property 227
        5.8   Estates in Real Property 227
        5.9   Leasehold Estates.................................. 230
                Case: Terri Johnson v. Scandia
                Associates, Inc. 231
                Case: Brenda Dean v. Richard Gruber 233
        5.10   Acquiring Title to Real Property............... 234
        5.11   Zoning... 236
                Case: Atlantic Richfield Company v.
                Harrisburg Zoning Hearing Board 237
        5.12   Review Cases....................................... 239
        5.13   Internet References 240

CHAPTER 6   **CRIMINAL LAW IN A BUSINESS SETTING** **243**

    6.1   Criminal Law 243

    6.2   Crimes.. 244

                Case: People v. Elsey 245

                Case: Com. v. Bedell 248

                Case: Commonwealth of Pennsylvania v. Matthews 252

                Case: Anthony Hankinson v. Wyoming 254

                Case: People v. Alejandro 255

                Case: U.S. v. Awada 258

    6.3   Criminal Liability for Business Entities 262

                Case: State v. Zeta Chi Fraternity.................. 263

    6.4   Problem Six—A... 264

                Case: North Dakota v. Smokey's Steakhouse, Inc. 266

    6.5   Police Investigation..................................... 271

    6.6   Questioning of a Suspect 271

                Case: Commonwealth of Pennsylvania v. Graham 272

    6.7   Problem Six—B... 273

                Case: Glenmore Morgan v. State of Maryland 274

    6.8   Search and Seizure...................................... 277

                Case: Missouri v. Cordell Mosby.................. 278

                Case: State v. Thomas Hoskins 280

    6.9   The Progress of a State Criminal Case 281

    6.10   The Progress of a Criminal Case in Federal Court.. 284

    6.11   The Grand Jury 285

                Case: In re Grand Jury Subpoena Issued to Galasso............................. 286

    6.12   Verdicts and Sentencing................................ 288

    6.13   Problem Cases... 291

    6.14   Internet References 292

CHAPTER 7   **REMEDIES AVAILABLE IN COURT** **297**

    7.1   An Overview.. 297

                Case: United States v. Parlavecchio 298

    7.2   Compensatory Damages 299

                Case: Suttle v. Landstar Inway, Inc. 301

    7.3   Punitive Damages 301

                Case: Whitney Houston v. New York Post Co., Inc. 302

7.4	Nominal Damages	303
	Case: ESPN, Inc. v. Office of the Commissioner of Baseball	304
7.5	Liquidated Damages	305
7.6	Problem Seven	306
	Case: Mary Martin v. Trans World Airlines, Inc.	307
7.7	Injunction	311
	Case: McDonald's Corp. v. Rappaport	312
7.8	Restitution	313
	Case: Thomas Mitchell v. William Moore	313
7.9	Recision and Reformation	314
	Case: Jeffrey Stambovsky v. Helen Ackley	315
7.10	Declaratory Judgment	316
	Case: Gianni Sport, Ltd. v. Metallica	317
7.11	Specific Performance	318
	Case: Montanile v. Botticelli	318
7.12	Problem Cases	319
7.13	Internet References	321

CHAPTER 8   CYBERLAW **323**

8.1	Introduction	323
8.2	Copyright Law	323
	Case: Lenz v. Universal Music Corp.	326
	Case: Playboy Enterprises, Inc. v. George Frena	327
8.3	Trademark Infringement	329
	Case: In re Chippendales USA, Inc.	330
8.4	Domain Names	332
	Case: WIPO Arbitration and Mediation Center, Gordon Sumner, a/k/a Sting v. Michael Urvan	336
	Case: WIPO Arbitration and Mediation Center, Madonna Ciccone a/k/a Madonna v. Don Parisi and Madonna.com	338
8.5	Trademark Dilution	339
	Case: Louis Vuitton Malletier S.A. v. Haute Diggity Dog, LLC	341
8.6	e-Defamation	343
	Case: Alexander Lunney v. Prodigy Services Company	344
	Case: Doe v. Friendfinder Network, Inc.	346

8.7	Problem Eight	348
	Case: *John Doe v. Franco Productions*	349
8.8	e-Privacy	353
	Case: *Romano v. Steelcase Inc.*	355
	Case: *Tammy Blakey v. Continental Airlines, Inc.*	359
8.9	e-Contracts	360
	Case: *M.A. Mortenson Co. v. Timberline Software Corp.*	362
8.10	Statute of Frauds	363
8.11	Review Cases	365
8.12	Internet References	367

CHAPTER 9   BUSINESS ORGANIZATIONS BY: S. JAY SKLAR, ESQUIRE   369

9.1	Introduction	369
9.2	Sole Proprietorship	369
9.3	Partnership	370
	Case: *Douglas Hillme v. Brent Chastain and C & H Custom Cabinets, Inc.*	371
9.4	Limited Partnership	377
9.5	Limited Liability Partnership	377
	Case: *Henry Chamberlain v. Charles Irving*	378
9.6	Family Limited Liability Partnership	379
9.7	Corporation	379
	Case: *Gilbert v. James Russell Motors, Inc.*	383
9.8	Subchapter S Corporation	385
9.9	Limited Liability Company	386
9.10	Franchises	386
	Case: *Sherman v. Master Protection Corp.*	388
9.11	Security Regulations and Investor Protection	390
9.12	Review Questions	394
9.13	Internet References	397

CHAPTER 10   EMPLOYMENT LAW, BY TONY MCADAMS   399

10.1	Introduction	399
10.2	Selection of an Employee	399
10.3	Problem Ten—A	403
	Case: *Fifth Club, Inc. v. Ramirez*	404
10.4	Liability	408
10.5	Hiring, Retention, Training and Supervision	410
	Case: *Yunker v. Honeywell, Inc.*	410

10.6	Minimum Wage	413
10.7	Workplace Hazards	415
10.8	Occupational Safety and Health Act	416
10.9	Workers' Compensation	419
	Case: Quaker Oates Co. v. Ciha	421
10.10	Rights of Privacy	424
10.11	Drug Testing in the Workplace	425
	Case: Smyth v. Pillsbury Co.	428
10.12	Employee Benefits and Income Maintenance	430
10.13	Unemployment Compensation	432
10.14	Problem Ten—B	435
	Case: Draper v. Unemployment Compensation Bd. of Review	436
10.15	At-Will Employees	439
	Case: Barrera v. ConAgra, Inc.	441
10.16	Immigration	443
10.17	Review Questions	444
10.18	Internet References	448

CHAPTER 11   INTERNATIONAL LAW BY: MICHAEL VALENZA, ESQ. 455

11.1	Introduction	455
	Case: United States of America v. David Kay and Douglas Murphy	458
11.2	International Organizations as Sources of Law	459
	Case: Hyundai Electronics Co., Ltd. et al. v. United States of America	463
11.3	Scope of International Transactions	464
11.4	Risks of International Commerce	465
11.5	Protecting Against the Risks of International Transactions	468
11.6	Principles of Foreign Contract Law	468
11.7	Documentary Transactions	471
11.8	INCO Terms	472
	Case: St. Paul Guardian Ins. Co. v. Neuromed Medical Systems & Support, Gmbh	473
11.9	Intellectual Property in the Global Environment	473
11.10	TRIPS	474
11.11	The Future of International Law	475
11.12	Problem Eleven	475
11.13	Review Cases	479
11.14	Internet References	480

CHAPTER 12   **THE JUDICIAL SYSTEM**..**483**

    12.1   The Federal Court System 483

    12.2   The 10 Worst Supreme Court Decisions.............. 488

    12.3   The State Court System 494

    12.4   The Jury System.. 497

    12.5   Jurisdiction... 499

                     Case: Severinsen v. Widener University......... 500

                     Case: Aero Toy Store, LLC v. Grieves............ 502

    12.6   Venue 504

                     Case: Gonzalez v. State 505

    12.7   Standing 507

                     Case: Halwill Music, Inc. v. Elton John......... 507

    12.8   Full Faith and Credit.. 508

                     Case: Embry v. Ryan 509

    12.9   Comity 510

                     Case: Hennedeld v. Township of Montclair 511

    12.10   Alternative Dispute Resolution........................... 512

    12.11   Problem Cases... 513

    12.12   Internet References 514

CHAPTER 13   **ETHICS AND THE LAW BY: TERRY ANN HALBERT, ESQ.** **517**

    13.1   An Overview of Ethics 517

                     Case: State of Montana v. Montana

                                Thirteenth Judicial District Court............. 518

                     Case: Wilson v. Athens-Limestone

                                Hospital 520

    13.2   Ethical Theories 522

    13.3   Problem Thirteen—A.. 524

    13.4   The Whistleblower... 529

                     Case: George Geary v. United States

                                Steel Corporation 530

    13.5   Ethics, Law and Privacy 533

    13.6   Drug Testing... 534

                     Case: Paul Luedtke v. Nabors Alaska

                                Drilling, Inc. 535

    13.7   Problem Thirteen—B... 539

    13.8   Sexual Harassment... 543

                     Case: Vivienne Rabidue v. Osceola

                                Refining Co. 545

    13.9   Problem Thirteen—C... 547

    13.10   Problem Cases... 551

    13.11   Internet References 552

APPENDIX   **555**

CASES LISTED ALPHABETICALLY

A

Aero Toy Store, LLC v. Grieves 502
Jo Laverne Alden v. The Estate of Elvis A. Presley 120
Alumni Ass'n. v. Sullivan 33
Margaret Andrews v. Richard Peters 189
Arya Group, Inc. v. Cher 136
Atcovitz v. Gulph Mills Tennis Club, Inc. 162
Atlantic Richfield Company v. Harrisburg Zoning Hearing Board 237

B

Barrera v. ConAgra, Inc. 441
Tammy Blakey v. Continental Airlines, Inc. 359
Virginia Brumley v. Pfizer, Inc. 204

C

Henry Chamberlain v. Charles Irving 378
Champion v. Dunfee 10
Coca-Cola Bottling Co. v. Hagan 187
Patricia Cochran v. Johnnie Cochran, Jr. 94
Com. v. Bedell 248
Commonwealth of Pennsylvania v. Graham 272
Commonwealth of Pennsylvania v. Matthews 252
Congini v. Portersville Valve Co. 18
Currie v. Phillips 21

D

Brenda Dean v. Richard Gruber 233
James DeFulio v. Spectaguard, Inc. 177
Doe v. Friendfinder Network, Inc. 346
John Doe v. Franco Productions 349
Draper v. Unemployment Compensation Bd. of Review 436

E

Embry v. Ryan 509
ESPN, Inc. v. Office of the Commissioner of Baseball 304

F

Farrell v. Whiteman 129
Fifth Club, Inc. v. Ramirez 404
Ford v. Applegate 160

G

Gaines v. Kelly 150
Garcia v. Grepling 185
Nancy Garrity v. John Hancock Mutual Life Insurance Company 192
Gary v. Dormire 57

George Geary v. United States Steel Corporation 530
Gianni Sport, Ltd. v. Metallica 317
Gilbert v. James Russell Motors, Inc. 383
Randy Giunto v. Florida Panthers Hockey Club, Ltd. 132
Michaelene Gon v. Dick Clark's American Bandstand 169
Gonzales v. Raich 67
Gonzalez v. State 505
Green v. Morris 79

H

Mark Hadfield v. Sam Gilchrist 225
Halwill Music, Inc. v. Elton John 507
Anthony Hankinson v. Wyoming 254
Hennedeld v. Township of Montclair 511
Douglas Hillme v. Brent Chastain and C & H Custom Cabinets, Inc. 371
Whitney Houston v. New York Post Co., Inc. 302
Hyundai Electronics Co., Ltd. et al. v. United States of America 463

I

In re Chippendales USA, Inc. 330
In re Estate of Wiley 107
In re Grand Jury Subpoena Issued to Galasso 286

J

Terri Johnson v. Scandia Associates, Inc. 231

K

Marvin Katko v. Edward Briney 82
Katzenbach v. McClung 61
Kent v. Sexton 92
Kevorkian v. Glass 197
Kimrey v. American Bankers Life Assurance Company of Florida 113
Klein v. Raysinger 17
Koller v. Rose 37

L

Lenz v. Universal Music Corp. 326
John Leonard v. Pepsico, Inc. 110
Roger Lindh v. Janis Surman 122
John Lowe v. California Professional Baseball 180
Paul Luedtke v. Nabors Alaska Drilling, Inc. 535
Alexander Lunney v. Prodigy Services Company 344

M

M.A. Mortenson Co. v. Timberline Software Corp. 362

Mary Martin v. Trans World Airlines, Inc. 307

McDonald's Corp. v. Rappaport 312

Darko Milicic v. Basketball Marketing Co., Inc. 128

Missouri v. Cordell Mosby 278

Thomas Mitchell v. William Moore 313

Montanile v. Botticelli 318

Glenmore Morgan v. State of Maryland 274

N

North Dakota v. Smokey's Steakhouse, Inc. 266

Norton v. Hawkinson 159

P

Pellman v. McDonald's Corporation 171

People v. Alejandro 255

People v. Elsey 245

Playboy Enterprises, Inc. v. George Frena 327

PNC Bank Corporation v. Workers' Compensation Appeal Board 24

Q

Quaker Oates Co. v. Ciha 421

R

Vivienne Rabidue v. Osceola Refining Co. 545

Raith v. Blanchard 85

Rekun v. Pelaez 173

Romano v. Steelcase Inc. 355

S

Sattler v. Sattler 105

Severinsen v. Widener University 500

Sherman v. Master Protection Corp. 388

Smyth v. Pillsbury Co. 428

Sokaitis v. Bakaysa 109

St. Paul Guardian Ins. Co. v. Neuromed Medical
    Systems & Support, Gmbh 473

Jeffrey Stambovsky v. Helen Ackley 315

State of Montana v. Montana Thirteenth Judicial District Court 518

State of Washington v. Boyd 31

State of Washington v. Sean Tyler Glas 12

State v. Thomas Hoskins 280

State v. Zeta Chi Fraternity 263

Suttle v. Landstar Inway, Inc. 301

Larry Swalberg v. Todd Hannegan 27

T

Mitchell Telega v. Security Bureau, Inc...176
Texas Beef Group v. Oprah Winfrey...199
Toffoloni v. LFP Publishing Group, LLC 194
Trinity Homes, L.L.C. v. Fang...117
Tual v. Blake 97

U

U.S. v. Awada...258
United States of America v. David Kay and Douglas Murphy 458
United States v. Martha Stewart...76
United States v. Parlavecchio..298
University of Montana v. Mark D. Coe 213

V

Laura Vetter v. Chad Morgan 190
Vigoda v. DCA Productions Plus Inc...202
Christopher Vincent v. Charles Barkley...201
Louis Vuitton Malletier S.A. v. Haute Diggity Dog, LLC.......................341

W

Wilson v. Athens-Limestone Hospital..520
Wilson v. Brawn of California, Inc. 146
WIPO Arbitration and Mediation Center, Gordon Sumner,
    a/k/a Sting v. Michael Urvan...336
WIPO Arbitration and Mediation Center, Madonna Ciccone,
    a/k/a Madonna v. Don Parisi and Madonna.com...............................338

Y

Yunker v. Honeywell, Inc..410

CHAPTER 1

LAW IN BUSINESS, AN OVERVIEW

**SECTION 1.1
INTRODUCTION**

Law is a dynamic force that is not capable of a single or simple definition. For instance, the Greek philosopher *Aristotle* believed that "law is a pledge that citizens of a state will do justice to one another." *Black's Law Dictionary* defines the term as "that which must be obeyed and followed by citizens, subject to sanctions or legal consequences." Regardless of how the term is defined, the law affects all aspects of life and establishes the parameters of acceptable conduct within our society. These rules can be created by the legislature, administrative regulations, or be imposed by court decree. While one may not always agree with the law, deviations from these mandates may result in both criminal and civil liabilities.

In the face of expanding government regulations and a litigation-oriented society, businesses must be cognizant of the legal implications of their actions. Seemingly minor violations of the law may have significant financial and emotional consequences. Million-dollar verdicts occur with some frequency in the United States, and the courts do recognize new or expanded theories of liability.

Law books tend to be theoretical and discuss the economic, sociological, and political framework within which the law operates. This text will examine the forces that shape the law and will provide the reader with the opportunity to observe the legal system in action. As the semester unfolds, the reader will follow the legal difficulties encountered by a local sports bar and its owners as they struggle to operate in today's complex business world at a profit. Students will learn of these legal controversies through a series of problems that the reader will be requested to help solve.

This text is also broken down into several segments. Part One will examine some of the basic principles of the law in the United States such as the evolution of our legal system and the doctrine of precedent. Part Two will expose the reader to the categories of private law—contracts, torts, property and family law. The final portion of the book will look at those laws that specifically affect the entrepreneur including how to form a business enterprise, employee rights, and the legal implications of dealing with international business transactions.

SECTION 1.2
THE STUDY OF LAW

The rules, regulations and judicial edicts that make up the legal environment in which businesses must operate can be difficult to understand. The law is not perfect, but it does establish a system of order and justice. What would automobile traffic be like if we didn't have a motor vehicle code to establish rules of the road? How could we be secure in our homes if we didn't have the threat of imprisonment for those who violate the sanctuary of those residences?

Unlike any other facet of life, the law operates in an adversarial setting. There are two sides to every dispute and one party must lose.

The law can be complicated because legal documents aren't easy to understand and seem to be filled with Latin phrases. Instead of simply saying a person has filed an appeal to the United States Supreme Court, this procedure is labeled a *Writ of Certiorari*. Precedent becomes *stare decisis* and legal papers are filled with wherefore's and hereinafter's.

Change is occurring, but reform takes time. More and more contracts are required to be written in easy-to-understand language. For instance, we now have "plain language" leases and authors of contracts are penalized by the courts who construe ambiguities in a document against the drafter.

This text will attempt to simplify the law by explaining how it affects business pursuits in both theory and practice. Legal terms will be translated into common English and a variety of contemporary legal issues will be explored. It is only through this type of learning process that one may gain a better appreciation of the American system of jurisprudence.

SECTION 1.3
THE COURTROOM

Judges are the final arbiters of legal disputes and the courtroom is like a stage filled with drama and suspense. It is through this forum that stories unfold with people's futures hanging in the balance. How are the business assets to be divided when the partners encounter irreconcilable differences which mandate the dissolution of the once successful enterprise? Who is to receive the name and location of the business when the partners are equal and the agreement is silent on these issues? The outcome is never certain until the verdict is announced.

There is no better place to start this educational experience than to introduce the players in the courtroom.

The master of ceremonies is the judge who sits facing the parties on an elevated platform. All are bound by the judge's rulings and the jurist oversees everything that occurs within the courtroom. The starting and concluding times of the hearing and legal determinations are within the province of the judge.

The directors in the drama are the attorneys. They orchestrate the presentation of evidence and determine the sequence of witnesses to maximize the impact of the testimony.

The parties to the suit are the plaintiff and the defendant. The plaintiff initiates the case, and the defendant is the one being sued. The easiest way to remember the difference is to look at the word "defendant." Note that the term contains "defend" in its spelling.

The positions of the parties in the courtroom is predetermined by custom. The party with the burden of proof, sits closest to the jury. In a civil case, the plaintiff has the burden of proof and in a criminal case, the government must prove that the accused is guilty of the crime. The other side of the courtroom is reserved for the defense or the party being sued.

The jury sits to the side of the judge and is segregated from all others in the courtroom. This is done to guard against tampering and undue influence. Jurors are instructed not to discuss the case with anyone and to refrain from contact with those involved in the dispute. Jurors are brought into and leave the courtroom separately from all the other parties. While the judge makes all decisions concerning the applicable law, the jury resolves the factual issues. For instance, the judge will decide whether it is improper for a motorist to enter an intersection after the traffic light has turned yellow, while the jury will make the factual determination as to whether the defendant actually entered the intersection on a yellow light.

As for the actual litigation, cases are tried by the presentation of evidence. Witnesses testify as to the facts and occasionally act as character witnesses. The witness stand is located next to the judge, and is in close proximity to the jury because of the importance of the stories being told. Witnesses may be sequestered during a trial so that they cannot ascertain the testimony of other parties. This excluding of a witness from the courtroom while others are being questioned is done to reduce the risk of collusion, inaccuracies and fabrication. This rule, however, does not apply to a plaintiff or defendant.

COURTROOM

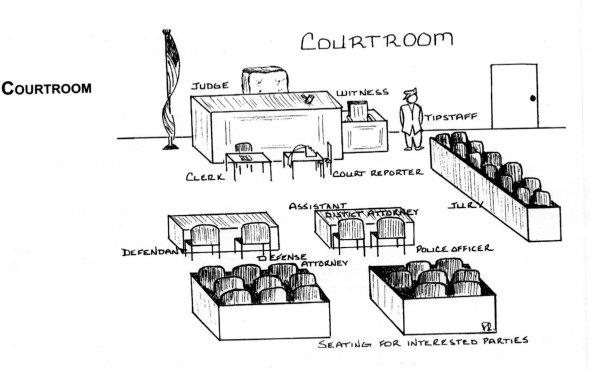

All dramas need an audience and trials are no different. Courtrooms are generally open to the public and spectators are seated in the back of the room.

As a theater needs a production crew, a courtroom needs a staff. A stenographer records everything that is said for appellate review. A court clerk keeps track of the exhibits, administers the oath to all who testify, and oversees the jury. Each judge also has a court officer who helps run the courtroom and assists the judge in the daily operation of the office.

SECTION 1.4
THE EVOLUTION OF
THE JURY TRIAL

The right to be judged by one's peers is so basic to a fair hearing that a trial by jury is constitutionally guaranteed. In turn, the power of a jury is immense. Did the defendant murder his wife and unborn baby? Did Martha Stewart lie to the federal authorities when they investigated her sale of ImClone Systems' stock just before the value of the stock plummeted? The jury decides these types of factual questions, and their answers determine the outcome of the case.

This right to a trial by one's peers is so engrained in the American system that it is part of the United States Constitution. In most cases, parties to a trial are entitled to have their fate decided by a collective group of people chosen from the county in which the case is being heard.

The evolution of the jury system is presented in the following article prepared by the **American Association for Justice** and which is reprinted with their permission:

The U.S. jury system has its origin in English history. Before juries, there were three general methods of "trial" in England. The first, the **wager of law**, simply required the accused person to take an oath, swearing to a fact. In those days, a person's oath carried great weight. In fact, the word "jury" derives from the term "jurare" which means to swear, or to take an oath. Those with good reputations who were accused of a crime only had to swear that they were innocent to be acquitted.

If others swore against the accused, however—in effect challenging the truth of the accused's oath—a **compurgation** was necessary. The accused had to bring in 11 supporters called **compurgators**, making 12 people in all who would be willing to take an oath on behalf of the accused. The **compurgators** did not swear that what the accused said was true. They served more as character witnesses, swearing that the accused was considered a credible person. If the accused was found guilty, the compurgators might also be punished because they were then implicated in the defendant's guilt.

An accused who was a repeat offender, or who was unable to find enough compurgators willing to swear to his good character, would be subjected to a **trial by ordeal**, some sort of physical test, the results of which were supposed to indicate guilt or innocence. Unfortunately, the trials were usually designed so that, in proving innocence, the physical ordeal often resulted in bodily harm or even death to the accused.

For instance, in a **trial by hot water**, a ring might be suspended by a string in a cauldron of boiling water, either wrist-deep or elbow-deep, depending upon the severity of the crime. The accused was first "cleansed" by prayer and fasting and then was instructed to reach into the boiling water to grab the ring. If the accused's hand and arm were burned, that was considered a sign of guilt. If not burned, the obvious miracle was treated as a sign of innocence.

In a **trial by cold water**, used in the American colonies at the time of the Salem witch trials, the accused was bound and placed in a body of water that had been purified by prayer. An accused who sank was considered innocent because the water would "accept" one who was pure; floating indicated that the accused's body was polluted by sin and the water was rejecting it. Apparently the object of this ordeal was not always to drown the innocent or the guilty—the accused might be removed from the water after sinking or floating for awhile.

There were various types of **trial by fire**. Some entailed having the accused show innocence by either walking across hot coals or holding a white-hot iron rod. In these trials, the accused was guilty if burned or innocent if not burned. Sometimes the test was not whether the person was burned, but how the burn healed after a certain period of time. For instance, if the burn healed well after a few days, it was a sign of innocence because the body was "clean." But if the wound showed signs of infection, it was considered a sign that the body was defiled by evil.

Not all trials by ordeal were so dramatic. For example, one trial consisted only of taking a large piece of bread from an altar and eating it. An accused who could eat the bread without difficulty was considered innocent; choking or gagging was thought to show an evil presence in the body rejecting the bread. Another less dramatic trial required the accused to wear a blindfold and choose between two pieces of wood, one of which had a cross drawn on it. If an accused selected the one with the cross, it was considered that divine intervention had proved innocence.

One common aspect of all trials by ordeal was that the outcomes were often a matter of chance or placed the accused in a "no-win" situation. To prove innocence, an accused had to risk death or serious bodily injury. Yet, since survival was often considered a sign of guilt, an accused lucky enough to survive the ordeal was often immediately judged guilty and put to death.

Most of these trials had a religious context and were conducted by clergymen or other church officials. Most were preceded by a purifying prayer for either the accused or the object used in the trial—water, bread, etc. If the trial required purification of the body before the ordeal, the accused was often sequestered and forced to fast and pray for up to three days prior to the trial.

These kinds of trials had no juries, and often citizens did not want to be chosen for "jury duty" as compurgators because they faced the possibility of punishment for "incorrect" verdicts. As trial by jury began to develop, the situation for the jurors did not improve much. When the courts were under royal control, the jurors were often punished if they decided against the king. Often, "incorrect" jurors had their property seized, were imprisoned, or were separated from their families as punishment for not "properly" fulfilling their duties as jurors. And since the jurors were still considered witnesses, they were also subject to punishment for perjury.

Trial by jury did not fully come into being until the trial by ordeal was abolished. The move to jury trial took longer for criminal matters than for civil cases, since trials by ordeal were used mainly to resolve common crimes or offenses against the king, the state, or the church. Corrupt rulers were known to "plant" witnesses or jurors to manipulate the outcomes of trials. In order to guard against this, the church began to support the principle that jurors should have no interest in the case at issue. With the church's influence, the courts began to insist on impartiality in jurors. The separation of the roles of witness and juror, and the desire for protection against royal manipulation, combined to spark the evolution of the system of trial with an impartial and unbiased jury.

New developments brought additional changes to the nature of the jury. For instance, when attorneys began to bring in witnesses to corroborate facts in a case, it was no longer necessary for the jurors to know the accused. And witnesses began to testify before the judge as well as the jury, not before the jury alone. Since both the judge and the jury were to hear the facts, it became more desirable for all persons to be at the same place, hear the same facts, and base their decisions solely upon the information presented in open court, instead of having some persons on the jury who knew more about the case than others. Gradually, juries came to decide only questions of fact, while judges ruled on questions of law.

By the time the colonists were settled in America, the right to **trial by jury** was considered essential. British rulers attempted to deny the colonists this right but were met by strong resistance. The importance and value the colonists placed on this right was clearly evidenced in the Declaration of Independence, and in the Sixth and Seventh Amendments to the U.S. Constitution. Today, the jury is a mainstay of the American legal system.[1]

SECTION 1.5
THE PLAYERS

PARK, BROWN & SMITH, P.C.
ATTORNEYS AT LAW
MEMORANDUM

To: All Law Clerks

FROM: Peter Smith, Esquire

RE: Biographical Sketches

My name is Peter Smith, and I am the managing partner of the law firm of *Park, Brown & Smith, P.C.* We are a multi-faceted firm which provides representation and counsel in all types of cases. We have been retained by Joseph Roberts to represent him in several disputes that have arisen with his neighbors. I am providing you with brief biographical sketches of the people whose legal problems you will hear about during the next few months.

Joseph and Estelle Roberts

After working in the construction field for a number of years, Joe Roberts decided to switch careers. Because of his love for sports and flare for cooking, Joe opened a sports bar with his next door neighbor, Donald Jones, M.D. The new venture is named Tyler's Sports Bar and Grill. Dr. Jones invested all of the start up money while Joe would run the business on a daily basis. The parties did not sign a partnership agreement memorializing the business arrangements between them, but they did hire an advertising agency to promote the sports bar and to create the following logo, which will be seen whenever you are asked to solve a problem on behalf of Tyler's Sports Bar and Grill.

Joe and his wife Estelle Roberts have been married for twenty-five years and have four children: Tony, Kathy, Brad and Greg.

Anthony Roberts

Joe and Estelle's son, Tony, is 23 years old. Throughout high school, Tony excelled in athletics and was the goalie on the soccer team. During his junior year, Tony took up football. His soccer background enabled him to become an outstanding place kicker, and his high school team went on to win a state championship.

Tony was offered a full-paid scholarship to play college football. During his last year at college, he set a number of school records for points and field goal accuracy. The various scouting combines rated him as one of the top kickers in collegiate football. He subsequently tried out for the Stallions, the latest professional football expansion team and was signed to a three-year contract.

Kathleen Roberts

Kathy is 16 years old and spends hours talking on the phone or surfing the internet. One might assume that she is a normal teenager texting, but Kathy has a serious problem. Ever since she started experimenting with drugs, her grades have gone from A's to F's and she has detached herself from the day-to-day life of her family. Whenever her parents try to communicate with her, Kathy reacts with great hostility. Since her parents increasingly avoid any sort of confrontation with her, Kathy's decline continues.

Peter Christopher

Peter Christopher is a retired Army officer and veteran of several military conflicts. Following his discharge from the service, Christopher opened a private investigation service specializing in undercover surveillance and industrial espionage. He lives next to the Roberts family but intensively dislikes his neighbors. He believes that the Roberts are undisciplined and uncouth. Needless to say, he and his next-door neighbors are constantly fighting.

Donald Jones, M.D.   Donald Jones always wanted to be a physician, and studied diligently to achieve this lofty goal. Upon graduating from medical school, he became a surgical resident at a hospital in Chicago. Following several years in a clinical rotation, he relocated to Philadelphia and is now a successful surgeon. Dr. Jones is Joe's other neighbor and silent partner in Tyler's Sports Bar and Grill.

Officer John O'Brien   John O'Brien is the oldest of five children. Both his father and grandfather were members of the police force, and it has always been John's ambition to follow in their footsteps. He graduated from college with a degree in criminal justice and secured a job as a police officer with a suburban police department. He is presently assigned to patrol the neighborhood in which Joe Roberts and his family live.

**SECTION 1.6
CASE ANALYSIS**

COMMON LAW AND STATUTORY LAW

The laws of the United States originate primarily by legislative enactment or by judicial decree. The creation of statutory law is the primary function of the legislature, whether it is on the federal, state, or municipal levels. These laws are designed to address specific problems in our society and to set forth rules to regulate areas of concern. This process is so important to the governance of the country that this law-making function is found in Article One of the United States Constitution.

The Constitution also empowers the judiciary with the authority to interpret the laws and to establish standards of care. This process is known as common law or judge-made law. The court is empowered to pass judgment on what type of conduct is proper and valued in our society. These pronouncements are based upon the judge's perception of what is in the best interest of the people given the political, sociological, and economic climate of the time. The court even has the power to review a law passed by the legislature to ensure its constitutionality or to ascertain whether certain conduct falls within the contemplation of the statute.

These judicial pronouncements are rendered in the form of written explanations called **opinions** so that the parties to the litigation and the general public may understand the basis for the court's resolution of the dispute.

The study of law requires a review of these court decisions in order to gain an appreciation as to how legal determinations are made, learn the rules that govern our conduct, and understand the factors that a judge weighs in rendering a decision.

Reading and understanding court decisions is an acquired skill that takes time to learn. This skill, however, is extremely important to master, as judicial decisions affect every aspect of our lives.

This chapter will introduce students to this judicial decision-making process. Initially, the reader will examine two unrelated decisions. The first case, **Champion v. Dunfee,** provides an example of the common law process or judge made law, and will demonstrate how the court arrives at a decision. The issue presented is whether a car's passenger owes a duty to prevent a visibly intoxicated driver from operating an automobile. The second case, **Washington v. Glas,** offers an illustration of statutory law and the difficulties that arise in applying an existing statute to problems that surface with new technology, a camera in a cell phone that was never contemplated when the law was enacted. The reader will learn about a term called upskirt voyeurism.

CHAMPION V. DUNFEE
398 N.J. SUPER. 112 (N.J. SUPER., 2008)

At issue is whether a passenger in a motor vehicle, which she neither owns nor controls, owes an affirmative duty to a fellow passenger to prevent a visibly intoxicated driver from operating his own automobile. Under the circumstances, we find no legal duty arises from the mere presence of a guest passenger who enjoys no special relationship to, and has not substantially encouraged the wrongful behavior of, the actual tortfeasor.

At around 7:30 p.m. on June 15, 2002, defendant Kakoda drove to David Dunfee's apartment in Bridgeton, New Jersey. She had been dating Dunfee for about two years. While at the apartment, she saw Dunfee consume two or three beers, although she herself did not drink any alcoholic beverages. Plaintiff arrived at the apartment sometime later, driven there by two friends who left shortly thereafter. At around midnight, plaintiff received a call from the two friends who had driven him to Dunfee's asking to meet them at a graduation party. Dunfee agreed to take plaintiff to the party.

The trio left Dunfee's apartment. There was no discussion as to who would drive. Dunfee drove his Chevy Camaro with (his girlfriend) in the front passenger seat and plaintiff seated in the rear. Dunfee showed no signs he was unable to drive the short distance (to the party) although he did appear to be "buzzed."

En route to the party, plaintiff chided Dunfee about the performance capabilities of his Camaro, comparing it to a friend's speedier Ford Mustang. As if to prove plaintiff wrong, Dunfee "started hauling tail." Kakoda repeatedly told Dunfee to slow down. First when he reached 70 m.p.h., Kakoda said, "That's enough, you proved your point." Then when Dunfee approached 100 m.p.h., Kakoda again told him to slow down. A third time, she cursed at him.

Within seconds, Dunfee hit a bump in the road, lost control of the car and crashed into a fence on the side of the roadway, severely injuring the plaintiff. A State Police investigation of the accident revealed that Dunfee was traveling at least 82 m.p.h., and Dunfee himself admitted speeding between 90 and 100 m.p.h. He also admitted having consumed an entire twelve-pack of beer prior to driving that evening. Indeed, Dunfee's blood alcohol level was .143.

Plaintiff sued Dunfee for negligence. Dunfee answered, and filed a third-party complaint against Kakoda alleging she had a duty to prevent Dunfee from operating his own vehicle.

Other jurisdictions have declined to hold passengers, who are neither owners nor custodians of the vehicle, responsible to third-parties for the tortious conduct of intoxicated drivers, absent either a special relationship to the tortfeasor, or substantial encouragement contributing to the tortfeasor's misconduct.

A special relationship exists where the occupant has some control over the driver, as where the driver is in the occupant's employ or where they are engaged in a joint enterprise or venture. This well-recognized exception to the general rule of passenger non-liability is also embodied in the Restatement (Second) of Torts, which provides:

> There is no duty so to control the conduct of a third person as to prevent him from causing physical harm to another unless (a) a special relation exists between the actor and the third person which imposes a duty upon the actor to control the third person's conduct. Such special relationships include parent-child; master-servant; landlord-tenant; and guardian-ward.

Thus, absent a special relationship, there is no duty to control a third person's conduct. Of course, the failure to exercise such control where reasonably necessary to his or her own safety may limit the plaintiff passenger's recovery against another where negligent driving caused the accident in which the plaintiff was injured. The other recognized exception to the rule of passenger non-liability is where the passenger substantially encourages or assists in the driver's tortious conduct. Correspondingly, liability has not been imposed where it was established that the passengers were merely companions who did nothing to substantially encourage or assist the driver in his or her voluntary consumption of alcohol and operation of the vehicle while intoxicated.

Governed by these legal principles, we conclude that Kakoda's conduct does not give rise to a legal duty owed plaintiff, her fellow passenger injured by Dunfee's conduct. It is undisputed that Kakoda did not own, operate, possess or otherwise exert custody over Dunfee's vehicle, which remained in Dunfee's control at all relevant times. Moreover, Kakoda never interfered with Dunfee's operation of the vehicle. Nor was she using Dunfee or the vehicle for her own purposes. She was merely a companion accompanying both plaintiff and Dunfee to a party.

Kakoda also bore no "special relation" to either the driver or injured passenger. Absent also is any proof that Kakoda encouraged or assisted Dunfee in the commission of the wrong or in any conduct leading up to it.

QUESTIONS FOR DISCUSSION

1. Would it have made a difference concerning the liability of the girlfriend if Dunfee was operating a car owned by his girlfriend at the time of the accident?

2. Would it have made a difference if Dunfee's father was a passenger in the car and the father had been sued by the injured plaintiff?

3. Would it have made a difference if Dunfee's girlfriend had supplied the beer?

The second case for review involves the cell phone camera, an engineering marvel that is so popular in today's society. As more and more of these mobile devices are purchased, a number of novel legal issues have surfaced involving such things as voyeurism, invasion of privacy, child security, and workplace espionage. Camera phones and small video cameras make it easy to take pictures or videos of an unsuspecting person, or to transmit images of workplace secrets across the internet. Some facilities, such as fitness centers, schools, and military installations have even barred these devices from their premises. In most cases, however, precautions have not been put into place so citizens must resort to existing laws for a remedy.

For example, in **State of Washington v. Sean Tyler Glas,** the court had to ascertain whether the criminal laws of Washington on invasion of privacy could be used to prosecute an individual who utilized a camera phone to take inappropriate pictures of unsuspecting women. This case is an example of statutory law.

STATE OF WASHINGTON v. SEAN TYLER GLAS
54 P.3D 147 (WASH., 2002)

Sean Glas and Richard Sorrells were each found guilty of voyeurism for taking pictures underneath women's skirts ("upskirt" voyeurism). Glas and Sorrells contend that Washington's voyeurism statute does not apply to their actions because it does not criminalize upskirt photography in a public place.

On April 26, 1999, Glas took pictures up the skirts of two women working at the Valley Mall. Mosier was working in the ladies' department at Sears when Glas caught her attention. Glas was lurking near her and acting suspiciously. Mosier saw a flash out of the corner of her eye and turned around to discover Glas squatting on the floor a few feet behind her. She later noticed a small, silver camera in his hand. Police confiscated the film, revealing pictures of Mosier's undergarments.

On July 21, 2000, Sorrells attended the Bite of Seattle at the Seattle Center with a video camera. Jang was standing in line to buy ice cream when she noticed Sorrells behind her. Jang thought that Sorrells had

his hand on her purse so she reacted and Sorrells fled from the line. A witness later informed police that she had observed Sorrells videotaping underneath little girls' dresses. Police viewed a copy of the videotape from Sorrells' camcorder and discovered images of children and adults, including Jang. Many of the images were taken from ground level, recording up the females' skirts.

Under **RCW 9A.44.115,** does a person have a reasonable expectation of privacy in a public place? Washington's voyeurism statute provides:

> A person commits the crime of voyeurism if, for the purpose of arousing or gratifying the sexual desire of any person, he or she knowingly views, photographs, or films another person, without that person's knowledge and consent, *while the person* being viewed, photographed, or filmed *is in a place where he or she would have a reasonable expectation of privacy.*

The statute defines a place where a person "would have a reasonable expectation of privacy" as either "a place where a reasonable person would believe that he or she could disrobe in privacy, without being concerned that his or her undressing was being photographed or filmed by another," or "a place where one may reasonably expect to be safe from casual or hostile intrusion or surveillance." Both Glas and Sorrells contend that the voyeurism statute was misapplied because the victims were in *public* places and therefore did not possess a reasonable expectation of privacy.

The voyeurism statute protects an individual "while the person… is in a *place* where he or she would have a reasonable expectation of privacy." **RCW 9A.44115(2)**. Thus, it is the physical location of the person that is ultimately at issue, not the part of the person's body.

California draws the closest parallel to the case presented here. In 1998, citizens in Orange County were subjected to three incidents of video voyeurism, including one case where the perpetrator followed several dozen women while he attempted to position a gym bag containing a hidden video camera between the woman's legs while she stood in line or shopped in a crowded store. Prosecutors determined that California's voyeurism statute was inadequate to cover these incidents. The statute provided:

> Any person who looks through a hole or opening, into, or otherwise views, by means of any instrumentality, including, but not limited to, a periscope, telescope, binoculars, camera, motion picture camera, or camcorder, the interior of a bathroom, changing room, fitting room, dressing room, or tanning booth, or the interior of

any other area in which the occupant has a reasonable expectation of privacy, with the intent to invade the privacy of a person or persons inside.

Significantly, the statute focused on the location of the incident and did not cover public places. In response, the California Legislature amended its statute, adding a subsection that focused on the nature of the invasion itself, rather than where the crime was committed. The supplemental subsection stated:

> Any person who uses a concealed camcorder, motion picture camera, or photographic camera of any type, to secretly videotape, film, photograph, or record by electronic means, another, identifiable person under or through the clothing being worn by that person, for the purpose of viewing the body of, or the undergarments worn by, that other person, without the consent or knowledge of that other person, with the intent to arouse, appeal to, or gratify the lust, passions, or sexual desires of that person and invade the privacy of that other person, under circumstances in which the other person has a reasonable expectation of privacy.

The key language "under circumstances in which the other person has a reasonable expectation of privacy" differs from the first subsection, which named the place where this privacy is expected, thus leaving the option open to include public places.

Both Glas and Sorrells engaged in disgusting and reprehensible behavior. Nevertheless, we hold that Washington's voyeurism statute does not apply to actions taken in purely public places and hence does not prohibit the "upskirt" photographs they took.

Pennsylvania's Invasion of Privacy statute is set forth in **18 Pa.C. S.§7507.1(a)** and provides:

> A person commits the offense of invasion of privacy if he knowingly views, photographs or films another person without that person's knowledge and consent while the person being viewed, photographed or filmed is in a state of full or partial nudity and is in a place where the person would have a reasonable expectation of privacy.

What would be the outcome of a criminal prosecution in Pennsylvania for "upskirt" voyeurism if the facts are identical to those presented in **State of Washington v. Sean Tyler Glas?**

The Pennsylvania House of Representatives has introduced an amendment to that state's invasion of privacy law. Would the following proposed amendment change your answer in an upskirt voyeurism case?

> A person commits the offense of invasion of privacy if he, for the purpose of arousing or gratifying the sexual desire of any person, knowingly does any of the following:
>
> 1. Views, photographs, electronically depicts, films or otherwise records another person without that person's knowledge and consent while that person viewed, photographed or filmed is in a state of full or partial nudity and is in a place where the person would have a reasonable expectation of privacy.
>
> 2. Views, photographs, videotapes, electronically depicts, films or otherwise records the intimate parts of another person, whether or not covered by clothing or undergarments, which that person does not intend to be visible by normal public observation without that person's knowledge and consent.

SECTION 1.7
ELEMENTS OF A
JUDICIAL OPINION

Most people are aware of the risks of driving a motor vehicle while intoxicated and newspapers are filled with tragic stories of innocent victims of such gross violations of the law. The police are also very aggressive in enforcing the laws involving drunk driving. Sobriety check points are routinely established; stiffer penalties have been imposed for conviction including mandatory jail time for repeat offenders and the blood/alcohol level establishing legal intoxication has been lowered to .08.

The Center for Disease Control estimates that nearly 18,000 people were killed in 2006 as the result of alcohol-related motor vehicle crashes and almost 1.5 million drivers were arrested for driving under the influence of alcohol or narcotics the year before. These violations, however, are not limited to the adult population. Underage drinking is a large problem and a number of alcohol related deaths have been reported on college campuses because of binge drinking or accidents following the consumption of liquor.

A variety of judicial and legislative pronouncements have been issued concerning these problems. This chapter will examine the development of the law in Pennsylvania concerning the liability of a social-host for providing alcoholic beverages to a guest. Cases will be presented on the issue of social host liability so that the reader can see how different rulings have emerged depending upon the fact patterns presented.

The first case deals with the liability of a social host to a third party who is injured by the negligence of an intoxicated guest involved in an automobile accident after leaving a party. Is it the consumption of alcohol by the guest or the furnishing of the alcohol by the social host that is the proximate cause of a subsequent accident?

The case is **Klein v. Raysinger** and this name is known as the **caption** since it identifies the parties to the lawsuit. In other words, Klein sued Raysinger so the former is known as the plaintiff. Raysinger is the defendant since he is the party being sued. When a case is appealed to a higher court, the names of the parties change. The person who appeals the decision is the **"appellant"** and the party against whom an appeal is filed is the **"appellee."**

The **citation** tells the reader how to locate the case. In this instance, the citation is 470 A.2d 507 (Pa., 1983). "A.2d" refers to the book that contains this decision, or in this case, the Atlantic Reporter. Court cases are published by West Publishing Company which entity has divided the country into regions for reporting purposes. The Atlantic Reporter contains the regional appellate decisions of those states on the Atlantic side of the United States and includes such jurisdictions as Pennsylvania, New Jersey, Delaware and Maryland, Connecticut, Maine, New Hampshire and Vermont. The first set of these books is contained in series one or A. and covers the years 1895 to 1938. A.2d refers to the second series of books and covers the time frame from 1939 until the present. By comparison, California decisions are published in the Pacific Reporter and court cases from Massachusetts and New York are found in the Northeast Reporter.

The first number in the citation is 470 and refers to the volume of the book that contains the decision, and 507 is the page number on which the case is published. The information in the parenthesis identifies the state and appellate court who heard the case. For instance, Pa. is the abbreviation for the Pennsylvania Supreme Court. A decision from the Pennsylvania Superior court would be Pa. Super. The last information in the citation is the year in which the case was decided or in this case 1983.

The next item that appears after the caption is the name of the judge who authored the opinion. On appeal, one judge writes the opinion or body of the case for the "majority" of the court. Because an appellate court consists of a panel of three or more judges, a decision reached by more than half of the judges constitutes the **"majority opinion."** A decision rendered by the majority is the law. A judge authors a **"dissenting opinion"** when he or she disagrees with the result reached by the majority—however, the dissent has no value as precedent. A judge may also write a **"concurring opinion"** when the jurist agrees with the outcome of the case but wants to note a difference in logic for reaching the decision.

SECTION 1.8
BRIEFING OF A CASE

Breaking a case down into its component parts simplifies a person's under-standing of the opinion. An opinion has four main parts:

1. The Action;   3. The Issue; and
2. The Facts;   4. The Opinion of the Court.

The Action — What kind of case is it? What remedy is being sought? For instance, does the case involve a criminal prosecution or a civil lawsuit for money damages?

The Facts — What happened? The reader should be concerned with the three *W's*: specifically, *Who* did *What* to *Whom?* The facts of a case are discussed in a narrative form.

The Issue — What question is presented to the court for it to decide?

The Opinion of the Court — First, the reader must ascertain what the court decided. In other words, how did the court answer the question posed in the Issue section? Second, and more importantly, what justification does the court provide for coming up with its answer? For example, what sociological, economic or political policies does the court use to justify its decision? Any dissenting or concurring opinions should also be noted in this section, but that discussion may be less detailed than the majority opinion.

An appellate court can affirm, reverse or remand the decision of a lower court. When a decision is **affirmed**, the appellate court determines that the lower court reached the correct decision. The appellate court **reverses** a decision when it finds that the lower court's decision was incorrect. A case may also be **remanded** to the trial court. This occurs when the appellate court finds that the trial judge committed an error in deciding the case, additional evidence must be obtained, or the lower court's decision must be clarified.

KLEIN V. RAYSINGER
470 A.2d 507 (PA., 1983)

McDermott, Justice.

On or about May 8, 1978, Michael Klein and his family were driving on the Pennsylvania Turnpike when they were struck in the rear by a vehicle driven by Mark Raysinger. Prior to the collision, Raysinger had been served alcoholic beverages at the home of the Gilligans. It is alleged that Raysinger was visibly intoxicated at the time he was served by the Gilligans, and that it was known that Raysinger would be driving. As a consequence, appellants' claim that the Gilligans are liable for the injuries they sustained in the accident.

This case is one of first impression in this jurisdiction. The Kleins' are requesting this Court to recognize a new cause of action in negligence, against a social host who serves alcohol to a visibly intoxicated person, whom the host knows, or should know, intends to drive a motor vehicle.

No social host who furnishes alcoholic beverages to any person shall be held legally accountable for damages suffered by such person, or for injury to the person or property of, or death of, any third person, resulting from the consumption of such beverages.

Ordinarily, a host who makes available intoxicating liquors to an adult guest is not liable for injuries to third persons resulting from the guest's intoxication. There might be circumstances in which the host would have a duty to deny his guest further access to alcohol. This would be the case where the host "has reason to know that he is dealing with persons whose characteristics make it especially likely that they will do unreasonable things." Such persons could include those already severely intoxicated, or those whose behavior the host knows to be unusually affected by alcohol. Also included might be young people, if their ages were such that they could be expected, by virtue of their youth alone or in connection with other circumstances, to behave in a dangerous fashion under the influence of alcohol.

Thus, the great weight of authority supports the view that in the case of an ordinary able bodied man, it is the consumption of the alcohol, rather than the furnishing of the alcohol, which is the proximate cause of any subsequent occurrence. This is in accord with the recognized rule at common law. We agree with this common law view, and consequently hold that there can be no liability on the part of a social host who serves alcoholic beverages to his or her adult guests.

Dissenting Opinion by Mr. Justice Manderino

Liquor dispensers who act negligently and cause harm should not be given any special privilege of immunity from liability. We do not give such immunity to automobile drivers. We do not give such immunity to drug dispensers. We do not give such immunity to homeowners. The establishment of a new immunity makes bad history. The combination of an intoxicated person and an automobile causes death and serious harm to many each day. Such victims are entitled to their day in court.

Can we declare as a matter of law that it is reasonable conduct to serve intoxicating liquors to a person who is in a state of visible intoxication? I think the question answers itself. In acting, a person is assumed to know what the reasonable man in the society knows. The common knowledge of the reasonable man certainly includes information concerning the effects of alcoholic beverages and the consequences of intoxication on human behavior. From the alleged facts, reasonable men could infer negligent conduct by the appellees.

As the court noted, its holding is a common law ruling in which the judges had to decide what they believed was proper and right under the circumstances. Simply put, they determined that there is no liability under Pennsylvania law on the part of a social host who serves alcohol to an adult guest. Would the result be the same, however, if the legislature issued a pronouncement on the subject or established a policy against furnishing liquor to certain classes of individuals such as children?

In 1972, the Pennsylvania legislature spoke on the issue of underage consumption of alcohol when it made it illegal for persons under 21 years of age to purchase or possess liquor. 18 Pa. C.S.A.§6308 provides:

(a) A person commits a summary offense if he, being less than 21 years of age, attempts to purchase, purchases, consumes, possesses or knowingly and intentionally transports any liquor or malt or brewed beverages.

The legislative purpose of this statute is clear so that the law punishes anyone under the age of 21 for the consumption of alcohol in any amount, regardless of the blood/alcohol level produced. In other words, the police are not required to show a specific blood/ alcohol level in children to establish its case. Will this statute change the result of social host immunity if the liquor is furnished to a minor? That is the issue in **Congini v. Portersville Valve Co.** in which the court had to decide whether this statute applied to an employer who supplied liquor to an employee at an office party who was under 21 years of age.

Congini v. Portersville Valve Co.
470 A.2d 515 (Pa., 1983)

McDermott, Justice.

This appeal arises from an action for personal injuries sustained by Mark Congini in an automobile accident. At the time of the accident, Mark Congini was eighteen years of age and an employee of Portersville. On December 22, 1978, Portersville held a Christmas party for its employees at which alcoholic beverages were served. Mark attended the party and, as a result of consuming an undisclosed amount of alcohol, became intoxicated.

Mark's car was parked at Portersville plant, which was the scene of the party, and Portersville, through one of its agents, had possession of the car keys. Although Portersville's agent was aware of Mark's intoxicated condition, the keys were given to Mark upon his request so that he could drive from the plant to his home.

While Mark was operating the car on the highway, he drove it into the rear of another vehicle which was proceeding in the same direction. As a result, Mark suffered multiple fractures and brain damage which have left him permanently disabled.

Appellants have alleged that defendant was negligent in providing Mark with alcoholic beverages to the point that he became intoxicated. This issue is similar to that raised in **Klein v. Raysinger, 470 A.2d 507 (1983),** i.e., the extent to which a social host can be held liable for injuries sustained by his guest to whom he has served intoxicating liquors. This case, however, differs in two respects: that the guest here was a minor; and that the plaintiff is the guest to whom the intoxicants were served, rather than a third person injured by a person who was served alcoholic beverages.

In **Klein v. Raysinger,** we held that there exists no liability on the part of a social host for the service of intoxicants to his adult guests. In arriving at this decision we relied upon the common law rule that in the case of an ordinary able bodied man, it is the consumption of alcohol rather than the furnishing thereof, that is the proximate cause of any subsequent damage.

However, our legislature has made a legislative judgment that persons under twenty-one years of age are incompetent to handle alcohol. Under 18 Pa.C.S.§6308, a person "less than 21 years of age" commits a summary offense if he "attempts to purchase, purchases, consumes, possesses or transports any alcohol, liquor or malt or brewed beverages." Furthermore, under 18 Pa.C.S.A.§306, an adult who furnishes liquor to a minor would be liable as an accomplice to the same extent as the offending minor.

This legislative judgment compels a different result than Klein, for here we are not dealing with ordinary able bodied men. Rather, we are confronted with persons who are, at least in the eyes of the law, incompetent to handle the affects of alcohol.

Section 6308 of the Crimes Code represents an obvious legislative decision to protect both minors and the public at large from the perceived deleterious effects of serving alcohol to persons under twenty-one years of age. Thus, we find that defendants were negligent in serving alcohol to the point of intoxication to a person less than twenty-one years of age, and that they can be held liable for injuries proximately resulting from the minor's intoxication.

Under our analysis, an actor's negligence exists in furnishing intoxicants to a class of persons legislatively determined to be incompetent to handle its effects. Thus, although we recognize that an 18-year-old minor may state a cause of action against an adult social host who has knowingly served him intoxicants, the social host in turn may assert as a defense the minor's "contributory" negligence. It will remain for the fact finder to resolve whether the defendant's negligence was such as to allow recovery.

Roberts, Chief Justice, concurring.

I join in the mandate of the majority allowing the complaint, which seeks recovery for injuries allegedly caused by the serving of liquor by a social host to a visibly intoxicated minor guest, to proceed to trial. The Liquor Code mandates that it is "unlawful ... for any licensee, or any employee, servant or agent of such licensee, or any other person, to sell, furnish or give any liquor ... or to permit any liquor… to be sold, or given, to any person visibly intoxicated...." The use of the language "any person visibly intoxicated" clearly manifests the Legislature's intention to prohibit the furnishing of alcoholic beverages to all visibly intoxicated persons, without regard to whether those persons are adults or minors.

Zappala, Justice, dissenting.

In **Klein v. Raysinger,** we held that no duty exists under the common law which would impose liability upon a social host who serves alcohol to an adult guest for conduct of the guest which results in injury to himself or to a third party. We recognized that it is the consumption of alcohol, rather than the furnishing of alcohol to an individual, which is the proximate cause of any subsequent occurrence.

In the instant case, however, the majority opinion concludes that liability of a social host may arise from the act of furnishing alcohol to a minor and that such liability may extend to harm suffered by the minor. By adopting this legal premise, the majority today is effectively overruling Klein and for that reason I must dissent.

I cannot agree, therefore, that liability should be imposed on a social host serving alcohol to a person under 21 based upon the rationale that minors are incompetent to handle alcohol. If it is consumption by an adult guest, rather than the furnishing of alcohol by a host, which is the proximate cause of subsequent occurrences, then it is not less compelling to conclude that it is a minor's voluntary consumption of alcohol which is the proximate cause of harm which results.

QUESTIONS FOR DISCUSSION:

1. The judges in Congini were identical to the judges who decided the Klein case. Do you agree that the statute applicable to underage drinking cited in Congini warranted a different result?

2. Do you agree with the dissenting judge who said that the majority was effectively overruling Klein by its decision?

3. Do you think that the court merely wanted to protect children by its decision?

4. Under this holding would a social host be liable for an injury if the adult served alcohol to a child but the minor was not visibly intoxicated?

Twelve years following the Klein and Congini decisions, the court was asked to decide yet another variation of social host liability. Up to this point, the court had held that a social host is not liable to a third party who is injured by an intoxicated guest but an adult who serves liquor to a minor will be responsible because the legislature has decided to protect both minors and the public at large from the ill effects of serving alcohol to persons under twenty-one years of age. What social policies and protections, however, come into play when a minor is the social host who serves liquor to another minor? Who will the law protect in this situation when both parties are incapable of appreciating the consequences of alcohol because of their tender years? That is the issue in **Currie v. Phillips.**

CURRIE V. PHILLIPS
70 D. & C. 4TH 401 (PA. COM. PL., 2005)

This action was commenced by J. Craig Currie, administrator of the estate of Robert Skaf. Plaintiff's complaint alleges that Skaf died after attending a party where he had consumed alcoholic beverages. The defendant, Phillips, owned the apartment building at 415 Taylor Avenue, Scranton, Pennsylvania and leased the premises to the additional defendants. At the time of Skaf's death, he was 20 years of age and a minor for alcohol consumption purposes.

Skaf's estate commenced the within action against Phillips as the owner of 415 Taylor Avenue, Scranton, Pennsylvania, where Skaf was found dead on April 28, 2002. Apparently, Skaf had gone to those premises to stay for the night, and during the early morning hours, he attempted to walk up a flight of stairs in which there were no handrails and apparently fell causing fatal injuries.

After service of the complaint, Phillips filed a writ of summons joining the additional defendants presenting claims against them for social host liability. The Phillips' joinder complaint avers that Potts was a tenant of 415 Taylor Avenue and on April 27, 2002, he sponsored the "Second Annual Beer Pong Tournament" with the other tenants which was held upon said premises. The attendees of the party were required to pay $5 to gain entrance to the event. Throughout the evening, the additional defendants provided nine kegs of beer to all party participants, including those under the age of 21.

The issue that must be clarified is whether a minor may be held liable for injuries sustained as a result of furnishing alcohol to another minor under the social host doctrine. The prevailing view on social host liability is found in **Kapres v. Heller, 640 A.2d 888 (Pa., 1994).** There the Supreme Court was confronted with the identical issue involving social host liability. In Kapres, the plaintiff was a student at Clarion University and attended three separate alcohol-related parties all hosted by minors. The plaintiff, who was 19 years old, ingested alcohol at all three parties, and while walking home, was struck by a vehicle and sustained numerous injuries. At the time of the accident the plaintiff had a blood alcohol content of .19. The plaintiff brought causes of action against the minor hosts who served him alcohol under the social host doctrine. He asserted that his intoxication proximately caused him to be hit by an automobile driven by an additional defendant. The minor defendants filed motions for summary judgment on the basis that they owed no duty to the minor plaintiff for injuries sustained as a result of his intoxication. In the opinion of the Supreme Court, Justice Cappy wrote, "it is more logical and consistent with the prevailing view on social host liability to find that one minor does not owe a duty to another regarding the furnishing or consumption of alcohol."

In Kapres, the court ultimately found that a plaintiff and defendant, who were both minors, were incompetent as a matter of law in handling alcohol. A minor is responsible under the law for his/her own actions in either furnishing or consuming alcohol. This notion was coupled with the standard set forth in **Klein v. Raysinger, 470 A.2d 507 (Pa., 1983)** where it addressed the idea of social host liability. In Klein, the court found that where an able bodied individual consumes alcohol, "it is the consumption of alcohol rather than the furnishing of the alcohol which is the proximate cause of any subsequent occurrence." The view accepted by the Klein court follows the common-law view.

There is an exception to the rule established in Klein which involves furnishing alcohol to a minor by an adult. This exception was established in **Congini v. Portersville Valve Company, 470 A.2d 515 (Pa., 1983).** The Supreme Court held that the rule in

Klein is inapplicable in those situations where an adult provides a minor with alcohol. The concept that a minor is incompetent to handle alcohol has necessitated the exception to the rule of Klein. The premise for the exception is grounded in insuring the safety of minors. Yet, the minor himself is not totally blameless because the Congini court further held that the minor's contribution to his/her injuries will also be taken into account. This holding brings us back to the assertions made in Kapres case where the court expands upon the theory in Klein whereby under the law minors are considered incompetent to handle alcohol. It is logic and consistency that led the Supreme Court to hold that one minor owes no duty to another minor under the guise of social host liability regarding the furnishing and consumption of alcohol. We too agree that a minor is not liable to another minor for injuries that might have been sustained as a result of the host minor's distribution of alcohol to another under the age of 21. Therefore, the pleadings establish that there are no material facts in dispute upon the issue of social host liability so it is proper to grant the additional defendant Potts' judgment on the pleadings.

SECTION 1.9
STATUS AND PROCESS

Status and process is a concept that makes judicial decisions a little easier to understand. The principle is quite simple. If one is able to ascertain who enjoys favored status with the law, it is often possible to predict the outcome of a case without even knowing the law.

Status and process requires an examination of the parties to the litigation. The outcome of the case will depend on whom the courts want to protect and what goals society wants to achieve.

For example, consider the institution of marriage. Does the law favor or frown upon marriage? Historically, the laws supported marriage and the outcome of a case was frequently decided to uphold that institution. From a sociological point of view, marriage serves three functions:

1. It is a way of regulating the struggle between men and women. This is amply reinforced during the marriage vows when one takes a spouse for better or for worse, and through sickness and in health.

2. The law recognizes marriage as the accepted way of producing children, albeit not the only way. A child born out of wedlock was frowned upon and labeled "illegitimate."

3. Marriage was favored since it offers a logical way of transferring assets from generation to generation. Assets are passed down to children and spouses rather than being given to the first person that arrives at the home of the decedent.

To prove that the law historically favored the institution of marriage, one merely has to think of how easy it is to become married and how difficult it is to obtain a divorce. Everyone is aware that a marital union can be created through a religious or civil ceremony. The law, however, went out of its way to establish marital relationships and had created the fiction of a common law marriage.

In **Hall v. Duster, 727 So.2d 834 (Ala. Civ. App., 1999),** the court outlined three general requirements for a common law marriage. First, the parties must have the capacity to marry. Next, they must agree to enter into a marital relationship, but no particular words are necessary to show a present agreement to marry. This is demonstrated in **In Re Estate of Garges, 378 A.2d 307 (Pa., 1977),** where the court stated:

> A marriage contract does not require any specific form of words. In particular, words of taking or explicit utterances, such as "I take you to be my wife" or "I hereby marry you" are unnecessary. All that is essential is proof of an agreement to enter into a legal relationship of marriage at the present time. For example, a marriage contract was found where a man gave a woman a ring and said, "Now you have the right and you are my wife," whereupon she replied, "That is fine, I love it."

Finally, the parties must consummate the marriage; that is, they must live in such a way as to gain public recognition that they are living as husband and wife. For instance, the fact that a man "made no comment" when introduced as a woman's husband was taken as an objective manifestation of an intent to be married. Sexual relations between the parties is also not an indispensable element of cohabitation.

The implications of these informal arrangements are dramatic. A common law marriage was just as valid as a religious or civil ceremony and required a formal divorce decree to dissolve.

What other institutions enjoy favor with the law? These groups would include children, incompetents, the government, and religious organizations to name a few. For instance, the government, its agencies, and high ranking officials enjoy immunity from suit in most cases because the law protects these types of entities. After all, the government and its agents represent the members of society and is funded by the taxpayers.

Status and process, however, requires that one analyze the institution as it exists at the time of the court decision. As times change, so do the institutions that the law protects. With regard to marriage, women were traditionally viewed as the weaker of the sexes. Therefore, women in the past were automatically awarded one-third to one-half of the husband's net income in a support proceeding. Following the Equal Rights movement, and the shifting of public opinion, the role of women in today's society has vastly changed. They are considered equal to men and have made significant inroads in the market place. It is now common to see a female doctor, lawyer, construction worker, police officer or soldier. This equality of the sexes has resulted in change in the support laws. The courts now examine the earning capacity of each person instead of making an automatic award to the wife. This has resulted in court decisions requiring wives to pay support to husbands and giving husbands custody of the children.

Traditional notions of marriage must be reexamined in view of the number of people who choose to cohabitate instead of becoming married. The U.S. Census Bureau estimates that unmarried couples make up about 5.5 million households with about 40 percent of those households having children. New terms are being coined to identify this growing group such as domestic partners who seek the same benefits afforded to their married counterparts. For example, a number of employers now offer benefits to this group with increasing frequency similar to those provided to a married couple. In view of this trend, has the concept of a common law marriage outgrown its usefulness?

Common law marriage was created because of the difficulties in obtaining a marriage license during the early years of this nation. Women were also considered the weaker partner and needed to be protected at all costs. In view of the current ease in obtaining a marriage license and the economic power of women, the continued validity of common law marriage is the issue in **PNC Bank Corporation v. Workers Compensation Appeal Board.**

PNC BANK CORPORATION v. WORKERS' COMPENSATION APPEAL BOARD
831 A.2D 1269 (PA. CMWLTH., 2002)

In this appeal, we are called upon to address the issue of the continued viability of common law marriages.

In 1997, Kretz filed a fatal claim petition alleging that he was the common law spouse of Stamos, who died in an airplane crash in 1994 while working for her employer. The nature of Kretz's relationship with Stamos was the subject of the hearings that followed before the Worker's Compensation Judge.

The doctrine of common law marriage was recognized by the United States Supreme Court as early as 1877. As settlement in America moved westward, common law marriages existed due to necessity. The country was sparsely populated, and travel difficult such that it was often difficult to have access to officials or clergy.

The vast majority of cases pondering the validity and desirability of common law marriage shared a common sociological backdrop: female economic dependency. Almost all common law marriage cases involved women in need of financial support, and most were initiated by female plaintiffs.

Common law marriage provided judges with a way to privatize the financial dependency of economically unstable women plaintiffs. By declaring a woman to be a man's wife or widow at common law, courts shielded the public from the potential claims of needy women, effectively deflecting those claims inward to a particular private, family unit.

Because claims for the existence of a marriage in the absence of a certified ceremonial marriage present a "fruitful source of perjury and fraud," Pennsylvania courts have long viewed such claims with hostility. Common law marriages are tolerated, but not encouraged.

Many sound reasons exist to abandon a system that allows the determination of important rights to rest on evidence fraught with inconsistencies, ambiguities and vagaries. The circumstances creating a need for the doctrine are not present in today's society. A woman without dependent children is no longer thought to pose a danger of burdening the state with her support and maintenance simply because she is single, and the right of a single parent to obtain child support is no longer dependent upon his or her marital status.

The fact that in today's world many couples choose to cohabit without any intention of being presently married only adds to the potential difficulties generated by common lack of public understanding as to what separates a common law marriage from mere cohabitation. Some persons may mistakenly believe they are common law spouses if they have lived with another for an extended period of time, particularly if they have children together. Others may assume that they can never be deemed married unless they have gone through the statutory formalities. When their understanding is challenged by dispute with their partners, third parties or government authorities, they may discover too late that they have forgone rights or undertaken responsibilities contrary to their intentions.

Moreover, uncertainty as to marital status has a far greater detrimental impact on third parties today than when the doctrine was created. At that time, persons contemplating business transactions with couples relied predominantly upon the creditworthiness and earning capacity of the husband. In twenty-first century commerce, third parties are entitled to know whether the men, women and couples with whom they contract are married or single, for that may significantly affect their rights. Statutory marriage provides a certain record if third parties chose to investigate; common law marriage may be impossible to ascertain or verify until some dispute brings about court proceedings.

This conclusion seems inescapable that recognizing as married only those who have duly recorded their union pursuant to the Marriage Law will greatly reduce the need for litigation to determine marital status. We must conclude that this court can no longer place its imprimatur on a rule which seems to be a breeding ground for such conduct and its attendant disrespect for the law itself.

Throughout the semester, you will be asked to solve a variety of legal disputes. The following is a problem dealing with the concept of status and process along with a suggested answer. When completing an assignment, please make sure that you answer all questions posed and explain your answer by citing to the appropriate case law. A one or two sentence response will not suffice.

SECTION 1.10
CHRISTOPHER
V. ROBERTS

SAMPLE PROBLEM

PARK, BROWN & SMITH, P.C.
ATTORNEYS AT LAW
MEMORANDUM

TO: All Law Clerks

FROM: Peter Smith, Esquire

RE: Kathy Roberts and the Purchase of Her Car

Kathy Roberts, a 16 year-old, related the following story to me.

Immediately after passing her driving test, Kathy decided she needed to buy a car. Unfortunately, she and her father, Joe Roberts, disagreed as to whether she was ready for what her father considered an "unnecessary extravagance." Joe had called his insurance agent and learned that the annual premium for insuring the car was more than what the automobile was worth.

Despite her father's objections, Kathy decided to secretly purchase a vehicle on her own. While walking home from school, she noticed that her next-door neighbor, Peter Christopher, had a *For Sale* sign in the window of a car parked in his driveway. The vehicle seemed perfect for Kathy's needs. The Honda was in good mechanical condition and Kathy was certain that her father would be favorably impressed with her conservative choice of transportation. Kathy contacted the neighbor and purchased the vehicle for $5,000.

When Kathy's father learned of the purchase, he exploded. "How dare you buy a car after I told you no." Kathy had never seen her father more outraged. Even her sweetest smile couldn't calm him down. Not only did he suspend her driving privileges, he even attempted to return the car to Christopher but the neighbor refused to take the car back, claiming that a "deal is a deal." Two days later, Kathy figured that her father had calmed down enough for her to start driving the vehicle. Unfortunately, Kathy was unable to negotiate a sharp turn a block from home and demolished the Honda. As she sat on the curb crying, the hubcap of the vehicle rolled by her. Since this was the only thing left of the car, she picked it up and walked home.

Kathy spent the rest of the day calling friends for advice. One girlfriend told Kathy that she could obtain the return of her money from Christopher since she was only sixteen. The girlfriend had her money refunded from a record club that she had joined when she was fifteen. Relying on this advice, Kathy approached her neighbor and demanded her money back. She even offered Christopher the return of the hubcap. After all, that was all that was left of the car. Christopher laughed and said that Kathy had entered into a valid contract and she had destroyed the car.

Please read **Swalberg v. Hannegan** and apply the case to Kathy's problem. You must decide the following:

1. Should Kathy be able to rescind the contract and get her money back from Christopher?

2. Does it matter that the only thing she can return to Christopher is the hubcap, or must she pay to have the car repaired before she can disaffirm the contract?

3. Did status and process play any part in the Swalberg decision? Explain your answer.

LARRY SWALBERG V. TODD HANNEGAN
883 P.2D 931 (CT. APP. UTAH, 1994)

In 1990, Hannegan contracted with Swalberg to purchase plaintiff's 1974 Ford truck for $2,500. Defendant's minority was apparently not discussed when the parties entered into the contract, and there is no allegation that defendant made any misrepresentation as to his age. Defendant paid plaintiff $640 and agreed to pay the balance three months later. Rather than paying the balance, however, defendant disaffirmed the contract on the basis of his minority. Plaintiff filed a complaint asking that the contract be enforced, or in the alternative, that the truck be returned and that defendant be held responsible for the reasonable value of his use of the truck or for the amount it depreciated while in defendant's possession.

Plaintiff argued that when defendant disaffirmed the contract, defendant did not properly "restore" the truck since he purchased it for $2,500 and returned it in a condition worth only $700. The court awarded $1,160, which was the remaining balance minus the value placed upon the truck in its returned condition.

The dispositive issue on appeal is whether a minor who disaffirms a contract is required to restore the full value of the property received under the contract. Defendant argues that the law does not require a disaffirming minor to restore the other party to his or her precontractual status. We agree.

Utah Code Ann. § 15-2-2 (1986) provides:

> A minor is bound not only for the reasonable value of necessities but also for his contracts, unless he disaffirms them before or within a reasonable time after he obtains his majority and restores to the other party all money or property received by him and remaining within his control at any time after attaining his majority.

This statute requires only that the property remaining within the minor's control be returned to the other party. The trial court held, however, that defendant was required to return the property in its original condition or be liable for the difference in value. This holding is clearly contrary to the provisions of this statute and case law.

In **Blake v. Harding, 54 Utah 158 (1919),** a minor sold a pony, harness, and buggy to an adult at an agreed value of $150, for which the adult delivered 3,000 shares of stock in a mining company. The minor later disaffirmed the contract and returned the stock to the adult. The minor sued to recover $150 since the adult had sold the pony, harness, and buggy. The jury was instructed that "if you believe that the contract was reasonable, and if you further find that the mining stock traded to the minor by the adult is now worthless, the minor is not entitled to recover in this action." A jury returned a verdict in favor of the adult. The Utah Supreme Court reversed the verdict and held that the jury instruction was in "direct conflict with our statute." The Supreme Court stated that this jury instruction would require the minor to place the adult in his precontractual status, which would "disregard and misapply the purpose of the law. The law is intended for the benefit and protection of the minor; and hence an adult, in dealing with a minor, assumes all the risk of loss."

Further, in **Harvey v. Hadfield, 13 Utah 2d 258 (1962),** a minor contracted with an adult to buy a house trailer. The minor paid $1,000 as a down payment without selecting a trailer. The minor later disaffirmed the contract, requesting the return of his money. When the adult refused to return the money, the minor brought an action against the adult. The trial court returned a judgment in favor of the adult. The Utah Supreme Court reversed the trial court, holding that the minor could recover the down payment without compensating the adult for the loss of a sale.

Section 15-2-2 requires that a disaffirming minor must only return the property remaining within his or her control. The court has interpreted this statute to allow a minor to effectively disaffirm the underlying contract without restoring the full value of the property received under the contract.

We find in favor of the defendant.

Name

Please Print Clearly

1. Should Kathy be able to rescind the contract and obtain her money back from Mr. Christopher? (Support your answer with case law.)

    Yes. Kathy should be able to obtain the return of her money even though the car has been destroyed. According to **Swalberg v. Hanegan,** the Utah Supreme Court merely requires a minor, when rescinding a contract, to return only the money or property remaining within his or her control. The child does not have to restore the parties to the status quo. The Court indicated that the purpose of this statute is for the benefit and protection of the minor; and hence an adult, in dealing with a minor, assumes the risk of loss.

    Assuming that Kathy Roberts lives in a place with a law similar to that in Utah, Kathy will be able to rescind the contract and get her money back. Typically, the law protects minors in their ability to enter into contracts, and merely requires that the minor return what is left from the contract. Kathy attempted to return the hubcap; the only property left in her possession, so she has properly rescinded the contract.

2. Does it matter that the only thing Kathy can return to Christopher is the hubcap, or must she pay to have the car repaired before she can disaffirm the contract?

    No, she does not have to pay to have the car repaired. Kathy fulfilled her requirements as a minor. The statute given to us to read merely requires a minor to return the money or property he or she has left, or in this case, the hubcap. Kathy is not required to have the car repaired.

3. Do you think that the concept of status and process played any part in the "Swalberg" decision? Explain your answer.

    Status and process played an important role in the Swalberg decision. Under the concept of status and process, minors enjoy favored status in the law, and when a class such as children enjoys this status, it becomes easy to predict the outcome of the case. All things being equal, when one party enjoys favored status, and the other does not, it becomes clear who will be the winning side.

SECTION **1.11**
PRECEDENT:
THE BACKBONE
OF **AMERICAN**
JURISPRUDENCE

Precedent is the process whereby judges apply the decisions and rules of prior cases to the case over which they are currently presiding. As Justice Cardoza stated in an essay entitled, *The Nature of the Judicial Process,* "We recognize that no judicial system could do society's work if it eyed each issue afresh in every case that raised it." The formal legal term for this concept is **stare decisis**. This doctrine forms the backbone of the American legal system and offers litigants certainty, predictability and uniformity in the application of the law. As noted in **In re Larry A. Deboer, 1999 WL 33486710** (Bankr. D. Idaho), stare decisis provides that when the court has once laid down a principle of law as applicable to a given state of facts, it will adhere to that principle and apply it in future cases where the facts are substantially the same. This principle has long been a cornerstone of common law.

Judges will generally follow precedent but are not bound to do so in every situation. A legal principle may be changed by the legislature and the court has the discretion to change the law as the social, political, or economic conditions change. Changes are also observed as members of the court, especially the United States Supreme Court, are replaced by jurists with different judicial or political philosophies.

A change in precedent may occur for a number of reasons including: (1) when the court is convinced that prior decisions are irreconcilable; (2) the application of a rule or principle has created confusion; (3) a rule of law has been inconsistently applied; (4) to correct a misconception in a decision; or (5) where the court believes that the reason for the law no longer exists, justice requires a change, and no vested property interests will be injured by the change. **Niederman v. Brodsky, 261 A.2d 84 (Pa., 1970).**

The reader has learned about upskirt voyeurism and how the Washington appellate court did not believe that its criminal laws on invasion of privacy applied to this improper activity. That case of **State of Washington v. Glas**, as set forth on page 12, was decided in 2002. The court again considered the issue of upskirt voyeurism in 2007. However, in the subsequent matter of **State of Washington v. Boyd**, the court reached a different conclusion. Please read the following case and ascertain why the court reached a different result and did not adhere to the precedent established by the earlier decision on the issue.

STATE OF WASHINGTON V. BOYD
137 WASH. APP. 910 (WASH. APP., 2007)

Boyd worked as a part-time custodian at Port Angeles High School. In April 2004, students began to hear rumors that he was trying to look up girls' skirts and take pictures. Two students saw him follow a girl, who was wearing a skirt, up the stairs as he held a camera. When the students got the girl's attention, Boyd turned around and pretended to pick something up, hiding the camera. The students reported the incident to the principal.

The camera contained several "upskirt" photographs of young female students. He claimed that he had brought the camera to school to take pictures of students misbehaving, but he admitted that he did not have any photographs of student misconduct. He also said he had never done anything like that before, that it was a "spur of the moment thing."

The police arrested Boyd and the State charged him with one count of voyeurism and five counts of attempted voyeurism. Each count alleged an incident involving a different girl.

Boyd first contends that the "intimate areas" portion of the voyeurism statute is unconstitutionally vague and overbroad. He argues that the meaning of "intimate areas" depends on the victim's subjective intent and that the statute criminalizes a substantial amount of protected speech.

Washington's voyeurism statute has survived constitutional challenge. See **Washington v. Glas, 147 Wash.2d 410**. But no case has analyzed the "intimate areas" provision, which the legislature added in 2003.

Prohibitions against voyeurism protect individual bodily privacy as well as intrusions into geographic areas where a person has a reasonable expectation of privacy. RCW 9A.44.115 (2)(b) provides:

A person commits the crime of voyeurism if, for the purpose of arousing or gratifying the sexual desire of any person, he or she knowingly views, photographs, or films ... [t]he intimate areas of another person without that person's knowledge and consent and under circumstances where the person has a reasonable expectation of privacy, whether in a public or private place.

The statute further defines "intimate areas" as "any portion of a person's body or undergarments that is covered by clothing and intended to be protected from public view."

Boyd claims that (the statute) is vague because whether conduct amounts to voyeurism depends on the victim's subjective intent. He argues that an area of the body or underclothing constitutes an "intimate area" only if the victim covers that area with the intent to protect it from public view. But he asserts, because different people may dress with different sensibilities, a person would have to guess whether viewing or photographing another would be prohibited by the statute. We disagree.

When a woman puts on clothing, she expresses her intent that certain areas of her body are not open to public view. The statute prohibits others from intruding into those covered areas. If the statute incorporates a subjective intent element, that intent is readily discernable to all viewers in the coverage the clothing provides. When a woman wears a skirt that reaches above her knees, she clearly expresses her intent that public eyes may not peer further into the covered areas. The statute provides sufficient guidance that reasonable persons will not be required to guess what conduct is prohibited.

Boyd suggests that because a person must intend to protect an intimate area from public view, the clothing alone insufficiently gives notice of what is prohibited. For example, he argues that a high school student and a prostitute may wear the same short skirt, but one will intend to keep her underwear hidden while the other will not.

But we construe the term "intimate areas" in the context of the entire statute. The unwanted viewing of intimate areas is prohibited only when it occurs under circumstances where the person has a reasonable expectation of privacy. RCW 9A.44.115(2)(b). Thus, when a student dons a skirt, the scope of her expectation of privacy depends on the circumstances. If she climbs a flight of stairs, she may reasonably

expect that people standing beneath her may incidentally glimpse parts of her body above the hemline. By wearing a skirt, she does not implicitly authorize others to attempt to view the hidden parts of her body.

In this case, the student victims all wore skirts that covered their underwear and thighs. Their choice of clothing put the public on notice that they intended to keep the covered areas private, and their expectation of privacy was reasonable. The testimony, and the photographs themselves, suggest that Boyd went to extraordinary lengths to position himself and his camera so that he could peer up the students' skirts. His conduct falls squarely within the statutory prohibition and we reject his vagueness challenge.

SECTION 1.12
SULLIVAN V. ROBERTS

PROBLEM ONE—A

PARK, BROWN & SMITH, P.C.
ATTORNEYS AT LAW
MEMORANDUM

To: All Law Clerks

FROM: Peter Smith, Esquire

RE: Kathy's Party

Joe and Estelle Roberts decided to celebrate their 25th wedding anniversary by spending the weekend at the New Jersey shore. After arriving at the Borgata Hotel and Casino and checking into their room, Joe called home to touch base with his 16 year old daughter who was spending the evening at home studying for an exam. Much to his surprise, Kathy answered the phone in a jovial mood with music blaring in the background. She obviously did not expect her father to be calling. It turns out that Joe's daughter had invited some of her friends over to the house for a party.

Mr. Roberts had a fit when he learned that some of Kathy's guests included a young man in whom they did not have a high level of trust. After a brief argument, Joe told Kathy that she and her friends better behave and not get into any trouble. He then hung up in a foul mood, went to one of the casino's bars and ordered several stiff drinks to settle his nerves. Joe just hated these confrontations with his daughter.

At three o'clock in the morning, the phone in Joe and Estelle's hotel room rung and it was Kathy. She was crying and told her parents that they needed to come home immediately because something horrible had happened. It turns out that some additional high school friends, including Brian Sullivan, stopped over that night when they learned that Mr. and Mrs. Roberts were not home.

Joe has a rather large bar in the family room that was stocked with all sorts of exotic liquor from his restaurant. This bar is the focal point of the room and has a large number of neon signs that illuminate the area. It turns out that Brian raided the bar that night and became highly intoxicated. He then left around midnight in an impaired condition and was involved in a tragic accident a mere one block from Joe's home that left the minor seriously injured. It turns out that Brian was speeding and smashed into a tree on the side of a road.

To make a long story short, Brian's parents have filed a lawsuit against Mr. and Mrs. Roberts and their daughter on behalf of their minor son, Brian. Please read the attached case of **Alumni Association v. Sullivan** and let me know if Kathy and her parents are liable for the injuries sustained by Brian Sullivan as the result of his consumption of liquor in the house owned by Mr. and Mrs. Roberts while they were down the shore.

ALUMNI ASS'N. V. SULLIVAN
572 A.2D 1209 (PA., 1990)

On December 7, 1983, appellant Unterberger, an eighteen-year-old freshman at Bucknell University, attended a party held in his dormitory and a second party hosted by the Kappa Chapter of Sigma Chi Fraternity at their fraternity house. At both parties alcohol was served and consumed by Unterberger. The owner of the neighboring fraternity house, Lambda Chi Alpha Fraternity, subsequently filed a claim against Unterberger and another alleging that the two had negligently caused a fire in the Lambda Chi Alpha house which resulted in over $400,000 in property damage. Unterberger filed a complaint to join Bucknell University, and Sigma Chi Fraternity as additional defendants, alleging that they were negligent in providing him, a minor, with alcoholic beverages at the parties he attended.

The trial court dismissed Unterberger's complaint. The trial court found that under **Congini v. Portersville Valve Co., 470 A.2d 515 (1983)**, Sigma Chi and Bucknell were not social hosts who knowingly served intoxicants to a minor.

Unterberger alleges on appeal that the Congini requirement that an alleged defendant *knowingly furnished* intoxicants to a minor is to be accorded a broad interpretation. He therefore claims that the court should have sustained his cause of action against parties who allegedly *should have known* that alcohol was being provided for minors on their premises.

The allegations as to the University simply state appellant resided in a campus dormitory designated for the occupancy of freshmen, and the University employed Resident Advisors and a Resident Director who knew, or should have known, of this activity. The allegations do not contend that any agent, servant, employee or other personnel of Bucknell was in any way responsible for supplying, serving, dispensing or otherwise furnishing alcoholic beverages to appellant. As to the allegations relating to Sigma Chi, it is asserted that the fraternity was the reputed owner of the property where the party was held. There are no allegations the fraternity had actual knowledge of the activities allegedly occurring at the local chapter or of the ability of the national body to control said activities. Appellant would have us find Bucknell had a duty to supervise private social functions held on the University campus to ensure no one under the age of twenty-one consumed alcoholic beverages. They also contend the national fraternal organization should have a similar responsibility to monitor the activities of its Chapters.

In **Klein v. Raysinger, 504 Pa. 141, 470 A.2d 507 (1983),** this Court refused to recognize a common law social host liability for serving alcohol to a visibly intoxicated person, whom the host knew, or should have known, intends to drive a motor vehicle.

In **Congini** we held that a social host was negligent in serving alcohol to the point of intoxication to a person less than twenty-one years of age, and that they can be held liable for injuries proximately resulting from the minor's intoxication. In arriving at this conclusion we emphasized that in Pennsylvania "our legislature has made a judgment that persons under twenty-one years of age are incompetent to handle alcohol," and we accepted that legislative judgment as defining a duty of care on the part of adults *vis-a-vis* their minor guests.

In **Congini,** an employee of Portersville Valve Company, Mark Congini, became intoxicated at the company's Christmas party but was given his car keys by a Portersville agent despite his inebriated condition. He sustained permanent injuries in the resulting car accident, and he sued his employer for providing him with liquor in violation of the Crimes Code. Under these facts, the Court found the company to be the host and deemed that it was negligent to serve alcohol to the point of intoxication to a person less than twenty-one years of age. In *Congini* the court employed the standard of *"knowingly furnishing"* intoxicating beverages to minors.

In the instant appeal it is argued that the *knowingly furnished* standard is overly restrictive; that we should adopt the standard *"knew or should have known."* The instant facts support no such conclusion. There are no allegations that either the fraternity or the University was involved in the planning of these events or the serving, supplying, or purchasing of liquor. The fact that the functions were held on property owned by appellees is of no consequence in light of their detachment from the events in question. Appellees' conduct is insufficient to establish them as social hosts for the purpose of finding potential liability.

The modern American college is not an insurer of the safety of its students. The authoritarian role of today's college administrations has been notably diluted in recent decades. Trustees, administrators, and faculties have been required to yield to the expanding rights and privileges of their students.

It is equally clear Sigma Chi fraternity is an inappropriate body from which to require the duty urged by appellant. By definition such organizations are based upon fraternal, not paternal relationships. National organizations do not have the ability to monitor the activities of their respective chapters which would justify imposing the duty appellant seeks.

We thus conclude that the modern perception of the relationships between the University and their students, and the respective units of fraternal organizations is totally antithetical to the heightened duty we are here being importuned to accept. Moreover, the increased cost which would enure to such bodies could seriously impede the mission of these institutions which serve a vital role in the development of our youth. We empathize with the victims and their families in these tragic situations, but experience does not establish a statistical basis which justifies such a sweeping change of our existing law.

Accordingly, the Order of the lower court is affirmed.

PROBLEM ONE—A
ANSWER SHEET

Name _____

Please Print Clearly

1. Are Mr. and Mrs. Roberts liable to Brian Sullivan under the theory of social host liability?

_____

_____

_____

_____

_____

_____

_____

_____

_____

2. Under the cases presented in Chapter One, is Kathy liable as a social host? After all, she is the one who had the party at her parent's home.

_____

_____

_____

_____

_____

_____

_____

_____

_____

_____

3. Should Mr. and Mrs. Roberts be held liable because they should have known that unsupervised children could or would drink the liquor in the game room?

_____

_____

_____

_____

_____

_____

_____

_____

_____

_____

_____

_____

_____

_____

_____

_____

_____

_____

_____

There is one other Pennsylvania case noteworthy of examination in the development of liquor liability law in this state. The reader has learned that there is no liability for a social host who serves liquor to an adult guest who becomes intoxicated. That holding, however, changes and liability will be imposed if the social host knowingly serves liquor to a minor. This exception occurs because of the courts' desire to protect children since they are incompetent to handle its affects. What happens if a party is held at the house of a homeowner by a third party and that adult is present at the time that liquor is served to a minor? That is the issue in **Koller v. Rose.**

KOLLER v. ROSE
5 PA. D. & C. 5TH 464 (PA. COM. PL., 2008)

On the evening of October 14, 2005, a party was held at defendant Neely's house. While defendant Neely was present at the time, the party was hosted by her nephew, Roth Neely, to whom she leased the basement of her home. Among others in attendance at the party was the defendant, Damian Rose, a minor, who consumed alcohol at the residence.

On his way home from the party, defendant Rose was involved in a car accident and struck the plaintiff, Terina Koller, a pedestrian. Plaintiff filed a complaint alleging, in part, that defendant Neely was negligent under the theory of social host liability.

Neely filed a motion for summary judgment alleging that there was no evidence that: (1) she knew a party was scheduled at her home; (2) she purchased, helped purchase, delivered, or distributed the beer which was consumed at the party; (3) she invited defendant Rose or any other individual to the party; or (4) she "knowingly furnished" alcoholic beverages to defendant Rose or any other individual at the party.

In **Congini v. Portersville Valve Company,** the Pennsylvania Supreme Court determined that a social host is negligent per se in serving alcohol to the point of intoxication to a person less than 21-years of age. In **Orner v. Mallick, 515 Pa. 132, 527 A.2d 521 (1987),** the court explained its decision in Congini:

In arriving at this conclusion we emphasized that in Pennsylvania our legislature has made a legislative judgment that persons under 21 years of age are incompetent to handle alcohol; and we accepted that legislative judgment as defining a duty of care on the part of adults vis-à-vis their minor guests.

(Thus), the Supreme Court employed the standard of "knowingly" furnishing intoxicating beverages to minors.

The Third Circuit Court of Appeals elaborated upon the Congini standard in **Fassett v. Delta Kappa Epsilon, 807 F.2d 1150 (3d Cir., 1986).** The Third Circuit held that a defendant who "knowingly" allows his or her premises to be used for the purpose of serving alcohol to minors may be liable even if the alcohol was provided by another individual.

In the instant matter, a genuine question of fact exists as to defendant Neely's liability as a social host. Neither party disputes the fact that defendant Neely did not supply any alcohol for the underage party. However, she was admittedly present at the party. Numerous witnesses saw defendant Neely interact with the underage children while they were drinking alcohol. Witnesses testified that defendant Neely talked with the minors and watched as they poured beer from the kegs. Defendant Neely was even seen carrying a cup of beer at one point. Furthermore, while the party originated in the basement apartment, it spread to the back porch and surrounding yard, which is part of defendant Neely's property that is not solely inhabited by her nephew.

Therefore, sufficient evidence exists to support a jury's conclusion that defendant Neely actually knew of alcohol consumption by minors on her premises. On that basis, summary judgment is not appropriate in this case.

SECTION 1.13 LEGAL RESEARCH[2]

The ability to do legal research can be a very helpful skill. While this type of research may seem intimidating, it can also become an intellectually rewarding experience once a person gets the hang of it. However, like other complex skills, it requires a basic understanding of the key resources and strategies which will enable a student to find the answers with the least amount of time and frustration.

Courts follow precedent so a judge will usually resolve a dispute in the same manner that previous courts within that jurisdiction have decided similar cases. The basic aim in conducting legal research, therefore, is to find a recorded instance of a suit that is similar to the matter of interest. This type of case is referred to as being "on point" or "on all fours" with the issue of the research. But a case is only on point if it is similar in relevant facts. Therefore, it is crucial to fully understand which facts are relevant, and which legal issues need to be answered.

Legal issues are the questions that must be decided by a court to resolve a particular conflict. In identifying these issues, the best starting point is to ask, what are the plaintiff's specific problems that bring this litigant to court in the first place? What is the person trying to achieve?

Once a person understands the facts and legal issues, the reader is ready to begin the assignment. This may require a trip to the law library. These facilities can seem intimidating at first but they become much less so once the researcher understands that publications fall into two basic categories; 1) primary sources and 2) secondary sources.

A **primary source** is the written law itself. These consist of the cases, statutes and legal decisions which can govern the fact pattern that a person is researching. Primary sources then fall into two subcategories, binding authority and persuasive authority. Binding authority is the writings which collectively form the law in the jurisdiction on a given subject. This would occur when the researcher finds a case in Pennsylvania exactly on point with the fact pattern of the problem that occurred in the Commonwealth. Finding these sources is the ultimate goal of most legal research. Persuasive authority is the law from other jurisdictions. For instance, a person conducting research on an issue under Pennsylvania law may find a case on point in New Jersey. While the

New Jersey case will not govern the issue that the person is researching, it can give a better understanding of that law and may be helpful in swaying a Pennsylvania court to rule a certain way when the authority in the jurisdiction being studied leaves an issue open to question.

Secondary sources basically consist of all other writings on the law, including such things as law review articles, treaties, restatements, digests, and encyclopedias. While these are not the law or binding precedent, they are extremely useful tools for finding and understanding the law, and are usually a good place to start legal research. The following are examples of secondary sources:

A. Legal Dictionaries

Law is chock full of unusual words and phrases which have a unique meaning in the legal world. The reader may feel that he or she can understand these phrases, but a **legal dictionary** is often a good place to make sure the meaning is right. While the easiest way to define terms may be through on-line legal dictionaries, such as those found at sites like Law.com (http://dictionary.law.com), the legal dictionaries available in the law library or bookstore are usually considered more authoritative.

B. Encyclopedias

Legal Encyclopedias are a good starting point for gaining a broad understanding of a legal issue. Some of these books are heavily annotated, meaning they provide lists of other sources that the reader will want to further consult. These annotations may lead directly to key primary sources on a given topic, or may list the main cases which other sources are likely to reference.

Encyclopedias are usually available for each state. For instance, Pennsylvania maintains two such sources; the *Pennsylvania Legal Encyclopedia and Summary of Pennsylvania Jurisprudence 2d.* In addition, there are also two national level encyclopedias; *Corpus Juris Secundum* (C.J.S.) and *American Jurisprudence 2d* (Am.Jur.2d). These books are arranged alphabetically by topic, so the researcher should start by looking for the topic in the index, which will then list more specific sub-topics along with the sections in which they can be found. Keep in mind that index lists subjects by their "section number" (abbreviated as §) rather than their page number. The section number will be found at the top of a page after the symbol §, while the page number is usually at the bottom.

C. Form Books

Courts can be picky about the format of legal documents that they will accept for filing. They often require a standardized form and specific information to help manage their dockets. In addition, the drafting of a contract or agreement can be a daunting task. In this regard, most states have at least one set of form manuals which will provide a brief discussion of the issues involved in drafting the document along with one or more examples of the necessary form. For instance, Pennsylvania lawyers and paralegals use the multi-volume book Pennsylvania Transaction Guide to draft a variety of legal documents. The co-editor of this book is Joseph Bongiovanni, an assistant professor in the Department of Legal Studies at Temple University.

D. Legal Periodicals

Most **legal periodicals** are published by bar associations or legal magazines, and generally come out on a monthly or bi-monthly basis. Aside from the American Bar Association Journal, most state law associations have their own journals. These periodicals discuss cutting edge issues that are of broad concern to the legal community. Still others periodicals deal with more specialized topics specific to different types of legal practice such as tax or litigation. These journals can usually be found at the reference desk of the law library. An example of this type of publication is the Pennsylvania Bar Quarterly.

E. Law Review Articles

Law review articles are usually published by law schools and provide very in-depth discussion of specific legal issues or important cases and statutes. While they are often written by law students, judges and attorneys may also contribute articles and they can form important contributions to the development of legal theory. Law review articles can be very helpful if the researcher knows little about an issue.

It sometimes makes sense to just take the assertions of an article at face value and not bother to review the footnotes. However, this should not be done when reading a law review article because the researcher would miss out on what's often the most valuable part. Law review articles are only written after extensive research. The footnotes will generally not be restricted to cases within a specific jurisdiction so they can still be helpful in finding cases from any jurisdiction.

F. Treatises

A **treatise** is dedicated to a single topic or area of law and describes the law in basic succinct paragraphs, often referred to as "black letter law." For instance, Prosser on Torts discusses legal issues common to tort law, such as negligence and proximate cause, while *Ohlbaum* on Evidence explains the basic rules of evidence in Pennsylvania. Treatises can be a good starting point for a very general discussion of the law on a given topic.

G. Restatements

Restatements are considered a form of treatise. They distill the rules of the common law as they have developed through numerous cases. Restatements explain that law in relatively simple paragraphs which cite to a wide variety of cases on the issue. While Restatements are a secondary source, and are not consider the law, some of these publications, such as the *Second Restatement of Torts,* are so influential that sections of them have been widely adopted by the courts as accurate statements of the law within that jurisdiction.

H. Digests

Digests are compilations that list the primary sources of case law by topic. Topics are listed alphabetically. Digests are available by state, region and court. Often the most useful digests are published by case law reporters, such as the West Case Law Reporter. To use one of these books you look up the topic in the index and find its "key number," then look up that number in the digest. The digest itself provides a list of cases dealing with that topic or issue, which in turn will lead the reader to relevant cases under the same number within the Case Law Reporter itself.

As for the very important primary sources of the law, these can be divided into two categories; case law or judge made law and statutory law or law made by the legislature.

1. Case Law

Case law refers to the written decisions issued by judges. When courts decide a case, the judges will often record a written "opinion" which recites the facts of the dispute, states the legal outcome and explains the court's reasoning. When a court with authority to establish precedent, such the United States Supreme Court, applies a legal rule to the facts, then the case forms a "holding." Under the rules of stare decisis, that holding will dictate the result in future cases within that jurisdiction that contain similar facts.

Many cases will be similar to the facts you are researching in some respects and different in others. The degree to which the relevant facts are similar to the issue being researched determines how much the case is "on-point" and how much force it will have under stare decisis for resolving the legal question at issue. In order to tell how "on-point" or relevant the case being examined is, it is a good idea to make a list of the similarities and differences between the case and the facts of a person's research. Such a list might look like the following:

Facts	**Client's Case**	**Published Case**
Similarities		
Differences		
Unknown		

This chart will allow a person to easily compare the cases. If there are many similarities and few differences, then it is more likely that the case is on-point. Keep in mind, however, that even one major difference can easily result in a case being "distinguished" from the case that the reader is concerned with. So once you notice a difference between the published case and the issue being researched, make sure you go back and carefully re-read the case to see how much weight the court gave to that different fact in reaching its conclusion. If the outcome of the case seemed to hinge on the one fact which is unlike your own case, then this case is most likely distinguishable and may be of little help.

Cases are collected in large volumes of books known as reporters. Most cases are reported in two reporters known as Westlaw and LEXIS. These are enormous computerized databases which offer the most efficient way to access a case, or allow a person to search for specific words, terms and phrases within the case itself. However, these databases can only be accessed with an account. For instance, some Universities make available to students LEXIS/NEXIS which databank contains a partial listing of court cases on a topic.

Cases are also published in written form by several different publishers and the same case may be found in multiple books. The larger states, such as Pennsylvania, New York, California, Florida and Texas publish their own state's appellate decisions in volumes known as the official reporters. Courts at each level within a state may also publish their decisions in simple chronological order in an official case reporter for that specific court. Other states have arranged for private publishing companies, such as West, to publish their cases in the appropriate regional reporter.

In addition to the written case reporters, many websites compile their own unofficial reporters, which can be accessed for free on the internet. One of the most widely used of these is FindLaw.com (available at www.findlaw.com/casecode), but others can be retrieved by going to an internet browser and typing in terms like "case law."

Cases decided by federal courts are compiled in their own federal reporters. The decisions of the federal district court will be published in the Federal Supplement and federal appellate decisions can be found in the Federal Reporter. The Supreme Court of the United States has its own opinions published in several different resources, such as the official Unites States Reports, the Supreme Court Reporter, which is an unofficial publication but provides editorial comments, and the Supreme Court Lawyers Edition, which is another unofficial version that provides further editorial comments.

2.   Statutory Law

Statutes, also referred to as Codes, are statements of the law passed by the legislative body of a given jurisdiction. After the federal and state constitutions, statutes are the highest expression of law within a jurisdiction. This means that if a statute directly contradicts a common law rule, then the statute trumps the case law unless the law is deemed unconstitutional.

Because statutes are often very complicated, legislators rely on the courts to interpret the statutes and flesh out their hidden meanings.

Federal statutes are passed by the United States Congress, while state statutes are passed by the state legislatures. Federal statutory law is found in the United States Code, while the statutory law of different states is found in the individual state codes. Statutes are also grouped together by subject matter and organized into "Titles" or "Chapters" devoted to different subjects, which are then further subdivided into section numbers.

The following is an example of a simple Pennsylvania statute on theft.

Title 18:	Crimes and Offenses
Article C:	Offenses Against Property
Chapter 39:	Theft and Related Offenses
Section 3921:	Theft by Unlawful Taking or Disposition

(a) MOVABLE PROPERTY — A person is guilty of theft if he unlawfully takes, or exercises unlawful control over, movable property of another with intent to deprive him thereof.

The citation for this statute is written as 18 Pa.C.S. § 3921(a) (2009), which indicates that the law is found in Title 18 of the Pennsylvania Consolidated Statutes, at Section 3921, paragraph (a), which is still in force as of 2009.

Statutes are often amended or updated by the legislature, so one cannot automatically assume that the statute in the book is the current law. To ascertain if the law is "current," the reader must check the "pocket part" for this volume of the code. The pocket part is a supplemental booklet which is inserted at the very end of the volume. Because they are removable, pocket parts can be replaced on a yearly or even quarterly basis so that the law in the volume is always kept up to date. Once the researcher finds the appropriate statute, he or she must examine the back of the volume and look up the same section in the pocket part for any changes in the law.

To decide whether the statute applies to the facts of a case, it's best to break the law down into its basic "elements" and write these out as a set of steps which are necessary pre-conditions required for the statute to apply. The following is a break-down of the elements present in the above statute:

A person is guilty of theft if he or she:

1) unlawfully takes, or exercise unlawful control,
2) over movable property,
3) when that property belongs to another, and
4) the person who takes it intends to deprive the other of such property

Every one of these elements must be present in the facts in order for this statute to apply. Thus, if the person has taken the property of another on a temporary basis with the intent to return it, the criminal has not theft under this section of the code.

The most useful codes for legal research are those which are annotated. These annotations contain case references which interpret the section of the code the researcher is examining. Cases are important because they not only demonstrate the application of the statute to given fact patterns, but they will often explain the law's meaning in language that is much easier to understand. Under the doctrine of stare decisis, once the statute is interpreted in a particular way by an appellate court, the lower courts within the jurisdiction are bound to follow that interpretation.

3. Legal Research on the Internet

The Internet has become a major source of information, communication, and even entertainment for people all over the world. Materials on a variety of subjects can be accessed at the touch of a key, including law-related topics. Court decisions, law review articles, and legislation are now instantly accessible.

A good start for legal research on the Internet is to visit a law-oriented directory or search engine. These resources can help you find subjects from different types of law to specific cases, legal news, and even U.S. Government sites. Several specific legal research sites are:

- **www.lawcrawler.com**
  Lawcrawler is a legal search engine that is powered by Alta Vista and allows for a comprehensive legal search on the topic of your choice.

- **www.findlaw.com**
  Findlaw is a legal subject index.

- **www.hg.org**
  Hieros Games has information on legal organizations, including every government in the world. This is a good research tool for those interested in practicing law.

- **www.ilrg.com**
  Internet Legal Resource Guide is a categorized index of over 3100 select websites in 238 nations, islands, and territories.

- **www.nolo.com**
  Legal Encyclopedia is a self-help center on the Internet.

- **www.lawguru.com**
  This useful tool contains answers to frequently asked legal questions and has many interesting links.

- **www.lectlaw.com**

   The *Lectric Law Library* contains practical links such as "Legal help for the poor" and "How to fight your traffic ticket."

- **www.legis.state.pa.us**

   This website allows access to information from the Pennsylvania legislature, including the text of bills and the history of the legislation.

- **www.fedworld.gov**

   This site provides access to the search engine of the federal government.

- **www.lawoffice.com**

   West Publications has created this link to allow the public to gain access to the profiles of law firms and attorneys around the country.

- **www.aclu.org**

   This is the official site for the American Civil Liberties Union and offers information on civil liberty controversies, such as lesbian and gay rights and women's rights.

- **www.uslaw.com**

   This comprehensive site covers all aspects of the legal field, including articles, current events, and chat rooms where you can submit questions to be answered by attorneys.

- **www.megalaw.com**

   This site discusses recent legal developments in the news and provides access to information in different legal fields, as well as information on state and federal court decisions.

- **www.itslegal.com**

   This site provides links to different legal topics, including real estate law, personal injury, credit and debt issues, family law, and employment law.

- **www.law.indiana.edu/v-lib**

   Indiana University School of Law-Bloomington's virtual law library allows searches about the legal field and provides links relating to the search.

- **www.law.com**

   The law.com connection features law-related articles and stories; summaries from local, state, and federal court decisions; law links, and other legal information.

- **www.prairielaw.com**

   Through articles, columns, and online discussions, this site offers information about the law including consumer concerns, crime, immigration and work related issues.

Now it's time to try one of these legal research tools. The Steven Spielberg movie, Amistad, is based upon an actual United States Supreme Court decision that decided the fate of African slaves who staged a shipboard revolt off the cost of Cuba in an attempt to gain their freedom. The slaves ended up in America, but Spain demanded their return in order to face criminal prosecution for the uprising. American abolitionists became involved in the frey and the matter ended up in the courts. In a landmark decision, our highest court established the principle that all people are "presumptively free" and entitled to the protections of American law. This holding granted the African slaves the freedom they desired in order to return to their homeland. The Amistad, 40 U.S. 518 (1841). If you wish to read the case or learn more about the story, you merely have to access the Internet. If you submit the term Amistad to a search engine, it will take you to a variety of stories and references on the topic. You can also access www.findlaw. com which will take you to the home page of Find Law, whose research engine scans court cases and other legal information on most legal topics. Go to the box marked Supreme Court and click on it. The Supreme Court decision in the Amistad case should be visible when the page opens. You may also gain access to the case by typing 40 U.S. 518 in the appropriate box.

More and more courts are placing their dockets and other court related information on the Internet. For instance, a person can access the records of the Philadelphia Court of Common Pleas by going to http://courts.phila. gov. Depending on the search, one may check the dockets of a specific case, conduct a judgment search involving a specific person, or conduct a litigation search involving a person's name.

For General Information on the Internet

- **http://info.isoc.org/guest/zakon/Internet/History/HIT.html**
  Hobbs' Internet Timeline provides information about the Internet, the people who use it, and online culture.

- **www.columbia.edu/~hauben/netbook**
  Netizens: On the history and Impact of Usenet and the Internet—this site contains a collection of essays about the history, nature, and impact of the Internet.

- **http://home.netscape.com/eng/mozilla/3.0/handbook**
  The *Navigator Handbook Online* provides detailed information on how to use netscape navigator.

Section 1.14
Internet Research
on Malpractice

Problem One—B

Park, Brown & Smith, P.C.
Attorneys at Law
M e m o r a n d u m

To: All Law Clerks

From: Peter Smith, Esquire

Re: Internet Research on Medical Malpractice

It has become very expensive to maintain a law library, so I am interested in learning how to conduct legal research on the internet. I have been told that many courts have posted their decisions on the web and a number of excellent search engines and websites provide answers to a variety of legal problems.

Park, Brown & Smith, P.C. has been consulted by a client who suffered a tragic loss as the result of the amputation of her foot due to the negligence of Dr. Jones. The client had a cancerous tumor on the right foot that required amputation. However, in the operating room, Dr. Jones became confused and mistakenly amputated the left foot. I believe this is a clear case of medical malpractice, and we should recover millions.

Please research the issue of medical malpractice on the internet. I want to learn if there are any legal resources on this topic. Let me know the results of your internet research and provide me with an explanation on how you uncovered the information. Print out two of these resources and attach the first page of each site to this assignment. Your research should not be confined to cases involving the amputation of a leg or foot.

PROBLEM ONE—B
ANSWER SHEET

Name

Please Print Clearly

1. Does the Internet have legal resources on the topic of medical malpractice? If so, please list and describe five of these resources.

_____

_____

_____

_____

_____

_____

_____

_____

2. Please explain how you found these resources. How many resources were there?

_____

_____

_____

_____

_____

_____

_____

_____

3. Please print out two of these references and attach the first printed page of each site to this assignment.

_____

_____

_____

_____

_____

_____

_____

_____

_____

_____

_____

_____

_____

_____

_____

_____

_____

**SECTION 1.15
REVIEW CASES**

1. A 16-year-old went to a local car dealer in order to purchase an automobile. When the salesman learned of the customer's age, he refused to sell the car unless the purchase was made by an adult. A few hours later, the minor returned with an adult that the child had just met. The salesman sold the car to the adult and then assisted the buyer in having the title transferred to the youth. A few days later, the 16-year-old returned with his father and attempted to rescind the contract. Will the car dealer be required to take the automobile back and return the money? **Quality Motors, Inc. v. Johnny Hayes, 225 S. W. 2d 326 (Ark., 1949).**

2. The mother of a mentally challenged female was concerned that her 15-year-old daughter would become pregnant without understanding the consequences. The mother filed a "Petition To Have A Tubaligation Performed On A Minor" with the court. Although there was no legal authority for the court to order the sterilization, the judge felt that the procedure would be in the best interest of the child in order "to prevent unfortunate circumstances..." The child was taken to the hospital under the pretext of having her appendix removed, and the tubaligation was performed. Several years later, the child married and attempted to become pregnant. At this time, she learned that she had been sterilized. As a result of her inability to have children, she sued the judge, claiming that he violated her constitutional rights. Under the concept of status and process, will the judge be immuned from suit for his actions? **Judge Harold Strump v. Linda Sparkman, 435 U.S. 349 (1978).**

3. The parties to a lawsuit attended a settlement conference before the trial judge. During a break, the judge confronted the plaintiff in the hallway, and in a loud, angry voice, yelled at the plaintiff that his settlement demand was "Bull - - - -", and if he thought that there was money in the case, the plaintiff had "s - - - for brains!" The judge then told counsel for the plaintiff that the client "had to deal with him and now he was their enemy." Sometime later, the judge was interviewed by a reporter about the incident and denied that he had acted improperly, despite the plaintiff's allegation. This made it appear as though the plaintiff was lying. Subsequently, the plaintiff filed suit against Judge Williams for his improper conduct. Will the judge enjoy immunity for his actions, or should he be held responsible for the outbursts? Do you see a difference between the statements that the judge made during the settlement conference as opposed to those he made to the reporter? **Robert Soliz v. Alexander Williams, III, 74 Cal. App. 4th 577 (1999).**

4. Charles Kuralt, the former "On The Road" correspondent with CBS, maintained a longtime and intimate relationship with Elizabeth Shannon. This relationship was kept secret because Kuralt was married; Kuralt was the primary source of financial support for Shannon at the time. In 1989, the television personality sent Ms. Shannon a letter indicating that in the event of his death, he wanted her to own the property in Montana which was used as their retreat. In 1994, Kuralt executed a will naming his wife and children as the beneficiaries of his Estate. The will said nothing about the Montana property. In 1997, Kuralt decided to transfer the property to Shannon. The transaction was disguised as a sale, but it was Kuralt's intention to give Shannon the money for the transfer. Prior to the completion of the sale, Kuralt become critically ill. While in the hospital, he wrote a letter to Shannon and enclosed a check to complete the transfer with a notation that it was his intent for her to inherit the Montana property. Before the transfer could take place, Kuralt died. Subsequently, conflicting claims were made against the Montana property by both Kuralt's family and Ms. Shannon. Who do you believe is entitled to the property? Does status and process play any part in your decision? In re: The Estate of Charles Kuralt, 2000 Mont. LEXIS 375 (2000).

Footnote: 1. Reprinted with permission from **"When Justice Is Up To You,"** 1992, by the American Association for Justice and the National Institute for Citizen Education in the Law.

2. This section on legal research was written by Avi Cohen, Esquire.

KEY TERMS

Affirmed

Appellant

Appellee

Article One of the Constitution

Briefing of a Case

Burden of Proof

Caption

Case Law

Citation

Codes

Common Law

Common Law Marriage

Compurgation

Concurring Opinion

Court Clerk

Defendant

Digests

Dissenting Opinion

Domestic Partnership

Encyclopedias

Form Books

Internet Research

Judge

Judicial Decree

Judicial Opinion

Jury

Law Review Articles

Legal Dictionaries

Legal Periodicals

Legislative Enactment

Lexis

Majority Opinion

Plaintiff

Precedent

Primary Source

Questions of Fact and Law

Remanded

Restatements

Reversed

Secondary Source

Social Host

Stare Decisis

Status and Process

Statutory Law

Treaties

Trial by Ordeal

Trial by Water and Fire

Voyeurism

Wager of Law

Westlaw

Witness

CHAPTER 2

CLASSIFICATIONS OF LAW

SECTION 2.1
PUBLIC LAW V.
PRIVATE LAW

The major classifications of law are public law and private law. **Public law** involves the rights of society, and those rights are usually represented by a governmental agency. An example of public law is the crime of murder. This criminal offense affects the right of all members of society to be safe and secure. The categories of public law are criminal law, constitutional law and administrative law.

Private law, on the other hand, involves matters between individuals, such as the leasing of an apartment, a claim against a doctor for making a mistake during surgery, or the purchasing of a new car. These matters are personal between the parties to the transaction or incident. The major classifications of private law are contract law, tort law, property law, and family law and the remedy is usually money.

SECTION 2.2
CRIMINAL LAW

A **crime** is a violation of those duties that an individual owes to his or her community and the breach of which requires the offender to make satisfaction to the public. As a result, a crime is a violation of the rights of society and not the individual victim of the crime. This distinction is immediately apparent when the victim of a crime does not want to prosecute the suspect. While the prosecutor will usually follow the victim's wishes, a district attorney can force a victim to testify against the accused if there is a compelling societal interest, such as in cases of child or spousal abuse or rape. Since the government is responsible for taking action against a criminal defendant on behalf of society, the caption of the case contains the name of the governmental unit, such as the "United States," "The State," or "The People" versus the defendant.

Criminal laws are established by the legislature and are broken down into different categories based upon one thing—the penalty for the offense. While each jurisdiction will differ on what crimes go into a specific category, these classifications are treason, felonies, misdemeanors, and summary offenses. **Treason** is defined in the United States Constitution because it is considered the most serious offense against the country. **Article III, Section 3** states that: "Treason against the United States shall consist only in levying war against them or in adhering to their enemies, giving them aid and comfort." A person cannot be convicted of treason unless two witnesses testify to the commission of the same overt act done to betray the United States, or if the accused confesses in open court. Because this burden of proof is so high, the government has prosecuted less than 100 cases involving treason in its history. Examples of people accused of being traitors include Benedict Arnold, Aaron Burr, Julius and Ethel Rosenberg, Anthony Cramer, and John Walker Lindh, the 20-year-old American who was captured while fighting for the Taliban. The penalty for treason can range from death to a minimum of five years in prison along with a fine of $10,000.

Although penalties for most crimes vary from state to state, a felony is a crime generally punishable by more than one year in jail. Examples include such offenses as murder, rape, burglary, and arson. A **misdemeanor** is usually punishable by less than one year in jail and includes such matters as assault, criminal trespass, and harassment. A defendant accused of a **summary offense** will generally be responsible for the payment of a fine, such as that which occurs with a traffic ticket.

The government has the burden of proving a defendant guilty **beyond a reasonable doubt**. This phrase has been interpreted to mean "fully satisfied," "entirely convinced," or "satisfied to a moral certainty." This is a very strict standard requiring the prosecutor to prove that the defendant actually committed the crime or **actus reus,** and that he or she had the necessary state of mind to commit the crime. This requisite state of mind, or criminal intent, is called **mens rea**. The legal system is concerned with what the defendant intended, knew, or should have known when he or she committed the offense.

There are various ways of proving mens rea. Criminal intent may be proved through an intentional, knowing, reckless, or negligent act. For example, in **Commonwealth of Pennsylvania v. Cheatham, 615 A.2d 802 (Pa. Super., 1992),** the court had to decide whether a seizure-induced-black-out caused by epilepsy was an involuntary act which relieved the driver of a car of criminal responsibility for a fatal motor vehicle accident. The driver was found guilty because he possessed the necessary mens rea to commit the offense. The court concluded that the driver clearly knew that he suffered from unannounced seizures and was ordered not to operate a car. By choosing to drive a motor vehicle, the motorist exhibited recklessness under the circumstances. A different resolution would occur, however, if a person causes an accident by suffering an unexpected heart attack. Mens rea would be lacking since the act would be involuntary and the accident unforeseeable.

Does a person's voluntary intoxication eliminate his or her ability to form the necessary mens rea to commit a crime when the statute specifically requires that the person commit the crime with knowing intent? That is the issue in **Gary v. Dormire**.

GARY V. DORMIRE
256 F.3D 753 (C.A. 8 MO., 2001)

David Gary visited his estranged wife to explore the prospect of reuniting. His efforts at reconciliation proved unsuccessful, and the conversation ended with Gary striking his estranged wife in the mouth. St. Louis police located the defendant's car several hours later and took up pursuit. Gary tried eluding police, and a high-speed chase ensued. The chase ended tragically when the defendant crashed into a police squad car barricade while traveling over one hundred miles per hour. He survived the crash. The police officer sitting in the squad car he struck was killed on impact. In a post-accident inventory of the Gary's car, police recovered empty and full beer cans and a bottle of hard liquor.

The state must prove every element of the crime beyond a reasonable doubt. However, in determining the defendant's guilt or innocence, (the jury was) instructed that an intoxicated condition from alcohol will not relieve a person of responsibility for his conduct.

According to the Missouri Supreme Court, there are two aspects to Missouri's rule on voluntary intoxication evidence. First, voluntary intoxication is not per se proof of inability to form a culpable mental state. Second, voluntary intoxication is irrelevant to the defendant's mental state. The statute "... places an intoxicated person on a level footing with a sober person as to the mental elements of an offense and places limits on the defense of diminished capacity due to intoxication."

Gary argues that evidence of voluntary intoxication was relevant to the issue of whether he acted "knowingly" and "after deliberation" under the State's charge of first-degree murder. A person commits the crime of murder in the first degree if he knowingly causes the death of another person after deliberation upon the matter. He claims a due process right to have the jury consider evidence of voluntary intoxication when determining whether he possessed the requisite mens rea to be found guilty beyond a reasonable doubt of first-degree murder.

We reject the defendant's argument that States must redefine the criminal offense to eliminate the mens rea element for voluntarily intoxicated defendants. Missouri treats voluntarily intoxicated individuals and sober individuals equally culpable for criminal activity. It accomplishes this by giving evidence of voluntary intoxication no relevance insofar as the mental elements of the crime are concerned. Because evidence of voluntary intoxication has no exculpatory relevance under Missouri law, a criminal defendant has no corresponding constitutional right to have the jury consider this evidence. The judgment of the district court will be affirmed (and the defendant's petition is denied).

SECTION 2.3
CONSTITUTIONAL LAW

The idea of a constitution to govern and protect the citizens of a country is not a novel idea. Ancient Rome was formed as a republic that granted certain fundamental freedoms to its citizens. King John of England approved the Magna Carta in 1297. This historic document provided that the people of England had certain fundamental rights that could not be abridged and the threads of this document are found in this country's Bill of Rights.

Following the Revolutionary War, the states decided to create a lasting document to govern the people of America. In the summer of 1787, fifty-five men gathered in secret session in Philadelphia to amend the Articles of Confederation, a document that joined 13 independent colonies into a loose confederation of states with a weak central government. An infirmed Ben Franklin was the oldest delegate at 81 and Jonathan Douglas was the youngest at 26. George Washington presided over the meetings, but Thomas Jefferson and John Adams were unable to attend. Rhode Island refused to send a delegation.

After much debate, the delegates agreed upon the United States Constitution, which document creates a strong centralized government whose primary purpose is to serve its citizens.

The document was then forwarded to the thirteen original states for ratification. One year later, the United States Constitution became the law of the land, and no federal or state law may conflict with that document. Today, the Constitution is the oldest written national constitution in effect. For instance, Italy did not become a democratic republic until 1948 at which time its constitution was enacted. Likewise, Japan did not create its constitution until after World War Two.

The Constitution is the most important legal document in American jurisprudence. It establishes the branches of the government, creates the fundamental rights of the people and protects them from unlawful governmental interference.

The Constitution is purposely written in broad and often vague terms so that it can adapt to changing times. This concept is called **constitutional relativity** and insures that this legal document will maintain its vitality. How does this occur? The courts continually interpret and apply the Constitution to current issues. This power of the judiciary was established by John Marshall, Chief Justice of the United States Supreme Court, in the landmark decision of **Marbury v. Madison, 1 Cranch 137 (1803).**

The application of constitutional relativity is demonstrated by the evolution of the **Fourth Amendment**. This Amendment provides:

> The right of the people to be secure in their persons, houses, papers, and effects, against unreasonable searches and seizures, shall not be violated, and no warrants shall issue, but upon probable cause.

How could this Amendment, which was adopted more than 200 years ago, have application to a police search of a computer's hard drive when this technology was clearly not within the contemplation of the drafters of the Constitution? Quite simply, the 4th Amendment does not identify what is to be searched but merely specifies that warrants must be issued upon probable cause. This allows the court to decide what is and is not subject to police searches over the course of time.

The Constitution of the United States starts with the following Preamble:

> We the people of the United States, in order to form a more perfect Union, establish justice, insure domestic tranquility, provide for the common defense, promote the general welfare, and secure the blessings of liberty to ourselves and our posterity, do ordain and establish this Constitution for the United States of America.

This introductory sentence provides the framework for the origins, purpose and beneficiaries of this historical document. The Preamble clearly reflects that the Constitution originates with the citizens and not with the states and its purpose is to form a better government that will insure fairness and protection of the people over time.

The body of the Constitution consists of seven **Articles** and twenty-seven **Amendments**. The framework of the document creates an intentional distribution of power. The framers realized the need for a Federal or National system rather than a loose confederation of states. They also realized the need to prevent a concentration of power in a single branch of the government. With this in mind, the drafters created a framework of limited government power through the concept of the separation of powers. The first three Articles of the Constitution apportion the power to run the country among the legislative, executive, and judicial branches of the government. Article I empowers the legislature to make the laws which the executive branch enforces pursuant to the authority granted to the President in Article II. Article III designates the judiciary as that branch of the government that interprets the Constitution.

Ratification of the Constitution by the original states was not a certainty because of the lingering doubt that a strong central government would infringe upon the individual rights of its citizens. In fact, some states ratified the Constitution only after noting that the document had to be amended to include a list of individual protections that people would enjoy from governmental interference.

This concern was addressed by James Madison two years after the ratification of the Constitution when he drafted the Bill of Rights. Twelve Amendments were proposed but only ten were adopted. These personal safeguards include the right to freedom of speech, protection of religion, and right to assemble. The Amendments also guarantee that people will be secure in their person, the government will not conduct unreasonable search and seizures, and no person shall be forced in a criminal case to testify against himself. Citizens are also guaranteed the right to a speedy and public trial by an impartial jury.

Over the years, these protections have generated a number of lawsuits that have tested the limits of what is meant by these personal freedoms. For instance, does the First Amendment protect the burning of the American Flag or hate speech that has the ability to incite a riot? Does the First Amendment protect religious groups from holding anti-gay protests at military funerals? Does the law against unlawful search and seizures prohibit the government from conducting warrant-less searches of computer hard drives and does a prohibition against cruel and unusual punishment prohibit the state from executing a defendant?

While many people think that the last Amendment to the Constitution granted 18-year-olds the right to vote, the 27th Amendment was passed in 1992 and provides:

> No law, varying the compensation for the services of the Senators and Representatives, shall take effect, until an election of Representatives shall have intervened.

In other words, the Constitution prohibits the legislature from granting itself a pay raise that is effective before those representatives run for re-election.

Passing an amendment to the Constitution is a very difficult task. This is amply demonstrated by the fact that over 11,000 amendments have been proposed since the Constitution's inception but only 27 have been adopted. Article V of the Constitution requires that an amendment be passed by two-thirds of each House and by three-fourths of the State Legislatures. The framers did not want the Constitution to be amended every time the population was impassioned by a controversial court decision or legal issue.

The call for an amendment to protect the American flag from desecration is a prime example of such constitutional politics. Whether an amendment to prevent the burning of a flag is necessary or appropriate has been the source of debate. To put the matter in the proper context, should an amendment have been passed to protect the American flag when the country could not agree on the passage of the Equal Rights Amendment which guaranteed equal rights for men and women? It is possible that a constitutional amendment to prevent flag burning may be adopted by appealing to the emotional support of the population. This, however, is the type of issue the framers hoped to avoid by making the amendatory process so difficult to fulfill.

Another proposed amendment that has sparked much discussion is an amendment to limit the terms of those in Congress. This proposal stems from disgruntled voters who believe that career politicians have lost touch with the American people and should not be allowed to stay in office for an indefinite period. The United States Supreme Court in **U.S. Term Limits Inc. v. Thornton** decided that a state cannot limit service in Congress without amending the Constitution. The Court stated that any change in term limits must not come by legislation adopted by Congress or an individual state, but through amendment procedures. The passage of such a constitutional amendment would require a two-thirds vote in the House of Representatives and the Senate, as well as ratification by thirty-eight states.

An important provision in the United States Constitution for the regulation of interstate business is the **Commerce Clause** found in Article 1. This provision authorizes Congress "To regulate Commerce with foreign Nations, and among the several States, and with Indian Tribes." As described by the United States Senate, this clause is one of the most far-reaching grants of power to Congress and covers all movement of people and goods across state lines. The Commerce Clause has permitted a wide array of federal laws, from the regulation of business to justifying minimum wage. The Clause has even been used to prohibit racial discrimination. The following is one of the landmark cases in the area.

KATZENBACH v. McCLUNG
379 U.S. 294 (1964)

Ollie's Barbecue is a family-owned restaurant in Birmingham, Alabama, specializing in barbecued meats and homemade pies, with a seating capacity of 220 customers. It is located on a state highway 11 blocks from an interstate. The restaurant caters to families and white-collar trade with take-out service for Negroes. It employs 36 persons, two-thirds of whom are Negroes.

In the 12 months preceding the passage of the Civil Rights Act, the restaurant purchased approximately $150,000 worth of food locally, $69,683 or 46% of which was meat that it bought from a local supplier who had procured it from outside the State. The restaurant has refused to serve Negroes in its dining room accommodations since its opening. The court below concluded that if it were required to serve Negroes it would lose a substantial amount of business.

The lower court also held that the Civil Rights Act could not be applied because the State of Alabama was not involved in the refusal of the restaurant to serve Negroes. As to the Commerce Clause, the court found that it was an express grant of power to Congress to regulate interstate commerce, which consists of the movement of persons, goods or information from one state to another; it found that the clause was also a grant of power to regulate intrastate activities, but only to the extent that action on its part is necessary or appropriate to the effective execution of its expressly granted power to regulate interstate commerce. The court concluded, however, that Congress had legislated a conclusive presumption that a restaurant affects interstate commerce if it serves or offers to serve interstate travelers or if a substantial portion of the food which it serves has moved in commerce. This, the court held, it could not do because there was no demonstrable connection between food purchased in interstate commerce and sold in a restaurant and the conclusion of Congress that discrimination in the restaurant would affect that commerce.

The Civil Rights Act commands that all persons shall be entitled to the full and equal enjoyment of the goods and services of any place of public accommodation without discrimination or segregation on the ground of race, color, religion, or national origin. Furthermore, any restaurant principally engaged in selling food for consumption on the premises' under the Act if it serves or offers to serve interstate travelers or a substantial portion of the food which it serves has moved in commerce.

Ollie's Barbecue admits that it is covered by these provisions of the Act but there is no claim that interstate travelers frequented the restaurant. The sole question, therefore, narrows down to whether the Act, as applied to a restaurant annually receiving about $70,000 worth of food which has moved in commerce, is a valid exercise of the power of Congress.

The record is replete with testimony of the burdens placed on interstate commerce by racial discrimination in restaurants. A comparison of per capita spending by Negroes in restaurants, theaters, and like establishments indicated less spending in areas where discrimination is widely practiced. Moreover, discrimination in restaurants had a direct and highly restrictive effect upon interstate travel by Negroes. This resulted because discriminatory practices prevent Negroes from buying prepared food served on the premises while on a trip, except in isolated and unkempt restaurants and under most unsatisfactory and often unpleasant conditions. This obviously discourages travel and obstructs interstate commerce for one can hardly travel without eating.

It goes without saying that, viewed in isolation; the volume of food purchased by Ollie's Barbecue from sources supplied from out of state was insignificant when compared with the total foodstuffs moving in commerce.

Article I confers upon Congress the power (t)o regulate Commerce among the several States' and the same Article grants it the power (t)o make all Laws which shall be necessary and proper for carrying into execution the foregoing Powers. This grant extends to those activities intrastate which so affect interstate commerce, or the exertion of the power of Congress over it, as to make regulation of them appropriate means to the attainment of a legitimate end, the effective execution of the granted power to regulate interstate commerce. Much is said about a restaurant business being local, but even if appellee's activity was local and though it may not be regarded as commerce, it may still be reached by Congress if it exerts a substantial economic effect on interstate commerce.

Here, Congress has determined that refusals of service to Negroes have imposed burdens both upon the interstate flow of food and upon the movement of products generally. But where we find that the legislators have a rational basis for finding a chosen regulatory scheme necessary to the protection of commerce, our investigation is at an end.

We must conclude that Congress had a rational basis for finding that racial discrimination in restaurants had a direct and adverse effect on the free flow of interstate commerce. Insofar as the Civil Rights Act is concerned, Congress prohibited discrimination only in those establishments having a close tie to interstate commerce, i.e., those, like the McClungs', serving food that has come from out of the State. We think in so doing that Congress acted well within its power to protect and foster commerce in extending the coverage of the Act only to those restaurants offering to serve interstate travelers or serving food, a substantial portion of which has moved in interstate commerce.

The judgment is therefore reversed.

The Constitution in Everyday Language

To better understand the rights guaranteed to citizens of the United States, it is important to review briefly the Constitution and its Amendments. The archaic language of this more than 200-year-old document is often difficult to understand, so the following summary is written in simplified language.

We the People of the United States establish this Constitution for the United States of America.

Article I	The power to make the laws of the United States will be given to Congress, which will consist of a Senate and House of Representatives.
Article II	All power to enforce and execute the laws of the United States will be given to an elected President and Vice President.
Article III	The power to interpret the laws of the United States will be given to the Supreme Court and other federal courts.
Article IV	Each state will enforce and recognize the laws, legal records, and results of lawsuits from every other state. No state shall discriminate against citizens from another state.
Article V	Congress may propose Amendments to the Constitution based upon a two-thirds vote of both Houses of Congress or two-thirds of the states can call a convention to propose Amendments. Three-fourths of the states must ratify the proposed change before it may become an Amendment to the Constitution.
Article VI	This Constitution, and the laws and treaties made under it, are the supreme law of the land.
Article VII	The Constitution became effective on September 17, 1787.

Amendments to the Constitution of the United States of America

Amendment I	Citizens have the right to freedom of religion, speech, press, and to assemble peaceably.

AMENDMENT II	Citizens have the right to bear arms.
AMENDMENT III	Citizens cannot be required to house soldiers in their homes during peace time.
AMENDMENT IV	Citizens are protected against unreasonable searches and seizures of both their person and property.
AMENDMENT V	No person can be tried twice for the same crime or be forced to testify against himself. A person's life, liberty, or property cannot be taken away by the government without going through the proper and fair legal procedures.
AMENDMENT VI	A defendant in a criminal trial is entitled to legal representation and must be provided with a speedy and public trial by an impartial jury.
AMENDMENT VII	Citizens are entitled to jury trials in civil cases involving more than twenty dollars.
AMENDMENT VIII	A court cannot impose cruel and unusual punishment or excessive bail on defendants.
AMENDMENT IX	Rights that are not specifically mentioned within the Constitution are held by the citizens.
AMENDMENT X	Rights that are not delegated to the federal government are reserved for the states and the citizens.
AMENDMENT XI	Citizens are not permitted to sue states where they are not residents.
AMENDMENT XII	The Electoral College will select the President and Vice President.
AMENDMENT XIII	Slavery and involuntary servitude is abolished.
AMENDMENT XIV	No state can make or enforce any law which will take away the privileges and immunities of citizens; nor deprive any person of life, liberty or property, without due process of law; nor deny any person within its borders the equal protection of its laws.
AMENDMENT XV	Citizens of all races and colors have the right to vote.
AMENDMENT XVI	Congress may tax income.
AMENDMENT XVII	When a Senator is required to leave office before his or her term in Congress expires, the governor of the Senator's state can appoint another to fill the position until the citizens of the state elect a new Senator.

Amendment XVIII	The manufacture, sale, or transportation of intoxicating liquors is prohibited. [REPEALED]
Amendment XIX	Both male and female citizens have the right to vote.
Amendment XX	The President and Vice President begin their terms January 20; Senators and Representatives January 3. If the President-Elect dies before being sworn in, the Vice-President-Elect becomes President.
Amendment XXI	The Eighteenth Amendment enforcing the prohibition of intoxicating liquors is repealed.
Amendment XXII	The President may not be elected more than twice.
Amendment XXIII	The District of Columbia is entitled to representation at the Electoral College.
Amendment XXIV	Citizens cannot be charged a fee in order to vote.
Amendment XXV	When the President cannot perform his official duties, the Vice President will assume the duties of the President. The President can be impeached upon a two-thirds vote of Congress.
Amendment XXVI	Citizens who are eighteen (18) years of age and older have the right to vote.
Amendment XXVII	Members of Congress cannot raise their pay while in office. Any law that provides for a pay raise for Congress cannot take effect until after the election, which follows the vote, granting the raise.

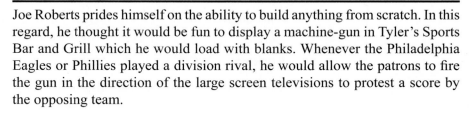

SECTION 2.4
JOE ROBERTS'
CONSTITUTIONAL
LAW PROBLEM

PROBLEM TWO—A

PARK, BROWN & SMITH, P.C.
ATTORNEYS AT LAW
MEMORANDUM

TO: All Law Clerks

FROM: Peter Smith, Esquire

RE: Joe Roberts' Constitutional Law Problem

Joe Roberts prides himself on the ability to build anything from scratch. In this regard, he thought it would be fun to display a machine-gun in Tyler's Sports Bar and Grill which he would load with blanks. Whenever the Philadelphia Eagles or Phillies played a division rival, he would allow the patrons to fire the gun in the direction of the large screen televisions to protest a score by the opposing team.

Mr. Roberts knew that it was against the law to buy a machine-gun so he built the weapon from scratch at his home's machine shop. Once Joe perfected the automatic weapon, he brought it to the bar and built an elevated platform to display his new toy. His idea was an immediate success and Philadelphia sports fans flocked to the bar on game day to participate in shooting down the opposing team. After a few weeks, the patronage at the bar tripled and people soon waited in line to get a chance to fire the gun which Joe affectionately named "Big Red."

The bar owner's marketing scheme blew up in his face one Sunday afternoon when a New York fan went into the bar to watch the Eagles play the Giants on television. This patron was harassed from the moment he walked into the bar wearing a Giant's jersey. At first, he thought the ribbing was just good natured fun but then things turned ugly. The Giants jumped out to a quick 14-point lead and the boos soon turned to profanity laced insults. But then the Eagles scored and "Big Red" came to life. A couple of Eagle's fans took turns firing the gun in the direction of the Giant's fan who had ducked under the table for cover.

After the initial bursts of fire, the stranger stood up screaming, reached into his pants pocket and held something in his right hand high in the air. Almost immediately, the laughter stopped and the patrons recognized the object being held aloft. It was a badge which identified the New York fan as a member of the Federal Bureau of Investigation.

Roberts quickly walked over to the FBI agent to make peace. However, the next thing Joe Roberts remembers is being thrown up against the bar and handcuffs being slapped on his wrist. Within minutes, Tyler's was swarming with cops, and Roberts was taken to jail and booked for possessing a machine-gun in violation of 18 U.S.C. § 922 (o). That statute makes it illegal for any person to transfer or possess a machine-gun except for:

A. a transfer to or by, or possession by or under the authority of, the United States or any department or agency thereof or a State, or a department, agency, or political subdivision thereof; or

B. any lawful transfer or lawful possession of a machine-gun that was lawfully possessed before the date this subsection takes effect.

The bar owner wishes to challenge his arrest as being unconstitutional and has sought our advice. Joe claims that he was very careful in making the gun. He only used local parts and the gun was made and assembled in Pennsylvania. It is also one of a kind since he destroyed the mold after he made the one machine-gun.

The only defense that comes to mind is that the federal government has no power to enforce the machine-gun law because this is purely a local matter. Also, Joe made the gun for his own use and never took any part in interstate commerce. I want to see if we can successfully challenge his prosecution on the basis that Congress does not have the power to forbid his possession of the weapon under the Commerce Clause because the gun never traveled in interstate commerce but rather was "home-grown."

Please read **Gonzales v. Raich** and tell me if Joe can be successfully defended.

GONZALES V. RAICH
545 U.S. 1 (2005)

California authorizes the use of marijuana for medicinal purposes. The question presented is whether the power vested in Congress by Article I, § 8, of the Constitution "[t]o make all Laws which shall be necessary and proper for carrying into Execution" its authority to "regulate Commerce with foreign Nations, and among the several States" includes the power to prohibit the local cultivation and use of marijuana in compliance with California law.

In 1996, California voters passed Proposition 215, now codified as the Compassionate Use Act of 1996. The proposition was designed to ensure that "seriously ill" residents of the State have access to marijuana for medical purposes.

Angel Raich and Diane Monson are California residents who suffer from a variety of serious medical conditions and have sought to avail themselves of medical marijuana pursuant to the terms of the Compassionate Use Act. Both women have been using marijuana as a medication for several years pursuant to their doctors' recommendation.

Monson cultivates her own marijuana, and Raich relies on two caregivers to provide her with locally grown marijuana at no charge.

On August 15, 2002, the federal Drug Enforcement Administration (DEA) came to Monson's home and after a 3-hour standoff, the federal agents seized and destroyed all of her cannabis plants.

Respondents brought this action against the Attorney General of the United States seeking injunctive and declaratory relief prohibiting the enforcement of the federal Controlled Substances Act (CSA), to the extent it prevents them from possessing, obtaining, or manufacturing cannabis for their personal medical use.

The question before us is whether Congress' power to regulate interstate markets for medicinal substances encompasses the portions of those markets that are supplied with drugs produced and consumed locally. Well-settled law controls our answer. The CSA is a valid exercise of federal power.

In 1969, Congress set out to enact legislation that would consolidate various drug laws on the books into a comprehensive statute, provide meaningful regulation over legitimate sources of drugs to prevent diversion into illegal channels, and strengthen law enforcement tools against the traffic in illicit drugs. That effort culminated in the passage of the Comprehensive Drug Abuse Prevention and Control Act of 1970.

In enacting the CSA, Congress classified marijuana as a Schedule I drug. By classifying marijuana as a Schedule I drug, the manufacture, distribution, or possession of marijuana became a criminal offense.

Respondents' argue that the CSA's prohibition of the manufacture and possession of marijuana as applied to the intrastate manufacture and possession of marijuana for medical purposes pursuant to California law exceeds Congress' authority under the Commerce Clause.

Our case law firmly establishes Congress' power to regulate purely local activities that are part of an economic "class of activities" that have a substantial effect on interstate commerce. See: **Wickard v. Filburn, 317 U.S. 111 (1942).** As we stated in Wickard, "even if appellee's activity be local and though it may not be regarded as commerce, it may still, whatever its nature, be reached by Congress if it exerts a substantial economic effect on interstate

commerce." When Congress decides that the total incidence of a practice poses a threat to a national market, it may regulate the entire class. In this vein, we have reiterated that when a general regulatory statute bears a substantial relation to commerce, the de minimis character of individual instances arising under that statute is of no consequence.

In Wickard, we upheld the application of regulations promulgated under the Agricultural Adjustment Act, which were designed to control the volume of wheat moving in interstate and foreign commerce in order to avoid surpluses and abnormally low prices. The regulations established an allotment of 11.1 acres for Filburn's 1941 wheat crop, but he sowed 23 acres, intending to use the excess by consuming it on his own farm. Filburn argued that even though we had sustained Congress' power to regulate the production of goods for commerce, that power did not authorize "federal regulation [of] production not intended in any part for commerce but wholly for consumption on the farm." Justice Jackson's opinion for a unanimous Court rejected this submission. He wrote:

> "The effect of the statute before us is to restrict the amount which may be produced for market and the extent as well to which one may forestall resort to the market by producing to meet his own needs. That appellee's own contribution to the demand for wheat may be trivial by itself is not enough to remove him from the scope of federal regulation where, as here, his contribution, taken together with that of many others similarly situated, is far from trivial."

Wickard thus establishes that Congress can regulate purely intrastate activity that is not itself "commercial," in that it is not produced for sale, if it concludes that failure to regulate that class of activity would undercut the regulation of the interstate market in that commodity.

In Wickard, we had no difficulty concluding that Congress had a rational basis for believing that, when viewed in the aggregate, leaving home-consumed wheat outside the regulatory scheme would have a substantial influence on price and market conditions. Here too, Congress had a rational basis for concluding that leaving home-consumed marijuana outside federal control would similarly affect price and market conditions.

More concretely, one concern prompting inclusion of wheat grown for home consumption in the 1938 Act was that rising market prices could draw such wheat into the interstate market, resulting in lower market prices. The parallel concern making it appropriate to include marijuana grown for home consumption in the CSA is the likelihood that the high demand in the interstate market will draw such marijuana into that market. While the diversion of homegrown wheat tended to frustrate the federal interest in stabilizing prices by regulating the volume of commercial transactions in the interstate market, the diversion of homegrown marijuana tends to frustrate the federal interest in eliminating commercial transactions in the interstate market in their entirety. In both cases, the regulation is squarely within Congress' commerce power because production of the commodity meant for home consumption, be it wheat or marijuana, has a substantial effect on supply and demand in the national market for that commodity.

The exemption for cultivation by patients and caregivers can only increase the supply of marijuana in the California market. The likelihood that all such production will promptly terminate when patients recover or will precisely match the patients' medical needs during their convalescence seems remote; whereas the danger that excesses will satisfy some of the admittedly enormous demand for recreational use seems obvious. Moreover, that the national and international narcotics trade has thrived in the face of vigorous criminal enforcement efforts suggests that no small number of unscrupulous people will make use of the California exemptions to serve their commercial ends whenever it is feasible to do so.

The case is remanded for further proceedings consistent with this opinion. It is so ordered.

ANSWER SHEET
PROBLEM TWO—A

Name

Please Print Clearly

1. Can the federal government regulate the possession of a machine-gun that was made wholly within Pennsylvania and was never part of interstate commerce?

_____

_____

_____

_____

_____

_____

_____

_____

2. Is it a defense that Joe's possession of the machine-gun was insignificant in the grand scheme of things? After all, he is just one person who possesses only one firearm.

_____

_____

_____

_____

_____

_____

_____

_____

_____

3. Will Joe be convicted for owning a machine-gun based upon **Gonzales v. Raich**?

_____

_____

_____

_____

_____

_____

_____

_____

_____

_____

_____

_____

_____

_____

_____

_____

_____

_____

_____

_____

SECTION 2.5
ADMINISTRATIVE LAW

As the United States has grown in population and complexity, the task of running the country has become extremely difficult, and the needs of the population too great for the legislative branch to handle on its own. In an effort to ease its burden, Congress has created administrative agencies to deal with specialized areas and has staffed the agencies with experts who know how to deal with the particular problems encountered in each area.

An **administrative agency** is a "governmental body charged with administering and implementing particular legislation." Administrative agencies have greatly increased in number over the past several decades in order to effectuate general policy mandates of the legislative and executive branches of the government at the national, state, and local levels. Administrative agencies are created through congressional action called **Enabling Acts.**

Administrative or regulatory law, therefore, is concerned with the legal rules and principles that regulate governmental agencies. These agencies are unique because they enjoy legislative, executive and judicial powers. As public agencies, they protect a public interest or sector instead of a private right or person.

Administrative agencies can exist at any level of the government including the federal, state and local levels. The following are examples of federal administrative agencies:

* *Environmental Protection Agency* (EPA). This agency is designed to protect human health and to safeguard the environment, including the air, water, and land upon which life depends. The **EPA** has been responsible for environmental safeguards such as the banning of DDT, which is used in pesticides and has been found to be a cancer-causing agent. They have also banned the use of lead in gasoline, limited discharges by factories of pollution into waterways, and established fuel economy standards for motor vehicles. The **EPA's** website is: **www.epa.gov**.

* *Securities and Exchange Commission* (SEC). This regulatory body is designed to protect investors and maintain the integrity of the securities market. This agency was created following the economic collapse in the 1930s. The **SEC** oversees the various stock exchanges, mutual fund markets, broker/dealers, and public utility-holding companies. The **SEC** is aggressive in its enforcement function and brings between 400 to 500 enforcement actions each year against individuals and companies that break the security laws. Examples of infractions include insider trading and providing false or misleading information about securities or the companies that issue them. The website for the **Securities and Exchanges Commission** can be found at: **www.sec.gov**.

- *Occupational Safety and Health Administration* (**OSHA**). The bureau is designed to reduce the number of safety and health hazards at work. **OSHA** regulates work environments to ensure that they are free from recognized hazards that are likely to cause death or serious physical harm to workers. This goal is accomplished through work place inspections and by establishing protective standards. Since this agency was created in 1970, the overall workplace death rate has been cut in half. The agency's website is: **www.osha.gov.**

- *Food and Drug Administration* (**FDA**). This agency protects the health of the public by monitoring products for safety, and helps safe and effective products reach the marketplace in a timely fashion. The *FDA* regulates the sale of food, drugs, medical devices, and radiation-emitting products such as cell phones, lasers, and microwaves. The agency's website is: **www. fda.gov**.

- *Federal Trade Commission* (**FTC**). The **FTC** enforces anti-trust and consumer protection laws. The bureau investigates and prosecutes unfair or deceptive business practices, seeks monetary damages for conduct detrimental to consumers, is responsible for the labeling of cigarettes with health-related warning labels, requires the labeling of ingredients for food, drugs, and cosmetic products, and regulates automatic teller machines. The agency's website is:
www.ftc.gov.

- *Federal Communications Commission* (**FCC**). This agency was created in 1934 and is responsible for regulating communications by radio, television, satellite, wire, and cable. It also oversees the nation's emergency alert system, which notifies the public about a local or national emergency. The **FCC's** website is: **www.fcc.gov.**

The functions of all these administrative agencies include the imposition of sanctions; licensing and other regulatory decisions; environmental and safety decisions; awards of benefits, loans, grants and other subsidies; inspections, audits, and approvals; and planning and policy-making.

Administrative agencies are unique because they are created with legislative, executive and judicial powers. An agency acts as a legislative body in the sense that it can issue rules and regulations. Its regulations are promulgated through a daily publication called the **Federal Register**. This power allows the agency to investigate alleged violations of the Act.

Administrative agencies also possess a judicial power called agency adjudication. Administrative hearings are very similar to court proceedings. Witnesses are heard and evidence is presented so that an administrative law judge can decide the case. Because agencies possess rule-making, adjudicating and investigative powers, they have been considered by some to be a fourth branch of government.

The theory behind the creation of administrative agencies is that the administrator's expertise allows them to resolve problems within a particular area or industry quickly and effectively. The administrator's expertise should lead to proper decisions in the problem areas, as opposed to improper decisions that might be handed down by Congress or the courts due to good intentions but inadequate knowledge.

Because administrative agencies are empowered to regulate and develop the law for a specific area, the scope of review of an agency's adverse determination is very limited. The courts often feel that agencies possess the expertise in their field. Thus, their decisions are rarely overturned unless they are arbitrary, capricious, or an abuse of discretion. Factual findings, however, are conclusive so long as they are supported by **"substantial evidence."** Under this standard, a finding will not be changed on appeal if it is supported by relevant evidence that a reasonable mind might accept as adequate to support a conclusion. This is a very difficult burden for an aggrieved party to overcome.

Martha Stewart gained notoriety as a "domestic diva" whose cooking, sewing, and home remodeling talents seemed endless. She was very successful in promoting her ideas and turned her talents into a multi-million dollar enterprise. In 2003, however, her world was turned upside down because of a stock scandal involving ImClone Systems, Inc. The Food and Drug Administration informed the corporation that its cancer drug, Erbitux, was not going to obtain FDA approval. Shortly before this news was released to the public, Stewart sold almost 4,000 shares of ImClone stock. By selling the stock one day before the news was made public, Stewart avoided losses of more than $45,000.

Following an investigation, the Securities Exchange Commission charged Ms. Stewart both civilly and criminally for violating the Security Act of 1933 dealing with insider trading. The court's disposition of the motion to have the criminal charges dismissed follows:

UNITED STATES V. MARTHA STEWART
NO. 03 CR. 717 (S.D. NEW YORK, 2004)

Defendant Martha Stewart has moved for a judgment of acquittal. The motion is granted with respect to Count Nine.

The criminal charges against Stewart arose from Stewart's December 27, 2001 sale of 3,928 shares of stock in ImClone Systems, Inc. ("ImClone"). Im-Clone's then-chief executive officer, Samuel Waksal, was a friend of Stewart's and a client of Stewart's stockbroker at Merrill Lynch, defendant Bacanovic. On December 28, 2001, the day after Stewart sold her shares, ImClone announced that the Food and Drug Administration had rejected the company's application for approval of Erbitux, a cancer-fighting drug that ImClone had previously described as its lead product.

The Indictment alleges that on the morning of December 27, 2001, Bacanovic learned that Waksal and several of his family members were selling their ImClone shares. Bacanovic allegedly instructed his assistant to inform Stewart of the Waksal's trading activity, and she sold her shares in response to that information. According to the Indictment, the defendants then lied about the real reason for Stewart's sale in order to cover up what was possibly an illegal trade. The defendants claimed that they had a standing agreement that Stewart would sell her position in ImClone if the stock fell to $60 per share.

The Indictment charges the defendants with conspiracy, obstruction of an agency proceeding, and making false statements to government officials. Count Nine of the Indictment charges Stewart, the CEO of Martha Stewart Omnimedia, Inc., ("MSLO") with fraud in connection with the purchase and sale of MSLO securities.

Stewart held approximately sixty percent of the shares of stock in MSLO. The jury could reasonably infer from this evidence that Stewart had a significant financial stake in MSLO. Stewart was also aware that certain activities could send a negative message to the market.

The prospectus for MSLO states that: "Our success depends on our brands and their value. Our business would be adversely affected if Martha Stewart's public image or reputation was tarnished. Our continued success and the value of our brand name depend, to a large degree, on the reputation of Martha Stewart."

A reasonable jury could infer from this evidence that Stewart was aware of the importance of her reputation to the continued health of MSLO. With respect to Stewart's state of mind, a jury could infer, based on the falling stock price and the news reports that Stewart believed that the price of MSLO was falling in response to the negative publicity about the SEC investigations.

The Government introduced evidence of the timing, context, and substance of allegedly false public statements which appeared in *The Wall Street Journal*.

Included in an article entitled "Martha Stewart Sold ImClone Stock," is the following paragraph: According to her attorney, Ms. Stewart's sale, involving about 3,000 shares of ImClone, occurred on December 26 or 27. The sale was executed, he said, because Ms. Stewart had a predetermined price at which she planned to sell the stock. That determination, made more than a month before that trade, was to sell if the stock ever went below $60, he said. At the time, the stock was trading at about $60.

The Government contends that a reasonable jury could draw inferences from the evidence that would permit it to find beyond a reasonable doubt that Stewart intended to deceive investors with her statement. Specifically, the Government argues that the evidence supports the inferences that Stewart was aware of the impact of the negative publicity about her ImClone trade on the market value of MSLO securities and on her personal wealth, and that Stewart deliberately directed her statements to investors in MSLO securities.

In viewing the evidence in the light most favorable to the Government, I hold that a reasonable juror could not find beyond a reasonable doubt that Stewart's purpose was to influence the market in MSLO securities.

The Government contends that intent can be drawn from the fact that *The Wall Street Journal* is "the most widely read financial publication in the na-

tion." Specifically, by making the statement to that newspaper, Stewart intended to influence investors with her statement. The Government presented no evidence that Stewart or her lawyer reached out to *The Wall Street Journal* as opposed to other publications. Thus, there is no evidence that Stewart chose the forum for the statement. The fact that *The Wall Street Journal,* as a financial publication, had an interest in an investigation into a stock trade by the well-known CEO of a public company does not evidence Stewart's intent.

For the foregoing reasons, defendant Stewart's motion for a judgment of acquittal on Count Nine of the Indictment is granted.

SECTION 2.6 CONTRACT LAW

We enter into a variety of contracts every day. However, because of their informal nature we rarely think of these agreements as contracts. Buying gas, getting lunch, taking public transportation, or buying a newspaper are examples of agreements entered into by the parties that represent valid contracts. Merely walk out of a restaurant without paying for lunch, and the legal significance of your actions will be quickly realized.

The courts face a dilemma, however, when asked to enforce a promise that seems social in nature. For instance, how should a court decide a case where a high school student sues her prom date who never showed up for the dance? Suppose the student bought a prom dress and had her hair done. Should a court allow her to collect damages from her date in the form of payment for her dress and beauty treatment? Is this the type of agreement that will give rise to an enforceable contract, or is it merely a social agreement?

A **contract** is the exchange of promises voluntarily made by the parties, which agreement is enforceable in court. While the terms may vary from bargain to bargain, five essential elements must be present. They are:

1. an offer
2. acceptance
3. consideration
4. capacity
5. legality

An offer is a proposal by one party (offeror) to the other (offeree) manifesting a willingness to enter into a valid contract.

An acceptance is the unconditional promise by a party to be bound by the terms of the offer. For example, the words "I accept your offer to purchase my car for $15,000" shows intent to be bound by the offer.

Consideration is the third element of a contract and refers to what each party gives up in return for the act or promise of the other. This is called the quid pro quo, or "bargained for exchange."

The courts will not usually disturb a contract freely entered into by the parties of similar bargaining power. Nevertheless, when one of the individuals does not have the capacity to fully understand the ramifications of the contractual obligation, mutual consent to bargain is lacking. The law provides protection to certain groups deemed to lack the capacity to contract. These include children, insane people, and intoxicated individuals.

The last element of a contract requires the purpose and subject matter of the agreement to be legal. A contract is illegal if its performance is criminal, tortuous or against public policy. For instance, a contract to purchase drugs or the agreement to reward a person for assaulting another are illegal contracts and void as a matter of law.

A contract also requires the parties to have a meeting of the minds concerning the material elements of a transaction. What happens if the parties are mistaken as to an element of their bargain? Should that provide the court with the ability to rescind the contract and restore the parties to their original positions? The Restatement (Second) of Contracts provides the following guidance:

When Mistake of Both Parties Make a Contract Voidable

> Where a mistake of both parties at the time of contract was made as to a basic assumption on which the contract was made has a material effect on the agreed exchange of performances, the contract is voidable by the adversely affected party unless he bears the risk of the mistake.

When Mistake of One Party Makes a Contract Voidable

> Where a mistake of one party at the time a contract was made as to a basic assumption on which he made the contract has a material effect on the agreed exchange of performances that is adverse to him, the contract is voidable by him if he does not bear the risk of the mistake, and

> a.   the effect of the mistake is such that enforcement of the contract would be unconscionable, or

> b.   the other party had reason to know of the mistake or his fault caused the mistake

Both When a Party Bears the Risk of a Mistake

> A party bears the risk of mistake when:

> a.   the risk is allocated to him by agreement of the parties, or

b. he is aware, at the time the contract is made, that he has only limited knowledge with respect to the facts to which the mistake relates but treats his limited knowledge as sufficient, or

c. the risk is allocated to him by the court on the ground that it is reasonable in the circumstances to do so.

The following case provides an illustration of the problems involving a mistake and when a party to the transaction can terminate or rescind the contract because of that mistake.

GREEN V. MORRIS
43 S.W.3D 604 (TEX. APP.-WACO, 2001)

What is a mistake? Can you presently have a mistaken belief about future events? What ever the answers to these questions may be in philosophy, the answer takes on a dollar and cents value in the law. The law tells us that a mistaken belief about future events is not the type of mistake that will allow someone

Jason Green was injured when he fell off the trunk of a car driven by his friend, Kerry Morris. Two days later, Jason died. He had incurred hospital bills of approximately $60,000. Jason's parents sued Morris. Morris had liability insurance of $100,000. Ultimately, the Greens unconditionally offered to settle the litigation within policy limits. It was accepted within the time provided.

Prior to the signing of the settlement documents, the hospital that treated Jason, Baylor University Medical Center, filed a hospital lien to perfect a security interest in the proceeds of the settlement. Settlement documents and a check were tendered to the Greens. The Greens refused to sign the release, asserting that because Baylor had filed a hospital lien, a mutual or unilateral mistake had been made that would allow them to avoid the settlement contract.

Morris filed a motion for summary judgment. The Greens responded that they would (not have settled) if they had known that Baylor would file a hospital

lien. The Greens assert that either a mutual or unilateral mistake made the contract voidable.

An agreement may be avoided where the parties contracted under a misconception or mistake of a material fact. Where a mutual mistake exists, the parties are entitled to rescind their contract and be restored to positions held before entering the contract. To avoid the contract, however, the parties must have acted under the same misunderstanding of the same material fact. The party seeking to avoid the contract has the burden of proof to show a mutual mistake. The elements of mutual mistake are: (1) a mistake of fact, (2) held mutually by the parties, and (3) which materially affects the agreed-upon exchange.

When mutual mistake is alleged, the task of the court is not to interpret the language contained in the contract, but to determine whether the contract itself is valid. If it can be established that a contract sets out a bargain that was never made, it will be invalidated.

Most of the cases and legal writers affirm the proposition that equitable relief will be granted against a unilateral mistake when the conditions of remediable mistake are present. These conditions generally are:(1) the mistake is of so great a consequence that to enforce the contract as made would be unconscionable, (2) the mistake relates to a material feature of the contract; 3) the mistake must have been made regardless of the exercise of ordinary care; and (4) the parties can be placed in status quo in the equity sense; in essence, rescission must not result in prejudice to the other party except for the loss of his bargain. There may be other circumstances, not relevant here, which will govern or influence the extension of relief, such as the acts and extent of knowledge of the parties.

[A]n error in predicting a future fact known to be uncertain is not the kind of mistake which will relieve a party from a contract. The Restatement of Contracts says: "Where the parties know that there is doubt in regard to a certain matter and contract on that assumption, the contract is not rendered voidable because one is disappointed in the hope that the facts accord with his wishes."

The Greens have characterized the summary judgment evidence as follows: 1) First, at the time of the (settlement) demand and its subsequent acceptance, no hospital lien was on file for any services rendered to Jason by Baylor. 2) Second, there is no dispute that Baylor could have secured its claimed lien by simply filing its written notice with the county clerk, thus attaching the lien to the proceeds of a settlement by an injured individual arising from an injury for which the person was hospitalized. 3) Third, it is undisputed that the Greens were keenly aware of Baylor's omission at both the time of their demand and its purported acceptance. 4) Fourth, it is also undisputed that the Greens would not have made the demand had written notice of a lien previously been on file. 5) Fifth, and finally, it is undisputed that the Greens, at no time prior to the demand, contemplated, or expected, to pay Baylor any share of the settlement proceeds.

However it is characterized, the Greens had made no mistake about the facts at the time that they (made the offer to settle) nor at the time that it was accepted by Morris. The Greens' only argument is that because Baylor filed a hospital lien after the settlement offer was accepted, thereby attaching a lien to roughly sixty percent of the settlement proceeds, the Greens should be allowed to avoid the settlement agreement. From the Greens' viewpoint, subsequent events have made their settlement less favorable than they had hoped. This is, at most, a mistake about future events. It is not a mistake of existing fact. It is not the type mistake that will allow a party to avoid a contract as a mutual or unilateral mistake.

SECTION 2.7
TORT LAW

A **tort** is a private or civil wrong against an individual for which the court will award money damages. The word "tort" is derived from the Latin term "torquer," meaning "to twist." Torts are classified into the categories of negligence or intentional torts. **Negligence** arises when one fails to act as a reasonable person under the circumstances. Four elements must be established to make out a case of negligence: (1) the defendant must owe a duty, (2) there must be a breach of that duty, (3) that negligence must be the proximate cause of the harm, and (4) damages must flow from the wrongful conduct. For example, a motorist is negligent when the driver loses concentration and unintentionally runs into another car. The motorist did not intentionally try to injure the driver of the second car, however, he will be responsible for money damages in causing the accident.

The plaintiff has the burden of proving all of these elements by the preponderance of the evidence. Suppose Joe Roberts is stopped at a traffic light when Peter Christopher loses control of his vehicle and rams the rear of Joe's car. The force of the impact propels Joe forward and he sustains a whiplash type injury. Is Christopher negligent? Christopher owed a duty to drive his car carefully and avoid hitting another vehicle. Christopher breached that duty by striking the rear of the Roberts' vehicle. Finally, the negligence of Christopher in the operation of the car was the proximate cause of Joe's neck injury causing him to incur medical expenses and conscious pain and suffering.

The last element of a negligence claim is damages. This is the amount of money awarded to an injured person as the result of the wrongful or improper conduct of the defendant. This recovery may take the form of compensatory and punitive damages.

The purpose of compensatory damages is to make an injured party whole by providing a sum of money that would return the aggrieved party to the same position as though nothing had happened. These damages must always have a reasonable relationship to the negligent act of the defendant and cannot be speculative.

When the wrongdoer purposely sets out to harm another, that conduct gives rise to an **intentional tort** and may result in the imposition of money damages. Theories of liability include actions for battery, assault, defamation, false imprisonment, and infliction of emotional distress.

Intentional torts are treated more seriously by the courts and verdicts frequently include an award of **punitive damages,** which sum is to punish the wrongdoer for his actions. These types of claims are generally not covered by insurance.

One must always be mindful, however, that the mere fact someone suffers a loss does not mean that he or she is entitled to recover money. The claimant must prove that another person was at fault in causing the harm and that the law recognizes a theory of liability.

For instance, in **Ali v. Gates, 1998 WL 317584 (W.D. N.Y.),** an individual instituted suit against Bill Gates and a number of others alleging that his constitutional rights were being violated by the defendants, who were trying to murder him through a Windows program hooked to his mind. This case was dismissed by the court because Mr. Ali failed to establish a recognized cause of action under the various theories he asserted in his lawsuit.

Can a person use force to protect his property or will the homeowner be civilly responsible if a trespasser is injured? That is the issue in the landmark case of **Katko v. Briney.**

Marvin Katko v. Edward Briney
183 N.W.2d 657 (Iowa, 1971)

The primary issue presented here is whether an owner may protect personal property in an unoccupied boarded-up farm house against trespassers and thieves by a spring gun capable of inflicting death or serious injury.

At defendants' request plaintiff's action was tried to a jury consisting of residents of the community where defendants' property was located. The jury returned a verdict for plaintiff and against defendants for $20,000 actual and $10,000 punitive damages.

Most of the facts are not disputed. In 1957 defendant, Bertha L. Briney inherited her parents' farmland. Included was an 80-acre tract in southwest Mahaska County where her grandparents and parents had lived. No one occupied the house thereafter.

There occurred a series of trespassing and house-breaking events with loss of some household items, the breaking of windows and "messing up of the property in general."

Defendants boarded up the windows and doors in an attempt to stop the intrusions. They had posted "no trespass" signs on the land. The nearest one was 35 feet from the house. Defendants set a "shot-gun trap" in the north bedroom where they secured it to an iron bed with the barrel pointed at the bedroom door. It was rigged with wire from the doorknob to the gun's trigger so it would fire when the door was opened. Briney first pointed the gun's trigger so an intruder would be hit in the stomach but at Mrs. Briney's suggestion it was lowered to hit the legs. Tin was nailed over the bedroom window. The spring gun could not be seen from the outside. No warning of its presence was posted.

Plaintiff worked regularly as a gasoline station attendant seven miles from the old house and considered it as being abandoned. He knew it had long been uninhabited. Plaintiff and McDonough had been to the premises and found several old bottles and fruit jars which they took and added to their collection of antiques. About 9:30 p.m. they made a second trip to the Briney property. They entered the old house by removing a board from a porch window which was without glass. While McDonough was looking around the kitchen area plaintiff went to another part of the house. As he started to open the north bedroom door the shotgun went off striking him in the right leg above the ankle bone. Much of his leg, including part of the tibia, was blown away.

Plaintiff testified he knew he had no right to break and enter the house with intent to steal bottles and fruit jars therefrom. He further testified he had entered a plea of guilty to larceny in the nighttime of property of less than $20 value from a private building. He stated he had been fined $50 and costs and paroled during good behavior from a 60-day jail sentence.

The main thrust of defendant's defense in the trial court and on this appeal is that "the law permits use of a spring gun in a dwelling or warehouse for the purpose of preventing the unlawful entry of a burglar or thief."

The overwhelming weight of authority, both textbook and case law, supports the trial court's statement of the applicable principles of law.

Prosser on Torts, Third Edition, pages 116-118, states:

> The law has always placed a higher value upon human safety than upon mere rights in property, it is the accepted rule that there is no privilege to use any force calculated to cause death or serious bodily injury to repel the threat to land or chattels unless there is

also such a threat to the defendant's personal safety as to justify a self-defense… Spring guns and other man-killing devices are not justifiable against a mere trespasser, or even a petty thief. They are privileged only against those upon whom the landowner, if he were present in person would be free to inflict injury of the same kind.

Restatement of Torts, section 85, page 180 states: "The value of human life and limb, not only to the individual concerned but also to society, so outweighs the interest of a possessor of land in excluding from it those whom he is not willing to admit thereto that a possessor of land has no privilege to use force intended or likely to cause death or serious harm against another whom the possessor sees is about to enter his premises or meddle with his chattel, unless the intrusion threatens death or serious bodily harm to the occupiers or users of the premises.

The facts in **Allison v. Fiscus, 156 Ohio 120, 100 N.E.2d 237, 44 A.L.R.2d 369,** decided in 1951, are very similar to the case at the bar. There, plaintiff's right to damages was recognized for injuries received when he feloniously broke a door latch and started to enter defendant's warehouse with intent to steal. As he entered a trap of two sticks of dynamite buried under the doorway by defendant owner was set off and plaintiff was seriously injured. The court held the question whether a particular trap was justified as a use of reasonable and necessary force against the trespasser engaged in the commission of a felony should have been submitted to the jury. The Ohio Supreme Court recognized plaintiff's right to punitive or exemplary damages in addition to compensation damages. The jury's findings of fact including a finding defendants acted with malice and with wanton and reckless disregard, as required for an allowance of punitive or exemplary damages, are supported by substantial evidence. We are bound thereby.

Affirmed.

Katko v. Briney clearly demonstrates that a person cannot use force that will inflict death or serious bodily injury in the protection of property. Human life is simply more important than property. In **Commonwealth v. Johnston, 263 A.2d 376 (Pa., 1970)** however, the court was confronted with the issue as to whether a person can use deadly force in order to protect human life. While the killing of another without justification is illegal, a killing is excusable if it is committed in self-defense. This will occur when **(1)** the slayer reasonably believes that he is in imminent danger of great bodily harm, **(2)** he has attempted to flee the harm, and **(3)** deadly force is the only way to protect human life.

While the use of a shotgun in the protection of property is clearly excessive force, is the owner of a store liable for an attack by a vicious dog that is allowed to roam the store at night in order to stop trespassers? Based upon the reasoning in **Katko v. Briney,** the store owner will be liable for the attack. The dog has been kept on the premises for the sole purpose of protecting property by inflicting serious harm to the intruder. Will liability, however, be imposed on a homeowner whose pet dog attacks a burglar that enters a home when no one is present? The answer is no. The dog is not kept at the family dwelling for the sole purpose of attacking people. Dogs are territorial and they will protect their master's home against an intruder.

Will the owner of a dog be liable if the animal bites a guest or if a large playful dog, that has a habit of jumping on people, knocks someone down? The law is well settled that a dog's owner will be liable for the actions of the pet if the owner knows or has good reason to know of the dog's dangerous or vicious propensities and fails to take reasonable measures to protect the guest from the pet's actions. The saying that "every dog is entitled to one bite" is not true. If a dog has displayed a vicious propensity in the past, the owner will be liable to another for a dog bite even if the animal has not bitten anyone previously. Likewise, the law imposes a duty of restraint on the owner of a dog when the owner knows of the animal's playful but dangerous propensity of jumping on people and knocking them down.

SECTION 2.8
ROSEMAN V. TYLER'S
SPORTS BAR AND
GRILL

PROBLEM TWO—B

PARK, BROWN & SMITH, P.C.
ATTORNEYS AT LAW
MEMORANDUM

TO: All Law Clerks

FROM: Peter Smith, Esquire

RE: The Dog Attack

Joe Roberts saw a story in a magazine that catered to the sports bar trade about a breeder in St. Louis who trained dogs to play ball. This prompted Mr. Roberts to come up with a marketing idea for Tyler's Sports Bar and Grill. He would buy a German Shepherd puppy from the breeder in which the dog would then be trained to play football. Joe's idea was to dress the dog in an Eagles uniform and allow the bar patrons to throw a football to the canine.

Joe bought the dog at a cost of $2,000 but had to wait months for delivery because the puppy had to be trained to play the gridiron game. The breeder worked diligently with the puppy and soon the dog was catching every football tossed his way. The dog was even taught to run with the ball to a make shift end zone and toss the pigskin up into the air as a parody of a touchdown celebration. The dog became so proficient with this task that he could toss the ball about 20 feet into the air and catch it on the way down.

Joe took possession of the eighty pound animal which he named "Banner" when it was 8 months old and brought the dog to Tyler's each day dressed in Eagles green. Joe even constructed an end zone in one corner of the bar complete with a goal post and bleachers where patrons could sit and drink while watching sporting events on large screen televisions.

Banner was an instant success. Joe sold replica NFL footballs at a tidy profit which purchases would entitle the patrons to toss the ball to the pooch who would then perform his end zone celebration. When he was finished, the German Shepherd would even pick up the football and bring it back to the person who initially threw it.

Things were going smoothly until a Monday Night Football game involving the Eagles and Redskins. This was also the first time the dog was asked to perform late at night and he seemed out of sorts from the commotion.

In any event, Banner was busy from the moment the game started and fans lined up to toss balls to the dog. By half time, Banner had retrieved more than 100 footballs and was exhausted. Unfortunately, the next toss did him in. Banner retrieved the thrown ball in the end zone but was way off target when he tossed it into the air as part of his end zone celebration. The errant ball landed in the end zone bleachers so Banner dutifully ran after the ball to retrieve it. He jumped over the bleacher wall and landed on the lap of Ira Roseman causing everything to go flying including a cup of hot coffee which scalded the patron. When the customer screamed from being burned, Banner became frightened and bit the customer.

Tyler's Sports Bar and Grill has been sued by Mr. Roseman and we have been asked to defend the bar. I have located the attached case which is the closet thing I could find to fit our fact pattern. Please read the case and let me know if Tyler's is liable to Mr. Roseman.

RAITH V. BLANCHARD
271 GA. APP. 723 (GA. APP., 2005)

Tracey Raith sued Grady and Jennifer Blanchard for damages she allegedly sustained when the Blanchards' dog bit her. The Blanchards subsequently moved for summary judgment. The trial court granted the motion, finding that the Blanchards lacked knowledge of the dog's temperament and that Raith assumed the risk of her injuries. Raith appeals, and for reasons that follow, we reverse.

The evidence shows that, on July 27, 2002, Raith and her husband attended a party at the Blanchards' home. At some point during the evening, Satchel, the Blanchards' Lhasa Apso dog, bit Raith on the lip while Raith was on her knees "at the dog's level," trying to pet the dog. Grady Blanchard and a party guest reported that Satchel growled at Raith as she

approached him at his level. Other persons at the party heard a growl, then turned to see Raith holding her lip.

Katherine Cherry, Raith's mother, testified that she spoke with Jennifer Blanchard after the incident. According to Cherry, Jennifer stated that "she should have warned [Raith] to stay away from the dog." Kathryn Blair, a neighbor of the Blanchards, also testified that prior to July 2002, she saw Satchel running loose in the street and picked him up. At that point, Satchel "went after" her face, trying to bite her. Blair dropped the dog, but Satchel "turned around and nicked at [her] hand" with his teeth, drawing a small amount of blood. Blair never mentioned the incident to the Blanchards. On another occasion in late 2001 or early 2002, Blair attended a party at the Blanchards' home and asked Jennifer where the dogs were. Jennifer responded that she did not allow the dogs in the house when company was there because Satchel could bite somebody.

The Blanchards disputed Blair's testimony, asserted that Satchel had not bitten anyone before he bit Raith, and claimed that they had never had a problem with him. Several individuals who occasionally cared for Satchel also offered testimony regarding his mild-mannered and friendly behavior.

A dog owner is liable for damages only if the owner has knowledge that the dog has the propensity to do the particular act which caused injury to the complaining party. **Wade v. American Nat. Ins. Co., 246 Ga. App. 458 (2000).** A plaintiff must show that the dog had the propensity to do the act and that the owner had knowledge of that propensity. Although this traditionally has been described as the "first bite rule," the rule does not literally require a first bite. Instead, the true test of liability' is the owner's superior knowledge of his dog's temperament.

The Blanchards argue, and the trial court found, that Raith presented no evidence that Satchel had previously exhibited vicious behavior or that the Blanchards possessed superior knowledge of such behavior. We disagree.

Raith offered evidence that Satchel bit or "nicked" Blair on the hand before July 2002, raising a question of fact regarding Satchel's propensity to bite. Furthermore, although Blair did not tell the Blanchards about this incident, Jennifer Blanchard's statement to Blair that she did not allow Satchel in the house with guests because he "could bite somebody," as well as her admission to Raith's mother that she should have warned Raith to stay away from Satchel, raise a jury question as to whether the Blanchards knew that Satchel had a propensity to bite. See: **Harper v. Robinson, 263 Ga. App. 727 (2003)** (plaintiff failed to show that dog had propensity to harm people where evidence demonstrated that dog had not previously bitten or attacked another person); **Supan v.**

Griffin, 238 Ga. App. 404 (1999) (although dog bite victim apparently presented no evidence that dog had previously bitten another person, dog owner's prior statement to neighbor that neighbor should do "whatever was necessary ... to keep [owner's] dogs from attacking and off of [neighbor's] property" raised genuine issue of material fact as to owner's knowledge of his dogs' tendency to attack humans); **Johnson v. Kvasny, 230 Ga. App. 162 (1998)** (trial court erred in granting summary judgment to dog owner in dog bite case because owner's statement to mother of bite victim that owner "knew that something like this would happen" provided some proof that owner knew of dog's propensity to inflict harm in the manner in which victim was injured).

We recognize that the Blanchards presented evidence that Satchel was friendly, well behaved, and had never caused a problem before he bit Raith. Construed favorably to Raith, however, the disputed evidence presents a jury question as to the Blanchards' superior knowledge of Satchel's temperament.

In granting summary judgment to the Blanchards, the trial court alternatively found that Raith assumed the risk of her injuries by continuing to interact with Satchel after he growled at her. Several people at the party reported that Satchel growled at Raith just before biting her. And Jennifer Blanchard testified that earlier in the evening, Raith told Jennifer that Satchel had growled when she tried to kiss him.

The defense of assumption of the risk "bars recovery when the evidence shows that the plaintiff, without coercion of circumstances, chooses a course of action with full knowledge of its danger and while exercising a free choice as to whether to engage in the act or not. To establish this defense, the Blanchards must show that Raith had actual knowledge of the danger that Satchel might bite her, understood and appreciated the risks associated with that danger, and voluntarily exposed herself to the risks. Whether a plaintiff assumed the risk is ordinarily a jury question, except in cases involving plain, palpable, and undisputed evidence.

The Blanchards argue that Raith assumed the risk as a matter of law by ignoring Satchel's growl and approaching him at his level. Under the law, however, barking and growling amount, at most, to what has been characterized as menacing behavior. Standing alone, such behavior does not demonstrate a vicious propensity or put a dog owner on notice that the dog will bite. We thus fail to see how Satchel's growl gave Raith actual notice, as a matter of law, that he might bite if she approached him.

Because a dog's growl does not put the dog owner on notice of the dog's propensity to bite, it can hardly be viewed as plain and palpable evidence that a third party actually knew about and appreciated the danger that the dog might bite. Accordingly, the trial court erred in granting summary judgment to the Blanchards on their assumption of the risk defense.

Judgment reversed.

ANSWER SHEET
PROBLEM TWO—B

Name   **Please Print Clearly**

1. Is the bar liable for the dog's actions in jumping into the stands and injuring Mr. Roseman?

_____

_____

_____

_____

_____

_____

_____

_____

2. Is it a defense that the dog was not vicious and never bit anyone before?

_____

_____

_____

_____

_____

_____

_____

_____

_____

_____

3. Does it matter that this was the first time the dog went into the end zone stands to retrieve the ball? Please explain.

_____

_____

_____

_____

_____

_____

_____

_____

_____

_____

_____

_____

_____

_____

_____

_____

_____

_____

_____

SECTION 2.9
PROPERTY LAW

Property law deals with the rights and duties that arise out of the ownership or possession of real property and personal property. **Real property** includes land and everything attached to the land. For instance, a building, a tree, or ground are all considered part of the realty. **Personal property** consists of all other property and would include a book, a car, money, or even a folding chair. In other words, personal property includes everything not attached to the land.

Personal property is further sub-divided into tangible and intangible property. **Tangible property** is a physical object, such as this textbook. **Intangible property**, on the other hand, is personal property that is not a physical object. The ownership of intangible property is usually evidenced by a legal document. Examples of such property include a patent or invention, a copyright for published material, or a trademark to identify a manufacturer or merchant's product.

The purchase of a home has certain inherent problems. Disputes frequently arise as to what was included in the sale. When the buyer inspected the home, a crystal chandelier hung in the foyer. At the time of settlement, a plastic fixture replaced the chandelier. The seller refuses to give the buyer the chandelier, claiming that it is a family heirloom worth several thousand dollars. The buyer maintains that the fixture was part of the realty since it was on display at the time the home was inspected. Who is correct? The answer will depend upon whether the item is real or personal property.

In **O'Donnell v. Schneeweis, 73 D. & C.2d 400 (Chester County Ct. of Common Pleas, Pa., 1975),** the court offered guidelines as to what constitutes a fixture that would be included in the sale of real estate. A **fixture** is an item of personal property which, by reason of its being attached to a building, becomes part of the real estate. In reaching this conclusion, the court noted that personal property used in connection with real estate falls into one of three classes.

First, furniture, such as a couch or table, always remains personal property; second, fixtures, or those things so affixed to the property that they cannot be removed without material injury to the real estate are considered real property; and third, those things which, although physically connected to the real estate, are affixed in such a manner that they may be removed without destroying or materially injuring the item to be removed. This third category of property becomes part of the realty or remains personal property, depending upon the intention of the parties at the time of annexation.

For example, wall-to-wall carpeting remains as a fixture, but a mirror or picture attached to a wall by a wire is considered personal property. If the mirror was affixed in such a way that it provided the impression that it was meant to be permanent, it would be considered a fixture that remained with the house. Such an example would include a mirror that was glued to the wall and could not be removed without causing damage to the wall.

The following case is an example of a dispute that can arise in the sale of a property and whether an item is part of the real estate or personal property that the former owner can remove without repercussions.

KENT V. SEXTON
1978 WL 217424 (OHIO APP. 5 DIST.)

This case involves the ownership of three chandeliers, two in the main lobby and one in the Matador Room, all in the Grandville Inn. The father of Sarah Sexton, Defendant-Appellant, owned and built the Grandville Inn. He died and she came into ownership. Two of the chandeliers were in the Grandville Inn when Sara Sexton came into ownership. She placed one of comparable likeness in the Matador Room. All three were replacements and the smaller chandeliers were preserved and stored in the Grandville Inn when they were removed and the new ones installed.

Subsequent to Sara Sexton's acquiring the assets of the Grandville Inn, the Grandville Restaurant, Inc. was formed and either Sara Sexton or the Grandville Restaurant, Inc. owned all the assets known as Grandville Inn.

A mortgage was given to secure a loan from the Newark Trust Company. A mortgage foreclosure action was filed in the Common Pleas Court, which found a balance due of $114,727. The mortgage was ordered foreclosed and the Grandville Inn was sold at auction to the highest bidder, E. Clark Morrow, trustee.

E. Clark Morrow, Trustee, conveyed the premises to Paul F. Kent, beneficiary. The mortgage indebtedness was paid to the bank and a surplus of $51,095.13 was paid to Grandville Restaurant, Inc. No reference was made in any of the foreclosure proceedings as to the three chandeliers.

Prior to the auction, Sexton did conduct Plaintiff-Appellee, Kent, through Grandville Inn as a prospective purchaser after it had been appraised. The chandeliers in question were in place. Other items being retained by Sara Jones Sexton were mentioned but nothing was said by anyone about the chandeliers being either reserved or going with the property. After showing the property to Plaintiff-Appellee and his son, and after the appraisal but prior to the sale at the Courthouse, Sexton had the three chandeliers removed by Holland Electric Company and took the three out of storage and had them installed in their former place.

There is no question that the three chandeliers were attached to the ceiling of the Grandville Inn and lighted by a wall switch. Plaintiff-Appellee, Kent, was not again shown the premises and first noticed after the sale that the chandeliers were missing. The instant action was commenced by Kent to have the chandeliers replaced in the Inn.

The trial court found the nature of the fixtures and their attachment to be such that by reason of their annexation to and use of association of the real property, they were a part thereof and declared Sexton estopped from claiming the three light fixtures.

The buyer, Kent, did, prior to sale, view the premises showed to him by Sexton. From the view he would have reason to believe that the fixtures were annexed as a part of the realty and the same were not included among the items which Sexton stated would be reserved.

Sexton's later removal of the chandeliers was an act which a person shown the property would not have reason to expect and the sale being at the Courthouse there was no opportunity to view the premises at the time and location of the bidding. For the reasons set forth, the judgment appealed from is affirmed.

SECTION 2.10
FAMILY LAW

The institution of marriage no longer enjoys the same favor that it did historically, and more and more couples are establishing family units without much formality or binding commitment. Regardless of how the family unit is created, issues regarding children, assets and benefits arise. **Family law** encompasses the rights, duties, and obligations involving marriages, civil unions, domestic partnerships, divorce, custody, child support, paternity, and other family related issues.

This category of private law is exclusively regulated by state law whose rules and regulations vary from jurisdiction to jurisdiction. There are, however, a number of basic concepts that remain constant.

A **marriage** is a contract between a man and a woman whereby they take each other to be husband and wife for life. Massachusetts was the first state that varied this definition by allowing people of the same sex to marry and New Jersey has held that same-sex couples must be afforded the same rights as married individuals. Washington, D.C., New Hampshire, Connecticut, Iowa and Vermont have also legalized same-sex marriages. New York, New Jersey and Rhode Island recognize same-sex marriages performed in other states. A handful of other jurisdictions recognize **domestic partnerships** in which an unwed couple, including those of the same sex, can acquire legal rights and protections. Usually this arrangement can only have legal standing if the parties register with the state by filing a Declaration of Domestic Partnership or similar document. While registration does not create a marriage, it does secure a number of rights such as the ability to collect insurance benefits from a partner's employer. It is anticipated that the Supreme Court will eventually decide the issue.

First time marriages have a 50% failure rate and the legal dissolution of a marriage is called a **divorce.** Historically, this dissolution could only be accomplished by an innocent spouse who had to prove that his or her partner was at fault in causing the termination of the marriage by engaging in cruel and barbarous treatment, desertion, indignities, adultery or some other type of conduct that caused the marriage to fail. This rigid requirement has changed and partners are now allowed to obtain no-fault divorces. For instance, Pennsylvania allows a couple to file for divorce if the marriage is irretrievably broken.

An **annulment** occurs when there is a legal impediment to a marriage so that the union is declared null and void from its inception. For example, this occurs when one of the parties is still married to another at the time of the subsequent marriage, impotence, insanity or fraud.

As part of a divorce proceeding, the court will occasionally award **alimony** and **child support.** These terms mean different things. Alimony refers to the legal obligations of an individual to provide periodic payments for the support and maintenance of the spouse or former spouse. On the other hand, child support is that sum of money awarded to the custodial parent or caregiver for the support of a minor child for such things as food, shelter, and medical expenses. The amount awarded will depend upon the financial resources of each parent. Some states, such as Pennsylvania, have enacted support guidelines which try to provide an objective and uniform way to establish the amount of money to be awarded by looking at the net monthly income of each parent.

Today's society has become more attuned to the financial consequence of a divorce so some couples enter into **prenuptial agreements.** This is nothing more than a contract entered into before the marriage or civil union that spells out the financial consequences if the union fails.

The term **palimony** was first coined in a suit between actor, Lee Marvin, by his live-in companion, Michelle Marvin. Even though the actor was still married to another woman, Michelle maintained that the parties had entered into an oral agreement when they started living together for the actor to pay support for the rest of Michelle's life. Palimony has now come to mean support and division of property given to a non-married partner based upon a contract entered into by the parties before they separate.

The following case involves a claim against the late Johnnie Cochran, Jr. for palimony based upon **Marvin v. Marvin, 18 Cal.3d 660 (1976).** The issue is whether the parties have to live together on a full-time basis to justify an award of palimony.

Patricia Cochran v. Johnnie Cochran, Jr.
89 Cal. App. 4th 283 (Cal. App., 2001)

This is the third appeal between appellant Patricia Cochran (appellant) and respondent Johnnie Cochran, Jr. (respondent) arising out of their long-term, nonmarital relationship.

Appellant and respondent began their relationship in 1966, at a time when respondent was still married to his first wife. Appellant later changed her surname to match respondent's. In 1973, the parties' son was born. In 1974, appellant and respondent bought a house in North Hollywood. Title was placed in both their names. Respondent also owned a home on Hobart Street. He and appellant split their living time between the two homes. Respondent stayed with appellant and their son at the North Hollywood

home from two to four nights a week. He kept clothes there and took meals at the house. Respondent held himself out to the world as appellant's husband. In 1978, respondent divorced his first wife.

In 1983, they experienced troubles after appellant learned respondent was unfaithful. On October 21, 1983, they signed a property settlement agreement. Pursuant to the agreement, respondent quitclaimed to appellant all his interest in their North Hollywood house. He agreed, among other things, to pay child support of $350 each month, and to provide medical and dental insurance for their son. The agreement was expressly limited to claims then existing. It did not include a release of future claims.

Within one to three weeks of signing the settlement agreement, respondent told appellant he wanted to keep things as they had been before. He also promised to care for her "financially, emotionally and legally" for the rest of her life. In return, she agreed to maintain their home and care for respondent and their son. After that time, he continued to live with appellant and her son "as he had before."

In 1985, respondent married his second wife. Between 1984 and January 1993, appellant worked for a company named Ipson. During those years, respondent helped pay for appellant's expenses. He gave her cash and paid her bills as needed. During those years, respondent "paid child support for their son and gave me money whenever I needed it."

At respondent's behest, on or about January 1993, appellant left her job at Ipson. After that, in accord with the support agreement, respondent provided regular, monthly support checks for appellant. Respondent also made direct deposits to appellant's bank account of between $3,500 and $4,000 each month. Respondent concedes he provided regular support for appellant after she left her job, but contends he agreed to do so at his son's request only until appellant got another job.

Respondent contends that the support agreement is unenforceable because he and appellant did not cohabitate, or live together. Viewing the evidence in appellant's favor, it appears that before entering the 1983 settlement and support agreements, respondent stayed at the North Hollywood house two to four nights a week. Appellant and the parties' son sometimes stayed at respondent's house on Hobart Street. Appellant stated that after respondent made his support promises, he continued to live with her as he had before. However, from her deposition testimony it is apparent that after respondent remarried in 1985, he stayed at the house less often.

The **Marvin** court held "that adults who voluntarily *live together* and engage in sexual relations are nonetheless as competent as any other persons to contract respecting their earnings and property

rights." **Marvin v. Marvin, 18 Cal.3d at 674.** So long as the agreement does not depend upon meretricious sexual relations for its consideration, or so long as that portion of the consideration may be severed from other proper forms of consideration, such agreements are enforceable.

In **Taylor v. Fields (1986) 178 Cal. App.3d 653 (1986),** the court seized upon the "live together" reference in Marvin to hold that a dead man's mistress, who never lived with the decedent, was not entitled to enforce their purported Marvin agreement. The Taylor court held that cohabitation was a prerequisite to recovery under Marvin. Because the appellant's agreement in Taylor rested upon an illicit sexual relationship for its consideration, it was not enforceable.

Taylor was followed by **Bergen v. Wood 14 Cal. App. 4th 854 (1993).** The plaintiff in Bergen had a long-term sexual relationship with the decedent, acting as his hostess and social companion. Though he had supposedly promised to support the plaintiff, they never lived together. The **Bergen** court noted that cohabitation was required under **Marvin** because from cohabitation flows the rendition of domestic services, which services amount to lawful consideration for a contract between the parties. We make the additional observation that if cohabitation were not a prerequisite to recovery, every dating relationship would have the potential for giving rise to such claims, a result no one favors." Citing both **Marvin and Taylor,** the **Bergen** court noted that recovery under Marvin "requires a showing of a stable and significant relationship arising out of cohabitation." Because the plaintiff never lived with her decedent, it was impossible to sever the sexual component of their relationship from other appropriate considerations.

Citing **Taylor** and **Bergen,** Johnnie Cochran contends that his relationship with appellant did not involve cohabitation, since the evidence showed that he spent as little as one night a week at appellant's house after their property settlement agreement was reached in 1983. As a result, he characterizes their relationship as no more than "dating." On the other hand, appellant relies on **Bergen's** statement that cohabitation was in order to establish lawful consideration through the performance of domestic services. Since appellant provided such services, she contends there was lawful consideration even absent cohabitation.

We conclude that the rationale of **Marvin** is satisfied by a cohabitation arrangement that is less than full-time. Both **Taylor** and **Bergen** considered claims by parties who served as the mistress or girlfriend of their respective decedents. Neither plaintiff had ever cohabitated with their respective decedents. Moreover, neither decision considered whether anything less than a full-time living arrangement was necessary to show cohabitation. By contrast, in the present case, when respondent supposedly entered the support agreement in November of 1983, he and appellant had shared a relationship for approximately 17 years. That relationship produced a son, whom they were raising together. They held themselves out to the world as husband and wife. Appellant legally changed her surname to respondent's. They had jointly owned their home until respondent quit-claimed his interest as part of their settlement agree-ment. Appellant performed a variety of domestic chores for respondent, including raising their son and maintaining the house. Respondent "spent family time there" and "slept there on a regular basis."

The purpose of **Marvin** was to permit parties to a significant and stable relationship to contract concerning their earnings and property rights. So long as the agreement does not rest upon illicit meretricious consideration, the parties may order their economic affairs as they choose. To require nothing short of full-time cohabitation before enforcing an agreement would defeat the reasonable expectations of persons who may clearly enjoy a significant and stable relationship arising from cohabitation, albeit less than a full-time living arrangement. Certainly the rationale of **Marvin** does not support such a result.

Here, the parties had shared a long-term, stable and significant relationship. In this context, evidence that they lived together two to four days a week both before and at the time they entered their **Marvin** agreement is sufficient to raise a triable issue of fact that they cohabitated under **Marvin**.

SECTION 2.11
VIOLATIONS OF PUBLIC
AND PRIVATE LAW

Can one incident give rise to a violation of both public and private law? The answer is yes. This is a frequent occurrence in situations involving criminal misconduct. For instance, an intoxicated person who is involved in an accident may be criminally prosecuted for drunken driving and sued civilly by the aggrieved party for personal injury. An election of remedies between public and private law need not be made, since both forms of action may be pursued. The government prosecutes the criminal case in the name of the State, and the aggrieved party is merely a witness. A civil lawsuit may be instituted for the same misconduct by the individual harmed to seek monetary compensation. Each suit is independent of the other.

This distinction is demonstrated by the Robert Blake criminal and civil trials. The former actor was criminally prosecuted in December of 2004 for the murder of his wife but was found not guilty. Following that acquittal, the three children of his wife filed a civil lawsuit against Blake to recover money for the wrongful death of their mother, Bonny Lee Bakley. Much of the same evidence used during the criminal prosecution was presented in the civil trial. However the lower burden of proof for a civil trial, by a preponderance of the evidence, allowed the jury to find the former actor responsible for the murder of his wife, and award her children $30 million dollars in damages.

Tual v. Blake
2008 WL 1838617 (Cal. App., 2 Dist.)

Robert Blake appeals a judgment awarding the administrator of the estate of his deceased wife, Bonny Lee Bakley, $30 million for her wrongful death.

Blake began acting as a child and performed in movies and on television for many years. He was single when he met Bakley in 1999, and they began a sexual relationship. Bakley lived in Little Rock, Arkansas at the time. She ran a mail-order business selling nude and seminude photographs of herself to older men and promising to meet them. She had three children. She was on probation and confined to the State of Arkansas.

Bakley visited Blake in Los Angeles for sexual liaisons. She also carried on a relationship with Christian Brando during the same time period. She had a previous relationship with Jerry Lee Lewis and had named a daughter Jeri Lee Lewis after him.

Bakley informed Blake that she was pregnant. Blake encouraged her to abort the pregnancy and offered to pay her $250,000 to do so, but she refused. Blake and Bakley visited a doctor together when she was three months pregnant. Blake then discontinued all contact.

Bakley gave birth to a baby girl in June 2000 and named the child Christian Shannon Brando. Bakley told her daughter that she selected that name to make Blake jealous. She later changed the name to Rosie Lenore Sophia Blake. Blake saw the baby shortly after she was born, during Bakley's visit to Los Angeles, and his attitude changed. A DNA test performed in September 2000 confirmed that Blake was the father.

Blake sought to obtain custody of the child. William Jordan, a private investigator hired by Blake, suggested that Blake encourage Bakley to leave the baby with Blake for a few days and that Blake not return the child. Accordingly, during Bakley's visit in September 2000, Blake suggested leaving Rosie at his house with an associate who was posing as a nurse while he and Bakley went out to eat. After Blake and Bakley left the house, Blake called the "nurse" and told her to take the baby to her own home. She complied. Blake later met with her, recovered the baby, and took the baby to his adult daughter's home.

(Eventually,) Blake and Bakley agreed to get married… (and they) ate dinner together at Vitello's Restaurant on May 4, 2001. They entered the restaurant and sat in a booth. Blake was carrying a gun and put it on the seat beside him under a sweatshirt. They left the restaurant together…Bakley was found in the passenger seat of Blake's car with gunshot entry wounds to her right cheek and right shoulder. The murder weapon, a German Walther pistol, was found in a landfill the next day after the contents of the dumpster were emptied there. Blake was arrested and prosecuted for murder and was acquitted of the murder count.

Blanchard E. Tual, as administrator of the Bakley estate, filed a complaint against Blake in April 2002, alleging wrongful death. The complaint alleges that he shot Bakley to death on May 4, 2001.

The trial began …(and) Blake testified that he and Bakley returned to the car after dinner. He quickly realized that he had left his gun in the restaurant and ran back to the restaurant. He entered by the front door, found the gun on the floor under the dinner table, put it in his pocket, and left by the front door. He returned to his car, opened the door and noticed that Bakley was slumped on the center console and appeared to be sleeping. He spoke to her, and shook her when she did not respond. Then he noticed blood, closed the car door, and ran for help.

Frank Minucci's testimony from Blake's criminal trial was read to the jury. Minucci is a former "street guy" who …(did) "a lot of bad guy stuff," until he met his wife, found God, and became a minister. He became an actor and performed the role of a mafia boss in Carlito's Way. Minucci testified that Blake once sent him $500 cash in an envelope and then another $500 and said that he had something for Minucci to do. Blake complained about a woman who Blake would break up with and then get back together with again, said that she was a "f'ing bitch" who was "doing filthy things," and that Minucci should scare her, and that he did not care how Minucci did it…He said that Blake was screaming about some broad that got him by the balls. She's saying the kid is his.… And I said to him, Bobby, what are you talking about? You want me to whack somebody. And I said, "If you're talking about whacking somebody, you got the wrong guy. I don't do these things anymore."

Blake denied asking Minucci to intimidate a woman, sending him $500, telling him that he had "something really heavy for him to do," telling him that "some broad" had him "by the balls," or discussing Bakley with him at all. Blake also denied other statements made by Minucci and stated that their conversations were very few and brief.

After several weeks of testimony and approximately two weeks of deliberations, the jury returned a verdict, finding that Blake had intentionally caused Bakley's death. The jury awarded the plaintiff $30 million.

A verdict may be vacated on a new trial motion because of juror misconduct that materially affected the substantial rights of a party. A party moving for a new trial on the ground of juror misconduct must establish both that misconduct occurred and that the misconduct was prejudicial.

Blake contends evidence of the following alleged misconduct requires a new trial: (1) juror Severson concealed a material fact during voir dire by failing to disclose her daughter's murder conviction and incarceration; and (2) juror Elias admitted that he could not hear a large part of the testimony due to his hearing impairment.

Evidence filed in support of the new trial motion showed that juror Severson's daughter had been convicted of second degree murder and was incarcerated at the time of trial. During voir dire, counsel asked, "is there any of you who have or were in trouble either civilly, like in this case, or criminally." Severson did not raise her hand. Counsel later asked, "Has anyone had any experience with the legal system that left them with a bad taste in your mouth, and that would include small claims?" Severson did not indicate that she had.

In our view, the record supports the trial court's conclusion that juror Severson's failure to disclose her daughter's conviction and incarceration in response to these questions was not misconduct. The questions regarding "problems with the law" and legal "troubles" related to those of the jurors themselves, rather than those of the jurors' family members. There is no evidence that Severson was implicated in her daughter's crime or that she suffered any threat of civil liability or criminal prosecution. The question regarding any "experience with the legal system" might include a juror's experience as the mother of a criminal defendant, but there is no evidence that Severson regarded her daughter's prosecution as unfair or that the experience undermined her confidence in the legal system or otherwise "left … a bad taste in [her] mouth."

A juror's inattentiveness is a form of misconduct that may justify a new trial. The duty to listen carefully during the presentation of evidence is among the most elementary of a juror's obligations. Each juror should attempt to follow the trial proceedings and to evaluate the strengths and weaknesses of the evidence and arguments adduced by each side so that the jury's ultimate determinations of the factual issues presented to it may be based on the strongest foundation possible.

Juror Elias's difficulty hearing the testimony was akin to a juror's inattentiveness in that it resulted in his missing some portions of the trial. We conclude that any misconduct in this regard was prejudicial only if it resulted in his missing material portions of the trial. Juror Elias's declaration that he "told other jurors that [he] was having difficulty hearing some of the testimony" at unspecified times during the trial did not establish that he missed important testimony, as opposed to testimony of little or no practical importance, and therefore establishes no substantial likelihood of prejudice and does not justify a new trial.

SECTION 2.12 REVIEW CASES

1. Lawmakers from Virginia have approved specialty license plates for a number of organizations for many years. However, the state legislature refused to allow the Sons of Confederate Veterans to obtain license plates that contained a rebel flag logo because it might offend African-Americans. Does this action by the lawmakers violate the Sons of the Confederate Veterans' First Amendment freedom of speech rights?

2. Morris released a computer program known as a "worm" on the internet which spread and multiplied, eventually causing computers at various educational institutions to crash or cease functioning. Morris was charged with violating the *Computer Fraud and Abuse Act* which punishes anyone who intentionally accesses, without authorization, a category of computers known as "federal interest computers," or prevents authorized use of information in such computers. Morris argues that the government did not prove that he had the necessary mens rea to have committed the computer crime since it was necessary for the government to show not only that (1) he intended the unauthorized access of a federal interest computer, but also (2) that he intended to prevent others from using it. The government argued that the criminal intent requirement required them to prove only one part of the crime. Which side do you believe is correct? **United States v. Robert Morris, 928 F.2d 504 (1991).**

3. Following the entry of a civil judgment against O.J. Simpson, Fred Goldman attempted to seize a grand piano at Simpson's home in order to help satisfy the multi-million dollar judgment. O.J. Simpson's mother testified that the piano was given to her as a gift in 1984. Although the grand piano was still in the football player's house, Simpson claimed that it belonged

to his mother, and that she was the only one who could play the musical instrument. Who do you think should obtain possession of this item of personal property? **Ronald Goldman v. O.J. Simpson, Los Angles Superior Court (Sept., 1997).**

4. Bernard Getz boarded a New York subway and sat down on a bench. Four individuals surrounded Getz and asked him for five dollars. Getz stood up and fired four shots striking the individuals that surrounded him. Getz told the police that two youths stood to his left and two stood to his right. After he was asked for the money, Getz said the four had smiles on their faces and they wanted to "play with me." While he did not think that any of the people had a gun, Getz had a fear of harm based upon prior experiences of being "maimed." Will Getz have any liability for using deadly force in either a criminal or civil context? **People of New York v. Bernard Getz, 68 N.Y.2d 96 (Ct. App. N.Y., 1986).**

SECTION 2.13
INTERNET REFERENCES

For more information on public and private law, see the following internet sites:

A. **Criminal Law**

- **www.fbi.gov/homepage.htm**
  The Federal Bureau of Investigation's website provides information on major criminal investigations, their most wanted-list, and crime reports.

- **www.thebestdefense.com**
  This criminal law firm's website provides information about various crimes and the judicial process.

- **www.talkjustice.com**
  At this site, a person can post notes on message boards about the criminal justice system and access "Cybrary," an online library which provides 12,000 links to different websites relating to criminal law.

- **www.law.indiana.edu/law/crimlaw.html**
  Indiana University School of Law at Bloomington provides downloads of short lectures on different aspects of criminal law, such as double jeopardy and being called as a witness in a criminal trial.

B. **Constitutional Law**

- **www.usconstitution.net/index.html**
  This site focuses on the U.S. Constitution and provides a general overview of this historic document, its history, and other related information.

- **www.supremecourtus.gov**
  The Supreme Court's official site is located at this address. It provides access to court opinions, rules, and other general information about the Supreme Court.

C. **Administrative law**

- **www.law.fsu.edu/library/admin.com**
  The American Bar Association's Administrative Procedure Database is located at this address. The site provides information about the organization, federal and state resources, and other related links.

D. **Contract Law**

- **www.ira-wg.com/library/contract.html**
  This site is devoted to issues involving contract law.

E. **Tort Law**

- **www.itslegal.com/infonet/injury/injurymain.html**
  This link provides answers to frequently asked questions about tort issues, specifically involving transportation accidents, injury to property, medical malpractice, and defamation.

- **www.prairielaw.com**
  This web address provides a general overview of personal injury claims and the law of torts. Information is provided about the statute of limitations, airline liability, products liability, and wrongful death.

F. **Property Law**

- **http://propertymart.net**
  Advertisements and other related links dealing with real estate may be accessed through this site

KEY TERMS

Acceptance

Administrative Agencies

Administrative Law

Alimony

Annulment

Article

Beyond a Reasonable Doubt

Bill of Rights

Burden of Proof

Capacity

Child Support

Commerce Clause

Compensatory Damages

Consideration

Constitutional Amendment

Constitutional Law

Constitutional Relativity

Contract

Crime

Criminal Intent

Criminal Law

Damages

Divorce

Domestic Partnership

Duty of Care

Family Law

Federal Register

Felony

Fixture

Intangible Property

Intentional Tort

Legality

Marriage

Mens Rea

Misdemeanor

Negligence

Offer

Palimony

Personal Property

Prenuptial Agreement

Private Law

Proximate Cause

Public Law

Real Property

Summary Offense

Tangible Property

Tort

Treason

CHAPTER 3

CONTRACTS

SECTION 3.1
INTRODUCTION

"A verbal contract isn't worth the paper it is written on."

–Samuel Goldwyn

People and businesses enter into a number of contracts each day unaware of the legal nature of their bargains. Routine activities such as purchasing supplies, paying an employee's salary, or offering health insurance to workers involve contractual obligations. A buyer of goods who demands the return of the purchase price because the product does not live up to expectations is really asserting a breach of contract claim.

A **contract** is the voluntary exchange of promises between two or more entities creating a legal obligation that is enforceable in court. Most agreements are informal but people do occasionally enter into written contracts for things such as the purchase of a car or a home. Business transactions tend to be more formal because of the use of preprinted forms, so more of these contracts are in writing. Regardless of the formality of the agreement or the purchase price, the following elements must be present in every contract:

1. Offer
2. Acceptance
3. Consideration
4. Capacity
5. Legality

The penalty for a breach of contract may range from nothing to substantial money damages. The contract may even dictate the consequences in the event of a breach of the agreement such as the forfeiture of the deposit or a set dollar amount. The contract may also specify how the dispute is to be resolved. For example, a contract may provide for binding arbitration or leave the parties to traditional court remedies, but specify the place where the lawsuit must be filed.

SECTION 3.2
KINDS OF CONTRACTS

For the most part, the law of contracts has developed based upon state law. These legal tenets may be part of the common law of a particular jurisdiction or may arise through various state statutes such as the **Uniform Commercial Code**. This is a uniform act that regulates the sale of goods and certain other commercial transactions.

Contracts may be characterized in several different ways. The agreement may be classified as a bilateral or unilateral contract, depending on the number of promises involved. Contracts may be expressed or implied, depending on how the terms of the contract are set forth. Contracts may also be classified as valid, void, voidable, or unenforceable, based on their validity and enforceability.

Unilateral and Bilateral Contracts

Although contracts involve at least two parties, not all contracts involve two promises. When one party makes a promise in exchange for an act, a **unilateral contract** is formed. For example, the promise of a reward for the return of a lost ring forms the basis of a unilateral contract. Many people may search for the object, but only the person who returns the ring will receive the money from the owner. Also, once the party to whom a unilateral offer has been extended starts to perform the requested act, that person must be given a reasonable time to complete the job. For instance, if a homeowner tells the neighbors that he will give $1,000 to the first person who paints his house and a neighbor starts painting the walls of the dwelling later in the day, the homeowner cannot revoke the offer.

A **bilateral contract** is created when the parties exchange mutual promises to do some future act. For example, if Joe Roberts promises to sell his pet bear to a zoo for $5,000 and the zoo promises to buy the animal, a bilateral contract is formed at that moment in time. Both the buyer and seller are bound by their promises and are under a legal obligation to perform under the terms of their agreement. If Joe subsequently changes his mind, the zoo may sue him for the loss of the bargain. Most contracts are bilateral and not unilateral.

Can a high school student sue her date if he stands her up for the prom? Is this agreement of the type that gives rise to an enforceable contract or is it merely a social engagement that only has moral significance? A student from Pennsylvania successfully sued her date when he was a no-show at her senior prom. The school district required all out-of-town prom dates to sign a written agreement to stay at the dance and see the student home after the prom. The judge ruled that the date's failure to attend the prom was a breach of contract and the high school student was awarded $548 for her dress and court costs.

When one party to a pending marriage has significant wealth, it is a common practice for the parties to enter into a prenuptial agreement concerning what will happen to the assets in the event of a divorce or death of a party. An agreement to marry dependant upon the execution of a prenuptial agreement, is an example of a unilateral contract. However, do these types of agreements have to be fair in their financial terms? That is the issue in **Sattler v. Sattler**.

SATTLER V. SATTLER
2008 WL 4613589 (TENN. CT. APP. 2008)

William Sattler and Linda Gay Sattler met at a party hosted by his neighbors. At the time, Mr. Sattler was 74 years old and Mrs. Sattler was 49. Upon first seeing her, Mr. Sattler immediately identified Mrs. Sattler as "a very nice looking lady" and he vigorously pursued her during the party. At the end of the evening, she gave him her phone number. Mr. Sattler continued to vigorously pursue Mrs. Sattler by dating her three to four times per week over the next two months.

A month after their first meeting, Mr. Sattler started talking about marriage. Mrs. Sattler expressed concern about quitting her job; he repeatedly told her he would give her "whatever she needed" to feel financially secure in marrying him. Soon thereafter, Mrs. Sattler walked into the bedroom and presented Mr. Sattler with a handwritten agreement she wrote for him to sign:

> After we are married, I promise to put in Gay's personal savings a substantial amount (minimum $50,000.00 year) every year as long as we are together…I agree that we will buy, remodel or build another home…I agree to put Gay's name on the house and in the event of my death it will be hers. In the event of a divorce it will remain 1/2 mine.

After reading it, Mr. Sattler signed the bottom of the handwritten document.

The parties were married in Hawaii. Unfortunately, their relationship began to deteriorate. After a year and a half of marriage, Mr. Sattler filed for divorce.

The issue is whether the writing in dispute constitutes a valid and enforceable agreement. We have determined it is not an enforceable agreement because it is an agreement entered into in contemplation of marriage concerning property owned by one of the future spouses; therefore, it must satisfy the requirements for antenuptial agreements under Tenn. (law) which it does not.

In Tennessee, such agreements are enforceable if entered into freely, knowledgeably, and in good faith, without the exertion of duress or undue influence. Accordingly, the issue is whether the purported unilateral agreement was entered into "knowledgeably and in good faith."

An agreement to marry gives rise to a confidential relationship and as such the parties to a given agreement "do not deal at arms' length and must exercise candor and good faith in all matters bearing upon the contract." Accordingly, it is appropriate that parties entering into such agreements do so with full knowledge of the holdings to which they are waiving any claim under state law.

The spouse seeking to enforce an antenuptial agreement must prove either that a full and fair disclosure of the nature, extent, and value of his or her holdings was provided to the spouse seeking to avoid the agreement or that disclosure was unnecessary because the spouse seeking to avoid the agreement had independent knowledge of the full nature, extent, and value of the proponent spouse's holdings.

Applying the foregoing, it is clear the parties never fully disclosed their assets, liabilities, and income. A schedule of their assets, liabilities, and income was not provided. The brief duration of their relationship prior to the execution of the agreement, a mere two months, did not afford Mr. Sattler the opportunity to independently gain a full and fair understanding of Mrs. Sattler's financial world. The circumstances surrounding the drafting and signing the document do not favor Mrs. Sattler's position. She drafted the handwritten document on a Sunday afternoon and presented it to Mr. Sattler unexpectedly for his signature, and he signed it immediately without the benefit of independent advice of counsel. We also note that the unilateral agreement is completely one-sided in that it only obligates Mr. Sattler's assets.

When the unilateral agreement was signed by Mr. Sattler, the parties were in a confidential relationship; therefore, each of them owed the other a duty to exercise good faith in all matters bearing upon the agreement. Moreover, we have concluded that Mrs. Sattler did not act in good faith because the unilateral agreement is wholly one-sided and in Mrs. Sattler's favor, she wanted the agreement in order to "punish him" if they divorced, and Mr. Sattler did not have the opportunity for an attorney to review the agreement and provide independent advice of counsel to him prior to executing the agreement.

For these reasons, we have determined the handwritten unilateral agreement is not a valid or enforceable agreement.

EXPRESS AND IMPLIED CONTRACTS

An **express contract** is one in which the parties spell out the specifics of their agreement in direct terms. The format of this type of contract may be written or oral. An apartment lease, bank loan or home purchase are examples of express contracts. These types of agreements are normally in writing and comprehensive in nature. Nevertheless, **express contracts** may be verbal, informal, and brief. For example, if you offer to sell this text to a classmate for $40 and the fellow student accepts your offer, an express contract has been formed.

Promises may also be inferred by the conduct of the parties in view of the surrounding circumstances. These contracts are **implied-in-fact** because it is reasonable to infer that the parties intend to create a contract by their conduct. For example, it is reasonable to expect a person who picks up and eats a banana in a grocery store to pay for the fruit.

Another type of implied contract is one **implied-in-law** or a **quasi-contract.** This type of contract arises in order to prevent unjust enrichment. For example, an emergency room physician who renders aid to an unconscious patient in the hospital must be compensated for those services. The court will order reimbursement from the patient on the basis of a contract implied-in-law, even though the patient never consented to the emergency room treatment.

In Re Estate of Wiley is an example of a contract implied-in-law. The plaintiff and her husband cared for the plaintiff's parents on a continuous basis until the parents died. The caregivers maintained that they were entitled to be compensated for their services since the decedents requested that care and indicated that they would pay their daughter and her husband for those services. The Estate refused to honor the claim and argued that services rendered by family members are gratuitous and not subject to compensation. While the existence of a family relationship between the parties raises a presumption that the services were gratuitous, a contract implied-in-law will be imposed to prevent an unjust result. In this case, however, the caregivers could not overcome that presumption by providing the appropriate evidence to demonstrate a firm agreement to pay them.

In re Estate of Wiley
2002 WL 31117197 (Mich. App. 2002)

Petitioners appeal the court's judgment granting respondent's motion for summary disposition. We affirm. Petitioners filed suit against decedent's estate, claiming that for several months they cared for decedent and her husband, petitioner's parents, on a continuous basis, and did so until both died. Petitioners claimed that the decedent requested the care and indicated that she would pay for the care. Petitioners sought compensation in the amount of $86,148.64 as the fair value of their services.

Respondent noted that a presumption exists that services rendered to a person by a family member are performed gratuitously, and contended the evidence did not raise a question of fact as to whether petitioners gave care to decedent in anticipation of payment or as to whether decedent expected to pay petitioners for the care.

A contract implied in law is an equitable obligation imposed to avoid an unjust result. A contract implied in law cannot be applied when a special relationship existed between the parties that gave rise to the presumption that the services in question were rendered gratuitously. However, a court may recognize a contract implied in fact when services were performed by a person who at that time expected compensation from another person who expected to pay for the services. The issue is a question of fact to be resolved in consideration of all the circumstances, including the type of services rendered, the duration of the services, the closeness of the relationship between the parties, and the express expectations of the parties. Whether a contract should be implied in fact between parties who had a special relationship is a question of fact.

Petitioners assert that reasonable minds could differ as to whether they rendered services to decedent in anticipation of payment and whether decedent accepted the services with the intent to pay for them. We disagree. The undisputed evidence showed that petitioners rendered services to both decedent's husband and to decedent for several months until their deaths. The existence of a family relationship triggered the presumption that these services were rendered gratuitously. Petitioners asserted that regardless of the presumption, a contract should be implied in fact because they rendered the services in anticipation of receiving payment, and decedent accepted the services in anticipation of paying for them.

However, petitioners could point to no evidence that showed that they and decedent agreed on an amount to be paid, what form payment would take, or when payment would be made. Petitioners' testimony established that on those few occasions when decedent mentioned the subject, they objected and insisted that the topic be reserved for a time when decedent's health had improved. Petitioners rendered the services under these conditions until decedent died. Petitioners' assertion that their claim is bolstered by the fact that decedent paid another, Karen Phillips, for care is inaccurate. The testimony of Karen Phillips' husband established that an insurance company, and not decedent, paid for that care.

The trial court did not err in finding that under the circumstances, a contract should not be implied in fact because reasonable minds could not differ as to whether petitioners rendered the services in anticipation of payment and decedent received the services in anticipation of making payment for them.

VALID, VOID, VOIDABLE, AND UNENFORCEABLE CONTRACTS

Contracts may be classified according to their validity and enforceability. A **valid contract** satisfies all of the requirements of a binding and enforceable agreement, and either party may seek court intervention to uphold the terms of the bargain.

A contract is **voidable** if one of the parties has the legal right to withdraw from the arrangement without liability. Until this right is exercised, however, the contract remains valid and enforceable. For example, a contract with a child is voidable at the minor's election, since the minor lacks capacity to enter into the agreement. Nevertheless, the adult is bound by the terms of the contract and may not use the child's lack of capacity as a reason to disaffirm the bargain.

A **void contract** occurs when the agreement lacks one or more of the essential elements of a valid contract and can be attacked by either party to the agreement. Examples of a void contract include an agreement to perform an illegal act, or a contract which lacks consideration. An agreement to buy someone's vote in an election demonstrates a void contract, which has no force or effect.

An agreement is **unenforceable** when it satisfies the technical requirements of a valid contract but will not be enforced by the court. This type of contract leaves the aggrieved party without a remedy. For instance, a contract for the sale of land must be in writing to be enforceable. The courts, therefore, will not enforce an oral promise to transfer realty.

People enter into many contracts on a daily basis, and most of these agreements are informal, and oral in nature, but still constitute enforceable contracts. In ascertaining the intent of the parties to an oral contract, one must consider not only the language used in forming the oral agreement, but also the circumstances surrounding the making of the arrangements, the motives of the parties, and the purposes which the parties sought to accomplish. The major problem with an oral agreement is proving the existence of the arrangement. When a dispute arises over an oral contract, the courts are required to assess the credibility of the parties in trying to ascertain the thoughts of the litigants, since they are not set forth in writing.

With the growing number of lottery games offered by the states and gambling casinos, stories occasionally surface about family members, friends or co-workers polling their money to buy lottery tickets or agreements made by people to share the winnings. Are these types of agreements enforceable or are they illegal betting contracts? That is the issue in **Sokaitis v. Bakaysa.**

Sokaitis v. Bakaysa
105 Conn. App. 663 (Conn. App., 2008)

On April 12, 1995, the plaintiff and the defendant, who are sisters, signed a written agreement. The agreement stated "this is a letter of agreement between the defendant and the plaintiff. This letter states that we are partners in any winning we shall receive, to be shared equally." On June 20, 2005, a winning Powerball lottery ticket, worth $500,000, was presented to the Connecticut lottery officials for payout. The winning ticket was presented by Joseph F. Troy, Sr., the brother of the parties, who indicated that he held the ticket jointly with the defendant. Lottery officials paid Troy and the defendant each $249,999. The defendant did not provide the plaintiff with any portion of the lottery winnings.

The plaintiff brought an action against the defendant for breach of contract. The plaintiff sought money damages equal to half of the defendant's Powerball winnings.

Section 52-553 (of the Connecticut Code) provides in relevant part: "All wagers, and all contracts of which the consideration is money or other valuable thing won, laid or bet, at any game, horse race, sport or pastime, and all contracts to repay any money knowingly lent at the time and place of such game, race, sport or pastime, to any person so gaming, betting or wagering, or to repay any money lent to any person who, at such time and place, so pays, bets or wagers, shall be void...."

The plaintiff argues that "the parties' agreement is not a 'wagering contract' because it is a mutual exchange of promises to share profits from legal forms of gambling." Furthermore, the plaintiff argues that "money... won... at any game" was not the consideration for the agreement. In contrast, the plaintiff argued that the consideration was, in fact, the exchange of promises to share equally in the proceeds from the legal activity. We agree with the plaintiff.

We conclude that § 52-553 was not applicable to the agreement between the plaintiff and the defendant. The statute makes void any wager or contract "of which the whole or any part of the consideration" is "money... won... at any game...." In the present case, the plaintiff and the defendant promised to share equally in any winnings they received from various forms of legalized gambling, including the lottery. They did not make promises that were induced by the consideration of "money... won... at any game...." Therefore, the consideration for the agreement was not the money that they won but rather their mutual promises to one another to share in any winnings they received. Consideration is "a benefit to the party promising, or a loss or detriment to the party to whom the promise is made..." Therefore, § 52-553 does not apply to the agreement between the plaintiff and the defendant because the consideration was not "money... won... at any game...."

Therefore, the (lower) court improperly granted the defendant's motion for summary judgment and improperly rendered judgment in favor of the defendant.

SECTION 3.3
THE ELEMENTS OF
A CONTRACT

Intent is a primary factor in ascertaining whether there is an agreement between the parties to enter into a contract. This element is determined by words, conduct, and the surrounding circumstances. The courts apply an objective or reasonable person's standard in ascertaining the intentions of the parties based upon the totality of the circumstances. For example, an offer made by an intoxicated person should not be taken seriously. Likewise, an offer made in jest, in which no reasonable person would conclude that an offer was made, fails the objective person's standard.

Leonard v. Pepsi Co., Inc. is a famous case involving the soft drink promotion, *Pepsi Stuff,* and the request by a consumer to purchase a military jet from Pepsi based upon a television advertisement. The television commercial highlighted various items that a person could purchase by drinking Pepsi products. The advertisement was shown on television following the release of the movie "Top Gun," and featured a high-school student flying a fighter jet to class since he was late for school and the roads were congested. The commercial ended with the beverage company offering to sell the plane for seven million Pepsi points. The court was required to ascertain whether Pepsi objectively made an offer to sell the military jet as part of its promotion, or whether the proposal was merely a humorous presentation that no reasonable person should have taken seriously.

JOHN LEONARD V. PEPSICO, INC.
210 F.3ᴿᴰ 88 (S.D. N.Y., 2000)

This case arises out of a promotional campaign conducted by the distributor of Pepsi. The promotion entitled "Pepsi Stuff," encouraged consumers to collect "Pepsi Points" and redeem these points for merchandise featuring the Pepsi logo. Plaintiff saw the Pepsi Stuff commercial that he contends constituted an offer of a Harrier Jet.

Whether the television commercial constituted an offer is the central question in this case. The commercial opens with the appearance of a teenager preparing to leave for school, dressed in a shirt emblazoned with the Pepsi logo. While the teenager preens, the subtitle "T-SHIRT 75 PEPSI POINTS" scrolls across the screen. Bursting from his room, the teenager strides down the hallway wearing a leather jacket. The subtitle "LEATHER JACKET 1450 PEP-SI POINTS" appears. The teenager opens the door of his house and puts on a pair of sunglasses. The drumroll then accompanies the subtitle "SHADES 175 PEPSI POINTS."

The scene then shifts to three young boys sitting in front of a high school building. The three boys gaze in awe as a Harrier Jet swings into view and lands by the side of the school building. Several students run for cover, and the velocity of the wind strips one hapless faculty member down to his underwear. While the faculty member is being deprived of his dignity, the voiceover announces: "Now the more Pepsi you drink, the more great stuff you're gonna get."

The teenager opens the cockpit of the fighter, holding a Pepsi. "[L]ooking very pleased with himself," the teenager exclaims, "Sure beats the bus," as the following words appear: "HARRIER FIGHTER 7,000,000 PEPSI POINTS."

Inspired by this commercial, plaintiff set out to obtain a Harrier Jet. Plaintiff consulted the Pepsi Stuff Catalog. The Catalog specifies the number of Pepsi Points required to obtain promotional merchandise.

The Catalog notes that in the event that a consumer lacks enough Pepsi Points to obtain a desired item, additional Pepsi Points may be purchased for ten cents each; however, at least fifteen original Pepsi Points must accompany each order.

Although plaintiff initially set out to collect 7,000,000 Pepsi Points by consuming Pepsi products, it soon became clear to him that buying Pepsi Points would be a more promising option. Through acquaintances, plaintiff ultimately raised about $700,000.

Plaintiff submitted an Order Form, fifteen original Pepsi Points, and a check for $700,008.50.

Defendant rejected plaintiff's submission and returned the check, explaining that:

> The item that you have requested is not part of the Pepsi Stuff collection. The Harrier jet in the Pepsi commercial is fanciful and is simply included to create a humorous and entertaining ad.

The general rule is that an advertisement does not constitute an offer. Advertisements and order forms are "mere notices and solicitations for offers which create no power of acceptance in the recipient." Under these principles, plaintiff's letter constituted the offer. There would be no enforceable contract until defendant accepted the Order Form and cashed the check.

Plaintiff's understanding of the commercial as an offer must also be rejected because the Court finds that no objective person could reasonably have concluded that the commercial actually offered consumers a Harrier Jet.

In evaluating the commercial, the Court must not consider what the commercial offered, but what an objective, reasonable person would have understood the commercial to convey.

Plaintiff's insistence that the commercial appears to be a serious offer requires the Court to explain why the commercial is funny.

First, the youth featured in the commercial is a highly improbable pilot, one who could barely be trusted with the keys to his parents' car, much less the prize aircraft of the United States.

Second, the notion of traveling to school in a Harrier Jet is an exaggerated adolescent fantasy.

Third, the number of Pepsi Points the commercial mentions as required to "purchase" the jet is 7,000,000. To amass that number of points, one would have to drink 7,000,000 Pepsi's (or roughly 190 Pepsis a day for the next hundred years–an unlikely possibility), or one would have to purchase approximately $700,000 worth of Pepsi Points. The cost of a Harrier Jet is roughly $23 million dollars, a fact of which plaintiff was aware when he set out to gather the amount he believed necessary to accept the alleged offer. Even if an objective, reasonable person were not aware of this fact, he would conclude that purchasing a fighter plane for $700,000 is a deal too good to be true.

In sum, there are two reasons why plaintiff's demand cannot prevail as a matter of law. First, the commercial was merely an advertisement, not an offer. Second, the tongue-in-cheek attitude of the commercial would not cause a reasonable person to conclude that a soft drink company would be giving away fighter planes as part of a promotion.

SECTION 3.4
OFFER

An **offer** is a proposal by one party (offeror) to the other (offeree) manifesting a willingness to enter into a valid contract. An offer has three requirements. It must be: (1) a definite proposal, (2) made with the intent to contract, and (3) be communicated to the party for whom the offer is intended.

For a proposal to be definite, the terms may not be vague or ambiguous. The offer should identify the subject matter of the transaction, the quantity, and the price of the object. If Joe Roberts informs a zoo that he is interested in selling his pet bear, and a zoo official replies, "We accept," a contract is not formed, since the parties failed to specify the price and other elements of the deal.

The second element of a valid offer requires the party who offers the proposal to intend to contract. Phases such as "Are you interested" or "Would you give me" are words of **preliminary negotiations**. Terms such as "I bid," "I will give you," or "My lowest price is," show a present intention to contract and constitute valid offers. An advertisement, however, is generally treated as a mere invitation to enter into discussions. It is not construed as an offer even though the ad contains a description of the item and the price. The justification for this rule is that the vendor never has an unlimited supply of the item for sale. This principle also applies to catalogs and circulars.

The final element of an offer requires it to be communicated to the offeree. In other words, the offeree must know of the proposal before it can be accepted. The mere fact that the offeree consents to identical terms of the offer does not create a contract if the person is unaware of the proposal. For example, an individual who returns a lost puppy to its owner unaware that a reward has been posted for the animal is not entitled to the reward. The good samaritan acted without knowledge of the offer so a binding contract is not formed.

Once a valid offer has been made, how long does that offer remain open? A rejection or counter-offer by the buyer terminates an offer. If in response to a $1,000 offer to sell a car, the buyer tenders $500, the original offer is terminated. An offer may also be revoked at any time before its acceptance, and an offer may terminate by its own terms. If a party is given five days to make a decision, the offer automatically terminates at the end of that five day period. An offer may also terminate if the subject matter of the bargain is destroyed before acceptance, if one of the parties dies, or if the proposal contract is deemed illegal.

SECTION 3.5
ACCEPTANCE

An **acceptance** is the unconditional promise by a party to be bound by the terms of the offer. Until this occurs, there has been no meeting of the minds. Also, a change in the proposal by the offeree constitutes a rejection of the offer and becomes a **counter-offer**.

The acceptance must follow the same format as the offer, and: (1) be made with the intent to contract, (2) be communicated to the offeror, and (3) be unconditional. An acceptance may occur by the return of a promise, the performance of an act, or by any other method of acceptance that is stated in the offer. In a bilateral contract, an offer to sell a car for $1,000 is accepted by the promise of the buyer to pay $1,000. In a unilateral contract, the offer is accepted by the performance of an act. For example, the individual who returns the lost item with knowledge of the reward has accepted the offer and is entitled to the money.

When a perspective insured submits an application to an insurance company for coverage, is that document an offer to contract in which the carrier has the decision to accept or reject or is it an acceptance of an offer that forms a binding contract? The answer depends on the nature of the negotiations and documentation. Generally, the customer makes the offer by submitting an application that the insurance company can accept or reject depending upon the risk. On the other hand, the insurance application can be phrased in such a manner that acceptance occurs automatically upon submission of the insurance form. In decided the answer to this question, the courts will apply an objective analysis. Would an objective person looking at the transaction have reasonable believed that a contract was formed by submission of the documentation? That is the issue in the following case.

KIMREY V. AMERICAN BANKERS LIFE ASSURANCE COMPANY OF FLORIDA
2008 WL 746999 (W.D. VA., 2008)

Melanie Kimrey brought this suit against American Bankers Life Assurance Company ("ABA") to recover damages for ABA's refusal to pay a claim on an accidental death insurance policy following the death of her husband in a traffic accident. ABA argues that the Kimreys were not covered under the policy because an insurance contract was not formed between ABA and Kimrey before her husband's death.

ABA offered "Accidental Death Insurance" to Kimrey and her husband in connection with the mortgage on their house. ABA inserted a document in the mortgage closing papers which carried the heading "Enrollment Form." ABA's enrollment form listed three steps to enroll, to insure the Kimreys against accidental death for the remainder of their mortgage: 1) check single or joint coverage; 2) complete non-shaded areas, including your signature, and 3) mail back the enclosed envelope.

The form stated that by enrolling, the customer would get "6 months of complimentary coverage," and noted that once enrolled, the insured would receive a certificate of insurance that contained his or her effective date of coverage. Nothing in the form suggested that the effective date would not be the date on which the completed form was mailed or that it would be a future date. Throughout, ABA referred to the form as an "enrollment form" and never as an application.

Kimrey completed and mailed the form on or about April 5, 2006. On April 22, 2006, Mr. Kimrey was killed in an automobile accident, and ABA denied coverage.

ABA argues that Kimrey's completed enrollment form was an offer to contract for insurance by Kimrey that could be accepted only by ABA issuing a certificate of insurance containing an effective date of its choice. Kimrey argues that the ABA enrollment form constituted an offer to insure, which she accepted by completing and mailing the form, with coverage beginning from that date. The court finds that a reasonable person in Kimrey's position would have believed that the ABA enrollment form was an offer of insurance which could be accepted by completing and mailing the form.

Virginia courts apply the objective theory of contract to determine whether an offer was made and whether that offer was accepted, forming a contract. Under the objective theory of contract an offer has been made if a reasonable person in the offeree's position, in view of the offeror's acts and words and the surrounding circumstances, would believe that the offeror has invited the offeree's acceptance. Where an offer has been made, Virginia courts apply the "mailbox rule" which provides that a contract is formed upon mailing the acceptance.

An insurance application is considered an offer to enter a contract which the insurer may accept or reject after determining whether the applicant is a desirable risk. This is so because, typically, an application is precisely that– an application that could be accepted or rejected. Under the objective theory of contract, a reasonable person would view an application as an offer subject to the insurer's acceptance, not the acceptance of an insurer's offer. But the paradigm can shift. The insurer could offer insurance that an offeree could accept. The insurer could market its insurance in such a way that a reasonable person in the offeree's position, in view of the offeror's acts and words and the surrounding circumstances, would believe that the offeror has invited the offeree's acceptance.

With these precepts in mind, the court concludes that Kimrey's complaint alleges the formation of a contract of insurance. A reasonable person in Kimrey's position would have believed that the ABA enrollment form was an offer that she could accept by completing and mailing the form. The ABA enrollment form outlined the terms of the offered policy: the coverage, the exclusions, and the amount of the benefits. No statement in the documents expressed or implied that coverage would not begin immediately. The enrollment form, with headings like "Why Wait? Enroll Today ...," left a reasonable person to understand that he had the power to accept this offer and that he would receive coverage by taking the prescribed steps, completing and mailing the form.

ABA argues that an applicant for life insurance is not covered until a policy is issued citing a line of Virginia cases. In each of these cases, however, the application was clearly identified as an application and nothing positioned it as an offer of insurance that could be accepted by the prospective insured. In each case ABA cites, the insurance application expressly stated that it was not binding on the insurance company and that coverage would not commence until a policy was issued. Further, the applicant still had to submit to a medical examination after his application before the insurer issued the policy.

For the reasons stated, the court finds that a reasonable person in Kimrey's position would have believed that the ABA enrollment form was an offer which she could accept by completing and mailing the form.

Suppose Joe Roberts receives an unsolicited package from a mail order company containing a DVD of his favorite movie. The video is accompanied by a letter, which states that if Joe does not want to purchase the movie, he merely has to return it in the envelope provided. Joe discards the letter but keeps the movie. Is he required to pay for the film?

The mail-order company will argue that by not returning the movie, Joe impliedly accepted the offer even though he never ordered the product. Is the vendor correct?

Generally, silence or inaction alone is not an effective acceptance. The offeror has no power to unilaterally impose silence as to the manner of acceptance.

Businesses that send unsolicited products in the mail to potential customers now run afoul of the law. The **Postal Reorganization Act** and various state statutes make it an unfair trade practice to send unsolicited products to a customer in the mail. In fact, these products are to be considered gifts that may be kept by the consumer without having to pay for them. The following is part of the Act:

39 U.S.C. § 3009(a) *Mailing of unordered merchandise*

(a) Except for:

  (1) Free samples clearly and conspicuously marked as such, and

  (2) Merchandise mailed by a charitable organization soliciting contributions, the mailing of unordered merchandise constitutes an unfair method of competition and an unfair trade practice.

(b) Any merchandise mailed in violation of subsection (a), may be treated as a gift by the recipient, who shall have the right to retain, use, discard, or dispose of it in any manner he sees fit without any obligation whatsoever to the sender. All such merchandise shall have attached to it a clear and conspicuous statement informing the recipient that he may treat the merchandise as a gift to him and has the right to retain, use, discard, or dispose of it in any manner he sees fit without any obligation whatsoever to the sender.

Silence may constitute an acceptance if the offeree remains silent with the intent to accept the offer or where a prior course of dealings between the parties has treated silence as an acceptance. For example, a party who has contracted with a record club to accept a compact disc on approval every month, may not sit back and keep the goods without paying for them.

Auctions are gaining in popularity. Commercial establishments, like Sotheby's and Christie's, have been around for years. The internet, however, has introduced auctions as a way of buying to the average person. For example, EBay has become the world's online marketplace where millions of items are traded each day. For instance, the company has estimated that its sales in 2011 will be about $10.6 billion. If a person makes the highest bid at an auction, is that bid an offer or an acceptance?

There are two ways to offer something for sale at auction: with and without reserve. If the auction is **with reserve,** the auctioneer is merely inviting people to make offers and no contract is formed until the gavel is struck. The auctioneer may reject the highest bid and remove the item from sale. The courts will treat this situation as though there has been no meeting of the minds. Auctions **without reserve** provide a different result with the highest bidder obtaining the product regardless of the bid. In fact, the seller may not withdraw the item once a legitimate bid is received. Auctions that fail to specify which method is to be used are presumed to be with reserve.

Construction, municipal, and service contracts are frequently awarded on the basis of **sealed bids.** Is the highest bidder making an offer or making an acceptance requiring the awarding of the contract? The rules for sealed bids are very similar to an auction with reserve. The request for bids is merely an invitation to negotiate and the bid constitutes an offer that can be accepted or rejected even if it is the highest one. No legal rights are formed until the bid is accepted.

An acceptance of an offer is valid only when it has been communicated to the offeror. Generally, the offer will dictate the medium, manner, and time by which the offer is to be accepted. For example, "you must call me by Friday if you wish to buy my car." The amount of time the offeree has to communicate the acceptance is generally as long as the offer remains open. If the offer does not specify the medium to be used, it is assumed that the acceptance is to be communicated by the same or similar medium as the offer was made.

This can create a problem if the parties are using the mail because of the time delay between dispatch of the acceptance and its receipt by the offeror. The courts have resolved the problem by making the acceptance of the offer effective on dispatch. This is known as the Mailbox Rule. In other words, acceptance of the offer takes place as soon as it is mailed and not when it is received by the offeror. Revocation of an offer, however, is effective on receipt.

What happens if the offer is not accepted by return mail but by a faster form of communication, such as by a telephone call or faxed message? Has a contract been formed? That is the issue in **Trinity Homes, L.L.C. v. Fang.**

TRINITY HOMES, L.L.C. V. FANG
2003 WL 22699791 (VA. CIR. CT., 2003)

The primary issue is the effect of an alleged facsimile transmission by Damon Stewart (Stewart), the agent for Trinity Homes, L.L.C. to T. H. Nicholson, III (Nicholson), the agent for Ching Fang of the Agreement for Purchase & Sale of Real Estate (Agreement) dated June 17, 2002.

Stewart alleges that he placed the Agreement in his facsimile machine, dialed the number for Nicholson, pushed the button to start the facsimile and then went on an errand. There are no phone records relative to the alleged transmission of the facsimile transmission by Stewart. Shortly after Stewart alleged forwarded the facsimile to Nicholson, he received a phone call from Nicholson indicating that the Defendant did not wish to sell the property nor enter into a contract with Trinity Homes for that purpose.

Initially, it is necessary to consider whether facsimile (fax) transmissions are similar to or should be treated the same as the Mailbox Rule in regard to the acceptance of a contract. The Mailbox Rule states that once an offeree has dispatched his acceptance, it is too late for the offeror to revoke the offer. The Mailbox Rule has been accepted in most American jurisdictions The Restatement (of contracts also) addresses the issue of the application of the Mailbox Rule to electronic communication in §64, which states: "Acceptance given by telephone or other medium of substantially instantaneous two-way communication is governed by the principles applicable to acceptances where the parties are in the presence of each other." This is, therefore, a two-prong test: (1) the communication must be "substantially instantaneous"; and (2) the communication must be two-way. The rationale of the Restatement's position is that when parties are conversing using substantially instantaneous two-way communication, they are, in essence, in each other's presence.

To be substantially instantaneous, the transmission must occur within a few seconds, or, at most, within a minute or two. For a communication to be two-way, one party must be able to determine readily whether the other party is aware of the first party's communications, through immediate verbal response or, when the communication is face-to-face, through nonverbal cues. Further, if a communication is not two-way, the offeror will not know exactly when the offeree accepts and may attempt to revoke the offer after the offeree has already sent his instantaneous acceptance to the offeror. In such a situation, the Mailbox Rule should continue to apply and the contract should be considered accepted upon dispatch of the offeree's acceptance.

In **Osprey LLC v. Kelly-Moore Paint Co., 984 P.2d 194 (Ok.,1999),** the plaintiff leased commercial property to the defendant. The lease required that the defendant provide notice of its intent to renew the lease at least six months prior to the expiration of the lease, and notice was to be given in writing and delivered personally or through registered first class mail. The defendant attempted to extend the lease by faxing a renewal letter on the last day of the notification period. The plaintiff denied receiving the fax, despite a fax record and telephone record confirming the transmission. Applying the Mailbox Rule, the court held that the faxed notice of the lease renewal was sufficient to timely exercise the lease renewal option because the notice was in writing, and the delivery of the notice by fax transmission served the same purpose of the authorized methods of delivery. The court stated specifically: "the fax log and telephone records show that the notice was properly transmitted to Osprey. Transmitting the fax was like mailing an acceptance under the Mailbox Rule, where an offer is accepted when it is deposited in the mail." ("The telegraph is considered an instantaneous form of communication but is only a one-way form to which the Mailbox Rule does apply.").

This Court concludes that the Mailbox Rule is applicable in the instant cause and thus the issue is one of fact-whether or not the facsimile transmission was actually forwarded or transmitted by Stewart to Nicholson.

Stewart's fax machine was apparently one of early vintage and provided no verification of the transmission to Nicholson. Unlike in the Osprey case, there was no fax log and/or telephone records to show that the fax was properly transmitted to Nicholson. Stewart cannot say with certainty if the fax actually went through other than to say that he placed the fax in the fax machine, turned it on and then left before viewing and/or verifying its transmission. Further, Stewart did not recall looking at the fax machine by or through which the Agreement allegedly was transmitted, when he returned later in the afternoon from his errand.

The burden is on the plaintiff to prove by preponderance of the evidence that the fax transmission of the Agreement was actually made and accomplished. The Court in considering the totality of the evidence and the totality of the circumstances finds and concludes that the burden has not been met nor satisfied and finds for the Defendant.

SECTION 3.6

CONSIDERATION

Consideration is what each party gives up in return for the act or promise of the other. This is called the quid pro quo, or "bargained for exchange." Two elements must be present to satisfy the requirement of consideration. It must appear that both parties intend to incur legal rights and liabilities, and the bargained for exchange must have legal value. For example, if a person purchases a slice of pizza from a vendor for $2.00, what is the consideration? The vendor is giving up a slice of pizza in exchange for $2.00. The consumer is giving up $2.00 and will receive a piece of pizza in return. This bargained for exchange is supported by consideration from both parties. If the merchant only has one slice of pizza left and the customer offers the vendor $20.00 in order to outbid three other customers, is the contract valid since the consideration is unequal? The value of the bargain does not have to be equal as long as fraud or undue influence is not present.

Several unique situations arise in which a contract appears to have been formed, but the agreement lacks consideration. Examples include an illusory promise, a moral obligation, and a contract supported by a past obligation.

An **illusory promise** is one in which the act of performance is left solely to the discretion of one party. The promisor has in effect agreed to do nothing but creates an illusion that mutual obligations were exchanged. For example, a person who agrees to purchase as many tickets to a concert as he wants, or a business which promises to sell as many books as it decides to release have agreed to do nothing.

A **moral obligation** is also insufficient consideration to support a contract. For instance, a parent's promise to give $1,000 to a child out of "love and affection" is not a valid contract.

Past consideration will not support a future promise since no consideration exists. This may be illustrated by the promise of a person on his deathbed to transfer land to a neighbor for the assistance rendered two years earlier is not a valid promise.

Not all individuals or businesses have sufficient credit to obtain a loan or merchandise on credit. Occasionally, a third person will be required to guarantee the obligation of the borrower in the event of a default. For instance, a college student may not have a sufficient credit history to finance the purchase of a new car, so the credit company will request a parent to co-sign the loan.

A co-signer may be considered either a surety or guarantor, depending upon the financial arrangement required by the lender. The primary difference between the two types of agreements is that a **surety** is primarily liable for the debt as though he or she borrowed the money. A **guarantor** is only secondarily liable. In other words, the creditor will look to the guarantor only after the debtor has defaulted and the creditor is unsuccessful in recovering the money from the borrower.

Is the promise of the third party to be responsible for the debts of another supported by consideration? These agreements are enforced on a variety of theories. Some jurisdictions find that the lender's extension of credit in reliance on the third party's promise to be responsible for the debt supplies the necessary consideration. Other courts rule that the consideration for the guaranty is supplied if the primary debtor receives a benefit from the promise such as the extension of credit. Some jurisdictions, such as New York, even hold that the mere signing of the agreement without more provides the necessary consideration and the court has to look no further.

Suppose a friend promises to give you $500 in celebration of your 21st birthday but fails to deliver the gift as promised. Will the court enforce the promise? The promise of a **gift** is not supported by consideration and is unenforceable. The party promising the gift has not incurred any liability for the promise nor has the person with the birthday given up anything of legal value for the promise. This deficiency, however, may be overcome by showing that the recipient of the promise relied upon the gift to his detriment. For example, a graduate who pledges one million dollars to a University's building fund will be bound by that promise if the educational institution starts construction on the new structure based upon that gift.

The following case involving Elvis Presley concerns the enforceability of a promise to make a gift.

Jo Laverne Alden v. The Estate of Elvis A. Presley
637 S. W.2d 862 (Tenn., 1982)

This is an action against the Estate of Elvis Presley to enforce a gratuitous promise to pay the mortgage on plaintiff's home by decedent but not consummated prior to his death. The Estate of Elvis Presley did not deny a promise was made by decedent but contended that plaintiff's reliance upon that promise following decedent's death constituted an unreasonable and unjustified action on her part.

Jo Laverne Alden is the mother of the former girl-friend of the late Elvis Presley. Presley was quite generous to several members of the Alden family including the plaintiff. Due to his close relationship with plaintiff's daughter, Presley became aware of plaintiff's desire to obtain a divorce. Presley offered to pay all expenses incurred in the divorce preceding, and to pay off the remaining mortgage on the Alden home.

As a result of these promises, plaintiff filed for divorce and a property settlement agreement was executed in which plaintiff paid her husband for his equity in return for a deed conveying all of his interest in the home to plaintiff. The mortgage at the time of the execution of the settlement agreement was $39,587.66, and it is this amount which is the subject of the present suit.

On August 16, 1977, Presley died suddenly leaving unpaid the mortgage indebtedness on the Alden home. On August 25, 1977, an attorney for the Presley Estate, informed plaintiff that the Estate would not assume liability for the mortgage.

The trial court held that decedent did make a promise unsupported by consideration to plaintiff, and the plaintiff and her husband suffered no detriment as she "wound up much better off after their association with Elvis Presley than either would have been if he had never made any promise to Jo Laverne Alden.

We concur in the reasoning of the lower court's findings that decedent did not make a gift of the money necessary to pay off the mortgage as there was no actual or constructive delivery.

The court relied upon definitions of promissory estoppel found in the *Restatement of Contracts.* "A promise which the promisor should reasonably expect to induce action or forbearance on the part of the promisee and which does induce such action or forbearance is binding if injustice can be avoided only by enforcement of the promise."

The reason for the doctrine is to avoid an unjust result. The limits of promissory estoppel are: (1) the detriment suffered in reliance must be substantial in an economic sense; (2) the substantial loss to the promisee in acting in reliance must have been foreseeable by the promisor; (3) the promisee must have acted reasonable in justifiable reliance on the promise as made.

In this State, settlement agreements between husband and wife are not binding until approved by the Court. The property settlement agreement that the Aldens entered into expressly provided that it was "subject to Court approval."

Accordingly, the plaintiff has shown that Presley's promise induced her to assume the mortgage as part of a property settlement agreement. However, the property settlement agreement was not binding upon plaintiff until approved by the court. The Estate's denial of liability for Presley's gratuitous promise before submission of the agreement to the court removed the element of detrimental reliance from the case. It follows, plaintiff's reliance on the promise to pay the mortgage was not reasonably justified and she suffered no loss as a result of justifiable reliance.

PARK, BROWN & SMITH, P.C.
ATTORNEYS AT LAW
MEMORANDUM

TO: All Law Clerks

FROM: Peter Smith, Esquire

RE: Tony Roberts v. Lillian Winter

During the off-season, Tony Roberts returned to his apartment in the Philadelphia area but he became restless and lonely. Being stuck in the city without his football teammates and friends caused Tony to miss his favorite night spots in Chicago, Dallas, and New York. One evening, the football player decided to visit a new night spot featuring exotic dancers which had developed a reputation for serving gourmet food. While eating his meal, Tony struck up a conversation with Lil Winter, one of the exotic dancers, who was eating dinner before the start of her performance.

As the nightclub was closing, Tony invited Lil to Dave and Buster's for some late night entertainment. The couple hit it off instantly and found that they had much in common. Following a two-month romance, Tony asked Lil to marry him and Lil accepted on the spot. They spent the rest of the night talking and planning their future together. When the jewelry store opened the next morning, Tony and Lil were their first customers. After an hour of looking at rings, Tony purchased a 2-carat flawless diamond ring in an antique platinum setting for $18,000.

Tony also took Lil to a car dealer where he replaced her 10-year-old Ford hatchback with a new Mustang. The car would provide Ms. Winter with dependable transportation to visit him during the football season.

Unfortunately, the couple had a falling out two months later. Lil felt that things were moving too quickly and she wasn't ready to give up her dancing career. Once Tony recovered from the initial shock of their breakup, he realized that he had spent more than $50,000 on the car and ring. Tony requested the return of these items but Lil refused claiming that they were unconditional gifts. Tony visited our office for advice. He maintains that the only reason he purchased the items was because Tony wanted his fiancée to be happy in their new relationship and future life together. Tony insists that the purchases were not unconditional gifts and only given in anticipation of their pending marriage. Since Lil canceled their engagement, Tony believes that he is entitled to the return of the ring and car.

Please read the case of **Lindh v. Surman**, and answer these questions:

1. Does Lil get to keep the ring?

2. Who gets to keep the car?

3. What role does fault have in determining which items are to be returned?

ROGER LINDH V. JANIS SURMAN
702 A.2D 560 (PA. SUPER., 1997)

This appeal requires resolution of whether the law should permit retention of an engagement ring by the donee, (the person receiving the gift) after the donor (the person giving the gift) of the ring breaks their engagement. The facts follow.

Rodger Lindh (Rodger) asked Janis Surman (Janis) to marry him on August 24, 1993. Janis accepted his proposal and Rodger gave Janis a diamond engagement ring worth approximately $21,000. Unfortunately, Rodger experienced misgivings about the impending marriage and requested the ring's return in October of 1993. Janis returned the ring. However, Janis and Rodger subsequently reconciled, and once again planned to marry. Rodger again gave the diamond ring to Janis and Janis wore it. Janis began to make wedding plans.

On March 20, 1994, Rodger unexpectedly informed Janis that he no longer loved her and broke their engagement. Rodger requested that Janis return the ring, but Janis refused. Litigation ensued. Rodger filed a civil action to recover the ring or its value.

Both Janis and Rodger agree that Pennsylvania follows the law of conditional gifts in engagement ring matters. They disagree over what condition renders the gift complete. Janis' position is that the conditional gift of an engagement ring is incident to the engagement itself. The condition attached to the gift is her agreement to marry Rodger. The condition of the gift thus satisfied, she should be entitled to retain the ring.

For his part, Rodger contends that his gift of the engagement ring to Janis was conditioned upon the marriage rather than her agreement to marry him. Because the condition, marriage, never took place, Rodger contends the trial court's award of the ring to him should be affirmed. We agree.

The law of conditional gifts is set forth in the Restatement of Restitution. With particular interest we note that engagement rings are treated differently from other *wedding* and/or *engagement gifts*:

Gifts Made in Reliance on a Relation.

Gifts made in the hope that a marriage or contract of marriage will result are not recoverable, in the absence of fraud. Gifts made in anticipation of marriage are not ordinarily expressed to be conditional and, although there is an engagement to marry, if the marriage fails to occur without the fault of the donee, normally the gift cannot be recovered. If, however, the donee obtained the gift fraudulently or if the gift was made for a purpose which could be achieved only by the marriage, a donor who is not himself at fault is entitled to restitution if the marriage does not take place, even if the gift was of money. If there is an engagement to marry and the donee, having received the gift without fraud, later wrongfully breaks the promise of marriage, the donor is entitled to restitution if the gift is an engagement ring, a family heirloom or other similar thing intimately connected with the marriage, but not if the gift is one of money intended to be used by the donee before the marriage.

We now turn to Pennsylvania cases, which apply the law of conditional gifts in antenuptial gift contests. We believe these cases make clear that in this Commonwealth, engagement rings are *conditional gifts*.

An early case, **Ruehling v. Hornung, 98 Pa. Super. 535 (1930),** reflects the Restatement's characterization of an engagement ring as a *conditional gift*. In Ruehling, the donor in contemplation of marriage presented his fiancée with a diamond ring, a diamond wristwatch, and a medallion. The question of who broke the engagement was in dispute and the donee refused to return the three items. In analyzing the status of the three gifts, this court set forth:

> [t]he contention of [the donor] appellant is that gifts to a person to whom the donor is engaged to be married, made in contemplation of marriage, are conditional; and that if the donee breaks the engagement the gifts or their value may be recovered by the donor.

We find no case in this State directly bearing on this question, but in (a law treaties) it is stated: 'A gift to a person to whom the donor is engaged to be married, made in contemplation of marriage, although absolute in form, is conditional; and upon breach of the marriage engagement by the donee the property may be recovered by the donor. But if the gift is made simply for the purpose of introducing the donor to the donee's acquaintance and to gain her favor, the property is not recoverable, although marriage does not ensue. So where a Christmas present is made by a man to his fiancée, it becomes her property and the subsequent breaking of the engagement does not entitle him to recover it back.'

Following a review of case law from other jurisdictions, the court stated:

It follows that in order to permit a recovery by plaintiff, it would be necessary to hold that the gifts were subject to the implied condition that they would be returned by the donee to the donor whenever the engagement was dissolved. Under such a rule the marriage would be a necessary prerequisite to the passing of an absolute title to a Christmas gift made in such circumstances. *We are unwilling to go that far, except as to the engagement ring.* Such a ring is given as a pledge or symbol of the contract to marry. We think that it is always given subject to the implied condition that if the marriage does not take place either because of the death, or a disability recognized by the law on the part of, either party, or by breach of the contract by the donee, or its dissolution by mutual consent, the gift shall be returned. It only becomes the absolute property of the recipient if the marriage takes place.

Hence, as far back as 1929, this court has adhered to the law of *conditional gifts* with respect to engagement rings. The retention of the gift is subject to the implied condition that marriage takes place and absent that occurrence, for whatever reason, it is impossible for the gift to become complete.

Pennsylvania jurisprudence merely follows basic principles of restitution found in gift law in awarding antenuptial property. While Rodger, the donor in this case, proposed marriage, the marriage between Rodger and Janis did not occur. Thus, we find the gift of the ring to Janis at the time of their betrothal was subject to an *implied condition* requiring its return if the marriage did not take place.

After careful analysis, we affirm the order of the trial court which denied Janis post-trial relief and awarded judgment in Rodger's favor.

ANSWER SHEET
PROBLEM THREE—A

Name _____

Please Print Clearly

1. Is Tony entitled to the return of the ring? Explain your answer.

_____

_____

_____

_____

_____

_____

_____

_____

_____

_____

_____

_____

_____

_____

_____

_____

_____

_____

_____

_____

2. Who is entitled to the car? Explain your answer.

_____

_____

_____

_____

_____

_____

_____

_____

3. What role does fault have in deciding who is entitled to the items?

_____

_____

_____

_____

_____

_____

_____

_____

SECTION 3.8
CAPACITY

The courts will usually not disturb a contract freely entered into by parties of similar bargaining power. Nevertheless, when one of the individuals does not have the **capacity** to fully understand the ramifications of the contractual obligation, mutual assent to bargain is lacking. In this regard, the law provides protection to certain groups deemed to lack the capacity to contract, such as children, insane people, and intoxicated individuals.

Contracts of a minor are voidable at the child's election. This means that the child may disaffirm the contract, but the adult is bound by the agreement. In order to disaffirm, the child does not have to return the adult to the status quo. The minor only has to return what is left of that purchased or received. In addition, a minor may ratify a contract upon reaching adult age. Ratification occurs when a child reaches maturity and expresses an intention to be bound by the agreement or fails to disaffirm the contract. For instance, a child who continues to drive a car that he purchased as a minor after reaching majority will be found to have ratified the contract.

Because of public policy considerations, a minor may not disaffirm certain types of contracts. These include contracts for necessities such as food and shelter, contracts with colleges or the armed forces, and agreements of minors involved in a business transaction.

Insane individuals, like minors, lack the capacity to enter into binding contracts. Individuals are considered insane when they are unable to understand the nature and consequences of their acts at the time they entered into an agreement. Mere psychological or emotional problems are not enough. It is also irrelevant whether mental illness, senility, alcohol, or drug abuse causes the insanity. The only requirement is that the individual must be incompetent at the time of entering into the contract.

A contract entered into by one who has previously been adjudged incompetent by the court is void. An adjudication of incompetency by the court is notice to the world that the person lacks the capacity to contract. Contracts entered into by persons claiming to be insane, but not adjudged insane by the court, are voidable. In the latter situation, it is the responsibility of the person claiming to be incompetent to prove that he or she was insane at the time of contracting.

Unlike a child, an incompetent cannot disaffirm the contract unless he can return the parties to the status quo. The exception to this rule is if the other party knows of the disability but still enters into the contract. In that event, the incompetent merely has to return what is left and does not have to return the parties to the status quo.

Darko Milicic v. Basketball Marketing Co., Inc.
2004 WL 1895074 (Pa. Super., 2004)

The Basketball Marketing Co., Inc. is in the business of marketing and sale of basketball apparel and related products. Darko Milicic, is an 18-year-old basketball player from Serbia, and the 2003 second overall draft pick by the Detroit Pistons.

The parties entered into an endorsement agreement when Milicic was just 16 years old, whereby the corporation would pay Milicic certain monies and products in exchange for Milicic's endorsement.

Although Milicic was virtually unknown in the United States at the time the agreement was executed, his status significantly changed when it was known he was likely to be a top five NBA draft pick. As one would expect, Milicic was then in a position to sign a more lucrative endorsement deal.

Four days after his 18th birthday, Milicic made a buy-out offer to the Basketball Marketing Co., which was refused. About six days later, Milicic sent the Basketball Marketing Co. a letter disaffirming the agreement. He began returning all monies and products he had received pursuant to the agreement.

The Basketball Marketing Co. refused to accept Milicic's letter as a negation of the agreement. On July 11, 2003, the Basketball Marketing Co. wrote letters to Adidas and Reebok who were believed to have offered endorsement contracts to Milicic. In the letters, the Basketball Marketing Co. informed the recipients that it was "involved in a contractual dispute" with Milicic and that the "agreement is valid and enforceable and will remain in force for several more years."

Pennsylvania law recognizes, except as to necessities, that the contract of a minor is voidable if the minor disaffirms it at any reasonable time after the minor attains majority. On July 1, 2003, eleven days after his 18th birthday, Milicic sent a letter withdrawing from the agreement to the Basketball Marketing Co. This letter was sent within a reasonable time after Milicic reached the age of majority and stated his unequivocal revocation and voidance of the agreement.

The Basketball Marketing Co.'s refusal to acknowledge Milicic's ability to disaffirm the contract is at odds with public policy. Because infants are not competent to contract, the ability to disaffirm protects them from their own immaturity and lack of discretion. It confounds the Court that the Basketball Marketing Co., a corporation of great magnitude, whose business may be said to be based in contract law, not only failed to have a guardian appointed for Milicic but as they have failed to produce any evidence that Milicic was represented by an attorney, the Court finds Milicic entered into this agreement without being advised of his rights.

Milicic was a child, living in a foreign country when he signed the agreement that the Basketball Marketing Co. drafted. The public policy consideration underlying the rule which allows a child to disaffirm a contract within a reasonable time after reaching the age of majority is that minors should not be bound by mistakes resulting from their immaturity or the over-bearance of unscrupulous adults.

Based upon the foregoing reasons, we hold that the Basketball Marketing Co. conduct in sending out the letters to its competitors did support a valid potential claim for intentional interference with prospective contractual relations.

SECTION 3.9
LEGALITY

The law requires that the purpose and subject matter of an agreement be legal in order for the contract to be valid. A contract is **illegal** if its performance is criminal, tortious, or against public policy. For instance, a contract to purchase illicit drugs or the agreement to reward a person for assaulting another are illegal contracts and void as a matter of law.

Illegal contracts are void and neither party may seek court intervention to enforce the obligation even when one party has performed the act or promise specified in the agreement. Courts will simply leave the parties where it finds them. For example, the court will not enforce a gambling debt between two friends over a football game. The court takes the position that its enforcement of the illegal transaction makes the judiciary an indirect participant in the wrongful conduct.

The categories of illegal contracts are much broader than one might suspect. For example, an unlicensed entity that performs a service requiring a license, such as a plumber or electrician, may be precluded from recovering a fee on the basis that the contract is illegal. Likewise, an attorney is not allowed to share a fee with one who is not a lawyer. This type of fee sharing is illegal and the rational is quite simple. A contrary ruling would permit a person to indirectly profit from an enterprise that he or she is directly not allowed to perform unless properly licensed. That is the issue in the following case.

FARRELL v. WHITEMAN
200 P.3D 1153 (IDAHO, 2009)

Damian Farrell sued Kent Whiteman to recover for architect services he rendered for Whiteman's condominium project in Ketchum. Whiteman asserted that Farrell was not entitled to be compensated because of his failure to comply with Idaho's architect licensing statutes. The district court awarded Farrell damages, and Whiteman appealed. We vacate the damage award.

Farrell, a Michigan-licensed architect, and Whiteman, a real estate developer, both Michigan residents, were friends for many years. Beginning in 2002, Farrell and Whiteman discussed the possibility of working together on a condominium project in Ketchum, Idaho. Farrell understood that he and Whiteman would be partners in the project and that

in exchange for his work–which included designing the building, securing site plan approval, overseeing the development of the construction documents, and working as the project architect–he would receive twenty-five percent of the project's profits. Whiteman testified that they discussed a partnership and profit-sharing arrangement, but never reached an agreement regarding how Farrell would be compensated for his architectural services.

Farrell worked on the project until the end of July 2004. Some of Farrell's work was performed in Michigan, where he held an architect's license. However, Farrell also performed some work in Idaho before he received his license to practice architecture in Idaho in February 2004.

In July, 2004, Whiteman terminated Farrell from the project. Even after the project was completed, Whiteman refused to pay Farrell for his work. Farrell filed suit and Whiteman defended based on Idaho's architect licensing statutes, claiming that because Farrell had not complied with them, the entire contract was illegal and unenforceable.

Whiteman contends that the implied contract was illegal because Farrell did not have a license to practice architecture in Idaho until midway through his work on the project.

Idaho has long disallowed judicial aid to either party to an illegal contract. An illegal contract is one that rests on illegal consideration consisting of any act or forbearance which is contrary to law or public policy. Generally, when the consideration for a contract explicitly violates a statute, the contract is illegal and unenforceable. In most cases, the court will leave the parties to an illegal contract as it finds them.

Idaho Code § 54-301 reads: "In order to safeguard life, and property, and to promote the public welfare, any person practicing architecture, in Idaho, shall submit evidence of his qualifications so to practice and be licensed." The code defines the "practice of architecture" as: rendering or offering those services in connection with the design, construction, enlargement, or alteration of a building or a group of buildings.

Since the consequences of a court finding a contract to be illegal are harsh, only those contracts which involve consideration that is expressly prohibited by the relevant prohibitory statute are void. Such statutes must be narrowly construed, and only those contracts violating express provisions will be deemed illegal.

Farrell admittedly performed some architectural services in Idaho before he was licensed. Although courts should interpret statutes narrowly when applying the doctrine of illegality, the lower court went too far in interpreting the statute to merely require architects to be licensed at "critical times." This language does not appear anywhere in the statute, and no case law supporting this interpretation was offered. The statute reads "any person practicing or offering to practice architecture ... in the state of Idaho, shall ... be licensed." This unambiguously requires anyone who practices any architecture in Idaho to be licensed. Because Farrell was not licensed to practice architecture in Idaho until February 17, 2004, the architectural services he rendered before then were done pursuant to an illegal contract.

Although Farrell's work performed while unlicensed was illegal, his actions after receiving his license were certainly legal. "Where a transaction is composed of both benign and offensive components and the different portions are severable, the unobjectionable parts are generally enforceable." In other words, the implied contract in this case is chronologically separable. It was proper to award damages to Farrell for the services he rendered after he received his license. Where the services are severable, a person should not be penalized for the services he performed in compliance with the law.

We vacate the district court's award of damages and remand for further consideration consistent with this opinion.

SECTION 3.10
ESTELLE ROBERTS
v. TRI-COUNTY
GOLF CLUB

PROBLEM THREE—B

PARK, BROWN & SMITH, P.C.
ATTORNEYS AT LAW
MEMORANDUM

TO: All Law Clerks

FROM: Peter Smith, Esquire

RE: Tri-County Golf Course

Estelle Roberts has a rather interesting problem. She agreed to play in a charity golf tournament at Tri-County Golf Club. To encourage golfers to join the event, a new and very expensive Mercedes was offered to anyone who hit a hole-in-one on the 8th hole. Estelle stepped up to the tee and hit her shot straight and true. The ball landed on the green and headed directly to the cup. When the golf ball was less than one inch away from the hole, the most amazing thing happened. A frog was hiding in the cup but became scared when he heard all of the noise. The frog jumped out of the hole just as the ball was about to drop in, brushing the ball aside. Because the golf course was in a wooded area surrounded by water, Tri-County had many animals on its property, but this was the first time that a frog had interfered with a golf shot. Estelle demanded her prize, and the golf club officials consulted with the tournament judge. This individual happened to be Dr. Leonard Mauro, who promptly denied Estelle's claim to the prize. Since the ball did not go into the hole, Mauro said the shot did not fulfill the terms of the offer. Mauro directed Estelle to shoot the ball over.

Joe Robert's wife wishes to sue the golf course in order to claim the prize. I have looked at the tournament's entry form that Estelle signed when she made her $500.00 donation to play in the event. That form notes: "Disputes concerning the winner of the tournament, the scoring of any round, or other issues involving a specific shot will be determined solely by the appointed judge whose decisions are final in all matters relating to the event." The signs promoting the tournament advertised that any person who shoots a hole-in-one on the designated hole will be awarded a new Mercedes.

Estelle claims that she is being denied the Mercedes since Dr. Mauro has a bias against the Roberts' family. This physician is currently engaged in litigation with Joe Roberts over a malpractice claim.

I have found one case that deals with the awarding of a disputed prize in a contest. Please read **Giunto v. Florida Panthers,** and let me know whether you think we will be successful in a claim against the golf course.

RANDI GIUNTO V. FLORIDA PANTHERS HOCKEY CLUB, LTD.
745 S.2D 1020 (FLA. APP., 1999)

Giunto completed a sweepstakes application for the "Coca-Cola/Blockbuster/ Florida Panthers Sweepstakes." The application contained contest rules (the "Entry Form Rules"). Pursuant to the Entry Form Rules, ten persons would be chosen to receive free tickets to one of ten different Florida Panthers home games. At the game, the ticket winner would be given a chance to win $1,000,000 by shooting a hockey puck across the ice "into and through a special small goal." Mr. Giunto was selected as one of the persons to have a try at the $1,000,000 prize.

Giunto appeared at the Florida Panthers game for his attempt at the prize. Just prior to his attempt, Mr. Giunto signed a Spectator Agreement to Participate ("SAP"). Included on the SAP was the requirement that in order for the contestant to win, the puck had to "pass completely through" the goal.

The target in this case was a piece of plywood placed in front of the hockey goal. At the bottom of the plywood sheet, a small slot had been created, somewhat larger than the hockey puck.

From a position of 118 feet from the hockey goal, Giunto took the contest shot. A videotape shows that the puck hit the corner of the small slot and rebounded from side to side. It did not go completely through the opening, but came to rest just slightly within the slot. A contest judge declared that the shot was unsuccessful.

Giunto sued the Sponsors for breach of contract alleging that he had successfully made the goal. Giunto contended that the controlling contest requirement was that the puck pass "into and through" the goal; that the SAP requirement that the puck pass "completely through" the goal was a nullity; and that "into and through" was satisfied if any part of the puck entered the opening, even if the puck did not pass completely through the opening.

The Sponsors claimed that Mr. Giunto's claims were barred because the contest judge had made the determination that Mr. Giunto did not successfully make the shot. The Entry Form Rules provided, "By participating in this sweepstakes, entrants agree to abide by and be bound by these official rules and the decisions of the judges, which are final in all matters relating to this sweepstakes." By submitting the application containing the Entry Form Rules, Mr. Giunto agreed to abide by the decision of the judges.

Other jurisdictions have held that "when a contestant agrees to be bound by the decisions of a tournament director or an awards committee, such decisions are final and binding on contestants absent evidence of fraud, gross mistake, or lack of good faith." **National Amateur Bowlers, Inc. v. Tassos, 715 F.Supp. 323 (D. Kan., 1989)** (holding that decisions of the tournament committee would be final, unless there was "fraud, intentional or gross mistake, or lack of good faith").

The contest judge determined that Mr. Giunto had not successfully made the hockey shot. There was neither pleading nor proof of fraud, gross mistake, or lack of good faith. When the puck entered the plywood slot but did not pass completely through it, the contest judge was required to decide whether Mr. Giunto had won under the contest rules. The judge's decision was binding on Mr. Giunto.

As to the question of whether the puck had to pass "into and through," or "completely through" the opening, Mr. Giunto signed the SAP which stated, "I understand that the Official Rules are as follows: The puck must pass completely through the target template." This document clearly informed Mr. Giunto, before he took his contest shot, that the judges would interpret "into and through" to mean "completely through" in order to win. The contest judge's ruling was in accordance with that interpretation.

ANSWER SHEET
PROBLEM THREE—B

Name _____ **Please Print Clearly**

1. What arguments can we advance on behalf of Estelle as to why she should be awarded the prize?

_____

_____

_____

_____

_____

_____

_____

_____

_____

2. What arguments will be raised by the country club?

_____

_____

_____

_____

_____

_____

_____

_____

_____

3. Based upon the Florida Panthers case, who should win? Please explain your answer so that I can inform Estelle of her legal rights.

_____

_____

_____

_____

_____

_____

_____

_____

_____

_____

_____

_____

_____

_____

_____

_____

_____

_____

_____

_____

_____

SECTION 3.11
STATUTE OF FRAUDS

Most contracts are informal and need not be in writing to be enforceable. The **Statute of Frauds** provides an exception to this basic rule. Based upon a seventeenth-century English law, known as the Act for the Prevention of Frauds and Perjuries, certain types of contracts must be in writing and signed by the individual against whom enforcement is sought. The purpose of this rule is to prevent perjured testimony in claiming the existence of an oral contract when one never existed.

The Statute of Frauds vary by state but the following types of agreements generally must be in writing:

1. Contracts that cannot be performed within one year;

2. Contracts involving the sale or lease of real estate;

3. Contracts to be liable for the debts of another; and

4. Contracts for the sale of goods over $500.00.

The writing itself need not follow a specific format or be a formal legal document. In fact, a binding contract may be pieced together through a series of letters or correspondence between the parties. Faxes, telegrams and Western Union Mailgrams also satisfy the requirements for a written contract.

As for the specific elements of the writing, the Statute of Frauds is satisfied if the documentation sets forth the basics of the agreement, such as the identity of the parties and the subject matter of the contract, and be signed.

In this age of electronic commerce, how is the Statute of Frauds satisfied in an Internet transaction? The **Electronic Signature in Global and National Commerce Act** was enacted by Congress in 2000 and provides that a signature, contract, or other record used in interstate or international commerce may not be denied legal effect because an electronic signature or electronic record was used in its formation. This means that a digital or electronic signature must be treated in the same manner as an inked signature on a piece of contract.

The Statute of Frauds is a flexible rule, and the courts recognize exceptions to the doctrine to prevent an injustice. For example, a party will be deemed estopped to deny the existence of an oral contract when the goods have been specially manufactured, the goods have been received by the buyer, or if the individual admits the existence of the agreement in a court document. An aggrieved party may also receive court help in the enforcement of an oral contract in order to prevent unjust enrichment to the defendant and a disproportionately harsh penalty upon the plaintiff.

ARYA GROUP, INC. V. CHER
91 CAL. RPTR. 2D 815 (CT. APP. CAL., 2000)

Arya Group, Inc. appeals from the order dismissing its action against Cher and the Inshallah Trust. Arya contends the trial court's ruling constituted an abuse of discretion because the allegations in Arya's complaint show Arya is entitled to relief under theories of breach of contract and unjust enrichment.

The material allegations of Arya's complaint, which we assume to be true for purposes of this review, may be summarized as follows. Cher is the beneficiary and trustor of the Inshallah Trust, which is the record owner of property in Malibu. In June 1996, representatives of Cher and the Inshallah Trust negotiated an oral agreement with Arya, whereby Arya was to design and construct a house on the Malibu property. Cher consented to pay Arya for Arya's provision of design, construction, general contracting and supervision services. She further agreed that Arya would "be paid progress payments upon periodic percentages of project completion." The parties' oral agreement was subsequently memorialized in a written contract, which was delivered to Cher in early October 1997. Cher never signed the contract, despite her promise to do so.

Between June 1996 and November 1997, Cher assured Arya that the contract would be honored and that Arya would receive full compensation for the construction services it provided under the contract. In fact, Arya did receive payment from Cher for a number of services it discharged under the contract.

Commencing in August 1997 Cher requested that Arya meet with Bussell, a designer who had previously worked with Cher on speculative residential projects. In the course of meeting with Bussell, Arya showed Bussell the plans and designs for the Malibu property. Unbeknownst to Arya, the meetings with Bussell were part of a plan by Cher (who had never intended to sign the contract with Arya or honor its terms) to induce Arya to divulge information relat-

ing to the Malibu property so Cher could terminate her contract with Arya without paying Arya for the services it had provided, and replace Arya as the general contractor.

In November 1997, Cher terminated her agreement with Arya, without paying the balance then due Arya. In addition, Cher contacted several of Arya's subcontractors in an effort to induce them to breach their contracts with Arya and work directly with Cher. They also misappropriated for their own use the plans, designs and drawings Arya had prepared, and had the permits issued to Arya transferred to Cher's name.

We are called upon to decide, whether Arya is precluded under Business and Professions Code section 7164 from pursuing a breach of contract claim as a result of its failure to secure a signed written contract for the construction of Cher's residence. Section 7164 reads: "Every contract, between an owner and a contractor, for the construction of a single-family dwelling to be retained by the owner for at least one year, shall be evidenced in a writing signed by both parties..."

Although the California Supreme Court acknowledged that, generally speaking, a contract made in violation of a regulatory statute is void, it stressed that the rule is not an inflexible one to be applied in its fullest rigor under all circumstances. The court noted that in compelling cases, illegal contracts will be enforced in order to avoid unjust enrichment to a defendant and a disproportionately harsh penalty upon the plaintiff. The court explained, "In each case, the extent of enforceability and the kind of remedy granted depend upon a variety of factors, including the policy of the transgressed law, the kind of illegality and the particular facts." **Asdourian v. Araze, 211 Cal. Rptr. 703 (Cal., 1985).**

It appears that Cher is a highly sophisticated home-owner with previous involvement in residential construction projects, that her legal representatives assisted her in negotiating the Malibu construction project agreement with Arya, that Arya had already completed a substantial amount of the work it contracted to perform when Cher terminated the parties' agreement, and that Cher would be unjustly enriched if she were not required to compensate Arya for the reasonable value of its work. Under these circumstances, we decline to hold that Arya's non- compliance with section 7164 absolutely forecloses it from seeking to enforce the oral agreement it purportedly made with Cher, which was allegedly memorialized in an unsigned written contract. On the other hand,

should it become apparent in the course of a trial that the facts are otherwise than as alleged, and are such as to place the case outside the exception to the general rules regarding enforceability of illegal contracts, our holding would not preclude Cher from reasserting her position about unenforceability of any agreement between her and Arya in the absence of a signed written contract.

Consequently, we hold that Arya may seek to enforce its contract claim against Cher to the extent Cher would otherwise be unjustly enriched as a result of her failure to compensate Arya for the reasonable value of its work on the Malibu construction project.

SECTION 3.12
MOVIE CONTRACT

PROBLEM THREE—C

PARK, BROWN & SMITH, P.C.
ATTORNEYS AT LAW
M E M O R A N D U M

To: All Law Clerks

FROM: Peter Smith, Esquire

RE: Movie Contract

I need your assistance with the soon to be released film, *"The Real Tragedy of Rock and Roll."*

The late John De Simone of Seattle, Washington, gained notoriety a number of years ago when he attempted to kill a famous singer who was considered one of the founders of rock and roll. The Seattle resident became psychotic as the result of medication he took for his health. During an acute episode, the decedent concluded that teenagers were being brainwashed by the singer's music, and the recording star had to be killed to stop that process.

The singer was in Seattle for a concert when De Simone put his plan in action. He loaded his car with explosives and drove to the concert hall. The load, however, was unstable and detonated two blocks away from the intended target. De Simone was killed, and several historic buildings in the Seattle underground were damaged.

With the passage of time, this incident has been largely forgotten but that is about to change. The surviving child of De Simone is a Seattle physician who went to medical school with my daughter. He learned that True Films, Inc.

had decided to make a movie about this incident. Because of my expertise in entertainment law, Dr. De Simone contacted me about the film project.

The doctor wanted me to stop the movie production about his father but that was not a viable legal option. My job, therefore, was to reduce the impact of the movie on the life of Dr. De Simone. With the threat of a lawsuit for invasion of privacy, I was able to achieve this goal by having the decedent's name changed in the film, and the movie was required to be shot in San Francisco as though the events occurred in that city.

Parts of the signed movie contract are as follows:

THIS AGREEMENT is made by and between True Films, Inc. ("Film Company") and Brad De Simone ("Son").

1. Film Company wishes to film and license for distribution the motion picture, *The Real Tragedy of Rock and Roll* ("Picture").

2. The Picture is to depict certain events in the life of John De Simone.

3. Son is a physician in the Seattle area and is concerned that the Picture may have a negative impact on his life because of the disclosure of private embarrassing facts about his family.

4. In exchange for the execution of this Agreement, the parties agree that:

    (a) No part of the Picture will be filmed in the Seattle area and the movie will depict all events as though they had happened in San Francisco.

    (b) All references to John De Simone in the movie and publicity about the film will be changed to "Tony Volpe."

    (c) The film will not mention or depict any member of John De Simone's family.

    (d) Son will be provided with a copy of the screenplay within ten days of the execution of this Agreement for review and editing.

5. Film Company further warrants that the Director of the Picture shall abide by the terms of this Agreement.

6. In consideration of the foregoing warranties, Son grants the Film Company the non-exclusive right to depict John De Simone in any manner consistent with the terms of this Agreement in the movie *The Real Tragedy of Rock and Roll.*

7. Son releases the Film Company from all liability, including any liability for libel, defamation, and invasion of privacy.

8. Son waives all equitable remedies that may be available to him for a breach of this Agreement including the issuance of an injunction, and any action

for specific performance of this contract, and he understands that his exclusive remedy shall be limited to the recovery of monetary damages.

Once this contract was signed, a discussion ensued about whether Dr. De Simone had any documents concerning his father. He searched the attic and found a suitcase filled with newspaper accounts and news clips of the incident. Dr. De Simone had mixed feelings about releasing the materials but was willing to consider the request. Because True Films was about to start production, the Director asked if he could review the items while the doctor decided what he wanted to do about the request.

A number of letters were exchanged between the film company and our client about the matter. Because of time deadlines, the Director used the materials in the film assuming that everything had been worked out. Our client initially granted permission to use the materials but then changed his mind. The master copy of the film is at the distributor and copies of the movie are ready for release to the theaters.

Dr. De Simone wants to block the showing of the film and hold True Films liable for the actions of the Director. I have pieced together the following sequence of events.

On August 12, 2009, Dr. De Simone mailed an offer to True Films allowing for use of the items in exchange for a $25,000 donation to the Mental Health Association of Seattle. The film company was given 10 days to accept the offer at which time the offer would automatically terminate.

On August 15, 2009, True Films received the letter from Dr. De Simone.

On August 16, 2009, Dr. De Simone changed his mind about granting permission to use the materials in the film. He thought the public would misconstrue his father's actions and not remember that the decedent had planned the events while in a psychotic state. Accordingly, Dr. De Simone mailed a second letter to the film company retracting the offer of August 12.

On August 18, 2009, True Films received the letter of revocation.

On August 19, 2009, the film company sent Dr. De Simone a letter accepting the offer, and immediately made a $25,000 donation to the Mental Health Association of Seattle.

On August 20, 2009, Dr. De Simone received the film company's letter of acceptance but ignored it because he had already sent the letter of revocation.

Dr. De Simone wants to know his rights. Is there a valid contract to use the materials in the film? Can he legally revoke his offer even though the doctor promised that the offer was to remain open for ten (10) days? What remedies does Dr. De Simone have against the film company and can he stop the release of the film by obtaining an injunction? Is the film company liable for the Director's actions?

Name

Please Print Clearly

1. Is there a valid contract to use the materials in the film?

_____

_____

_____

_____

_____

_____

_____

_____

_____

2. Can the doctor properly revoke the offer even though he stated that the offer was to remain open for ten (10) days?

_____

_____

_____

_____

_____

_____

_____

_____

3. What remedies does Dr. De Simone have against the film company and can he stop the release of the film by obtaining an injunction?

_____

_____

_____

_____

_____

_____

_____

_____

_____

4. Is the film company liable for the Director's actions in including the materials in the film?

_____

_____

_____

_____

_____

_____

_____

_____

_____

SECTION 3.13
UNIFORM
COMMERCIAL CODE

The **Uniform Commercial Code** is the most complete of the uniform laws in the United States. The purpose of the Code is to make uniform the laws involving commercial transactions in each state such as the law of sales, banking, secured transactions and other business contracts. Over the years, the provisions have been modified but the same basic scheme exists. The Uniform Commercial Code is broken down into the following nine articles:

ARTICLE	TITLE
Article One	General Provisions
Article Two	Sales
Article Two-A	Leases
Article Three	Negotiable Instruments
Article Four	Bank Deposits
Article Four-A	Fund Transfers
Article Five	Letters of Credit
Article Six	Bulk Transfers and Sales
Article Seven	Documents of Title
Article Eight	Investments Securities
Article Nine	Secured Transactions

The Code is not involved with real estate transactions but with personal property such as merchandise. Because of the Code's requirement of good faith and reasonableness, a number of the provisions will be different than the general rules of contract law.

This section shall be limited to a review of some of the provisions in Article Two which deal with the sale of goods. Because this uniform law is a legislative mandate, it is important to see how certain terms are defined in the Code. The following are a few of the relevant definitions:

A **consumer** refers to an individual who enters into a transaction primarily for personal, family, or household purposes.

A **good** means all things that are movable at the time of identification to a contract for sale. The term includes future goods, specially manufactured goods, growing crops, and other identified things attached to realty.

A **seller** means a person that sells or contracts to sell goods.

A **sale** consists in the passing of title from the seller to the buyer for a price.

A **merchant** is a person that deals in goods of that kind or otherwise holds itself out by occupation as having knowledge or skill peculiar to the practices or goods involved in the transaction.

A **buyer in the ordinary course of business** refers to a person that buys goods in good faith, without knowledge that the sale violates the rights of another person in the goods, and in the ordinary course from a person in the business of selling goods of that kind.

A **bill of lading** refers to a document evidencing the receipt of goods for shipment issued by an entity engaged in the business of transporting or forwarding goods.

A. Entrustment

Joe Roberts decided to surprise his wife for their 25th wedding anniversary by secretly taking her engagement ring to the jeweler to have it reset in a new wedding band. Joe picked out a platinum setting which complemented her original stone by surrounding it in alternating diamonds and emeralds. Because the ring had to be specially made, Joe left his wife's stone with the jeweler hoping that she would not miss the ring while it was being reset. The owner returned two days later as instructed but the merchant could not locate the gem anywhere in the store. It turns out that the jeweler mistakenly sold the diamond with the new setting to another customer. Because of the sentimental value of the ring and the horrible mistake made by the merchant, can Mr. Roberts obtain the return of the ring from the buyer?

The Uniform Commercial Code provides in Section 2-403 that any **entrustment** of the possession of goods to a merchant who deals in goods of that kind gives that entity the power to transfer all rights of the entruster to a buyer in the ordinary course of business.

Three reasons have been articulated in support of this Code provision: (1) it protects the innocent buyer who believes the merchant has legal title to the goods because the items are in the merchant's possession; (2) the clause is based on the idea that the entruster is in a better position than the innocent buyer to protect against the risk of the dishonesty or mistake of the dealer; and (3) the principle of entrustment facilitates the flow of commerce when buyers in the ordinary course of business are involved.

Would the same result occur if a person brings her car to the gas station to have a flat tire repaired only to have the mechanic sell the car to a different customer? The gas station is not in the business of selling automobiles so the original owner would be able to demand its return.

B. Risk of Loss

Ascertaining who bears the **risk of loss** is important when the goods are damaged or lost. Surprisingly, the answer does not depend upon who owns the goods. In the absence of an agreement, Section 2-509 of the UCC governs who has the risk of loss and the answer depends upon such factors as whether the seller is a merchant, how the goods are to be delivered, or if a warehouse is involved.

Where the contract requires the seller to ship the goods, the risk of loss will pass to the buyer when confirming goods are delivered to the carrier. This is known as a **shipment contract**. On the other hand, if the agreement requires the seller to deliver the items to a specified destination, the risk of loss does not pass until the items have been delivered to that destination. This is known as a **destination contract**. For instance, Tyler's Sports Bar and Grill orders 100 cases of imported beer from a vendor in Baltimore and the terms are "F.O.B. Shipment." The beer is picked up by an independent trucking company at the seller's place of business but the bottles are destroyed in transit when the vehicle is in an accident. Who has the risk of loss? Since this is a shipment contract, so long as the seller delivered confirming goods to the trucking company, the risk of loss passes to the buyer as soon as the items were given to the trucking company. On the other hand, if the contract called for the beer to be sent "F.O.B. Destination," then the risk of loss remains with the seller until confirming goods are delivered to Tyler's place of business in Philadelphia.

A different set of rules apply if the merchandise is stored at a warehouse owned by a third party. This third person is known as a **bailee**. When goods held by a bailee are the subject of a **bill of lading**, the risk of loss passes to the buyer upon possession of these documents. If the items, however, are not covered by documents of title, the risk of loss passes to the purchaser only when the third person acknowledges the buyer's right to possession of the goods. In international trade, it is common for merchandise to be sold through bills of lading. The seller of a product will provide a bank with the documents of title which will then be given to the buyer upon payment for the goods. The paperwork will allow the buyer to go to the warehouse and obtain possession of the merchandise. This insures that international transactions go smoothly. For instance, if the beer company ships its alcoholic drinks to a refrigerated warehouse owned by the city of Philadelphia for distribution throughout the tri-state area, when a bar places an order for the imported beer, it will receive the bill of lading from the bank after paying for the goods. So, when Tyler's orders 100 cases of beer, the owner of the bar must go to the bank, pay for the beer and obtain the bill of lading. After Tyler's performs these steps but before the beer can be picked up, the roof of the warehouse collapses and the beer is destroyed. Who has the risk of loss? Since the merchandise was stored in a warehouse and the buyer has taken possession of the documents of title, the risk of loss has passed to the buyer.

The last rule on risk of loss covers that situation where the goods are in possession of the seller and the buyer is to pick them up at the store. In this case, the risk of loss passes to the customer on receipt of the goods if the seller is a merchant; otherwise the risk passes to the buyer on tender of delivery. Returning to the bar, Tyler's needs two large screen televisions so the manager goes to an electronics store and buys them. After paying for the items, he learns that the boxes will not fit into his small pickup truck. The merchant agrees to hold the television while the buyer secures a larger truck. In the interim, a fire occurs at the store and the goods are destroyed. Under Section 2-509 of the Uniform Commercial Code, the electronics store bears the risk of loss since the goods have not been delivered. On the other hand, if the seller is not a merchant, the risk of loss passes as soon as the goods are tendered to the buyer. This only requires the seller to make the goods available to the buyer and to give the buyer notification reasonably necessary to enable him to take delivery. For instance, if the manager of Tyler's buys his next door neighbor's large screen television and asks the seller to hold the item until the next week, the risk of loss passes to the buyer at the point of sale.

WILSON V. BRAWN OF CALIFORNIA, INC.
132 CAL. APP. 4ᵀᴴ 549 (CAL. APP., 2005)

Brawn markets clothing through its catalogs and over the Internet. When a customer places an order, Brawn packages it and holds it at its warehouse, where it is picked up by a common carrier and delivered to the customer, using an address provided by the customer. At all times, the terms of Brawn's mail order form required the customer to pay the listed price for the goods purchased, plus a delivery fee and a $1.48 "insurance fee."

Plaintiff purchased items from Brawn's catalogue, each time paying the insurance fee. On February 13, 2002, he brought suit against Brawn, contending that in charging the fee, Brawn violated the Unfair Competition Law. Plaintiff's suit was premised on the theory that by charging customers an insurance fee, Brawn suggested to them that they were receiving a special benefit–insurance against loss in transit–when in fact, customers did not need insurance against loss in transit because Brawn already was required to pay for that loss as a matter of law.

Uniform Commercial Code Section 2509 sets forth the general rules for determining which party bears the risk of loss of goods in transit. Where the contract requires or authorizes the seller to ship the goods by carrier (a) If it does not require him to deliver them at a particular destination, the risk of loss passes to the buyer when the goods are delivered to the car-

rier; but (b) If it does require him to deliver them at a particular destination and the goods are then duly tendered while in the possession of the carrier, the risk of loss passes to the buyer when the goods are duly so tendered as to enable the buyer to take delivery.

Under this Article the "shipment" contract is regarded as the normal one and the "destination" contract as the variant type. The seller is not obligated to deliver at a named destination and bear the concurrent risk of loss until arrival, unless he has specifically agreed so to deliver, or the commercial understanding of the terms used by the parties contemplates such a delivery. It follows that a contract is not a destination contract simply because the seller places an address label on the package, or directs the carrier to "ship to" a particular destination. Thus a "ship to" term has no significance in determining whether a contract is a shipment or destination contract for risk of loss purposes."

It is not at all uncommon for a contract to shift the risk of loss to the buyer at the point at which the seller delivers the goods to a common carrier, while calling for the seller to pay for delivery and insurance. The Commercial Code recognizes this type of contract in its provisions pertaining to the term "C.I.F." The term C.I.F. means that the price includes in a lump sum the cost of the goods and the insurance and freight to the named destination. The C.I.F. contract is not a destination but a shipment contract with risk of subsequent loss or damage to the goods passing to the buyer upon shipment if the seller has properly performed all his obligations with respect to the goods. Delivery to the carrier is delivery to the buyer for purposes of risk and title. In a standard "C.I.F." contract, the buyer bears the risk of loss in transit even though the cost of insurance is rolled into the purchase price and is in fact paid by the seller. By breaking out the cost of insurance, and requiring the buyer to pay it, Brawn's mail order contracts even more clearly place the risk of loss in transit on the buyer.

Other evidence is consistent with the conclusion that Brawn intended the contracts to be shipment contracts. Brawn's own insurance covers goods lost while in Brawn's possession, but it does not cover goods destroyed or lost after the goods left Brawn's physical possession. Brawn pays California use tax, rather than sales tax, on the theory that the goods were "sold" when they left Brawn's place of business, located outside of California. Brawn records the revenue for the goods sold at the point of shipment, and removes the goods from its inventory at the time of shipment.

In sum, nothing in Brawn's conduct, and nothing in the delivery or insurance terms of Brawn's mail order forms, suggests that it was offering anything other than a standard, C.I.F.-type shipment contract, which the customers agreed to when they used Brawn's mail order form to purchase goods.

C. Requirement of Good Faith

The law of contracts provides that an agreement which lacks an important term, such as price or quantity, will not be enforceable because of indefiniteness. So, a contract between neighbors for the sale of a car that fails to specify the price is not enforceable. It is missing a key element of the contract.

That is not the result under the Uniform Commercial Code which requires that every contract impose an **obligation of good faith** in its performance or enforcement. For instance, Section 2-204 provides that even though one or more elements of a contract are missing, an agreement for the sale of goods is valid and will not fail for indefiniteness if the parties intended to make a contract. The courts will simply fill in the gaps by ascertaining what is commercially reasonable under the circumstances. This is demonstrated in the following example. If an appliance company contracts with a television manufacturer for the purchase of 100 large screen televisions that must be delivered two weeks before Super Bowl Sunday but nothing is said about the cost, the Code mandates that the price will be what is reasonable at the time of delivery of the merchandise.

D. Consideration

Consideration is an essential element of every contract. If a party offers to sell his racing car for $25,000 and tells the buyer that he has one week to make up his mind, this offer can be revoked anytime before acceptance. The promise to keep the offer open for one week is not supported by consideration. This result changes under the Code if one of the parties to the contract is a merchant. Section 2-205 states that an offer by a merchant to buy or sell goods in a signed writing which gives assurances that it will be held open is not revocable, for lack of consideration, during the time stated or if no time is stated for a reasonable time not to exceed three months.

**SECTION 3.14
AGENCY**

Businesses act through their **agents** whether it is an employee or third party and these agents have the power to enter into contracts on behalf of their **principals**. Agency law deals with these relationships and in what context an agent can bind a principal. Examples of agents include sports or music representatives, employees, realtors, public adjusters, buying agents, auctioneers, and attorneys.

The Restatement (Third) of Agency provides that an agency relationship is created "when one person (the "principal") manifests assent that another person (the "agent") shall, subject to the principal's right of control, have power to affect the principal's legal relations through the agent's acts and on the principal's behalf." These relationships are generally created by the mutual agreement between the principal and agent and can be expressed or implied. Examples of an expressed agency include when an attorney represents an injured party in a personal injury claim based upon the signing of a contingent fee agreement and when a realtor lists and sells a person's home upon the signing of a listing agreement. An agency relationship, however, can also be created by the actions of the parties without the necessity of a formal contract. This type of implied agency can occur in an employment situation such as when a sales clerk has the power to bind the store on a customer purchase even though there is no written contract that expressly provides that power.

An agent's duties and obligations to the principal are usually governed by the terms of a written agreement. Nevertheless, an agent acts in a position of trust which allows the principal to relax the care and vigilance ordinarily used. Therefore, an agent may not act in her own self-interests and she owes the principal a duty of loyalty and good faith. A sports agent, for instance, cannot make a deal with a team to sign one player at a lower salary so that another player the agent represents can obtain a higher salary or better deal.

An agent is clothed with authority to act on behalf of the principal and to enter into contracts to bind her master. This authority may be express, implied or apparent. **Express authority** is established by written or spoken words that signify the principal has delegated authority, and the agent has accepted that grant of power to act on behalf of he master. An attorney handling a personal injury claim pursuant to a contingent fee agreement would have the power to hire an investigator to interview witnesses, obtain the client's medical records and to take photographs of the accident scene. These tasks will be spelled out in the fee agreement.

The parties do not always spell out all of the details of the agencies and there will be situations when the agent must exercise discretion. Do those actions which are contained in the agency agreement or conversations between the principal and agent bind the principal? This concept is known as implied authority and consists of those actions which are reasonably necessary and proper for the agent to carry out the terms of the agency and which are not prohibited by the agreement. An attorney would be authorized to obtain the services of an accident reconstruction expert in the investigation of a claim even though the agreement is silent on this issue since that is a reasonable necessary and proper expense.

Apparent authority involves those situations where the master's conduct would lead a reasonable person to conclude that the agent is clothed with authority to act on the master's behalf. An agent with apparent authority can bind the principal to a contract even though that contract may exceed the principal's grant of authority or express instructions to the contrary. The manager of a bar would have the apparent authority to bind her employer to the purchase of an exotic beer that costs $10 a bottle even though the employee was given specific instructions not to buy any beer that costs more than $1 a bottle unless the seller was aware of this limitation.

Gaines v. Kelly raises the question as to whether a mortgage broker acts on behalf of a bank in order to bind that institution under the theory of apparent authority or whether the broker is merely a middleman.

GAINES V. KELLY
235 S.W.3D 179 (TEX., 2007)

In this appeal, we must determine whether representations, allegedly made by a mortgage broker that a loan would be funded, may be attributed to a lender for purposes of a borrower's claim against that lender.

In December 1998, Roger Kelly signed an Agreement with Robert Thompson, acting on behalf of Commercial Realty Advisors, Inc., to assist him in obtaining financing for a 31-acre tract in Texas. Although Kelly did not own the property, he held an option to purchase the property and needed financing.

Thompson approached Russell Gaines, an officer of Southwest Guaranty Mortgage Corp., about a loan for Kelly, providing Gaines with preliminary information about the proposed transaction. Gaines in turn provided Thompson with a loan application that Thompson delivered to Kelly. Kelly completed the application and returned it to Thompson, who delivered it to Gaines.

Kelly's attorneys pressed Gaines for a loan commitment because of the imminent expiration of Kelly's option on the property. On December 23, Southwest Guaranty issued a thirty-day loan commitment conditioned upon receipt of a title report.

When the subsequent title report indicated that Kelly did not have an ownership interest in the tract, Gaines asked for additional documentation concerning Kelly's ownership and the pre-sold lots. Kelly's attorneys, however, insisted that Southwest Guaranty fund the loan, and, when Gaines declined, Kelly promptly filed suit.

In his fraud claim, Kelly alleged that Thompson told him during the application process that the loan was a "done deal" and that he relied on this false statement to his financial detriment.

An agent's authority to act on behalf of a principal depends on some communication by the principal either to the agent or to the third party. The evidence clearly substantiates Thompson's authority to deliver the loan documents to Kelly. There is no evidence, however, that Thompson had actual authority to negotiate the loan, and thus the question is whether he had apparent or implied authority to do this.

Apparent authority is based on estoppel, arising "either from a principal knowingly permitting an agent to hold himself out as having authority or by a principal's actions which lack such ordinary care as to clothe an agent with the indicia of authority, thus leading a reasonably prudent person to believe that the agent has the authority he purports to exercise. The principal's full knowledge of all material facts is essential to establish a claim of apparent authority based. Moreover, when making that determination, only the conduct of the principal is relevant. Thus, to determine an agent's apparent authority, we examine the conduct of the principal and the reasonableness of the third party's assumptions about authority.

Kelly submits that he reasonably believed that Thompson possessed apparent authority in this case similar to that of the agent in **Walker Insurance Services v. Bottle Rock Power Corp., 108 S.W.3d 538 (Tex. App., 2003).** Walker sued Bottle Rock, a California power company, for a fee that was to be paid if a bond was acquired under specific time constraints. At issue was whether the alleged agent, Arlie Beane, had apparent authority to negotiate or contract with Walker on behalf of the power company. The court of appeals concluded that he did have the authority, noting that most of the negotiations were conducted through Beane and that his efforts were "accepted and ratified" by Bottle Rock. Moreover, Wilson testified that "one of Bottle Rock's directors confirmed his understanding of Beane's authority to act and negotiate on its behalf." On this evidence, the court concluded that Beane was no mere middleman but rather Bottle Rock's "point man" for obtaining the bond on its behalf. Kelly likewise suggests that Thompson was no mere middleman in his dealings with Gaines, but the evidence is otherwise.

Initially signing as Kelly's mortgage broker, Thompson located Southwest Guaranty as a possible lender, brought the parties together, and facilitated the paperwork for the loan. There is no evidence, however, that Thompson had any role in the negotiations. Instead, the evidence indicates that Thompson acted merely as a middleman.

In further contrast to **Walker Insurance Services,** the evidence in this case consists almost entirely of acts or statements attributed to the alleged agent, Thompson, rather than to the principal, Gaines. Declarations of the alleged agent, without more, are incompetent to establish either the existence of the alleged agency or the scope of the alleged agent's authority. Instead, apparent authority must be based on the acts of the principal and is limited to the scope of responsibility that is apparently authorized.

Gaines testified that he gave loan documents to Thompson for delivery to Kelly because Thompson said that he "would be the best bird dog to get it done." Gaines also testified that Thompson solicited the loan on behalf of Southwest Guaranty. There were also blank loan forms on Southwest Guaranty letterhead in Thompson's office.

Gaines' testimony clearly indicates that Gaines used Thompson as an intermediary to deliver loan documents and facilitate the transaction. But evidence that Thompson brought the parties together, delivered the paperwork, and assisted in its completion is not evidence that Gaines authorized or acquiesced in Thompson's representation that the loan was "a done deal." Nor is the existence of blank Southwest Guaranty loan forms in Thompson's office evidence that Thompson had authority to commit funds. The record does not show that Thompson was authorized to fill in the loan forms, there is no evidence he was authorized to sign them on Southwest Guaranty's behalf thus rendering them "a done deal."

Kelly complains that Thompson, acting for Gaines, fraudulently misled him into believing that the loan was "a done deal." Thus, the relevant issue is whether Thompson's agency included the authority to commit Gaines and Southwest Guaranty to the loan.

Because an agent's authority is presumed to be coextensive with the business entrusted to his care, it includes only those contracts and acts incidental to the management of the particular business with which he is entrusted. The evidence here fails to raise a fact issue about whether Thompson's agency included the apparent authority to commit the funds or obligate Gaines to terms other than those agreed to in the parties' contract, and thus Thompson's alleged assurance that the loan would close cannot be imputed to Gaines or Southwest Guaranty. Accordingly, we render judgment that Kelly takes nothing.

1. Story promised his nephew $5,000 if he would refrain from drinking liquor, using tobacco, swearing, or playing cards until he became 21 years of age. The nephew fulfilled the terms of this promise and requested the money upon becoming 21. This request was refused on the basis that the contract lacked consideration. Did the nephew provide legal consideration for the promise so that he may be awarded the money? **Hamer v. Sidway, 27 N.E. 25 (N.Y., 1891).**

2. Pemerton accepted an invitation to appear on "The Jerry Springer Show." In exchange, she received airfare from Tennessee, and her expenses were paid for two days in Chicago. Prior to the show's taping, she signed a document entitled "Jerry Springer Consent and Release" which provided that any dispute arising out of her appearance on the show would be resolved by binding arbitration with the American Arbitration Association. Pemerton sued Springer in state court for the injuries she received when her arch enemy burst from behind the scenes and beat Pemerton about the head and shoulders during the taping. Pemerton claims that Springer promised not to invite her assailant to the studio. Pemerton asserts that the Release does not cover the assault. She claims that it merely covers disputes arising out of the production of the show. Does the arbitration agreement cover this claim for personal injury? **Tracy Pemerton v. Jerry Springer, 1995 W.L. 579465 (N.D. Ill., 1995).**

3. Following the murder of Gianni Versace in front of his South Beach home, the FBI offered a reward leading to the "arrest and conviction of Andrew Cunanin." A dock attendant at a marina saw an individual who fit Cunanin's description on a nearby house boat. He notified the authorities, and the FBI surrounded the house boat containing Cunanin. Following a volley of gun shots, Cunanin was found dead inside the vessel. Since Cunanin was never brought to trial, is the dock worker entitled to the reward since he did not provide information leading to the "arrest and conviction" of the fugitive?

4. Turilli operates the Jessie James Museum and contends that the man buried as Jessie James in 1882 was an imposter. He claims that Jessie James lived for many years thereafter under the alias of J. Frank Doulton. Turilli offered a $10,000 reward "to anyone who could prove me wrong." The widow of the desperado's son, maintained that Jessie James was shot and killed by Robert Ford who pleaded guilty to the murder. Ms. James submitted affidavits to Turilli which noted that **(1)** the James Family Bible recited the death of Jessie James in 1882; **(2)** the outlaw's mother often stated that she identified the body of her son; **(3)** a boyhood neighbor of Jessie James swore that he went to the James home right after the shooting and identified the body; and **(4)** Jessie James' own son declared that when he

was seven years old, he heard the fatal shot and saw his father die in his mother's arms. Has the daughter-in-law of Jessie James presented sufficient evidence to fulfill the terms of the offer? **Stella James v. Lou Turilli, 473 S.W. 2d 757 (Mo. App., 1971).**

5. Great Entertainment Merchandise (GEM) purchases merchandising rights from various performing artists before they go on tour. Vince Neal of Motley Crue entered into negotiations with GEM to transfer his merchandising rights to the manufacturer in order for GEM to produce various memorabilia for the upcoming concert tour. In anticipation of the licensing agreement, Neal incorporated a "loan out" company. This type of entity is standard in the music industry so that artists can take advantage of certain tax incentives. Neal then transferred his merchandising rights to the "loan out" company, who in turn, assigned those rights to GEM. GEM paid $1 million to the company based upon 800,000 paid concert attendees. Neal also entered into a contract with GEM agreeing to use his best abilities to discharge the obligations undertaken by the artist. The actual attendance was well below the projected numbers. Therefore, GEM requested that Neal pay back part of the money on the basis that the separate agreement signed by the musician was a guarantee agreement. Neal counters that the clause merely guaranteed that he would use his best efforts to perform for 800,000 attendees. Is Neal responsible to pay back the money on the basis that he guaranteed the obligations of the "loan out" company? **Great Entertainment Merchandising, Inc. v. Vince Neal, 1996 U.S. Dist. Lexis 8973 (N.Y., 1996).**

6. At the start of his employment with Douglas and Lowmenson, Anderson was given an employee handbook which described a progressive disciplinary policy. After three years on the job, Anderson was fired because a box of company pencils were found in his pickup truck. Anderson sued the employer for breach of contract, claiming that they did not follow the progressive disciplinary policies outlined in the handbook for unauthorized possession of company property. These progressive discipline policies merely required a written notice for the first offense. Can an at-will employee be discharged at any time, or is an employer bound by the terms of the employee handbook? **Terry Anderson v. Douglas & Lowmenson Company, 540 N.W. 2d 277 (Ia., 1995).**

The following internet references offer more information on contract law, including breach of contract and remedies.

- **www.law.cornell.edu/topics/contracts.html**
  The Legal Information Institute gives a good overview of contract law with federal and state materials and recent Supreme Court decisions.

- **www.loc.gov**
  The Library of Congress website provides online links to an extensive menu of topics concerning contract law and contains documents, photos, movies, and sound recordings from American history.

- **www.uchastings.edu**
  This reference provides a link to a research project on the nature and enforceability of electronic contracts.

- **www.ilrg.com/forms.html**
  This site gives examples of different types of contracts.

KEY TERMS

Acceptance

Bailee

Bilateral Contract

Bill of Lading

Buyer in the Ordinary
    Course of Business

Capacity

Cause of Business

Consideration

Consumer

Contract

Contract Implied-in-Fact

Contract Implied-in-Law

Co-Signer

Counter Offer

Destination Contract

Electronic Signature in Global
    and National Commerce Act

Entrustment

Express Contract

Gift

Good

Guarantee

Guarantor

Illegal Contract

Illusionary Promise

Implied Contract

Implied-in-Fact

Implied-in-Law

Legality

Liquidated Damages

Merchant

Moral Obligation

Obligation of Good Faith

Offer

Past Consideration

Postal Reorganization Act

Preliminary Negotiations

Quasi-Contract

Quid Pro Quo

Risk of Loss

Sale

Seller

Shipment Contract

Silence as Acceptance

Statute of Frauds

Surety

Unenforceable Contract

Uniform Commercial Code

Unilateral Contract

Valid Contract

Void Contract

Voidable Contract

CHAPTER 4

TORTS

SECTION 4.1
THE LAW OF TORTS

"That great principle of the common law...declares that it is your duty to use your own rights as not to cause injury to other people."

Sir Charles Williams
Grey v. North Eastern Rail Co.
48 L.T.R. 905 (1883)
"The Quotable Lawyer"

A **tort** is a private civil wrong committed against another for which the law provides an award of money damages. That wrong may also give rise to criminal charges for which the remedy is incarceration. The law of torts establishes standards of conduct for different types of activities ranging from the driving of a car to owning an animal. These standards are established by either the legislature or by the courts.

There are three types of civil wrongs in a business setting: unintentional, intentional, and strict liability. An unintentional tort is conduct that was not intended or planned by the performer but whose actions have harmed another. A driver who negligently operates a motor vehicle thereby causing an accident is an example of this category. An intentional tort is one that the wrongdoer does on purpose and includes such things as defamation, invasion of privacy, battery, and false imprisonment. Strict liability is that responsibility imposed upon a business regardless of the care exercised or the precautions taken to prevent the harm. Such liability may arise from the ownership of a dangerous animal such as a pet bear or by selling a defective product such as a new car whose brakes fail.

Recoverable damages include lost wages, medical expenses, harm to property, and pain and suffering.

SECTION 4.2
NEGLIGENCE

Negligence, generally speaking, is the failure to do what a reasonable person would do under the circumstances. While this definition may seem vague, several principles do emerge. The mere happening of an accident is not negligence. Rather, four elements must be present in order to establish an actionable claim:

1. A duty must be owed;
2. There must be a breach of that duty;
3. The negligence must be the proximate cause of the harm; and
4. The aggrieved party must sustain damages.

The plaintiff has the burden of proving all four elements by the preponderance of the evidence. Suppose Joe Roberts is stopped for a traffic light when the driver of a delivery truck loses control of his vehicle and rams the rear of Joe's car. The force of the impact propels Joe forward, and he sustains a whiplash type injury. Is the truck driver negligent? Yes. The truck driver owed a duty to drive his vehicle carefully and avoid hitting another vehicle. He breached that duty by striking the rear of the Roberts car. Finally, his negligence was the proximate cause of Joe's neck injury causing him to incur medical expenses and conscious pain and suffering. Not all cases, however, are so easy to prove, so a more detailed examination of each element of negligence is required.

SECTION 4.3
DUTY OF CARE

Duty of care establishes the type of behavior a person must exhibit in a given situation. The basic rule is that a person must conform to the standard of care of a "reasonable person under the circumstances." This duty can vary from case to case depending upon the age of the person, his or her expertise, and the specific situation.

Generally, the law does not make a distinction concerning the standard of care between adults of different ages. A 65-year-old man will be held to the same standard of care in driving a car, as a person 16 years of age. That standard of care is simply the "average driver." A professional, however, is held to a higher standard of care when he or she is engaged in a professional capacity. This claim is called malpractice and the defendant is held to the standard of care of the average professional. For example, a neurosurgeon who makes a mistake during surgery is held to the standard of care of the average neurosurgeon and not to the standard of care of the average person performing surgery—or even the average physician. The neurosurgeon has been selected because of this individual's specialized skill, so the doctor must possess and utilize the appropriate expertise of the average neurosurgeon.

Children develop differently each year of their lives. There is a vast difference in the motor and intellectual skills between a child of six and a child of twelve. Therefore, minors are held to a different standard than that of the average adult. A minor is held to the standard of care of a child of similar age, intelligence, and experience. The exception to this rule is when a child engages in adult activity, such as the driving of a car, operating a boat, or the flying of an airplane. In those cases, children are held to the standard of care of the average person.

The age of majority varies from state to state and country to country. In the United States, adulthood can legally begin anywhere between 18 to 21 depending upon the jurisdiction. A youth in Japan, however, achieves majority at 20 while a child in Italy is considered an adult at 18.

The case of **Norton v. Hawkinson** involves the determination of the proper standard of care of a 13-year-old child driving a car which was given to her by the child's 18-year-old sister. One of the issues in the case is negligent entrustment. This is a concept that refers to the responsibility of a person in lending a car to an incompetent driver. The complication in this litigation is that both the driver and supplier of the vehicle were minors.

NORTON V. HAWKINSON
2001 WL 32788 (MINN. APP., 2001)

Appellant, the trustee for the estate of Rhya Hawkinson, challenges the court's determination that the adult standard of care applies to a child operating a motor vehicle in the context of comparing the child's fault to the fault of the entrustor in a negligent entrustment action.

Thirteen-year-old Rhya Hawkinson was killed in a one-vehicle accident when she lost control of the vehicle she was driving. Jill Hawkinson, Rhya's 18-year-old sister, gave Rhya permission to drive her vehicle to the family's mailbox at the end of a quarter-mile-long driveway, but Rhya drove past the mailbox to a nearby farm. Rhya accelerated to 60 miles per hour on a gravel road. The vehicle fishtailed and went into a ditch. Rhya was ejected from the vehicle and suffered fatal head injuries.

The Estate of Rhya Hawkinson brought this wrongful death suit against Jill Hawkinson, alleging negligent entrustment of the vehicle to a minor.

Appellant asserts that this is a case of first impression and that a failure to apply the child standard of care to Rhya would render the doctrine of negligence entrustment meaningless. We disagree.

When engaged in activities appropriate to her age, experience, and wisdom, a child is judged by the standard of care of a child of similar age, experience, and maturity. In the operation of an automobile, airplane, or powerboat, however, a minor is held to the same standard of care as an adult. The rationale for this exception was that bystanders cannot know whether the operator of an automobile, airplane, or

powerboat is a minor or an adult and cannot protect themselves against "youthful imprudence."

Although that the purpose of applying the adult standard is to protect third parties, the Minnesota Supreme Court has clarified that the adult standard applies not simply to child-defendants but unequivocally in all circumstances where a child operates a vehicle. The standard of care of a child is only proper when minors are "engaged in activities appropriate to their age, experience, and wisdom, operating a motor vehicle not being one of such activities.

A minor-entrustee has a cause of action for negligence entrustment despite the minor's own fault. The adult standard of care to the child-driver does not lessen the negligence of the entrustor.

Cases from other jurisdictions cited by the parties have all rejected the proposal to use a different standard for comparing a child-driver's fault with an entrustor's fault. See **Keller v. Kiedinger, 389 So.2d 129, 133 (Ala., 1980)** (applying adult standard of care to child-driver to determine contributory negligence); **Daniels v. Evans, 224 A.2d 63, 66 (N.H., 1966)** (applying adult standard of care to child-driver to determine contributory negligence). The trustee presents no reason to upset nearly 40 years of precedent in holding minors operating automobiles, airplanes, powerboats, or in some cases, guns, to an adult standard of care. The district court correctly determined that the adult standard of care applies to Rhya's conduct in this case.

Affirmed.

Establishing a duty of care is an essential element in every claim for the tort of negligence. This duty can differ depending upon the circumstances. In carrying out the duties of one's trade, a professional is held to a higher standard than an average person and a child is generally held to a lower standard of care than an adult. It is not always possible, however, to establish that a duty of care is owed to a person just because an individual is harmed by the actions or lack of actions of another.

The practice of medicine is a collaborative effort with many physicians frequently providing input on the care of a patient. In this context, each physician owes a duty to exercise care in the rendering of services. Does a duty arise, however, if a treating physician asks a colleague to merely look at a patient's diagnostic films and to provide an opinion? That is the issue in **Ford v. Applegate.**

FORD V. APPLEGATE
2003 WL 22000379 (CAL. APP. 2 DIST., 2003)

Erin Ford appeals a grant of summary judgment in favor of defendant, Gregory Applegate, M.D., in an action for medical malpractice.

In April 1999, Ford, a high school basketball player, fell during a game and injured her knee. Ford was seen by Dr. McKeever for evaluation. Ford underwent an MRI of her right knee. The film was interpreted by Dr. Eto. Dr. Eto's impression was that there were changes in the anterior cruciate ligament suggesting a strain or partial tear.

On July 30, 1999, Dr. McKeever asked Dr. Applegate to look at Ford's film. Dr. Applegate reviewed the MRI and found Ford's "anterior cruciate ligament is fully intact." Dr. McKeever included that finding in Ford's medical record. Dr. McKeever then diagnosed Ford's condition as a strain, rather than a tear.

However, Ford, in fact had a partial tear. According to Ford, Dr. Applegate's interpretation led to a delayed diagnosis of the tear, which went from a partial tear to the complete tear of the anterior cruciate ligament.

Ford filed this action against Drs. Applegate and McKeever alleging they were negligent in their diagnosis and treatment, causing her injuries and damages.

Dr. Applegate filed a motion for summary judgment on the ground there was no physician-patient relationship between him and Ford giving rise to a duty of care. Dr. Applegate asserted he never met, saw, examined or treated Ford, he never billed Ford or her insurance company for any care or treatment, he never prepared any medical reports, records or billings in reference to her, and he had no medical chart on her.

Ford contends a physician who is asked to consult in order to assist in making a diagnosis owes a duty of care to the patient and can be sued for medical malpractice.

Negligence is conduct which falls below the standard established by law for the protection of others against unreasonable risk of harm. In the medical malpractice context, liability arises where there is a relationship of physician-patient between the plaintiff and the defendant doctor; the relationship gives rise to the duty of care.

The practice of medicine is a collaborative endeavor. A radiologist, for example, reviews films some clinician has ordered, and a pathologist analyzes a tissue specimen or fluid another doctor has put into a container destined for the laboratory. Such physicians, like other health care providers who engage in serving as consultants in the care of other doctors' patients, as by performing diagnostic services or providing care of one form or another, become subject to liability for lapses committed in such services, if, of course, a physician-patient relationship has come into existence.

No physician-patient relationship arose between Dr. Applegate and Ford, where Dr. Applegate simply provided a colleague with an informal opinion but did not bill for his services, write a report or otherwise undertake to serve as Ford's physician. There is no indication in the record that Dr. Applegate ever billed Ford or her insurance company for any care or treatment. He did not prepare any medical reports, records or billings in reference to her, and he had no medical chart on her. The imposition of liability in these circumstances "would not be prophylactic" but instead counter-productive by stifling efforts at improving medical knowledge, and by extension, patient care.

For these reasons, we conclude that Dr. Applegate's rendering of an informal opinion to a colleague was insufficient to give rise to a physician-patient relationship and a duty of care owed to Ford.

Does the law impose a duty upon a person to go to the aid of another in trouble? The cases are well documented of people who turn their back on victims of crimes, the injured and the sick. This conduct is morally and ethically reprehensible but is it actionable in a civil lawsuit? Generally, there is no legal duty to aid or protect another.

The law, however, does require a person who harms another or places another in a position of peril to go to that individual's assistance. A legal duty is also imposed where a special relationship exists between the parties. For example, a parent must go to the aid of a child, a spouse must help the other spouse, and an employer must protect an employee.

Must a physician, however, stop and render emergency aid to the victim of a car accident that he or she did not cause? Despite the doctor's specialized training, the answer is no. Physicians are reluctant to become involved because of the fear of being sued for medical malpractice. To encourage healthcare professionals to render emergency help, however, many states have passed **Good Samaritan Statutes**, which impose liability only in the event of gross misconduct.

The following law is an example of a Good Samaritan Statute:

> Any physician or any other practitioner of the healing arts or any registered nurse, licensed by any state, who happens by chance upon the scene of an emergency or who is present when an emergency occurs and who, in good faith, renders emergency care at the scene of the emergency, shall not be liable for any civil damages as a result of any acts or omissions by such physician or practitioner or registered

nurse in rendering the emergency care, except any acts or omissions intentionally designed to harm or any grossly negligent acts or omissions which result in harm to the person receiving emergency care.

This limited immunity also extends to a lay person rendering emergency aid if that individual possesses a current certificate evidencing the successful completion of a course in first aid or basic life support sponsored by the American National Red Cross or a similar organization. A lay person will not enjoy the protection of the Good Samaritan statute if the emergency aid extends beyond one's specialized training. For instance, a person trained in CPR cannot perform open-heart surgery or administer intravenous drugs to regulate the rhythm of the heart.

The Good Samaritan law is created by statute so one must always look at the applicable state law to see how it is phrased and whom it covers. While the protections afforded by these laws are normally limited to those who are medically trained, some legislatures have granted immunity to non-medically trained people when it comes to Automated External Defibrillators or AED devices. These portable units are designed to diagnose and treat certain heart conditions when the heart muscle goes into cardiac arrest. Because these devices come with instructions and are relatively easy to use Pennsylvania, for example, gives immunity to those who attempt to save a person's life by using an AED device even though he or she may not be medically trained. This exception was used in **Atcovitz v. Gulph Mills Tennis Club, Inc.** to try and impose a duty upon a tennis club for not keeping such a life saving device on its premises.

ATCOVITZ V. GULPH MILLS TENNIS CLUB, INC.
812 A.2D 1218 (PA., 2002)

On January 16, 1996, Jerry Atcovitz suffered a stroke, secondary to a heart attack, while playing tennis at the Gulph Mills Tennis Club. Within a minute of his collapse, two tennis club members administered cardiopulmonary resuscitation and called for an ambulance. Approximately ten minutes later, emergency medical technicians arrived and administered a series of defibrillation shocks with an AED and transported Atcovitz to a hospital. Although he survived the incident, Atcovitz sustained severe and permanent injuries.

Atcovitz sued Gulph Mills for negligence. Specifically, they claimed that, "had Gulph Mills possessed an AED device and used it on Atcovitz promptly, his injuries would have been significantly less. In its defense, Gulph Mills asserted that, at the time of Atcovitz's injury, its employees would not have been permitted by law to use an AED.

The court addressed the effect of the "AED Good Samaritan Act," which provides "Good Samaritan civil immunity" for use of an AED in certain instances. It specifically provides immunity for untrained individuals who, in good faith, use an AED in an emergency as an ordinary, reasonably prudent individual would do under the same or similar circumstances. Although the AED Good Samaritan Act was enacted after Atcovitz's injuries, the court found that its passage evinced the Legislature's desire that use of AEDs not be restricted solely to trained professionals.

Here, we must focus our analysis on the threshold element of duty. Only therein may we resolve the fundamental question of whether the plaintiff's interests are entitled to legal protection against the defendant's conduct.

A duty, in negligence cases, may be defined as an obligation, to which the law will give recognition and effect, to conform to a particular standard of conduct toward another. There is a duty if the court says there is a duty; the law, like the Constitution, is what we make it. Duty is only a word with which we state our conclusion that there is or is not to be liability; it necessarily begs the essential question. When we find a duty, breach and damage, everything has been said.

The Legislature's enactments and the ensuing regulations reveal that acquisition, maintenance, and use of an AED, along with AED training requirements, are highly regulated. Where our lawmakers have so thoroughly considered the statewide application and implications of a subject, this Court must refrain from imposing additional requirements upon that legislation.

Looking first to the EMS Act, the Legislature aspired to assure readily available and coordinated emergency medical services of the highest quality to the people of Pennsylvania. The implication of the Legislature's exclusion of untrained laypersons from the EMS Act and its regulations is to preclude unqualified and untrained individuals from administering emergency medical services using an AED. It would be absurd for the governmental system charged with rendering effective emergency medical care to hinder the delivery of that care using AEDs through the system, while ordinary citizens would be duty-bound to acquire, maintain, and use AEDs free from any regulation by the Department of Health.

The AED Good Samaritan Act, which was adopted two years after Atcovitz sustained his injuries, provides civil immunity for *trained* users of AEDs and requires that "expected users shall complete training in the use of an AED. As an *exception* to that general rule, the AED Good Samaritan Act provides civil immunity to untrained individuals who, *in good faith,* use an AED in an emergency as an ordinary, reasonably prudent individual would do under the same or similar circumstances. Significantly, the AED Good Samaritan Act defines "good faith" as including "a reasonable opinion that *the immediacy of the situation is such that the use of an AED should not be postponed until emergency medical services personnel arrive* or the person is hospitalized."

Thus, the AED Good Samaritan Act merely creates an exception for imposing liability on an untrained individual who uses an AED in limited emergency situations; it does not *authorize* its use by any such individual. Indeed, the exception applies only to instances where emergency medical services personnel are unavailable. In addition, it does not indicate that the Legislature aimed to dispense with the regulations governing the training and use of AEDs. Simply, the existence of a civil immunity provision for Good Samaritans who use an AED in an emergency situation cannot impose a duty on a business establishment to acquire, maintain, and use such a device on its premises.

The AED Good Samaritan Act does not impose a duty upon Gulph Mills to acquire, maintain, and use an AED. Plaintiff does not cite any other case, statute, or regulation that would have imposed such a duty on Gulph Mills at the time of Atcovitz's injuries in January 1996. Because Gulph Mills did not owe a duty to carry an AED, Appellees could not have established a *prima facie* claim of negligence. We reverse the order of the Superior Court and affirm the trial court's grant of summary judgment in favor of Gulph Mills.

What duty does an owner or possessor of land owe to a person who comes upon the premises? The answer will depend on whether the individual is a trespasser, licensee, or business visitor.

A **trespasser** is one who comes upon the premises of another without consent and with no legal right to be on the property. For instance, a burglar is a trespasser. The only obligation a land-owner or possessor of property owes to a trespasser is to avoid injuring the person through willful and wanton misconduct. Suppose Joe Robert fills his pool with piranhas to keep trespassers out of the water. Will Joe be liable if someone climbs over the fence, dives into the water, and is attacked by the man-eating fish? According to **Katco v. Briney**, discussed in Chapter Two, the answer is yes. The conduct of Joe Roberts is willful and wanton.

Because of the need to protect very young children, the **attractive nuisance doctrine** has been created to safeguard youngsters who trespass on the land of another that contains an inviting, but dangerous condition. For example, if the land contains a dangerous condition that will naturally attract young children to it, the possessor of land owes a duty to eliminate or protect the minor from that risk. A swimming pool is considered such an attraction and property owners are mandated to erect fences around their pools.

A **licensee** is a person who comes on the property of another with the owner's consent or with the legal right to be on the land. The most common type of licensee is a social guest or a person walking on the sidewalk. The owner or possessor of land is liable to a licensee for a defect on the property that the owner or possessor of land knew of or should have known of, and the guest is not likely to discover. For example, if the owner of a house is having the basement steps repaired and fails to warn the licensee of the repairs, the owner is liable if the guest falls. On the other hand, a thief who breaks into the same house and falls down the basement steps will not collect damages from the homeowner, since the failure to warn the thief is not willful and wanton misconduct.

A **business visitor** is one who enters the premises for a business purpose. A person who goes to a department store is a business visitor. In these circumstances, the landowner or possessor of land is liable for a defect that he knew of or should have known of, and the visitor is not liable to discover. While this standard seems to be the same as that owed to a licensee, the difference is that the business establishment owes a duty to make a reasonable inspection of the premises to make sure it is safe for the business visitor.

Businesses open to the public, such as department stores, theaters, and food markets, are particularly susceptible to having debris strewn on the floor. The proprietor of such a business must maintain the premises in a reasonably safe condition. The mere fact that a harmful condition may exist on the property, however, does not establish negligence on the part of the store owner. The injured patron must prove that the dangerous condition existed for such a sufficient period of time that a reasonable inspection would have discovered the problem. For instance, a puddle of milk on the floor of a supermarket that is partially dried, filled with footprints, and contains shopping-cart wheel marks would establish constructive notice on the part of the merchant of the dangerous situation. After all, this condition could only occur after a lengthy passage of time. On the other hand, a puddle of white milk that was not created by the actions of the merchant and is not soiled in any way would indicate a very recent spill for which the supermarket will have no liability.

SECTION 4.4
TYLER'S SPORTS
BAR AND GRILL

PROBLEM FOUR—A

PARK, BROWN & SMITH, P.C.
ATTORNEYS AT LAW
MEMORANDUM

TO: The Law Clerks

FROM: Peter Smith, Esquire

RE: Estate of Robert Jones v. Tyler's Sports Bar and Grill

As you know, Joe Roberts has an interest in Tyler's Sports Bar and Grill. In order to create an identity, Tyler's only serves poultry that has been specially bred by the Pennsylvania Dutch to reduce its fat content. The chicken and turkey are also served with the skin removed, thereby eliminating unnecessary calories. In any event, Mr. Roberts called me this morning with his latest crisis. It seems that a customer died in the Sports Bar while eating the grilled chicken special and Tyler's has received a letter of representation from an attorney threatening suit. Roberts conveyed the following facts to me:

Donny Jones was a frequent customer at the restaurant and always ordered the grilled chicken special. Two weeks ago, Jones entered the Sports Bar but seemed out of sorts. His clothes were disheveled and he was unshaven. He staggered to his usual table and reeked of liquor. His normal food order was delivered and Jones bit into a piece of chicken. All of a sudden, Jones seemed to get sick. His face changed colors; he grabbed his throat, and slumped over in his chair. A fellow customer screamed at the sight, and Joe Roberts ran over to the table. The owner checked the customer's vital signs, and noted that Jones' pulse was weak and irregular. Joe immediately called for an ambulance which arrived in minutes. The paramedics' efforts to save Jones, however, were to no avail, and he died. An autopsy determined the cause of death to be an obstruction to the decedent's airway caused by a chicken bone that had become lodged in the decedent's throat. The coroner's report further noted that Jones had a blood/alcohol content of 0.24% which is well above the legal limit for intoxication. Finally, the pathologist opined that it is not unusual for an extremely intoxicated person to choke to death on food.

Joe has learned that a physician was in the restaurant during the incident and did nothing to help out. In fact, Jones was a patient of this surgeon. When questioned by the police as to why he didn't assist the choking victim, the doctor stated that he was eating dinner and was tired after playing a full day of golf in the sun.

The attorney for the Estate of Mr. Jones claims that the bar did not exercise reasonable care to save its customer. It is asserted that not only should Joe have used the "Heimlich" maneuver on the customer, but the restaurant's staff knew that Jones had ordered chicken so the manager should have looked into the decedent's mouth to make sure that nothing was lodged in the customer's throat.

I am not sure if the lawyer also sent a letter to the surgeon about the physician's failure to help his patient. If the attorney does not name the physician in the lawsuit, I will join the doctor into the lawsuit as an additional or third party defendant. At least the owner of Tyler's attempted to help the decedent while the doctor continued to eat his food unconcerned with the health of his patient.

Please discuss the issues and defenses on behalf of all parties. Will the family of the decedent be successful in recovering money from either Tyler's or the doctor?

ANSWER SHEET
PROBLEM FOUR—A

Name   **Please Print Clearly**

1.   What duties did the bar owe to the decedent?

_____

_____

_____

_____

_____

_____

_____

_____

_____

_____

_____

_____

_____

_____

_____

_____

_____

_____

_____

_____

_____

2. What duty did the surgeon owe to his patient?

_____

_____

_____

_____

_____

_____

_____

_____

3. Who will win the lawsuit? Explain your answer in detail.

_____

_____

_____

_____

_____

_____

_____

_____

_____

_____

_____

**SECTION 4.5
BREACH OF DUTY**

The second element of a negligence action is quite simple. If a duty is owed, and a person fails to fulfill that obligation, a **breach of duty** has occurred. For example, a property owner owes a duty to a business visitor to make the property safe. This includes the obligation to inspect the premises on a reasonable basis. If a business establishment does not inspect its facility, and a business visitor is injured because a broken bottle or wet spot on the floor is not cleaned up in sufficient time, the store owner has breached its duty of care.

MICHAELENE GON V. DICK CLARK'S AMERICAN BANDSTAND
1996 WL 785533 (OHIO APP. 10TH DIST.)

Gon filed a complaint against Dick Clark's American Bandstand & Grill. Ms. Gon alleged Dick Clark's created and/or had actual or constructive knowledge of a dangerous condition and failed to remedy or warn of such dangerous condition. As a result of such alleged dangerous condition, Ms. Gon slipped and fell and sustained injuries.

In general, a shopkeeper owes a business invitee a duty of ordinary care in maintaining the premises in a reasonably safe condition so that its customers are not unnecessarily and unreasonably exposed to danger. However, a business owner is not an insurer of the customer's safety.

Where the injury is due to a hazardous condition not created by the business owner, the plaintiff must show the business owner had, or should have had, notice of the hazard for a sufficient time to enable the owner to remove it or warn patrons about it. Evidence of the length of time the hazard existed is necessary to support an inference that an owner had constructive notice.

At trial, therefore, Gon would have to show either: Dick Clark created the hazardous condition and failed to warn of it or otherwise failed to exercise ordinary care with regard to such condition, or the hazardous condition was created by someone else and Dick Clark had notice of such or in the exercise

of reasonable care should have had notice of such condition for a sufficient time to enable Dick Clark to remove it or warn patrons of it.

The record establishes the following: Ms. Gon went to Dick Clark's restaurant with three of her friends. It was very busy, and Ms. Gon and the party were told there would be a wait. Ms. Gon and her friends entered the bar. Two of Ms. Gon's friends were behind her and another friend was in front. Ms. Gon walked toward the booths to look at a display case. The next thing she knew, Ms. Gon had fallen to the floor.

Ms. Gon does not know what made her slip. Ms. Gon looked down at the floor to see why she had fallen but stated, "It was just as any other floor is at the time, but I just had no idea why this had happened to me." Ms. Gon testified that at the time, she did not know what caused her to fall, but she later formed the opinion that "it probably was some sort of a wet spot in the vicinity of the bar area that I walked through." Ms. Gon had no water on her hands or clothes.

Gon contends Dick Clark created the dangerous condition that consisted of a slippery floor. In support of this argument, Gon points to evidence that the area where Ms. Gon fell was a high traffic area and that the service bar, where ice, sinks, coolers and a soda gun were located, was within four feet of where Ms. Gon fell.

Gon's arguments consist largely of conclusions that have little if no basis in fact. First, there is simply no evidence that Dick Clark created a hazardous condition. Ms. Gon has no idea what she slipped on but believes, after hearing stories of prior incidents and knowing an employee wiped up a wet spot after she fell, that she must have slipped on a wet spot. Ms. Gon herself testified that she believes she slipped on a wet spot, not on a slippery floor itself.

There was no evidence of what exactly this wet spot was. The wet spot was not directly at the service bar area. While we do not require plaintiffs to have direct evidence showing how a hazard occurred, it would be unreasonable for this court to presume that whenever there is a wet spot on the floor of a restaurant, it was caused by the owner or occupier. Without more evidence in this case, we cannot infer that the restaurant caused the wet spot.

SECTION 4.6
PROXIMATE CAUSE

Proximate cause requires that there be a reasonable connection between the negligence of the defendant and the harm suffered by the plaintiff. The fact that a party is careless and another suffers an injury is not by itself enough to impose liability. Rather, the negligent conduct must be a substantial factor in causing the harm. For instance, a surgeon who leaves an instrument in a patient's abdomen following surgery has obviously breached the duty of exercising reasonable medical care. The patient's need for additional surgery to remove the medical instrument would be directly related to the doctor's malpractice.

The driver of a car traveling 90 m.p.h. down the opposite side of the road is negligent. Suddenly, a wheel from an airplane flying overhead falls off and kills the passenger in the speeding automobile. While the driver of the car is operating the vehicle in a negligent fashion, that negligence is not the proximate cause of the passenger's death. The falling wheel from the airplane is the substantial factor in causing the harm.

Obesity has become a major health issue in today's society with nearly twice as many overweight children than there were twenty years ago. McDonald's Corporation aggressively targets youngsters in their marketing campaigns and makes their stores children-friendly in order to entice families to visit their restaurants.

Fast food products offered by McDonald's come at a nutritional price. Super-sized french fries weigh in at 610 calories and 29 grams of total fat. A Big Mac tips the scales at 590 calories with 34 grams of fat. Topping off a meal with a Nestle Crunch McFlurry adds an additional 630 calories and 24 grams of fat. However, this information generally is not readily available in the restaurants or on the food wrappers. For the most part, consumers have no idea of the ingredients or nutritional value of what they order.

A class action lawsuit was filed against McDonald's on behalf of overweight children alleging that the fast-food chain is engaged in deception in the making and selling of its products and that this wrongful conduct has caused the minors who consume McDonald's products to harm their health by becoming obese.

McDonald's objected to the lawsuit and claimed that the plaintiffs failed to establish a causal connection between their obesity and the consumption of McDonald's fast food products. The court's ruling is contained in **Pellman v. McDonald's Corporation.**

PELLMAN V. MCDONALD'S CORPORATION
237 F. SUPP. 2D 512 (S.D. N.Y., 2003)

The plaintiffs have alleged that the practices of McDonald's in making and selling their products are deceptive and that this deception has caused the minors who have consumed McDonalds' products to injure their health by becoming obese.

Americans spend more than $110 billion on fast food each year, and on any given day in the United States, almost one in four adults visit a fast food restaurant.

Today there are nearly twice as many overweight children and almost three times as many overweight adolescents as there were in 1980. Obese individuals have a 50 to 100 percent increased risk of premature death from all causes.

The plaintiffs allege five causes of action as members of a class action of minors who have purchased and consumed McDonald's products. Count III sounds in negligence, alleging that McDonald's acted negligently in selling food products that are high in cholesterol, fat, salt and sugar when studies show that such foods cause obesity and detrimental health effects.

Plaintiffs argue that McDonalds' products have been so altered that their unhealthy attributes are now outside the ken of the average reasonable consumer. They point to McDonalds' ingredient lists to show that McDonalds' customers worldwide are getting much more than what is commonly considered to be a chicken finger, a hamburger, or a french fry.

McDonald's argues that Count III should be dismissed because the plaintiffs may not as a matter of

law allege that the unhealthy attributes of McDonalds' products were the proximate cause of their obesity and other health problems.

In order to show proximate cause, a plaintiff must establish that the defendant's conduct was a substantial cause in bringing about the harm. The issue of proximate cause may be determined as a matter of law where no reasonable person could find causation based on the facts alleged in the complaint. E.g., No reasonable person could find probable cause based on the facts in the Complaint without resorting to "wild speculation."

First, the Complaint does not specify how often the plaintiffs ate at McDonald's. The class action proposed by plaintiffs could consist entirely of persons who ate at McDonald's on one occasion. As a result, any number of other factors then potentially could have affected the plaintiffs' weight and health.

Second, McDonald's points out that articles on which plaintiffs rely in their Complaint suggest that a number of factors other than diet may come into play in obesity and the health problems of which plaintiffs complain. Obesity is a complex multifactorial disease developing from interactive influences of numerous factors—social behavioral, physiological, metabolic, cellular, and molecular in addition to cultural and genetic factors.

As a result, in order to allege that McDonalds' products were a significant factor in the plaintiffs' obesity and health problems, the Complaint must address these other variables and, if possible, eliminate them or show that a McDiet is a substantial factor despite these other variables.

Because the Complaint fails to allege that the danger of the McDonalds' products were not well-known and fails to allege with sufficient specificity that the McDonalds' products were a proximate cause of the plaintiffs' obesity and health problems, Count III shall be dismissed. Leave is granted to replead all claims.

SECTION 4.7
DAMAGES

The last element of a claim is **damages**. This is the amount of money awarded to an injured person as the result of the wrongful or improper conduct of the defendant. This recovery may take the form of compensatory and punitive damages.

The purpose of compensatory damages is to make an injured party whole by providing a sum of money that will return the aggrieved party to a position as though nothing had ever happened. These damages must always bear a reasonable relationship to the negligent act of the defendant, and cannot be speculative. In a tort action, the damages should place the injured party in as substantially good a position as that occupied before the injury. These damages, however, are not always easy to quantify. While one may quantify the amount of lost wages, how much is a broken arm worth? Would it matter if the injured party is a painter or professional quarterback?

Reasonable people can differ on the value of a case but the following elements may be considered in arriving at a dollar figure: medical expenses, lost wages, property damages, and pain and suffering.

Pain and suffering is the most controversial of the recoverable items because it is subjective and cannot be calculated with mathematical certainty. The value of each case will also change depending upon the circumstances. For instance, if the victim of a broken arm makes a good recovery after six weeks, the case will have one value. If the injury, however, results in a permanent impairment in the person's range of motion with continuing pain upon elevating the arm, it is worth a much larger sum of money.

Punitive damages may be claimed if the conduct of the wrongdoer is outrageous. In that event, the law will punish the party by awarding an additional sum of money to prevent the conduct from ever occurring again. For instance, an automobile accident that occurs because the driver simply failed to see a stop sign is insufficient to give rise to punitive damages. Punitive damages, however, will be awarded if the accident was caused by a driver's intoxication.

**SECTION 4.8
DEFENSES TO A
NEGLIGENCE ACTION**

Even though a defendant is negligent, an injured party's own conduct may preclude recovery. Two defenses to a negligence action are contributory negligence and assumption of the risk.

Contributory negligence is the failure of the plaintiff to act as a reasonable person under the circumstances. A driver who fails to stop for a red light is negligent. While the operator of the vehicle with the green light has the right of way, that driver may not blindly proceed through the intersection without first looking to the left and right. If the two vehicles collide, and neither driver looked for the other, they are both negligent. Since the individual who went through the red light bears the bulk of the liability, can the other motorist collect damages? No. A plaintiff may not recover if he or she has any degree of contributory negligence even if that fault is 1% of the responsibility for the accident. Only a handful of jurisdictions follow this harsh rule such as North Carolina, Virginia, Alabama, Maryland and the District of Columbia.

Most jurisdictions find this principle too harsh and have adopted a modified concept called **comparative negligence**. Basically, as long as the plaintiff's negligence is not greater than that of the defendant, the plaintiff may recover damages, but the verdict will be reduced by the percentage of the plaintiff's negligence. In other words, if the plaintiff is found to be 30% at fault and the verdict is $10,000, the award will be reduced to $7,000.

If the plaintiff and defendant are found to be equally at fault, the plaintiff will receive one-half of the verdict, since the plaintiff's negligence is not greater than that of the other responsible party. If the plaintiff, however, is found to be 51% at fault, the claimant will receive nothing, since his negligence is greater than that of the defendant.

REKUN V. PELAEZ
976 A.2D 578 (PA. SUPER., 2009)

Tiffany Rekun, the Administratrix of the Estate of Neil Rekun, filed suit against Carl Pelaez after Neil Rekun was killed while riding a motorcycle when hit by Pelaez. Ultimately, the parties agreed to binding arbitration before former Judge Thomas Raup. Judge Raup found Neil Rekun 60% negligent and Carl Pelaez 40% negligent and determined the damages to be $800,000.

Under Pennsylvania's Comparative Negligence Act, a plaintiff cannot recover if he or she is more than 50% negligent. See 42 Pa.C.S.A. § 7102(a). Rekun argues that the language the parties had agreed on (in the arbitration agreement), "comparative fault," did not include a bar on recovery if a plaintiff was more than 50% negligent, just a proportionate reduction (of the award).

On March 12, 2008 Judge Raup found Neil Rekun 60% negligent and Pelaez 40% negligent and determined the damages to be $800,000. Pelaez appeals, claiming that the principles of comparative fault and comparative negligence are one and the same and because Rekun was found to be 60% negligent judgment should be entered in favor of Pelaez.

We find that several factors weigh in favor of barring Rekun from recovery when he was 60% at fault: The history of the negotiations was that traditional comparative negligence principles would apply, barring a plaintiff from recovery if he or she is more than 50% negligent. The Comparative Negligence Act provides:

> In all actions brought to recover damages for negligence resulting in death or injury to person or property, the fact that the plaintiff may have been guilty of contributory negligence shall not bar a recovery by the plaintiff or his legal representative where such negligence was not greater than the causal negligence of the defendant or defendants against whom recovery is sought, but any damages sustained by the plaintiff shall be diminished in proportion to the amount of negligence attributed to the plaintiff.

Additionally, our courts have used the terms "comparative negligence" and "comparative fault" interchangeably, intending them to mean the same thing.

Rekun's attorney stated in the November 27, 2005 letter that "comparative fault" would apply, and as there is no statute or case law that defines comparative fault separate from comparative negligence, common sense says that the parties agreed to apply the standard principles of comparative fault/comparative negligence. In fact, Rekun's attorney, to clarify his use and interpretation of the term "comparative fault," only explains how it will affect the maximum amount recoverable. He states: "The way you have it phrased is that comparative fault would apply to policy limits and not to the award, which ... is subject to the cap." If Rekun's counsel meant to deviate from the traditional principle of comparative negligence–i.e. allow Rekun to recover even where it is found that Neil Rekun was 51% or more negligent-one would expect that Rekun's attorney would have clearly set out the terms, instead of discussing policy limits and the cap on damages.

Finally, when the words of a contract are clear and unambiguous, the intent of the parties is to be discovered from the express language of the agreement. Where ambiguity exists, however, the courts are free to construe the terms against the drafter and to consider extrinsic evidence in so doing.

As Rekun's counsel was the party who drafted the final contract, we shall construe the terms against him, as the drafter. Thus, we find that the parties agreed that the finding of comparative negligence would apply to the entire award, which would then be capped at $100,000. Because Judge Raup found Neil Rekun to be 60% negligent, Rekun is barred from any recovery.

Case remanded with directions to confirm the arbitration award and enter judgment in favor of Pelaez.

The second defense to a negligence action is **assumption of the risk**. If the plaintiff knows of the danger but voluntarily exposes himself to the harm, the plaintiff will be barred from recovery. For example, if a person jumps over an open manhole instead of walking around it, he will have assumed the risk of injury if he falls into the unguarded hole.

Over the years, a number of lawsuits have been filed for injuries to spectators at sporting events who are hit by flying objects such as baseballs or hockey pucks. This type of claim is generally unsuccessful because the risks are well known and inherent to the event. Most people who attend baseball games are aware that foul balls are hit into the stands on a regular basis. The allure of catching one of these errant balls is also part of the fun of attending the game.

To reinforce the awareness of the danger for purpose of assumption of the risk, the reverse side of an event ticket will contain a warning concerning the danger of flying objects leaving the playing field. The awareness of this danger is reinforced when the announcer repeats the warning over the public address system both before and during the game. For instance, the hockey ticket provided by the Philadelphia Flyers provides on the reverse side:

> Pucks flying into spectator areas can cause serious injury. Be alert when in spectator areas, including after the stoppage of play. If injured, notify an usher for directions to medical station. Ticket holder assumes all risks and dangers of personal injury and all other hazards arising from or related in any way to the event for which this ticket is issued, whether occurring prior to, during or after the event, including, specifically (but not exclusively), the danger of being injured by hockey pucks and sticks, and other spectators or players or by thrown objects. Ticket Holder agrees that the Spectrum Arena Limited Partners, the National Hockey League, Comcast - Spectacor, L.P., the Philadelphia Flyers, the playing teams, the players and the officers, employees and agents of each are expressively released by Ticket Holder from claims arising from or in any way related to the foregoing causes...

Before and during the game, the Flyers' announcer also warns fans about the danger of pucks leaving the playing surface and that fans should be vigilant of this risk at all times.

Does a fan, however, assume the risk of injury when she is injured while other fans wildly chase a foul baseball that goes into the stands or by a football that sails over the end zone safety net and into the seats? In other words, should the management of a stadium be liable for failing to protect a fan from the unruly actions of people who will do anything, including knocking people over, in their pursuit of a souvenir ball? This is the issue in the following case.

MITCHELL TELEGA V. SECURITY BUREAU, INC.
719 A.2D 372 (PA. SUPER., 1998)

Mitchell Telega and his wife, Karen, attended a Pittsburgh Steelers football game on December 6, 1992. For approximately two years, the Telegas were season ticket holders whose seats were located in Section 41, the pie-shaped end-zone section of the stadium behind the Steelers' goalpost. During the last quarter of the game, the Steelers' kicker attempted a field goal. The football was catapulted through the uprights of the goalpost, over the stadium net designed to catch it, and into the stands. Mr. Telega, who saw the ball coming his way, stood up in front of his assigned seat, extended his arms, and cleanly fielded the football. When he attempted to sit down, Mr. Telega was thrust from his seat and trampled face first into the cement aisle by aggressive fans who stripped him of the souvenir ball. Mr. Telega suffered numerous injuries from this attack, including facial lacerations, a sprained shoulder and arm resulting in extensive physical therapy, and a broken nose that required surgery.

Prior to this incident, the Telegas and other patrons seated in the end zone section of the stadium lodged complaints with the stadium's Guest Relations Office and security personnel concerning the lack of security and crowd control in their seating area during field goal and extra point attempts. They often complained that the football regularly clears the catch net, lands in the stands, and causes a disturbance among the fans, resulting in a danger to the welfare of the patrons seated in their section.

Appellants filed a complaint asserting a cause of action in negligence against Security Bureau, Inc. alleging that the defendants breached a duty of care owed to Mr. Telega by, failing to supervise security guards at the Stadium and failing to regulate crowd control in the end-zone seating area.

Our courts have long refused to grant recovery for injuries sustained by amusement patrons, which were caused by a risk inherent in the activity in question. The Court has also denied recovery where a spectator at a stockcar race track was struck by one of the racing vehicles while he was standing in the unprotected "pit" area of the track; the patron admitted that his presence in the pit area was unauthorized and that collisions in this area were common.

The question before this Court is whether a spectator will be held to assume as inherent in the game the risk of being attacked by displaced fans if he catches a soaring football. We believe not.

The risk involved here is unlike the risk of being struck by an errant puck while a spectator at a hockey game, falling down or being bumped by other skaters at a roller skating rink, or being hit by a batted ball during baseball tryouts. Contrary to the instant matter, these cases involve risks that are inherent in the activity itself and are specific to the activity at any appropriate venue. They are, therefore, as a matter of law, risks assumed by the spectators and participants who patronize the amusement facilities. It is not a matter of universal knowledge that an onslaught of displaced fans is a common, frequent or expected occurrence to someone catching a souvenir football. Therefore, it cannot be said that the injuries suffered by Mr. Telega resulted from a risk that any spectator would be held to anticipate and against which an amusement facility has no duty to protect. Certainly this matter would compel a different result had Mr. Telega been injured by the aerial football itself rather than the displaced fans intent on obtaining it.

Therefore, the trial court committed an error of law and we must reverse.

SECTION 4.9
IMPUTED NEGLIGENCE

Imputed negligence or vicarious liability means that because of a special relationship that exists between the parties, one person can be held liable for the negligence of the other. The classic example of such a relationship is that of employer and employee. Even though the employer has done nothing wrong, he or she will be responsible for the torts of their employees that were committed within the scope of the employment. For example, a bus company will be liable for an accident caused by the negligence of a bus driver. However, the bus company will generally not be liable for the assault of a customer by a bus driver since an assault is beyond the scope of the employment.

An employer will also not be liable for the torts of an **independent contractor**. An independent contractor is one who undertakes to perform the act requested on his own and is not subject to the control of an employer. If a professional sports team charters an airplane to fly the team to its next game, the airline is an independent contractor and not an employee of the sports franchise. The team exercises no control over how to fly the plane, and the team would not be liable for the torts of the pilot if the plane crashes, even though it hired the airline.

JAMES DeFULIO v. SPECTAGUARD, INC.
FEBRUARY TERM, 1990 #6199 (C. P. PHILA., 1990)

On May 16, 1988, Plaintiff James DeFulio was climbing a fence to enter Veteran's Stadium (the Stadium) to see a Pink Floyd concert. He did not have a ticket. As Plaintiff neared the top of the fence he was climbing, he used his hand to grasp the ledge of concrete platform above him. Testimony revealed that a security guard who was standing on the platform stepped on Plaintiff's hand causing him to fall 15 feet to a concrete concourse and fracture both ankles.

Plaintiff brought the instant suit against Spectaguard, Inc. (Spectaguard) and Electric Factory Concerts, Inc. (Electric Factory) alleging that they were vicariously liable for the guard's actions.

Spectaguard employed the security guard in question and one of the duties was to prevent people who did not have tickets from entering the Stadium. Following a trial, the jury found in favor of Plaintiff in the amount of $165,000 and against Spectaguard and Electric Factory.

Under the doctrine of respondeat superior, the negligence of an employee may be imputed to the employer. **Fitzgerald v. McCutcheon, 410 A.2d 1270 (Pa. Super. Ct., 1979).** However, before an employer will be held liable for an employee's actions, it must be determined that the employee's actions occurred within the course and scope of his employment. Pennsylvania courts have adopted the Restatement (Second) of Agency Section 228 in determining whether an employee's conduct is done within the scope of employment:

1. Conduct of a servant is within the scope of employment if, but only if:

    a. it is of the kind he is employed to perform;

    b. it occurs substantially within the authorized time and space limits;

    c. it is actuated, at least in part, by a purpose to serve the master, and

d. if force is intentionally used by the servant, the use of force is not unexpected by the master.

Defendants conceded that the guard's conduct occurred within the authorized time and space and that it was "arguably actuated by a purpose to serve his employer." However, Defendants argue that there was no evidence that the guard's conduct was of the kind he was employed to perform. Further, Defendants argued that there was no evidence that the force used by the guard (in stepping on Plaintiff's fingers) was "not unexpected" by Spectaguard.

Pennsylvania Courts have addressed the issue of whether an employee's action is unexpected by the employer and not of the kind he is employed to perform.

It is, in general, sufficient to make the master responsible that he gave to the servant an authority, or made it his duty to act in respect to the business in which he was engaged when the wrong was committed, and that the act complained of was done in the course of his employment. The master, in that case, will be deemed to have consented to and authorized the act of the servant, and he will not be excused from liability, although the servant abused his authority, or was reckless in the performance of his duty, or inflicted an unnecessary injury in executing his master's orders.

The law, as applied to the facts of the instant case, supported the jury's finding that the guard's actions occurred within the scope of his employment. First, there was evidence that the guard's conduct was of the kind he was employed to perform. Specifically, the guard was employed, in part, and authorized by Spectaguard to make contact with and prevent entry to the Concert by people who did not have tickets. Since Plaintiff was climbing the Stadium's fence, it surely appeared obvious to the guard that Plaintiff was the sort of person that Spectaguard paid its employees to make contact with and keep out of the concert. Secondly, the conduct in question occurred within the authorized time and space limits. Without question, it occurred at the concert and on stadium grounds. Thirdly, the guard's actions served the purpose of Spectaguard by preventing an individual whom did not have a ticket from entering the stadium. Finally, regarding the force employed, Spectaguard's incident report from the night in question evidenced the fact that guards ejected people from the concert including people who did not have tickets and who climbed the fences surrounding the Stadium. The guard showed a lack of judgment but such conduct does not necessarily extinguish an employer's liability. Under the instant circumstances it was within the province of the jury to determine whether the guard's conduct was not unexpected by Spectaguard and whether Spectaguard and Electric Factory could he held liable for the tortuous conduct of the guard.

Defendants' request is denied.

PARK, BROWN & SMITH, P.C.
ATTORNEYS AT LAW
MEMORANDUM

To: All Law Clerks

FROM: Peter Smith, Esquire

RE: Joe Roberts v. The Stallions

For Joe Roberts' birthday, his son obtained a " Press Pass" for his father to attend the Stallions opening football game. Joe was ecstatic since he had never seen Tony play in a live professional football game. Roberts stood on the sidelines next to the Stallions' bench and told everyone that his son was the place-kicker. As a special treat, Tony had arranged for some of the Stallions' cheerleaders to give his father a birthday cheer. During the beginning of the second quarter, the cheerleaders started to sing Happy Birthday to Joe who was speechless.

Unfortunately, the game was still being played, and the Stallions' 250-pound fullback caught a pass and was pushed out of bounds. The player's momentum carried him into Joe, who had his back to the field as he watched the cheerleaders. Mr. Roberts was violently knocked to the ground and broke his right leg in three places.

Joe Roberts wishes to file suit against the Stallions for negligence in not protecting him against being hit by a football player as he stood on the sidelines. Joe contends the team should not have issued a sideline pass if it was dangerous for an individual to stand there. I am sure the Stallions will argue that Joe assumed the risk of being injured. Does a person normally assume the risk of being hurt by a football player when the spectator is standing ten yards off the field? Based upon **Lowe v. California League of Professional Baseball**, can Joe prevail in a suit against the Stallions since Joe was watching the cheerleaders at the time he was hurt? Are the Stallions responsible for the actions of their cheerleaders in diverting Joe's attention from the game? I suspect the team will argue that the cheerleaders exceeded their duties by engaging in a private cheer. Please refer to **DeFulio v. Spectaguard, Inc.,** which is set forth immediately before this problem, in order to ascertain whether the cheerleaders were acting within the scope of their employment with the Stallions.

JOHN LOWE V. CALIFORNIA PROFESSIONAL BASEBALL
56 CAL. APP.4TH 112 (CAL., 1997)

John Lowe was seriously injured when struck on the left side of his face by a foul ball while attending a professional baseball game. The game was being played at "The Epicenter," home field of the Rancho Cucamonga Quakes.

The Quakes, at their home games, feature a mascot who goes by the name of "Tremor." He is a caricature of a dinosaur, standing seven feet tall with a tail, which protrudes out from the costume. Tremor was performing his antics in the stands just along the left field foul line. Tremor was behind plaintiff and had been touching him with his (Tremor's) tail. Plaintiff was thereby distracted and turned toward Tremor. In the next moment, just as plaintiff returned his attention to the playing field, he was struck by a foul ball before he could react to it. The case was resolved in the trial court by summary judgment entered in favor of the defendant.

In the action, filed after his injury, plaintiff's complaint was styled in a single count, a refreshing example of clear and concise pleading. The key charging allegations were contained in two paragraphs:

1. On said date and some time after the stated time and after the seventh inning, 'Tremor' the Quake's mascot, came up into the stadium in the area where plaintiff and his group were seated. Tremor was accompanied by an usher as he performed antics and entertained the crowd. Tremor is a person who wears a dinosaur costume with a long protruding tail. As John Lowe sat in his assigned seat, he was facing forward and looking toward the playing field when suddenly, and without warning or his consent, his right shoulder was touched by the tail of Tremor's costume. As he turned to his right to see who, or what, was touching him, baseball play had resumed and a batted ball, believed to be a foul

ball, hit the plaintiff on the left side of his face breaking multiple facial bones.

2. The Left Terrace Section, where the plaintiff was seated with his group, is located northwesterly of the left field foul ball territory, and in the direct line of foul balls passing west of the third base line. Tremor's antics and interference, while the baseball game was in play, prevented the plaintiff from being able to protect himself from any batted ball and foreseeably increased the risks to John Lowe over and above those inherent in the sport.

These deposition excerpts provide an insight into how plaintiff was injured:

Q. *Where was the mascot at the time that the foul ball was hit?*

A. **Directly behind me.**

Q. *How long had the mascot been directly behind you at the time you were hit?*

A. **I would say probably two minutes.**

Q. *Did any part of the mascot's costume or person touch you before you were hit?*

A. **Yes.**

Q. *And what or how were you touched by this mascot?*

A. **With his tail.**

Q. *When did that occur in relationship to when you were hit by the ball?*

A. **Well, during that approximate two-minute span he was doing his act. And I felt this bam, bam, bam, on the back of my head and shoulders, and I turned around to see what he was doing.**

Q. *And when you turned around and looked, what did you see?*

A. Well, I noticed that he was doing his antics to the crowd that was in the immediate area. And I saw that as he was turning his body, his tail was hitting me.

Q. *Where were you looking at the moment the ball was hit?*

A. I had just turned my head towards the field as the ball arrived.

Q. *And in terms of timing, was it almost instantaneous that you turned your head to the field and got hit?*

A. Yes.

Q. *Where were you looking immediately before you turned your head toward the field?*

A. Up at Tremor.

Q. *And at that time you were looking at Tremor immediately before turning your head back to the field and getting hit, was the reason that you were looking at Tremor that his tail had just tapped you on the shoulder again and you turned around and looked?*

A. Yes.

The dispositive issue in this case then is whether the mascot's antics and their resulting distraction of the plaintiff operated to increase the inherent risks assumed by a spectator at a baseball game. In this regard, it is well established that defendants generally do have a duty to use due care not to increase the risks to a participant over and above those inherent in the sport. The rule is no different in instances involving spectators.

The key inquiry here is whether the risk which led to plaintiff's injury involved some feature or aspect of the game, which is inevitable or unavoidable in the actual playing of the game. In the first instance, foul balls hit into the spectators' area clearly create a risk of injury. If such foul balls were to be eliminated, it would be impossible to play the game. Thus, foul balls represent an inherent risk to spectators attending baseball games, and such risk is assumed. Can the same thing be said about the antics of the mascot? We think not. Actually, the declaration of the person who dressed up as Tremor, recounted that there were occasional games played when he was not there. In view of this testimony, as a matter of law, we hold that the antics of the mascot are not an essential or integral part of the playing of a baseball game. In short, the game can be played in the absence of such antics. Moreover, whether such antics increased the inherent risk to plaintiff is an issue of fact to be resolved at trial.

We note further, under the holding in **Neinstein v. Los Angeles Dodgers, 185 Cal. App. 3d 176,** absent any distraction by the mascot, that plaintiff could have assumed the risk. Justice Compton, writing in Neinstein, observed that the plaintiff "voluntarily elected to sit in a seat which was clearly unprotected by any form of screening. She was sufficiently warned of the risk by common knowledge of the nature of the sport. The Dodgers were under no duty to do anything further to protect her from the hazard."

However, in *Neinstein*, there was no mascot bothering the plaintiff and thus distracting her attention from the playing field. Thus, *Neinstein* is readily distinguishable.

Based upon the foregoing analysis, we hold that the trial court improperly granted the motion for summary judgment.

ANSWER SHEET
PROBLEM FOUR—B

Name

Please Print Clearly

1. Did Joe Roberts assume the risk of his injuries? Explain your answer.

_____

_____

_____

_____

_____

_____

_____

_____

_____

_____

_____

_____

_____

_____

_____

_____

_____

_____

_____

2. Will the Stallions be held liable for the actions of the cheerleaders?

Generally, parents are not held liable for the torts of their children unless a parent is directly at fault, if the child is acting as the agent of the parent at the time of the harm, or if the parent participates in or encourages the improper act. For instance, a parent will be held liable if he or she leaves a loaded gun on the table and a young child shoots someone with the weapon. Liability attaches because the parent is negligent in leaving the gun unattended and not because of the parental relationship.

Some states have passed laws to hold parents liable for the torts of their children in specific instances. The following statute is the law in Pennsylvania:

23 Pa. C.S.A. Section 5502 —Liability of Parents

Any parent whose child is found liable or is adjudged guilty by a court…of a tortuous act shall be liable to the person who suffers the injury to the extent set forth in this chapter.

23 Pa. C.S.A. Section 5505—Monetary Limits of Liability

Liability of the parents under this Chapter shall be limited to:

1. The sum of $1,000 for injuries suffered by any one person as a result of the tortuous act or continuous series of tortuous acts.

2. The sum of $2,500 regardless of the number of persons who suffer injury as a result of one tortuous act or continuous series of tortuous acts.

Are the parents of a school bully liable for the child's actions in harming a classmate? That is the subject of the following case:

Garcia v. Grepling
561 S. E.2d 868 (Ga. App., 2002)

Anthony Garcia was severely injured after Charles Grepling and Kevin Lanterman attacked him at a high school party. Garcia brought this action against Grepling and Lanterman seeking a recovery of damages for injuries sustained in the assault. Garcia also named Grepling's father as a defendant, charging him with liability under a theory of negligent supervision of his minor son.

It is well settled that unless changed by statute, parents are not liable for the torts of their minor children merely because of the parent-child relationship.

When liability exists, it is based on a principal-agent or a master-servant relationship where the negligence of the child is imputed to the parent, or it is based on the negligence of the parent in some factual situation such as allowing the child to have unsupervised control of a dangerous instrumentality.

Recovery has been permitted where there was some parental negligence in furnishing or permitting a child access to an instrumentality with which the child likely would injure a third party. In those cases in which the parent did not furnish the dangerous instrumentality to the child, the standard for imposing liability upon a parent for failing to prevent the child's action is whether the parent knew of the child's proclivity or propensity for the specific dangerous activity.

Garcia's argument is that the father may be held liable because he was put on notice of a dangerous proclivity or propensity by his son to commit such an assault. According to Garcia, such notice was provided to the father as a result of two prior incidents resulting in his son's suspension from school. In our opinion, the undisputed facts underlying the prior incidents were insufficient to charge Grepling's father with knowledge of a propensity to engage in the "specific dangerous activity" resulting in Garcia's injuries. Both Grepling and another student involved in the first incident were suspended from school af-

ter the other student challenged Grepling to a fight which he accepted by knocking the other student to the ground and then walking away. In the second incident, Grepling was suspended for pushing one student, spitting on another, and using foul language and inappropriate gestures during the taping of a video for a student project. Because these incidents consisted of rather typical schoolyard altercations in which no one complained of any injuries, knowledge of them was insufficient to charge the father with vicarious liability for the tortuous conduct of his son here.

Because the undisputed facts of this case entitle Grepling's father to judgment as a matter of law, the trial court did not err in granting his motion for summary judgment.

SECTION 4.11
INTENTIONAL TORTS

When the wrongdoer purposely sets out to harm another, that conduct gives rise to an intentional tort and may result in the imposition of money damages. Theories of liability include actions for a battery, assault, invasion of privacy, defamation, infliction of emotional distress, and false imprisonment.

Intentional torts are treated more seriously by the courts and verdicts frequently include awards of both compensatory and punitive damages, which sum is to punish the wrongdoer for his actions. Punitive damages are generally not covered by insurance and remain the personal responsibility of the actor.

SECTION 4.12
INFLICTION OF
EMOTIONAL DISTRESS

A person who by extreme and outrageous conduct intentionally or recklessly causes severe emotional distress to another is liable to that person for any bodily harm that may result from the emotional distress. The outrageous conduct must go beyond the bounds of normal decency and be considered as intolerable in a civilized community.

For instance, racial slurs in the workplace can be actionable as was the case where a sheriff called a co-officer a "jungle bunny," or when a physician spoke to a female employee in an unwelcome "lewd" and "sexual" manner. However, a debt collection agency was found not to have committed the tort of infliction of emotional distress where its employees made six phone calls over a three month period and told the debtor that they were "no better than lying thieves or sponges" and that the creditor was going to "sue your asses" or "sue the hell out of you." The court felt that the language used by debt collector's employees was not so atrocious as to be utterly intolerable in a civilized community. Likewise, liability does not extend to mere insults, indignities, threats, annoyances, or petty oppression.

People are very squeamish when it comes to finding unnatural things in food. Over the years, a variety of food cases have arisen in which foreign substances have been found in food ranging from a mouse inside a bottle of soda to finding chewing gum in a salad. **Coca-Cola Bottling Co. v. Hagan** deals with whether two individuals who consumed a can of soda that appeared to contain a condom can succeed in a suit for inflection of emotional distress because they believed they could contact the AIDS virus.

COCA-COLA BOTTLING CO. V. HAGAN
813 SO.2D 167 (FLA. APP. 5 DIST., 2002)

The plaintiffs, Hagan and Parker, consumed some of the contents of a bottle of Coca-Cola which tasted flat. Upon inspection, it appeared to have a foreign object floating in it which they assumed was a "used condom." Neither investigated nor had the contents of the bottle been examined. They did give the bottle to Coca-Cola for analysis. It was inspected and analyzed by a chemist and manager of Coca-Cola Quality Assurance Department. He concluded that although on visual inspection the foreign object appeared to be a condom, it was "to a scientific certainty" a mold.

Recovery of damages for consuming a part of a bottle of Coca Cola containing a mold is possible. However, virtually all of the damages established by the plaintiffs related to their fear they had been exposed to the AIDS virus and we conclude they established no valid basis for this fear.

Hagan and Parker established that after drinking part of the contents of the can of Coke, they were to seek treatment for protection against AIDS, including tests for HIV, immediately and again six months later. They testified they were fearful their possible exposure to AIDS would damage their child care

business and reputations. They were embarrassed and humiliated because others knew about their possible exposure to this dreadful disease. They were fearful that they could, in the indefinite future, contract AIDS, and this fear of becoming HIV positive interfered with one plaintiff's marital relations. Recognizing that the plaintiffs' fear of contracting AIDS was the basis and essence of their damage claim, the trial court ruled and so instructed the jury that their recovery for emotional distress should be limited to the time beginning with their drinking the Coca-Cola to six months later when they received a negative HIV test. He concluded that after that time, the plaintiffs' fears of contracting AIDS would not be reasonable because there was no scientific basis to substantiate their emotional upset beyond that point.

The fear of AIDS cases in which recovery has been permitted for negligent infliction of emotional distress and upset alone, require as a threshold, a showing by the plaintiff that the fear is reasonable. The great majority of cases say this means the plaintiff must show that the virus was present, and that the contact between the material containing the virus and the plaintiff was a medically and scientifically accepted channel for the transmission of the disease.

The plaintiffs failed to establish the foreign item in the bottle was a used condom. But for purposes of argument only, even if they had established that fact, they failed to establish the virus was present. Only a very small percentage of the general population is HIV positive or has AIDS and the mere presence of semen would not be enough.

Without such showings or proofs, a plaintiff's fear of contracting AIDS is unreasonable as a matter of law and not a legally compensable injury. As a matter of public policy, the allowance of such lawsuits without the threshold proofs discussed above could lead to an explosion of frivolous litigation, opening as some courts say a "Pandora's box" of AIDS phobia claims.

We conclude that the judgment being appealed in this case must be reversed because the plaintiffs failed to establish a basis for an award of damages based on fear of getting AIDS.

SECTION 4.13
ASSAULT AND BATTERY

A **battery** is the intentional touching of the body of another or an object closely associated with the body in an offensive or harmful manner. Mere recklessness or negligence on the part of the actor is insufficient. The tortfeasor must, in fact, have intended to cause the harm.

An offensive touching is as objectionable as a harmful touching. For example, the uninvited touching of the body of another or an unappreciated kiss is as actionable as a punch in the mouth. There are times, however, when an intentional touching will not be deemed a battery. For instance, consent is a defense to a battery which permission may arise by words or implication. A person who engages in sports or play impliedly consents to the usual touching associated with that sport. For example, professional football is a violent sport in which players frequently are injured because of the severity of the impact. If a star running back is injured while being tackled by five members of the opposing team, he cannot sue the opposing players since the tackle is part of the game. The Cincinnati Bengals, however, were required to defend a lawsuit brought by a Denver Bronco who was intentionally hit in the back of the head by a Cincinnati player following an intercepted pass. The court ruled that the general customs of football do not approve the intentional punching or striking of other players. **Jack Hackbart v. Cincinnati Bengals, Inc., 601 F.2d 516 (1979).** Likewise, a hockey player who intentionally strikes another player in the head with a hockey stick commits a battery. Marty McSorley committed such a transgression in October of 2000 while playing for the Boston Bruins. At the end of the game, McSorley purposely struck Donald Brashear on the side of the head with his hockey stick causing the player to fall to the ice temporarily losing consciousness.

Professional boxing is a violent and vicious sport in which one of the primary goals is to knock out the opponent as quickly as possible. The biting of Evander Holyfield's ear by Mike Tyson during their heavyweight bout, however, was not a usual touching of the sport and would constitute a battery.

A consensual touching may be a battery if the consent is procured by fraud. For example, a party who touches the arms and legs of a woman on the fraudulent misrepresentation that he is a doctor is responsible for a battery.

A person's motives in initiating the touching are also not relevant. A hostile intent or a desire to harm the victim is not required. Rather, it is the intent to bring about a result that establishes a battery. For instance, in **Andrews v. Peters**, a co-employee jokingly tapped the back of the knee of another worker causing her to fall to the ground. While the co-employee did not intend to cause any harm by his prank, he did intend to tap the back of the woman's leg, which constituted a battery.

Margaret Andrews v. Richard Peters
330 S. E.2d 638 (Ct. App. N.C., 1985)

The facts, briefly stated, are as follows. The plaintiff, Margaret H. Andrews, was injured when her co-employee, August Richard Peters, III, walked up behind her at work and tapped the back of her right knee with the front of his right knee, causing her knee to buckle. Andrews lost her balance, fell to the floor, and dislocated her right kneecap. Andrews instituted this action against Peters for intentional assault and battery.

Peters alleges that there is no evidence that he intended to injure Andrews. As summarized in Peters' brief:

[Peters] testified that he did not intend to be rude or offensive in tapping [Andrews] behind her knees. He stated that the same thing had only moments before been done to him by a co-worker and that it struck him as fun. Peters' contention ignores the nature of the intent required for an intentional tort action.

The intent with which tort liability is concerned is not necessarily a hostile intent, or a desire to do any harm. Rather it is an intent to bring about a result which will invade the interests of another in a way that the law forbids. The defendant may be liable although intending nothing more than a good-natured practical joke, or honestly believing that the act would not injure the plaintiff, or even though seeking the plaintiff's own good. Peters does not deny that he intended to tap Andrews behind the knee. Although tapping Andrews' knee was arguably not in and of itself a harmful contact, it easily qualifies as an offensive contact. "A bodily contact is offensive if it offends a reasonable sense of personal dignity." **Restatement**, Section 19. There is no evidence of consent to the touching. We hold that the trial court did not err in denying Peters' motions for a directed verdict. Vacated and remanded for further proceedings consistent with this decision.

An **assault** is an act intended to put another in fear of an immediate battery. To commit an assault, it is not necessary that the tortfeasor actually intend to cause an offensive or harmful touching upon the body of another. Rather, it is sufficient that the person intends to cause only a fear of such contact. Pointing a gun at a person and saying, "I am going to kill you" is an assault. However, a gunman who points his weapon at another with the warning, "I would kill you on the spot if this gun didn't make so much noise" has not committed an assault. The victim has not been placed in fear of an immediate touching.

The National Highway Traffic Safety Administration has determined that more than 41,000 people die each year in traffic accidents and two thirds of these fatalities are the result of road rage. This recent phenomena defines a situation where an angry driver intentionally harms or threatens another operator or passenger because of some perceived driving indiscretion. According to CNN, there are a number of reasons for road rage. Congested highways cause tailgating and near-collisions, and there is the great urgency for drivers to quickly reach their destinations. Also, some people are transformed from passive citizens into aggressive and discourteous drivers. While criminal charges are the obvious remedy against the aggressive operator, civil lawsuits for assault are finding there way into the courts. The following case is an example.

LAURA VETTER V. CHAD MORGAN
22 KAN. APP.2D 1 (KAN. CT. APP., 1995)

Vetter was injured when her van ran off the road after an encounter with a car owned by Morgan and driven by Dana Gaither. Vetter stopped her van at a stoplight. Morgan and Gaither drove up beside Vetter. Morgan began screaming vile and threatening obscenities at Vetter, shaking his fist, and making obscene gestures in a violent manner. According to Vetter, Gaither revved the engine of the car and moved the car back and forth while Morgan was threatening Vetter. Vetter testified that Morgan threatened to remove her from her van and spat on her van door when the traffic light turned green. Vetter was frightened and thought Morgan was under the influence of drugs or alcohol. She was able to write down the license tag number of the car. Morgan stated he was trying to amuse his friends, who were laughing at his antics.

When the traffic light changed to green, both vehicles drove forward. According to Vetter, after they had driven approximately 10 feet, the car driven by Gaither veered suddenly into her lane, and she reacted by steering her van sharply to the right. Vetter's van struck the curb, causing her head to hit the steering wheel and snap back against the seat, after which she fell to the floor of the van.

Assault is defined as an intentional threat or attempt, coupled with apparent ability, to do bodily harm to another, resulting in immediate apprehension of bodily harm. No bodily contact is necessary. There was evidence of a threat in this case. Vetter testified that Morgan verbally threatened to take her from her van. Ordinarily, words alone cannot be an assault. However, words can constitute an assault if together with other acts or circumstances they put the other in reasonable apprehension of imminent harmful or offensive contact with his person. The record is sufficient to support an inference that Morgan's threat and the acts surrounding it could reasonably put someone in Vetter's position in apprehension of imminent or immediate bodily harm. Morgan's behavior was so extreme that Vetter could reasonably have believed he would immediately try to carry out his threat.

The record also supports an inference that Morgan had the apparent ability to harm Vetter. Although Vetter's van was locked and the windows rolled up, the windows could be broken. The two vehicles were only six feet apart, and Morgan was accompanied by two other males. Although Vetter may have had the ability to flee by turning right, backing up, or running the red light, her ability to prevent the threatened harm by flight or self-defense does not preclude an assault. It is enough that Vetter believed that Morgan was capable of immediately inflicting the contact unless prevented by self-defense, flight, or intervention by others. The trial court erred in concluding there was no evidence that Vetter was placed in apprehension of bodily harm. Whether Morgan's actions constituted an assault was a question of fact for the jury.

SECTION 4.14
INVASION OF PRIVACY

A person has the right to be left alone. An unwarranted intrusion upon this right constitutes an **invasion of privacy**. Wiretapping of a neighbor's telephone, taking improper and revealing photographs of an unsuspecting neighbor in a state of undress, calling a divorced spouse every fifteen minutes, or disclosing private embarrassing facts about another are actionable wrongs.

Truth is not a defense to an invasion of privacy. For example, the disclosure at a party that the host was a prostitute twenty years earlier is highly offensive and a private matter. Even though the information is true, that fact would not protect the disclosing party from liability.

A growing number of employers provide workers with computers and e-mail accounts. These accounts are sometimes monitored by the business to make sure that an employee is not using the e-mail system for personal reasons during working hours or to guarantee that the computers are not being used for improper purposes such as the transmission of harassing or pornographic messages. In **Garrity v. John Hancock Mutual Life Insurance Company**, the court had to decide whether the practice of monitoring the e-mail of employees constituted an invasion of privacy.

NANCY GARRITY V. JOHN HANCOCK MUTUAL LIFE INSURANCE COMPANY
2002 WL 974676 (D. MASS., 2002)

Plaintiffs, Nancy Garrity and Joanne Clark, were employees of John Hancock Mutual Life Insurance Company for twelve and two years respectively, until their termination. According to the defendant, plaintiffs regularly received on their office computers, sexually explicit e-mails from Internet joke sites and other parties, including Mrs. Garrity's husband, which they then sent to co-workers. These facts are undisputed: A fellow employee complained after receiving such an e-mail. Hancock promptly commenced an investigation of plaintiffs' e-mail folders, as well as the folders of those with whom they e-mailed on a regular basis. Hancock determined that plaintiffs had violated its E-Mail Policy, which states, in relevant part:

- Messages that are defamatory, abusive, obscene, profane, sexually oriented, threatening or racially offensive are prohibited.

- The inappropriate use of E-mail is in violation of company policy and may be subject to disciplinary action, including termination of employment.

- All information transmitted, or contained in the company's E-mail systems is the property of John Hancock. It is not company policy to intentionally inspect E-mail usage. However, there may be situations that necessitate company review of E-mail messages and other documents.

- Company management reserves the right to access all E-mail files.

During plaintiffs' employment, defendant periodically reminded its employees that it was their responsibility to know and understand the e-mail policy. In addition, defendant warned them of several incidents in which employees were disciplined for violations. Plaintiffs assert that the e-mail policy is almost impossible to locate on Hancock's internet system, and even harder to decipher. In addition, they contend that the reminders sent by defendant during plaintiffs' employment did not accurately communicate its e-mail policy. They also dispute defendant's characterization of the e-mails in question as sexually explicit, or in any way in violation of the policy language. Upon review of the e-mails in question, however, there can be no question that they are sexually explicit within the meaning of defendant's e-mail policy. Regardless, plaintiffs assert that Hancock led them to believe that these personal e-mails could be kept private with the use of personal passwords and e-mail folders. Their complaint sets forth a claim based on invasion of privacy.

Plaintiffs' state that "it is uncontested that Ms. Garrity, Mr. Garrity and Ms. Clarke believed that the personal e-mail correspondence they sent and received was private." While that may be true, the relevant inquiry is whether the expectation of privacy was reasonable. Any reasonable expectation on the part of plaintiffs is belied by the record and plaintiffs' own statements. According to deposition testimony, Mrs. Garrity and Ms. Clark assumed that the recipients of their messages might forward them to others. Likewise, Mr. Garrity testified that the e-mails he sent to his wife would eventually be sent to third parties. Although there is a dearth of case law on privacy issues with regard to office e-mail, **Smyth v. Pillsbury Co., 914 F. Supp. 9 (E. D. Pa., 1996)** is instructive here. In Smyth, the court held that even in the absence of a company e-mail policy, plaintiffs would not have had a reasonable expectation of privacy in their work e-mail.

Both Mrs. Garrity and Ms. Clarke admit that they knew defendant had the ability to look at e-mail on the company's internet system, and knew they had to be careful about sending e-mail. Nevertheless, they claim that their e-mails were private because the company had instructed them on how to create passwords and personal e-mail folders.

Even if plaintiffs had a reasonable expectation of privacy in their work e-mail, defendant's legitimate business interest in protecting its employees from harassment in the workplace would likely trump plaintiffs' privacy interests. **Title VII of the Civil Rights Act of 1964** requires employers to take affirmative steps to maintain a workplace free of harassment and to investigate and take prompt and effective remedial action when potentially harassing conduct is discovered. Accordingly, defendant's motion for summary judgment is allowed.

The tort of invasion of privacy may arise in a variety of situations, including:

- Unwarranted publicity;

- Intrusion into a person's private life;

- Disclosure of a private embarrassing fact; and

- Use of a person's name or likeness for another's financial gain.

Invasion of privacy is defined as the right of an individual to be left alone and to lead a life that is free from unwarranted publicity. This right, however, has its limitations. The right of privacy does not forbid the use of information that is of public benefit, nor does it extend to information which the public has the right to know.

Based upon these concepts, the life of a public figure, such as a politician, actor, musician, or athlete, is newsworthy, so great latitude is afforded concerning disclosures of personal information about these famous individuals.

Over the years, a number of cases have arisen where the name, voice or likeness of a well-known person is used to promote a commercial venture without the celebrity's permission. For instance, Johnny Carson successfully sued a toilet manufacturer who dubbed a new product, "Here's Johnny Portable Toilet," after the entertainer's trademark introduction. Bette Midler recovered money from Ford Motor Company when the car manufacturer made a commercial showing a singer doing a Better Midler impersonation. This type of exploitation gives rise to the tort of invasion of privacy, which claim may be advanced by alleging: **(1)** the defendant's use of the plaintiff's identity; **(2)** the use of the plaintiff's name or likeness for the defendant's benefit; **(3)** the lack of consent to use the plaintiff's name or likeness; and **(4)** a resulting injury.

Toffoloni v. LFP Publishing Group, LLC
572 F.3d 1201 (C.A. Ga., 2009)

Maureen Toffoloni is the mother and the administrator of the estate of Nancy Benoit. Benoit and her son were murdered by her husband, Christopher Benoit. Christopher Benoit then committed suicide. Prior to her death, Benoit was a model and professional woman wrestler. Christopher Benoit was a well-known professional wrestler.

Approximately twenty years before her death, Benoit posed nude for photographer Mark Samansky. Toffoloni alleges that, immediately after the shoot, her daughter asked Samansky to destroy the photographs and believed that Samansky had destroyed them. However, Samansky kept a video, from which he extracted nude and partially nude photographic stills of Benoit. Samansky conveyed the photographic stills to LFP, which published them in the March 2008 issue of Hustler magazine.

Toffoloni brought suit against LFP seeking damages for violation of Benoit's right of publicity. Georgia recognizes a right of publicity to protect against the appropriation of another's name and likeness without consent and for the financial gain of the appropriator whether the person whose name and likeness is used is a private citizen, entertainer, or a public figure who is not a public official. Violation of the right of publicity is a tort.

The tort of invasion of privacy protects the right to be free from unwarranted publicity, or the unwarranted appropriation or exploitation of one's personality, the publicizing of one's private affairs with which the public had no legitimate concern. From this right to be free of the public's illegitimate gaze, the law extrapolated a right of publicity-a right to control if, when, and under what circumstances one's image is made public and subject to scrutiny.

Georgia first recognized the right of publicity in **Cabaniss v. Hipsley, 114 Ga. App. 367 (1966).** The court held that the plaintiff, who was an exotic dancer, could recover from the Atlanta Playboy Club for its unauthorized use of her photograph in an entertainment magazine advertising the club. The court explained that appropriation does not require the invasion of something secret, secluded or private pertaining to plaintiff, nor does it involve falsity. It consists of the appropriation, for the defendant's benefit, use or advantage, of the plaintiff's name or likeness. The interest protected is not so much a mental as a proprietary one, in the exclusive use of the plaintiff's name and likeness as an aspect of his identity.

The Restatement (Second) of Torts, however, tempers the right of publicity, providing that: no one has the right to object merely because his name or his appearance is brought before the public, since neither is in any way a private matter, and both are open to public observation. It is only when the publicity is given for the purpose of appropriating to the defendant's benefit the commercial or other values associated with the name or the likeness that the right to privacy is invaded.

Thus, the Restatement clarifies that the right of publicity does not attach to that which is open to public observation. Accordingly, the right of publicity must attach to that which is not open to public observation and is appropriated for the commercial benefit of another. The rationale for protecting the right of publicity is the straight-forward one of preventing unjust enrichment by the theft of good will. No social purpose is served by having the defendant get free some aspect of the plaintiff that would have market value and for which he would normally pay.

The Georgia courts have adopted a "newsworthiness" exception to the right of publicity. Where an incident is a matter of public interest, or the subject matter of a public investigation, a publication in connection therewith can be a violation of no one's legal right of privacy.

Toffoloni argues that she should be allowed to sue for damages incident to the publication of nude pictures of her deceased daughter because those photographs were published against her express direction and were violative of her daughter's right of publicity. LFP responds that it published an article on the life, career, and tragic death of Benoit, which "includes comment on the modest beginnings of Ms. Benoit's career, and is accompanied by images of Ms. Benoit from that time." LFP argues that the article and related images are of substantial public interest and are therefore newsworthy.

It seems clear that had LFP published the nude photographs of Benoit by themselves—i.e., without a corresponding news article, the publication would not qualify within the newsworthiness exception. While one who is a public figure or is presently newsworthy may be the proper subject of news or informative presentation, the privilege does not extend to commercialization of his personality through a form of treatment distinct from the dissemination of news or information. The nude photographs impart no information to the reading public.

Here, however, LFP published the photographs alongside a biographical piece on Benoit's career.

The magazine cover advertises "WRESTLER CHRIS BENOIT'S MURDERED WIFE NUDE." The table of contents lists "NANCY BENOIT Exclusive Nude Pics of Wrestler's Doomed Wife." Neither the cover nor the table of contents makes any reference to the accompanying article. The article is entitled "NANCY BENOIT Au Naturel: The long-lost images of wrestler Chris Benoit's doomed wife." The title and page frame, which reads "EXCLUSIVE PICS! EXCLUSIVE PICS!," comprise about one-third of the first page. A second third of the page is devoted to two nude photographs of Benoit. The final third of the page discusses. The second page of the article is entirely devoted to photographs, displaying eight additional photographs of Benoit. The heart of this article was the publication of nude photographs-not the corresponding biography.

LFP's brief biography of Benoit's life, even with its reference to her youthful pursuit of modeling, is merely incidental to its publication of her nude photographs. Therefore, the biographical piece cannot suffice to render the nude photographs newsworthy.

LFP may not make public private, nude images of Benoit simply because she once wished to be a model and was then murdered. The photographs bear no relevance-let alone "substantial relevance"-to the matter of legitimate public interest. On these facts, were we to hold otherwise, LFP would be free to publish any nude photographs of almost anyone without their permission, simply because the fact that they were caught nude on camera strikes someone as "newsworthy." Surely that debases the very concept of a right to privacy.

We hold that these photographs do not qualify for the newsworthiness exception to the right of publicity. Accordingly, we reverse and remand for further proceedings.

SECTION 4.15
DEFAMATION

Over two thousand years ago, the Roman Empire expressed its displeasure for the uttering of false statements about another. The Twelve Tablets, the foundation for the ancient laws of Rome, provided: "If any person has sung or composed against another person a song such as was causing slander or insult.... he shall be clubbed to death." A case for libel also played a part in the history of this country and the development of the law on defamation. In 1734, John Peter Zenger, a newspaper publisher, was arrested for voicing his opposition to the colonial governor of New York. Zenger efforts did not go unnoticed. He was tried for seditious libel. He was defended by Andrew Hamilton and the not guilty verdict brought about the principle of freedom of the press.

A statement is **defamatory** if it is false and tends to harm the reputation of another or to lower him in the estimation of the community. There are two categories of defamation: libel and slander.

Libel involves the publication of defamatory matter by written or printed words. **Slander**, on the other hand, is a defamatory communication that is verbal or oral in nature. Merely saying something defamatory to the aggrieved party is insufficient regardless of the false nature of the communication. In order for the defamatory comment to be actionable, it must be conveyed to a third person. This is called publication.

In the case of defamation, the truth of the matter communicated is an absolute defense. If the defendant can prove that what was said or written was true, a suit for defamation will fail. The mere expression of an opinion is also not defamatory.

Employers are often thrust into a difficult situation when they are requested to complete a job reference for a prior employee. A poor rating can result in the failure of the worker to obtain the new job. This scenario can trigger a defamation action.

In addition to truth being a defense to defamation, certain situations give raise to the defense of privilege. Privilege exist in two different forms: absolute and qualified. For instance, defamatory statements made in open court or during a debate in a legislative body, such as Congress, enjoy absolute privilege and protect the speakers from being liable for defamation. On the other hand, a qualified privilege exists if the publisher believes that he or she has a duty to speak out, or that to speak out is necessary to protect either his or her interests, or those of third person. Examples of qualified privileges include a job reference provided by a former employer or the reports of a credit agency. This qualified privilege, however, can be lost if statement is made in bad faith.

Kevorkian v. Glass explores the law with respect to the liability of an employer who provides a poor job reference to a potential employer of a former worker.

KEVORKIAN V. GLASS
913 A.2D 1043 (R.I., 2007)

Kevorkian is a licensed practical nurse who began working for the Pawtuxet Village Nursing and Rehabilitation Center (Pawtuxet Village) in 1989. In April 1994, plaintiff was suspended from work for three days for insubordination. Glass, the director of nursing at the center, alleged that plaintiff had failed to dispense necessary medication to patients. Kevorkian disputed her employer's allegation, and, unwilling to continue to work under the shadow of such accusations, she resigned and announced that she had secured new employment elsewhere.

Approximately two years after she resigned, Kevorkian, contacted Mercury Medical, a placement agency for nurses. Mercury Medical asked Kevorkian if Pawtuxet Village could be contacted for a reference. Kevorkian agreed, and a document entitled "Reference Form" was faxed to Glass. Glass left the document largely incomplete, but she did fill out three parts of it before faxing it back to Mercury Medical. First, she checked a box marked "very good" for the category "appearance;" second, she answered "no" to the question "[W]ould you rehire?" and, finally, she wrote that the reason she would be unwilling to rehire Kevorkian was because of "unacceptable work practice habits."

After Glass submitted the reference form, Kevorkian began attending interviews with prospective employers set up by Mercury Medical. Perplexed that none of those facilities offered to hire her, Kevorkian began to suspect that she had received a poor reference from Pawtuxet Village. When she discovered the contents of Glass' reference, Kevorkian decided to file suit.

Plaintiff filed a one-count complaint alleging that, by using the phrase "unacceptable work practice habits" in the context of a work reference, defendant had defamed her by "circulating a libelous and slanderous job reference form to prospective employers."

Counsel for defendant argued that (1) the statement "unacceptable work practice habits" is not capable of a defamatory meaning; and even if the statement is capable of such meaning, and (2) defendant's publication of that statement to Mercury Medical was protected by a statutory privilege set forth in G.L.1956 § 28-6.4-1(c).

To succeed in an action for defamation, the plaintiff must prove: (1) the utterance of a false and defamatory statement concerning another; (2) an unprivileged communication to a third party; (3) fault amounting to at least negligence; and (4) damages.

General Laws 1956 §28-6.4-1(c) provides:

> An employer that, upon request by a prospective employer or a current or former employee, provides fair and unbiased information about an employee's job performance is presumed to be acting in good faith and is immune from civil liability for the disclosure and the consequences of the disclosure. The presumption of good faith is rebuttable upon a showing that the information disclosed was: (1) Knowingly false; (2) Deliberately misleading; (3) Disclosed for a malicious purpose; or (4) Violative of the current or former employee's civil rights under the employment discrimination laws.

In the realm of defamation, privileges exist in two different forms: absolute and qualified. Here, we deal only with the latter. The major difference between the two types of privilege is that a qualified privilege may be lost in situations in which the publication exceeds the scope of the privilege or is the fruit of improper motivation. For example, a qualified privilege may be lost when the publication of an allegedly defamatory statement is induced by spite or ill will-also known as malice. Absolute privileges, on the other hand, are not subject to such limitations. A qualified privilege exists if the publisher makes the statements in good faith and reasonably believes that he has a legal, moral or social duty to speak out, or that to speak out is necessary to protect either his own interests, or those of third person[s], or certain interests of the public.

In **Swanson v. Speidel Corp.**, **110 R. I. 335 (1972),** a case factually similar to the matter now before us, we held that a former employer's communication to a prospective employer with regard to the work characteristics of a former employee was protected by a qualified privilege. In that case, we said that: "the public interest requires that the protection of the privilege be accorded to a communication by a former employer to a prospective employer with regard to a former employee's work characteristics where the publisher acts in good faith and has reason to believe that to speak out is necessary to protect his own interests, or those of third persons, or certain interests of the public."

The qualified privilege can be overcome, however, when the plaintiff proves that the person making the defamatory statements acted with ill will or malice.

When it enacted § 28-6.4-1(c), the General Assembly created a statutory qualified privilege for former employers' communications to prospective employers concerning former employees.

Here, defendant's statement that plaintiff had "unacceptable work practice habits" clearly was covered by the § 28-6.4-1(c) privilege. The defendant is a former supervisor of plaintiff who, at the request of both plaintiff and a placement agency provided information about plaintiff's work performance while she was employed at Pawtuxet Village. Clearly, when she received an inquiry about Kevorkian from a prospective employer, Glass had a qualified privilege to reveal her dissatisfaction with plaintiff's work during the time she worked at Pawtuxet Village. Thus, a presumption of good faith attached to defendant's publication and the burden of rebutting that presumption shifted to plaintiff.

Plaintiff argued that defendant's statement was made for a malicious purpose, thereby removing it from the scope of the privilege. However, we conclude that plaintiff did not meet the burden imposed on her by directing the court to specific facts that raise a genuine issue about whether defendant made the publication for a malicious purpose.

After a review of the record, the plaintiff has pointed to no facts that show that defendant's publication of the defamatory remark was motivated by malice toward plaintiff.

We affirm the judgment of the Superior Court, and return the record of this case to it.

Even though a communication is false, an action for defamation will only be successful if the statement actually harms the reputation of another so as to lower the individual in the estimation of the community or to deter others from associating or dealing with that person. Therefore, an individual who believes that he has been defamed must be readily identifiable by and associated with the statement. This is known as the "of and concerning" requirement and creates a problem when a class of people are the subject of the false statement. For instance, if a newspaper publishes an article that the students at a particular college are unruly drunks and bores, the individual students at the school will fail in a defamation action since they are not sufficiently identified in the article.

Likewise, the statement that all politicians are liars and crooks is not actionable since no one individual has been singled out so the "of and concerning" requirement has not been satisfied.

The "of and concerning" requirement was the issue in a case against Oprah Winfrey when she aired a story about Mad Cow Disease entitled "Dangerous Food." The talk show host was sued by the Texas Beef Group over the program's contents.

TEXAS BEEF GROUP V. OPRAH WINFREY
11 F. SUPP. 2D 858 (M. D. TEXAS, 1998)

On March 20, 1996, British Health Minister Stephen Dorrell announced that a committee of scientists had linked a deadly, degenerative brain disease in cattle known as Bovine Spongiform Encephalopathy (BSE) with fatal human disorder known as Creutzfeldt-Jakob Disease (CJD). Minister Dorrell announced that consumption of beef was "the most likely explanation" for this new variant.

BSE is commonly referred to as "Mad Cow Disease." BSE is an infectious neurological disorder of cattle whose rapid spread in some countries is believed to have caused by the feeding of certain infected cattle and sheep tissues to cattle in the form of "ruminant" derived protein supplements. Cattle are ruminant animals.

On April 16, 1996, The Oprah Winfrey Show broadcast a program entitled "Dangerous Food" which included a segment on Mad Cow Disease.

The show began with a discussion of Mad Cow Disease in England. A guest for this segment was Beryl Rimmer, from England, whose granddaughter was in a coma suffering from a form of CJD. Ms. Rimmer believed that her granddaughter contracted CJD from eating a hamburger tainted by Mad Cow Disease.

The second segment considered the question, "Could it happen here?" Guests in connection with that segment included... Defendant Howard Lyman, a former cattle rancher-turned-vegetarian who is executive director of the Humane Society's Eating With Conscience campaign. Lyman stated that the United States is at risk of an outbreak similar to that in England, if the practice continued. The program did not mention Texas or name any of the Plaintiffs.

The Plaintiffs are cattlemen operating in the Panhandle of Texas. Plaintiffs claim that the "Dangerous Food" show was "nothing more than a 'scary story', falsely suggesting that U.S. beef is highly dangerous because of Mad Cow Disease and that a horrible epidemic worse than Aids could occur from eating U.S. beef." Plaintiffs claim that Defendant Lyman is "a vegetarian activist and lobbyist, with an agenda to wipe out the U.S. Beef industry..." Plaintiffs contend that the April 16, 1996, broadcast of The Oprah Winfrey Show caused beef markets to "immediately" crash and that they were damaged thereby.

A defamation claim requires proof that the defendant in question published to a third person... a false statement of defamatory fact that was "of and concerning" the Plaintiff in question with the required degree of fault which proximately caused damage to the reputation of the Plaintiff in question. **Rosenblatt v. Baer, 383 U.S. 75, 81, 86 S.Ct. 669, 673, 15 L.Ed.2d 597 (1966).**

The Court held in *Rosenblatt* that the jury could not find liability without evidence that the published statement "was made specifically of and concerning" the plaintiff. Texas law imposes the same "of and concerning" standard before a plaintiff can state a defamation claim "the settled law requires that the false statement point to the plaintiff and to no one else."

Texas law on defamation is: "A libel is a defamation expressed in written or other graphic form that tends to blacken the memory of the dead or that tends to injure a living person's reputation and thereby ex-poses the person to public hatred, contempt or ridicule, or financial injury or to impeach any person's honesty, integrity, virtue, or reputation or to publish the natural defects of anyone and thereby expose the person to public hatred, ridicule, or financial injury." The action for defamation is to protect the personal reputation of the injured party.

Even if a statement on the program could be construed to meet the definition of defamation, it cannot meet the "of and concerning" requirement. None of the Plaintiffs were mentioned by name on the April 16, 1996 Oprah Winfrey Show. Plaintiff Paul Engler testified that the statements made were about him "as well as the rest of the cattle feeding industry." Engler also testified that there are "about a million" cattlemen in the United States and that the states of Kansas and Colorado have feeding operations similar to Cactus Feeders in Texas.

The Texas Court of Appeals has held that an individual may not recover damages for defamation of a group or class in excess of 740 persons of which he is a member. Therefore, Plaintiffs have failed as a matter of law to meet their burden of establishing the "of and concerning" element of the defamation cause of action.

Accordingly, the Court grants Defendant's Motion for Judgment as a matter of law made at the close of Plaintiffs' case on the defamation claim.

SECTION 4.16
FALSE IMPRISONMENT

False Imprisonment is the unlawful detention of a person against his or her will in a specific area. This tort is defined as the intentional and wrongful infliction of confinement against a person's will without consent or legal authority. The confinement may result from acts or words which the person fears to disregard. By implication, it is required that a person being detained be aware of the confinement, and that the actor intended to confine the victim. Simple examples include kidnapping, or the improper imprisoning of a person for a crime that the accused did not commit.

A person detained in a department store who has been falsely accused of stealing merchandise may sue the store for false imprisonment if the business establishment acted without just cause in its actions.

Consider the following case regarding a claim for false imprisonment against former basketball players Charles Barkley and Jayson Williams. A patron in a bar claimed that the basketball players falsely accused him of threatening Mr. Williams with a knife resulting in his arrest for aggravated assault. The charges were dismissed when the basketball players failed to appear in court as witnesses.

CHRISTOPHER VINCENT V. CHARLES BARKLEY
644 N. E.2D 650 (ILL. APP., 1996)

Plaintiff Christopher Vincent seeks his day in court after a tough night in a Chicago bar.

This complaint was brought against Jayson Williams and Charles Barkley. Vincent alleged that Williams hit him over the head with a beer mug while they were out "socializing." Williams asserted the defense of self-defense.

Vincent further claimed that Williams and Barkley falsely accused Vincent of threatening Williams with a knife. Vincent was arrested and charged with aggravated assault. The case was stricken when Williams and Barkley failed to appear in court. Based on these facts, Vincent sought recovery for false imprisonment.

Vincent alleged that Williams and Barkley conspired together to fabricate a fictitious story about Vincent threatening Williams with a knife. This story, Vincent said, was a cover-up for Williams' unprovoked attack on the plaintiff. When the police came to the bar to investigate a report of a fight, Williams and Barkley, in furtherance of their plot, informed the police of this fictitious threat. Based upon this information, Vincent was arrested, charged with aggravated battery, and confined in jail for approximately twelve hours before he was released on bail.

To state a cause of action for false imprisonment, the plaintiff must allege that his personal liberty was unreasonably or unlawfully restrained against his will and that defendants caused or procured the restraint. An unlawful arrest by an officer, caused or procured by a private person, is the same as an arrest by the private person. For liability to attach to the private person, however, the arresting officer must have relied solely on the information given to him by the private party when making the arrest.

It is clear to us that Vincent's complaint, on its face, states a cause of action for false imprisonment. Defendants argue that the trial court, by taking judicial notice of the police report that had been attached to plaintiff's prior complaint (but later withdrawn), could find that the officer did not arrest Vincent based solely on information given by them. This report indicated that two female witnesses gave the investigating police officers the "same info" given by the defendants.

This police report is not a "source of indisputable accuracy." It is an inadmissible hearsay document of unproved verity.

But even if judicial notice of this document were taken, it would not negate Vincent's allegation that defendants caused or procured his arrest. The report merely indicates that two other witnesses gave the police the "same info" given by defendants. The report does not say whether the witnesses' statements were based on direct observation of the incident or exactly what information they corroborated. This hearsay report, vague and general, should not be a substitute for direct, testimonial evidence.

For these reasons, the plaintiff's factual allegation that defendants, in conspiracy with one another, falsely and maliciously caused or procured his arrest are sufficient to withstand the motion.

SECTION 4.17
TORTUOUS INTERFERENCE WITH A CONTRACT

The tort of **interference with a contract** has its origins in a 150-year-old case involving an opera singer who attempted to breach her performance contract with one theater in order to sing at another facility. In **Lumley v. Gye**, the court in England found that liability may attach for the wrongful and malicious interference with a contract.

This cause of action stabilizes business relationships since a party that wrongfully interferes with an existing contract or a future business opportunity may face economic sanctions.

To maintain a viable claim for tortuous interference with a contract, the following five elements must be present:

1. An enforceable contract;

2. The defendant's awareness of that contractual relationship;

3. The defendant's intentional inducement to breach the contract;

4. A wrongful interference by the defendant to breach the agreement; and

5. Actual damages.

VIGODA v. DCA PRODUCTIONS PLUS INC.
741 N.Y.S.2D 20 (2002)

Plaintiffs, as members of a rock band called "Groovelily," entered into a one-year agreement with defendant DCA Productions Plus Inc. (DCA) to act as plaintiffs' personal manager in exchange for a percentage of the band's professional revenue. Defendant's services were to include career counseling in addition to acting as a booking agent. Plaintiffs reserved the right to terminate the agreement, which

they did on June 2, 1999. At that time, DCA had already submitted an application on plaintiffs' behalf to have them perform at the Great Lakes Showcase of the National Association for Campus Activities (NACA). For a performer to appear at a NACA showcase, the performer must be represented by an agent who is an NACA member.

After plaintiffs terminated their agreement with DCA, plaintiffs advised DCA that they wished to continue with DCA as their booking agent. Following negotiations, however, the parties were unable to agree on terms, and the plaintiffs signed with another booking agent who had formerly worked for DCA. Under NACA rules, there can only be one booking agent for a performer and an act selected for the showcase may be eliminated if the agency submitting it no longer represents the act. Although NACA had responded to DCA's application on behalf of plaintiffs with a "Letter of Intent," NACA further required that one signed copy must be received by NACA to guarantee plaintiffs' appearance at the showcase.

When DCA learned that one of its former employees had become the booking agent for plaintiffs, DCA informed NACA that DCA no longer represented plaintiffs. NACA removed plaintiffs from the showcase. Plaintiffs commenced the present action seeking damages for tortious interference with contractual relations.

Tortious interference with contract requires the existence of a valid contract between the plaintiff and a third party, defendant's knowledge of that contract, defendant's intentional procurement of the third party's breach of contract without justification, actual breach and damages. The NACA Letter of Intent was not a binding contract since it contained an explicit condition precedent for the obligations under the contract to arise, namely that it must be signed and returned by a certain date to guarantee plaintiff's appearance. Even if we were to view the Letter of Intent as having created contractual obligations, defendants' failure to sign and return it did not constitute a breach of contract. NACA rules required that a performing act only have one agent and that the agent who procured the act's appearance remain as agent. DCA merely informed NACA that plaintiffs were no longer represented by DCA, a fact created by plaintiffs. The predictable consequence of plaintiffs' decision was that NACA removed them from the showcase. DCA breached no contractual duty to plaintiffs and procured no breach of a contractual relationship between plaintiffs and NACA.

Section 4.18 Products Liability

Nearly everyone has heard of Stella Lieback and her lawsuit against McDonald's over a cup of hot coffee. Lieback is the elderly lady who was scalded by hot McDonald's coffee that she had placed between her legs in a moving car. The woman was awarded nearly three million dollars by a jury who found the coffee to be defective because McDonald's brewed the hot beverage at a temperature that far exceeded the temperature of a normal cup of coffee. This case is an example of the law of products liability.

Section 402A of the Restatement (2nd) of torts, more commonly known as the law of products liability or strict liability, holds sellers of defective products liable for the harm caused to the user, consumer, or his property. This is the case even though the seller has exercised all possible care in the preparation and sale of the product.

The law of products liability has developed in response to society's changing attitude towards the relationship between the seller of a product and the consumer. Basically, the courts have abandoned the principle of caveat emptor and have made the supplier of a product a virtual guarantor of its safety. This insures that manufacturers who place a defective product in the marketplace will be responsible for the costs of injuries resulting from the defect rather than by the injured person who is powerless to protect himself.

Defective products include those things that contain a manufacturing defect, lack of a proper warning, or a defect in the product's design making it unsafe to a user or consumer.

The law of product liability provides that:

1. One who sells any product in a defective condition unreasonably dangerous to the user or consumer or to his property is subject to liability for physical harm thereby caused to the ultimate user or consumer, or to his property, if

    a. the seller is engaged in the business of selling such a product, and

    b. it is expected to and does reach the user or consumer without substantial change in the condition in which it is sold.

2. The rule stated in Subsection (1) applies although

    a. the seller has exercised all possible care in the preparation and sale of his product, and

    b. the user or consumer has not bought the product from or entered into any contractual relation with the seller.

Over the years, the courts have found the seller of a defective product to include anyone in the chain of distribution from the manufacturer to the retailer. Lessors, such as renters of cars, trucks, or heavy equipment, have also been held to be sellers for purposes of products liability law.

Virginia Brumley v. Pfizer, Inc.
149 F. Supp. 2d 305 (S. D. Tex., 2001)

This is a product liability action involving Viagra, a medication manufactured by Pfizer for the treatment of erectile dysfunction. Earnest Brumley died of cardiac complications after taking his first dose of Viagra and engaging in sexual intercourse with his wife.

At the time of his death, Mr. Brumley was 49 years old and had "ongoing symptomatic coronary artery disease" including "angina [chest pains] on a regular basis." Before he was prescribed Viagra, Mr. Brumley would sometimes have to stop during sexual activity to take nitroglycerin to alleviate his chest pains.

The Estate of Earnest Brumley filed suit against Pfizer, alleging that Mr. Brumley died as a result of his use of Viagra. They assert claims of (1) strict products liability and (2) negligence.

Pfizer asserts that there is no evidence of a product defect; and that Pfizer provided an adequate warning of the cardiac risk associated with its product.

In order to recover under the theory of strict liability, a Plaintiff must establish (1) the defective and unreasonably dangerous condition of the defendant's product; and (2) a causal connection between such condition and the plaintiff's injuries. A product is defective if it is (1) unreasonably dangerous as manufactured, (2) unreasonably dangerous as designed, or (3) unreasonably dangerous because adequate warnings or instruction were not provided.

A product may be unreasonably dangerous if a manufacturer fails to warn of a foreseeable risk arising from the use of the product, and the lack of adequate warnings or instructions renders an otherwise adequate product unreasonably dangerous.

In this case, Plaintiffs contend that Pfizer failed to communicate adequately the level of risk inherent in Viagra for a person with Mr. Brumley's medical history. Pfizer moves for summary judgment on the ground that it adequately warned Mr. Brumley's treating physician, Dr. Brackin, of the risks of Viagra for patients with heart disease.

The package insert that Pfizer included with Viagra at the time Dr. Brackin prescribed Viagra to Mr. Brumley states in relevant part:

Warnings:

There is a potential for cardiac risk of sexual activity in patients with preexisting cardiovascular disease. Therefore, treatments for erectile dysfunction, including Viagra, should not be generally used in men for whom sexual activity is inadvisable because of their underlying cardiovascular status.

Physicians should discuss with patients the potential cardiac risk of sexual activity in patients with preexisting cardiovascular risk factors. Patients who experience symptoms (e.g., angina pectoris, dizziness, nausea) upon initiation of sexual activity should be advised to refrain from further activity and should discuss the episode with their physician.

Plaintiffs assert that the first warning is inadequate because it is labeled **"PRECAUTION,"** instead of **"WARNING."** Plaintiffs submit testimony from Dr. Brackin that a "warning" increases a physician's awareness level generally. The Court fails to see a material difference between the words "warning" and "precaution", when both are intended to alert physicians not to an inherent risk caused by Viagra itself, but to an inherent risk in sexual activity in patients with heart disease. It is undisputed that the cardiac risk that sexual intercourse poses to patients with heart disease is the same risk that any vigorous physical activity would pose to such patients.

Dr. Brackin testified that had he been made aware of the information in the current package insert, he would have ruled out Viagra for Mr. Brumley. A physician who is aware of his patient's heart disease is cognizant that the patient is at risk both during sexual intercourse and during any other strenuous exercise, and neither version of the Viagra package insert contains any language that would delude a physician into thinking that Viagra would lessen this risk.

Dr. Brackin was aware both of Mr. Brumley's heart condition as well as the cardiac risk inherent in physical exertion. Dr. Brackin provided Mr. Brumley with specific warnings about what to do if he suffered an angina attack during sexual intercourse. The (Pfizer) warning addressed the specific circumstances in which Mr. Brumley suffered a fatal heart attack. Plaintiffs simply have not submitted any evidence that creates a genuine issue of material fact that either version of the Viagra insert contained an inadequate warning.

Courts have found that it is reasonable for the manufacturer to rely on the health care provider to pass on its warnings, because the provider understands the propensities and dangers involved in the use of a given drug, and as the prescriber, he stands between the drug and the consumer. Nevertheless, the warning to the physician must still be adequate, and if "the warning to the intermediary is inadequate or misleading, the manufacturer remains liable for injuries sustained by the ultimate user." The Court concluded above that there is no evidence the warning was inadequate.

The evidence shows that Dr. Brackin was aware that his patient should not have been prescribed Viagra in the first place. It also is undisputed that an angina patient with chest pains is in immediate need of the use of his nitrates and that the Viagra insert that Dr. Backin had available when he prescribed Viagra for Mr. Brumley listed use of nitrates "in any form" as a contraindication.

For the foregoing reasons, Plaintiffs' claims are dismissed.

QUESTIONS FOR DISCUSSION:

1. Should a manufacturer of a microwave be strictly liable for failing to warn a consumer that a cat should not be dried in the appliance?

2. Should a manufacturer of a lawn mower be strictly liable when a person is injured when he uses a lawn mower to trim his hedges?

SECTION 4.19 REVIEW CASES

1. Hustler Magazine featured a "parody" of an advertisement for Campari Liqueur entitled "Jerry Falwell talks about his first time." While the parody was modeled after an actual Campari advertising campaign, the Hustler ad clearly played to the sexual double entendre of the subject, "first times." Copying the layout of the Campari ads, Hustler's editors chose this conservative religious official as their featured celebrity and drafted an alleged "interview" in which Falwell states that his "first time" was during a drunken incestuous rendezvous with his mother in an outhouse. Falwell sued Hustler Magazine for defamation and infliction of emotional distress. Hustler defended the claim on the basis of the First Amendment and the fact that Falwell is a public figure. Who should win the case? **Hustler Magazine v. Jerry Falwell, No. 87-1278 (U.S., 1986).**

2. Dustin Hoffman is a highly successful and recognizable motion picture actor. He has a strong policy of not endorsing commercial products for fear that he will be perceived in a negative way which would suggest that his career is in decline. Los Angeles Magazine published a photograph of Hoffman as he appeared in the movie "Toostie," and, through computer software, altered the photograph to make it appear as though the actor was wearing a contemporary silk gown designed by Richard Tyler and high-heeled shoes created by Ralph Lauren. Underneath the picture was the quote: "Dustin Hoffman isn't a drag in a butter-colored silk gown by Richard Tyler and Ralph Lauren heels." Hoffman sued the magazine for invasion of privacy for their commercial use of his name and likeness in

a commercial venture. Is the magazine liable for the altered photograph of the actor or is it merely a parody for which no liability would attach? **Dustin Hoffman v. Capital City/ABC, Inc., 33 F. Supp. 2d 867 (1999).**

3. Schick and his father were playing golf with two other people. Schick teed off from the 16th hole and was followed by two other golfers, including his father. Subsequently, Verloito teed off and sliced his drive into the woods on the right, but the ball did not go out of bounds. Schick and his father then walked to their golf cart in front of the tee assuming that Verloito would play his second shot from the woods. Instead, the golfer unexpectedly hit a second shot from the tee, striking Schick in the face. Did Schick assume the risk of his injuries for being hit by a ball on the golf course? **Jeffrey Schick v. John Verloito, 744 A.2d 219 (N.J. Super., 2000).**

4. Linda Matarazzo attended an Aerosmith concert at Madison Square Garden. She was injured during the concert by an unknown patron who struck her in the nose as she attempted to return to her seat. Matarazzo sued Aerosmith on the grounds that the group's music encourages violence and their concerts attract "crazies" who are particularly drawn to this type of message. Warner Brothers Records was also sued under the theory that Warner Brothers willfully, intentionally, and deliberately aided and abetted Aerosmith in attracting such "crazies" to their concerts by promoting and selling records and tapes of the group's music. Should Aerosmith and Warner Brothers be responsible for the injuries sustained by the plaintiff? **Linda Matarazzo v. Aerosmith Productions, Inc. 1989 W.L. 140322 (S.D. N.Y., 1989).**

5. Debbie Tay had been a frequent guest on the Howard Stern show before her death at the age of 28. She was a topless dancer whose claim of having had sexual encounters with females from outer space earned her the nickname of "Space Lesbian." Tay was cremated and her ashes were given by the family to her friend, Chaunce Hayden, who appeared on the Stern Radio Show with a box containing some of the remains. Stern played prior video clips of Tay's appearances on the program and then shook and rattled the box containing the decedent's remains. Stern even handled some of the bone fragments. These actions prompted a lawsuit by Tay's next-of-kin against Stern for infliction of emotional distress. Can the family hold Howard Stern responsible for the way he handled the decedent's ashes on his television show? **Jeffrey Roach v. Howard Stern, 653 N.Y.S. 2d 532 (S. Ct., 1996).**

6. Fisher and Segal composed the classic '50s' tune "When Sunny Gets Blue." Dees requested permission to use part of the composition in order to create a comedic version of the song but permission was refused. A few months later, Dees released a comedy tape entitled, "Put It Where the Moon Don't Shine." One cut on the release was, "When Sonny Sniff's

Glue." The parody was an obvious take-off on the composers' song and copied the first six of the composition's thirty-eight bars of music—its recognizable main theme. In addition, the remake changed the opening lyrics from "When Sunny gets blue, her eyes get gray and cloudy, then the rain begins to fall," to "When Sonny sniffs glue, her eyes get red and bulgy, then her hair begins to fall." The composers sued Dees for defamation, claiming the new version of the song associated the composition with obscene, indecent and offensive words. Will Dees be responsible for the parody? **Marvin Fisher v. Rick Dees, 794 F.2d 432 (9th Cir., 1986).**

SECTION 4.20
INTERNET REFERENCES

For more information about the topics in this Chapter, see the following Internet sites:

- **www.lawguru.com/auto.html**
  For information on automobile accidents.

- **www.itslegal.com/infonet/injury/injurymain.html**
  Answers to frequently asked questions about tort law, including transportation accidents, injuries to property, medical malpractice, and defamation are provided at this address.

- **www.prairielaw.com/articles/article.asp?channelid=22&articleid=1371**
  A general overview of the law of personal injury is located at this web address.

- **www.lectlaw.com/tmed.html**
  This site offers practical information about medical malpractice, civil litigation, and standards of care.

- **www.ashcraftandgerel.com**
  A law firm that specializes in tort law has created this website. It provides general information about the subject, and maintains a library of articles on the law of torts, including materials on medical malpractice, and automobile accident litigation.

- **www.legalaidman.com**
  Practical information about personal injury claims, including what to do after an accident and the litigation process, is offered at this website.

- **http://encarta.msn.com/index/conciseindex/17/0170400.htm**
  Encarta Encyclopedia provides an overview of the law of negligence at this address, including the burden of proof in a civil case.

Key Terms

Adult Activity
Assault
Assumption of the Risk
Attractive Nuisance Doctrine
Battery
Breach of Duty
Business Visitor
Comparative Negligence
Contributory Negligence
Damages
Defamation
Duty of Care
Electronic Communication
    Privacy Act
False Imprisonment
Good Samaritan Statute
Imputed Negligence
Independent Contractor

Infliction of Emotional Distress
Intentional Tort
Interference with a Contract
Insanity
Invasion of Privacy
Liability of Parents
Libel
Licensee
Negligence
Products Liability
Proximate Cause
Slander
Substantial Factor
Tort
Tortuous Interference with
    a Contract
Trespasser
Vicarious Liability

CHAPTER 5

PROPERTY LAW

BY: BARBARA SCHNELLER, ESQ.
AND SAMUEL D. HODGE, JR., ESQ.

"Land is, like any other possession, by natural right wholly in the power of its present owner; and may be sold, given or bequeathed, absolutely or conditionally. But natural law would avail little without the protection of the law."

–Samuel Johnson

SECTION 5.1
INTRODUCTION

Property law deals with those rights and duties that arise out of the ownership or possession of real and personal property. In turn, **real property** consists of the land going from the center of the earth to the heavens and everything permanently attached to the land. For instance, a building, tree or driveway are considered part of the realty. This area of jurisprudence is also known as **real estate** law. **Personal property** is everything else and includes such things as a car, books, clothes, and furniture, as well as bank accounts, stocks, bonds, patents, and copyrights. Property law defines and enforces the rights and responsibilities that accompany these interests in all forms of property.

SECTION 5.2
OWNERSHIP

Ownership is often viewed as a bundle of rights. Owners have certain rights with respect to their property: they may use it, prevent others from using it, lend it to someone else, sell it, give it away, or destroy it. **Title** refers to the right of ownership. A person who has title to property has all of the rights of ownership. But the idea of title, in a legal context, is more abstract. Courts are often asked to determine who, among several contenders, has ownership rights to a given piece of land. A **quiet title** action is used for this purpose. The court listens to the facts presented by everyone who has a claim to the real property and decides who the owner is, i.e., who has title.

Property can be owned by many types of entities such as businesses, individuals, partnerships, trusts, cooperatives and even religious or other charitable organizations. It is also subject to division thereby giving a number of people ownership in the same asset. This has required the creation of specialized terms to explain the ways property may be owned or possessed.

It is customary to use **documents of title** to prove ownership, for example, title to a car, a "deed" to a house, or a "bill of sale" for merchandise.

Conveyancing is the term used for the processing and transferring of title between the owner of real estate and the buyer. This transfer generally occurs at a real estate settlement where the seller signs a deed conveying the appropriate interest in the property to a third person. On the other hand, items of personal property are usually conveyed by the mere delivery of the item to another.

A. Sole Ownership

The simplest form of title is **sole ownership** in which one person enjoys the bundle of rights and liabilities that accompany property. A deed to land will reflect this fact by referring to the owner as a single man or single woman. This type of ownership, however, is not limited to real estate. A business owned by one person is labeled a **sole proprietorship** and there is no distinction between the person's personal and business assets. In other words, the liabilities of the business are also the liabilities of the individual. Since the property is owned and controlled by one person, the assets will generally pass upon the owner's death to whomever the owner desires or by intestate succession if there is no will. Interstate succession means that the property will pass to the decedent's heirs according to an established hierarchy. For instance, if there are no children, the property will pass to the surviving spouse. If there are surviving children, the property is divided between the spouse and children.

B. Concurrent Ownership

It is common for people to jointly own assets with one another. The law calls this **concurrent or joint ownership** and it occurs when the title to property is shared by two or more people. The most common forms of concurrent ownership are **tenancy in common,** and **joint tenancy with the right of survivorship**. Both forms give the co-owners essentially equal rights to the property. Each owner, however, has given up the right of exclusivity, meaning one owner cannot prevent his co-owner(s) from using the property.

The difference between a tenancy in common and joint tenancy deals with what happens when one co-owner dies. In a tenancy in common, if one co-owner dies, his share will pass to his heirs. In a joint tenancy, the right of survivorship means that if one co-owner dies, his share will pass to the surviving co-owner. Thus, if Joe Roberts and Peter Christopher have a joint bank account as tenants in common, either of them may make deposits or withdraw funds. If Joe dies, his share will pass to his heirs, usually the family, and Peter will keep his one-half share. If, on the other hand, Joe and Peter are joint tenants with the right of survivorship, and Joe dies, his share will automatically pass to Peter who becomes the sole owner of the bank account. When property is owned concurrently as joint tenants with the right of survivorship, the co-owners forfeit their individual right to "alienate," or dispose of, the property as they wish at the time of death. The property is automatically transferred to the survivor and does not become part of the estate.

It is sometimes unclear whether property is owned as a joint tenancy or as a tenancy in common. When a dispute arises over the form of ownership, courts scrupulously examine the documents of title to determine what type of ownership was specified by the co-tenants or, if the language is ambiguous, what the parties intended. For example, the Pennsylvania legislature has solved this problem by providing that unless the owners clearly state that the co-tenancy is a "joint tenancy with the right of survivorship," it will be considered a tenancy in common.

As the following case shows, the court's decision on how to classify ownership may be crucial in determining how much a creditor can force a debtor to repay.

UNIVERSITY OF MONTANA V. MARK D. COE
704 P.2D 1029 (MONTANA, 1985)

This case involves an execution on a bank account to recover student loans under the National Direct Student Loan Program.

The appellant, Mark D. Coe, a former Montana University student, took out a series of student loans under the National Direct Student Loan Program, amounting to $6,437.30. He defaulted on the loans and made only one payment of $20. The University brought suit and obtained a partial summary judgment in the sum of $6,437.30.

Through one of several executions, the University levied against the joint checking account of Mark Coe at the First Bank-Western Montana, Missoula. The savings account was in the name of "Tammerly or Mark D. Coe," which at the time of execution had a balance of $3,179.23. Tammerly Coe requested the Bank not to release the funds, claiming that the funds did not belong to Mark Coe, but rather belonged to her and to Jordan Coe, brother to Tammerly and Mark.

Tammerly Coe and her brother, Jordan contend that they deposited the money in the bank and that their brother, Mark, deposited no funds whatsoever. However, one of the exhibits presented to the District Court was a copy of the signature card of the account which listed the names of Tammerly Coe or Mark D. Coe, along with their addresses, which stated that Mark was "the owner of a joint checking account with his sister." Jordan Coe did not sign this account, nor does his name appear on the signature card though he claims he owns $2,000 of the funds in the account. Jordan alleges he gave that amount to Tammerly for safe keeping on his behalf. Tammerly claims the remainder of the funds, less the $2,000 deposited by her brother Jordan, belong to her and that Mark Coe never made a deposit.

The question is whether this is a joint account or a tenancy in common with no survivor. This Court in **Ivins v. Hardy, 179 P.2d 745,** held that a tenancy in common is created whenever the instrument bringing an estate of two or more persons into existence does not specifically state that the estate created is other than a "tenancy in common." The facts situation concerning the signing of the signature card in **Casagranda v. Donahue** and this case are different. The card signed in the joint account in **Casagranda** specifically said:

> "The undersigned hereby open an account in your bank as joint tenants and not as tenants in common, and, upon the death of either or any of us, all monies then in this account shall be paid to the survivor or survivors as his, her, or their individual property."

Under the facts in **Casagranda**, we held that the savings account became the individual property of respondent upon the decedent's death. Right of survivorship cannot be defeated by the executrix of decedent's estate, and any attempt to satisfy the general devises in a will.

In the case at the bar, the signature card signed by Tammerly D. Coe or Mark D. Coe noted:

> "The undersigned depositor, whose bank account is described on the reverse side, hereby appoints the person(s) whose specimen signature(s) appears above, agent(s) of the undersigned with respect to said bank account with the authority specified in the Bank's posted General Rules and Regulations Governing Bank Accounts."

We find that the major distinguishing characteristic of a joint tenancy as opposed to a tenancy in common is a right of the survivor of each of the co-tenants. We hold, under the facts of this case, that this is a tenancy in common and that the creditor, University of Montana, is entitled to one-half, not the total amount levied against the account currently being held by the Clerk of the Court of the Fourth Judicial District.

SECTION 5.3
THE JOINT
BANK ACCOUNT

PROBLEM FIVE

PARK, BROWN & SMITH, P.C.
ATTORNEYS AT LAW
MEMORANDUM

TO: All Law Clerks

FROM: Peter Smith, Esquire

RE: The Joint Bank Account

Joe Roberts and Donald Feelgood decided to open a joint savings account with their golf partner, Osgood G. Huntingdon, so they could put away their gambling money. Feelgood and Huntingdon informed Joe that they would open the joint account since Joe was busy. Feelgood and Huntingdon signed the bank papers which noted that all three were joint tenants of the account. Nothing further was specified. Joe deposited $5,000 into the account. Feelgood and Huntingdon made similar deposits.

About two weeks later, Huntingdon visited Las Vegas and was quite successful at the slot machines and soon accumulated $500 in quarters. He then cashed in this change for silver dollars so he could play the progressive slot machine. Ten spins later, Huntingdon drew three cherries and won $100,000. He supplied the casino with his social security number and wire-transferred the funds to the newly created bank account. Unfortunately, Huntingdon's luck ran out that evening when he was struck and killed by a car while crossing Las Vegas Boulevard.

Joe was devastated by the news. Mr. Roberts' day grew even bleaker when he was served with a subpoena to appear at a support hearing initiated by a woman who claims that Joe is the father of her five-year-old boy.

Mr. Roberts failed to attend the paternity hearing so the court imposed a retroactive support order for $50,000 and ordered Joe to pay $2,000 a month in future support payments.

Wanting to keep this embarrassing matter from his wife, Joe wrote a check for $54,000 from the joint account. This sum represented the retroactive support obligation and two months of future payments.

When the attorney for the Estate of Osgood Huntingdon learned of the transaction, he sued Roberts to prevent future withdrawals from the account. The lawyer also requested a judgment against Joe for $54,000 which represented the sum our client had already withdrawn from the account. The Estate claimed that Joe was merely entitled to his original $5,000 deposit. In the alternative, the attorney suggests that Joe has a tenancy in common and is only entitled to one-third of the account's balance.

It is our position that Mr. Roberts is a joint tenant with the right of survivorship, thus entitling him to one half of the money at the time of Mr. Huntingdon's death. The remaining 50% should automatically go to Feelgood. Based upon **University of Montana v. Coe,** which is set forth earlier in this Chapter, answer the following questions:

1. Who should win? Please explain your answer.

2. What are the advantages and disadvantages of a tenancy in common?

3. What purpose do you think a joint tenancy with the right of survivorship serves?

ANSWER SHEET
PROBLEM FIVE

Name _____

Please Print Clearly

1. Who should win? Please explain your answer.

_____
_____
_____
_____
_____
_____
_____
_____
_____

2. What are the advantages and disadvantages of a tenancy in common?

_____
_____
_____
_____
_____
_____
_____
_____
_____

3. What purpose do you think a joint tenancy with right of survivor serves?

_____

_____

_____

_____

_____

_____

_____

_____

_____

_____

_____

_____

_____

_____

_____

_____

_____

_____

_____

_____

_____

C. Other Kinds of Concurrent Ownership

Married people enjoy a special form of co-ownership designed to protect the marital assets from creditors and to insure an easy transition of the property to the surviving spouse upon a tenant's death. Most states recognize a **tenancy by the entirety**, which is similar to a joint tenancy because it carries the right of survivorship. It differs from a joint tenancy, however, in that neither spouse can convey his or her interest in the property without the other. In other words, each spouse owns a 100 percent interest in the property and cannot dispose of the asset without the consent of the other. Because each spouse owns 100 percent of the property, a creditor of one spouse is unable to seize the joint asset. Sophisticated creditors, such as banks and mortgage companies, are aware of this rule and require both spouses to sign the loan documentation even though only one spouse may receive the money.

Husbands and wives have historically been viewed as one, so in the absence of clear evidence to the contrary, property owned by a married couple is held as a tenancy by the entireties. For instance, a deposit in a bank account which is opened in the name of a "husband and wife," or a "husband or wife" creates a tenancy by the entirety with all of the benefits relating to entirety ownership irrespective of how the joint account is designated.

During the duration of the marriage, either spouse has the presumptive power to act for both, so long as both spouses share in the proceeds. Neither spouse, however, may take the property for his or her sole use unless the other spouse consents. There have been numerous cases over the years where one spouse secretively withdraws money from an entireties bank account and then deposits the funds in a different bank account solely under that person's name. This is a common tactic when a divorce is contemplated. Since this type of unilateral severance works a hardship to the other, the courts have found that the unauthorized transfer destroys the tenancy by the entireties and will order the funds to be divided in half regardless on how the funds were generated. Two elements must exist in order for a court to find that such an "implied mutual agreement" has severed a tenancy by the entireties. A misappropriation by one spouse must occur (the offer), and the other spouse must file a suit for an accounting, division or other appropriate relief (the acceptance).

A handful of jurisdictions, especially in the West, are community property states including Arizona, California, Louisiana, Nevada, New Mexico, Texas, Washington and Wisconsin. A community property state regards all property acquired during the marriage, with the exception of that obtained through gift or inheritance, as being owned jointly by the couple. For example, a house or pension in the name of one spouse will be considered the asset of both.

As with a tenancy by the entirety, neither spouse can convey separately his or her interest without the consent of the other. In some states, community property will pass to the surviving spouse if one dies. In others, the deceased spouse's interest will pass to his or her heirs. Both a tenancy by the entirety and community property rights will be terminated or severed by a divorce. In that event, property is automatically transferred to a tenancy in common with each owning a one-half interest. These forms of co-ownership apply to both real and personal property.

D. Encumbrances

As a sole owner or co-owner, it is possible to give up one or more of the rights of ownership. In property law, this is called an **encumbrance**. An encumbrance is any right or interest that someone has in another's real property. For example, if a homeowner rents her house, she has given the tenant the rights of possession and use during the term of the lease. The title to the real property is, therefore, encumbered: she still owns the house but no longer has all of the rights of ownership because she has given some to the tenant for the term of the lease. Another example is a mortgage or lien on a property. For instance, a bank obtains an interest in the parcel of land until the loan is repaid and a business or person who makes improvements to the land of another obtains a mechanics lien until the work is paid in full.

On the other hand, an **easement** is the granting of the right to use a part of the land by an entity that does not own the land. A common example is the grant of an easement to a utility company to bury gas, electric and telephone lines on the owner's property. Easements run with the land on transfer so they constitute restrictions on the property and the new owner must honor the easement.

SECTION 5.4
PERSONAL PROPERTY

Various legal terms are used to describe items of personal property. **Chattel**, an old English word for cattle, has come to mean all forms of personal property: tangible; or intangible. As the reader may remember from Chapter Two, **tangible personal property** refers to a physical object. Personal property that is both tangible and movable is called a **good**. An automobile is an example of a good. **Intangible property** gives the owner a right rather than a physical object of independent value. For example, the owner of a share of stock in a company has certain rights, such as the right to receive dividends and the right to vote for the corporation's officers. But there is no physical object that goes with it, aside from the stock certificate that says the investor owns a share of the corporation. Other forms of intangible personal property include patents, trademarks, and copyrights.

**SECTION 5.5
ACQUIRING TITLE TO
PERSONAL PROPERTY**

Personal property may be acquired by purchase, gift, production or possession. The most common way to acquire ownership of personal property is to purchase it. A **purchase** is the transfer of title from one owner to another for payment or compensation. State law governs the purchase and sale of goods as noted in Chapter Two. The states have adopted Article 2 of the Uniform Commercial Code, a lengthy catalog of rules that details the rights and responsibilities of sellers and buyers of goods. Federal and state laws, including the Securities Exchange Act and Articles 3 and 4 of the Uniform Commercial Code regulate the purchase and sale of intangibles.

Personal property may also be acquired by gift, a transfer of title to property without payment or compensation. A **gift** may be made **inter vivos**, which means while the donor is alive, or it may take effect upon death under the terms of a will or the laws of inheritance. There are three requirements for an inter vivos gift to be valid: **(1)** the donor must intend to make a gift of the property; **(2)** the donor must deliver the property to the donee; and **(3)** the donee must accept the property. If the gift is valid, all the rights of ownership pass from the donor to the donee. For example, a gift is completed when a person hands a present to another during the holiday season and the recipient takes the package.

A **gift causa mortis** is the transfer of personal property made in contemplation of one's approaching death. It requires the same elements of a normal gift plus the fact that it was done by the donor in anticipation of imminent death. A gift causa mortis is revocable anytime prior to the donor's death and the gift fails if the person recovers. For instance, if a heart attack victim tells his best friend to take his gold Rolex watch moments before he dies, the gift is complete at that time and the time piece does not pass under the decedent's will. Also, no writing or consideration is necessary to support a gift causa mortis. Because of the chances of fraud, however, proof of a gift causa mortis must be clear and convincing.

Personal property may also be acquired by **production**. A person who takes scraps of fabric and creates a quilt owns the quilt because she has created or produced it by her labor. Similarly, the author of a book owns the copyright to the book because she has produced it. She may, however, transfer those rights to a publisher in order to have the book published.

Possession is another means of acquiring personal property. Historically, if one captured or killed a wild animal, he acquired title to the animal. If, however, he captured or killed the animal while he was trespassing on someone else's property, the owner of the land would acquire title to the animal. Today, state gaming statutes typically provide that the state owns and retains title to the wild animals captured or killed within its borders unless the animal was hunted or trapped pursuant to state laws regulating hunting, trapping, and fishing.

If personal property has been abandoned by its owner, title may be acquired by anyone who finds it. **Abandoned property** is that which has been discarded and the owner has no intention of claiming it. Abandoned property also includes property that was lost and its owner has given up all attempts to find it. An example would be a broken television put out for trash collection by its owner and then a junk dealer picks it up and repairs the television set. The junk dealer is now the lawful owner of the repaired television set. As with wild animals, if the abandoned property was discovered while the finder was trespassing, the landowner will acquire title to the property.

Abandonment of property requires intent plus an act that manifests a conscious purpose and intention of the owner neither to use nor to retake the property into his possession. An intention to discard property may be inferred from convincing evidence or it may be shown by conduct inconsistent with an intention to continue the use or ownership of the asset. The actual motive behind the abandonment is not a factor. Mere nonuse of the item, or lapse of time without claiming the property, however, is not enough to constitute abandonment. An exception to this rule protecting the rights of landowners is the doctrine of **treasure-trove**.

This form of property carries with it the thought of antiquity; the treasure must have been hidden or concealed so long as to indicate that the owner is probably dead or unknown. Treasure trove is money, gold, silver, or bullion that has been found buried in the earth or hidden in a private place. If the owner of the treasure-trove is unknown, the finder will acquire title as against the owner of the land where it is found.

If property has merely been lost or mislaid, the person who lost or misplaced the item retains title. **Lost property** is that which the owner has involuntarily and accidentally parted with and does not know where to find it. If someone finds lost property, he does not acquire title to it as against its rightful owner. The finder will, however, have better title to the property than anyone other than the rightful owner. For example, the finder of a wallet that contains identification must return it to the rightful owner, or be guilty of conversion. If the wallet contains no identification, but the owner learns that the wallet has been found and requests that it be returned, the finder must do so.

Most states have statutes that govern lost property. These statutes typically provide that if a finder of lost property turns it over to the appropriate authority and the loss is advertised, then the finder will acquire title to the property if the item is not claimed. This is the case even against the original owner if its rightful owner does not claim the property within a specified period of time.

Does a police officer who finds a bundle of money obtain ownership of the cash? This is the issue in **In re Funds in Possession of Conemaugh Tp. Sup'rs, 753 A.2d 788 (Pa., 2000)** where the court noted that police officers are held to a higher standard than ordinary citizens. It is part of an officer's duties to guarantee the protection of lost property and to investigate whether the item is evidence of a crime and whether the owner can be located. If the law permitted a police officer to retain lost property, then the law enforcement official might be encouraged by such a policy to conduct a sham or less than complete investigations in order to insure that no crimes would be unearthed and the true owners would never be located.

Mislaid property has been voluntarily and intentionally placed somewhere by the owner and forgotten. This would occur if someone leaves a textbook in the back seat of a friend's car and can't remember where he left it. The friend does not acquire title to the book but becomes an involuntary bailee and has a duty to take care of the book for the owner.

SECTION 5.6 BAILMENTS

A **bailment** occurs when the owner of personal property gives possession of the item to someone else, usually for a particular purpose. The owner is called the **bailor**, and the person temporarily in possession of the item is the **bailee**. The bailor continues to have title to the property but has given up some of the rights of ownership, possession and use, to the bailee.

Bailments can be placed into three categories: **(1)** for the sole benefit of the bailor, e.g., when someone takes care of a friend's dog as a favor; or when a friend forgets her gloves at another's house; **(2)** for the sole benefit of the bailee, e.g., when someone lends a car to a friend so the friend may get to work; and **(3)** for the mutual benefit of the bailor and the bailee, e.g., renting a car, taking clothes to the cleaner, or shipping a package. Mutual benefit bailments are the most common. Typically one party receives monetary compensation for supplying a good or service to the other. Such a bailment occurs when a person leaves a car at a parking garage. A bailment, however, only transfers possession and not ownership in the property. The transfer does not provide the person who takes possession of the asset, with the right to use it. For instance, a parking garage employee may not use a patron's car to run an errand.

Bailments have three elements: **(1)** the item must be personal property; **(2)** the property is delivered into the possession of another; and **(3)** the property is delivered pursuant to an agreement, which may be either expressed or implied.

Although the rights and responsibilities of the bailor and bailee may be specified in an agreement, there are certain rights and duties implied by law. The bailee has the right to temporarily possess and use the property for the purposes of the agreement. In addition, the bailee has a right of compensation. Usually the amount of compensation will be expressed in the agreement. For example, if a customer takes a jacket to the cleaners, the shop owner will be entitled to the cost of providing the cleaning service. Even if the amount of compensation is not expressly agreed upon, the bailee will have the right to receive a reasonable amount if it is a mutual benefit bailment. If the bailor does not pay the bailee's fee, the bailee may retain possession of the item until the bill is paid. This is called a **bailee's lien**. Thus, the cleaner can keep the jacket until the bill is paid, or a gas station may retain a car until the repair bill has been satisfied.

A bailee also has certain duties with respect to the item. For instance, the bailee has the duty to take reasonable care of the item. If the bailee fails to exercise reasonable care of the property entrusted to him, he will be liable for damages. The bailee also has the duty to return the item at the end of the bailment.

If there is an express agreement between parties, the bailee can limit her liability, either by a set dollar amount or by type of risk. For example, when one takes film to be developed, it is common for the developer to limit its liability to the replacing of the film if the film is lost or destroyed. This type of limitation of liability is generally valid if it is conspicuous, and the bailor has notice of the limitation.

A bailor also has certain rights and responsibilities with respect to the bailment. The bailor has the right to have the property returned in the same condition or as altered, pursuant to the terms of the agreement. Any service provided by the bailee must be performed in a workmanlike manner. The bailor is responsible to notify the bailee of any known or discoverable defects in the property. If the bailor fails to do so, she will be responsible for any injuries that result. For example, if someone rents a car with defective brakes, and the renter is injured in an accident as a result of that defect, the car rental company would be liable for the injuries.

Municipalities, businesses, and property owners have become very protective of their parking areas. Many have contracts with towing services to remove any vehicle which has been parked in a spot without authorization. What kind of bailment arises when a car is towed to a storage facility because it was illegally parked and is damaged while in the possession of the bailor or towing company? That is the issue in **Hadfield v. Gilcrest**.

MARK HADFIELD V. SAM GILCHRIST
538 S.E.2D 268 (S.C., 2000)

Gilchrist owns a motor vehicle towing service and maintains a storage facility for the retention of the towed vehicles.

Hadfield went to retrieve his Lincoln Continental from the parking spot where his wife parked the vehicle. The parking spot was on private property owned by Allen Saffer. Hadfield's wife parked the vehicle on Saffer's property without permission. The vehicle was not in the parking spot when Hadfield arrived as Saffer had called Gilchrist to have the vehicle removed.

Gilchrist towed Hadfield's car to his storage facility. Gilchrist maintained a chain link fence around the storage area and had an employee on the lot around the clock. The employees' duties included periodically leaving the office to check on the storage area which was some distance away from the office.

Upon Hadfield's arrival to pick up his car, he paid the fees. When he went to the storage area to collect his vehicle, Hadfield discovered the vehicle had been extensively vandalized. The vandals entered the storage area by cutting a hole in the fence.

Hadfield's attempts to persuade Gilchrist to pay for the damages were futile. Hadfield left the vehicle on Gilchrist's lot as he could not afford to repair it. After more than 60 days elapsed, Hadfield sold the vehicle for $1,000.

A bailment is created by the delivery of personal property by one person to another in trust for a specific purpose.

Bailments are generally classified as being for **(1)** the sole benefit of the bailor; **(2)** the sole benefit of the bailee; or **(3)** the mutual benefit of both. Bailments which benefit only one of the parties, the first and second classifications, are often described as gratuitous.

A gratuitous bailment is one in which the transfer of possession or use of the bailed property is without compensation. For instance, a gratuitous bailment arises if the bailment is undertaken as a personal favor.

By contrast, a bailment for the mutual benefit of the parties arises when one party takes the personal property of another into his or her care or custody in exchange for payment or other benefit.

Although a bailment is ordinarily created by the agreement of the parties, the agreement of the parties may be implied, and the bailment may arise by operation of law. Such a constructive bailment arises when one person has lawfully acquired possession of another's personal property, other than by virtue of a bailment contract, and holds it under such circumstances that the law imposes on the recipient of the property the obligation to keep it safe and redeliver it to the owner.

Gilchrist argues he towed the vehicle pursuant to the **Charleston Municipal Ordinances,** and the ordinances are for the sole benefit of the vehicle owners. Accordingly, he contends, the relationship created is a gratuitous bailment. We disagree.

We conclude a constructive bailment, for the mutual benefit of Hadfield and Gilchrist, was created.

After finding a bailment for mutual benefit exists in this case, we must determine whether Hadfield is entitled to damages.

The degree of care required of a bailee for mutual benefit is the degree of care which would be exercised by a person of ordinary care in the protection of his own property.

The burden of proof in this case rests first upon the bailor, Hadfield, to prove a prima facie case. He must show: **(1)** the goods were delivered to the bailee in good condition; and **(2)** they were lost or returned in a damaged condition. When the bailor, Hadfield, has so proven, the burden is then shifted to the bailee, Gilchrist, to show that he has used ordinary care in the good's storage and safekeeping.

Hadfield testified regarding the "nice" condition of his vehicle prior to it being towed, and the damage to his vehicle. Thus, Hadfield made out his prima facie case. The burden then shifted to Gilchrist to show that he used ordinary care in protecting the vehicle while in his care.

Gilchrist impounded the cars in a storage lot surrounded by a chain link fence. The person on duty spent time in the office and only visited the storage lot to check on it. The vandal cut a hole in the fence and broke into six to eight cars on the night in question.

The fact the guard was not on duty at the impound lot and, considering the only other security for the vehicles was the chain link fence, the trial judge could have concluded Gilchrist failed to exercise ordinary care.

We rule that where a city ordinance is utilized as the legal justification for taking possession of a vehicle on private property, the entity lawfully acquiring possession of the property becomes a constructive bailee as a matter of law. We also conclude the burden of proof in a constructive bailment case rests first upon a bailor to prove a prima facie case and, once so proven, the burden shifts to the bailee to show the use of ordinary care in the storage and safekeeping of the property. Accordingly, the order of the lower court is affirmed in favor of the plaintiff and he is awarded $4,030 in damages.

Pennsylvania has enacted legislation dealing with the removal of a motor vehicle that has been illegally parked on private property. That law is contained in the Motor Vehicle Code which provides:

(b) (1)   No person shall park or leave unattended a vehicle on private property without the consent of the owner or other person in control of the property except in the case of emergency or disablement of the vehicle, in which case the operator shall arrange for the removal of the vehicle as soon as possible.

(b) (2)   The provisions of this subsection shall not apply to private parking lots unless such lots are posted to notify the public of any parking restrictions and the operator of the vehicle violates such posted restrictions.

(c)   The owner or other person in possession of any property on which a vehicle is parked or left unattended in violation of the provisions of subsection (a) may remove or have removed the vehicle at the reasonable expense of the owner of the vehicle. Such person who removes or has removed a vehicle left parked or unattended in violation of the provisions of subsection (b) shall have a lien against the owner of the vehicle, in the amount of the reasonable value of the costs of removing the vehicle plus the costs of storage. If storage charges are not set by the municipality, a maximum of $25 per day may be charged for storage.

SECTION 5.7
REAL PROPERTY

Real property consists of land and everything attached to the land. Thus, the owner of a parcel of real estate owns the land itself, any minerals such as oil, ore, or gems located under the ground, the air space above the land, and the buildings, plants and trees attached to the land. Ownership comprises the bundle of rights that allow someone to possess, use, exclude others, encumber or alienate the real estate. There might be a sole owner or there may be co-owners who share the rights of ownership.

The purchase of a home has certain inherent problems. Disputes frequently arise as to what was included in the sale. When the buyers looked at a home before they agreed to purchase it, an elegant crystal chandelier hung in the foyer. At the time of settlement, however, the chandelier had been replaced by a plastic fixture. The seller refuses to give the buyers the chandelier claiming that it is a family heirloom worth several thousand dollars. The buyers maintain that the fixture was part of the realty since it was on display at the time the home was inspected. Who is correct? The answer will depend on whether the item is real or personal property. If the item is found to be real property, it will be part of the sale.

SECTION 5.8
ESTATES IN
REAL PROPERTY

The word **estate** is used in the law of real property to refer to a person's interests or rights concerning land. There are several types of estates; the most common is **fee simple absolute**. Its name derives from the same root as "fief" or "feudalism" because the concept of fee land ownership descends from the feudal system. Originally, the term denoted land that was held by a "free holder" in exchange for certain rights or duties paid to the superior lord. In fact, the property system used today—estates in land and tenancy—evolved from the feudal systems in England and France.

The fee simple absolute estate is the most complete form of ownership of real property. It includes the rights to possess, use, exclude others, encumber and alienate the property. It is not, however, totally unrestricted ownership because the government still retains certain rights in privately owned property.

For example, the government has the right to regulate an owner's use of the property through zoning laws that prescribe which areas of a community may be used for residential, commercial, or industrial purposes. Although the owner of the land owns the airspace above it, the United States government has passed various statutes that allow the public to use that airspace for air traffic and commerce.

The government also has the right to tax real property. Typically, each parcel of property is taxed based on its value. If the owner does not pay the tax, the government will place a tax lien on the property. The tax lien is a form of encumbrance that allows the government to have the property sold at a sheriff's sale to satisfy the unpaid tax bill.

Finally, the government has the right of eminent domain. That is, the right to take private property for a public purpose. However, the Fifth and Fourteenth Amendments to the United States Constitution require the government to pay just compensation to the private property owner whose land is taken by eminent domain.

The power of eminent domain should be exercised only in the mode and manner, prescribed by the legislature and the taking must be for a public purpose with just compensation. A government entity, however, is forbidden from taking a person's land for the purposes of conferring a private benefit on another citizen and the government is not allowed to take property under the mere pretext of a public purpose, when its actual purpose is to bestow a private benefit. A recent controversy in this area is whether a governmental entity may take property on behalf of a private party who plans on using the land for a public purpose. That was the issue in **Kelo v. City of New London, 545 U. S. 469 (2005)** where the Supreme Court ruled that the use of the powers of eminent domain to advance redevelopment by a private developer and to increase tax revenues for an economically distressed area met the "public use" requirement of the Constitution.

As for condemned property owned by a commercial establishment, the income from the business operation is not one of the factors that go into calculating the value of the property for the public taking. Instead, the fair market value of the land is the proper measure of damages. The owner, however, may receive business dislocation damages if that business cannot be relocated without substantial loss of patronage.

Other than the fee simple absolute, there are lesser estates in which the title holder of the real property does not enjoy the unrestricted right of ownership. These include the **fee simple defeasible** and the **life estate**. The fee simple defeasible estate, also known as a conditional or qualified fee, conveys all of the rights of ownership so long as the owner complies with a certain condition. For example, if an owner gives her real estate to a church to be used for church purposes, the church receives all of the rights of ownership but the use of the property is restricted to church purposes. If the church attempts to use the property for any other reason or attempts to alienate the property, the real estate will revert back to the original owner, or her legal heirs if she is no longer living. The owner, therefore, is said to retain a **reversionary interest** in the property.

A **life estate** conveys an ownership interest that is limited to the life of the person holding it. The holder of the life estate has all the rights of possession, use, and exclusivity. When that person dies, however, the estate reverts back to the original owner or his heirs or other grantees. They hold the future interest in the property, called the **remainder**.

For example, a person may convey property to her children while retaining the right to reside in the home as long as she wants. Such an interest, however, must be done through a deed which carves out the life estate for the grantor.

The remaindermen have the right to receive the property without diminution in value. This right imposes a duty on the life tenant not to allow or commit waste, through the deterioration, destruction, or material alteration of the property. Waste may include cutting timber for more than household purposes, removing subsurface minerals, and not maintaining the property. If the life tenant commits waste, the remaindermen may seek an injunction to prevent the wasteful conduct.

An **estate at sufferance** refers to the lowest interest one can have in real property. This term deals with a person who retains possession of real estate with no title. For example, a tenant who continues to remain in the property after a lease has expired will be considered to have an estate at sufferance. If the tenant pays rent after the expiration of the lease and the landlord accepts that rent, this acceptance converts an estate at sufferance into an estate at will. An **estate at will** is an estate created not by the consent, but by the doctrine of laches or actions of the owner in accepting the rent.

In recent times, new terms have been coined to describe interests in real estate. For example, a **condominium** refers to a multiunit structure where the resident owns the unit that he or she occupies together with an interest in the common areas. Usually, these units are run by a condominium association that levies monthly fees against the owners for the upkeep of the common areas. Condominiums will also have bylaws that govern the operation of the association and establish rules and regulations that the owners of the units must follow for the common good. On the other hand, a **housing cooperative** is an entity that owns real estate but allows a person to use the premises. The resident does not own the unit that he or she occupies and no deed is issued. Rather, the housing cooperative issues stock to the resident which gives the person the right to occupy one housing unit, to use the common amenities, and the resident has a say in the operation of the cooperative. This type of estate is very similar to a lease. Also, the housing cooperative will meet and decide if a perspective resident is to their satisfaction.

A leasehold estate is commonly called a **lease**. As mentioned earlier, a lease is an encumbrance upon the property: the landlord is the owner of the property and he has a fee simple absolute estate. But the landlord has given the tenant the exclusive right to possess and use the property.

In Pennsylvania, a lease for a term of more than three years must be in writing. As for which party is required to make the repairs to the leased premises, one must examine the written lease since that document will usually specify who is responsible for the repairs. For example, the lease may specify that all repairs under $100 are the responsibility of the tenant and all other repairs are the responsibility of the landlord unless caused by the conduct of the tenant. If the contract is silent on the issue or if the parties are operating under an oral lease, the owner of the property is usually responsible for those things that are attributable to ordinary wear and tear. On the other hand, if the tenant causes the damage, the renter may be responsible to fix it.

Many states have enacted **housing codes** that set minimal standards for apartments. Example provisions include the providing of heat between October and May, providing hot and cold water, and exterminating insects and rodents. Tenants also have obligations under a housing code such as the disposing of trash in a sanitary manner.

SECTION 5.9
LEASEHOLD ESTATES

The rights and responsibilities of the **lessor** (landlord) and the **lessee** (tenant) are usually specified by a written lease agreement. Even in the absence of a written lease, the law provides certain rights and responsibilities. The tenant receives the rights to exclusively possess and use the real estate by the landlord's covenant of quiet enjoyment. In other words, the landlord promises that he will not disturb the tenant's possession and use of the property. If the landlord, or anyone working for the landlord, unreasonably disturbs the tenant's enjoyment of the property, the tenant will have the right to sue for damages, or the lessee may elect to terminate the lease under the doctrine of constructive eviction. A constructive eviction occurs whenever the landlord breaches its duties to the extent that the tenant's use and possession of the premises is impossible or extremely difficult. A landlord may enter the premises for reasonable purposes, such as to do maintenance and repair, but many leases require the landlord to give the tenant reasonable notice of such entry unless there is an emergency.

A residential tenant also has the right to insist that the premises be fit for human habitation. This right is contained in the landlord's **implied warranty of habitability**, which the law requires to be a part of all residential leases. This warranty, however, does not apply to leases of property for commercial purposes. Lack of heat during winter months, no hot or cold running water, a substantial leak in the roof or pest infestation to the extent it may injure the health of the residents, are examples of defects which render the premises uninhabitable. If the premises are not habitable, a constructive eviction has occurred allowing the tenant to sue the landlord for damages or recession of the lease.

Many states have passed statutes that provide additional remedies for a breach of the warranty of habitability. These remedies include the withholding of rent and the placing of money into an escrow account, or repairing the defect and deducting the cost of the repairs from the rent. Before engaging in these self-help remedies, the tenant is usually required to give the landlord notice of the problem and an opportunity to repair it. In addition, many local housing ordinances provide that a violation of building and housing codes constitutes a breach of the warranty of habitability.

TERRI JOHNSON V. SCANDIA ASSOCIATES, INC.
717 N.E.2D 24 (IND., 1999)

Scandia Associates, Inc. owns and operates an apartment complex through its agent Oxford Management, Co. Terri Johnson sued Scandia and Oxford after suffering physical injuries caused by an electric shock she received when simultaneously touching two kitchen appliances while cooking in her apartment.

Asked whether a warranty of habitability is implied in the residential leasehold contract, we hold that a landlord could be found liable to his tenant on a breach of implied warranty, at least where there was a housing code and city inspectors had cited the landlord with multiple violations.

A warranty is a promise relating to a past or existing fact that incorporates a commitment by the promisor that he will be responsible if the facts are not as manifested. Habitability means reasonably fit for occupation as a dwelling. Thus, when a landlord warrants habitability, the warranty is an affirmative declaration of the apartment's fitness for habitation, that is, as a dwelling place.

When a landlord enters a lease agreement with her tenant, she voluntarily confers certain rights upon the tenant, such as possession and quiet enjoyment for a specific term. She does this in consideration of the tenant's promise to pay rent, not to waste the property, and not to "holdover" beyond the term. The landlord agrees to this legal relationship after balancing the costs and benefits, and the same is true for the tenant.

In light of these considerations, we conclude that a warranty of habitability is a landlord's promise to convey to a tenant an apartment suitable for living, and breach of which promise occurs when a landlord fails to tender a suitable apartment.

When a landlord warrants his property to be suitable for living and then breaches that promise by conveying an unsuitable apartment, the tenant's remedy may take several forms, including conveyance of a suitable property, recision and reformation of the agreement while the tenant retains possession, recision of the contract, or damages at law.

Johnson complains that her apartment was not suitable for living because its fixtures unexpectedly released an electric current and, second, that her injuries were foreseeably caused by the breaching condition. She does not allege whether the defect was present at the time of entry or arose after taking possession, nor does she have any contention about giving Scandia notice of the defect.

Indiana's law governing the landlord-tenant relationship has developed a warranty of habitability. The warranty derives from the agreement between the tenant and the landlord and may be express or implied. The existence of an implied warranty may be proven through evidence of the parties' course of dealing or performance and by evidence of ordinary practices in the trade. Where the warranty is express, consequential damages for injury to the person may be available as a remedy. Where the warranty is implied-in-fact, however, consequential damages may not be awarded because personal injury is outside the parties' contemplation. Johnson's complaint does not aver facts tending to show that Scandia warranted the apartment's habitability or that her injury was reasonably foreseeable within a warranty of habitability.

For these reasons, we find in favor of the defendants.

The tenant's right to use and possession, however, are not unlimited. The tenant may not create a nuisance that would interfere with other tenants' rights of quiet enjoyment. The tenant also has a duty not to commit waste by abusing, destroying, or altering the premises. If the tenant causes a problem that renders the premises uninhabitable, it will be the tenant's responsibility to repair it.

The primary right of the landlord is to receive rent; if the tenant does not pay it, the landlord may evict the renter. Most states require the landlord to give the tenant notice (frequently 30 days) to vacate the premises. If the tenant does not move out, the landlord may sue. If the tenant has no defense, such as breach of the implied warranty of habitability, the court will order the tenant to vacate the premises within a reasonable time (e.g., 10-30 days). If the tenant still refuses to move out, the landlord may request the sheriff to forcibly remove the tenant from the premises.

The tenant has a corresponding duty to pay rent for the term of the lease, which means that if the tenant leaves before the term has expired, she is still responsible to pay the rent, unless the landlord is able to lease the premises to someone else. The landlord has a duty to mitigate damages by attempting to lease the property; if he is unable to find a suitable new tenant, however, the original tenant will be liable for the rent until the end of the lease term.

In a residential lease, the landlord has a duty to maintain and repair the premises pursuant to the warranty of habitability. If a defective condition renders the property unfit for human habitation and causes an injury to the tenant or a guest, the landlord will be liable.

The law also imposes upon the landlord a duty to maintain common areas in a reasonably safe condition. A common area is used by some or all tenants— sidewalks, parking lots, entrance ways, halls, stairs, and elevators, and remains under the control of the landlord. If a tenant or guest is injured in a common area because the landlord has failed to maintain it in a safe condition, the landlord is liable for negligence. Some written leases contain an **exculpatory clause,** which provides that the landlord is not liable for injuries sustained upon the leased premises, whether due to the landlord's negligence or some other cause. Exculpatory clauses are not enforceable in residential leases because they violate the public policy that people need a safe place to live. In commercial leases, however, exculpatory clauses may be enforceable if the tenant is aware of and knowingly agrees to the clause.

Dean v. Gruber deals with a landlord's duty to make repairs under an oral lease.

BRENDA DEAN V. RICHARD GRUBER
978 S.W.2D 501 (MO. APP., 1998)

On November 15, 1993, Ms. Dean fell and sustained injuries while walking down the driveway at 5139 Swope Parkway. At the time, she was visiting her sister, Cynthia Gorman. Ms. Dean claims that her fall was caused by a loose handrail.

Approximately four months prior to Ms. Dean's fall, Ms. Gorman rented the single-family dwelling from Mr. Gruber. The lease was a verbal month-to-month agreement. Gorman states that the only entrance to the premises was the driveway and, because of the condition of the driveway, the lack of lighting at night, and the slope of the driveway, it was necessary to use the handrail to enter and exit the residence. Gorman also states that she noticed the handrail was loose shortly after moving in, and reported the problem to Gruber's employees, but that no repairs were made. Additionally, Ms. Gorman stated that at the time of the verbal rental agreement, she and Gruber agreed that all repairs would be made by the landlord. Gruber's employees were at the house to repair the plumbing, a toilet, a screen door, and a clogged basement drain.

Gruber stated that he was not aware that the hand railing was loose or in a dangerous condition until after Dean's fall, and that "at no time during the tenancy of Cynthia E. Gorman did she report... any dangerous condition of the hand railing, driveway or lighting, of which plaintiff complains" and at no time did he "promise Gorman to fix or repair any reported dangerous condition of the hand railing."

The general rule is that a landlord does not owe a duty to his tenant, and is not liable for personal injuries received by a tenant or by a tenant's invitee, caused by dangerous conditions of the premises. Exceptions to the rule include: (1) when the landlord had knowledge of a dangerous condition, which condition is not discoverable by the tenant, and the landlord fails to make disclosure; (2) when the injury occurs in a common area; and (3) when a landlord is responsible for making repairs, but negligently fails to do so. The tenant argues that exceptions two and three are applicable here.

This was a single-family home with a driveway which is for the exclusive use of the tenant of the homeowner and her invitees. The driveway was not a common area used by more than one tenant. Thus, the common area exception to the general rule of landlord non-liability is inapplicable.

Next, Dean contends that Gruber maintained control of the premises such that he was responsible for making repairs. A landlord is under no obligation to a tenant to repair unless there is a contract which creates a duty to repair. However, where the landlord retains partial control over the leased premises for the purpose of making repairs, the landlord is then obligated to make such repairs and to keep the premises in a reasonably safe condition for the intended use.

Although Dean contends that when she rented the premises from Gruber they agreed that he would make all repairs, such evidence alone does not create a duty. There must be something more from which a jury could infer that under the agreement the tenant gave up and surrendered his right to exclusive possession and control and yielded to the landlord some degree or measure of control and dominion over the premises.

Determination of whether the amount of control a landowner exerts is sufficient to incur liability turns largely on the extent to which the landowner permits the tenant to treat the premises as belonging to the tenant. Viewing all the factual inferences in favor of Dean, there are no facts alleged which would allow a jury to infer Gruber's control of the premises that would demonstrate a duty for him to make repairs. Gruber did not retain a key, or reserve the right to inspect the premises, except with the permission of the tenant. The fact that Gruber may have made repairs to the property prior to the injury does not establish control absent other evidence. There is no assertion of general supervision by Gruber over the premises in order to make the repairs. As a result, the trial court correctly determined that Gruber was entitled to judgment as a matter of law. Judgment affirmed.

Section 5.10 Acquiring Title to Real Property

There are several ways to acquire title to real property: by gift, adverse possession, or purchase. One may acquire title by gift, either inter vivos or testamentary. For an inter vivos gift, a deed will be prepared transferring title to the land from the donor to the donee. As with personal property, a valid gift requires the donor to intend to give the property, that the donor delivers it, and that the donee accepts it. Because real property cannot be delivered physically, delivery of the deed is the symbolic transfer of possession.

A **testamentary gift** of land is one given by a will. For example, a parent may leave real property to a child by will. If the owner of real estate dies without a will, the property will be given to the decedent's legal heirs. This is called intestate succession. If there are no legal heirs, the property will be transferred to the state under a doctrine called **escheat**, which means that real property lacking an individual competent to inherit it, the property will revert to the state.

Title to real property may be acquired by **adverse possession**. Adverse possession requires a person claiming title to the real estate to possess and use it for a statutory period of time which varies from 5 to 30 years, depending on the state. There are five elements required to acquire title by adverse possession; the claimant's use must be: **(1)** adverse or hostile, which means that the claimant is using the property without the owner's permission; **(2)** actual, meaning the claimant is using the real estate in an appropriate fashion; **(3)** open, visible or notorious, which means that the claimant's use of the land is visible to the community to see; **(4)** exclusive, which signifies the claimant is asserting the right to exclude others (the land is not being used by the public at large); and **(5)** continuous for the statutory period, meaning that the claimant has continued to use the land for the statutory period without being ejected by the rightful owner.

To prevent adverse possession, the record owner must affirmatively act to interrupt the adverse possessor's use of the property. The owner cannot sit passively by, knowing of the adverse use. For example, a homeowner who erects a fence 5 feet onto his neighbor's property may end up owning that extra piece of land if the trespass goes unchallenged for the appropriate number of years.

In Pennsylvania, the law requires that the possession be uninterrupted for 21 years and possession of the property must be visible. In other words, the use of the land must be open for all to see. Nevertheless, adverse possession does not apply to the land owned by the government.

By far, the most common way to acquire title to real property is to purchase it. The legal process of purchasing a home usually begins when the buyer and seller enter into an Agreement of Sale for the purchase of real property.

The Agreement of Sale specifies how much money is to be paid for the property and when the money is to be paid. In addition, the Agreement presumes that the buyer will secure financing. The mortgage contingency clause provides that if the buyer is unable to secure financing, she may terminate the agreement and receive a full refund of any deposit that has been given to the seller or the realtor, as the seller's agent. After both parties have signed the Agreement, the buyer will apply for a mortgage with a bank or mortgage company. If the lender approves the application, it will lend the money to the buyer at settlement. The collateral or security for the loan is a mortgage on the real estate purchased by the buyer. A **mortgage** is a lien that allows the lender to have the property sold at a foreclosure sale if the buyer does not repay the loan. A mortgage holder can also insist that its interests in the property be protected. For instance, it is common for a mortgage company to require that the owner pay the real estate taxes into an escrow account that will be maintained by the mortgage company to insure that the taxes are paid currently.

The agreement normally provides that the seller will convey good and marketable fee simple title to the buyer. A title is marketable if it is free from reasonable doubt as to its validity or if it conveys all the rights of ownership. A title that is encumbered by liens would not be marketable unless the liens were removed.

After the Agreement is signed, the buyer will usually arrange for a search of the title by a lawyer, or more commonly, by a title insurance company, to be sure that the seller can convey a marketable fee simple title. If the seller cannot convey such a title, the buyer may terminate the Agreement and receive a full refund of his deposit money.

The agreement will specify what items are attached to the property as fixtures and are therefore included in the sale. If any of these items are not to be included in the sale, or if there are additional items which are to be included, the parties must state this either in the "Special Clauses" section or by an addendum or rider to the agreement.

A standard agreement will generally provide for remedies in the event the buyer defaults. If the buyer breaks the agreement and refuses to purchase the property for a reason other than the buyer's inability to obtain financing or the seller's inability to convey marketable title, the seller's most common remedy is to keep the buyer's deposit money as liquidated damages. Liquidated damages are an amount of money agreed upon as damages prior to a breach of the contract. In this case, it is the amount of the buyer's deposit. If the seller breaches the agreement by refusing to convey the property to the buyer, the buyer's usual remedies are either: to seek specific performance, which is to sue the seller to convey the property; or to rescind the contract, which is to sue the seller for a return of his deposit and any other money expended to perform his duties under the Agreement (such as a loan application fee).

If all goes smoothly after the agreement is signed, the buyer can obtain a mortgage loan, and the seller can convey marketable title, at which point, the parties will have a closing or settlement, the consummation of the transaction. The buyer will pay the purchase price to the seller, and the seller will deliver a deed, which conveys fee simple title to the buyer. At that point, all the rights and responsibilities of ownership will belong to the buyer.

SECTION 5.11
ZONING

As our country, particularly the more populated cities began to develop in a haphazard way, the desire for orderly planning arose. As a result, local governments, often with input from the citizens, created codes which specified areas for development as residential, commercial and industrial areas. This process is known as **zoning** and is defined by the federal government as the public regulation of land and building use to control the character of a place. One may remember that at one time in Philadelphia, no building was allowed to be taller than the hat of William Penn on the top of City Hall. This is known as a height restriction.

After a landmark decision by the United States Supreme Court in 1926 found that zoning codes were constitutional, these codes began to be adopted in many communities. Although similar, there were, and still are, differences to reflect the character of the city or town and what a good scheme is for a specific area.

The different designations are further divided. For instance, within the Residential Districts, some places are limited to single family dwellings while others permit multi-family units including duplexes and apartments. Likewise, the Industrial Districts are divided into light and heavy uses. The amount, area, or lot size, is also specified within each district.

One problem with these codes is what to do with uses of property that were already in place when the new regulations were adopted, but are now in conflict with the zoning classification. In order to protect the property rights of these owners, they are permitted to continue their existing use, and to pass it on to family or purchasers of their property. This is referred to as a nonconforming use. Often the codes provide that if a **nonconforming use** ceases for a certain period of time, usually from one to three years, that nonconforming use is lost. The property must then confirm to the new zoning code designation.

In addition to nonconforming uses, a zoning board is created to hear cases where the owner of property can show that for some reason related to the property, such as shape, size, or type of building, the owner cannot conform to the code. The board is then empowered to give that property owner a **variance** to permit a use not designated in the code. The standards for a variance are usually strict and never granted just because the property owner would make more income by not complying with the code.

From time to time, a legislative body, such as City Council or the Township Commissioners, adds to or changes the code. They also shift zoning classification when changes to a neighborhood or new uses occur. The legislative body cannot make such changes for just one property as a favor to the owner. The area in question must be large and the change must be in keeping with the surrounding area. Otherwise, the change may be challenged as **spot zoning** which is not permitted. Zoning and land use planning are supposed to go together. Most large cities have a comprehensive plan which is prepared by professional land planners who staff a planning commission. Smaller towns have planning boards made up of citizens from the area that perform a particular task.

There has been a movement with gasoline service stations to expand their product offerings to more than the sale of gasoline. A number of establishments have converted their gas stations into mini-markets. This simple conversion can run afoul of laws in the areas which are not zoned for such a use. That is the issue in **Atlantic Richfield Company v. Harrisburg Zoning Hearing Board** where the court had to decide if a mini-mart is just an expanded use of a gas station which previously sold candy bars, cigarettes and sodas to its customers.

ATLANTIC RICHFIELD COMPANY V. HARRISBURG ZONING HEARING BOARD
18 D. & C. 3D 564 (PA. COM. PL., 1981)

Food and fuel, the prime participants in our unprecedented inflationary spiral, are locked in a territorial conflict which, impinging on certain zoning restrictions, necessitates a judicial delineation. Apparently feeling that "fill her up" should apply to tummy as well as tank, the Atlantic Richfield Company seeks to expand its service station at Second and Verbeke Streets in the city of Harrisburg into a mini-market. The zoning administrator denied its application for a permit. An appeal from his decision was denied by the zoning hearing board and the matter is now before this court.

The zoning hearing board based its denial on the principal grounds that to permit Atlantic Richfield to operate a grocery store would add a second nonconforming use to the property. Since 1923 when the gasoline and service station began operation, the area has become more restrictive and is now classified an RPO zone which permits only residential and professional offices. Following marketing studies which identified this location as desirable as a convenience store, appellant proposed to remove the auto lifts, close off the service bay, delete the service and repair functions entirely and convert the building into a 24 hour mini-market having only self-service gas pumps.

The applicant contends that its proposal is permissible under the Codified Ordinances of Harrisburg which provide that a nonconforming use may continue as the "same" use or be "expanded" into other portions of the building for increased trade. We cannot see the operation of the proposed grocery store as a continuation of the same use. Since its inception, this station has been operated as a traditional full-service gas station. While there have been incidental sales in the office portion of the building of such items as cigarettes, soda, candy, flashlight batteries, aspirin and a limited supply of snacks, they were merely offered as a convenience for motorists and can be viewed only as incidental to the primary purpose of providing gasoline and auto repairs and service. While you can buy a hot dog and a cup of coffee at Penn State's Beaver Field, it's still a football stadium and not a restaurant. In **Reinert v. Weisenberg Zoning Board, 48 Pa. Commonwealth Ct. 519 (1980),** an applicant who "merely worked on and tinkered with his own automobiles and those of his friends without charge" was not permitted to claim this nonconforming use entitled him to establish a complete automobile repair shop. If more is needed, one need only consider the extensive physical alterations proposed for the conversion of the property to a grocery store.

The applicant also asserts that its proposal is simply an expansion of a previous nonconforming grocery use. This argument would be attractive if the use as an existing grocery store had been established. Appellant did present testimony that 15 percent of its current sales are of non-gasoline items, although inspection by the zoning officer throws this into serious doubt. Nor can we accept appellant's projection that a full grocery store line as it contemplates would result only in a 22 percent total sales ratio of non-gasoline items. The oil industry is not noted for its philanthropic gestures and one can hardly imagine all this bother for an anticipated 7 percent increase in sales.

The past sales of non-gasoline items do not, under the evidence, justify or create a presumption that they were always part and parcel of the primary use. It appears that they were really incidental sales, made in the fashion of the old time gasoline stations, which are now being transformed into an argument that the grocery store was always there, you just couldn't see it. The policy of the law is to restrict closely nonconforming uses and to strictly construe provisions which provide for their continuance.

And finally a nonconforming use cannot be expanded unless applicant's proposed use will not be detrimental to or tend more greatly to alter the character of the neighborhood. The zoning hearing board, acting with proper discretion, determined that the introduction of a convenience grocery store would defeat the recent efforts to upgrade the neighborhood. The board cited substantial rehabilitative and restorative efforts being undertaken in this district. The existence of these efforts combined with the neighboring corridor of various "commercial" enterprises including two grocery stores obviates the need for a retail enterprise in this particular neighborhood.

The board was also justifiably concerned about the safety, health and welfare of the citizens. It found that existing traffic patterns on North Second Street create a significant flow of automobiles particularly "circuit" riders who parade around this area and would be further attracted by the presence of an all-night convenience store.

For all the above reasons, we feel that the board committed no error of law; hence, no mini-market.

SECTION 5.12 REVIEW CASES

1. Chavez conveyed his interest in a piece of real estate to himself and his spouse as tenants by the entirety after a lawsuit had been filed against him by Premier Property. Later that year, a judgment was entered against Chavez for $190,000. When Premier learned of the transfer, it moved to set aside the conveyance as being a fraudulent conveyance to defeat the rights of a creditor. Can a debtor transfer property to the other spouse in anticipation of the entry of future judgment in order to defeat the rights of the creditor? **Premier Property Management Inc. v. Claudia Chavez, 728 N.E.2d 476 (Ill., 2000).**

2. Bloomfield Club Recreation Association sued the builder of a housing complex for breach of implied warranty of habitability with respect to certain commonly held facilities within their residential development. The builder had created a declaration of covenants agreed to by each homeowner when they purchased their homes that granted each owner a right of easement to use the common areas, including the clubhouse in the development. The homeowner, however, said the clubhouse was uninhabitable because of defective workmanship. Does the implied warranty of habitability apply to non-residential construction, such as a clubhouse or is it limited to an occupied residence? **Bloomfield Club Recreation Association v. The Hoffman Group, Inc., 712 N.E.2d 330 (Ill., 1999).**

3. Hamilton and Morris were guests at a dinner party where alcoholic beverages were served throughout the evening. Hamilton removed her wrist watch and placed it on the kitchen counter. About midnight, the lights in the house went off and Hamilton left the kitchen. Morris saw the watch on the counter and picked it up so that it would not be misplaced. Unfortunately, Morris could not remember where she put the watch for safekeeping. Hamilton sued Morris, alleging that Morris was the bailee of the watch and that she negligently lost it while it was in her possession. Morris, however, contended that she was a gratuitous bailee and only owed a slight duty of care. Was a bailment created when Morris took possession of the watch? If so, what type of bailment was created, and will Morris be responsible for losing the watching? **Andrea Morris v. Marsha Hamilton, 302 S.E.2d 51 (Va., 1983).**

4. During his lifetime, the decedent had a romantic relationship with Sharon Clark. During the winter months, they traveled to Florida with a camper. They continued this ritual on an annual basis. The trailer was registered in both of their names. The decedent also maintained a bank account in which he added Clark's name to the account. That account, however, did not have survivorship language on the signature card in the event of the death of Mr. Donahue. How much of the decedent's property is Clark entitled to with respect to the trailer and bank account? **Estate of John Donahue v. Sharon Clark, 692 N.Y.S.2d 225 (N.Y. App., 1999).**

5. Rodman was an employee of the Horse Shoe Casino. As an employee, she was required to park her car in an employee's parking lot. One night, her car was stolen from the Casino lot. Employees of the casino were required to park their vehicles in this special lot and they were forbidden to park in the guest parking lot which was much closer to their place of employment. What type of bailment was created and who should win the case? **Robinson Property Group, Ltd. v. Debra Rodman, 1998 Miss. LEXIS 359 (Miss., 1998).**

SECTION 5.13
INTERNET REFERENCES

For more information on the materials in this Chapter, see the following sites on the Internet:

A. Real Estate

- **www.propertymart.net**
  This company site provides information about real estate, including advertisements about available properties and various related links.

- **www.realtor.com**
  Realtor.com helps prospective home buyers find houses for purchase all over the country. The site also has a reference library relating to real estate matters and offers information about buying, selling, and other important issues regarding real property.

- **www.realestate.com**
  This site discusses home buying, selling, and financing. Specific information is offered on the real estate professional, lending services, appraisers, and service providers.

- **www.vamch.com/reinfo.html**
  This site provides a detailed glossary of real estate and mortgage terms.

- **www.parealtor.org**
  The Pennsylvania Association of Realtors maintains this site devoted to real estate news, consumer information, and updated information regarding real estate legislation.

- **www.legalwiz.com/contract**
  An attorney explains the basics of the real estate contract at this site.

- **www.yahoo.com/Government/Law/Property**
  Yahoo's search engine on property law is located at this address, and a person can use it to search through many subjects concerning real estate. For instance, a person can learn about the disposition of property by will.

B. Intellectual Property

- **www.expresssearch.com/inventor**
  Information about the patent process is offered at this site.

- **www.patentcafe.com**
  This site offers information about patents, including articles and frequently asked questions on the topic; it also discusses other intellectual property issues, such as trademarks and copyrights.

- **www.patents.com**
  The law firm of Oppedahl & Larson, LLP, maintains this site which is dedicated to information on intellectual property.

C. Estate Planning

- **http://evans-legal.com/dan**
  Information relating to estate planning is provided at this address, and issues discussed include wills, trusts, and inheritance tax.

- **www.virginiaweber.com/eplan.htm**
  This site provides answers to frequently asked questions about estate planning.

- **www.estateattorney.com**
  Articles and information about decedent's estate and estate planning is offered at this site, which is maintained by a Pennsylvania estate-planning attorney.

D. Leasing

- **www.pa.landowners.org**
  The Pennsylvania Landowners' Association maintains this site which provides information about the organization and current articles of interest dealing with land for rent.

- **www.nolo.com/encyclopedia/articles/lt/agreement_faq.html**
  Nolo's Legal Encyclopedia provides general information about leases and rental agreements at this address.

KEY TERMS

Abandoned Property
Adverse Possession
Bailee
Bailee's Lien
Bailment
Bailor
Chattel
Concurrent Ownership
Condominium
Conveyancing
Deed
Eminent Domain
Encumbrance
Escheat
Estate
Estate at Sufferance
Exculpatory Clause
Fee Simple
Fee Simple Absolute
Gift
Gift Causa Mortis
Good
Housing Code
Housing Cooperative
Implied Warranty of
    Habitability
Inter Vivos
Joint Tenancy

Lease
Lessee
Lessor
Life Estate
Lost Property
Mislaid Property
Nonconforming Use
Ownership
Personal Property
Property
Purchase
Quiet Title
Real Property
Remainder
Reversionary Interest
Right of Survivorship
Sole Ownership
Spot Zoning
Tenancy by the Entirety
Tenancy in Common
Testamentary Gift
Title
Treasure-Trove
Uniform Commercial Code
Variance
Waste
Zoning

CHAPTER 6

CRIMINAL LAW IN A BUSINESS SETTING

**SECTION 6.1
CRIMINAL LAW**

"The real significance of crime is in its being a breach of faith with the community of mankind."

Joseph Conrad
Lord Jim, 1900

As a general rule, an individual can engage in any type of conduct that he or she wishes unless the law specifically prohibits those actions. The legislature, however, will intercede whenever necessary to regulate and prohibit conduct that society deems inappropriate.

A **crime** is an offense against society as determined by the legislature or considered a public wrong that carries the punishment of imprisonment or some other public sanction. Crimes number in the thousands, and specific definitions will vary from jurisdiction to jurisdiction. The offense is investigated by law enforcement officials who usually file the criminal charges against the accused, and a governmental agency, such as the District Attorney or United States Attorney, prosecutes the defendant. These crimes range from felonies to summary offenses.

The United States Department of Justice maintains statistics on the categories of crimes committed each year in this country. The most frequently charged offenses deal with non-violent crimes and make up about three-fourths of all arrests. Drug trafficking and other drug related crimes constitute the single largest category of all arrests and make up 36% of the total arrests made in the United States. Violent crimes account for one-fourth of all arrests and assault and robbery lead this category. The Southern states have the highest rate of violent crimes and account for 42% of all such crimes committed in this country.

Crimes against businesses retard economic prosperity. Some people, however, consider these types of offenses to be "victimless" crimes because of the perception that commercial entities can absorb the losses or have insurance.[1]

Burglary, robbery, shoplifting, employee theft, and fraud costs businesses billions of dollars annually. Crime can be particularly harmful to small commercial establishments, which lose both customers and employees when crime and fear take their toll on a neighborhood. For instance, when small businesses are victims of crime, they often change their hours of operation, raise their prices to cover the losses, relocate outside of the community, or simply close.[2] As for crimes by employees, they are 15 times more likely to steal from an employer than customers do and shoplifting costs vendors $9.5 to $11 billion annually.[3]

On the other hand, the public is not immune from the criminal and unscrupulous acts of businesses. From Bernard Madoff to Enron, the news is replete with stories of corporate wrongdoing, improper accounting practices, and stock manipulation. Illegal actions perpetrated in a business setting are generally classified as **white collar crimes**. This Chapter will explore some of these crimes and will examine several of the constitutional rights commercial establishments enjoy against unwarranted governmental intrusions.

SECTION 6.2 CRIMES

Crimes against businesses take many forms. The following are some of the more common offenses.

BURGLARY

According to the FBI, more than two million burglaries occur each year and two-thirds of these offenses are of residential structures. Burglars invade homes primarily during the day through forcible entry while business structures are usually entered at night. The average loss per illegal entry is a little more than $1,700. The Northeast has the fewest number of burglaries while the South has the highest rate for these crimes. As for what month has the highest burglary rate, that distinction goes to July. February has the fewest.

The definition of burglary has changed over time. In common law, **burglary** was defined as the breaking and entering of a building at night with the intent of committing a felony. Since the purpose of this law is to allow people to be secure in their homes, should it matter whether the offense occurs during the day or night? The modern definition of burglary provides that a person is guilty of this crime if he enters a building or occupied structure with the intent to commit a crime unless the premises are open to the public. The distinction of committing the crime between the day or night has been eliminated, as well as the requirement of breaking and entering. For instance, a person who enters a business premise while it is closed to steal something commits the crime of burglary.

By way of comparison, England defines burglary as the entry into "any building, part of a building, inhabited vehicle or vessel with the intent to steal, cause grievous bodily harm, criminal damage, or to commit rape."

Burglary is a crime in and of itself and does not require the substantive offense to be committed by the criminal. For example, if a person breaks into a home to steal a rare painting, but the painting is no longer there, the individual is still guilty of burglary.

Is a defendant's entry into separately secured offices, and dormitory rooms in the same building a single offense or multiple burglaries? That is the issue in **People v. Elsey.**

PEOPLE V. ELSEY
97 CAL. RPTR. 2D 269 (CAL. APP. 3 DIST., 2000)

Central Valley Intermediate School (CVI) was scheduled to hold its Medieval Festival. In preparation, tables and chairs for the festival's culminating "feast," a lunch for 500 guests were borrowed and set up on Thursday night.

Joe Brouillard, the principal at CVI, contacted Statewide Security to guard the borrowed items. Two guards from Statewide Security, defendant and Richard Maddox, arrived at 10:00 p.m. on Thursday. Principal Brouillard gave them a set of keys so that they could use the staff room, where there were restrooms, a telephone, and a soda machine. Although the keys also afforded entry into all of the rooms on the school campus, defendant and Maddox were not given permission to enter any other room.

The school's physical layout consists of an older building in one corner, three different wings connected with a fourth wing that runs north and south, and three new portables on the east south side.

About midday on Friday, the food service clerk informed Brouillard that lunch money collected from the students was missing from her desk. Later that day, Brouillard also learned that money was missing from classroom 10 and that classroom 16 had been broken into.

Maddox, who pleaded to one count of burglary in exchange for a grant of probation, testified that he and defendant had devised a plan to take items from rooms in the school and pawn them.

The two men first used a key to open the locked door of classroom 16, from which they took three knives and two rifles. Maddox and defendant next entered two connecting classrooms, classrooms 7 and 8, through the locked outside door to classroom 7. They entered the second classroom through the closed, but unlocked, connecting door between the classrooms, after moving a large roll of paper that

was in front of the door. They took a tool kit from each classroom.

In a pretrial motion, the People set forth their theory of the case: Defendant was guilty of six burglaries because he burgled six separate areas, each of which required a separate entry. Defendant urges that there was but one burglary because only a single school was entered and "it is irrelevant that the school burgled was made up of multiple buildings and portables."

Burglary in California, as defined in Section 459, provides:

> Every person who enters any house, room, apartment, tenement, shop, warehouse, store, mill, barn, stable, outhouse or other building... with intent to commit any felony is guilty of burglary.

Thus, the plain language of the statute supports the trial court's instruction that entry into each room constitutes a separate burglary. California cases have concluded that entry into any type of room with the requisite intent constitutes a burglary. If entry into a "room" within a building can constitute a burglary, it would appear to follow that entry into multiple rooms with such intent would support multiple charges of burglary. Indeed, California courts have affirmed separate burglary convictions for entry into separate rooms in a single structure, whether it be student dormitory rooms within interconnected buildings, or separately leased and locked offices in a small office building.

There is no doubt that if the premises had been located in three separate buildings defendant could have been punished for three separate burglaries; he is not entitled to two exempt burglaries merely because his victims chose the same landlord. If the rule were otherwise, a thief who broke into and ransacked every store in a shopping center under one roof, or every apartment in an apartment building, or every room or suite in a hotel, could claim immunity for all but one of the burglaries thus perpetrated.

Defendant argues that different rooms within the school were not separate dwelling places, and so therefore, entering into each was not a separate burglary. Accordingly, the issue facing us is whether defendant's entry into separately secured classrooms and an office, largely in separate buildings, should be treated any differently than separate dormitories or leased premises in single or interconnected structures. The plain language of the statute, prohibiting entry into "any" house, room, or other building with burglarious intent, would support the conclusion that each entry with the requisite intent constituted a separate burglary.

Based on the record before us, the occupants of each classroom or office at CVI had a separate expectation of protection against an unauthorized entry. The office and classrooms at CVI were assigned to different people, locked to the outside, and located to a great extent in separate buildings on the school campus. Defendant entered five of the six rooms from the outside through doors that were kept locked to the outside. The evidence was that teachers had a reasonable expectation of protection against intrusion with respect to each individual classroom.

Accordingly, both the plain language and the underlying purpose of the burglary statute support convicting defendant of separate burglaries for each entry into a secured room assigned to a different person and largely located in a different building on the CVI school campus, as long as he had the requisite intent.

How would you answer the following questions?

1. If a person breaks into a car to steal the radio, does it constitute burglary?

2. If a person enters a mobile home to assault the occupants, is this burglary?

3. If a person enters a department store while it is open in order to steal a coat, is this burglary?

CRIMINAL TRESPASS

Has a person committed a crime if he or she purposely comes onto the land of another but has no intent to commit a crime? For example, is it a crime if a camper discovers a home in the woods and enters the structure to take a shower or if one climbs over a fence of a business property to go hunting on that land?

Criminal trespass laws have been enacted to protect the unlawful intrusion onto real estate. The crime occurs when a person enters the land of another without permission or with no legal right to be there. For instance, some states make it a crime if a person:

1. Enters, gains entry by subterfuge or surreptitiously remains in any building or occupied structure; or breaks into any building or occupied structure or separately secured or occupied portion thereof, or

2. Knowing that he is not licensed or privileged to do so, enters or remains in any place as to which notice against trespass is given by:

    i.   actual communication to the actor;

    ii. posting in a manner prescribed by law or reasonably likely to come to the attention of intruders;

    iii. fencing or other enclosure manifestly designed to exclude intruders; or

    iv. an actual communication to the actor to leave school grounds as communicated by a school, center or program official, employee or agent or a law enforcement officer.

THEFT RELATED CRIMES

Consider the following cases to ascertain if there is a common thread. In 1980, two men rigged the Pennsylvania State Lottery by placing counterfeit balls in the machine insuring that 666 would be the winning number. A bank clerk mistakenly deposited ten thousand dollars into a customer's checking account which was promptly withdrawn by the recipient. A person gave his ATM card to a co-worker to withdraw $20 from his checking account as a loan. Instead, the co-worker withdraws $500. A person walked into a jewelry store and sold a new $9,000 Rolex watch to the merchant for $100. The common thread in these cases is that they are all examples of theft related offenses.

The Federal Bureau of Investigation determined that over seven million theft related crimes were committed in 2002 with an estimated loss of $4.9 billion dollars in property. These figures represent a very sizable portion of the total crimes committed during the year with theft related offenses ranging from larceny to receiving stolen property.

Larceny is the taking and carrying away of property that belongs to another without the owner's consent and with the intention of depriving the owner of the goods permanently. Because this crime requires the person to take possession of and carry away the item, the offense does not apply to real estate or intangible property.

Most people have heard of the terms "petit larceny" and "grand larceny." The distinction between these crimes merely involves the value of the item stolen. For instance, Virginia classifies a theft of something having a value of $200 or more as grand larceny while an item with a value of less than $200 is petit larceny.

Embezzlement is the act by which someone takes ownership of property that has been entrusted to him with the fraudulent intent to deprive the owner of the property. For instance, embezzlement occurs when a bank teller fraudulently changes the deposits so she can take some of the money. While embezzlement is closely aligned with theft, there is a critical difference. An embezzler is lawfully entrusted with the property as opposed to a thief who improperly obtains possession of the asset.

Embezzlement has no financial boundaries. The amount taken can be small or large. The crime can be as minor as a store clerk pocketing a few dollars from the register to executives of a large company falsely transferring millions of dollars of corporate funds into their personal bank accounts. Depending upon the scale of the wrongdoing, embezzlement may be punishable by large fines and jail time.[4]

Robbery consists of all of the elements of larceny with one additional requirement. The taking must be accomplished by force or the threat of force.

The Federal Bureau of Investigation reports that most robberies occur on streets and highways and firearms are used almost half of the time. The average dollar value of the items taken per robbery is $1,230.

The force needed to accomplish a pick-pocket is not the type ordinarily required for robbery. If a weapon is used, however, the crime will be considered robbery. For instance, a purse snatch in which the victim is knocked to the ground is considered robbery.

COM. V. BEDELL
954 A.2D 1209 (PA. SUPER., 2008)

On December 7, 2005, at a SEPTA station, Bedell snatched a wallet from the victim's hand and fled. The victim was using the wallet to support a note that he was writing. Following the theft, the victim chased and caught up to Bedell who then threw the wallet back to the victim. Upon inspecting the wallet, the victim realized that Bedell had removed forty dollars. The victim resumed his chase and after finding Bedell again, notified the police of his whereabouts. Officer Silberstein arrived at the scene and the victim informed him of Bedell's presence at the scene. Officer Silberstein and the victim approached Bedell, who removed forty dollars from his person, handed it to the victim and stated "Here ... we're cool, right?" The police arrested Bedell. The Commonwealth charged Bedell with robbery.

On May 8, 2006, Bedell entered a guilty plea to the charge. On November 6, 2006, Bedell filed a Petition seeking to withdraw his guilty plea on the ground that trial counsel was ineffective for failing to fully advise him that he had a valid defense to robbery.

The Crimes Code defines robbery as follows: A person is guilty of robbery if, in the course of committing a theft, he ... physically takes or removes property from the person of another by force however slight. Any amount of force applied to a person while committing a theft brings that act within the scope of [the] robbery ... statute. This force may be actual or constructive. Actual force is applied to the body; constructive force is use of threatening words or gestures, and operates on the mind. The degree of actual force is immaterial, so long as it is sufficient to separate the victim from his property in, on or about his body.

Here, Bedell argues that there was no struggle between the victim and himself and he did not use or threaten any force other than the force necessary to actually remove the wallet. Bedell asserts that because he did not use any force against the victim, there was no factual basis for the plea and his counsel unlawfully induced him to plead guilty to a crime he did not commit. The Commonwealth argues that the facts of the case support a conviction because there was some force applied in taking the wallet and the victim was aware of the taking and the force used to do so. While our Supreme Court has not addressed this specific issue, we conclude that there was a factual basis for the crime of robbery. Specifically, our Courts have distinguished between cases where a person is able to remove property from a victim by stealth and those cases where the victim is aware of the removal and any force required to do so in determining whether the evidence is sufficient to support a robbery conviction.

In **Commonwealth v. Brown, 484 A.2d 738, 741 (Pa., 1984)** the defendant, who grabbed a purse hanging off of the victim's arm and ran away with it, was convicted of robbery. Our Supreme Court affirmed the conviction stating the following:

> The force used in taking the purse from the victim's arm was a harmful touching of the person, accompanied with sufficient force to compel the victim to part with the conscious control of her property, and supports a robbery. This conduct substantially differs from the case of the thief who merely takes the property of another with intent

permanently to deprive him thereof, using no force or threat of force on the victim-like the pickpocket.... Such conduct is nonviolent, poses no threat to the victim who is unaware of the taking, and is accordingly graded less severely than robbery. A victim who is aware of the taking of property from his person is apt to reflex action to protect himself and his property and thus may be injured by the felon.

For this reason, robbery has always been considered a greater harm against society because violence is caused or threatened. The ordinary citizen has the right to go about his way free from the fear of attack to his person from those who would deprive him of control over his goods. That right is violated even by the slight tug on the arm by the purse thief who must use force to wrench the purse from the arm of the victim without regard to her safety. Accordingly, we find that the evidence was sufficient to establish robbery.

By way of contrast, in **Commonwealth v. Smith, 481 A.2d 1352 (Pa. Super., 1984),** the defendant was convicted of robbery after removing a pack of cigarettes from the pocket of a blind person who was unaware of the removal. Our Court reversed the robbery conviction, concluding that the evidence was insufficient to support conviction because the defendant removed the property by stealth and not by force.

Here, Bedell took the wallet out of the victim's hand and ran away with it. The victim was fully aware of the taking, which had been accomplished with some force, however slight. We conclude that Bedell used force to take the wallet, and, therefore there was a basis for the guilty plea.

A person commits the crime of **receiving stolen property** if he or she intentionally obtains or disposes of property of another knowing that it has been stolen, or believing that it has probably been stolen.

Generally, the person prosecuted for receiving stolen property is the "fence" and not the original thief. The thief cannot be convicted of receiving stolen property he already has in his possession.

The government has the burden of proving each element of this crime. Knowledge that the item was stolen can be established by circumstantial evidence; however, that knowledge may not be inferred solely from the unexplained possession of recently stolen merchandise. The test of knowledge is a subjective one, and the operative question is whether the defendant knew from the circumstances surrounding the possession that the property had been the subject of a theft.[5] For instance, a person who purchases a 48 inch, high definition television from the back of a truck for $100 is going to be hard pressed to convince the fact finder that the buyer did not suspect the item was stolen.

As a sign of our dependence on the Internet, states have added the offense of **electronic fencing.** This crime occurs when one uses the Internet to sell property gained through unlawful means. This variation of receiving stolen property is demonstrated by Illinois Public Act No. 94-179 which provides:

> A person commits the offense of electronic fencing when he or she uses or accesses the Internet with the intent of selling property gained through unlawful means knowing that the property was stolen. A person who unknowingly purchases stolen property over the Internet does not violate this provision.

This crime is aimed at penalizing those who take possession of stolen merchandise. The court looks at the circumstances behind the transaction to decide the criminal intent of the person who obtained the goods.

According to the National Crime Prevention Council, **retail theft** is committed by people of every age, race, sex, social and economic background, and about 25% of those who get caught are between the ages of 13 and 17. The offense is so commonplace that it costs businesses about $10 billion dollars a year. Customary tools of the trade include umbrellas, baby carriages, newspapers and diaper bags. When questioned as to why the person committed this crime, a common response is that the individual was bored and had nothing better to do or that peer pressure played a role in this crime.[6]

Common synonyms for this illegal activity are "five-finger" discounts and shoplifting. A person is guilty of this offense if he carries away or transfers any merchandise offered for sale with the intention of depriving the merchant of such items without paying the retail value for the product. Retail theft also encompasses the altering of a label or price tag in order to purchase the product at a discounted price or the removal or destruction of a security tag with the intent of depriving the merchant of the full purchase price. In a number of jurisdictions, retail theft statutes provide more severe penalties for theft from retail businesses than for theft from other parties.

Identity theft is a recent phenomenon that involves using the victim's personal information to obtain a financial advantage such as the misappropriation of a credit card or money from a bank account. Criminals have even assumed the unsuspecting person's identity to obtain a fraudulent driver's license or to apply for a job. In fact, the United States Postal Authority estimates that nearly 10 million people are the victims of identity theft at the cost of about 5 billion dollars.

In 1998, Congress enacted the **Identity Theft and Assumption Deterrence Act** by making it a crime to misuse the personal identifying information of another. A number of states have followed suit by passing similar legislation. For example, Wisconsin provides that: "Whoever intentionally uses or attempts to use any personal identifying information or personal identification documents of an individual to obtain credit, money, goods, services or anything else of value without the authorization or consent of the individual and by representing that he or she is that individual, is guilty of a felony."

It is not necessary to break into someone's home to steal a person's private information. For instance, some thieves engage in "shoulder surfing" which involves watching an unsuspecting victim punch in a password on an automated teller machine or by listening in on a conversation while the person discloses a credit card number over the telephone. Some criminals even engage in "dumpster diving" by looking through discarded trash for copies of checks, or credit card statements. A recent expansion of this crime has occurred with the Internet. People frequently receive spam e-mails requesting personal information under a false pretense and people unwittingly provide that data.[7]

Victims of identity theft need to take four protective steps as quickly as possible after learning of the problem. Contact each of the three major credit reporting agencies and place a fraud alert on your credit card report. These agencies are as follows:

1. Equifax
    P.O. Box 749241
    Atlanta, GA 30374-0241

2. Experian
    P.O. Box 9532
    Allen, TX 75013

3. TransUnion
    Fraud Victim Assistance Division
    P.O. Box 6790
    Fullerton, CA 9283-6790

Once a fraud alert is issued, the credit agency will provide a free copy of your credit report if requested. Review that document carefully and check to see if any inquiries have been made about your credit history from companies that you have not contacted or accounts you did not open. If fraudulent information is discovered, request that it be removed.

The next step in the process of protecting and restoring your credit history is to notify credit card companies and banks in writing about the problem. If you discover an improper entry on an account, file a written dispute with the company and immediately close the account. Also, file a complaint with the police in the location where the identity theft took place and obtain a copy of the police report or report number. Finally, contact the Federal Trade Commission and file a complaint online at www.consumer.gov/idtheft.[8]

The following case deals with the crime of receiving stolen property and the application of the inference of guilty knowledge that may be drawn from the unexplained possession of recently stolen goods.

COMMONWEALTH OF PENNSYLVANIA v. MATTHEWS
632 A.2D 570 (PA. SUPER., 1993)

William Murphy discovered that his home had been burglarized. Among the items taken were the keys to his automobile. The car had also been stolen.

A few days later, Officer Bush spotted Matthews driving the stolen car. Bush asked Matthews to produce his driver's license and owner's registration. Matthews was unable to produce either. The officer then informed Matthews that the vehicle had been reported stolen.

At trial, Matthews testified that he had rented the car from Charles Lewis in exchange for two "rocks" of crack cocaine. Matthews testified that he needed the car in order to perform a plumbing job at the home of Edward Thorton, and, at the time he was stopped by Officer Bush, he was on his way to return the car to Charles Lewis.

It is undisputed that the vehicle showed no physical manifestations of theft, such as signs of forced entry, broken ignition system or obliterated vehicle identification number.

In order to obtain a conviction for receiving stolen property, the Commonwealth must prove beyond a reasonable doubt that the property was stolen, the defendant was in possession of the property and the defendant knew the property was stolen or had reason to believe the property was stolen.

A permissible inference of guilty knowledge may be drawn from the unexplained possession of recently stolen goods. The mere possession of stolen property, however, is insufficient to permit an inference of guilty knowledge. There must be additional evidence, circumstantial or direct, which would indicate that the defendant knew or had reason to know that the property was stolen.

In this case, we find that the evidence presented by the Commonwealth was insufficient to establish that Matthews knew or had reason to believe that the vehicle in question had been stolen. Matthews was cooperative with the police; the car showed no physical signs that it had been stolen; and, Matthews offered an explanation for his possession of the vehicle at trial which was consistent with his statement to police at the time of his arrest. Accordingly, we reverse the judgment of sentence for receiving stolen property.

CONSPIRACY

In July of 2004, the FBI shocked the American public by indicting the chairman of Enron Corporation and other officers for perpetrating one of the largest corporate frauds in this country's history. They were charged with overseeing a massive scheme to "cook the books" and to create the illusion that Enron was a robust, growing company with limitless potential when Enron was an increasingly troubled business kept afloat only by a series of deceptions." The charged crimes for this deception were **conspiracy** and fraud.[9]

Labeled by the court more than 80 years ago as the "darling of the modern prosecutor's nursery," **conspiracy** is an all encompassing crime that allows the government to file charges against anyone who has participated in the planning or committing of a crime and to hold each liable for the actions of the other. For example, the following is Pennsylvania's definition of a conspiracy:

A person is guilty of conspiracy with another person or persons to commit a crime if with the intent of promoting or facilitating its commission he or she:

1. agrees with such other person or persons that they or one or more of them will engage in conduct which constitutes such crime or an attempt or solicitation to commit such crime; or

2 agrees to aid such other person or persons in the planning or commission of such crime or of an attempt or solicitation to commit such crime.

3. No person may be convicted of conspiracy to commit a crime unless an overt act in pursuance of such conspiracy is alleged and proved to have been done by him or by a person with whom he conspired.

4. It is a defense that the actor, after conspiring to commit a crime, thwarted the success of the conspiracy, under circumstances manifesting a complete and voluntary renunciation of his criminal intent.

Conspiracy is a separate crime from the actual offense that is to be committed. The agreement to commit the crime does not have to be in writing and can be informal. In fact, a mere tacit understanding is sufficient and each participant becomes the agent of the other for purposes of criminal responsibility.

ANTHONY HANKINSON V. WYOMING
47 P.3D 623 (WYO., 2002)

Anthony Hankinson was convicted of conspiracy to commit aggravated assault and battery. He submits this appeal contending that there is not sufficient evidence to sustain the conviction.

Hankinson and Lester Poague got drunk on July 25, 2000. They decided to go to the business owned by Daryl Coast and give him a beating, because of grievances against Coast. After drinking most of the day, Hankinson and Poague went to Coast's place of business and broke in the door. Once inside, they looked for Coast because they wanted to "kick his ass." Because Coast was a much bigger man than Poague, Poague had armed himself with an axe handle. However, Coast was not at his business, so the two vandals scattered business papers and poured fingernail polish on a credit card machine. Hankinson subsequently was charged with burglary, attempted assault and conspiracy.

The central thrust of Hankinson's appeal is that he was too drunk to have formed the intent to conspire with Poague and, to the extent they discussed a "plan" to beat up Coast using the axe handle, it did not rise to the level of a conspiracy, as that word is viewed in the context of the criminal law.

In **Jasch v. State, 563 P.2d 1327 (Wyo., 1977),** we defined a conspiracy as an agreement between two or more persons to do an unlawful act. The crime of conspiracy is complete when an agreement has been made and overt acts are performed to further the unlawful design. A conspiracy is completed when an agreement has been made and some overt act is performed in furtherance of the conspiracy. A mere tacit understanding will suffice, and there need not be any written statement or even a speaking of words, which expressly communicates agreement.

If it is established that a conspiracy existed and that the Defendant was one of its members, then the acts and declarations of any other member of such conspiracy in or out of such Defendant's presence, done in furtherance of the objects of the conspiracy, and during its existence, may be considered as evidence against such Defendant.

Whether or not Hankinson was so drunk that he could not form the requisite intent, and whether Hankinson actually engaged in a conspiracy to commit the crime of assault and battery on Coast, were questions for the jury. There was evidence that suggested that Hankinson was relatively lucid on the night of the crime. During the crimes, Hankinson had to make decisions and take actions that required some presence of mind, even if those actions were only the basest form of stupidity. In light of this evidence, the jury could reasonably have inferred that Hankinson acted with specific intent, even though there was a great deal of evidence to indicate that Hankinson was drunk. Likewise, though the agreement that Poague and Hankinson made to assault Coast was crude and ill conceived, the jury could reasonably have inferred that a conspiracy was present. Hankinson's argument focuses on his own view of the facts, rather than that view which might have been taken by reasonable jurors. The Judgment of the district court is affirmed.

WHITE COLLAR CRIME

Illegal actions perpetuated in a business setting are generally classified as **white-collar crimes**. It has been estimated that the dollar loss from this offense is larger than all other crimes put together. In fact, the figure has been placed at a staggering $400 billion dollars a year and the crime is on the rise. While there is no one exact definition for this offense, the Federal Bureau of Investigation has defined white collar crime as "...those illegal acts which are characterized by deceit, concealment, or violation of trust and which are not dependent upon the application or threat of physical force or violence." This catch-all phrase includes computer fraud, health care fraud, securities fraud and insider trading, counterfeiting, theft of trade secrets, embezzlement, and tax evasion. The problem is so pervasive that the FBI estimates that white-collar crime accounts for 4% of all reported crime with the majority of these offenses being for fraud, counterfeiting, and forgery. The National White Collar Crime Center has determined that one in every three American households has been victimized by white-collar crimes. While individuals are the largest group of victims, businesses, financial institutions, governments, religious organizations, and other public entities have all been victimized.

Because of the difficulty and expense in uncovering white-collar crime, as well as the public's low tolerance for corporate wrongdoing, the state and federal governments have become more aggressive in prosecuting these cases. Some legislative bodies have even increased the penalty for white collar crime by imposing mandatory jail time. California is an example of a state that now imposes a minimum jail sentence for anyone convicted of economic or white collar crime. The rationale for this mandate is discussed in **People v. Alejandro.**

PEOPLE V. ALEJANDRO
28 CAL. 4ᵀᴴ 481 (CAL., 2002)

On April 18, 1997, a complaint was filed charging defendant with the theft of a trade secret. It was further alleged that the loss exceeded $2.5 million. Defendant pleaded no contest to the theft charge, a charge based upon evidence that he had printed out confidential design specifications for certain computer chips on the last day of his employment as an electrical engineer at Digital Equipment Corporation. Defendant objected to the potential application of **Section 1203.044** to his sentence.

Defendant stands convicted of theft, specifically a violation of **Section 499c**, which provides: "Every person is guilty of theft who, with intent to deprive or withhold the control of a trade secret from its owner, or with an intent to appropriate a trade secret to his or her own use or to the use of another, does any of the following: steals, takes, carries away, or uses without authorization, a trade secret."

The trial court determined that **Section 1203.044** applies to such a theft. This statute, entitled The

Economic Crime Law, requires that a defendant who is convicted of certain theft offenses and is granted probation shall be sentenced to at least 90 days in the county jail as a condition of probation.

The Legislature declared in enacting **Section 1203.044:** "Major economic or white collar crime is an increasing threat to California's economy and the well-being of its citizens. The Legislature intends to deter that crime by ensuring that every offender, without exception, serves at least some time in jail. White collar criminals granted probation too often complete their probation without having compensated their victims or society. Probation accompanied by a restitution order is often ineffective because county financial officers are often unaware of the income and assets enjoyed by white collar offenders. Thus, it is the Legislature's intent that the financial reporting requirements of this act be utilized to achieve satisfactory disclosure to permit an appropriate restitution order. White collar criminal investigation and prosecutions are unusually expensive. These high costs sometimes discourage vigorous enforcement of white collar crime laws by local agencies. Thus, it is necessary to require white collar offenders to assist in funding this enforcement activity."

We observe that the term "white collar crime" is a relatively broad one and is not limited to losses involving cash or cash equivalents. It generally is defined as "a nonviolent crime usually involving cheating or dishonesty in commercial matters. Examples include fraud, embezzlement, bribery, and insider trading." **Black's Law Dict. (7th ed.,**

1999). The Legislature has applied the term "white collar crime" to fraud and embezzlement in **Section 186.11,** a statute that provides for enhanced prison terms for recidivists committing these offenses when the offense involves a pattern of "taking more than one hundred thousand dollars." Like the crime of theft, fraud and embezzlement are not limited to the unlawful acquisition of cash or cash equivalents. Indeed, frequently fraud and embezzlement simply are methods by which a charged theft is accomplished.

Because the crime of theft includes a wide range of property and the term "white collar crime" has a broad meaning, we find it improbable that the Legislature intended to address only the theft of cash or cash equivalents in adopting The Economic Crime Act. It is far more reasonable to conclude that the Legislature intended the provision to apply to all thefts of property of a particular value. Any other interpretation would permit many white collar thieves to continue to receive light probationary sentences and to evade strict restitution requirements. From the usual meaning of the terms used in **Section 1202.044,** the purpose of the enactment, and the Legislature's parallel use of the same terms in other statutes, one must conclude that **Section 1203.044** is not limited to thefts of cash or cash equivalents.

We find it clear from the words employed in **Section 1203.044** and the declaration of intent accompanying its enactment, that **Section 1203.044** does not apply solely to thefts of cash or cash equivalents, but rather that it addresses thefts of property, including trade secrets, exceeding specified values.

Do the words "payola" or "kickback" sound familiar?" These terms refer to the crime of **bribery.** This crime is the act of offering something of value to another with the intent of influencing that person's opinion or to have something done in return by that entity. Bribery arises in a number of contexts such as influencing a juror's vote, paying a police officer to disregard a traffic ticket or influencing the awarding of a contract. Over the years, a number of politicians have been convicted of this crime. For instance, Congressman Randy

Cunningham resigned from Congress in 2005 after pleading guilty to taking more than $2 million in bribes from government contractors. One of the most famous bribery cases, however, involved a sting operation known as Abscam. The FBI set up a dummy business which was said to represent an Arab Sheik that offered bribes to a variety of politicians to influence their actions. The result of this undercover investigation was the conviction of seven members of Congress, a member of the New Jersey legislature, and several members of Philadelphia City Council for bribery.

In the fall of 2005, House Majority leader Tom DeLay resigned from Congress after being indicted by a grand jury for illegally funneling campaign contributions to the Republican National Committee. His alleged crime was **money laundering.**

Money laundering is not something new. Some say the term originated with organized crime's ownership of laundromats during the days of Al Capone. Criminals were in possession of large sums of cash from extortion, prostitution, and gambling. They needed to show a legitimate source for these funds so this was accomplished by purchasing legitimate businesses that could commingle the illegal earnings with the revenues received from these businesses. Laundromats were chosen because they were cash businesses, so the crime naturally became known as money laundering.[10]

This crime is contained in a Federal statute entitled the **Money Laundering Control Act.** The basic design of money laundering is to conceal the real source of illegally obtained money by having a third party claim ownership to the currency. This is a frequent tool used by terrorists, drug traffickers, organized crime, and corrupt politicians so that the source of illegally obtained money cannot be traced.

The statute is rather complex and the following is part of the federal law:

Whoever with the intent:

  (A) to promote the carrying on of specified unlawful activity;

  (B) to conceal or disguise the nature, location, source, ownership, or control of the property believed to be the proceeds of specified unlawful activity; or

  (C) to avoid a transaction reporting requirement under State or Federal law;

conducts or attempts to conduct a financial transaction involving property represented to be the proceeds of specified unlawful activity, or property used to conduct or facilitate specified unlawful activity, shall be fined, or imprisoned for no more than 20 years, or both.

A person charged with money laundering does not have to commit the crime which generated the illegal revenue. Rather, the charge applies to the person who disposes of the cash or hides its true origination. **U.S. v. Awada** demonstrates this point.

U.S. v. Awada
425 F.3D 522 (C. A. Minn., 2005)

Awada was indicted following an investigation into a large-scale gambling ring operated by Douglas Sabby. Sabby was a bookmaker, taking bets on various sporting events. Concerned that the assets of his illicit activity would come to the attention of the federal government, Sabby took pains to veil his gambling operation. For instance, Sabby's cellular telephone was not registered in his name, and he would pay and collect from his bettors through intermediaries.

Sabby testified that, because most illegal gamblers do not want to leave a paper trail, they would generally pay him in cash. However, one bettor, John Boss, found himself several hundred thousand dollars in debt to Sabby, and tired of the scrutiny associated with making large-sum withdrawals from his financial accounts to pay Sabby in cash. Sabby accommodated Boss by letting Boss write several checks, made out to "cash." Boss gave Sabby a number of $5,000 checks made out in this fashion at the same time. Sabby did not have a bank account of his own, as he sought to hide the assets of his enterprise.

Sabby was a patron of Awada's bar and restaurant. Awada was one of Sabby's bettors, and thus knew he was a bookmaker. Sabby brought several of the $5,000 checks from John Boss to Awada's bar, seeking to have Awada cash them. The checks were not endorsed by Sabby, and no marking on the checks connected Sabby to them. Awada had never met Boss, the person from whose account the checks were drawn. Awada cashed Boss's checks as requested by Sabby, commingling them with his legitimate busi-

ness proceeds when he later deposited them into his business account. Awada was subsequently indicted for twelve counts of money laundering.

To sustain a money laundering conviction, the government must prove that the defendant conducted a financial transaction designed to conceal the proceeds of a "specified unlawful activity." The transaction or transactions that created the criminally-derived proceeds must be distinct from the money laundering transaction, because the money laundering statutes criminalize transactions in proceeds, not the transactions that create the proceeds.

After reviewing the evidence, we are convinced that Awada was properly convicted. The indictment specifies the unlawful activity from which the criminal proceeds derived was "an illegal gambling business." Conducting an illegal gambling business is a felony under federal law, and thus is a predicate offense sufficient to support the "specified unlawful activity" element of the crime of money laundering. The money laundering allegations concerned *proceeds* of the illegal gambling business; they did not comprise the illegal gambling business. Further, the record contains more than sufficient evidence that an illegal gambling business did exist. Sabby and many of his accomplices testified that Sabby conducted a large-scale, long-running, bookmaking operation.

Money laundering is a financial transaction crime involving the proceeds of some other crime; there is absolutely no requirement that a money laundering defendant also be involved in the underlying

7059

crime. That Awada was not a conspirator in Sabby's gambling ring does not exempt him from liability for laundering the proceeds of that illegal activity.

Awada further asserts that the evidence at trial was insufficient as to the scienter element of the crime. We disagree. The government was required to prove that Awada performed financial transactions (the check cashing) knowing that the transactions were designed "to conceal or disguise the nature, the location, the source, the ownership or the control of the proceeds of the specified unlawful activity." Although Awada never directly admitted such knowledge and Sabby testified that he never made his concealment plan

explicit, reasonable jurors could infer Awada was aware of what he was doing. Awada knew Sabby was a bookmaker since Awada himself placed bets with Sabby. Awada cashed a number of $5,000 checks for Sabby, all of which were from an unknown third party, made out to "cash," and not endorsed by Sabby. Even Awada himself admitted that he suspected the checks came from one of Sabby's losing customers. Accordingly, we find that a jury could reasonably conclude that Awada knew he was laundering the funds of Sabby's gambling enterprise, and that the transactions were undertaken with the intent to conceal the nature of that enterprise.

Many people have heard of **insider trading** and the news contains stories about this problem. For instance, the former CEO of Qwest Commutations was convicted of this charge for selling the company's stock at a profit of $176 million before the firm's financial collapse. And, who can forget the well publicized case against the CEO of Enron Corporation because of that firm's accounting fraud that showed tremendous profits which were not an accurate reflection of the firm's financial status. Even Martha Stewart was involved in an insider trading scandal, in her case concerning the sale of ImClone stock. So, what is this crime?

According to the Securities and Exchange Commission, insider trading occurs when corporate insiders, such as officers, directors, and employees, buy or sell stock in their own companies. Illegal insider trading, however, refers to the buying or selling of a security, in breach of a relationship of trust and confidence, while in possession of information that has not yet been made public about the stock.[11]

Examples of insider trading complaints filed by the SEC include:

- Corporate officers, directors, and employees who traded the corporation's securities after learning of significant, and confidential corporate developments;

- Friends, business associates, family members, and other "tippees" of such officers, directors, and employees, who traded the securities after receiving confidential information;

- Employees of law, banking, brokerage and printing firms who were given confidential information in order to provide services to the corporation and then traded those securities;

- Government employees who learned of such confidential information because of their employment by the government; and

- Other persons who misappropriated, and took advantage of confidential information concerning their employers.

Because insider trading undermines investor confidence in the securities markets, the SEC has treated the detection and prosecution of insider trading as one of its enforcement priorities.[12]

There are two theories of insider trading: the "**classical theory**" and the "**misappropriation theory**." The classical theory imposes liability on corporate insiders who trade on the basis of confidential information obtained by reason of their position within the business. This responsibility is based on the idea that a corporate insider breaches a duty of trust and confidence to the stockholders of the corporation. On the other hand, the misappropriation theory, imposes liability on "outsiders" who trade on the basis of confidential information obtained by reason of their relationship with the person possessing such information, usually a person on the inside of the corporation. Liability under the misappropriation theory is based on the notion that the outsider breaches "a duty of loyalty and confidentiality" to the person who shared the confidential information with him. Not only are the insider and outsider forbidden from trading on the basis of the confidential information they have received, they are also forbidden from "**tipping**" such information to someone else who, being fully aware that the information is confidential, does the trading. In other words, the people are forbidden from doing indirectly what they are forbidden from doing directly.[13]

Assume for a moment that Tyler's Sports Bar and Grill has concluded that it can dramatically increase its revenues by putting a microbrewery in its business establishment. This project will cost $250,000 so Tyler's needs a loan for this expenditure. The problem is that the bar's financial statements will not justify the loan. The expenses exceed the revenues which is why Tyler's wants to install a microbrewery. The solution is to change the financial statements to reflect larger revenues. Joe Roberts reasoned that it is only the bank; not the government who will receive the inaccurate information. Also, the bar will have no trouble repaying the loan so everything will work out. Well, things didn't play out exactly as Roberts planned. The bank requested backup documentation to support the loan application. They wanted to see the bar's tax returns and daily revenue logs. Has Roberts and the bar done anything criminal by "cooking the books?"

It is a federal crime to make a false statement to a financial institution in order to secure a loan. The offense is **making a false statement to a bank.** The law provides that anyone who knowingly makes a false statement of a material fact or overvalues property for the purposes of inducing a bank to take action shall be guilty of this offense. The penalty is a fine not to exceed $1,000,000 or imprisonment of a term not to exceed 30 years, or both.

In order to be convicted, the government must prove (1) that the defendant made a false statement or willfully overvalued land, property, or security, and (2) made the statement for purposes of influencing the action of financial institution upon application, commitment, or loan. These statements can be made orally or in writing, and whether the bank relied upon the false information is irrelevant. It is enough that the false statements are of the type that would disturb the balance of facts that would otherwise be available to the bank. The justification for this federal law is that false statements given to insured banks have the potential to mislead the government's auditors charged with maintaining the federal standards. After all, the government's interest in maintaining the vitality of its federal deposit insurance programs for banks mandates that all material false statements violate the federal law, even when they are given with the knowledge, consent or duplicity of a bank officer.[14]

Have you ever heard of **"bankruptcy fraud?"** Bankruptcy offers protection to a debtor by offering a fresh start or the ability to repay the obligations over a period of time. An entity that is overwhelmed with debts can turn to the bankruptcy courts for help in which assistance comes in a variety of ways. A **Chapter 7 bankruptcy** is known as a straight bankruptcy because it extinguishes or liquidates the debts. A bankruptcy trustee will collect all of the non-exempt property of the debtor and pay the creditors with those proceeds. The person will then be discharged in bankruptcy which means that the debts have been extinguished so the person can start over with a clean slate. A business, however, may not wish to liquidate its assets and go out of business. A **Chapter 11 bankruptcy** is known as reorganization and allows the debtor to regain solvency by seeking an adjustment of the obligations, either by reducing the debts or by extending the time for repayment. This allows the entity to stay in business while repaying the debts under a court approved plan. A **Chapter 13 bankruptcy** is known as a wage earner's plan since it allows individuals with regular income to develop a plan to repay all or part of their debts. The advantage of this bankruptcy is that it allows individuals to save their homes from foreclosure.[15]

Unfortunately, not all those who seek bankruptcy protection are honest in their disclosures. The Department of Justice estimates that 10 percent of all bankruptcy petitions contain some element of fraud. This undermines public confidence in the system, and taints the reputation of honest citizens seeking protection under the bankruptcy statutes.

The crime of **bankruptcy fraud** covers this situation and provides:

A person who having devised a scheme or artifice to defraud:

1. Files a bankruptcy petition;

2. Files a document in a bankruptcy proceeding; or

3. Makes a fraudulent representation, claim, or promise concerning a bankruptcy

shall be fined or imprisoned not more than five years, or both.

Bankruptcy fraud takes several forms: (1) when a debtor conceals assets to avoid forfeiting them, (2) when individuals file false or incomplete bankruptcy forms; (3) when a person files numerous times, either by using real information in several states or by using false information; or (4) when a court-appointed trustee is bribed. The FBI has primary investigative jurisdiction over bankruptcy frauds.[16]

SECTION 6.3
CRIMINAL LIABILITY FOR
BUSINESS ENTITIES

Even though corporations are distinct entities from their stockholders, officers and employees, a general rule has emerged that corporations can be liable for the criminal acts of its employees committed within the scope of their employment and with the intent to benefit the business. Criminal liability arises under the doctrine of **respondeat superior**. This result is only logical since a corporation is not a natural person who can engage in actions independently. It can only act through the efforts of agents and employees.

The scope of a corporation's criminal responsibility can only be determined by looking at the laws in the particular jurisdiction where the offense occurred. For instance, Congress may impose criminal liability on a corporation for the mere doing of the proscribed act wholly unrelated to actual or constructive knowledge of the event. Application of this principle is found in the public welfare crimes, such as distribution of harmful drugs, or narcotics, where injury to the public comes from the act or thing without regard to the antecedent circumstances, motivation or conduct. The actions also don't have to be by a top executive. The corporation may be criminally bound by the acts of subordinates, or even menial employees.[17]

A corporation can be convicted of a crime when the offense is committed by an agent acting within the scope of her employment such as a bar employee serving alcohol to a minor. An employee is acting within the scope of her authority if: (1) the employee has authority to do the particular corporate business which was conducted criminally; (2) the employee was acting, at least in part, in furtherance of the corporation's business interests; and (3) the corporate management has authorized, tolerated, or ratified the criminal acts.

Criminal liability has been found even where the corporation has published instructions and policies which are violated by the employee. Such instructions and policies when violated by its employees do not insulate the entity from criminal liability. Instead, the corporation must place the acts outside the scope of a worker's employment by adequately enforcing its rules.[18] A corporation can also be criminally responsible for the actions of its employees and agents even if it expressly instructed the person not to engage in that criminal conduct, so long as the agent acted within the scope of his or her authority.[19]

STATE V. ZETA CHI FRATERNITY
696 A.2D 530 (N.H., 1997)

The defendant, Zeta Chi Fraternity, appeals its conviction on the charges of selling alcohol to a person under the age of twenty-one.

The defendant, a corporation and fraternity at the University of New Hampshire, held a "rush" at its fraternity house to attract new members. Andrew Strachan, a nineteen-year-old guest at the fraternity party, testified that at some point during the evening he learned that beer was available from a soda machine. He made his way to an apartment in another part of the fraternity house where the machine was located, waited in line with three or four other people, and purchased three to five cans of beer. Strachan also testified that he noticed someone making change for the machine. The fraternity's secretary testified that the fraternity members voted not to provide alcohol at the rush and that they moved the vending machine that contained beer to a separate apartment in another part of the fraternity house for the rush. He also testified, however, that the fraternity had control over the vending machine and its proceeds and that only fraternity members would have an interest in making change for the machine.

The defendant argues the evidence was insufficient to convict it of selling alcohol to a person under the age of twenty-one. Specifically, the defendant contends that the testimony of the State's sole witness that he bought beer from the vending machine was uncorroborated; that even if the jury could find that beer was purchased from the machine, the State failed to prove that the defendant was responsible for the sale; and that the State failed to prove that the defendant acted recklessly.

The defendant argues that the State failed to prove that the defendant caused alcohol to be sold to Strachan. The defendant asserts that because the fraternity voted not to provide beer at the rush and the soda machine was moved from the main area in the fraternity house to a separate apartment at the back of the house, the defendant did not have control over the machine, and, therefore, could not have caused the sale of alcohol from the machine. Essentially, the defendant is arguing that the individuals responsible for making the beer available for sale to Strachan were not acting on behalf of the corporation or within the scope of their authority. We begin by noting that the only defendant in this case is a corporate entity. A corporation is a jural person, but not a person in fact. It is an artificial creature, acting only through agents. A corporation may be held criminally liable for criminal acts performed on its behalf by agents or employees acting within the scope of their authority or employment. The criminal conduct need not have been performed, authorized, ratified, adopted or tolerated by the corporation's directors, officers or other high managerial agents in order to be chargeable to the corporation.

In fact, a corporation can be convicted for actions of its agents even if it expressly instructed the agents not to engage in the criminal conduct. The agents, however, must have been acting within the scope of their actual or apparent authority. Actual authority can be either express or implied. Express authority exists when the principal explicitly manifests its authorization for the agent to act. Implied authority is the "reasonable incident or construction of the terms of express authority or results from acquiescence by the principal in a course of dealing by the agent. Apparent authority, on the other hand, exists where the principal so conducts itself as to cause a third party to reasonably believe that the agent is authorized to act. It is the rare case in which the corporate leadership explicitly authorizes its agents to engage in criminal conduct.

Evidence at trial indicates that the defendant had control over the apartment in which the vending machine was located, even though it had voted to make the apartment separate from the fraternity house. More importantly, however, witnesses testified that the defendant had control over the soda machine; that only the defendant had an interest in the proceeds from the machine; that only fraternity members had keys to the apartment in which the machine was located; that someone was making change for the machine;

and that no one would have an interest in making change except a member of the fraternity. We believe that from these facts the jury could reasonably have found that an agent of the defendant sold beer from the vending machine and that this agent was acting on behalf of the corporation and within the scope of his authority.

The defendant next argues that the evidence was insufficient for the jury to find that the defendant acted recklessly, the mens rea charged in the indictment. Because the defendant is a corporation, its mental state depends on the knowledge of its agents.

The corporation is considered to have acquired the collective knowledge of its employees and is held responsible for their failure to act accordingly.

In this case, the jury could reasonably have found that the defendant acted recklessly from the facts that about 150 guests, many of them under the age of twenty-one, were at the rush party that had been widely publicized on campus; that it was the defendant's vending machine; that only fraternity members had keys to the apartment in which the machine was located; that party guests gained access to the machine; that someone was making change; and that a number of people were waiting in line to use the machine.

SECTION 6.4
TYLER'S LIQUOR
PROBLEM

PROBLEM SIX—A

PARK, BROWN & SMITH, P.C.
ATTORNEYS AT LAW
MEMORANDUM

To: All Law Clerks
FROM: Peter Smith, Esquire
RE: Criminal charges against Tyler's Sports Bar and Grill for underage drinking

---

Joe Roberts called me about a problem at his business establishment. Criminal charges have been filed against Tyler's Sports Bar and Grill for underage drinking, and Joe is really upset because the bar does everything it can to prevent this from happening. These are the facts.

Tyler's has an aggressive policy against underage drinking and it posts signs throughout the bar warning people under 21 years of age not to order drinks. The employee's manual devotes three pages to the topic including the rule that all young people in the bar must be carded. In fact, employees are told in no uncertain terms that if he or she serves alcohol to a person under 21, the worker will be fired. Employees are also required to attend classes on how to spot underage drinkers. These policies are then reinforced in the monthly staff meetings Mr. Roberts holds on bar issues.

Last Friday night, Tyler's was lively and filled to capacity. People were standing five deep at the bar and the tables were stuffed with extra chairs to accommodate the overflow crowd. The reason for the packed house was that Tyler's was sponsoring a mechanical bull riding contest and people came from all over for the $5,000 cash prize that was being offered to the winner of the event. A sports talk show was also broadcasting live from the bar and several sporting events were being shown on the large screen televisions. It was sheer madness. Tyler's had never had a crowd like this before.

Tyler's was understaffed and the bar was having trouble keeping up with the food and beverage orders. Joe's wife had volunteered to help out in the kitchen and Tony Roberts, Joe's oldest son, happened to be in town so Tony was asked to help out. Tony had been trained as a bartender a few years earlier and had helped his dad once or twice before.

During the evening, Tony waited on a table which ended up containing some acquaintances from college. Tony had not seen them for years so he spent a few minutes talking about mutual friends and classes they had taken together. Tony didn't bother to card his former classmates because he knew they were of proper age. After all, they had all graduated from college together two years earlier and Tony had gone to a few bars with some of them while in school. These individuals turned out to be great customers. They ordered food and drinks continually and several participated in the bull riding contest. Tony even introduced Mr. Roberts to his former college friends and told his father about some of their college pranks. Mr. Roberts wished the guests well and thanked them for patronizing Tyler's. However, he excused himself because Joe wanted to keep an eye on the customers to make sure no one was intoxicated and to insure that the younger customers were being carded.

About one o'clock in the morning, investigators from the state's liquor control board paid a surprise visit to the bar and carded everyone. Much to the horror of Mr. Roberts, two of the people at the table containing his son's friends were underage. It turns out that one of Tony's former classmates was brilliant and had started college at age 14. The state investigators discovered that this individual and his girlfriend were only 20 years old. The police immediately arrested the two patrons and Tyler's received a criminal citation for serving liquor to minors. Mr. Roberts told me that he assumed his son had carded the people at the table so he did not personally inquire as to their ages.

Our client is devastated by the bad press the arrests have generated. Tony has even told the state investigators that he would accept full responsibility for what happened that night, stating that the bar and his father were faultless. Nevertheless, the corporation has been criminally charged for the violations.

North Dakota v. Smokey's Steakhouse, Inc. is the only case I could find even remotely on point. I know it is from a different state but the law is very similar to the one in this jurisdiction. Please let me know if Tyler's Sports Bar and Grill is criminally liable for the innocent mistake.

North Dakota v. Smokey's Steakhouse, Inc.
478 N. W. 2d 361 (N.D., 1991)

Smokey's Steakhouse, Inc., appealed from a judgment of conviction for allowing a person under the age of twenty-one to remain on the premises where alcoholic beverages were being sold. We affirm.

Smokey's is a restaurant and bar located in West Fargo. During an inspection of the premises, members of the West Fargo Police Department found Patricia Ingberg and Nicole Huether, both age twenty, in separate parts of the bar portion of the business. The women were arrested for being in a bar while underage.

Smokey's was cited and a trial was held at which the arresting officers and the two women testified. Both women stated that they were in the bar portion of Smokey's premises, that no Smokey's employee asked them for proof that they were of legal age, and that they were served an alcoholic beverage purchased by another patron. Accordingly, the court found Smokey's guilty of a single count of violating section 5-02-06, NDCC.

Smokey's contends that the State offered insufficient proof of the offense because a corporate defendant cannot be convicted for the willful criminal act of an employee acting outside the scope of her employment. Specifically, Smokey's argues that Loretta Frison intentionally served her underage sister, Pa-

tricia Ingberg. There is no culpability requirement in the statute under which Smokey's was convicted. A corporation can be convicted of a strict liability crime when the offense is committed by an agent acting within the scope of her employment. An employee is acting within the scope of her authority, for criminal law purposes, if: (1) the employee has authority to do the particular corporate business which was conducted criminally; (2) the employee was acting, at least in part, in furtherance of the corporation's business interests; and (3) the corporate management has authorized, tolerated, or ratified the criminal acts. A corporation is not insulated from criminal liability merely because it published instructions and policies which are violated by its employee; the corporation must place the acts outside the scope of an employee's employment by adequately enforcing its rules. Whether the corporation's enforcement measures are adequate is a question of fact.

Here, one of the employees working at the time of the police inspection, Loretta Frison, was the sister of Patricia Ingberg, one of the two minors the police found in the bar portion of Smokey's. Frison said she was not aware that her sister was underage. As a bartender, Frison was employed to serve alcoholic beverages and to determine the ages of patrons of the bar. While a supervisor testified that all Smokey's employees are instructed not to serve minors or to allow them to remain on the premises, no evidence of measures taken to enforce those instructions was offered. No employee checked the age of either Ingberg or Huether. The women arrived separately and were not together in the bar. Both women admitted being in the bar in excess of five minutes and receiving alcoholic beverages purchased by another patron. The trial court could infer from this, and other, evidence that Frison was not acting willfully when her underage sister and another minor were allowed to remain in the bar. The court could also infer that Smokey's had inadequately enforced its policy against serving minors so that the act of any employee who allowed Ingberg and Huether to remain on the premises without proving that they were of legal age was an act done within the scope of employment. The evidence is sufficient to sustain the conviction.

Smokey's also contends that it was entitled to the statutory defense under section 5-01-08.2, NDCC, which provides:

> The establishment of the following facts by a person making a sale of alcoholic beverages to a person not of legal age constitutes prima facie evidence of innocence and a defense to any prosecution therefore:

1. That the purchaser falsely represented and supported with other documentary proof that he was of legal age to purchase alcoholic beverages.

2. That the appearance of the purchaser was such that an ordinary and prudent person would believe the purchaser to be of legal age to purchase alcoholic beverages.

3. That the sale was made in good faith and in reliance upon the representation and appearance of the purchaser in the belief that the purchaser was of legal age to purchase alcoholic beverages.

Smokey's argues that the fact that Nicole Huether appeared to be of legal age entitles it to this statutory defense. Smokey's misreads the statute. Reading the statute as a whole, it is clear that the three subsections do not present separate defenses. The false representation described in subsection (1) and the appearance of the purchaser described in subsection (2) are necessary elements of the good-faith sale described in subsection (3). All three subsections must be satisfied in order to qualify for the single statutory defense established in section 5-01-08.2, NDCC. Neither Ingberg nor Huether made a false representation to an employee of Smokey's; neither woman was asked for proof that she was of legal age to be in a liquor establishment. The trial court properly concluded that Smokey's was not entitled to use the "good faith" statutory defense.

The judgment of the county court is affirmed.

ANSWER SHEET
PROBLEM SIX—A

Name

Please Print Clearly

1. Can Tyler's beat the charges by showing the many steps that the bar uses to prevent underage drinking?

_____

_____

_____

_____

_____

_____

_____

_____

_____

_____

_____

_____

_____

_____

_____

_____

_____

_____

_____

2. Will we be successful in asserting that we have a defense under Section 5-01-08.2? After all, Tony honestly believed that the patrons were of proper age.

_____

_____

_____

_____

_____

_____

_____

_____

_____

3. Please explain what you think will be the outcome of the case against Tyler's Sports Bar and Grill.

_____

_____

_____

_____

_____

_____

_____

_____

_____

SECTION 6.5
POLICE INVESTIGATION

Most crimes result in a police investigation in order to ascertain the identity of the perpetrator or to develop enough information to bring criminal charges. This process requires the police to examine the crime scene, question witnesses or to look at documentary evidence such as the books and records of a business.

While justice demands that the culprit be apprehended, the government must not violate the constitutional rights of the suspect or business entity.

SECTION 6.6
QUESTIONING
OF A SUSPECT

Nearly everyone has seen a movie or television show in which a police officer reads a suspect his rights as the person is being handcuffed. Is this something that has been added to the film for drama or is a law enforcement agent really mandated to tell the suspect that he has the right to remain silent? **Custodial interrogation** by the police is considered inherently coercive so the Supreme Court has mandated specific procedures to be followed in obtaining statements. More specifically, the Fifth Amendment provides that no person may be compelled to be a witness against himself. This fundamental guarantee is the basic cornerstone of the **Miranda Warnings.** If a person is the subject of custodial interrogation, the police must inform the suspect that he or she has the right to remain silent, that anything he or she says can and will be used against the individual in court, and the accused has the right to have a lawyer present during the questioning. If the accused cannot afford counsel, the government will supply an attorney for free.

Custodial interrogation has been defined as "questioning initiated by law enforcement officers after a person has been taken into custody or otherwise deprived of his or her freedom of action in any significant way." Custody is much broader than being incarcerated for purposes of the Miranda Warnings. A suspect must be told of his right to remain silent if his freedom of movement or liberty is significantly restricted. In practical terms, the issue is whether the suspect is free to walk away from the interrogation. If not, the suspect must be read his rights. For example, a suspect is considered in custody while in the back of a police car or while in bed and surrounded by the police. Interrogation, on the other hand, involves more than merely asking the suspect questions about routine information such as the person's name and address. The questions must focus on the crime to trigger the reading of the warnings.

How broad is the Fifth Amendment right against self-incrimination? The courts have ruled that this guarantee does not protect an individual from being fingerprinted or photographed, since these procedures are not testimony.

A breathalyzer is a common police tool to ascertain if a person is legally impaired while operating a motor vehicle. A blood/alcohol level of .08 or greater certainly incriminates the driver. **Commonwealth v. Graham** discusses whether the Fifth Amendment protects a person from having the results of the test being admitted into court where the defendant alleges that his consent to the breathalyzer was coerced.

COMMONWEALTH OF PENNSYLVANIA V. GRAHAM
703 A.2D 510 (PA. SUPER., 1997)

In this appeal we decide whether a provision of the Motor Vehicle Code is constitutional that permits the Commonwealth to introduce into evidence the fact that a defendant refused to be tested for alcohol or drugs where the defendant is charged with driving under the influence.

The fatal automobile accident occurred on August 2, 1994. On that evening, appellant was driving northbound on Interstate 95, weaving back and forth between lanes at an estimated speed of seventy miles per hour. As appellant made one of his abrupt lane changes, his vehicle collided with another vehicle. Several persons were seriously injured, and one person was killed.

After the accident, Sergeant Stieber noticed that appellant was agitated, had difficulty standing and had a strong odor of alcohol on his breath.

Lieutenant Nestel administered the "one leg stand" and the "walk and turn" tests, neither of which appellant could successfully complete. Appellant was then transported to police headquarters where Officer Waerig told appellant that the rights provided by **Miranda v. Arizona, 384 U.S. 436, 86 S.Ct. 1602, (1966),** do not apply to chemical testing, and if the accused refuses to consent, his driver's license will be suspended for one year. Appellant agreed to submit to the breathalyzer test.

The results of the breathalyzer test revealed that the alcohol level of appellant's blood was within the legal limit. An analysis of appellant's blood revealed the presence of cocaine metabolite, marijuana and marijuana metabolite.

Appellant argues that the results of his blood test should not have been admitted at trial. He maintains that his consent to the blood test was invalid because the officer coerced him to incriminate himself in violation of his Fifth Amendment rights. He asserts that he consented to the test only because he was afraid of the inferences the fact finders would draw if they learned he refused to take the blood test. He contends that such consent deprived him of his right not to incriminate himself.

The United States Supreme Court has made it clear that a defendant does not have a constitutional right to refuse blood tests. **Schmerber v. California, 384 U.S. 757, 86 S.Ct. 1826, 16 L.Ed.2d 908, (1966).** While blood test evidence may be "an incriminating product of compulsion," such evidence in no way implicates an accused's *testimonial* capacities and therefore, its admission does not offend the privilege against self incrimination embodied in the Fifth Amendment. The Court noted that the Fifth Amendment privilege relates to testimony or communication from an accused. The privilege does not prevent the police from using the accused's body or blood as physical evidence when it is material.

Because it is clear that appellant had no constitutional right to refuse the blood test, the Motor Vehicle Code does not burden appellant's constitutional rights by allowing evidence of his refusal to consent to be admitted at trial. As such, a defendant's consent to a blood test after being informed that his refusal could be admitted at trial, is valid and not coerced.

SECTION 6.7
COMMONWEALTH
V. CHRISTOPHER

PROBLEM SIX—B

PARK, BROWN & SMITH, P.C.
ATTORNEYS AT LAW
MEMORNDUM

To: All Law Clerks

From: Peter Smith, Esquire

Re: Commonwealth v. Peter Christopher
In Court Identification

Kathy Roberts often stays after school to workout. The wrestling team is usually there practicing but they were away at a match on the evening in question.

Kathy was so busy exercising that she didn't notice the presence of a stranger—at least not until it was too late. Kathy first realized that she wasn't alone when she looked up and saw what appeared to be a shark staring back at her. When she looked again, she realized it was a man with a tattoo of a shark on his left shoulder. The strange thing was that he was wearing a ski mask. Before she had time to realize what was happening, she was assaulted and her pocketbook was stolen.

Kathy was extremely troubled by the incident. She could not stop thinking about the tattoo, since she knew she had seen the image before. To her shock and amazement, Kathy realized that she knew her assailant. It was her next door neighbor, Peter Christopher. He had a tattoo of a shark on his shoulder, and he intensely disliked her family.

Ms. Roberts reported her suspicions to the police and their investigation led to the arrest of Peter Christopher on a variety of criminal charges. During the second day of trial, the District Attorney requested Peter Christopher to stand before the jury and remove his shirt so the panel could ascertain whether the defendant had a tattoo of a shark on his shoulder. The defense vigorously objected to this in-court identification, claiming that it would violate Christopher's Fifth Amendment rights against self-incrimination. The issue before the court concerns these identifying marks on the defendant's shoulder. The Fifth Amendment guarantees that no person shall be compelled to testify against himself. According to **Morgan v. State**, can the District Attorney compel Christopher to remove his shirt to show the jury his shoulder? Why would this type of in-court identification violate (or not violate) the Constitution?

GLENMORE MORGAN V. STATE OF MARYLAND
558 A.2D 1226 (MD. APP., 1989)

We are called upon to decide whether requiring a defendant to don an article of clothing in the courtroom in front of the jury so that the jury may see if the article of clothing fits violates his privilege against self-incrimination under the 5th Amendment.

In the case before us, Glenmore Morgan, defendant, was charged with possession of cocaine with intent to distribute, possession of cocaine and possession of controlled paraphernalia. During a jury trial, the court required the defendant to put on a jacket seized by officers of the Montgomery County Police Department pursuant to a search warrant.

At the time the search warrant was executed, defendant and two other men were present in the living room of the residence. After the two other men retrieved their coats, Morgan queried, "What about my jacket?" When asked by the police if a jacket located on the loveseat in the living room was his, Morgan hesitated before responding, "No." Police search of the jacket revealed a small quantity of cocaine, a beeper, keys to the residence and a key to a safe in the kitchen. During a search of the safe, the police discovered bottles of inositol powder, several baggies, razor blades, measuring spoons, a box containing a grinder, and twenty-three grams of cocaine. Morgan was convicted on all charges.

The Fifth Amendment of the United States Constitution provides: "No person... shall be compelled in any criminal case to be a witness against himself." Defendant contends that the court's order requiring him to put on the jacket in front of the jury violated his constitutional right against compelled self-incrimination.

The Court of Appeals in **Andrews v. State** upheld a trial court order restraining Andrews from shaving his head or facial hair until the conclusion of this trial. Purportedly, he had changed his appearance immediately after the crime in question by shaving his head and beard. The trial court order was designed to prevent the defendant from defeating "legitimate avenues of identification" by disguising his appearance.

In **Schmerber v. California, 384 U.S. 757 (1966),** the Supreme Court stated that the privilege against compelled self-incrimination "protects an accused only from being compelled to testify against himself or otherwise provide the State with evidence of a testimonial or communicative nature..." Requiring a defendant to put on an article of clothing, simply does not constitute an act compelling a testimonial or communicative response. The fact that an article of clothing fits may give rise to a inference of ownership, which under the facts of any given case could be incrimination, is not a communicative response from the defendant.

By granting the prosecutor's request to order the defendant to don the coat in the presence of the jury, the trial court compelled the defendant to disclose nothing of his personal knowledge. This is not communication within the meaning of the Fifth Amendment. Moreover, it is of no consequence that the defendant declined to take the stand to testify on his own behalf; his physical display simply does not constitute "testimony."

In this case, the trial court order requiring defendant to don a coat, which admittedly contained incriminatory evidence, to determine whether it fit him did not constitute a compulsion to elicit communicative or testimonial evidence from the defendant.

Judgment affirmed.

ANSWER SHEET
PROBLEM SIX—B

Name

Please Print Clearly

1. According to **Morgan v. State,** can the District Attorney compel Christopher to remove his shirt to show the jury his tattoo? Explain your answer.

_____

_____

_____

_____

_____

_____

_____

_____

_____

_____

_____

_____

_____

_____

_____

_____

_____

_____

_____

_____

_____

2. Why would this type of in court identification violate or not violate Christopher's constitutional rights? Explain your answer.

_____

_____

_____

_____

_____

_____

_____

_____

_____

_____

_____

_____

_____

_____

_____

_____

_____

_____

_____

SECTION 6.8
SEARCH AND SEIZURE

A truck driver was stopped by the police for a traffic violation. A drug-detecting dog was then walked around the commercial vehicle while another officer wrote the traffic ticket. The canine soon became agitated alerting the police to the presence of drugs. A search of the trailer yielded several hundred pounds of marijuana. Is there anything unconstitutional with allowing a police dog to randomly walk around a person's vehicle? This example raises the issue as to what constitutes a police search.

The **Fourth Amendment** prohibits unlawful **search and seizure** and requires that all warrants be issued upon probable cause. This protection against over-zealous police conduct usually requires a police officer to appear before a judge to establish **probable cause** for the issuance of a search warrant. Probable cause, however, is not defined in the Constitution. Over the years, the courts have determined probable cause to exist when the information on which the warrant is based is such that a reasonable person would believe that what is being sought will be found in the location to be examined. The judge, however, may consider the opinion of an experienced law enforcement officer in making the probable cause determination for a search warrant. An affidavit based on mere suspicion, or stating a conclusion with no supporting facts, however, is insufficient. If the court is satisfied that sufficient evidence exists to issue a warrant, that document must be specific as to the location and evidence that is the subject of the search warrant.

The general test to determine whether a warrant is needed by the police to conduct a lawful search and seizure is to ascertain whether the person or business had a reasonable expectation of privacy. If the entity enjoyed a reasonable expectation of privacy, a warrant must be obtained before the search can be undertaken. For example, a person has an expectation of privacy that the police will not search his private locker at work, but the police would not need a warrant to seize a gun that a person is brandishing while walking down the street.

The police may also seize property that has been discarded or abandoned since there is no longer an expectation of privacy.

Missouri v. Cordell Mosby
94 S. W.3d 410 (Missouri Ct. App., 2003)

On September 2, 2001, Officer C. Barbosa was on patrol and observed the defendant while the defendant was sitting on the steps in front of a dwelling at 500 E. Armour. Officer Barbosa testified that there was a "No Trespassing" sign posted on the dwelling. Officer Barbosa exited his vehicle and approached the defendant who then attempted to walk away. The officer observed the defendant drop a beige rock-like substance on the ground between two cars. The beige rock-like substance was recovered. It was later field tested with positive results for cocaine.

The State's claim that Mosby lacked standing to challenge the seizure of the cocaine and the handgun was because he did not have any legitimate expectation of privacy with regard to those items. In order for the defendant's Fourth Amendment rights to be violated or for the defendant to have standing to assert a violation of those rights, the defendant must have a legitimate expectation of privacy in the place or thing searched. To determine whether a criminal defendant has a legitimate expectation of privacy in the place or thing searched, the defendant must have an actual subjective expectation of privacy in the place or thing searched and this expectation must be reasonable or legitimate.

The Fourth Amendment, in protecting against unreasonable searches and seizures, do not give the courts general supervision over police practices and conduct. Evidence is excludable only if it has been obtained through an unreasonable search and seizure. In order to have standing to complain, a defendant must have a reasonable expectation of privacy related to that property *at the time of the allegedly improper search and seizure.*

Mosby has never asserted that he had any legitimate expectation of privacy in the public street where the clear plastic bag was located or in the stairwell where the white plastic bag was located. Indeed, there is no reasonable expectation of privacy subject to Fourth Amendment protection where the public at large is welcome.

Law enforcement officers do not violate the Fourth Amendment by merely approaching a person on the street and asking questions. Consequently, even when law enforcement officers have no basis for suspecting a particular individual, they may ask to see the person's identification and request consent to search, so long as they do not convey that compliance with those requests is required. Nothing in the record supports a finding that the officer exceeded these bounds.

We next turn to whether the record could support a finding that Mosby had a legitimate and reasonable expectation of privacy related to the two bags and their contents at the time he was seized. Officer Barbosa saw Mosby drop that bag on the ground between two cars while Mosby was attempting to walk away from the officer.

When property is abandoned, the constitutional protections against unreasonable search and seizure no longer apply, because those protections are designed to protect one's person and dwelling. Therefore, a person has no standing to complain of the search or seizure of property that he has voluntarily discarded, left behind, or otherwise relinquished his interest so that he no longer retains a reasonable expectation of privacy with regard to it at the time of the search or seizure. Where, as here, an individual drops, throws, or otherwise discards contraband while being followed or pursued by a police officer, the contraband is deemed to have been abandoned, and Fourth Amendment protections no longer apply.

Police generally need a **search warrant** when there is a reasonable expectation of privacy. There are, however, a number of exceptions to this rule. The police are not required to obtain a search warrant in the following situations:

1. **Plain View:** If the subject of the search is readily observable, in other words, in plain view, there is no reasonable expectation of privacy. For instance, if marijuana is growing in one's backyard and is visible from the sidewalk, the police do not need a search warrant to seize the plants. An improper search, however, will occur if the police peer into a basement window, and with the aid of a flashlight uncover contraband, since the homeowner would have a reasonable expectation of privacy against this type of intrusion.

2. **Emergency:** If the time delay in obtaining the warrant will defeat the ends of justice, the police can engage in the search without the warrant. Vehicle searches generally fall within this exception since vehicles are mobile and can avoid the police by merely being driven away. The police, however, must still have probable cause for the search. If the vehicle is towed to the police station and impounded, a search warrant will have to be obtained in order to conduct a lawful search since the vehicle is no longer mobile. The emergency situation would no longer be present, since the car would be in the possession of the authorities.

3. **Search Incident to an Arrest:** Police officers can search a defendant and the area within that person's immediate reach for weapons and other contraband. This exception was established to protect the public from possible harm.

4. **Hot Pursuit:** If the police are pursuing a suspect who is fleeing the scene of a crime, they may make a reasonable search of the area looking for the suspect.

5. **Consent:** The police are not required to obtain a search warrant when a suspect consents to a search. The consent, however, must be freely and voluntarily given, and not be coerced by law enforcement officials. Certain third parties may also consent to a search. For instance, parents may allow the police to search a child's room, and a school principal is authorized to allow the police to search student lockers at the educational institution. While a roommate may allow the police to search the common areas in an apartment, a landlord does not have the authority to allow the police to search the leased premises without a search warrant.

6. **Search Incident to a General Police Measure:** Border and custom searches are allowed to prevent the entry of illegal aliens and contraband. Custom agents can check everyone's luggage regardless of the existence of probable cause. Other examples include searches of passengers at the

airport, and individuals can be required to pass through a metal detector before being allowed to enter a courtroom. Both of these measures are designed to protect the safety of the public. The police, however, may not selectively discriminate against a particular racial group under the auspices of conducting a search incident to a general police measure. For example, the police may not stop young African-American males on the New Jersey Turnpike merely because the individual may match a racial profile.

7. **Stop and Frisk:** Police officers may conduct "pat-down" searches when there is probable cause to believe that a crime is about to occur and the suspect may possess a weapon. If the police find contraband during the "pat-down" that is instantly recognizable by feel, it may be seized without a warrant. This seizure is called **plain feel**. This exception has the potential for abuse, so courts generally require that the officers present very specific facts that lead to a conclusion of probable cause.

STATE V. THOMAS HOSKINS
2002 WL 1453811 (OHIO APP., 2002)

Officer Martin and his partner witnessed a vehicle driving with its passenger door wide open. The officers stopped the vehicle for possible violations of ordinances pertaining to driving in traffic with an open door and reckless driving.

Because of the high incident of drug and gun activity in the vicinity in conjunction with the passenger door being open, both officers approached the vehicle. Officer Martin, trained to watch the occupant's hands for signs of danger, noticed Hoskins' right hand placed down the front of his pants. Concerned Hoskins was concealing or reaching for a gun, Officer Martin ordered Hoskins out of the car, handcuffed him, and conducted a pat down search for the presence of weapons.

During the pat down, Officer Martin felt an object he immediately identified as crack cocaine in the area of Hoskins' right thigh near the area where his hand had been. Officer Martin retrieved the object, which was determined to be a baggie of crack cocaine.

Hoskins argues the trial court erred by denying his motion to suppress the crack cocaine found on his person following the traffic stop. We disagree.

Our first query is whether the police officers justifiably stopped the vehicle in which Hoskins rode. Under **Terry v. Ohio**, a police officer may make a brief, investigatory stop of an individual without probable cause if the officer reasonably suspects the individual is, or has been, involved in criminal activity. This standard for evaluating the officer's conduct is objective: would the facts available at the moment of seizure or search warrant a man of reasonable caution in the belief that the action was appropriate?

As Hoskins argues, the police lacked a reasonable suspicion to stop him. Nevertheless, reasonable suspicion of criminal activity sufficient to stop the vehicle in which he was riding existed because of the observed violations of Cleveland ordinances.

In determining the propriety of the Terry search, the question is whether the officer had a reasonable, objective basis for frisking the defendant after ordering him out of the car.

When Officer Martin approached the vehicle he noticed Hoskins' right hand placed down the front of his pants in a posture leading him to believe Hoskins was hiding or retrieving a weapon. Further, this incident occurred in an area Officer Martin recognized as a high drug area where shootings have occurred. Also, in Officer Martin's experience, driving with an open car door is indicative of an attempt to dispose of drugs or weapons. Based upon the totality of these circumstances, we conclude Officer Martin had a reasonable, objective basis for conducting a Terry search of Hoskins.

In **Minnesota v. Dickerson**, the United States Supreme Court adopted the "plain feel" doctrine. In doing so, the Supreme Court stated: "If a police officer lawfully pats down a suspect's outer clothing and feels an object whose contour or mass makes its identity immediately apparent, there has been no invasion of the suspect's privacy beyond that already authorized by the officer's search for weapons.

Here, the record establishes that Officer Martin, during the course of a lawful Terry search, discovered what he immediately determined to be crack cocaine. Because the contraband was in "plain feel," Officer Martin did not violate Hoskins' constitutional right to be free from unreasonable searches. The crack cocaine discovered on Hoskins' person was admissible into evidence.

**SECTION 6.9
THE PROGRESS
OF A STATE
CRIMINAL CASE[20]**

1. **The Obligations of Crime Victims and Witnesses**: A victim or witness to a crime is expected to report the crime to the police, and to testify in court about what happened. The police will take a statement and file a *criminal complaint*, which is a statement of facts about the crime and later becomes the basis of the formal charges against the accused. After the complaint is drafted, a judge will issue a warrant for the offender's arrest or a summons commanding the accused to appear for a preliminary hearing.

2. **Preliminary Arraignment**. In cases where the offender is arrested he or she, now called the *defendant*, appears within hours for a preliminary arraignment, which is held before the district justice in the district where the offense occurred or at the Roundhouse if the crime occurred in Philadelphia. It is not necessary that a victim appear for the preliminary arraignment.

    One of the purposes of this hearing is to set *bail*. Bail is a means of insuring that the defendant will continue to appear at scheduled court appearances. In setting bail, the judge considers such factors as the seriousness of the crime, the circumstances of the defendant, his age, employment status, etc., and whether the accused is likely to flee if released. Bail may take several forms, but it usually involves the use of money or property of the defendant or someone on his behalf along with the promise of the defendant to remain available. If the defendant fails to appear for a scheduled court appearance, the court may issue a bench warrant for the defendant's arrest and order revocation or forfeiture of bail.

STATE CRIMINAL PROCEDURE

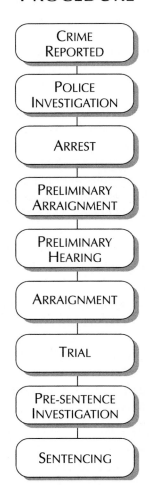

CRIME REPORTED

POLICE INVESTIGATION

ARREST

PRELIMINARY ARRAIGNMENT

PRELIMINARY HEARING

ARRAIGNMENT

TRIAL

PRE-SENTENCE INVESTIGATION

SENTENCING

The preliminary arraignment is also held to advise the defendant of his or her constitutionally guaranteed rights and to set a date for preliminary hearing. At the end of the preliminary arraignment, the defendant is released on bail or placed under confinement.

3. **Preliminary Hearing:** This hearing is held before the District Justice or a Municipal Court Judge in Philadelphia, and is usually the First Hearing at which the victim or witness will be called to appear. The purpose of the hearing is to determine whether there is probable cause that the defendant committed the offense or offenses charged. A police officer or prosecutor asks questions of witnesses and sometimes of the defendant. Counsel for the defendant may conduct cross-examination. It is important to remember that this hearing is not to determine guilt; only whether it is more likely than not that the defendant committed the crime charged. If the Judge determines that the defendant probably committed the offense, the case is bound over for further proceedings in the Court of Common Pleas. If no probable cause has been established, the defendant is released and the case is over.

4. **Arraignment**: When a case is bound over to Common Pleas Court, the records and transcripts from the earlier proceedings are sent from the District Justice to the appropriate county courthouse. Once the Court Clerk amasses a file, and the District Attorney draws up an *information*, which is a formal list of charges against the defendant, the accused appears in court for the arraignment.

    The purposes of arraignment are to insure the defendant's awareness of the formal charges against him, to determine whether he has a lawyer, to establish time periods for the filing of various motions, and to set a date for a trial. An arraignment is very informal, often conducted without the defendant being present, since he or she may forego or "waive" formal notice of the charges in the information. The presence of a victim or witness is not necessary at the arraignment.

5. **Trial**: After thirty days have passed since the arraignment, the case may be scheduled for trial. Once a specific date, time, and courtroom are assigned, the defendant is notified, and witness subpoenas are dispatched in the mail. A witness should receive a subpoena to appear in court about a month before trial. Unless the case is *continued*, or postponed to a later date, the case is called before the court at the designated time.

    Many cases are resolved prior to trial. Often the defendant decides to plead guilty. When this happens, or when the case is postponed, the witness should be contacted by the District Attorney's Office and be informed that his or her presence for the date listed in the subpoena will be unnecessary.

When a case does proceed to trial, the trial may take place before a judge and jury or just before a judge. In jury trials, the jury decides factual questions based on the evidence and on the law as provided by the judge. In other words, the jury decides what actually happened on the occasion in question and then renders a decision on the defendant's guilt or innocence. This is called the *verdict*. In non-jury or *bench* trials, the judge decides both factual and legal questions.

A trial consists of several phases. After a jury is picked, the prosecution makes an *opening statement*. The purpose of this statement is for the prosecutor to describe what the evidence will prove. The defense makes its opening statements, either right after the Commonwealth's or at the beginning of the defense case. After opening statements, the Commonwealth presents its *case in chief*. That is, the prosecutor calls witnesses and puts on evidence aimed at establishing the defendant's guilt. This is the phase at which a witness will testify if needed. After the prosecution concludes, or *rests*, the case for the defense is presented. After all the evidence has been heard, each side is permitted to make a *closing speech* to the jury. In these speeches, the attorneys argue to the jury how and why the evidence supports their view or theory of the case, asking respectively for verdicts of guilt and innocence. Afterwards, the judge *charges* the jury, explaining what law they must consider in reaching a verdict. The jury deliberates until it reaches a verdict. Once a decision of guilt or innocence is made, the verdict is announced and the court makes it final by pronouncing a *judgment* on the verdict. The trial is now concluded.

6. **Sentencing:** In cases where the defendant pleads guilty, sentencing is usually immediately imposed by the court. In other cases, a future date for sentencing is set by the court. Sometimes the court orders the filing of a *pre-sentence investigation report*. The purpose of the report is to advise the court of the circumstances of the defendant which could affect the type of sentence to be imposed. The Commonwealth and the defense may ask for punishment of greater or lesser severity. The court considers these arguments, the contents of the pre-sentence investigation report, as well as any input made by the victim, and then pronounces sentence on the defendant. Sentencing may call for fines, imprisonment, or both. In addition, the defendant is required to pay court costs and, whenever feasible, to make restitution to victims for lost or damaged property or other financial losses. The sentence is carried out by the offices of parole or probation.

SECTION 6.10
THE PROGRESS OF A
CRIMINAL CASE IN
FEDERAL COURT

An arrest may be initiated following a grand jury presentment or by a complaint and warrant.

The Fifth Amendment of the Constitution guarantees that "no person shall be held to answer for a capital, or otherwise infamous crime unless by presentment or indictment by a grand jury…" The **grand jury indictment** is utilized to determine that probable cause exists, that a crime has been committed, and that the target of the investigation probably did commit the crime. A grand jury consists of twenty-three people, and a majority vote is required to indict. The proceedings are conducted in secret, and a witness does not have the right to have counsel present.

Following indictment, a bench warrant is issued for the arrest of the suspects, and they are brought before a Federal Magistrate for an Initial Appearance.

Federal prosecutions can also be initiated by a complaint and warrant. This method is used when immediate arrest is necessary because of fear of flight by the suspect. The Complaint is prepared by the United States Attorney with the assistance of a federal law enforcement agent who narrates the facts of the case. A judge then examines the document, and a federal agent must be present to attest to its veracity. By issuing the warrant, the Court determines that probable cause exists for arrest.

Federal arrestees are often detained in local detention centers where cells are reserved and paid for by the federal government. An initial hearing is held promptly after the defendant's arrest. If a defendant is arrested on a weekend, he will be brought in for the initial hearing on the next business day following his arrest. At the initial hearing, bail is set, the defendant is advised of his rights, and legal counsel is appointed if the defendant has none.

If the arrest was made pursuant to a grand jury indictment, the case proceeds to arraignment where the charges are read, pleas are entered, and a trial date is selected. If the arrest is made pursuant to the complaint and warrant procedure, a grand jury indictment will follow unless waived and replaced with an information (formal list of charges). The arraignment follows in either case within thirty days of the arrest, and the trial occurs within seventy days of the initial appearance. This is required by the Speedy Trial Act. Fewer cases go to trial in the federal system, since 95% of federal criminal cases are resolved through guilty pleas.

FEDERAL CRIMINAL PROCEDURE

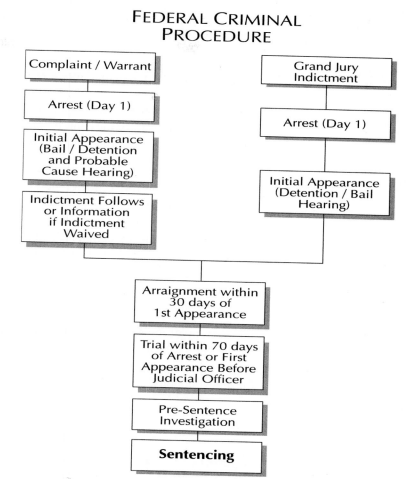

The grand jury is a group of people chosen from the same pool of citizens used to select trial jurors but it serves a very different function. The **grand jury** determines whether there is probable cause to believe that a crime was committed and that a specific person or persons committed it. If the grand jury finds that probable cause exists, it will then return a written statement of the charges called an **indictment**. After that, the accused will go to trial.

The grand jury normally hears only that evidence presented by an attorney for the government which tends to show the commission of a crime. The grand jury must determine from this evidence, and usually without hearing evidence for the defense, whether a person should be tried for a serious federal crime, referred to in the Bill of Rights as an **infamous crime**. An infamous crime is one which may be punished by imprisonment for more than one year. As a general rule, no one can be prosecuted for a serious crime unless the grand jury decides that the evidence it has heard so requires. In this way, the grand jury operates both as a "sword," authorizing the government's prosecution of suspected criminals, and also as a "shield," protecting citizens from unwarranted or inappropriate prosecutions. A person may, however, waive grand jury proceedings and agree to be prosecuted by a written charge of crime called an **information**.

The major portion of the grand jury's work is concerned with evidence brought to its attention by an attorney for the government. The grand jury may consider additional matters otherwise brought to its attention, but should consult with the United States Attorney or the court before undertaking a formal investigation of such matters. This is necessary because the grand jury has no investigation staff, and legal assistance will be necessary in the event that an indictment is voted.

It should be kept in mind that a federal grand jury can take action upon federal crimes that have been committed within the district in which it has been impaneled. Furthermore, a federal grand jury is not authorized to investigate situations involving the conduct of individuals, public officials, agencies or institutions that the grand jury believes is subject to mere criticism rather than a violation of federal criminal statutes. Its concern must be devoted solely to ascertaining whether there is probable cause to believe that a federal crime has been committed and to report accordingly to the court.

The secrecy of the grand jury is demonstrated in the following case in which the attorney for the parties under investigation was subpoenaed to testify before the grand jury but not allowed to see the document or learn the reasons for that subpoena.

IN RE GRAND JURY SUBPOENA ISSUED TO GALASSO
389 N. J. SUPER. 281 (N.J., 2006)

Appellant was the attorney for a social club where illegal gambling activity had allegedly been conducted. A Grand Jury subpoenaed him to testify and produce documents in connection with an investigation of the club. Based in part on a certification of the chief assistant prosecutor submitted ex parte for in camera review, the Law Division judge denied appellant's motion to quash the subpoena.

Appellant represented a number of persons involved in the formation of a social club, known as the 5th Street Club, LLC (the club), to be located in Dover. On December 30, 2004, a detective from the Morris County Prosecutor's Office received a facsimile transmission from appellant, consisting of a three-page letter from appellant to the owners of the club. In the letter, appellant opined that although members of the club had the option to wager on the gaming activities conducted there, such as air hockey, billiards, bridge, chess, darts, foosball, gin rummy, ping pong, pinochle, and poker, the "activities carried out at the 5th Street Club [did] not violate the law, because the Club [was] not acting as a gambling resort." Club members would be permitted to wager on the outcome of games played there as long as "no one, including the Club, act[ed] as a bookmaker," and so long as appellant's "client [did] not profit or receive remuneration for any bet or wager [placed] ... by the individual members."

On August 30, 2005, the grand jury indicted (the owners of the club) on counts of conspiracy, and maintaining a gambling resort. On October 31, 2005, the grand jury issued a subpoena ordering appellant to appear before it to testify and bring documents in connection with his representation of the club. After appellant moved to quash the subpoena, the State asked the court to review in camera an certification prepared by the prosecutor. Appellant then moved to compel access to the certification.

The grand jury has always occupied a high place as an instrument of justice, serving the dual purpose of determining whether an accused should be subjected to trial, while simultaneously safeguarding citizens against arbitrary, oppressive and unsupported criminal proceedings. It also operates as an independent investigatory body, free from the constraints of the rules of evidence and procedure. A grand jury is entitled to engage in an exhaustive investigation. Because the grand jury's task is to inquire into the existence of possible criminal conduct and to return only indictments that are well founded, its investigative powers are necessarily broad. Courts grant leeway to a grand jury's decision to conduct an investigation and issue subpoenas; the grand jury itself is the best judge of what evidence it deems necessary in the pursuit of its investigation.

Bringing these principles to bear, (we look at the court's) order denying appellant's motion to compel access to the ex parte certification submitted to the court by the State. While we may not disclose the specifics of the certification, it describes the nature of the grand jury investigation, details the reasons the State required appellant to testify, and provides facts supporting those reasons. The certification reveals facts pertaining to an ongoing investigation to determine if individuals not yet indicted could be criminally culpable and whether additional charges were warranted. The State believes that publication of the specific facts contained in the certification could impair the investigation.

Federal courts of appeals have held that a court may consider the government's ex parte submission in order to preserve the secrecy of the grand jury proceedings and have rejected due process argument[s] to the contrary. These courts have done so confident that the [trial] courts will vigorously test the factual and legal bases for any subpoena. The federal decisions permitting the use of ex parte certifications in the grand jury context are predicated on the secrecy afforded grand jury proceedings. New Jersey, too, recognizes the need for secrecy in grand jury proceedings. It has long been recognized that the proper function of the State's grand jury system depends upon the secrecy of the proceedings. Secrecy ensures that witnesses will testify fully, without fear of retribution or inducement; ensures that grand jurors will deliberate freely and openly; prevents targets of a grand jury investigation from fleeing; and protects innocent persons whose names have been mentioned in connection with a grand jury investigation, but who have not been, and may never be, charged.

In this case, the court inspected the certification in camera and allowed appellant and the defendants to argue their positions regarding the certification and the issuance of the subpoena. This procedure was sufficient to test the sufficiency of the ex parte certification. Indeed, the prosecutor could have opposed the motion to quash simply on his representations, without the necessity of providing the court with formal proof.

We affirm the trial judge's denial of appellant's motion seeking access to the ex parte certification.

**SECTION 6.12
VERDICTS AND
SENTENCING**

At the completion of a criminal trial, the fact finder may return with a variety of verdicts, including: **(1)** Not guilty; **(2)** Guilty; **(3)** Not guilty by Reason of Insanity; and **(4)** Guilty but Insane.

The verdicts of **not guilty** and **guilty** are easy to understand. If the defendant is found innocent, the case is over and the accused may not be prosecuted again for the same crime.

This result is mandated by the **double jeopardy** clause contained in the Fifth Amendment which provides: "nor shall any person be subject for the same offense to be twice put in jeopardy of life or limb." This concept is such a basic tenant of civilized law whose origins can be traced back to the ancient Roman Empire where it was proclaimed that the "governor should not permit the same person to be again accused of a crime of which he has already been acquitted."

The premise of the double jeopardy is to protect people against three distinct risks: **(1)** a second prosecution for the same offense after acquittal, **(2)** a second prosecution for the same offense after conviction, and **(3)** multiple punishments for the same offense.

As the reader may remember from Chapter Two, it is not a violation of the double jeopardy clause if both criminal charges and a civil lawsuit are brought against a person for the same event. On rare occasions, a person may even be prosecuted in both federal and state courts for the same act based on the logic that the state and federal governments are separate sovereigns. The Rodney King trial is a classic example. A California jury found the Los Angeles police officers involved in the filmed assault not guilty. The defendants were then successfully prosecuted in federal court for violating King's constitutional rights.

The idea of a defendant being found insane in response to a crime is not a novel idea. It was first introduced in England during the late 1800's and it continues to be a viable verdict. The fact finder is the ultimate judge of a person's mental capacity, and if the jury is convinced that the defendant was mentally ill at the time of the commission of the crime, they may return with a verdict of **not guilty by reason of insanity** or **guilty but mentally ill.** A person will be found not guilty by reason of insanity if he or she does not know the difference between right and wrong because of a defective thought process caused by mental illness. If a jury concludes that a person is insane at the time of the crime, the defendant will be sent to a mental institution instead of prison. Once the individual regains his sanity, he will be released from the mental facility.

Guilty but mentally ill offers the jury an "in-between" verdict. The defendant is still responsible for his criminal conduct, but is provided treatment for the mental illness. Only a minority number of states have adopted this approach including Pennsylvania and Delaware. Juries who determine that the accused suffered from a psychiatric disorder that left him with insufficient willpower to choose whether to commit the act or refrain from doing it, may return with a verdict of guilty but mentally ill.

The distinction between "not guilty by reason of insanity" and "guilty but mentally ill" lies in the degree of mental illness. The verdict of not guilty by reason of insanity reflects a finding that the defendant is so mentally impaired that he lacks the ability to appreciate the wrongfulness of his criminal conduct. A person who is guilty but mentally ill appreciates the inappropriateness of his conduct but due to a psychiatric disorder, lacks sufficient willpower to choose whether to do a particular act or refrain from doing it.

Perhaps the reader may remember John DuPont and his killing of an Olympic wrestler who trained at the DuPont estate. The accused admitted that he shot the athlete but claimed that he was insane at the time. The defendant introduced evidence to show that his paranoia resulted in his installing razor wires in the walls to prevent people from hiding there, and he had excavators dig on his property in search of underground tunnels that he thought led to his home. On the day of the incident, DuPont walked up to the wrestler, asked the athlete if he had a problem with the defendant, and then shot the man three times with a .44 Magnum revolver. The jury found that the multimillionaire suffered from a mental disease process but it was not severe enough to prevent DuPont from understanding the difference between right and wrong. He was found guilty but mentally ill and sentenced to thirteen to thirty years in jail.

If the defendant is found not guilty, the case is concluded. The government can generally not appeal an adverse determination because of the concept of double jeopardy. If the defendant is found guilty, however, the case proceeds to the sentencing phase of the trial, which phase rarely takes place immediately following conviction.

There is usually a short delay to allow counsel to file post-trial motions and for the court to conduct a background check on the defendant. Rarely, does the jury participate in the sentencing aspect of the trial except in capital murder convictions.

The idea of punishment for a crime is not novel and can be traced back to historical times. Most people are aware of the biblical reference by Matthew of "an eye for an eye and a tooth for a tooth." This quote is often used as the justification for retribution against a criminal which punishment is also thought to be a deterrent. That famous quote, however, is not the only reference in the bible for punishment. For instance, the bible also states that "he that killeth any man shall surely be put to death" or "he that killeth a beast shall make it good; beast for beast."

The Bureaus of Justice Statistics estimates that nearly 2.2 million people are confined in prisons across the United States and this figure represents a 33-year continuous rise in the prison population which makes this country number one in the world in people that are incarcerated at any given time. In fact, 1 out of every 136 people in this country is incarcerated despite a falling crime rate.[22]

Judges have a degree of discretion in the types and lengths of sentences that may be imposed in order for the penalty to fit the crime.

Punishment can range from incarceration to non-reporting probation or community service. Jail time remains the most frequent penalty with 72% of defendants being incarcerated for serious felonies while 25% receive probations.[23]

Prison sentences are usually indeterminate with a minimum and maximum term of incarceration. For instance, a defendant will be sentenced to five to ten years in a state penitentiary. This range allows the prisoner to be paroled after the minimum time period if he has been a model prisoner and has shown evidence of rehabilitation.

Mandatory sentencing is the legislature's attempt to take away the sentencing decision from the judge so that people who commit certain types of crimes will be treated the same. For example, committing a crime with a gun, selling drugs within a school zone, and the commission of three separate felonies will result in the imposition of mandatory jail time. Proponents of mandatory sentencing believe that it acts as a deterrent since it sends a clear message to criminals that they will face real prison time if they commit certain types of crimes. Not everyone, however, is sold on the idea since it removes the discretion from the judge in cases with extenuating circumstances and it does not consider the role of a particular defendant in the crime.

Judges can be creative in their sentences, and the newspapers occasionally contain stories about the more unusual punishments. For instances, novel penalties have included sex offenders being castrated, defendants having to put bumper stickers on their cars advertising their crimes, and a rap fan who was forced to listen to Wayne Newton's music for violating a sound ordinance.

Regardless of whether the penalty seems excessively harsh or whimsical, they involve the same issue. Does the punishment violate the person's constitutional rights on the basis that is it humiliating or barbaric?

The **Eighth Amendment** prohibits punishment that is cruel and unusual. This guarantee is frequently asserted by a defendant in response to a prison term that seems excessively harsh, or a penalty that seems a little too creative. The Constitution does not define what constitutes cruel and unusual punishment but is clear that the guarantee is intended to limit those entrusted with the sentencing power. Courts have interpreted the clause to mean that the penalty must be proportionate to the crime. That determination changes with evolving standards of decency but it is directed to punishments that *shock the conscious of civilized man.*

SECTION 6.13
PROBLEM CASES

1. Three packages containing more than $500,000 fell out of the back of an armored truck. Morant, an individual walking down the street, retrieved and carried away the bags. The money was not returned immediately nor were the police notified that the money had been located. A couple of days later, the armored truck company posted a $75,000 reward, and Morant came forward with the money in order to claim the reward. Has this individual committed the crime of theft by retaining the money until a reward was posted?

2. The police suspected that Gindlesperger was growing marijuana in his basement. An officer aimed a thermal detection device at the home from the street in order to measure the heat emissions coming from the defendant's house. The temperature of the home was felt to be consistent with marijuana production activities. Did the warrantless search of the house, with a thermal detection device, constitute an unlawful Search and Seizure? **Commonwealth of Pennsylvania v. Gregory Gindlesperger, 706 A.2d 1316 (Pa. Super., 1997).**

3. The police set up a road block as part of a program to interdict drunk drivers. Schavello, who was driving towards the road block, made a U-turn in order to avoid police contact. He was then stopped by the police a short distance away, and alcohol was detected on his breath. Schavello failed a field sobriety test and was arrested for driving under the influence of alcohol. Is avoiding a road block sufficient probable cause to stop a motor vehicle when it makes a U-turn without any further suspicion by the police of illegal activity? **Commonwealth of Pennsylvania v. Schavello, 734 A.2d 386 (Pa., 1999).**

4. The manager of an apartment building was making yearly repairs and maintenance inspections. The date of these inspections were posted throughout the building. During his examination of one of the units, the manager observed drugs on the kitchen table and immediately contacted the police. The manager then led the officers into the apartment with a pass key. The police observed five plastic bags containing crack cocaine on the kitchen table. Based upon their observations, one officer left the apartment in order to obtain a search warrant. The other officer remained behind and arrested Davis when he entered the apartment. The lease agreement provided: "Landlords and anyone allowed by the landlord, may enter the leased unit after first notifying tenant." Was the entry by the police into the apartment without a search warrant legal? **Commonwealth of Pennsylvania v. Curtis Davis, 743 A.2d 946 (Pa. Super., 1999).**

SECTION 6.14
INTERNET REFERENCES

To learn more information about the topics in this chapter, see the following internet references:

A. Criminal Law

- **www.talkjustice.com**
  A person is able to post messages at this location about the criminal justice system and can access Cybrary, an online library which provides 12,000 links to different websites relating to criminal justice.

- **www.law.indiana.edu/law/crimlaw.html**
  This site by Indiana University School of Law in Bloomington allows a user to download short speeches about different aspects of criminal law, such as double jeopardy and being called as a witness.

- **www.thebestdefense.com**
  Information about specific crimes and the process of a criminal case is offered at this criminal law firm's website.

- **www.softport-co.com/safety/home.html**
  The Los Angeles County Sheriff presents an article on how to prevent a home burglary at this location.

- **www.usdoj.gov**
  The United States Department of Justice provides information on criminal justice programs and initiatives, as well as other information on the United States criminal justice system.

- **www.fbi.gov**
  The Federal Bureau of Investigation's site provides information and statistics on crime, including FBI investigations, international crime, wiretapping, electronic surveillance, and economic espionage.

B. Miranda Warnings

- **www.courttv.com/legalhelp/lawguide/criminal/91.html**
  This site provides general information about Miranda Warnings and its history.

C. Search and Seizure

- **www.supreme.findlaw.com/constitution/amendment04/**
  The Constitutional Law Center provides a variety of information relating to the law of Search and Seizure at this site, including the history, cases, and statutes concerning this Amendment.

D. Grand Jury

- **www.archive.abcnews.go.com/sections/us/DailyNews clinton_jury.html**
  ABC News has created this link to explain the inner workings of the grand jury system.

- **www.udayton.edu/~grandjury**
  This site explains how the federal and state grand jury systems work.

E. Sentencing

- **www.sentencing.org**
  This is the site for the Coalition for Federal Sentencing Reform, and it provides articles, history, and links to relevant sites.

Footnotes:

1. Business Crime Prevention Report, The Sonoma County Economic Development Board, http://www.sonoma-county.org/edb/pdf/2002/bcp_report.pdf.

2. Workplace Safety-Small Business Crime Prevention, Philadelphia Police Department, http://www.ppdonline.org/prev/prev_work_smallbiz.php.

3. Small Business Security Tips: Internal Employee Theft Prevention, ADT Security Services, Inc.

4. Embezzlement, Investopedia, http://www.investopedia.com/terms/e/embezzlement.asp.

5. **Barnett v. State, 834 N.E. 2d 169, (Ind. App., 2005).**

6. Shoplifting Statistics & Tactics: 75% of Adults Are Guilty of the Five Finger Discount, The People's Media Company, http://www. associatedcontent.com/article/183545/shoplifting_statistics_tactics_75_of.html.

7. Identify Theft and Identify Fraud, www.usdoj/gov/criminal/fraud/idtheft.html.

8. Fighting Back Against Identify Theft: Deter, Detect, Defend, www.ftc.gov/bcp/edu/microsites/idtheft/consumers/defend.html.

9. Former Enron Chairman and Chief Executive Kenneth L. Lay Charged with Conspiracy, Fraud, and False Statements, Department of Justice, July 8, 2004.

10. Billy Steel, Money Laundering – A Brief History, http://www.laundryman.u-net.com/page1_hist.html.

11. Insider Trading, Securities and Exchange Commission, http://www.sec.gov/answers/insider. htm.

12. *Id.*

13. **S.E.C. v. Yun, 327 F.3d 1263 (C.A. 11th Fla., 2003).**

14. **U.S. v. Greene, 670 F. Supp. 337 (M.D. Fla., 1987).**

15. See: http://www.uscourts.gov/bankruptcycourts/bankruptcybasics/process.html.

16. White-Collar Crime, Operation Targets Bankruptcy Fraud, http://www.fbi.gov/page2/ oct2006/bankruptcy101806.htm.

17. **Standard Oil of Texas v. United States, 307 F.2d 120 (1962).**

18. **State v. Smokey's Steakhouse, Inc., 478 N.W. 2d 361 (N.D., 1991).**

19. Dietz, et al., Corporations, 18B Am. Jur. 2d Section 1841.

20. This summary has been partially reproduced from the "Victim's Rights Handbook" written by the District Attorneys' Office of both Bucks and Montgomery Counties and has been reproduced with their permission.

21. This has been reprinted in part from a manual entitled "Handbook for Federal Grand Jurors," published by the Administrative Office of the United States Supreme Court. Washington, D.C. 20544.

KEY TERMS

Arraignment

Arrest

Bail

Bankruptcy Fraud

Bribery

Burglary

Chapter 7 Bankruptcy

Chapter 11 Bankruptcy

Chapter 13 Bankruptcy

Classical Theory

Conspiracy

Crime

Criminal Complaint

Criminal Trespass

Custodial Interrogation

Eighth Amendment

Electronic Fencing

Embezzlement

Expectation of Privacy

Federal Rule of Criminal
  Procedure

Fifth Amendment

Fourth Amendment

General Police Measure

Grand Jury

Guilty

Guilty but Insane

Hot Pursuit

Identity Theft

Indictment

Innocent

Insanity

Insider Trading

Larceny

Making a False Statement

Malice Aforethought

Mandatory Sentencing

Misappropriation Theory

Miranda Warnings

Money Laundering

Not Guilty by Reason of Insanity

Overt Act

Plain Feel

Plain View

Polygraph

Preliminary Arraignment

Preliminary Hearing

Premeditation

Pre-Sentence Investigation

Probable Cause

Receiving Stolen Property

Respondeat Superior

Retail Theft

Robbery

Search and Seizure

Search Incident to a General
  Police Measure

Search Incident to an Arrest

Search Warrant

Sentencing

Speedy Trial Act

Stop and Frisk

Theft

Trial

Typing

White Collar Crime

CHAPTER 7

REMEDIES AVAILABLE IN COURT

SECTION 7.1
AN OVERVIEW

If a person is injured in an automobile accident or breaches a contract to buy a new car, what damages might be awarded? This topic deals with **judicial remedies** and is the subject of this chapter.

Judicial remedies may be divided into two categories; remedies at law and remedies in equity. **Remedies at law** developed from common law and generally result in an award of money damages. These damages are categorized as compensatory, punitive, nominal, and liquidated.

When remedies at law are inadequate, a party may seek **equitable relief**. Some scholars refer to this principle as the *irreparable harm* requirement. Developed in the Chancery Court of ancient England, **equity** allows the court to fashion a remedy to do what is just where traditional rules of law would produce an unfair result. Equitable remedies may either prohibit one from performing specified acts or require specific actions to be taken by a party. This relief can include an injunction to force employees to return to work or specific performance to require a party to go through with the sale of a unique item, such as a Picasso painting. The forms of equitable relief include restitution, reformation, injunctions, declaratory judgments, and specific performance. A party who violates an equitable decree may be held in contempt of court and be subject to the payment of fines and possible imprisonment.

JUDICIAL REMEDIES	
LAW	**EQUITY**
Compensatory	Injunction
Punitive	Reformation
Nominal	Restitution
Liquidated	Declaratory Judgment
	Specific Performance
	Recession

While there is a constitutional right to trial-by-jury in lawsuits at common law, no corresponding right exists in equity cases. Recently, however, the courts have started to disregard the distinction between these two categories of remedies, and award both legal and equitable relief in the same piece of litigation.

Since the concept of equity attempts to do what is right, the courts have developed maxims or guiding principles in decided matters. One of the oldest doctrines is that a person who requests the court to exercise its equitable powers must come before the judiciary with clean hands and keep them clean throughout the course of the proceeding.

This principle is demonstrated in **United States v. Parlavecchio.** This case involves a fight over the frozen sperm of a reputed New York mobster. Mr. Parlavecchio, an inmate at Allenwood Federal Correctional Institution, was part of a conspiracy to funnel seminal fluids to his wife so that she could conceive his child through artificial insemination. After Mrs. Parlavecchio pled guilty to participating in the scheme, she requested the court to exercise its equitable powers by ordering the government to return the sperm of her imprisoned spouse to her. The court refused to intercede because the wife was part of the illegal activity and did not have clean hands.

UNITED STATES V. PARLAVECCHIO
192 F. SUPP. 2D 349 (M.D. PA., 2002)

On December 13, 2000, a federal grand jury returned a 10-count indictment charging John Alite, Antonino Parlavecchio and Maria Parlavecchio with conspiracy. John Alite and Maria Parlavecchio pled guilty to Count 6 and Antonino Parlavecchio, the husband of Maria Parlavecchio, pled guilty to Count 7 of the indictment. Mrs. Parlavecchio was sentenced to a one-year term of probation.

On February 1, 2002, Mrs. Parlavecchio filed a motion for return of property pursuant to **Federal Rule of Criminal Procedure 41(e)**. The presentence report filed in this case reveals that the following facts are undisputed. In furtherance of the conspiracy, Mrs. Parlavecchio provided toiletries, foodstuffs and cryogenic sperm preservation kits to her husband through Troy Kemmerer who was employed as a correctional officer at the prison. It was part of the conspiracy that in exchange for receiving $5,000, Mr. Kemmerer would obtain the sperm kits from Mrs. Parlavecchio and deliver the kits to Mr. Parlavecchio. Mr. Parlavecchio would then fill the sperm preserva-

tion kits with his seminal fluids and the kits would be returned to Mr. Kemmerer who would transport the kits from the prison to Mrs. Parlavecchio. Mrs. Parlavecchio would thereafter transport the kits or cause them to be transported to a Park Avenue Fertility Clinic in New York City. On or about October 2, 2000, Mrs. Parlavecchio directed that the seminal fluids be forwarded to her gynecologist. One of the purposes of the conspiracy was to enable Mrs. Parlavecchio to conceive a child by her husband through artificial insemination.

Federal Rule of Criminal Procedure 41(e) provides:

Motion for Return of Property. A person aggrieved by an unlawful search and seizure or by the deprivation of property may move the district court for the return of the property on the ground that such person is entitled to lawful possession of the property...

A basic principle applicable to this case is that one requesting the court to exercise its equitable powers must come into court with "clean hands." **Gaudiosi v. Mellon, 269 F. 2d 873 (3d Cir.,1959)**. No principle is better settled than the maxim that he who comes into equity must come with clean hands and keep them clean throughout the course of the litigation, and that if he violates this rule, he must be denied all relief whatever may have been the merits of his claim. The Court of Appeals in Gaudiosi further stated that "[p]ublic policy not only makes it obligatory for courts to deny a plaintiff relief once his unclean hands are established but to refuse to even hear a case under such circumstances."

Mrs. Parlavecchio is not entitled to equitable relief. The ultimate crime in this case was bribery, i.e., the illegal payment of money in exchange for receiving seminal fluids from Mrs. Parlavecchio's husband.

The fruits of the crime for Kemmerer was the cash he received. From the other perspective, the fruits of the crime for Mrs. Parlavecchio were the seminal fluids she obtained in exchange for the cash she paid. Each of the parties to the illegal transaction gained something to which they were not legally entitled and which was the result of the criminal activity: Kemmerer received the cash and Mrs. Parlavecchio received the seminal fluids.

To permit Mrs. Parlavecchio to recover the illegally obtained seminal fluids would constitute judicial approval of her criminal activities and reward her for her crime. We will not use our equitable powers to aid a wrongdoer. Mrs. Parlavecchio's motion for return of property will be denied.

SECTION 7.2 COMPENSATORY DAMAGES

Compensatory damages are the most common type of award given to an aggrieved or injured party. The purpose of compensatory damages is to award a sum of money that will return an aggrieved party to the status quo as though nothing ever happened. That is, these damages compensate a party for loss or injury in order to make the person whole.

In a tort action, the damages should place the injured party in as substantially good a position financially, emotionally, and physically as that occupied before the injury. Such damages, however, may be difficult to quantify.

Examine the malpractice case of Joe Roberts, which was brought as a result of a surgical sponge that was left in his stomach. How much money should Joe receive for the doctor's mistake? The most obvious damages include the recovery of out-of-pocket expenses, such as:

1. medical expenses; 2. lost wages; and 3. property damage.

It is without question that Joe can recover the medical expenses he incurs by having to undergo a second operation. He may also recover the wages that he loses by being out of work while he recovers from the surgery.

When these items are added together, Joe will be reimbursed for all of his out-of-pocket expenses. Financially, he will be returned to the same position that he was in before he had to undergo the second surgery. Has Joe, however, been fully compensated for the doctor's mistake?

Another item of recovery, known as **pain and suffering**, is allowed in personal injury actions and is the most controversial because of its subjective nature. For instance, Joe is entitled to be compensated for the anguish and discomfort he has had to endure because of the doctor's carelessness in leaving a sponge in his abdomen as well as the pain associated with having to undergo additional surgery.

Pain and suffering is not as easy to calculate as other forms of damages that can be reduced to a mathematical certainty. Pain and suffering is subjective, and the value of each case will vary depending upon the circumstances. For instance, if Joe makes a speedy recovery from the second surgery with no ill effects, his pain and suffering will be worth far less than if he suffers from the residuals of the incident for the rest of his life. As a rule of thumb, it is not uncommon to see a claimant receive three to ten times the out-of-pocket expenses in the form of pain and suffering damages.

Damages in a contract action should place the injured party in the position he or she would have occupied had the contract not been breached. In other words, the plaintiff is entitled to receive the benefit of its bargain. Suppose Joe Roberts contracts with Dr. Jones to purchase the physician's boat for $20,000. On the day Joe learns that Jones breached the contract, the market value of the boat is $22,000. Joe is entitled to the difference between the contract price and the market price, or $2,000. What if Joe can purchase a comparable boat for $21,500 within a reasonable time after the breach? He would be entitled to the difference between the cover or purchase price and the contract price or $1,500.

Joe Roberts is also entitled to any **special damages** that were caused by the breach. Special damages are limited to those losses that are foreseeable, reasonably certain, and unavoidable. For example, if Dr. Jones knew that Joe needed the boat for a charter-fishing business, which business has generated profits of $10,000 each summer for the past five years, the physician will be responsible for Joe's lost profits.

If Joe is the breaching party, what can the aggrieved seller recover? Suppose the contract price was still $20,000, but the boat's market value had slipped to $19,000 on the scheduled date of contract performance. Jones' lost benefit would be the difference between the contract price and the market price or $1,000. If the seller can resell the boat, the damages will be the difference between the contract price and the resale price.

The following case illustrates the problem with collecting special damages. Even though a party clearly breaches a contract, unless that defendant has knowledge of the circumstances from which such damages might arise, items like lost profits can not be recovered.

SUTTLE v. LANDSTAR INWAY, INC.
2009 WL 1297470 (S.D., TEX.)

Suttle and Dai are partners in G & B. In April 2006, Plaintiffs purchased the CNC Machine at issue in this case for $10,000 "as-is, where-is, with all faults." Plaintiffs bought this machine from Delphi Automotive North America (Delphi) in an online auction. Plaintiffs did not physically see the machine before they bid on and purchased it. They did, however, view several photos of the CNC Machine. Plaintiff Dai then contacted Avxa Freight Logistics (Avxa) to arrange for the transportation of the CNC Machine from Delphi's Dayton, Ohio location to G & B's address in Houston, Texas. On October 13, 2006, Landstar transported the CNC Machine from Delphi to G & B. The shipping document completed by Delphi declares that the machine's extended value is $10,000. Plaintiffs allege that Landstar failed to adequately tarp the CNC Machine for transportation and that, during transport, the machine sustained rain damage which made it "unsafe and unmarketable."

Defendant contends that Plaintiffs' claims for damages in the form of lost profits and lost income are claims for special damages and are not recoverable under the facts of this case.

Plaintiffs had entered into an agreement with and had paid Defendant to protect and cover the machine with a tarp from weather elements and other debris while transporting the machine from one destination [Dayton] to another [Houston] for them. Additionally, Plaintiffs owned the CNC Machine at issue as they had purchased it several months earlier in an auction.

Defendant contends that Plaintiffs cannot recover damages for lost profits or lost income because Defendant did not have notice of these special damages prior to or at the time the bill of lading was issued. General damages are those that are foreseeable at the time of contracting. Special damages are those unusual or indirect costs that, although caused by the defendant's conduct in a literal sense, are beyond what one would reasonably expect to be the ordinary consequences of a breach. Typically, a plaintiff cannot recover special damages in a breach of contract action absent actual notice to the defendant of special circumstances from which such damages might arise.

When Dai contacted Avxa to arrange for the shipment of the CNC Machine, he only provided Avxa with the machine's physical size and weight. Plaintiffs never provided Avxa or Defendant with actual notice of the intended use of the CNC Machine prior to or at the time the bill of lading was issued. It was not until Plaintiffs submitted their (lawsuit) that they asserted a claim for special damages, specifically lost profits on the operation of the CNC Machine. Accordingly, the Court finds that Plaintiffs' claim for special damages must fail.

SECTION 7.3 PUNITIVE DAMAGES

Punitive or exemplary damage is exactly what its name implies. A sum of money is awarded to punish the wrongdoer and to send a message to others not to engage in the same type of conduct. This penalty is a United States doctrine that has not gained recognition in other parts of the world. Historically, punitive damages are not allowed in breach of contract claims. Rather, they are more commonly awarded in tort actions where the defendant has engaged in outrageous, malicious, or gross misconduct. For example, an automobile accident that occurs as the result of a party's mere negligence in going through a traffic light is insufficient to give rise to punitive damages. In order for punitive damages to be awarded, the accident would have had to be caused by the defendant being intoxicated, the driver intentionally going through a red light, or the wrongdoer driving at a speed far in excess of the speed limit in a school-crossing zone.

Punitive damage awards are unpredictable and can be staggering, since the jury is allowed to consider the net worth of the defendant in their calculations. According to a CNN survey of jury verdicts, a California jury punished Philip Morris by awarding a lung cancer patient 28 billion dollars, and a Missouri jury ordered a pharmacy to pay over 2 billion dollars to a woman with ovarian cancer whose medication was diluted by the drugstore. The record for punitive damages, however, was rendered in Florida where a 144 billion-dollar punitive damage award was entered against the tobacco industry.

An award of punitive damages is the exception rather than the rule. The New York Times published a study analyzing verdicts across the country. The article noted that punitive damages are awarded in only four percent of the cases and they are proportionate to the amount of compensatory damages.

State governments have the authority to regulate punitive damages and the Due Process Clause prohibits the imposition of grossly excessive or arbitrary awards against a tortfeasor. In fact, the Supreme Court has established the following guidelines to consider when looking at a punitive damage award: (1) the degree of reprehensibility of the defendant's misconduct; (2) the disparity between the actual or potential harm suffered by the plaintiff and the punitive damages award; and (3) the difference between the punitive damages awarded by the jury and the civil penalties authorized or imposed in comparable cases.

WHITNEY HOUSTON v. NEW YORK POST CO., INC.
1997 WL 10034 (S.D. N.Y., 1997)

Whitney Houston commenced this libel action after defendant New York Post falsely reported that she had been hospitalized following an overdose of diet pills. She seeks compensatory damages of $10,000,000 and punitive damages of $50,000,000.

On Friday, June 25, 1993, David Miller, a reporter for the Post, received an anonymous phone call claiming that Houston had overdosed on illegal drugs and had been admitted to the hospital at which the caller was employed. Miller called Florence Anthony at her home in an effort to confirm the story. After receiving the message on Saturday morning, Anthony phoned Regina Brown to confirm the report knowing that Brown, a former publicist for Houston, maintained close contacts with members of the plaintiff's family. Defendant alleges that Brown agreed to make some calls in an effort to confirm the story, and that Brown told Anthony of plaintiff's use of diet pills and of her depression. Anthony claims that she made several attempts to confirm the story, calling plaintiff's public relations firm and receiving no answer, attempting to call Lois Smith, plaintiff's publicist, but not being able to obtain her phone number, and finally calling plaintiff's company, Nippy, Inc., receiving no answer.

After speaking with Brown, Florence Anthony phoned Hoffman at the Post and relayed to him what Brown had allegedly told her. Hoffman started working on the article on Sunday, June 27, 1993. He phoned the Mount Sinai Hospital in Miami, which refused to either confirm or deny that Houston had been treated there. Hoffman reviewed the Post's file of articles about plaintiff, some of which contained information about plaintiff's recent struggle controlling her weight. Hoffman then wrote the Article, which was published the next day.

The article stated that plaintiff had been hospitalized because she "overdosed on prescription diet pills" after having been severely depressed about her weight. It further stated that the overdose caused plaintiff to suffer an acute heart arrhythmia. In fact, plaintiff was performing that evening in Washington, DC. She neither overdosed nor was admitted to Mount Sinai Hospital. Defendant has admitted to the falsity of the article, and indeed printed a conspicuous correction on June 30, 1993.

Houston argues that the article is defamatory because "it implied to the average reader that plaintiff was so depressed and despondent that she attempted to take her life by overdosing on diet pills. Second, plaintiff argues that the article is defamatory in that it "had a tendency to injure plaintiff in her profession since it implied, a mere matter of days before she was to begin an extensive tour, that she was mentally and physically unable to perform."

Plaintiff contends that the defendant did not adequately investigate the story prior to publication. Defendant contends that they made a number of efforts to contact the plaintiff and her representatives, but those attempts were unsuccessful. Defendant says that it relied on corroborating information supplied by Regina Brown. Brown now denies the statements attributed to her.

Under New York state law, punitive damages in a libel action are appropriate where there are "circumstances of aggravation and outrage, such as spite or malice, or a fraudulent or evil motive on the part of the defendant and where plaintiff makes a showing, by clear and convincing evidence, that the wrongdoing was "intentional and deliberate." Even if every material fact is construed in a light most favorable to plaintiff, Houston, fails to meet this burden. In publishing the article, defendant omitted the most unsavory aspects of the anonymous tip, such as alleged use of illegal drugs. Moreover, within 48 hours, defendant published a conspicuous, clear, and lengthy correction. These facts, and the complete absence of any compelling evidence of evil motive presented by the plaintiff, make it clear that no reasonable person could find that the article was published with the type of personal hatred or ill will required to sustain a claim for punitive damages in a libel action. Thus, the plaintiff's punitive damages claim is dismissed.

SECTION 7.4
NOMINAL DAMAGES

Have you ever heard of a verdict of one dollar? **Nominal damages** arise when a technical wrong has been committed but no actual harm has resulted. Courts will acknowledge the legal rights of the complaining party, but will award a trivial or nominal sum of money to the injured party. It is as if the court or jury is saying "Technically, a tort has been committed but so what?" By awarding normal damages, the fact finder is reinforcing the principle that the defendant's conduct is contrary to established law.

For example, if a motorist carelessly opens a car door into the side of a parked vehicle, causing a small dent on an already blemished and rusty 1995 Chevy, a cause of action for negligence can be successfully maintained. However, it is likely that the court will award a token sum of money or nominal damages since there has been no real harm to the aging automobile.

One of the better known cases involving nominal damages arose in a suit filed by the defunct United States Football League or USFL against the NFL for a violation of the Sherman Antitrust Act. The floundering USFL claimed damages of 567 million dollars which, when trebled according to antitrust laws, would total more than 1.7 billion dollars. Following a 48 day trial, the jury returned with a verdict of $1 which was then multiplied by 3 to arrive at an award of $3. While the jury believed that the NFL was technically guilty of an antitrust violation, the fact finders were not impressed that the USFL would have survived under any circumstance.

The following case involves a suit between ESPN and the National Baseball League over the breach of contract by the television network not to show baseball games on Sunday nights in September. The case discusses the burden of proof in showing damages with the necessary certainty.

ESPN, Inc. v. Office of the Commissioner of Baseball
76 F. Supp. 2d 416 (S.D. N.Y., 1999)

ESPN breached its 1996 telecasting agreement with Baseball when it preempted six baseball games scheduled for Sunday nights in September 1998 and September 1999 without the prior written approval of Baseball. ESPN broadcast NFL football games rather than the previously scheduled baseball games on those six nights.

Baseball claims that it has been damaged in an amount "believed to exceed millions of dollars" as a result of ESPN's breach of the 1996 Agreement.

ESPN seeks to preclude Baseball from introducing testimony of its alleged monetary damages. ESPN contends that "there is no factual basis to support any claim for monetary damages arising from these perceived injuries, and that such claims are the product of speculation and guesswork."

It is well-established that a plaintiff must prove the existence of damages with certainty in order to recover for breach of contract. Although it is true that "[w]hen the existence of damage is certain, and the only uncertainty is as to its amount, the plaintiff will not be denied recovery of substantial damages," but even then the plaintiff must show "a stable foundation for a reasonable estimate" of damages.

During discovery, ESPN served Baseball with interrogatories regarding its claims for monetary damages. Among other things, ESPN asked Baseball to "state the amount of monetary damages you seek in this action and explain the basis for the computation of your claim." Baseball responded as follows: "Baseball has not quantified the amount of damages it has sustained by reason of ESPN's willful refusal to carry baseball games as required by the 1996 Agreement."

Nowhere in its response does Baseball set forth any specific dollar amount of monetary damages other than its estimate that damages are "believed to exceed millions of dollars."

Finally, this Court held oral argument on ESPN's motion to preclude damages evidence. During that argument, this Court specifically asked counsel for Baseball whether Baseball had any "concrete proof of monetary harm." Counsel for Baseball was unable to show "any loss of sponsorship, any loss of advertising, or any loss of ancillary sales or ticket sales." As counsel for Baseball conceded: "We have not shown specific losses your Honor, we agree with you there. What we have said is we believe it did affect us."

Baseball has failed to adequately demonstrate either the fact of damages or the amount of damages. Put simply, Baseball's subjective belief that the amount of damages is "significant" does not meet any of the required proofs set forth under New York law. To the contrary, under New York law, a claim of damages for loss of reputation and future profits must be "reasonably certain."

Although Baseball is not entitled to an award of money damages, it may still receive nominal damages. It is a well-settled tenet of contract law that even if the breach of contract caused no loss or if the amount of the loss cannot be proven with sufficient certainty, the injured party is entitled to recover, as nominal damages, a small sum fixed without regard to the amount of the loss, if any. Accordingly, I will instruct the jury that if Baseball proves its breach of damages claim, it is entitled to an award of nominal damages.

SECTION 7.5
LIQUIDATED DAMAGES

The parties to a contract can agree in advance on the amount of damages that will be paid in the event of a default or breach of contract. These amounts are known as **liquidated damages** and are appropriate when the damages are uncertain or difficult to prove. The stipulated sum should be a reasonable forecast of the damages, although the plaintiff may end up recovering more or less than the actual loss. If the liquidated amount is unreasonable and grossly disproportionate to the actual loss, a court may refuse to uphold the agreement. The fact that the actual damages suffered by the aggrieved party end up being less than the damages specified in the contract is not fatal so long as the stipulated sum was reasonable at the time the contract was formed. Liquidated damage clauses have even been enforced when no real damages have been suffered.

A common example of a liquidated damage clause is contained in an Agreement of Sale for real estate. Such a clause requires the forfeiture of the buyer's deposit or down payment in the event of a default by the purchaser. The following is a sample liquidated damages clause:

> In the event of a breach of this agreement by the Buyer, all deposits and other sums paid by the Buyer on account of the purchase price shall be retained by the Seller as liquidated damages for such breach.

Air travel is the subject of several liquidated damage clauses unilaterally imposed by the governments of the world to stimulate the expansion of airline routes to all parts of the globe. This protection was created by the **Warsaw**

Convention which limits the recovery of compensatory damages in personal injury actions against an airline in international travel. Limitations on recovery have also been imposed for property damage claims such as those that result from lost or damaged luggage.

Additional protection can be obtained by purchasing insurance from a private company. Such insurance is not affected by the limitation of the carrier's liability under the Warsaw Convention, any tariff, or the plane ticket.

Would an airline be allowed to limit its liability for damages for a domestic flight between two U.S. cities? That is your next assignment, since the firm has received a new case on this issue. As usual, Mr. Smith will provide you with more information.

SECTION 7.6
ROBERTS V.
EASTCOAST
AIRLINES

PROBLEM SEVEN

PARK, BROWN & SMITH, P.C.
ATTORNEYS AT LAW
MEMORANDUM

TO: All Law Clerks

FROM: Peter Smith, Esquire

RE: Limitation of Liability of an Airline for Lost Luggage

Joe Roberts is a big fan of "The King." While a youth, Mr. Roberts spent some of his time in Nashville because of his love of music. One night, he went to hear the cover band, "Love Me Tender" at a bar in the rural countryside. The lead singer looked familiar but Joe couldn't place him. Our client waited around until the group was finished their set and approached the singer. "You are great!" exclaimed Joe as he asked the singer for an autograph. To his amazement, the musician gave Joe his guitar and autographed it with the name, "The King."

Two years ago, our client's guitar was appraised by Sotheby's, the famous auction house, for $50,000.

Joe recently booked a trip sponsored by fans of "The King." For a mere $200, a person can travel to Memphis and visit the spots where "The King" grew up, owned his famous home, and recorded his tunes. After booking the trip, our client received the travel tickets from East Coast Airlines. This start-up company offers inexpensive plane fares because it utilizes retired pilots and offers a "no-frills" operation. Joe checked his guitar at the airline counter along with the rest of his luggage. During the flight, however, the plane encountered unexpected turbulence which caused the baggage in the cargo bay to shift, crushing the guitar.

Joe is devastated by the damage to the valuable instrument and wishes to sue the airline for $50,000. East Coast, however, claims that its liability is limited to $2,500.

I have reviewed the plane ticket and found the following notice on the reverse side:

NOTICE OF BAGGAGE LIABILITY LIMITATION

Liability for loss, delay or damage to checked baggage is limited as follows, unless a higher value is declared in advance and additional charges are paid: $2,500 per passenger.

This limitation of liability seems unjust considering the airline's negligence and the actual value of the musical instrument. The terms of the Warsaw Convention are not applicable to this case since this flight was purely domestic. My preliminary research has uncovered an old case on point. Please read **Martin v. Transworld Airlines, Inc.** in order to ascertain whether the limitation of liability clause asserted by East Coast Airlines is enforceable.

MARY MARTIN V. TRANS WORLD AIRLINES, INC.
280 A.2D 642 (PA. SUPER., 1972)

Mary Martin brought suit to recover $2,200, the stipulated value of wearing apparel contained in a piece of luggage which was lost in transit when the plaintiff was traveling on defendant's airline from New York City to Pittsburgh.

The plaintiff had checked her baggage at the East side terminal at 42nd Street, New York City, and then proceeded to the airport. The agent of the defendant gave the plaintiff a baggage claim check which recited on its front: "Baggage checked subject to the tariffs indicating limitations of liability contained therein." A similar notice was also printed on the airline ticket.

In addition to the above notices, there were notices posted in bold-face type and prominently displayed in the baggage wells at the East Side terminal and at the airline ticket counter and also at the passenger boarding gates which bore the following notation:

"Tariff regulations limit airline liability for baggage to actual value not to exceed:

Domestic	$250
International	$495

unless higher valuation declared in advance and appropriate charges paid."

Similar signs were posted at the Pittsburgh airport in the baggage wells, at the ticket counter, and at boarding gates.

The plaintiff did not declare any valuation on any of her luggage. One bag was missing. She had testified that she didn't read the small print on her ticket and the baggage check, didn't see the posted signs, and had no knowledge of the limitations. Mary Martin denied knowledge of the limitations, although in her profession as a singer, she was a seasoned traveler.

Under the Civil Aeronautics Act, an airline Carrier may, by tariff, limit its liability and such tariff is valid even though loss of property is the result of the company's negligence. The tariff provisions are part of the contract, and it is the duty of the passenger to declare the higher valuation and pay the higher rate if he wished protection in excess of the limited amount.

This Court held in a similar case:

> The requirement that a passenger must be offered a fair opportunity to choose between higher or lower liability before an interstate carrier can limit recovery for loss of baggage to an amount less than the actual loss sustained does not require that the passenger be actually informed that a choice of rates is available.

> The appellant had ample opportunity to discover there was a choice of rates available. The baggage check which she received made reference to the tariff regulations under which the baggage was transported. In addition, the appellee had signs posted in the bus terminal referring to the limitations of liability for checked bags and advising how travelers could increase their protection.

Unlimited liability or even common law liability for negligence would seriously affect the economic life of a transportation industry already subsidized by government to insure its healthy operation. Unlimited liability would be an open invitation to fraud.

It should be noted that the United States courts have never permitted airlines to limit their liability with regard to injury and death actions on domestic flights. The Civil Aeronautics Board has always permitted limitations on baggage liability. The Second Circuit Court has held that tickets must be delivered to the traveler "in such a manner as to afford him a reasonable opportunity to take protection against the limited liability."

Even if we were to hold that notice on the baggage check and ticket was in too small print to bring notice home to the traveler, it would not dispose of the conspicuous signs in the baggage wells, ticket office, and the boarding gates, which not only gave notice of the filing of tariffs but advised of the right to file for a higher valuation. In addition, the record shows Martin was a seasoned traveler and had many opportunities to see the posted signs, and it is highly unlikely that she had no knowledge of the value limitation on luggage and her choice to pay a fee for higher valuation. A person may not be heard to say she did not see what should have been clearly visible to her.

This record had overwhelming evidence that such notice was given to Martin. Therefore, judgment is entered in favor of the plaintiff and against the defendant in the amount of $250, the amount as limited by the filed tariff.

ANSWER SHEET
PROBLEM SEVEN

Name

Please Print Clearly

1. Are such liquidated damage clauses enforceable?

_____

_____

_____

_____

_____

_____

_____

_____

_____

_____

_____

_____

_____

_____

_____

_____

_____

_____

_____

_____

_____

_____

2. What policy considerations support the enforcement of such clauses?

_____

_____

_____

_____

_____

_____

_____

_____

3. What is required for the clause to be enforced?

_____

_____

_____

_____

_____

_____

_____

_____

_____

_____

SECTION 7.7
INJUNCTION

An **injunction** is an equitable order issued by the court directing a person to do something **(mandatory injunction)** or to refrain from doing something **(prohibitory injunction)**. Injunctions are further classified as: permanent, preliminary, and temporary restraining orders ("TRO").

A **permanent injunction** is the final resolution of a dispute issued after a full hearing of all relevant factors. In granting this type of injunction, the court will evaluate the adequacy of a remedy at law, the enforceability of the decree, and the comparative hardship to the parties.

A **preliminary injunction** is granted as an emergency measure before a full hearing on the merits of the dispute can be held. The plaintiff must provide notice to the defendant of the proceeding, and the court will conduct an informal hearing to review the issue. If the plaintiff demonstrates that irreparable harm will result without such an order, the court will grant the temporary injunction to maintain the status quo prior to a final determination of the dispute.

A **TRO** is an ex parte injunction, or an injunction granted without notice to the defendant. Because the court initially hears only the plaintiff's side of the case, it will grant the order if the need for relief is so urgent that there is no time for a hearing. The plaintiff must also establish that an irreparable harm will occur. Since there is no notice to the defendant, the court weighs factors more heavily against the plaintiff. These proceedings must be followed by a full hearing on the merits of the dispute.

Injunctive relief is a tool frequently used by employers or the government to regulate the conduct of employees on strike. For instance, a prohibitory injunction can be obtained to limit the number of pickets at a facility or to prohibit violent conduct of striking employees.

Does a court of equity, however, have the power to order striking employees to return to work? In the absence of a law or provision in the collective bargaining agreement to the contrary, the court will not order striking workers to return to the job place unless the health, welfare and safety of the public is threatened.

The following case deals with whether McDonald's, the fast food giant, can obtain an injunction prohibiting its landlord from leasing empty space to an International House of Pancakes franchisee since the lease between the landlord and McDonald's prohibited the using of the shopping center space for the operation of another "fast food" restaurant.

McDonald's Corp. v. Rappaport
532 F. Supp. 2d 264 (Mass., 2008)

McDonald's Corporation asserts that the Highlander Plaza shopping center is violating a restrictive covenant contained in a lease between McDonald's and the shopping center. Specifically, McDonald's challenges Highlander Plaza's legal authority to lease space to an International House of Pancakes franchisee for the operation of an IHOP on the premises.

Defendants own Highlander Plaza, a shopping center which has located within it a variety of stores and restaurants. In 1993, McDonald's entered into a twenty-year lease with Defendants to open a new McDonald's restaurant in the shopping center. The lease contains a covenant not to compete provision that restricts the landlord as follows:

> Landlord covenants and agrees that no property within two (2) miles of the perimeter of the Demised Premises shall, during the term of this Lease be leased, or occupied as a so-called fast food restaurant, food service establishment, drive-in or walk-up eating facility.

In 2007, the Ground Round restaurant in Highlander Plaza closed. Defendants entered into an agreement to lease the space to Salem Pancakes, Inc., a company that intended to operate an IHOP franchise.

McDonald's sought to enjoin Defendants permitting the installation of an International House of Pancakes restaurant on the premises.

The standard for issuing a permanent injunction requires the court to find that (1) plaintiffs prevail on the merits; (2) plaintiffs would suffer irreparable injury in the absence of injunctive relief; (3) the harm to plaintiffs would outweigh the harm the defendant would suffer from the imposition of an injunction; and (4) the public interest would not be adversely affected by an injunction.

This court must determine the coverage of the restrictive covenant in the lease. McDonald's asserts that the restrictive covenant applies to all "food service establishments," arguing that the words "so-called fast food" modify only "restaurant." Defendants assert that the covenant applies only to "fast food" restaurants, with the phrase "so-called fast food modifying all of the elements that follow [in the clause]."

At trial, Defendants presented compelling evidence that the Parties intended the clause to restrict Highlander Plaza's ability to lease property in the shopping center to other "fast food" restaurants only, not all "food service establishments." As a result of such evidence, this court concludes that the restrictive covenant applies to fast food only.

Specifically, Defendants demonstrated that McDonald's originally sought a broad restrictive covenant, one that prohibited Highlander Plaza from renting to all other food service establishments. During negotiations, however, Highlander Plaza did not accept such a sweeping covenant. Gary Markoff, counsel for Highlander who participated in the negotiations, stated that Highlander was trying to "give as narrow an exclusive as possible." As a result, Highlander only agreed to restrict its ability to lease to other fast food restaurants. After negotiations, McDonald's accepted the narrower restriction. Accordingly, Markoff added "so-called fast food" to modify the entire covenant:

The evidence is more than sufficient for this court to conclude that the clause applies only to fast food. In addition, however, restrictive covenants are restraints on the alienability of land, and traditional rules governing these restraints add further support to this conclusion. The Supreme Court of Massachusetts has noted that restrictions on land are disfavored, and they in general are to be construed against the grantor and in favor of freedom of alienation. More specifically, any ambiguity in a restrictive covenant must be resolved in favor of the "freedom of land from servitude," meaning the less restricted use.

Here, a narrower interpretation of the covenant results in increased alienability of the premises. Although the lease does not define "so-called fast food," the Parties do not dispute that IHOP is a full service, family style restaurant.

Because the restrictive covenant in the lease applies only to fast food restaurants, and IHOP is not a fast food restaurant, the covenant did not prohibit Defendants from leasing the former Ground Round space to the IHOP franchisee, Salem Pancakes. Accordingly, Plaintiff's request for injunctive relief is DENIED.

SECTION 7.8
RESTITUTION

Restitution is designed to prevent one party from unfairly benefiting at the expense of another. This remedy has the advantage of either returning the property that is in the defendant's possession to the injured party or providing monetary relief. Money damages are measured by the sum that the defendant has been unjustly enriched. Not only must the defendant return the aggrieved party to the status quo, but the wrongdoer must also return any profits that he has earned by the use of the property.

THOMAS MITCHELL v. WILLIAM MOORE
729 A.2D 1200 (PA. SUPER., 1999)

Thomas Mitchell and William Moore first met in 1980; the two men quickly developed a romantic relationship. Moore resided in Elverson, Pennsylvania and Mitchell in South Carolina. In the spring of 1981, Mitchell accepted Moore's invitation to spend his "off season" at Moore's Chester County farm. By 1985, Mitchell had permanently moved to Elverson, where he resided at Moore's farm without paying rent. Among other things, Mitchell took care of the farm animals. In 1990, Mitchell enrolled at Penn State University for graduate studies. As a result of his academic schedule, he was unable to maintain the farm. Soon thereafter, the parties' relationship soured; Mitchell moved out of Moore's residence in June of 1994.

In 1995, Mitchell sought restitution for the services he rendered to Moore throughout the thirteen years the two men lived together on the farm. In his complaint, Mitchell alleged that Moore had: promised him compensation for his services rendered to maintain and operate his farm, agreed to compensate him for his help in running an antique cooperative (co-op) that Mitchell had purchased, and promised him future compensation and the devise of property in a will and codicil.

Mitchell's claim for restitution lies upon the theory of unjust enrichment. Where unjust enrichment is found, the law implies a contract, which requires the defendant to pay to the plaintiff the value of the benefit conferred. The elements necessary to prove unjust enrichment are:

1. benefits conferred on defendant by plaintiff;

2. appreciation of such benefits by defendant; and

3. acceptance and retention of such benefits under such circumstances that it would be inequitable for defendant to retain the benefit without payment of value.

Both parties concur that when Mitchell moved into Moore's home on a full-time basis, Moore paid many of Mitchell's bills, including car payments, card charges, and phone bills. Moreover, Moore claims that Mitchell became part of his own family; Mitchell, himself, admits to having celebrated all the major holidays with Moore's immediate family and received gifts from them on special occasions.

In order to prove that the defendant had been unjustly enriched by plaintiff's actions and services, there must be convincing evidence that plaintiff's services were not gratuitous.

We first note that Mitchell had complete access to a large farm house where he lived rent-free. The amount of benefits that plaintiff received from living at Moore's farm rebuts any presumption that the benefit conferred upon Moore was unjust.

Furthermore, the defendant testified that the plaintiff himself suggested that he move in with the defendant because he could not afford to rent an apartment on his own. He, as well as the defendant, thought such potential living arrangement would give the two men more time to foster their relationship. In fact, upon learning of plaintiff's potential job opportunity in nearby Lancaster, Pennsylvania, the defendant anticipated that the two parties would be able to grow closer in a permanent "live-in" situation—another indication that there existed no expectation of payment for plaintiff's voluntary work on the defendant's farm.

While Mitchell would characterize the nature of the parties' relationship as a type of business venture between partners, the evidence indicates a very different aspect of their lives. As Mitchell, himself, testified, he had a "romantic or sexual aspect to his relationship with Dr. Moore." Furthermore, the parties conducted themselves around the home like parties in a loving relationship; they shared household chores, cooked dinners for each other, bestowed gifts upon one another, attended events together, and shared holidays and special occasions with Moore's family.

After a review of the record in this case, we cannot find that the defendant benefited unjustly from plaintiff's services.

SECTION 7.9 RECISION AND REFORMATION

A contract can be **rescinded** if it is voidable, such as those agreements procured through misrepresentation, fraud, duress, undue influence, or impossibility. In that case, each party must return the property they have received from the other.

Suppose, however, that the contract between the parties is valid but it fails to express the real intent of the parties because of a mistake or ambiguity in language. In that event, a party can seek the equitable remedy of **reformation** in order to modify the written agreement to reflect their real intentions.

For example, suppose a seller orally agrees to transfer 120 acres of land to a buyer, but the written deed conveys only 100 acres. The buyer can request that the court reform or change the contract to reflect the sale of 120 acres of land.

The remedy of rescission is not easily granted. A court must be satisfied with the fact that the breach of contract is material and willful, or at least substantial and fundamental enough to strongly defeat the object of the parties in making the contract. The aggrieved party must also show that the normal remedy for breach of contract, in the form of monetary damages, is inadequate. Rescission has the effect of canceling the contract, thereby excusing future performance and requiring the return of all monies advanced.

Would a house that is reputed to be haunted allow the buyer to rescind the sale? That is the issue in **Stambovsky v. Ackley**. Where the condition created by the seller materially impairs the value of the contract and is peculiarly within the knowledge of the seller or is unlikely to be discovered by the buyer, non-disclosure of a material fact constitutes grounds for recession.

JEFFREY STAMBOVSKY V. HELEN ACKLEY
572 N.Y.S. 2D 672 (N.Y., 1991)

Plaintiff, to his horror, discovered that the house he had contracted to purchase was widely reputed to be possessed by poltergeists, reportedly seen by defendant seller and members of her family on numerous occasions over the last nine years. Plaintiff promptly commenced this action seeking rescission of the contract of sale.

The unusual facts of this case, clearly warrant a grant of equitable relief to the buyer who, as a resident of New York City, cannot be expected to have any familiarity with the folklore of the Village of Nyack. Not being a "local," plaintiff could not readily learn that the home he had contracted to purchase is haunted. Whether the source of the spectral apparitions seen by defendant seller are parapsychic or psychogenic, having reported their presence in both a national publication (Readers' Digest) and the local press, defendant is estopped to deny their existence and, as a matter of law, the house is haunted. More to the point, however, no divination is required to conclude that it is defendant's promotional efforts in publicizing her close encounters with these spirits which fostered the home's reputation in the community. The house was included in a five-home walking tour of Nyack and described in a November 27 newspaper article as "a riverfront Victorian (with ghost)." The impact of the reputation thus created goes to the very essence of the bargain between the parties, greatly impairing both the value of the property and its potential for resale.

From the perspective of a person in the position of plaintiff, a very practical problem arises with respect to the discovery of a paranormal phenomenon: "Who you gonna' call?" as a title song to the movie "Ghostbusters" asks. Applying the strict rule of caveat emptor to a contract involving a house possessed by poltergeists conjures up visions of a psychic or medium routinely accompanying the structural engineer and Terminix man on an inspection of every home subject to a contract of sale.

The doctrine of caveat emptor requires that a buyer act prudently to assess the fitness and value of his purchase and operates to bar the purchaser who fails to exercise due care from seeking the equitable remedy of rescission. It should be apparent, however, that the most meticulous inspection and the search would not reveal the presence of poltergeists at the premises or unearth the property's ghoulish reputation in the community. Therefore, there is no sound policy reason to deny plaintiff relief for failing to discover a state of affairs which the most prudent purchaser would not be expected to even contemplate.

Where a condition which has been created by the seller materially impairs the value of the contract and is peculiarly within the knowledge of the seller or unlikely to be discovered by a prudent purchaser exercising due care with respect to the subject transaction, nondisclosure constitutes a basis for rescission as a matter of equity.

In the case at bar, defendant seller deliberately fostered the public belief that her home was possessed. Having undertaken to inform the public-at-large, to whom she has no legal relationship, about the supernatural occurrences on her property, she may be said to owe no less a duty to her buyer. Where, as here, the seller not only takes unfair advantage of the buyer's ignorance, but has created and perpetuated a condition about which he is unlikely to even inquire, enforcement of the contract is offensive to the court's sense of equity. Application of the remedy of rescission is entirely appropriate to relieve the unwitting purchaser from the consequences of a most unnatural bargain.

SECTION 7.10 DECLARATORY JUDGMENT

If a person's rights are uncertain or disputed, an aggrieved party may request the issuance of a **declaratory judgment** to clarify the uncertainty. As the court noted in **Chanos v. MADAC, LLC, 903 N.Y.S.2d 506 (N.Y., 2010)**, "the primary purpose of a declaratory judgment is to stabilize an uncertain or disputed jural relationship with respect to present or prospective obligations."

For example, suppose a twice-married man dies leaving life insurance to his "wife" without specifying which spouse is the recipient of the insurance. Either his former spouse or his current wife may request a declaratory judgment in order to ascertain who is entitled to the property. When the court renders a decision on the issue, it will be a final determination of the problem between the parties.

Courts are specific about the conditions that must exist before they will entertain a declaratory judgment. An actual case or controversy must be present that requires court intervention. This fact is demonstrated in **Gianni Sport, Ltd. v. Metallica**, which case involved the use of the name Metallica by a manufacturer on clothing tags. Metallica is also the name of a famous rock group that specializes in heavy metal music, and the band was not happy with the inclusion of their moniker on the tag. The court refused to hear the lawsuit, since the clothing manufacturer had stopped using the Metallica mark by the time the lawsuit was filed.

GIANNI SPORT, LTD. V. METALLICA
2000 WL 1773511 (S.D. N.Y., 2000)

Gianni Sport, Ltd. seeks a judgment declaring that it does not infringe any rights defendant Metallica may have in the "Metallica" mark.

Gianni manufactures clothing. Metallica is a band that specializes in a type of music called "heavy metal." The dispute between the two parties arose when Metallica learned that Gianni was using the term "Metallica" on hang tags for a line of its women's clothing. Metallica demanded that Gianni cease and desist from use of the mark and that it provide Metallica with information about sales of its allegedly infringing products. Gianni did not believe any confusion between Gianni's exclusive clothing and Metallica's products was possible.

Metallica argues that because Gianni stopped using the term Metallica prior to filing this declaratory judgment action, Gianni fails to present an actual case and controversy. In trademark declaratory judgment actions, the actual-case-and-controversy standard has two elements. First, the defendant, Metallica must have created a real and reasonable apprehension of liability on the part of the plaintiff. Second, the plaintiff must have engaged in a course of conduct which has brought it into adversarial conflict with the defendant.

A substantial controversy between Gianni and Metallica exists regarding whether Gianni has infringed Metallica's rights. The controversy is immediate and real, not hypothetical. The activity at issue has taken place.

When deciding whether to entertain a declaratory judgment action, a court considers the litigation situation as a whole. First, this action does not further the purpose of the Declaratory Judgment Act. The Declaratory Judgment Act's fundamental purpose is to allow a plaintiff not certain of his rights to avoid accrual of avoidable damages, and to afford him an early adjudication without waiting until his adversary should see fit to begin suit, after damage has accrued. Gianni brought suit after committing the alleged infringement. Gianni has stopped using the term Metallica, and there is no suggestion that it intends to resume the use of the word "Metallica" even if it prevails here. Any damages that are due have already accrued. Therefore, Gianni will not "avoid the accrual of avoidable damages" by means of this action.

Not only does Gianni's claim fall beyond the scope of the Declaratory Judgment Act's purpose, but it was also filed in apparent anticipation of Metallica's California suit. Gianni's counsel states in his affidavit that if litigation was inevitable, we preferred that it take place where Gianni does business and keeps all its records, in New York.

Gianni filed this suit in anticipation of Metallica's California suit. Gianni's use of the Declaratory Judgment Act to gain a procedural advantage and preempt the forum choice of the plaintiff to the coercive action, weighs in favor of dismissal.

Gianni argues that the court is required to hear its declaratory judgment action because the action would serve a useful purpose in clarifying and settling the legal relations in issue, or terminate and afford relief from the uncertainty, insecurity, and controversy giving rise to the proceedings. The action will not serve the Declaratory Judgment Act's purpose of preventing the accrual of avoidable damages. In addition, this suit is not necessary to clarify and settle the legal relations or afford relief from uncertainty, insecurity and controversy. The pending action in California will provide Gianni the opportunity to resolve the issues raised in the instant action.

For the reasons stated above, Metallica's motion to dismiss this declaratory judgment action is granted.

SECTION 7.11
SPECIFIC PERFORMANCE

Specific performance is an equitable remedy for breach of contract that is used when money damages are inadequate to make the aggrieved party whole. If a court orders specific performance, it simply tells a defendant to do that which he or she has contractually promised. Courts generally prefer to award money damages for a breach of contract. Nevertheless, the court will enforce the terms of a contract by requiring performance when the goods are unique and cannot be purchased elsewhere.

Montanile v. Botticelli deals with whether the sale of rare baseball cards is the type of item that gives rise to the equitable remedy of specific performance.

MONTANILE v. BOTTICELLI
2009 WL 196423 (E.D., VA.)

Montanile brought suit against Botticelli for events originating with Botticelli's unsuccessful attempt to purchase vintage baseball cards from Montanile. Montanile's complaint claimed that Botticelli had her falsely arrested and then maliciously prosecuted.

On or about July 16, 2006, Botticelli ordered six vintage baseball cards from Montanile, at the cost of $7,800. Montanile insured and shipped the cards to Botticelli via UPS on August 30, 2006. Botticelli declared that he never received the cards. Montanile alleges that UPS failed to properly deliver the package. She states that she told Botticelli she had filed a claim for the misplaced package with UPS and that the matter would be settled civilly by a refund when UPS remitted the funds.

Botticelli met with the police department in Fairfax County, Virginia and secured a warrant for Montanile's arrest. He accused Montanile of obtaining money by false pretenses. Montanile was subsequently arrested, jailed for two weeks in New Jersey, and then extradited to Virginia, where she was released after posting bail. The charges against her were ultimately dismissed. Montanile seeks $5 million in compensatory damages and $5 million in punitive damages against Botticelli.

Botticelli submitted a Counterclaim against Montanile requesting specific performance of their agreement. The Counterclaim alleges that Montanile paid Botticelli for the six baseball cards with a check in the amount of $7,820, which Montanile cashed. For weeks, Botticelli did not receive the cards. He e-mailed Montanile numerous times and requested a tracking number for the shipment. Montanile responded first by telling Botticelli that his shipment was still being processed, then that the package was scheduled to ship later in the week, and later, when Botticelli threatened to ask for a refund, that she was waiting "for payments to clear our bank" and that the package should have been on its way.

When, approximately six weeks after ordering the baseball cards, Botticelli told her that he was planning to meet with the police because he had not received the cards and Montanile was ignoring his e-mails and phone calls, Montanile told him that the package had not yet shipped because she was still waiting for one card to arrive. The next day, Montanile e-mailed Botticelli to tell him that the package had shipped. The following day, Botticelli received a sealed, empty box. He e-mailed Montanile to request an immediate refund. Montanile never delivered the baseball cards and did not refund the $7,820. Botticelli alleges that Montanile never actually possessed the baseball cards.

Botticelli's claim for specific performance requests the tender of the six rare baseball cards he ordered in the condition in which they were advertised at the time of sale. Montanile moved to dismiss the Counterclaim. This motion is before the Court.

Botticelli's counterclaim requests specific performance of the agreement that he and Montanile reached: that he would pay $7,820 for six vintage baseball cards. He claims to have no adequate remedy at law because the baseball cards are rare, highly unique, and specialized goods. Botticelli requests "specific performance of the agreement ... that Plaintiff tender the six rare baseball cards in the condition advertised at the time of sale."

Specific performance is an equitable remedy that may be considered where the remedy at law is inadequate and the nature of the contract would allow specific enforcement without great practical difficulties. A remedy at law is not adequate if it is partial; instead, an adequate remedy at law must reach the end intended, and actually compel a performance of the duty in question. Specific performance is addressed to the reasonable and sound discretion of the court. A contract must be complete and certain and the essential elements of price and terms of sale must have been agreed upon before a court of equity will specifically enforce the contract.

Here, Botticelli has alleged that the parties entered into a "valid and enforceable agreement for the sale, delivery and purchase of the six rare baseball cards," that he performed by paying for the cards, and that Montanile failed to perform by never sending him the cards. Looking at the face of the Counterclaim, it appears that Botticelli has pled a claim for specific performance.

Montanile suggests that the issue is "moot" because she will reimburse the defendant as soon as UPS pays her the insurance proceeds for the lost baseball cards. Montanile's promise that she will refund Botticelli's money at some point in the future does not serve to make the issue of specific performance moot. First, Botticelli's claim requests specific performance, not a refund. Second, he has pled facts sufficient to allege that Montanile did not perform the contract. Montanile's statement that she will refund the payment at some indefinite point in the future-depending on the outcome of a pending insurance dispute-has no bearing whatsoever on the merits of Botticelli's claim, which alleges that a breach of contract has already occurred. Montanile's statement that Botticelli will be reimbursed after UPS pays her does not make Botticelli's claim against her moot. The Court will not dismiss the claim for specific performance.

For the foregoing reasons, the Court will deny Plaintiff's Motion to Dismiss Defendant's Counter-claim.

SECTION 7.12
PROBLEM CASES

1. The New York Yankees told the City of New York that they were going to play their home opening series with the Detroit Tigers in Denver instead of at Yankee Stadium. The City of New York filed for injunctive relief to prevent the implementation of that agreement with the City of Denver. The facts show that after extensive renovations to Yankee Stadium were made by the City, it was discovered that there were certain structural flaws in the bleachers in right and left field. Additional permanent repairs were scheduled to be made between the close of the last baseball season and the opening game of the new season. Those plans were done with the approval of the Yankees. Nevertheless, the Yankees requested a guarantee that the repairs would be completed in a timely manner at the start of the

new baseball season. The City stated that under the worse case scenario, only 1,000 to 2,000 seats would be unavailable for the Yankees' home opener. Nevertheless, this information led to the Yankees scheduling their home opener in Denver. Is the City of New York entitled to an injunction to prevent the Yankees from playing in Denver even though the repairs had not been completed but only 2,000 seats would have been unavailable for the Yankees home opener? **City of New York v. New York Yankees, 458 N.Y.S. 2d 486 (N.Y., 1983).**

2. Brett Michaels and Pamela Anderson Lee sought a Temporary Restraining Order to prevent the dissemination of a videotape in which Michaels and Lee had a registered copyright. The videotape showed the two high profile plaintiffs engaging in sexual intercourse. Internet Entertainment Group, Inc., claimed that it obtained the videotape from a purported "agent" of Michaels, who allegedly sold the tape to the Internet Entertainment Group for $15,000. Will Michaels and Lee be successful in blocking the distribution of the tape since IEG obtained a copy of the videotape from a third person? Will the distribution of the tape cause irresponsible harm? **Pamela Lee Anderson v. Internet Entertainment Group, Inc. 5 F. Supp. 2d 823 (C.D. Cal., 1998).**

3. The State of Washington enacted an "Erotic Sound Recordings Statute" which subjected all distributors of sound recordings to civil and criminal proceedings for distribution to minors of "erotic material." A number of recording artists filed a declaratory judgment against the state in an attempt to have the court determine that the statute violated their substantive due process right. Is a declaratory judgment a proper action in order to invalidate a statute which is believed to be unconstitutional? **Soundgarden v. Bikenberry, 871 P. 2d 1050 (Wash., 1994).**

4. Star Magazine published an article about Rodney Dangerfield entitled, "Vegas Casino Accuses Candy Shack Funnyman; Rodney Dangerfield Swills Vodka by the tumblerful, smokes pot all day and uses cocaine." Dangerfield sued Star Magazine for defamation and requested punitive damages. The purpose of punitive damages is to punish the wrongdoer, and this is accomplished by awarding money based on the net worth of the defendant. Star Magazine's statement of operation for the fiscal year reflected a net loss. Dangerfield, however, argued that the financial condition of Star's parent owner is relevant to the tabloid's financial condition and should have been disclosed to the jury. Is the comedian correct? **Rodney Dangerfield v. Star Editorial, Inc., 25 Media L. Rep. 1379 (9th Cir., 1996).**

For more information on nominal damages, see the following internet reference:

- **www.seyfarth.com/practice/labor/articles/ll_1221.html**
  An article about a Supreme Court decision regarding nominal damages is located at this address.

KEY TERMS

Compensatory Damages	Prohibitory Injunction
Declaratory Judgment	Punitive Damages
Equity	Recision
Injunction	Reformation
Judicial Remedies	Remedies at Law
Liquidated Damages	Remedies in Equity
Mandatory Injunction	Restitution
Nominal Damages	Specific Performance
Permanent Injunction	Temporary Restraining Order
Preliminary Injunction	Warsaw Convention

CHAPTER 8

CYBERLAW

SECTION 8.1
INTRODUCTION

The internet has had a profound impact on the lives of many people with more than one billion individuals going online each day. Billions of dollars in business are transacted annually with this technology. People frequently purchase products online and booking a vacation over the internet has become routine. In fact, e-commerce revenues topped one trillion dollars in 2004 with the United States accounting for more than half of this figure. A new worldwide communications system has also emerged with e-mail transmissions, instant messages, text messaging, Black Berrys and the World Wide Web. In fact, mobile eCommerce revenues in the US alone are projected to reach $23.8 billion by 2015. A primary driver to this increase in electronic communication is Smartphone ownership and corresponding mobile internet use. In terms of online purchase of physical goods, a rising trend in using handsets is anticipated to research products, compare prices and buy online while the consumer is out shopping or traveling.[1]

The emergence of this new technology, however, has not been without its share of legal questions such as whether a person may use something posted on a website without violating the copyright laws; may an employer monitor the e-mail accounts of its employees; and whether a person can defame another through an internet posting? The internet may be a relatively new phenomenon but the protection of a person's right is not. The courts simply apply traditional principles of property, contract, and tort law to answer the myriad of legal issues involving electronic commerce and e-mail communications.

The logical place to start a discussion concerning the law of the internet is with an examination of the basic principles of intellectual property. This area of the law deals with creations of the mind and includes copyrights, patents and trademarks.

SECTION 8.2
COPYRIGHT LAW

A **copyright** is the legal protection given to the creator of an original work and the recognized symbol for copyright is ©. Examples of such literary and artistic endeavors include a song, book, computer program, video game and musical to name a few.

The owner of a copyright enjoys a number of valuable property rights, including the exclusive ability to reproduce and distribute copyrighted materials, display the work publicly, or create a derivative product, such as the development of a screenplay from a novel. Surprisingly, it is not necessary to register the materials with the United States Copyright Office in order to secure legal protection. Federal registration merely creates an official record of the copyright. Protection takes effect as soon as the work of authorship is recorded in some fashion–from writing it down on a piece of paper to storing the information on a computer disc.

The unauthorized distribution of a copyrighted work constitutes an **infringement** and allows the registered owner of the copyright to seek legal redress, including the recovery of monetary damages, attorneys fees, and court costs. A willful violation of a copyright, such as the "bootlegging" of music for resale, or counterfeiting expensive handbags, may also result in criminal prosecution.

The **Copyright Act** does allow a person to use protected materials without permission under very limited circumstances. This exception is called "fair use" and permits the utilization of a copyrighted work for the restricted purpose of criticism, comment, news reporting, teaching, scholarship, or research. The standard for judging whether the purpose of a copyrighted work is a "fair use" is based upon four factors:

1. The purpose and character of the use, including whether such application is of a commercial nature or is for non-profit educational purposes;

2. The nature of the copyrighted work;

3. The amount and substantiality of the portion used in relation to the copyrighted work as a whole; and

4. The effect of the use upon the potential market for the copyrighted work.

A book review or the quoting of a passage from a book for a term paper would be an example of "fair use" of copyrighted material. However, the photocopying of a text book for resale to other students would be a copyright infringement.

As noted by the United States Copyright Office the distinction between fair use and infringement may not always be clear and easily defined. There is no magic amount of words, lines, or paragraphs that may safely be used without permission. Also, merely acknowledging the source of the copyrighted material does not substitute for obtaining permission.[2]

The 1961 Report of the Register of Copyrights on the General Revision of the U.S. Copyright Law provides a series of examples that courts have regarded as fair use: "quotation of excerpts in a review or criticism for purposes of illustration or comment; quotation of short passages in a scholarly or technical work, for illustration or clarification of the author's observations; use in a parody of some of the content of the work parodied; summary of an address or article, with brief quotations, in a news report; reproduction by a library of a portion of a work to replace part of a damaged copy; reproduction by a teacher or student of a small part of a work to illustrate a lesson; reproduction of a work in legislative or judicial proceedings or reports; incidental and fortuitous reproduction, in a newsreel or broadcast, of a work located in the scene of an event being reported."[3]

The safest approach is to always obtain permission from the copyright owner before using copyrighted material. The Copyright Office, however, is unable to grant this permission. When it is not possible to obtain permission, the utilization of copyrighted items should be avoided unless the doctrine of fair use would clearly apply to the situation.[4]

Would the reader anticipate a copyright problem involving a mother's use of "Let's Go Crazy" by Prince as background music to a thirty-second video of her son dancing? Universal, the administrator of the Prince composition has filed suit against the parent maintaining that the video violates copyright law. It has been predicted that this litigation may help define the limits of "fair use" in the digital age.[5]

As for the allegations in the suit, counsel for the mother argued that the video was "noncommercial and transformative" and she only used a small portion of the song so that there is "no plausible market harm" to Prince. Universal countered that there's no such thing as "obvious" fair use, and copyright holders aren't required to consider fair use before sending a notice to stop the use of the perceived infringement. It also maintained that the video in question was not an obvious fair use exception.[6]

It appears that sending "takedown notices" from some large copyright holders to remove content from user-generated-content sites such as YouTube has become a standard practice. An attorney for Universal, who testified in the baby video case, noted that "at times Universal had to ask YouTube to remove hundreds of videos per week," and that during a two month period in 2007 alone more than one-thousand videos posting were removed based on Prince's music copyrights. Other copyright administrators have left alone videos utilizing their materials on YouTube, which typically offers to split ad revenue with copyright owners on videos that incorporate copyrighted music or video.[7]

The Prince music case has become very contentious with multiple motions being filed by the parties. The following case deals with a motion filed by Universal to dismiss the claim of the mother.

LENZ v. UNIVERSAL MUSIC CORP.
2008 WL 962102 (N.D. CAL., 2008)

On February 7, 2007, Plaintiff Stephanie Lenz, using the screen name, "edenza," videotaped her toddler son dancing in the family's kitchen to a song entitled "Let's Go Crazy" by an artist known at the time the song was recorded as Prince. Lenz uploaded the video from her computer to an Internet video hosting site, YouTube.com ("YouTube"). YouTube is a web site that provides "video sharing" or "user generated content." She titled the video "Let's Go Crazy." Lenz alleges that she posted the video for her friends and family to enjoy.

Universal owns the copyright to "Let's Go Crazy". Universal allegedly sent a takedown notice pursuant to the Digital Millennium Copyright Act ("DMCA") demanding that YouTube remove the "Let's Go Crazy" video because of an alleged copyright violation. YouTube removed the video and sent Lenz an email notifying her that it had done so in response to Universal's accusation of copyright infringement. Lenz sent YouTube a DMCA counter-notification demanding that her video be re-posted because it did not infringe Universal's copyrights. The "Let's Go Crazy" video was re-posted by YouTube on the YouTube website about six weeks later.

On July 24, 2007, Lenz filed the instant action seeking redress for Universal's alleged misuse of the DMCA takedown process, its accusation of copyright infringement, and its alleged intentional interference with her contractual use of YouTube's hosting services. Universal moved to dismiss the complaint.

Lenz claims that the DMCA notice Universal sent to YouTube concerning her "Let's Go Crazy" video violated 17 U.S.C. § 512(f).FN3 Section 512(f) that provides:

Any person who knowingly materially misrepresents under this section that material or activity is infringing shall be liable for any damages, including costs and attorney's fees, incurred by the alleged infringer ... as the result of the service provider relying upon such misrepresentations in removing or disabling access to the material or active claims to be infringing. 17 U.S.C. §512(f)

Lenz's complaint states that: "On information and belief," Universal knew or should have known that the video did not infringe any Universal copyrights on the date it sent the notice to YouTube. Lenz also asserts that her posting was "a self-evident non-infringing fair use under 17 U.S.C. § 107." Universal argues that Lenz does not properly plead the mental state required by § 512(f) as interpreted by the Ninth Circuit. Universal contends that §512(f) applies only where the party sending a notice has the subjective mental state of "actual knowledge" that it is making a material misrepresentation.

Congress included an expressly limited cause of action for improper infringement notifications, imposing liability only if the copyright owner's notification is a knowing misrepresentation. A copyright owner cannot be liable simply because an unknowing mistake is made, even if the copyright owner acted unreasonably in making the mistake, Rather, there must be a demonstration of some actual knowledge of misrepresentation of the party of the copyright owner. Juxtaposing the "good faith" provision of the DMCA with the "knowing misrepresentation" provision of that same statute reveals an apparent statutory structure that predicated the imposition of liability upon copyright owners only for knowing misrepresentations regarding allegedly infringing websites.

Universal argues that Lenz's complaint alleges an objective reasonableness, and that accordingly, Lenz's section 512(f) claim be dismissed.

Here, it is undisputed that the song "Let's Go Crazy" is copyrighted, and Universal does not concede that the posting is a fair use. Lenz fails to allege facts from which such a misrepresentation may be inferred. Lenz also fails to allege why her use of "Lets Go Crazy" was a "self-evident" fair use. Accordingly, Lenz's first claim will be dismissed, with leave to amend.

Playboy Enterprises, Inc., has achieved a great deal of notoriety for its magazine and product lines, and the publisher has been very aggressive in protecting its name and merchandise from unauthorized use. In fact, several lawsuits have been filed by this adult entertainment company dealing with claims of misappropriation of their property rights through various internet applications.

Playboy Enterprises, Inc. v. George Frena involves a case in which the defendant was accused of infringing on Playboy's copyright to a number of photographs from its magazine. The pictures of Playboy models were posted on the defendant's website for any of the site's paying customers to view and download. Frena admitted that the photographs were copied from Playboy materials, but he asserted the defense of "fair use" in order to negate any copyright violation. While the actual infringement by the defendant was minor in nature, the court found Frena liable for a copyright violation. The federal court judge noted that if this type of conduct became widespread, it would adversely affect Playboy and deny the publisher of considerable revenue.

PLAYBOY ENTERPRISES, INC. V. GEORGE FRENA
839 F. SUPP. 1552 (M.D. FLA., 1993)

George Frena operates a computer bulletin board service, Techs Warehouse BBS ("BBS"), that distributed unauthorized copies of Playboy's copyrighted photographs. For a fee, or to those who purchase certain products from Frena, anyone with an appropriately equipped computer can log onto BBS. Once logged on, subscribers may browse through different BBS directories to look at the pictures.

The **Copyright Act of 1976** gives copyright owners control over activities of commercial value. There is no dispute that Defendant Frena supplied a product containing unauthorized copies of a copyrighted work.

Defendant Frena argues that the affirmative defense of "fair use" precludes a finding of copyright infringement. "Fair use" describes limited and useful forms of copying and distribution that are tolerated as exceptions to copyright protection.

The **Copyright Act** mandates four factors which courts shall consider in determining fair use:

[T]he fair use of a copyrighted work. . . for purposes such as criticism, comment, news reporting, teaching, scholarship or research, is not an infringement of copyright. In determining whether the use made of a work in any particular case is a fair use, the factors to be considered shall include:

1. the purpose and character of the use, including whether such use is of a commercial nature or is for nonprofit educational purposes;

2. the nature of the copyrighted work;

3. the amount and substantiality of the portion used in relation to the copyrighted work as a whole; and

4. the effect of the use upon the potential market for or value of the copyrighted work.

Defendant Frena's use was clearly commercial. BBS was provided to those paying twenty-five dollars ($25) per month or to those who purchased products from Defendant Frena.

The second factor is the "nature of the copyrighted work." The copyrighted works in this case are in the category of fantasy and entertainment. Therefore, the second factor works against Frena's fair use defense.

Regarding the third factor, the amount and substantiality of the portion of the copyrighted work used, the Supreme Court has directed a qualitative evaluation of the copying of copyrighted work. That is, a small degree of taking is sufficient to transgress fair use if the copying is the essential part of the copyrighted work.

By pirating the photographs for which Playboy has become famous, Defendant has taken a very important part of Playboy's copyrighted publications.

The fourth factor, the "effect of the use upon the potential market for or value of the copyrighted work," is "undoubtedly the single most important element of fair use, since a proper application of fair use does not impair materially the marketability of the copied work." This factor poses the issue of "whether unrestricted and widespread conduct of the sort engaged in by the defendant would result in a substantially adverse impact on the potential market for or value of the plaintiff's present work." 3 Melville B. Nimmer, *Nimmer on Copyright* § 13.05[A], at 13.102.61-62 (1993).

Obviously, if this type of conduct became widespread, it would adversely affect the potential market for the copyrighted work. Such conduct would deny Playboy considerable revenue to which it is entitled for the service it provides.

Defendant Frena infringed Plaintiff's copyrights; specifically, the 170 image files in question in 50 of Plaintiff's copyrighted magazines. Plaintiff's Motion for Partial Summary Judgment is granted.

Playboy Enterprise, Inc. v. George Frena has become the landmark decision in this area and its rationale has continued to be followed in subsequent cases. For instance, **Sega Enterprises, Ltd.** successfully sued the owner of a bulletin board service for allowing copyrighted Sega video games to be made available to bulletin board subscribers.

**SECTION 8.3
TRADEMARK
INFRINGEMENT**

Federal trademark law is regulated by the **Lanham Act** which defines a **trademark** as a word, name, symbol or slogan which identifies the origins of a product or service from those of a competitor. The recognized symbol for trademark is ™. For instance, "Scotch" is a trademark for tape manufactured by 3M, and "Crest" is a form of toothpaste distributed by Proctor and Gamble. Four interconnected circles is the symbol for Audi automobiles, and "You deserve a break today" is a slogan registered to McDonald's. These trademarks are synonymous with a specific product and its reputation in the market place. Only the owner of a trademark may use the name or symbol on the product it was intended to identify.

A **trademark infringement** occurs when there is a likelihood of confusion as to the source, origin, or sponsorship of a product in a commercial environment. Elements that will be examined in order to determine whether there is a likelihood of confusion between the products include:

1.   Product similarity, including sight, sound, and meaning;

2.   Strength of the trademark as demonstrated by the amount of consumer recognition and degree of advertising;

3.   Evidence of actual confusion among consumers; and

4.   Similarities of channels used to market or sell the product.

Pepsi could not market a soda line called "Koka-Kola" and feature a polar bear sipping the soft drink. This would constitute a trademark infringement because of the obvious likelihood of confusion with Coca-Cola. Similarly, a fast-food restaurant specializing in fried chicken could not open a store named Kansas Fried Chicken and feature an elderly gentleman with a beard advertising the product under the banner "KFC."

Trademarks are categorized according to their inherent distinctiveness and degree of protection afforded by the law. In descending order of importance, these marks are: **(1)** fanciful, **(2)** suggestive, **(3)** descriptive, and **(4)** generic.

A **fanciful mark** consists of made-up words which serve as a product's brand name, such as Kodak, Sunoco, Cisco, and Pepto-Bismol. Because these marks are inherently distinctive, they receive the greatest protection against infringement.

A **suggestive mark** requires imagination in order to figure out the nature of the product which the mark represents. Ocean Spray, Handiwipes, Orange Crush, and Chicken of the Sea are examples of words which do not easily disclose the nature of the product which they represent. Through advertising, however, the public is able to associate the mark with a specific product. This category of trademark is also considered inherently distinctive and entitled to protection.

A **descriptive mark** does not identify the source of the goods. Rather, it describes some feature or characteristic of the product, such as Instant Hot, Quick Print, All Season, or No-Fat. This type of mark will not receive protection unless the term has achieved a secondary meaning. That distinction occurs when the public recognizes a particular mark as an indicator of quality. For instance, Rita's Water Ice has achieved a secondary meaning that everyone associates with water ice, even though Rita is a person's first name which would not normally be protected.

A **generic mark** enjoys no protection under the **Lanham Act,** since it merely describes a type of product regardless of its source. Examples include shredded wheat, pub, aspirin, cellophane, and orange juice.

It is not always easy to figure out which category is the proper fit for a mark, which frequently forces a party to seek court intervention when a trademark infringement is suspected.

The Chippendales are an adult entertainment group for women that dress in a provocative fashion while wearing tuxedo-wrist cuffs and a bowtie collar. This costume has become their brand of dress. However, is this brand so distinctive that it can be registered and protected under the trademark laws or is it merely a costume used by dancers in the entertainment world that it common? That is the issue in the following case.

In re Chippendales USA, Inc.
2010 WL 3894246 (C.A. Fed., 2010)

Chippendales USA, Inc. appeals a decision of the refusal to register the "Cuffs & Collar Mark" as inherently distinctive.

Chippendales, is in the business of providing adult entertainment services for women. In 1979, Chippendales performers began wearing tuxedo-wrist cuffs and a bowtie collar without a shirt as part of their act. This costume, referred to as the "Cuffs & Collar," was featured prominently in Chippendales' advertising and performances over the past several decades.

Chippendales filed an application seeking to register the Cuffs & Collar mark as inherently distinctive for "adult entertainment services, namely exotic danc-

ing for women," in the nature of live performances. Chippendales claimed that it was entitled to a registration on the ground that the mark was inherently distinctive. The examining attorney for the United States Patent and Trademark office ("PTO") refused to register the Cuffs & Collar because the mark was not inherently distinctive.

A mark is not inherently distinctive if it or a variation thereof, is in common use. The Trademark Trial and Appeal Board (Board) concluded that the Cuffs & Collar was a common basic shape design, because it is not unusual for exotic dancers to "wear costumes or uniforms which are ... revealing and provocative." The Board also concluded that the Cuffs & Collar was not unique or unusual in the particular field of use, because costumes generally are common to the field of exotic dancing. Alternatively, the Board concluded that the Cuffs & Collar mark was not unique or unusual because it was inspired by the ubiquitous Playboy bunny suit, which included cuffs, a collar and bowtie, a corset, and a set of bunny ears.

In general, trademarks are assessed according to a scale which evaluates whether word marks are "fanciful," "suggestive," "descriptive," or "generic." Word marks that are fanciful or suggestive are inherently distinctive. Descriptive marks that acquire secondary meaning may also qualify for protection, while generic marks generally cannot qualify for trademark protection at all.

The question is whether the PTO erred in holding that the Cuffs & Collar mark is not inherently distinctive. The three relevant factors that the Board considered are: "whether the ... [m]ark is a common basic shape or design," "whether it is unique or unusual in the particular field," and "whether it is a mere refinement of a commonly-adopted and well-known form of ornamentation for a particular class of goods viewed by the public as a dress or ornamentation for the goods or services." A finding that any one of these factors is satisfied may render the mark not inherently distinctive.

The first factor essentially asks whether the trade dress is common generally: for example, does it employ a basic shape or design such as a letter or geometric shape? The second factor asks whether the symbol is common in the particular field of use. The third factor asks whether or not the mark is a mere refinement of or variation on (an existing one) within the relevant field of use.

The Board did not err in concluding that the Cuffs & Collar mark is not inherently distinctive. The question is whether the Cuffs & Collar mark constitutes "a mere refinement of a commonly-adopted and well-known form of ornamentation for a particular class of goods." That test is satisfied if the Cuffs & Collar mark is a mere variant or refinement of a particular costume. The Board found the Cuffs & Collar mark not inherently distinctive because of the existence of the pervasive Playboy mark, which includes the cuffs and collar together with bunny ears.

The Playboy bunny suit, including cuffs and a collar, was widely used for almost twenty years before Chippendales' first use of its Cuffs & Collar. The Cuffs & Collar mark is very similar to the Playboy bunny costume, although the Cuffs & Collar mark includes no bunny ears and includes a bare-chested man instead of a woman in a corset. While the Playboy clubs themselves did not involve exotic dancing, the mark was registered for "operating establishments which feature food, drink and entertainment." Additionally, the pervasive association between the Playboy brand and adult entertainment leads us to conclude that the Board did not err in considering the mark to be within the relevant field of use. Thus, the Playboy registrations constitute substantial evidence supporting the Board's factual determination that Chippendales' Cuffs & Collar mark is not inherently distinctive.

We conclude that the Board's determination that the Cuffs & Collar mark was not inherently distinctive is supported by substantial evidence.

For fans of *Who Wants to be a Millionaire*, do you know the name of the company that was started in 1985 under the moniker, *Quantum Computer Services,* and has become the world's leader in interactive services with thirty million subscribers who transmit 450 million e-mails and 1.5 billion instant messages a day? If your final answer is *America on Line,* you are correct. For many years, "You've Got Mail" has greeted AOL users whenever a member has a new message. At the same time that this folksy voice is heard, the icon of a yellow envelope emerging from an old-fashioned mailbox appears, which provides the visual notice of a new message.

In 1998, AT&T added e-mail to its AT&T World Net Service along with a "You Have Mail" window which, like AOL, included an old-fashioned U.S. mailbox logo. This prompted a lawsuit from AOL for trademark infringement. The court held that the phrase "You've Got Mail" consisted of common English words used as a mark for their ordinary meaning, so that the phrase cannot be appropriated by AOL for their exclusive use. Numerous computer books and other internet providers describe the receipt of e-mail with variations of the "You Have Mail" theme. Therefore, the court reasoned that the words are generic and cannot be protected. The court also found that AOL's "Buddy List" and "Instant Message" designations are generic marks that anyone may use. **America Online, Inc. v. AT&T Corp., 64 F. Super. 2d 549 (E.D. Va., 1999).**

The United States Patent and Trademark Office maintains a website that allows a person to conduct an online search of its data bank to see if a name has already been registered. Their address is: **www.uspto.gov.**

SECTION 8.4
DOMAIN NAMES

The name of a business has very important marketing implications and can determine the success or failure of a business venture. With the growing popularity of the internet, companies strive to obtain a **domain name** or website that is identical to or similar with their product line or business identity. After all, logic dictates that a customer will try to locate a website by logging onto a name that is similar to the name of the company that the customer is seeking to find.

It is estimated that more than 196 million domain names have been registered worldwide, and these cyberspace addresses are the equivalent of physical street addresses. Aboutdomains.com notes that a domain name is an entity's own cyber-estate that has value depending upon its contents and address. Every domain name contains two or more elements separated by periods or "dots." The last part of the address is the top level domain and includes abbreviations such as .com, .net, .org, .edu, .biz, .info, .mil, and .gov. These designations are made according to the purpose of the website. For instance, ".edu" is associated with an educational institution, and ".gov" refers to a governmental affiliation. The information to the left of this identifier is the second-level domain.

Domain names have become so widely accepted that they are now featured on billboards, in magazines, and on business cards.

While businesses that do not compete against each other can share variations of a similar name, only one entity can register a specific domain name. For instance, the name "eagles" may refer to a football team, rock group, investigative service, wildlife refuge, or the Boy Scouts. However, only one of these entities may be assigned the domain name **www.eagles.com.** Therefore, trademark disputes involving domain names have been the source of a great deal of litigation.

Domain names are assigned on a first-come, first-served basis without any type of investigation by the registering company of whether the name violates a prior trademark.

This absence of a monitoring system has encouraged a number of entrepreneurs to register the domain names of well-known companies or individuals in the hope of exacting a financial reward when the trademark owner or famous person wishes to use the name as an internet address. Others purposely register misspellings or variations of a name, anticipating that the site will be frequented by people who incorrectly type the address or who are unaware of how to properly spell the domain name. Since the enterprise is paid by advertisers for each visit or "hit" to the site, this practice can be financially rewarding. This "bad faith" intent to profit from the reputation of another person's name is called "cyberpiracy" or "cybersquatting."

In order to protect businesses and consumers against the improper registration of domain names and to promote the growth of electronic commerce, Congress enacted the **Anticybersquatting Consumer Protection Act.** This legislation makes it difficult for entrepreneurs to lay claim to a domain name that is similar to a well-known person, company, or product line for the purpose of receiving a windfall profit.

Testimony was presented during the Congressional hearings on this piece of legislation to illustrate some of the many abuses that have surfaced involving domain names. For instance, when Mobile and Exxon went public with their proposed merger, an individual registered every possible variation of a resulting domain name, including **"mobil-exxon.com," "exxon-mobil.com,"** and **"mobilexxon.com."** Similarly, a representative of Warner Brothers reported that the company was asked to pay $350,000 for the rights to the domain names of **"warner-bros-records.com"** and **"warnerpictures.com."**

The **Anticybersquatting Consumer Protection Act** prohibits the registration or use of a domain name that is identical to, confusingly similar with, or dilutive of a trademark or name of another with the bad faith intent to profit from the goodwill of that mark. Not only may the cyberpirate lose the ownership of the domain name, but the entrepreneur may be required to pay actual damages to the aggrieved party, such as lost profits, or statutory damages in an amount no less than $1,000 and not exceeding $100,000 per domain name. These damages can increase quickly, to surprisingly high amounts.

One of the major ways in which cybersquatters can profit from domain names is through online advertisements, which is a thriving business. Advertisers pay between 10 and 25 cents each time an internet user clicks on one of their ads posted on a website, and according to the Interactive Advertising Bureau Internet, advertising revenues in the U.S. during the first six months of 2010 were $12.1 billion. This figure included banner ads, rich media, digital video and sponsorships.[8] **Electronics Boutique Holding Corp. v. Zuccarini, 54 U.S.P.Q. 2d 1705 (E.D. Pa., 2000)** involved a cypersquatter who improperly registered the domain name "Electronics Boutique" in a variety of misspellings in order to generate advertising revenue from each site visit. Statutory damages in the amount of $500,000 were awarded to the plaintiff in this case, along with legal costs, because of this improper registration.

Mr. Zuccarini was sued a second time by a different domain name owner who objected to the defendant's tactics in registering names that were similar to his website address. In 2001, a Federal Court of Appeals in **Shields v. Zuccarini** found in favor of a graphic artist who marketed cartoons under the name joecartoon.com. Zuccarini registered five variations of the plaintiff's website address: joescartoon.com; joecarton.com; joescartons.com; joescartoons.com; and cartoonjoe.com. Visitors to a Zuccarini website were greeted by advertisements for other sites and for credit card companies. People were also "mouse-trapped," meaning that they were unable to exit the site without clicking through a succession of advertisements. The court found the work of the graphic artist to be famous and entitled to protection under the Anti-Cybersquatting Consumer Protection Act. The defendant was found to have purposely registered a series of names that were confusingly similar to that of the plaintiff for the sole purpose of diverting customers for profit. The magnitude of the problem was revealed by the testimony of Zuccarini himself who admitted that he owned more than three thousand web sites and earned between $800,000 and $1,000,000 a year from their use.

The Anticybersquatting Consumer Protection Act should send a clear signal to those entrepreneurs who improperly register a domain name by letting them know that they will be held accountable for their actions.

The **Internet Corporation for Assigned Names and Numbers (ICANN),** a non-profit corporation, is recognized by the United States government as the business which coordinates the management of the Internet's domain-name system and IP address numbers. It was created in 1998 by a broad coalition of Internet's business, academic, technical and user communities. Its core mission includes ensuring a secure and stable global internet. All those who register a domain name with this corporation are required to submit disputes to an approved dispute resolution service, or they must file a lawsuit against the domain-name holder in a court of proper jurisdiction. If the parties proceed to arbitration, either side may litigate an adverse determination in court. ICANN is located at **www.icann.com.**

The **World Intellectual Property Organization (WIPO)** is the leading dispute resolution service for disagreements arising out of the registration and use of internet domain names. This international organization has rendered hundreds of decisions involving domain names disputes dealing with a number of Fortune 500 companies and celebrity personalities. This organization's influence and the magnitude of the problem involving the use of domain names is demonstrated by the number of arbitration claims filed. In 1999, only one case was in dispute while in only part of 2010, the number of claims rose to 2,272. For instance, Julia Roberts brought a claim against Russell Boyd over his registration of the domain name **"juliaroberts.com,"** and she was successful in obtaining a transfer of the Internet address. The Arbitration Panel found that Boyd had improperly registered not only the domain name of Ms. Roberts, but that of several other famous movie and sport stars as well. **Julia Fiona Roberts v. Russell Boyd, WIPO Case No. D2000 - 0210.** Pizza Hut successfully retrieved the name **"pizzahut.org"** from an entrepreneur who registered the name in bad faith. **Pizza Hut v. R. J. Inc., WIPO Case No. D2000 - 0939.** The World Wrestling Federation was awarded the names of **"www.wwf.com"** and **"www.stonecold.com,"** even though these domain names had been previously registered to Matthew Bessette. The Arbitrators found that the domain names were confusingly similar to the marks **"WWF.com"** and **"stonecold.com." World Wrestling Enterprises, Inc. v. Matthew Bessette, WIPO Case No. D2000 - 0256.**

Yet all domain name disputes are not this easy to resolve. In order to obtain a disputed domain name, the complainant must prove three elements:

1. That the disputed domain name is identical or confusingly similar to the trademark or service mark to which it has rights;

2. That the respondent has no rights or legitimate interests with respect to the domain name; and

3. That the disputed domain name has been registered and is being used in bad faith.

One way to insure that an entity does not choose an improper domain name is to hire a professional service to determine if the contemplated name creates a conflict with an existing business. For example, an article published by Harvard Law School recommends the commissioning of a domain search organization such as Thompson and Thompson. This business can locate domain names that are similar to the name selected. I-Watch is a useful service that alerts users to when a new name is registered that may interfere with an existing domain name or trademark.

The Attorney General's Office of the United States has also become involved in domain name disputes and will seize control of a website's name that violates the law.

What comes to mind when a reader hears the word "sting"— a bee, a wrestler, a professional woman's basketball team, a junior hockey league team in St. Louis, or an elaborate confidence game involving undercover police? Gordon Sumner is a world-famous musician and recording artist who has used the name "Sting" for more than twenty-five years. When Sumner went to register the domain name **"sting.com,"** he found that the marker had already been registered, so he filed a claim with WIPO in order to retrieve the name. The Arbitration Panel denied his request, because the mark was not the singer's real name, and the term has various meanings in the English language. That decision follows.

WIPO ARBITRATION AND MEDIATION CENTER
GORDON SUMNER, A/K/A STING v. MICHAEL URVAN
CASE NO. D2000-0596 (2000)

---

1.   The Parties

1.1   The Complainant is Gordon Sumner, professionally known as "Sting." The Respondent is Michael Urvan, of Marietta, Georgia.

2.   The Domain Names and Registrar

2.1   The domain name, the subject of this Complaint is "sting.com."

3.   Factual Background

Complainant's Activities and Trademarks

3.1   In his Complaint, the Complainant asserted he is a world-famous musician, who has, for over twenty years, rendered high-quality musical services under his name, trademark and service mark STING.

3.2   The Respondent asserted that there are 20 trademark registrations of the word STING in the US, but none of them are registered by the Complainant. The word STING is a common word in the English language, and so registration of it as a domain name is not a violation of the Uniform Policy.

Respondent's Activities

3.3   During February of 2000, and again during May of 2000, the Respondent offered to sell the domain name to the Complainant for $25,000.00.

3.4   The Respondent registered the domain name in July 1995, approximately 5 years before this dispute was commenced.

4.   Parties' Contentions

The Complaint

4.1   The Complainant contends that each of the three elements specified in paragraph 4(a) of the Uniform Policy are applicable to the domain name which is the subject of this dispute.

4.2   In relation to element (i), the Complainant contends that the domain name is identical to the Complainant's unregistered trademark and service mark STING.

4.3   In relation to element (ii), the Complainant contends that the Respondent has no rights or legitimate interests in the domain name in issue.

4.4   The Complainant contends that evidence of bad-faith registration and use is established by the following circumstances. First, the Respondent offered to sell the domain name to the Complainant for $25,000. Secondly, the Respondent has used the domain name to link to the "Gun-Brokers.com" website. Thirdly, because the Complainant's STING mark has a strong reputation and is world-famous, the Respondent can make no good faith use of the domain name.

The Response

4.5   The Respondent admits that he registered the domain name "sting.com." However, the Respondent challenges the Complainant's claim to owning the STING mark, and exclusively associated with the Complainant and so entitled to protection against dilution.

5. Discussion and Findings

Domain name Identical or Confusingly Similar to Complainant's Mark

5.1   This Administrative Panel finds that the Complainant is a world-famous entertainer who is known by the name STING.

5.2   Although it is accepted that the Complainant is world-famous under the name STING, it does not follow that he has rights in STING *as a trademark or service mark*. Unlike the personal name in **Julia Fiona Roberts v. Russell Boyd,** the personal name in this case is also a common word in the English language, with a number of different meanings.

Domain Name Registered and Used in Bad Faith

5.3   The Complainant has not satisfied this Administrative Panel that the Respondent registered and is using the domain name in bad faith. The Respondent admitted that he offered to sell the domain name to the Complainant, but only after the Complainant solicited that offer. Although this evidence is *consistent* with the Complainant's contention that the Respondent acquired the domain name primarily for the purpose of selling it to the Complainant, this evidence does not *prove* that. This evidence is equally consistent with the Respondent's contention that he acquired the domain name five years ago in good faith.

6. Decision

6.1   This Administrative Panel decides that the Complainant has not proven each of the three elements in paragraph 4(a) of the Uniform Policy in relation to the domain name which is the subject of the Complaint.

What comes to mind when the reader thinks of the word "Madonna"— a religious icon, the entertainer, or a hospital? Pop star Madonna initiated a claim against Dan Parisi over the right to use the internet address "Madonna.com." Madonna has used her first name professionally for entertainment purposes for more than twenty years, and is the owner of a U.S. Trademark Registration for the name. Parisi paid $20,000 to purchase the registration for the disputed domain name and began operating it as a pornographic website. A WIPO Arbitration Panel ordered Parisi to transfer the domain name to Madonna, as it is her real name and has become synonymous in the minds of the public with the singer and her activities in the entertainment field; and the only plausible explanation for Parisi's actions was an intentional effort to trade upon the fame of Madonna's name for commercial gain.

WIPO Arbitration and Mediation Center
Madonna Ciccone a/k/a Madonna v. Don Parisi
and Madonna.com
Case No. D2000-0847 (2000)

1. The Parties

The Complainant is Madonna Ciccone, an individual professionally known as Madonna. The Respondent is **"Madonna.com,"** the registrant for the disputed domain name, located in New York or Dan Parisi, the listed contact for the domain name.

2. Factual Background

Complainant is the well-known entertainer Madonna. She is the owner of U.S. Trademark Registrations for the mark MADONNA for entertainment services and related goods.

Respondent is in the business of developing websites. On or about May 29, 1998, Respondent, through its business Whitehouse.com, Inc., purchased the registration for the disputed domain name for $20,000. On or about June 8, 1998, Respondent began operating an "adult entertainment portal website."

The word *"Madonna"* has the current dictionary definition of the Virgin Mary or an artistic depiction of the Virgin Mary, and is used by others as a trademark, trade name, and personal name.

3. Parties' Contentions

A. Complainant

Complainant contends that the disputed domain name is identical to the registered and common law trademark MADONNA in which she owns rights. She further contends that Respondent obtained and used the disputed domain name with the internet to attract internet users to a pornographic website for commercial gain based on confusion with Complainant's name and mark.

B. Respondent

Respondent claims that Complainant cannot show a legitimate interest in the domain name because Respondent (a) made demonstrable preparation to use the domain name for a bona fide business purpose; and (b) holds a bona fide trademark in the word MADONNA in Tunisia.

4. **Discussion and Findings**

A. **Lack of Rights or Legitimate Interests in Domain Name**

Complainant has presented evidence tending to show that Respondent lacks any rights or legitimate interest in the domain name. Respondent's claim of rights or legitimate interests is not persuasive.

Respondent has failed to provide a reasonable explanation for the selection of Ma-donna as a domain name. We find that name was selected and used by Respondent with the intent to attract for commercial gain, Internet users to Respondent's website by trading on the fame of Complainant's mark.

5. **Decision**

We find in favor of the Complainant. The disputed domain name is identical or confusingly similar to a trademark in which Complainant has rights; Respondent lacks rights or legitimate interests in the domain name; and the domain name has been registered and used in bad faith. Therefore, we decide that the disputed domain name **madonna.com** should be transferred to the Complainant.

The policy and rules of the World Intellectual Property Organization for domain name disputes, as well as the arbitration decisions rendered by this organization, may be found at: **www.arbiter.wipo.int/domains/index.html.**

SECTION 8.5
TRADEMARK DILUTION

Trademark infringement provides a clear remedy when someone adopts a name that is confusingly similar to a competing product. Can a merchant, however, utilize a well-known name to promote an unrelated product line? Coca-Cola is famous as a leading manufacturer of soft drinks. Enormous sums of money are spent to promote the consumption of this beverage. A clothing manufacturer hoping to cash in on the Coca-Cola name, develops a line of jeans called "Coca-Cola Blue." There is little chance of a consumer confusing the sale of pants with the purchase of a Diet Coke. Nevertheless, Coca-Cola can maintain that its image is being diluted by the sale of an unrelated product that uses the name Coca-Cola on the grounds that the clothing line could blur the public's instantaneous recognition of the beverage manufacturer.

This type of problem is remedied by the **Federal Trademark Dilution Act,** which was enacted to protect the owner of a famous mark from dilution regardless of the likelihood of confusion between the products.

In determining whether a name is distinctive and famous, the courts may consider such factors as:

A. The degree of distinctiveness of the mark;

B. The duration and extent of use of the mark;

C. The duration and extent of advertising the mark;

D. The geographic extent of the trading area in which the mark is used;

E. The channels of trade for the goods or services;

F. The degree of recognition of the mark in the trading areas used by the mark's owner and against whom the injunction is sought;

G. The nature and extent of use of similar marks by third parties; and

H. Whether the mark was registered.

Congress limited the application of the Federal Trademark Dilution Act to only those marks that are famous such as Pepsi, McDonald's, and Nike. An important advantage of the law is that the owner of the famous mark does not have to show actual competition between its product and that of the defendant. In other words, a firm that improperly uses a famous mark in an unrelated industry has still violated the law. For example, a clothing manufacturer that creates a line of summer dresses called Pepsi Lite has diluted the trademark of the soda company even though clothing has nothing to do with a soft drink.

The Federal Trademark Dilution Act defines dilution to mean the "lessening of the capacity of a famous mark to identify and distinguish goods or services, regardless of the presence or absence of (1) competition between the owner of the famous mark and other parties, or (2) likelihood of confusion, mistake, or deception."

Must there be proof of an actual economic injury to the trademark or is a technical violation of the Act sufficient to trigger the awarding of damages? That was the issue in a 2003 case that reached the Supreme Court of the United States. Victor Mosley opened a woman's lingerie and adult gift store named "Victor's Little Secret" much to the chagrin of Victoria's Secret. Mosley advertised the store's opening in a weekly magazine with the following advertisement: "GRAND OPENING. Just in time for Valentine's Day!" The ad featured "Intimate Lingerie for every woman," "Romantic Lighting," "Lycra Dresses," and "Adult Novelties/Gifts." The lingerie giant filed a lawsuit against Mosley for using a name that would tarnish and dilute the famous Victoria's Secret mark. The United States Supreme Court was unimpressed with the claim and found that a violation of the Act requires a showing of actual dilution of the mark, and not just the likelihood of dilution. This burden can only be established by objective proof of an injury to the economic value of the trademark.

To counter this decision and its high burden of proof, Congress revised the Federal Trademark Dilution Act in 2006 to make it clear that a plaintiff needs only show that the a defendant's mark is *likely* to cause dilution or blurring by tarnishment of a famous mark, regardless of the presence or absence of actual or likely confusion of competition or of an actual economic injury.

Most people can immediately identify Louis Vuitton products and their design In fact, the French company spends millions of dollars each year to advertising the uniqueness and sophistication of its luxury handbags and accessories. Also, no one would question the company's aggressive efforts to prevent others from infringing on their trademark by making "spin-offs" or counterfeit copies of their products. Louis Vuitton prominently displays a notice on its website that it has a zero tolerance policy against counterfeiting. For example, in 2004, there were to over 13,000 legal actions, more than 6,000 raids, over 947 arrests and the seizure of fake printing cylinders.[9] However, is it a trademark violation for a company to manufacture and distributes dog toys and bones called "Chewy Vuitton"? That is the issue in the following case.

Louis Vuitton Malletier S.A. v. Haute Diggity Dog, LLC
507 F.3d 252 (C.A. 4th, 2007)

Louis Vuitton Malletier (LVM) manufactures luxury handbags and accessories and commenced this action against Haute Diggity Dog, LLC, a corporation that sells pet products alleging trademark infringement. Haute Diggity Dog manufactures plush toys on which dogs can chew. The particular Haute Diggity Dog chew toys in question are small imitations of handbags that are labeled "Chewy Vuiton" and mimic LOUIS VUITTON handbags.

Haute Diggity Dog, LLC, sells a line of pet chew toys and beds whose names parody elegant high-end brands of products. These include– Chewy Vuiton (LOUIS VUITTON), Chewnel No. 5 (Chanel No. 5), Furcedes (Mercedes), Jimmy Chew (Jimmy Choo), Dog Perignonn (Dom Perignon), Sniffany & Co. (Tiffany & Co.), and Dogior (Dior). Haute Diggity Dog's "Chewy Vuiton" dog toys loosely resemble miniature handbags and undisputedly evoke LVM handbags of similar shape, design, and color. In lieu of the LOUIS VUITTON mark, the dog toy uses "Chewy Vuiton"; in lieu of the LV mark, it uses "CV"; and the other symbols and colors employed are imitations, but not exact ones, of those used in the LVM Multicolor and Cherry designs.

To prove trademark infringement, LVM must show that Haute Diggity Dog's use is likely to cause confusion. To determine whether the "Chewy Vuiton" product line creates a likelihood of confusion, we have identified several nonexclusive factors to consider: (1) the strength or distinctiveness of the plaintiff's mark; (2) the similarity of the two marks; (3) the similarity of the goods or services the marks identify; (4) the similarity of the facilities the two parties use in their businesses; (5) the similarity of the advertising used by the two parties; (6) the defendant's intent; and (7) actual confusion. These factors are not always weighted equally, and not all factors are relevant in every case.

Because Haute Diggity Dog's arguments with respect to the factors depend on whether its products are successful parodies, we consider first whether Haute Diggity Dog's products are indeed successful parodies of LVM's marks.

For trademark purposes, a parody is defined as a simple form of entertainment conveyed by juxtaposing the irreverent representation of the trademark with the idealized image created by the mark's owner. A parody must convey two simultaneous-and contradictory-messages: that it is the original, but also that it is not the original and is instead a parody. This second message must not only differentiate the alleged parody from the original but must also communicate some articulable element of satire, ridicule, joking, or amusement. Thus, a parody relies upon a difference from the original mark, presumably a humorous difference, in order to produce its desired effect.

When applying the criteria to the facts of this case, the "Chewy Vuiton" dog toys are successful parodies of LVM handbags and the LVM marks and trade dress used in connection with the marketing and sale of those handbags. The pet chew toy is obviously an irreverent, and indeed intentional, representation of an LVM handbag, albeit much smaller and coarser.

At the same time, the "Chewy Vuiton" dog toy is not the "idealized image" of the mark created by LVM. The differences are immediate, beginning with the fact that the "Chewy Vuiton" product is a dog toy, not an expensive, luxury Louis Vuitton handbag. Thus, "Chewy Vuiton" is not Louis Vuitton ("Chewy" is not "LOUIS" and "Vuiton" is not "VUITTON," with its two Ts); CV is not LV; the designs on the dog toy are simplified and crude, not detailed and distinguished. In short, the Haute Diggity Dog "Chewy Vuiton" dog toy deliberately conjures up the famous LVM marks and trade dress, but at the same time, it communicates that it is not the LVM product.

We conclude that the criteria are amply satisfied and that the "Chewy Vuiton" dog toys convey "just enough of the original design to allow the consumer to appreciate the point of parody," but stop well short of appropriating the entire marks that LVM claims.

Finding that Haute Diggity Dog's parody is successful, however, does not end the inquiry into whether "Chewy Vuiton" creates a likelihood of confusion. Haute Diggity Dog concedes that its marks are designed to be somewhat similar to LVM's marks. But that is the essence of a parody-the invocation of a famous mark in the consumer's mind, so long as the distinction between the marks is readily recognized. While a trademark parody necessarily copies enough of the original design to bring it to mind as a target, a successful parody also distinguishes itself and, because of the implicit message communicated by the parody, allows the consumer to appreciate it.

The differences are sufficiently obvious and the parody sufficiently blatant that a consumer encountering a "Chewy Vuiton" dog toy would not mistake its source or sponsorship on the basis of mark similarity. It is obvious that a "Chewy Vuiton" plush imitation handbag, which does not open and is manufactured as a dog toy, is not a Louis Vuitton handbag. LVM markets Louis Vuitton handbags through high-end fashion magazines, while "Chewy Vuiton" products are advertised primarily through pet-supply channels. "Chewy Vuiton" toys and Louis Vuitton products are neither sold nor advertised in the same way.

Recognizing that "Chewy Vuiton" is an obvious parody and applying the factors, we conclude that LVM has failed to demonstrate any likelihood of confusion. Accordingly, we affirm the judgment in favor of Haute Diggity Dog on the issue of trademark infringement.

SECTION 8.6
E-DEFAMATION

E-mail has clearly established itself as an effective method of communicating with other parties. People around the world have created e-mail addresses in order to receive and send messages. The transmission of the communication, however, can only be accomplished by the use of an online service such as America Online, Inc., Comcast, Verizon, or Prodigy.

Defamatory messages transmitted through the internet occur with some frequency, likely as the result of the impersonal and less formal nature of internet communications. Users often do not practice the same discretion and caution in sending instant messages or e-mails as when composing and mailing letters, and because e-mail messages lack voice contact, they are often less personal than telephone conversations. Web identities and e-mail addresses also provide internet users with a sense of anonymity in message-writing and web chats, which increases the likelihood that inappropriate statements will be made, and because of the ease with which duplicate copies of messages can be sent to others, more people are being exposed to false or inappropriate statements than would normally occur with the mailing of a letter.

A lawsuit for a defamatory e-mail transmission is still based upon established tort principles. The sender of the communication will be responsible if: **(1)** the transmission is false **(2)** it harms the reputation of another and **(3)** it is communicated to a third person. Therefore, the liability of the author of the defamatory internet transmission will be no different than if that communication was sent through the mail, posted on a billboard, or written in a newspaper. A more difficult issue concerns the liability of the e-mail service which is used to transmit the defamatory note. Publication of a false statement is a necessary element of a claim for defamation, and only the party or parties who publish the message can be subject to liability. In this way, a newspaper who prints a defamatory story written by a freelance reporter is liable for the false comment just as though it had authored the story itself. An internet service is also considered a publisher, since they took part in the distribution of the message. **Zeran v. America Online, Inc., 129 3rd 327 (4th Cir., 1997).** But should an internet service be held responsible for a false message because its server is used to transmit the defamatory communication? Unlike a newspaper or telegraph company whose publication of the false material can only occur through the direct participation of a representative of the company, an e-mail provider is similar to a telephone company that exercises no editorial control over the transmission. While newspapers can be responsible as the publisher of a defamatory comment, a telephone company is not liable. The responsibility of an internet service provider for defamation is the issue in **Lunney v. Prodigy Services Company.** In finding that an Internet service provider has no responsibility for the transmission of a defamatory message, the court concluded that the internet company had not participated in the preparation of the message, exercised any discretion or control over its content, or in any way assumed editorial responsibility.

ALEXANDER LUNNEY V. PRODIGY SERVICES COMPANY
1996 U.S. DIST. LEXIS 17090 (N.D. CALIF., 1996)

Usurping the name of Alexander Lunney, an imposter opened a number of accounts with Prodigy Services Company (Prodigy). The imposter posted two vulgar messages in Lunney's name on a Prodigy bulletin board and sent a threatening, profane electronic mail message in Lunney's name to a third person. Lunney has sued Prodigy, asserting that he has been stigmatized by being falsely cast as the author of these messages. The issue is whether Prodigy may be held liable for defamation. For the reasons that follow, we hold that the complaint against Prodigy was properly dismissed.

After opening several membership accounts with Prodigy under slightly different variants of the name Alex or Alexander Lunney, the imposter transmitted an e-mail message, under Lunney's name, to a local scoutmaster. The subject line of the message read **"How I'm Gonna' Kill U;"** the body was vulgar in the extreme. After receiving the e-mail, the scoutmaster alerted the police and they readily accepted Lunney's innocence in this episode.

Lunney sued Prodigy, claiming that Prodigy was derelict in allowing the accounts to be opened in his name, and was responsible for his having been stigmatized and defamed.

Lunney's defamation action is grounded in established tort principles. Although they were fashioned long before the advent of e-mail, these settled doctrines accommodate the technology comfortably.

As distinguished from e-mail communication, there are more complicated legal questions associated with electronic bulletin board messages, owing to the generally greater level of cognizance that their operators can have over them. In some instances, an electronic bulletin board could be made to resemble a newspaper's editorial page; in others it may function more like a "chat room." In many respects, an ISP bulletin board may serve much the same purpose as its ancestral version, but uses electronics in place of plywood and thumbtacks.

Lunney argues that because Prodigy, in its membership agreements, reserves for itself broad editorial discretion to screen its bulletin board messages, it should be liable as a publisher of such messages. Prodigy argues that while it reserves the right to screen its bulletin board messages, it is not required to do so, does not normally do so and, therefore, cannot be a publisher of electronic bulletin board messages posted on its system by third parties.

Even if Prodigy "exercised the power to exclude certain vulgarities from the text of certain bulletin board messages," this would not alter its passive character in "the millions of other messages in whose transmission it did not participate," nor would this compel it to guarantee the content of those myriad messages. In this case, Prodigy was not a publisher of the electronic bulletin board messages.

Lunney appealed this adverse determination to the United States Supreme Court, but the Justices refused to hear the appeal. This action by our top judiciary allows the New York appellate court decision to remain in place as valid law.

The **Communications Decency Act** was enacted by Congress in 1996 because of its desire to protect interactive computer services from the growing number of lawsuits being filed against internet providers as the result of the improper conduct of its customers. The legislature found that a growing number of Americans rely on this interactive media for an array of educational, political, cultural, and entertainment services. To promote the continued development of the internet, Congress concluded that immunity from suit was needed. As the court noted in **Zeran v. America Online, 129 F. 3ʳᵈ 327 (4ᵗʰ Cir., 1997):**

> Congress' purpose in providing immunity was evident. The amount of information communicated via interactive computer services is staggering. The specter of tort liability in an area of such prolific speech would have an obvious chilling effect. It would be impossible for service providers to screen each of their millions of postings for possible problems. Faced with potential liability for each message republished by their services, interactive computer service providers might choose to severely restrict the number and type of messages posted. Congress considered the weight of the speech interests implicated and chose to immunize service providers to avoid any such restrictive effect.

Section 230 of the Communications Decency Act indicates that "no provider or user of an interactive computer service shall be treated as the publisher or speaker of any information provided by another information content provider." In other words, a computer service has no responsibility to an injured party for the transmission of a defamatory message simply because its network is used to transmit the false message.

The protection afforded by this statute is so broad that America Online was found to have no liability for defamatory comments contained in the *Drudge Report,* even though AOL paid Matt Drudge to include his investigative report on its service. The report provides the exclusive writings of this internet journalist with links to many online news sources. America Online was not a passive party to the defamatory transmission. Rather, it actively advertised the Report by issuing a press release which made "clear the kind of material Drudge would provide to AOL subscribers –gossip and rumor –and urged potential subscribers to sign onto AOL in order to obtain the benefits of the Drudge Report." **Blumenthal v. Drudge 992 F. Supp. 44 (D. D.C., 1998.)**

The Federal Court of Appeals in 2003 reaffirmed the grant of immunity to internet providers in **Carafano v. Metrosplash.com**. Star Trek fans may remember Ms. Carafono as the actress, Chase Masterson, who played Leeta on *Deep Space Nine*. In an identity theft case, an unknown person created a dating profile for the actress on Matchmaker.com that was sexually suggestive, threatening, and contained Carafano's home address and telephone number. Carafano sued the dating service for the disclosure of her personal information.

Matchmaker.com countered by asserting immunity under the Communications Decency Act as a provider of an interactive computer service. The appellate court dismissed the lawsuit and noted that Congress made a clear policy choice by refusing to impose tort liability on companies that serve as intermediaries for the injurious messages posted by others.

In 1997, the Supreme Court limited the application of the Act by striking down that part of the law that prohibited the transmission of indecent or patently offensive materials over the internet. The continued immunity for internet providers, however, was unaffected by this ruling.

A second clause in the Communications Decency Act provides that no civil liability will attach if the internet service makes a good faith effort to actively police access to obscene, violent, harassing, or otherwise objectionable material on its site. In other words, this provision will protect an internet service provider that wishes to affirmatively oversee or edit information posted on its bulletin board or website service.

The immunity afforded by the Communications Decency Act is quite broad. However, does the law protect the operator of an adult web site in which an advertisement by a person purporting to be looking for other "swingers" was falsely placed? That is the issue in **Doe v. Friendfinder Network, Inc.**

DOE V. FRIENDFINDER NETWORK, INC.
540 F. SUPP.2D 288 (D. N.H., 2008)

The plaintiff has sued Friendfinder Network, Inc. and others arising out of the placement of allegedly false and unauthorized personal advertisements about her on their websites and others. The defendants move to dismiss the plaintiff's claims on the grounds that they are barred by the Communications Decency Act.

The defendant operates a number of "web communities" where members can meet each other through online personal advertisements, including "AdultFriendFinder.com," which bills itself as "the World's Largest Sex and Swinger Personal Community." In June 2005, a profile of a female member under the screen name "petra03755" was created on the AdultFriendFinder site. The profile identified the member as a recently separated 40-year-old woman who was seeking "Men or Women for Erotic Chat/E-mail/ Phone Fantasies and Discreet Relationship."

The plaintiff alleges she had nothing to do with creating the profile and that she does not engage in the "promiscuous sexual lifestyle" or the "perverse" sexual activities it describes. The plaintiff does not know the true identity of the user who created the profile-only that he or she accessed the AdultFriendFinder website through the Dartmouth College computer network. The plaintiff complains that the defendants did nothing to verify the accuracy of any of the information posted.

After the plaintiff contacted the defendants about the offending profile, they agreed to remove it. As a result, when other members thereafter attempted to access the profile, the site displayed the message, "Sorry, this member has removed his/her profile." The plaintiff asserts that this message was itself false in communicating that she was a member of the service and that the profile had been hers in the first place. She further faults the defendants for doing nothing to inform other users that the profile "had in fact been bogus and false."

The plaintiff claims a variety of harm: damage to her reputation; further alienation from her husband, embarrassment, loss of "important employment opportunities" and emotional distress, including anxiety over the lingering effect of the false profile, which has allegedly necessitated psychological treatment.

Under the Communications Decency Act ("CDA"), no provider or user of an interactive computer service shall be treated as the publisher or speaker of any information provided by another information content provider. The CDA further dictates that no cause of action may be brought and no liability may be imposed under any State or local law that is inconsistent with this section. These provisions bar state law claims against interactive computer services for publishing content obtained from another information content provider.

CDA Section 230 immunity should be broadly construed so as to effectuate what it identified as Congress's policy choice not to deter harmful online speech through the route of imposing tort liability on companies that serve as intermediaries for other parties' potentially injurious messages. To achieve this goal, the court reasoned, § 230 immunity extends beyond publisher liability in defamation law to cover any claim that would treat [a service provider] as the publisher, regardless of the plaintiff's theory of action.

This immunity plainly extends to a number of the acts and omissions alleged in the plaintiff's complaint. The plaintiff does not question that each of the defendants qualifies as a "provider or user of an interactive computer service" within the meaning of § 230. Thus, because the only role the defendants played in the initial appearance of the profile was as the publisher of information supplied by "petra03755," the plaintiff cannot call the defendants to answer for that under state law.

The bar on publisher liability also extends to the plaintiff's charges that certain features of the Adult-FriendFinder service facilitated the submission of false or unauthorized profiles. Imposing liability on that basis would eviscerate Section 230 immunity. § 230 bars the plaintiff's claims that the defendants acted wrongfully by encouraging the anonymous submission of profiles or by failing to verify that a profile corresponded to the submitter's true identity. The plaintiff offers no argument to the contrary.

A service provider's immunity as a publisher also extends to its "exercise of a publisher's traditional editorial functions" with respect to third-party information, "such as deciding whether to publish, withdraw, postpone or alter" it. A number of courts have reasoned that construing the CDA more narrowly would frustrate what they see as one its primary objectives by discouraging service providers from voluntarily regulating third-party contributions to their websites. Rather than risking lawsuits over allegedly failed efforts toward that end, these courts have reasoned, service providers would simply disallow-or allow-all third-party speech regardless of content, transforming the Internet into a highly sterile-or highly polluted-medium, in contravention of the policies the Act was explicitly intended to further.

Under the CDA, the plaintiff cannot recover from the defendants.

SECTION 8.7
THE EMBARRASSING
INTERNET
PHOTOGRAPHS

PROBLEM EIGHT

PARK, BROWN & SMITH, P.C.
ATTORNEYS AT LAW
MEMORANDUM

To: All Law Clerks

FROM: Peter Smith, Esquire

RE: Embarrassing Photographs

Tony Roberts contacted the firm about an incident that occurred in the locker room following the Stallions clinching of a playoff spot. With five seconds remaining on the clock, the team lined up to kick a fifty-yard field goal. When the ball was snapped, the quarterback faked the kick and threw a pass to an open receiver, who walked into the end zone. The Stallions erupted in wild jubilation. The players continued their celebration in the locker room as they dressed and talked to the reporters.

This crazy scene was witnessed by a ten-year-old fan who had won a drawing to be the team's mascot for the day. Little Aaron Berman was in awe as he snapped picture after picture with his dad's digital camera. The next day, Aaron wrote an essay about his experience and sent the message in an e-mail to his friends along with the photographs of the players. Unfortunately, the pictures showed some of the players in various stages of undress. Things got out of hand when Aaron's uncensored shots were e-mailed around the country. Tony learned of this delicate problem and called hoping that we could stop the distribution of the pictures on the Internet. I immediately contacted the Internet service providers, who either ignored my calls or claimed that there was nothing they could do. This response is unacceptable. I am sure Internet service providers have the technology to trace the path of the photographs from Aaron's computer and to put a stop to the distribution of these pictures. They could also send a message to its subscribers to honor the privacy of the players by deleting the unauthorized images.

I would like to file a lawsuit against the Internet service providers whose sites were used to transmit the pictures. Read **Joe Doe v. Franco Productions** and let me know the answer to the following questions:

1. What arguments may we make on behalf of the Stallions against the Internet service providers?

2. What defenses will the Internet service providers raise to our lawsuit?

3. Who should succeed in the case? Please explain your answer so I will know whether the case is worth pursuing. If helpful, you may include materials from this chapter on "Defamation and the Internet."

JOHN DOE V. FRANCO PRODUCTIONS
2000 WL 816779 (N.D. ILL., 2000)

The Plaintiffs were intercollegiate athletes who, without their knowledge or consent, were videotaped in various states of undress by hidden cameras in restrooms, locker rooms, or showers. The resulting videotapes were sold by various means, including websites hosted by Genuity.net and TIAC.net that included still images of the Plaintiffs taken from the videotapes. They instituted this action to obtain monetary damages and injunctive relief for intrusion into the Plaintiffs' seclusion against the alleged producers and distributors of the videotapes, and against defendants GTE Corporation and GTE Internet (together "GTE"), the respective successors to Genuity.net and TIAC.net. The Court dismissed Plaintiffs' previous complaint, finding that GTE was a service provider and therefore immune from suit under the **Communications Decency Act, 47 U.S.C. §230 ("CDA").** After the Court granted leave to amend, Plaintiffs filed their amended complaint. They re-alleged their previous claims, this time making their allegations against GTE in their capacity as website host. Presently, GTE moves this court to dismiss the amended complaint against them.

Plaintiffs assert that they are seeking to hold GTE liable for their "own conduct" in "knowingly failing to restrict content" under *§230 (c)(2). Section 230(c)*

(2) provides immunity to those who restrict or enable restriction to objectionable material. Thus, Plaintiffs reason because GTE did not restrict or enable restriction to objectionable material, they are not entitled to immunity under this section. However, what Plaintiffs ignore is that by seeking to hold GTE liable for their decision not to restrict certain content, it is seeking to hold them liable in a publisher's capacity.

The **CDA** creates federal immunity against any cause of action that would hold computer service providers liable for information originating from a third party. Immunity under the **CDA** is not limited to service providers who contain their activity to editorial exercises or those who do not engage in web hosting, but rather, "Congress… provided immunity even where the interactive services provider has an active, even aggressive role in making available content prepared by others." **Blumenthal v. Drudge, 992 F. Supp. 44, 52 (D.D.C., 1998).**

By offering web hosting services which enable someone to create a web page, GTE is not magically rendered the creator of those web pages. *See 47 U.S.C. (C)(1).*

For the reasons set forth above, the Court grants Defendant GTE's motion to dismiss.

ANSWER SHEET
PROBLEM EIGHT

Name _____

Please Print Clearly

1. What arguments my we make on behalf of the Stallions in order to assert a cause of action against the internet service providers?

_____

_____

_____

_____

_____

_____

_____

_____

_____

2. What defense will the internet service providers raise to our lawsuit?

_____

_____

_____

_____

_____

_____

_____

_____

3. Who should succeed in winning the case? Please explain your answer
    so I may know whether the case is worth pursuing. If helpful, you may
    include materials from the subsection of the book on "Defamation and the
    Internet."

_____

_____

_____

_____

_____

_____

_____

_____

_____

_____

_____

_____

_____

_____

_____

_____

_____

_____

_____

_____

SECTION 8.8
E-PRIVACY

The internet has opened new avenues of communication for millions of people. From e-mail transmissions to researching the purchase of a product, this electronic information super highway has something for everyone. The technology, however, comes with a price—an intrusion into the user's privacy. A personal message sent to another can be duplicated with little effort and sent to hundreds of people. The online ordering of a product may result in the disclosure to a third person of personal information, such as a telephone, credit card, or social security number. Visits to the World Wide Web leave a digital trail which can be retrieved by a merchant or marketing service. Even a person's e-mail account at work may be monitored by an employer.

Whether the offending conduct is actionable will frequently depend on whether the intrusion is substantial and highly offensive to a reasonable person or if legislation is in place to prohibit the conduct in question.

People have the right to be left alone and to enjoy their privacy. This principle has its foundation in the Bill of Rights and has long been recognized as a common law tort. For instance, **the Restatement (Second) of Torts** defines invasion of privacy as:

> One who intentionally intrudes, physically or otherwise, upon the solitude or seclusion of another or his private affairs or concerns, is subject to liability for invasion of his privacy, if the intrusion would be highly offensive to a reasonable person.

Placing a small video camera in the ceiling of the bathroom at work would be a substantial and highly offensive intrusion into a person's privacy. Likewise, repeated and unwarranted telephone calls at all hours of the day and night to a former spouse would be actionable.

This tort will have equal application in the world of electronic commerce when a cause of action arises in one of the following contexts:

1. Misappropriation of a person's name or likeness for another's financial gain;

2. Disclosure of a private embarrassing fact;

3. Publicity that places a person in a false light; and

4. An unreasonable intrusion upon a person's privacy.

The right of privacy specifically protects a person against the commercial exploitation of that individual's name, likeness or image without permission. This tort is sometimes called **appropriation**. A picture of a couple holding hands in the park which is captured by a photographer cannot be used on the cover of a romance novel without the couple's permission. Likewise, a person's name or likeness may not be commercially exploited merely because that individual is famous. For instance, Bette Midler successfully sued Ford Motor Company for its unauthorized use of a singer who imitated Midler's voice in a commercial in order to promote the sale of a car. The court noted that when a distinctive voice of a professional singer is known and is deliberately imitated in order to sell a product, the seller has misappropriated what is not theirs and has committed the tort of invasion of privacy. **Bette Midler v. Ford Motor Corporation, 849 F.2d 460 (9ᵗʰ Cir., 1988).**

The twenty-first century has seen the explosion of the phenomenon known as social networking. Social networking refers to a grouping of individuals into specific groups, like small rural communities or a neighborhood subdivision. It is most popular online because the internet contains millions of people who are looking to meet others, to gather and share information and experiences about sports, cooking, movies, developing friendships or professional alliances or topics. The topics and reasons are endless.[10]

Facebook is a well-known social networking website with more than 175 million users. Facebook users are given unique usernames and passwords to access their own user profiles as well as the profiles of their "friends." Users may send messages to each other through the Facebook website, either by e-mail or by postings made on a user's wall.[11]

MySpace.com is another popular Web-based social network which also allows a member to create of an online profile that serves as a medium for personal expression, and can contain photographs, videos, and other information about the person that he or she wishes to share with other MySpace.com users. Members have complete discretion regarding the amount and type of information that is included in a personal profile. Members can choose the degree of privacy they desire regarding their profile; that is, they determine who among the MySpace.com membership is allowed to view their profile.[12]

Despite the privacy settings available to users, how protected is this information? That is the issue in the next case where a defendant in a personal injury lawsuit asked the court to issuance an order allowing them to access the plaintiff's MySpace and Facebook accounts.

Romano v. Steelcase Inc.
907 N.Y.S.2d 650 (N.Y. Supp., 2010)

Plaintiff claims she sustained permanent injuries as a result of the incident and that she can no longer participate in certain activities or that these injuries have effected her enjoyment of life. However, contrary to Plaintiff's claims, Steelcase contends that a review of the public portions of Plaintiff's MySpace and Facebook pages reveals that she has an active lifestyle and has traveled to Florida and Pennsylvania during the time period she claims that her injuries prohibited such activity. In light of this, Defendant served Plaintiff with a Notice for requesting authorizations to obtain full access to Plaintiff's current and historical records on her Facebook and MySpace accounts. Plaintiff has refused to provide the requested authorizations.

Both Facebook and MySpace are social networking sites where people can share information about their personal lives, including posting photographs and sharing information about what they are doing or thinking.

The information sought by Defendant is both material and necessary to the defense of this action and/or could lead to admissible evidence. In this regard, it appears that Plaintiff's public profile page on Facebook shows her smiling happily in a photograph outside the confines of her home despite her claim that she has sustained permanent injuries and is largely confined to her house and bed. In light of the fact that the public portions of Plaintiff's social networking sites contain material that is contrary to her claims and deposition testimony, there is a reasonable likelihood that the private portions of her sites may contain further evidence such as information with regard to her activities and enjoyment of life, all of which are material and relevant to the defense of this action.

To permit a party claiming very substantial damages for loss of enjoyment of life to hide behind self-set privacy controls on a website, the primary purpose of which is to enable people to share information about how they lead their social lives, risks depriving the opposite party of access to material that may be relevant to ensuring a fair trial. To deny Defendant an opportunity access to these sites not only would go against the liberal discovery policies favoring pre-trial disclosure, but would condone Plaintiff's attempt to hide relevant information behind self-regulated privacy settings.

Production of Plaintiff's entries on her Facebook and MySpace accounts would not be violative of her right to privacy, and any such concerns are outweighed by Defendant's need for the information. New York courts have yet to address whether there exists a right to privacy regarding what one posts on their on-line social networking pages such as Facebook and MySpace. Whether one has a reasonable expectation of privacy in e-mails and other writings that have been shared with others has been addressed by New Jersey, in **Beye v. Horizon Blue Cross Blue Shield of New Jersey.** In this regard, the court stated that "[t]he privacy concerns are far less where the beneficiary herself chose to disclose the information." At issue in Beye, were on-line journals and diary entries of minor children who had been denied health care benefits for their eating disorders.

Plaintiff has no legitimate reasonable expectation of privacy. In this regard, MySpace warns users not to forget that their profiles and MySpace forums are public spaces, and Facebook's privacy policy set forth, inter alia, that:

> When you use Facebook, certain information you post or share with third parties,

such as personal information, comments, messages, photos, videos may be shared with others in accordance with the privacy settings you select. All such sharing of information is done at your own risk. Please keep in mind that if you disclose personal information in you profile or when posting comments, messages, photos, videos, or other items, this information may become publicly available.

Thus, when Plaintiff created her Facebook and MySpace accounts, she consented to the fact that her personal information would be shared with others, notwithstanding her privacy settings. Since Plaintiff knew that her information may become publicly available, she cannot now claim that she had a reasonable expectation of privacy. The materials including photographs contained on these sites may also be relevant to the issue of damages and may disprove Plaintiff's claims. Without access to these sites, Defendant will be at a distinct disadvantage in defending this action.

Defendant's motion for an Order granting Defendant access to Plaintiff's current and historical Facebook and MySpace pages and accounts, including all deleted pages and related information, is hereby granted.

In 1983, moviegoers were exposed to a fictitious story of a teenage hacker who gained unauthorized access to the country's computerized missile defense system and nearly triggered a nuclear war. *War Games* was entertaining, but given the level of computer technology at the time, its plot was farfetched at best. But unfortunately, this fictional account of breaking into a sophisticated computer system from a remote location has become an unpleasant reality. System security is now a paramount concern, and safeguards to minimize unauthorized access to computer mainframes include the use of passwords, fire walls, and encryption programs.

The **Electronic Communications Privacy Act** was enacted in 1986 to expand the scope of the federal wiretap laws by making the hacking into a computer a crime. The Act provides the primary statutory protection against the interception of electronic communications, including e-mail transmissions. Penalties can be either criminal or civil, and the legislation applies to the improper conduct of both the government and private sectors. Generally, the legislation prohibits **(1)** the intentional interception, use, or disclosure of electronic communications obtained during transmission; and **(2)** the improper accessing of stored electronic communications on a system used by the public. These protections are broad enough to cover hackers as well as disclosures of e-mail messages by a public internet service provider such as America Online or Prodigy to a third party.

Even though a person deletes an e-mail message from the hard drive or relies upon an internet service to automatically delete messages after a certain number of days, a copy of that communication still exists. Internet service providers routinely create a back-up file of all communications.

This type of stored electronic data can be lawfully reviewed by an internet service provider for such things as marketing or quality assurances purposes. The stored messages, however, may not be disclosed to a third party without a sheriff's sale or search warrant.

The protections afforded by the **Electronic Communications Privacy Act** were found to have been violated when AOL voluntarily disclosed to the Navy, the name of a sailor who listed his marital status as "gay" in his screen profile. In issuing an injunction to block the sailor's involuntary discharge, the court noted that the Navy's inquiry directed to an AOL service representative, in order to learn the sailor's identity, was "likely illegal" under the Act. **Timothy McVeigh v. Cohen, 983 F. Supp. 215 (D.D.C., 1998).** As the court stated:

> The **ECPA,** enacted by Congress to address privacy concerns on the Internet, allows the government to obtain information from an online service provider– as the Navy did in this instance from AOL–but only if **(1)** it obtains a warrant or **(2)** it gives prior notice to the online subscriber and then issues a subpoena or receives a court order authorizing disclosure of the information in question.

It must be noted, however, that immediately following 9/11, then President Bush signed into law the **USA Patriot Act** which allows a service provider that reasonably believes a third party is in imminent danger of bodily harm to disclose that information to a law enforcement agent.

The Electronic Communications Privacy Act also provides no protection against the disclosure of an electronic message by the recipient of the communication. This type of disclosure must be covered by other principles of law, such as the breach of a confidential relationship or invasion of privacy.

Consider the following work-place issue: Michael Smyth figured he was safe and could talk with impunity while using his employer's e-mail. After all, his employer repeatedly assured the Pillsbury workers that all e-mail messages on the company's electronic communications system could not be intercepted or used against an employee as grounds for termination. In response to e-mail messages from his supervisor which Smyth opened on his home computer, Smyth decided to provide his supervisor with some "editorial input" concerning the sales management team. He threatened to "kill the backstabbing bastards" and referred to the planned holiday party as the "Jim Jones Koolaid Affair." These creative efforts of expression were not well received by Pillsbury after they intercepted Smyth's private e-mail messages. The company exercised its own creative efforts of expression when Pillsbury terminated the worker's employment, despite the company's prior assurances of message confidentiality. **Michael Smyth v. Pillsbury Company, 914 Supp. 97 (E.D. Pa., 1996).**

This case clearly raises the question as to whether an employer can monitor the e-mail accounts of employees without violating invasion of privacy principles. Employers have legitimate reasons for wanting to monitor the electronic communication accounts provided to their employees. Good business practice dictates that the e-mail accounts of workers be reviewed for such things as illegal activity, sexual harassment in the work place, disclosure of trade secrets, productivity and quality control. Employers can even use programs which automatically scan their e-mail systems for violations of company policy, such as the viewing of pornographic materials, online betting or playing the stock market while on company time.

Generally, it is not considered an invasion of privacy for an employer to monitor its e-mail system. The employer's need to regulate its e-mail takes precedent over privacy interests of the worker. The Electronic Communications Privacy Act also allows monitoring of employee communications if the electronic communication service is used in the ordinary course of business or if the monitoring takes place with the employee's consent. For instance, businesses routinely implement privacy statements informing its employees that the employer reserves the right to review company-supplied e-mail accounts for quality assurance purposes.

What ever happened to Mr. Smyth's suit against Pillsbury in view of the company's repeated assurances of e-mail confidentiality? The court was still unimpressed with the former employee's claim and found that the actions of Pillsbury did not invade the plaintiff's privacy. The court noted:

> We do not find a reasonable expectation of privacy in e-mail communications voluntarily made by an employee to his supervisor over the company's e-mail system notwithstanding any assurances that such communications would not be intercepted by management. Once plaintiff communicated the alleged unprofessional comments to his supervisor over an e-mail system which was apparently utilized by the entire company, any reasonable expectation of privacy was lost.

> Even if an employee had a reasonable expectation of privacy in the contents of his e-mail communications over the company e-mail system, we do not find that a reasonable person would consider the defendant's interception of these communications to be a substantial and highly offensive invasion of his privacy. The company's interest in preventing inappropriate and unprofessional comments or even illegal activity over its e-mail system outweighs any privacy interest the employee may have in those comments.

The Supreme Court of New Jersey in **Blakey v. Continental Airlines, Inc.,** has now placed employers on notice that business owners may incur financial liability if they fail to monitor a company-sponsored electronic communication system once the employer knows or has reason to know that the system is being used to transmit inappropriate comments.

TAMMY BLAKEY V. CONTINENTAL AIRLINES, INC.
751 A.2D 538 (N.J., 2000)

Blakey, a pilot for Continental Airlines, became that airline's first female captain to fly an Airbus. Shortly after qualifying to be a captain, Blakey complained of sexual harassment and a hostile working environment based on conduct and comments directed at her by co-employees. In February 1991, she complained to Continental's management concerning pornographic photographs and vulgar gender-based comments directed at her that appeared in the workplace, specifically in her plane's cockpit and other work areas.

From February to July 1995, a number of Continental's male pilots posted derogatory and insulting remarks about Blakey on the pilots online computer bulletin board called the Crew Members Forum ("Forum"). The Forum is accessible to all Continental pilots and crew member personnel through the Internet provider, CompuServe. Continental requires that pilots and crew "access" the Forum in order to learn their flight schedules and assignments.

In December 1995, Blakey filed this complaint against Continental and the pilots alleging defamation, sexual harassment/hostile work environment, business libel, and intentional infliction of emotional distress.

The question is whether the Forum is the equivalent of a cork bulletin board in the pilots' lounge or a work-related place in which pilots and crew members continue a pattern of harassment.

The Court recognized that harassment by a superior that takes place outside of the workplace can be actionable. The fact that the electronic bulletin board may be located outside of the workplace does not mean that an employer may have no duty to correct off-site harassment by co-employees. Conduct that takes place outside of the workplace has a tendency to permeate the workplace.

Our common experience tells us how important the extensions of the workplace are where the relations among employees are cemented. If an "old boys' network" continued in an after-hours setting, where belittling conduct edges over into harassment, what exactly is the outsider (whether black, Latino, or woman) to do? Keep swallowing the abuse or give up the chance to make the team?

Employers may not disregard the posting of offensive messages on company or state agency e-mail systems when the employer is made aware of those messages.

To repeat, employers do not have a duty to monitor private communications of their employees; employers do have a duty to take effective measures to stop co-employee harassment when the employer knows or has reason to know that such harassment is part of a pattern of harassment that is taking place in the workplace and in settings that are related to the workplace.

The matter is remanded to the Law Division for further proceedings in accordance with this opinion.

Subsequently, the court in **Dyer v. Northwest Airlines Corp.** clarified the scope of the Electronic Communications Privacy Act by dismissing a lawsuit against Northwest Airlines for disclosing the names, addresses, credit card numbers, and travel itineraries of its passengers to the government. The court determined that the airline was not a provider of electronic communication services within the terms of the Act and was not subject to the disclosure restrictions of the law.

SECTION 8.9
E-CONTRACTS

In the course of a day, we enter into a variety of transactions that have legal consequences. Whether it is taking the train to school, buying lunch from a vendor, or purchasing a sweater in a department store, our interactions with others can create binding contracts.

As discussed previously, a contract is the voluntary exchange of a promise between two or more people that constitutes a legal obligation that is enforceable in court. These agreements may be contained in a highly technical written document, or they may be casual arrangements which are not reduced to writing. The necessary elements of a valid contract however, are the same regardless of the formality of the transaction. Each contract must contain the following:

1. **Offer**—An offer is a proposal by one party to another manifesting an intention to enter into a valid contract. The three essential elements of a valid offer are **(a)** intent to contract; **(b)** definiteness of the terms; and **(c)** the offer must be communicated.

2. **Acceptance**—An acceptance in an agreement by the offeree to be bound by the terms of the offer.

3. **Consideration**—Consideration is the bargain for exchange between the parties. While the consideration doesn't have to be economical in nature, it must have legal value, such as the performance of a service, or surrendering a legal right.

4. **Capacity**—The parties to the contract must have the legal capacity to enter into the transaction. This provision is designed to protect those who are incapable of making legal decisions, such as children and the mentally infirm. Such individuals may disaffirm a contract, but the competent party remains legally bound to fulfill the contract's terms. This type of transaction is called a voidable contract.

5. **Legality**—The purpose of the contract must be legal; thus the agreement cannot require the commission of a crime or the performance of a tort.

The Internet has forced businesses to ponder how they can form legally binding contracts in e-commerce transactions but the answer is simple. Traditional principles of contract law have equal application to internet transactions. The only difference with an internet contract is the introduction of a new set of terms, such as "click-wrap agreements" and "digital signatures."

For instance, the online purchase of a computer printer from Amazon.com is no different than buying a computer printer from the nearest Best Buy electronics store, as the same principles of contract law will apply to both transactions. The offer and acceptance is the agreement to buy the printer, whether it is accomplished by placing the item in an online shopping cart and checking out, or by carrying the printer to the cashier in the store. The consideration, or *quid pro quo*, is the exchange of the printer by the seller for the requested cash price. The contract is perfectly legal, and as long as the buyer is over 18, the parties have the capacity to contract.

Online auctions are becoming an increasingly popular way to find unusual or hard-to-locate items. To be a player, however, one must understand how the auction actually works. The key is simple and generally involves the following question: Is the highest bid an offer which the seller can choose to accept or reject, or is the highest bid an acceptance of the seller's offer which forms a binding contract?

Consider the following problem: It is your parents twenty-fifth wedding anniversary, and you want to buy them something special. You find an original Woodstock poster signed by the artist at an online auction site. You make the highest bid for the rock-and-roll memorabilia, but at the end of the auction, the seller refuses to give you the poster. He claims that the poster is worth five times the amount of the bid. Who wins? The resolution depends upon whether the internet auction was "with reserve" or "without reserve." If the online transaction is "without reserve," the seller is required to sell the item, regardless of the final bid price, because the highest bid constitutes the acceptance.

However, if the auction was "with reserve"–meaning that the seller conducted the auction with a specific minimum price in mind–the seller is not obligated to complete the transaction regardless of the bids placed, since the bid was an offer which the seller could accept or reject. Most auctions are "with reserve," and the sale does not take place until the bidding has closed, and the seller accepts the bid. To learn more about the rules for online actions, see: **www. pages.ebay.com/help.**

Computer software may be obtained by downloading the program from the internet or by installing the software from a CD. In each case, the software is accompanied with a license that limits the buyer's remedies in the event that the software does not work properly.

A **clickwrap license** will accompany the installation of a program from the web. The user is required to click through a series of screens before the program can be successfully installed. These screens contain non-negotiable terms and conditions imposed by the seller. Most people do not read these materials and merely click "I accept" to the questions, since it is the only way to advance the installation.

A **shrinkwrap license** receives its name from the fact that computer software bought in a store is packaged in a cellophane shrinkwrap. When the box is opened, the CD is contained in an envelope that includes a printed license. By opening the envelope or by using the software, the buyer agrees to be bound by the terms of the license.

These licenses are generally enforced by the courts even though they favor the software company, limit the buyer's rights in the event of a software problem and are seen by the user for the first time after the software has been purchased.

In **Mortenson v. Timberline Software Corporation,** the Washington Supreme Court had to decide whether to enforce the terms of a shrinkwrap license that limited the buyer's damages to the cost of the software program. Mortenson had used Timberline's software to prepare a construction bid but because the program did not work properly, the bid was almost $2 million dollars lower than it should have been. Mortenson sued the software company to recover its full losses and the limitation on damages contained in the license was asserted by Timberline Software Company as a defense to the suit.

M.A. MORTENSON CO. V. TIMBERLINE SOFTWARE CORP.
998 P.2D 305 (WASH., 2000)

This case presents the issue of whether a limitation on damages enclosed in a "shrinkwrap license" accompanying computer software is enforceable against the purchaser of the licensed software. M.A. Mortenson Company, Inc. (Mortenson), a general construction contractor, purchased licensed computer software from Timberline Software Corporation (Timberline). After Mortenson used the program to prepare a construction bid and discovered the bid was $1.95 million less than it should have been, Mortenson sued Timberline for breach of warranties alleging the software was defective.

All Timberline software is distributed to its users under license. The full text of Timberline's license agreement was set forth on the outside of each diskette pouch and the inside cover of the instruction manuals. The first screen that appears each time the program is used also references the license and states:

NEITHER TIMBERLINE NOR ANYONE ELSE WHO HAS BEEN INVOLVED IN THE CREATION, PRODUCTION OR DELIVERY OF THE PROGRAMS SHALL BE LIABLE TO YOU FOR ANY DAMAGES OF ANY TYPE. TIMBERLINE'S LIABILITY FOR DAMAGES IN NO EVENT SHALL EXCEED THE LICENSE FEE PAID FOR THE RIGHT TO USE THE PROGRAMS.

Mortenson utilized Timberline's Precision Bid Analysis software to prepare a bid for a project at Harborview Medical Center in Seattle. On the day of the bid, the software allegedly malfunctioned multiple times. After Mortenson was awarded the Harborview Medical Center project, it learned its bid was approximately $1.95 million lower than intended.

Although no Washington case specifically addresses the type of contract formation at issue, a series of recent cases from other jurisdictions have analyzed shrinkwrap licenses. See **Hill v. Gateway 2000, Inc., 105 F.3d 1147 (7th Cir.),** cert. denied, **522 U.S. 808 (1997); ProCD, Inc. v. Zeidenberg, 86 F.3d 1447 (7th Cir., 1996).**

In **ProCD,** which involved a retail purchase of software, the Seventh Circuit held software shrinkwrap license agreements are a valid form of contracting, and such agreements are enforceable unless objectionable under general contract law, such as the law of unconscionability. **ProCD, 86 F.3d at 1449-52.** The court stated, "a notice on the outside, terms on the inside, and a right to return the software for a refund if the terms are unacceptable, may be a means of doing business valuable to buyers and sellers alike."

In *Hill,* the customer ordered a computer over the telephone and received the computer in the mail, accompanied by a list of terms to govern if the customer did not return the product within 30 days. The court held the terms of the "accept-or-return" agreement were effective, stating, "competent adults are bound by such documents, read or unread." *Hill,* **105 F.3d at 1149.**

The question in *ProCD* was not whether terms were added to a contract after its formation, but how and when the contract was formed—in particular, whether a vendor may propose that a contract of sale be formed, not in the store or over the phone with the payment of money or a general "send me the product," but after the customer has had a chance to inspect both the item and the terms. *ProCD* answers "yes," for merchants and consumers alike. *Hill,* **105 F.3d at 1150.**

We find the approach of the *ProCD* and *Hill courts* persuasive. We, therefore, hold the terms of the license were part of the contract between Mortenson and Timberline, and Mortenson's use of the software constituted its assent to the agreement, including the license terms. The terms of Timberline's license were either set forth explicitly or referenced in numerous locations.

The terms were included within the shrinkwrap packaging of each copy of the Precision Bid Analysis software; they were present in the manuals accompanying the software; they were included with the protection devices for the software, without which the software could not be used. The fact the software was licensed was also noted on the introductory screen each time the software was used.

We affirm the trial court's order of summary judgment of dismissal.

In 2004, a Federal District Court in **Mortgage Plus, Inc. v. Docmagic, Inc**. reviewed the existing case law involving end-user licenses, and concluded that clickwrap and shrinkwrap agreements are routinely upheld as valid and enforceable contracts.

SECTION 8.10 STATUTE OF FRAUDS

Most agreements do not have to be in writing to be enforced by the courts, and oral agreements can be just as valid as formal written contracts. For instance, most consumer purchases at department stores, supermarkets, or home repair centers are not transacted with signed, written documents; rather, they are informal transactions. The **Statute of Frauds**, however, requires that certain types of agreements be in writing and be signed by the parties to the contract. This includes contracts for the sale of land, the sale of goods worth more than five hundred dollars, and contracts which cannot be performed in less than one year.

The required writing may be contained in a letter, invoice, telegram, contract or even a faxed transmission which contains one or both signatures of the parties. The signing of the document is also important, since it authenticates the writing and shows the intent of the parties to be bound by the terms of the agreement. In the online environment, however, the correspondence between the parties is electronic and does not generate a paper trail. This presents a problem with e-commerce transactions that must be in writing in order to comply with the Statute of Frauds.

When you purchase an item online from a retailer, your order is quickly confirmed by the vendor in an e-mail with a confirmation number and tracking number. But these return messages are not sent as a courtesy. Rather, they represent the seller's attempt to create a written record as evidence of compliance with the Statute of Frauds and to insure the validity of the order.

Because of the importance of electronic commerce, a number of states have passed legislation to validate electronic contracts and signatures. For example, New York tackled the problem by enacting the **Electronic Signature and Records Act** that provides that an electronic signature may be used in place of a signature affixed by hand. The law further provides that the "use of an electronic signature shall have the same validity and effect as the use of a signature affixed by hand." These statutes, however, are not uniform in approach and create uncertainty in the business world.

Congress remedied the situation in 2000 by enacting the **Electronic Signatures in Global and National Commerce Act,** which is also known as E-SIGN. The legislation should have a profound impact on internet transactions by making them the equivalent of a signed paper contract. This compliance with the Statute of Frauds is achieved by providing that a signature, contract, or other record relating to a digital transaction may not be denied legal effect solely because it is electronic in nature. Examples of electronic signatures include a personal identification number used to access a person's on-line account with a business, such as amazon.com or e-bay, a typed or automatic signature that is affixed at the end of an e-mail, or something that is encrypted. Therefore, businesses may now proceed with their online contracts secure in the knowledge that their agreements will be enforced by the courts across the land.

It is important to note that while the Electronic Signatures in Global and National Commerce Act eliminates the barriers to transacting business electronically, consumers still enjoy the full protection of the law available to them with paper contracts. Also, no person can be forced to enter into an electronic contract, and they may continue to do business in the traditional fashion.

The United States is not the only country to consider electronic signatures and internet contracts. The law firm of Baker and McKenzie maintains a website that summarizes how the nations of the world have responded to this issue.

For example, Japan has enacted the **Electronic Signatures and Certification Services** that is designed "to promote the diffusion of information using electromagnetic electronic methods and information processing through securing the smooth utilization of electronic signatures... by the presumption of the genuine... authenticity of electromagnetic records... and the prescription of other necessary matters concerning electronic signatures."

<table>
<tr><td>

**SECTION 8.11
REVIEW CASES**

</td><td>

1. Jcom, Inc. operated a website that catered to the sale of adult entertainment services. The company used the trademark "Barbie's Playhouse" on their website, along with a doll-like figure that resembled the form of a Barbie doll. The address of the website was **"www.jcomlive.com/barbie. htm."** Mattel brought suit against JCom., Inc., under the *Lanham Act* for the defendant's violation of the Barbie trademark and under the Federal Trademark Dilution Act. Will Mattel be successful? **Mattel, Inc. v. JCom, Inc. 1998 U.S. Dist. LEXIS 16195 (S.D. N.Y., 1998).**

2. America Online publishes updated stock quotations on a continual basis. This data is supplied by independent third parties who monitor the various stock exchanges. On several occasions, AOL posted incorrect information concerning the stock price and share value of Ben Ezra, Weinstein & Co., Inc. This prompted a lawsuit by the firm against AOL for defamation and negligence. Is the internet service liable for the posting of the misinformation about the value of the firm's stock, or are they protected by the Communications Decency Act? **Ben Ezra, Weinstein & Co., Inc. v. America Online, Inc., No. 99-2068 (10th Cir., 2000).**

3. An entrepreneur operated a website under the domain name **"www. Painewebber.com."** Visitors to the site would automatically be linked to a pornographic website. Painwebber, Inc., filed an injunction against the website operator to enjoin them from using the internet domain name. Did the website operator violate the Anticybersquatting Consumer Protection Act? **Paine Webber, Inc. v. www.painwebber.com, 1999 U.S. Dist. LEXIS 6551 (E.D. Va., 1999).**

4. Comedy III Productions has the exclusive right to the exploitation of the trademarks and images of the Three Stooges. But prior to Comedy III's exclusive rights, companies that were affiliated with Robert Walsh possessed a license to sell Three Stooges merchandise. That prior agreement explicitly warned the licensees that they had no right to continue selling Three Stooges products after the expiration of the agreement. Yet following the expiration of that license, a Robert Walsh-controlled company made available for sale on the internet a "Golf With Your Friends Embroidered Golf Shirt," which incorporated the images of the Three Stooges. Does the website's advertising of the Three Stooges products by a Walsh-affiliated

</td></tr>
</table>

company violate any rights possessed by Comedy III Productions? Will Comedy III Productions be successful under the Lanham Act for a trademark infringement? **Comedy III Productions, Inc. v. Robert C. Walsh, Jr., et al., 1996 U.S. Dist. LEXIS 5710 (S.D. N.Y., 1996).**

5. AOL offers a wide variety of "chatrooms," where its users can converse through messaging. One such chatroom was used by a subscriber to display and sell photographs of an eleven-year-old boy who had engaged in certain sexual acts with the subscriber. While the adult pled guilty to criminal charges, the parents of the minor sought to hold AOL liable for the transmission of the photographs, because their internet chatroom was used. Is AOL responsible for the transmission of the photographs over their system, or are they protected by the Communications Decency Act? **Jane Doe v. America Online, Inc., Case No. 97-25-87 (Fla. Dist. Ct. App., 1999).**

6. Microsoft Network is an online computer service that utilizes a clickwrap license, that prospective members must agree to if they wish to use the MSN internet site. The membership agreement appears on the computer screen in a scrollable window next to two blocks that provide the choices, "I agree" or "I don't agree." The agreement, among other things, requires any user who wishes to bring suit against Microsoft Network to file the claim in the State of Washington. Caspi brought a class-action lawsuit against the internet service provider in New Jersey because of an increase in the membership fees attributable to a change in the service plan. Will Microsoft be successful in having the case dismissed from the New Jersey court because Caspi's choice of jurisdiction violates the clickwrap agreement? **Caspi v. Microsoft Network a/k/a MSN, L.L.C., 732 A.2d 528 (N.J. Super., 1999).**

SECTION 8.12
INTERNET REFERENCES

For more information on Internet law, see the following sites:

- **www.phillipsnizer.com** *or* **www.perkinscoie.com**
  Both Internet sites provide summaries of court decisions on Cyberlaw. Cases are arranged by issue and the sites are maintained by law firms that specialize in intellectual property.

- **www.gigalaw.com**
  This site provides articles on various Internet law issues.

- **http://legal.web.aol.com**
  AOL provides legal information and court opinions on Cyber-law issues.

Footnotes:

1. "US Mobile ECommerce Revenues Set to Rise to $23.8 bn in 2015," cellular-news, http://www.cellular-news.com/story/42841.php (Last visited October 30, 2010).

2. "Fair Use," United States Copyright Office, http://www.google.com/search?q=fair+use&btnG=Search&hl=en&sa=2 (Last visited October 30, 2010).

3. *Id.*

4. *Id.*

5. Joseph Mullin, "The 'Dancing Baby' Lawsuit Will Shape Future of Fair Use," paid Content.org., http://paidcontent.org/article/419-the-dancing-baby-lawsuit-will-shape-future-of-fair-use/ 2 (Last visited October 30, 2010).

6. *Id.*

7. *Id.*

8. "Internet Ad Revenues Break Records, Climb to More Than $12 Billion for First Half of 10," IAB, http://www.iab.net/about_the_iab/recent_press_releases/press_release_archive/press_release/pr-101210. (Last visited November 12, 2010.)

9. See http://www.louisvuitton.com/info/fake/index.html (Last visited October 30, 2010).

10. "What Is Social Networking?," Social Networking, http://www.whatissocialnetwork-ing.com. (Last visited on November 14, 2010.)

11. **Facebook, Inc. v. Wallace,** 2009 WL 3617789.

12. **Doe v. MySpace, Inc.,** 528 F.3d 413 (C.A.5 Tex., 2008).

KEY TERMS

Anticybersquatting
    Consumer Protection Act
Appropriation
Clickwrap Agreement
Communications Decency Act
Copyright
Cyberlaw
Descriptive Mark
Digital Signature
Domain Name
e-Contracts
e-Defamation
e-Privacy
e-Sign
Electronic Communications
    Privacy Act
Electronic Signature and
    Records Act
Electronic Signatures in Global
    and National Commerce Act

Fair Use
Fanciful Mark
Federal Registration
Federal Trademark Dilution Act
Generic Mark
Infringement
Internet
Internet Corporation for
    Assigned Names & Numbers
Invasion of Privacy
Lanham Act
Online Auction
Shrinkwrap License
Statute of Frauds
Suggestive Mark
Trademark
Trademark Dilution
Trademark Infringement
World Intellectual
    Property Organization

CHAPTER 9

BUSINESS ORGANIZATIONS

By: S. Jay Sklar, Esquire

SECTION 9.1
INTRODUCTION

Remind people that profit is the difference between revenue and expense. This makes you look smart.
–Scott Adams

Individuals do not always have the foresight to properly plan their business operations for success or failure. What may start out as a hobby with the business being housed in a garage may expand into a multi-million dollar enterprise that is ill prepared to cope with success.

This chapter will explore the various organizational forms that an entrepreneur may utilize in starting a business from a sole proprietorship to a limited liability company. Each form has its own advantages, disadvantages and tax consequences. Choosing the correct form of organization is a critical first step and should be made in consultation with an attorney and accountant. Considerations include the cost in bringing the business to life, the liability of its owners, management issues and dissolution. The reader needs to keep in mind that no one form is automatically "better" than any other. They each have aspects that might be appropriate at a particular time in the development of a business.

SECTION 9.2
SOLE PROPRIETORSHIP

A. Creation

The **sole proprietorship** is the least expensive, most simple and common business to form. It has one owner who usually operates the business under his or her name. There can be many employees but only one owner who has personal liability for all of the business debts and obligations. A sole proprietorship is also not expensive to establish. The owner does not need the permission of a governmental agency in order to open the business but may be required to obtain a business license or permit in the county of operation. The owner may be required to file a **fictitious name registration** if the entrepreneur wishes to do business under a name other than his or her own. An example of a fictitious name registration would be Joe Roberts doing business at Tyler's Sports Bar and Grill.

B. Liability

The sole proprietorship has the greatest risk to the owner since the liability for the debts of the business is unlimited and the entrepreneur's personal assets can be seized to satisfy the business obligations. The entrepreneur may attempt to limit the exposure of personal assets to the creditors by holding all property jointly with the spouse. As one may remember from the chapter on Property Law, the assets of a husband and wife are considered owned as tenancy by the entireties and cannot be seized by a creditor for the debts of one spouse. The owner may also reduce the risk of suit from a customer who is injured on the premises or by use of a defective product sold by the merchant by obtaining the appropriate liability insurance.

C. Tax Implications

The simplicity of the sole proprietorship is further evidenced by the fact that the owner keeps all of the profits from the business operation and pays personal income tax on them on what is known as a Schedule "C." A separate tax return is not filed as is done with a corporation so there is no issue of double taxation. The opportunity to raise capital, however, is limited to the owner's personal resources or by obtaining a loan.

D. Termination

The business operation terminates whenever the owner stops doing business and no separate forms have to be filed with the government putting the company out of business. Since the owner is the business, it terminates upon the proprietor's death.

SECTION 9.3
PARTNERSHIP

A. Creation

A **partnership** is an association of two or more entities to carry on a business as co-owners. The partners will share in the profits and losses of the enterprise on an equal basis unless there is an agreement setting forth some other arrangement. This type of enterprise is not limited to individuals and can include members who are corporations, groups of people or companies. No magic words are needed to create a partnership and the parties do not need a written agreement even though that is strongly recommended in order to avoid conflicts over the business operation. In fact, a partnership can arise by implication. For instance, two or more people who join together to operate a business may be deemed to have formed a partnership regardless of their intent or failure to realize that a partnership has arisen.

Three essential elements are examined to determine if a partnership has been created:

1. The sharing of profits and losses by two or more people is prima facie evidence of a partnership. In other words, the law will assume that a partnership has been created if there is a sharing of profits. The burden then shifts to the persons involved in the business to show that they were not partners;

2. A joint ownership of the assets of the business; and

3. An equal right in the management of the enterprise.

The following case discusses the elements that create the existence of a partnership when a written agreement has not been made setting up the partnership.

DOUGLAS HILLME V. BRENT CHASTAIN AND C & H CUSTOM CABINETS, INC. 75 S.W.3D 315 (MO. APP. S.D., 2002)

Chastain appeals from the order finding that a partnership existed between Chastain and Hillme.

A partnership is defined as an association of two or more persons to carry on as co-owners of a business for profit. A partnership has also been judicially defined as a contract of two or more competent persons to place their money, effects, labor and skill, or some or all of them, in lawful commerce or business and to divide the profits and bear the loss in certain proportions. The partnership agreement may be written, expressed orally, or implied from the acts and conduct of the parties. The intent of the parties is the primary factor for determining whether such a relationship exists. The required intent necessary to find a partnership existed is not the intent to form a partnership, but the intent to enter into a relationship, which in law constitutes a partnership.

A partnership agreement may be implied from conduct and circumstances of the parties and the parties are not required to know all the legal implications of a partnership. A voice in the management of the partnership business, a share of the profits of the partnership business, and a corresponding risk of loss and liability to partnership creditors are all indications of a partnership.

The record shows that Chastain and Hillme had each worked for a period of time at Classic Cabinets, a cabinet making shop. Hillme had worked there for about four years and had eight or nine years experience in cabinet making. Chastain had also worked for the same concern and for the most part performed staining, finishing and installation work.

In April of 1997, Chastain and Hillme made the decision to go into business together. Hillme testified that they both agreed to divide the workload, profits, expenses, and losses equally, that is on a "50/50" basis. No written partnership agreement was executed. Each drew a flat and equal amount of pay each week. According to Hillme, any money left over they agreed to let accumulate in the partnership account.

Hillme wrote a check for the purchase of plywood and Chastain also contributed monies for the venture. Chastain rented a building and purchased some woodworking equipment. He also negotiated the rent for the building. Both spent time cleaning the building and prepared to move into the building. Hillme purchased furnace parts to heat the building. Both contributed tools and equipment to the business. A business insurance policy was obtained. The parties named the business "C & H Custom Cabinets." The "C" stood for Chastain's last name and the "H" stood for Hillme's last name.

During the day-to-day operation, Chastain ran errands and applied stain and finish to cabinets. Hillme's time was generally spent building the cabinets. Chastain was also in charge of paying bills and scheduling installations. A checking account for the business was opened at "Central Bank." The name shown on their checks was "C & H Cabinets." It was Hillme's understanding that as business partners, they were both owners of the jointly held account at the bank. Both issued checks from the account and each carried the concern's checkbook on occasion.

In 1997, Chastain and Hillme decided their business required a cargo trailer for hauling cabinets to the installation site. They discussed the purchase and both went to a vehicle dealer to select one. According to Hillme, it was his understanding that the cargo trailer was to be paid out of the partnership account. A bank loan was initially obtained for the purchase of the cargo trailer. Both Chastain and Hillme personally signed the note for the loan. Unbeknownst to Hillme, title to the cargo trailer was placed in Chastain's name only. Hillme also stated that it was not until after his lawsuit had commenced that he had found out how the title to the cargo trailer was held.

Hillme further testified that in October of 1998, a Dodge pickup truck was purchased. Hillme related that funds generated by the partnership were used for this purpose and he understood that the vehicle was to be a partnership vehicle. According to Hillme, Chastain informed him that once the 1994 pickup truck was paid for, the partnership would buy Hillme a pickup truck. However, the pickup truck was not titled in the name of the business. Rather, it was titled in Chastain's name. Once again, Hillme testified it was only after the lawsuit was filed that he first learned that the pickup truck was titled solely in Chastain's name.

According to Hillme, Chastain showed him the business records for 1997 and gave Hillme tax documents for the 1997 tax year so that Hillme could file his individual return. Each of the parties claimed half of the business expenses, such as utilities, and each claimed half of the gross income. At trial, Chastain claimed that Hillme was a subcontractor and then an employee. Significantly, Chastain's 1997 tax return did not show that he had paid Hillme either as an employee or as contract laborer. Indeed, as previously set out for the tax year involved, Chastain split the expenses of the business with Hillme.

Eventually, disagreements over management caused Hillme to open his own cabinet making business some time in 1999. By then Hillme had become aware of Chastain's claims that they were not partners.

In his appeal, Chastain maintains the trial court erred in finding that a partnership existed between himself and Hillme. Chastain asserts that Hillme failed to demonstrate the necessary elements of a partnership, such as co-ownership of business assets, mutual rights of control of the business, an agreement in fact, and the right to share in profits and duty to share in losses. We disagree.

While each evidentiary factor standing alone may not show a partnership, it is clear that the combination of the following probative factors is supportive of the trial court's conclusion that a partnership was created by Chastain and Hillme in 1997.

The factors we note are the following: The name of the business was based on each party's last name, all of the advertising included each party's name and home telephone number, the day-to-day operation of the business relied on each one's specialized skills—Hillme's greater experience in cabinet making and Chastain's accounting and management skills, and each party co-signed the note for the cargo trailer. Additionally, Hillme had a voice in the management of the partnership. This is evidenced by his "veto" of using partnership assets for the construction of an additional shop building. Furthermore, during the first year of the partnership in 1997, each divided equally the income and expenses generated through the business.

We cannot say that the trial court erred in finding that a partnership existed between Chastain and Hillme. Sufficient evidence in the record supports the trial court's judgment. The trial court's judgment is affirmed.

B. Management

The Partnership Agreement usually sets forth the rights and duties of the partners. If there are no provisions in the agreement to the contrary, the law imposes certain rights and duties between the partners. For instance, all partners have an equal right to participate in the management of the business' affairs. This right, however, can be limited or altered by the partnership agreement whereby one or more partners may have a greater role in the operation of the enterprise. A majority vote is usually needed for the approval of most daily operational aspects of partnership operations but unanimous consent of the partners may be required for certain significant actions such as the admission of a new partner or the purchase of a major asset. The following is a partial listing of some of these types of circumstances:

- Altering the essential nature of the partnership business

- Amending the partnership agreement

- Admitting new partners

- Entering into a wholly new business

- Assigning partnership property for the benefit of creditors

- Disposing of partnership goodwill

- Entering a confession of judgment or submitting a claim to arbitration

- Engaging in any action that would make it impossible to carry out the partnership's business

As for the duty of loyalty and good faith dealings, each partner has the duty to devote his or her time, skill and energy to the partnership's business. This is not a separately commensurable activity, unless otherwise agreed. Basically, the partners' "pay" is their share of the profits. The partnership books and records must also be made available to all partners.

Partners act in a fiduciary relationship to each other. This requires the utmost degree of trust and loyalty among them and they must act for the benefit of the partnership and not for their individual benefit. As the court stated in **Leff v. Gunter 33 Cal.3d 508 (1983):**

A partnership establishes a fiduciary relationship, and partners are held to the standards and duties of a trustee in their dealings with each other. In all proceedings connected with the conduct of the partnership, every partner is bound to act in the highest good faith to his co-partner and may not obtain any advantage over him in the partnership affairs by the slightest misrepresentation, concealment, threat or adverse pressure of any kind.

C. Liability

Like the sole proprietorship, the partners have unlimited liability for the debts of the business. Each is liable for the full debts of the business. A creditor, however, must first seek satisfaction of the debt out of the partnership assets. If this fails to satisfy the obligation, the creditor may then advance a claim against any single partner or all of the partners for the remaining partnership obligations. This is known as **joint and several liability**. While it may seem unfair that the creditor can go after one partner over another, the owner who pays a partnership debt may sue the other partners for reimbursement. This is known as **indemnification**.

Each partner is also an agent for the partnership and other partners. This means that one partner can bind the others on business matters with third parties even if those actions exceed the person's authority. For instance, a partner who buys a car in the partnership's name will bind the other partners to that contract even if the partnership agreement states that no one partner may make a purchase for the business that exceeds $1,000 without the consent of the others.

D. Taxation

A partnership is not a taxable entity. Rather, the profits of the business are apportioned to each partner who pays personal income tax on his or her share. The partnership, however, is required to file an information return each year with the Internal Revenue Service showing such things as income, deductions, gains, and losses but it pays no taxes. Rather, the partnership "passes through" the profits or losses to the individual partners who file a Schedule K-1. In this way, each partner includes his or her share of the partnership's income or loss on that person's personal tax return. On the other hand, partners are not employees and are not issued a W-2 tax form.

E. Termination

When certain events occur, the partnership will **terminate** such as at the expiration of the term of the partnership, the business objectives have been reached or the partners by agreement terminate the operation. For instance, the partnership agreement can provide that the business will operate for a set period of time at which point it will terminate. If no fixed time is specified, the partnership is one at will in which any partner at any time can dissolve the business without violating the agreement. The following is a sample clause in a partnership agreement concerning the termination of the business:

> The term of this partnership shall continue from the date of this Agreement until the death, retirement, or withdrawal of all partners or until the partnership is terminated as provided in this Agreement.

A change in the relationship of the partners that signals an unwillingness or inability to carry on the partnership, dissolves that relationship and leads to a termination of the entity. Such a termination is a two-stage process. The first step is the **dissolution** process, which means that a partner ceases to be associated with the venture and the second step is known as the winding up. This involves the collecting and distribution of the partnership assets. At the completion of the winding up, the partnership's existence is terminated.

As a sole proprietorship terminates upon the death of the owner, a similar principle applies to a partnership. The original partnership will automatically terminate upon the death of any owner.

There is also a distinction between the power to dissolve the partnership and the right to dissolve the business. Since a partnership is a voluntary agreement to act together, any partner has the power to dissolve the partnership but may not have the right to terminate the business without incurring legal liability to the others.

If liquidation occurs following the death of a partner, there is a fiduciary duty upon the remaining partners to act without delay and act in good faith to the estate of the deceased partner.

The intent to dissolve must be communicated to all partners. This notice can be by word or act.

The leaving partner must give notice to third parties who have dealt with the partnership, if he or she wants to be relieved from the future obligations of the remaining partners. Actual notice must be given to all those who have extended credit to the partnership, otherwise a public notice is sufficient.

After dissolution and notice, the partners cannot create new obligations for the partnership. Instead, the partnership moves to the second step in the termination process known as **winding up.** Current obligations must be concluded and the business wound up, i.e. collect assets, pay debts and accounts of each partner for the value of their interest.

Once the assets of the partnership have been accumulated, they are distributed in the following order:

- Third party creditors are paid first.

- Refund of loans made to or for the firm by the partners is then made.

- The capital contributions made by the partners are refunded.

- The balance of the assets is distributed to the partners in proportion to their shares in the venture.

Savvy business partners usually provide for a **Buy-Sell Agreement** in their partnership agreement which document creates a process in advance, on how the remaining partners are to buy out the leaving partner. Procedures for calculating value and payout method are predetermined. In case of death of a partner, this agreement can also provide for life insurance to be used to pay the estate of the deceased partner, the value of that person's interest.

If Tyler's Sports Bar and Grill was established as a partnership, the following would be a sample partnership agreement:

THIS PARTNERSHIP AGREEMENT is entered into between the following:

Joseph Roberts, 2605 Sandy Road, Philadelphia, Pa. and Donald Jones, 1534, Rydal Street, Philadelphia, Pa.

The above-named persons agree that they shall be become partners in business and conditions of this partnership are as follows:

1. The partnership's name shall be: Tyler's Sports Bar and Grill.

2. The principal place of business of the partnership shall be: *523 Water Avenue, Philadelphia, Pa.*

3. *Purpose* - The business of the partnership is to sell food and alcoholic beverages.

4. *Term* - The partnership shall continue until dissolved by mutual agreement of the partners.

5. *Capital contribution and distribution of profits and losses shall be as follows*:

     Joseph Roberts $10,000
     Donald Jones $10,000

     The profits and losses of the partnership shall be divided between the partners equally.

6. *Control* - Each partner shall have equal rights in the management and conduct of the business.

7. *Dissolution* - In the event of retirement, bankruptcy, or death, of a partner, the remaining partners shall have the right to continue the business under the same name.

Section 9.4
Limited Partnership

A. Creation

A **limited partnership** is a business entity that consists of one or more general partners and one or more limited partners. This form of enterprise is generally used to raise revenue since the liability of the limited partner is restricted to that person's investment and the limited partner has no say in the management of the operation. This type of entity is common in real estate development projects and the film industry.

This business form requires the filing of a **Certificate of Limited Partnership** with the state that contains the name of the partnership along with the words "limited partnership" in the title. The names and business addresses of each general partner will also be listed in the certificate.

B. Management

The business must be run by the general partners without the active participation from the limited partners.

C. Liability

The liability of a limited partner is restricted to that person's investment. The general partners, however, continue with unlimited liability. This benefit can be lost by a limited partner if that individual becomes involved in the affairs of the business. In that event, the person will have unlimited exposure.

If the limited partnership is organized in an improper manner and the limited partners discover this fact and fail to withdraw or amend the certificate, the limited partner can be held personally liable by the partnership's creditors.

D. Dissolution

A limited partnership is dissolved for the same reasons, and in much the same manner, as a general partnership. However, the death or bankruptcy of a limited partner does not dissolve the partnership.

Section 9.5
Limited Liability
Partnership

A. Creation

The **limited liability partnership** (LLP), a relatively new concept, is a hybrid between a partnership and corporation. It has been designed specifically for professionals, such as lawyers, doctors and accountants, to avoid personal liability for the malpractice of the other partners. Not all states, however, recognize this type of entity.

This business form must be registered with the state as a limited liability partnership and the name of the business must include a designation like company, limited, or limited liability company. For instance, it is common to see the firm use the initials "LLP" in order to notify others of the nature of the organizational form. In addition, the company is required to file a certificate of annual registration each year.

B. Management

Unlike a limited partner, those in a limited liability partnership manage the business on a routine basis.

C. Liability

The major advantage of this business form is that the partners are not personally liable for the malpractice claims of the other partners and, in some states, are not liable for the debts of the partnership. This is why it is called a hybrid since its owners enjoy the immunity of stockholders of a corporation.

When more than one partner is negligent, such as when a claim is made against a negligent partner and that person's supervisor, there is a question as to how liability is to be shared. Some states provide for proportionate liability, i.e. a separate determination of the negligence of each partner.

HENRY CHAMBERLAIN V. CHARLES IRVING
2006 WL 3290446 (CONN. SUPER., 2006)

This is a breach of contract action brought by Henry and Mary Chamberlain against the defendant, attorney Charles J. Irving. The plaintiffs filed their complaint alleging that the defendant's bill for $13,680 breached the fee agreement, which stated that fees were not to exceed $1,000. On May 30, 2006, the defendant filed an answer alleging that he was a limited liability partner at all times.

General Statutes § 34-327(c) provides in relevant part: "[A] partner in a registered limited liability partnership is not liable... for any debts, obligations and liabilities... arising in contract... arising in the course of the partnership business while the partnership is a registered limited liability partnership." This statute protects partners in a registered limited liability partnership from personal liability.

To establish that he is not personally liable under this statute, the defendant submits as evidence (1) the firm's certificate of standing with the secretary of state indicating the firm's existence as a registered limited liability partnership; (2) an affidavit from Garon Camassar, a partner of the law firm, attesting that the defendant practiced law as a partner during the time period at issue in the present case; and (3) an assortment of pleadings and other papers filed on the plaintiffs' behalf during the course of representation, all bearing the firm's name, "Irving, Dubicki & Camassar, LLP."

Also submitted is the fee agreement between the parties written in the form of a letter addressed to the plaintiffs. It states in relevant part: "To confirm our office discussion... it is my understanding that, should you decide to engage the services of this *law firm, we* would be representing each of you… Legal fees would be charged at the rate of $125.00 per hour for partners' time and $75.00 per hour for *associate attorneys'* time ... Should you see fit to engage the services of this law firm, I would look forward to working with you in this matter." At the top and centered, the agreement's letterhead contains the following in bold, conspicuous letters: "IRVING, DUBICKI & CAMASSAR." Below the firm name is: "ATTORNEYS & COUNSELORS AT LAW," followed beneath by the firm's address.

The plaintiffs' memorandum in opposition prints out that there is no "LLP" designation in the fee agreement. Henry Chamberlain states that he never met with attorneys Camassar and Dubicki, that he was unaware that he was dealing with a limited liability partnership, and that the defendant never "specifically represented" to him that he was a limited liability partner.

The court finds first that there is no genuine issue as to whether the defendant's firm represented the plaintiffs under the fee agreement. The agreement's terms-its words and their context-give rise to no conclusion other than that the firm, not the defendant individually, is agreeing to provide legal representation. The letterhead's omission of "LLP" is insignificant for that reason. Second, nowhere does § 34-327 condition its protection of partners on whether a third party knows that he or she is dealing with a limited liability partnership. This entitles the defendant to judgment as a matter of law.

For the above foregoing reasons, the defendant's motion for summary judgment is hereby granted.

SECTION 9.6
FAMILY LIMITED
LIABILITY PARTNERSHIP

A **family limited liability partnership** (FLLP) is a relatively new phenomenon in which the partners are related to each other. This type of partnership is recommended by a number of tax professionals as an estate planning tool especially for a client who has a great deal of wealth. Basically, the owner transfers the specified assets or property to the partnership made up of family members. The owner then supervises the partnership as the general partner and the family members are the limited partners. In this way, the property is removed from the person's estate even though the previous owner continues to use and manage the property.

SECTION 9.7
CORPORATION

A. Creation

A **corporation** is a separate and distinct entity apart from its owners. This allows the corporation to own assets, borrow money, hire employees and enter into contracts. By being its own person, the owners of the business, known as stockholders, are able to reduce their personal exposure for the debts and liabilities of the corporation.

A corporation is a creature of state law and those wanting to form a corporation are required to file **Articles of Incorporation** with the appropriate state office and pay a fee. The following information must be included in the Articles of Incorporation:

- Corporate Name

- Nature and Purpose

- Duration

- Capital Structure

- Internal Organization

- Registered Office

The name of the business is an important marketing tool for the business and great care is usually exercised in its selection. That name, however, cannot be the same or similar to an existing corporation or mislead as to the nature of the corporate business. The name must also end with a corporate denominator such as inc., co. or corp. For instance, if Tyler's was created as a corporation, it would be identified as Tyler's Sports Bar and Grill, Inc.

The nature and purpose requirement can usually be set forth as "for all legal purposes" in order not to restrict the corporation in the future as to the type of business it will conduct.

The duration of the corporation can be for a specific term of years or perpetual.

Capital structure refers to the classes and numbers of shares of stock that will be issued by the new entity.

Internal organization refers to the management structure of the company and the registered office is the address within the state where the corporation can be served with legal process and papers are to be mailed.

Once this information is ascertained and the Articles of Incorporation form completed, it is signed by the incorporators and sent to the appropriate state office. The papers will then be processed and the incorporators will receive a **Certificate of Incorporation**. This is the corporation's "birth certificate."

ARTICLES OF INCORPORATION
Tyler's Sports Bar and Grill, Inc.

We, the undersigned, persons acting as incorporators under the Pennsylvania Business Corporation Act, adopt the following Articles of Incorporation for such Corporation:

Article I

The name of the corporation is: *Tyler's Sports Bar and Grill, Inc.*

Article II

The purpose for which the corporation is organized is to engage in all aspects of the sale of food and alcoholic beverages. The corporation shall further have unlimited power to engage in and do any lawful act concerning any and all lawful business for which corporations may be organized under the Pennsylvania Business Corporation Act and any amendments thereto.

The corporation shall have authority to issue One Hundred Thousand (100,000) shares of stock which stock shall be of one class only, which shall be common, voting stock.

Article IV

The address of the corporation's initial registered office shall be:

1500 John F. Kennedy Boulevard, Philadelphia, Pa. 19102

The corporation's initial registered agent at such address shall be:
Peter Smith, *Esquire*

Article V

The names and addresses of the Incorporators are:

Joseph Roberts, 2605 Sandy Road, Philadelphia, Pa.
Donald Jones, 1534, Rydal Street, Philadelphia, Pa.

In Witness Whereof, Joseph Roberts and Donald Jones of Tyler's Sports Bar and Grill, Inc., have executed these Articles of incorporation and say: That they are all incorporators herein; that they have read the above and foregoing Articles of Incorporation; know the contents thereof and that the same is true to the best of their knowledge and belief, excepting as to matters herein alleged upon information and belief and as to those matters they believe to be true.

B. Continuity

Since the corporation is its own person, its status is not changed by the death or sale of stock by a shareholder.

C. Management

A corporation can engage in any act or enter into any contract available to a natural person in order to accomplish the purposes for which it was created. The corporation has express powers as delineated in the Certificate of Incorporation, By-Laws and resolutions of the Board of Directors. A corporation also has the implied power to perform all acts reasonably appropriate and necessary to carry out its corporate purposes.

Responsibility for the overall management of the corporation is with the **Board of Directors** who are elected by the shareholder. In turn, the Board of Directors selects the **corporate officers,** such as the president or treasurer, who are responsible for the day-to-day operation of the business. The Directors, however, have a duty to supervise the activities of the officers selected by them to run the corporation.

The members of the Board of Directors are fiduciaries of the corporation. However, no single Director can bind the corporation. The Board holds formal meetings with recorded minutes that must be in compliance with the firm's by-laws. The Board can also delegate some of its functions to an Executive Committee of the Board and various committees can be formed to deal with a specific issue such as compensation, auditor selection and nominating new members to the Board.

Directors cannot use corporate funds or inside information to their own advantage. These problems usually arise in the areas of competing with the corporation, usurping a corporate opportunity, doing business with the corporation, abusing minority shareholders or seizing control of the corporation.

The **Business Judgment Rule** guides the conduct of the Directors. They must use their best judgment in making decisions for the corporation. However, they are not insurers of the corporation's business success. If a decision is made that does not turn out well for the corporation, generally there is no cause of action against the Directors if they exercise their best judgment even if a "wrong" decision was made.

D. Liability

The shareholders own the corporation but they are not personally liable for the payment of corporate debt in the absence of a personal guarantee. Their only risk is the investment made in the corporation in the nature of purchasing stock in the business. While shareholders are not personally responsible for corporate debt or corporate actions, a Court could find responsibility by **piercing the corporate veil.** This occurs when there is fraud, under capitalization, intermingling of the business assets or disregarding the corporate entity such as what might occur when the business commingles the business assets with those of the stockholders.

Shareholders must approve major changes in corporate authority, such as amendments to the Articles of Incorporation, and they must approve a merger or dissolution or the sale of a substantial part of the corporate assets.

A shareholder has the right to inspect and copy the corporate books and records but such an inspection can be limited if it is for the purpose of corporate espionage, trade secret violations or harassment.

E. Taxation

The major disadvantage of a corporation is one of double taxation. Federal and state governments tax the corporate profits. However, the share of profits or dividends passed on to shareholders is taxed again on their personal tax returns.

The following case deals with an attempt to pierce the corporate veil in order to hold the stockholders liable for the debts of the business.

GILBERT V. JAMES RUSSELL MOTORS, INC.
812 SO.2D 1269 (ALA. CIV. APP., 2001)

James Russell Motors, Inc. ("JRM"), sued G & W Auto Sales, Inc. ("G & W"), and John Gilbert and his wife Lori Gilbert, who were shareholders of G & W. In its complaint, JRM sought to pierce G & W's corporate veil and impose on the Gilberts personal liability for G & W's debt to JRM. The trial court entered a judgment that pierced the corporate veil, and held the Gilberts both liable for the actions of the corporation.

In December 1997, the Gilberts and Lee Wood formed G & W to buy and sell automobiles. Wood contributed his experience in the automobile trade; Wood had exclusive responsibility for buying and selling the used automobiles. The Gilberts contrib-uted $22,000 in initial capital, and they later contributed an additional $3,600 to G & W to pay taxes.

Wood obtained business licenses for G & W, and he began buying and selling automobiles. The Gilberts opened two business bank accounts in the name "G & W Auto Brokers." G & W used one account for its regular business operations and the other account for a tax account. After all of these actions were taken, the Gilberts contacted an attorney about incorporating the business.

On February 4, 1998, the Gilberts and Wood executed articles of incorporation. The articles of incorporation named Lori Gilbert, John Gilbert, and

Wood as the incorporators of G & W. On February 5, 1998, the Gilberts and Wood filed G & W's articles of incorporation thereby forming G & W Auto Brokers, Inc.

On February 5, 1998, the date of G & W's incorporation, the shareholders held a corporate meeting, at which they adopted bylaws and elected officers. The minutes of the first shareholders' meeting indicate that stockholder certificates were delivered to G & W's shareholders. G & W's corporate minutes further reflect that the shareholders elected John Gilbert as president, Wood as vice president, Lori Gilbert as treasurer, and Michelle Wood as secretary.

On or about April 29, 1998, Wood, on behalf of G & W, took possession of three motor vehicles from Steve Dyas Autoshine, Inc., the predecessor to JRM. The total amount of G & W's transaction with Steve Dyas Autoshine was $24,275. G & W satisfied $7,600 of that amount. A balance remained of $16,675; that balance is the basis of this litigation.

Wood testified at his deposition that the Gilberts were not aware of the transactions between G & W and Steve Dyas Autoshine. Wood had accepted the three automobiles from Steve Dyas Autoshine and had sold the automobiles to individuals; Wood did not pay Steve Dyas Autoshine for the three automobiles. It does not appear that Wood actually deposited the money he received for the sale of those automobiles into either of G & W's bank accounts. Wood's testimony further indicates that on more than one occasion, Wood took money from G & W without the Gilberts' knowledge. In doing so, Wood accepted cash for automobiles he sold from G & W's stock, but he did not deposit that money into either of G & W's bank accounts. Wood also admitted that he lied to the Gilberts about transactions that did not actually take place.

A corporation is a legal entity that exists separate from its shareholders, and its actions and obligations are to be considered separately from those of its shareholders. The corporate structure is intended to protect shareholders and officers from liability

arising from the operation of the corporation. The ability to pierce a corporate veil and impose personal liability on the corporation's shareholders furnishes a means for a complainant to reach an individual upon a cause of action that otherwise would have existed only against the corporation. Piercing the corporate veil to impose personal liability on a corporation's shareholder is not a power that is exercised lightly.

The Alabama Supreme Court has set out the following circumstances in which it would be appropriate to pierce the corporate veil: 1) where the corporation is inadequately capitalized; 2) where the corporation is conceived or operated for a fraudulent purpose; or 3) where the corporation is operated as an instrumentality or alter ego of an individual or entity with corporate control.

The Gilberts argue that the record contains no evidence indicating that G & W was a "sham" corporation; they also argue that JRM presented no evidence of fraud on their part. G & W was created to buy and sell. The evidence suggests that G & W did in fact buy used automobiles and sell them to various businesses and individuals, including JRM. JRM argued to the trial court that G & W was created for a fraudulent purpose, namely to protect the Gilberts from liability that might arise from wrongful acts by Wood. However, the use of the corporate form to shield shareholders from personal liability is not a fraudulent purpose. In the absence of fraud, the corporate structure protects an individual from liability for the actions of the corporation. A legitimate primary purpose of any corporation is to limit the liability of its shareholders. JRM presented no evidence indicating that the Gilberts engaged in any fraudulent conduct. We agree that JRM presented no evidence to support a conclusion that the Gilberts had a fraudulent purpose in their conception of, or in their operation of, G & W.

JRM also argued that G & W did not comply with corporate formalities required by the Alabama Business Corporation Act. The evidence indicates without dispute that G & W was operated in accordance with its stated purpose, that of buying and selling used automobiles. In addition, the record contains evidence indicating that G & W was formed and registered in compliance with the provisions of the Alabama Business Corporation Act; that articles of incorporation and bylaws were adopted, that officers were elected, that common stock was issued, that corporate meetings were held, and that corporate records were maintained. The trial court received into evidence G & W's articles of incorporation, its bylaws, and minutes of the initial shareholders meeting, bank-account records, tax records, and employment-withholding records. Our supreme court has affirmed a judgment refusing to pierce a corporate veil even though the shareholders had failed to comply with all corporate formalities. Our review of the documents presented suggests that G & W substantially met the requirements of a corporate entity.

We cannot say the evidence regarding G & W's compliance with corporate formalities is sufficient to demonstrate that the Gilberts operated G & W as a "sham" corporation, or that the evidence supports a conclusion that G & W's corporate veil should be pierced on this basis.

The Gilberts also argue that they did not operate G & W as an alter ego or instrumentality of themselves. In order to prove that G & W was an alter ego or instrumentality of the Gilberts, JRM would have to present evidence indicating: 1) that the Gilberts had complete control and domination of G & W's finances, policy, and business practices, so that at the time of the challenged transaction G & W had no separate mind, will, or existence of its own; 2) that the Gilberts misused that control; and 3) that the Gilberts' misuse of that control was the proximate cause of harm or unjust loss to JRM.

JRM presented evidence indicating that it dealt only with Wood when it engaged in business with G & W. The Gilberts and Wood testified that Wood conducted the day-to-day operations of G & W. The evidence in the record indicates that, by having sole check-writing authority, the Gilberts controlled only the expenditures from G & W's bank accounts; the record indicates that Wood made many, if not all, of the deposits into G & W's bank accounts. No evidence indicates that the Gilberts knew of Wood's inappropriate activities with regard to the business or that they condoned those activities. The evidence in the record does not support a conclusion that the Gilberts had complete control of G & W, that they misused any control that they did have, or that any misuse they allegedly exerted proximately caused harm to JRM. We cannot say that the record contains evidence that would support a piercing of G & W's corporate veil for that reason.

We agree with the Gilberts that the evidence in the record is not sufficient to support an order piercing the corporate veil so as to impose personal liability on the Gilberts. We must reverse the judgment of the trial court.

SECTION 9.8 SUBCHAPTER S CORPORATION

A corporation can choose to be treated as an "S Corporation" as that term is defined by the Internal Revenue Code. The distinction for this type of corporation is that the profits are passed on directly to the shareholders and taxed to them, as profits would be in a partnership. Since the corporation pays no taxes, this type of entity eliminates the issue of double taxation that normally arises with a corporation.

In order to form a Subchapter S corporation, several qualifications must be met. The corporation must be a domestic corporation formed in a particular state and the entity must be a stand-alone company. In other words, it may not be a member of an affiliated group of corporations. The shareholders must be individuals, estates or certain trusts and there are a maximum number of shareholders allowed. Currently, that number is 100 and no shareholder can be a non-resident alien. If these conditions are met, the business can file Form 2553 with the Internal Revenue Service. This form is known as an Election by a Small Business Corporation and requires each shareholder to sign the form consenting to the business being treated as a Subchapter S corporation.

SECTION 9.9
LIMITED LIABILITY COMPANY

A. Creation

A **limited liability company** is a new, but popular type of business venture that does exactly what its name implies—it offers limited liability to its owners who are also known as members. It is less formal than a corporation in that the business does not have to maintain minutes and hold formal meetings of its owners.

To form a limited liability company (LLC), the Articles of Corporation must include information similar to corporate Articles of Incorporation. The business name must also include the designation at the end of LLC. For jurisdictional purposes, an LLC is a citizen of every state where its members are citizens.

B. Advantages and Disadvantages

A limited liability company is a hybrid form of a business enterprise that offers the limited liability of the corporation with the tax advantages of a partnership. In addition, the members of the venture are taxed as a sole proprietorship, unless they elect to be taxed as corporations.

Members of the limited liability company decide how to operate the business but an operating agreement does not need to be in writing. In a member managed LLC, all owners participate in management. In a manager managed LLC, the members designate a group of persons (member or not) to run the firm.

SECTION 9.10
FRANCHISES

According to Franchise Consultants, Inc., **franchises** account for about 50% of all retail sales in the United States and employ more than 15 million people. Entrepreneurs like them because the franchise has instant name recognition and assistance in running the business. People immediately know what is sold at McDonald's or Dunkin Donuts and the retailer receives start up training and advertising help. What then, is a franchise? It is an arrangement in which the owner of a trademark, trade name or copyright allows another to offer its products for sale or use in a geographic area. The key parties to this arrangement are the **franchisor** or owner of the business idea and **franchisee** or owner of the store offering the item to the public.

Several types of franchise arrangements have emerged over the years. A **distributorship** involves a manufacturing concern that licenses a dealer to sell its product such as an automobile dealership. A **chain style business operation** is one in which the franchisee operates the business under the name of the franchisor and must follow standardized methods of operation. This is the classic fast food operation such as McDonald's or Burger King. The last is a **manufacturing or processing plant franchise** where the franchisor provides the franchisee with an essential ingredient or formula to make a particular product such as a Coca Cola bottling plant.

The franchise agreement is a contract and is governed by state and federal statutes that regulate these types of contracts. For example, the Automobile Dealers Franchise Act and the Petroleum Marketing Practices Act deal with problems that can arise in automobile and gasoline franchise operations. The Federal Trade Commission also requires the (1) disclosure of material facts to all prospective franchisees in the business arrangement at the earlier of the first face-to-face meeting or ten business days before any money is paid or an agreement is signed in connection with the investment, and (2) the franchisor must give investors a copy of its standard-form franchise and related agreements at least 5 business days before their signing.

The franchise agreement is important because it spells out the terms of the relationship including the payment for the franchise, the purchase of products from the franchisor and the costs for advertising. The agreement will also discuss whether business premises are to be leased or purchased, the location of the franchise, sales quotas, record keeping responsibilities, and employee training. The franchiser may even require the franchisee to buy supplies from the franchisor.

There are several factors that can cause the termination of a franchise arrangement. For instance, the franchise contract may have a set term, such as ten years, and there can be a "termination for cause" clause that allows the franchise license to be revoked such as for none payment of fees to the franchisor, failure to follow the rules established by the home office or upon the death, disability or insolvency of the franchisee.

The franchisor and franchisee must also act in good faith and fairly deal with each other at all times. This is the issue in the following case.

SHERMAN V. MASTER PROTECTION CORP.
2002 WL 31854905 (CAL. APP. 6 DIST.)

Master Protection Corporation (MPC) is in the business of selling and servicing fire protection equipment under the trade name "FireMaster." In 1987, Michael Sherman purchased an MPC franchise for $40,000, and in 1991, he purchased a second franchise for $60,000. The franchise agreements provided that the purchase price was equivalent to the approximate gross sales from the previous year. In each case, Sherman signed a promissory note for the entire purchase price. The franchise agreements gave the franchisee the right to sell and service FireMaster fire extinguishers to MPC's customers within particular geographical territories, and to use MPC's trade name and service mark. In addition, MPC agreed to provide certain support services to its franchisees. The franchise agreements provided that the franchisee could sell or assign its rights under the agreement to a bona fide purchaser, subject to MPC's right to approve such a sale. When Sherman purchased his franchises, MPC's portable fire extinguishers were all sold and serviced by franchisees operating under territorial franchises similar to those purchased by Sherman.

In 1994, MPC management decided to phase out the franchise program in favor of an employee-based service operation. MPC did not inform its franchisees of this decision. A phase-out plan was drafted whereby MPC would stop selling new franchises and would repurchase existing franchises only at the "end" of the phase-out and only if necessary to keep the franchises from reselling to others. In January of 1995, MPC established a field service employee program and began hiring increasing numbers of employees to perform field services, including the sales and servicing of fire extinguishers formerly referred exclusively to the franchisees. MPC projected that its future mode of doing business would be with a "100% employee based field work force."

Sherman filed this complaint containing five causes of action: 1) violation of franchise investment law; 2) breach of the franchise agreement; 3) breach of the implied covenant of good faith and fair dealing; 4) breach of fiduciary duty; and 5) fraud.

As to the second cause of action for breach of the franchise agreements, the court found that MPC had breached the agreements when its employees sold and serviced fire extinguishers within Sherman's territories "resulting in a misappropriation of work." The court fixed damages at $11,697.49. As to the third cause of action for breach of the implied covenant of good faith and fair dealing, the trial court found that MPC's decision to phase out the franchise program was more than simply a decision not to sell any more franchises. It also involved a decision to make it difficult for franchisees to sell or assign their franchises, a decision not to repurchase any of the franchises and a decision to replace the franchisees with employees. The trial court found this conduct constituted a breach of the implied covenant of good faith and fair dealing. The trial court further found that as a result of MPC's conduct, "[Sherman's] franchises have become unsalable." The court awarded damages of $258,679, representing the purchase value of the franchises based on the gross sales for the previous year, as per the parties' franchise agreement.

MPC contends that there was no wrongful conduct shown that was contrary to any express or implied term of the franchise agreements. MPC argues that nothing in the franchise agreements guaranteed the longevity of the franchise program or prevented MPC from making what was essentially a business decision to discontinue the franchise program and move to an employee-based operation. Therefore it could not be a breach of the covenant of good faith and fair dealing to do so since the covenant exists merely to prevent one contracting party from unfairly frustrating the other party's right to receive *the benefits of the agreement actually made.* These principles, MPC argues, prevent a finding of a breach of implied covenant because MPC did not act contrary to any provision in the contract.

Breach of a provision in the contract, however, is not a necessary prerequisite to finding a breach of the covenant of good faith and fair dealing. Rather, the question is whether the conduct, even though not expressly prohibited, is nevertheless "contrary to the contract's purposes and the parties' legitimate expectations. The covenant of good faith is implied as a supplement to express contractual covenants to prevent a party from engaging in conduct that frustrates the other party's rights to the benefits of the agreement.

Here, the evidence showed that one of the intended benefits of purchasing a franchise was to build equity for resale. The franchise agreements provided for a right to sell the franchise and further provided that MPC had the right of first refusal. The franchisee was required to meet minimum increases in annual sales, and the purchase price of the franchise at any given time was determined based on the previous year's approximate gross sales. Thus, the agreements clearly contemplated that the franchises would increase in value over time. In 1992, MPC's President, Robert Wiles, issued a mission statement to all franchisees emphasizing MPC's "commitment to fair and ethical dealings with our ... franchise owners."

MPC argues that the court erred by finding that the phasing out of the franchise program was a breach of the covenant of good faith and fair dealing. This somewhat misstates the court's finding. The wrongful conduct found by the trial court was "more than simply a decision not to sell any more franchises." Rather, it was the way MPC went about implementing its decision. Without informing its franchisees of a management decision affecting their livelihood, MPC began hiring increasing numbers of employees to perform field services within the franchised territories and in competition with the franchisees. MPC

made it difficult for franchisees to sell or assign their franchises. In addition, MPC refused to repurchase franchises. The court found that such conduct was a breach of the covenant of good faith and fair dealing in that it frustrated plaintiff's expectations and injured "plaintiff's right to receive the fruits and benefits of his franchise agreements." We believe this falls within the legal parameters of the theory of breach of the covenant of good faith and fair dealing.

The court found that MPC's conduct rendered Sherman's franchises "unsalable," and awarded Sherman damages representing the "full amount of the probable sales value of [Sherman's] franchises, but for defendant's conduct." This amount was the equivalent of the previous year's gross annual sales, which was the method of setting the price of an MPC franchise as per the parties' franchise agreement. MPC argues that "unsalability" was an erroneous legal standard on which to base an award of damages.

The court's finding that Sherman's franchises had become "unsalable" was supported by substantial evidence in the record. Other franchise owners testified that they had made efforts to sell their franchises back to MPC or to employees of MPC, with no success. In some cases, MPC discouraged the buyers or blocked the sales by withholding approval. Sherman testified that he was not aware of any franchise owner in the San Jose area who had been able to resell his franchise since 1994. Out of eight or nine franchise owners in this area, there were only three left and none of the others had gotten anything for their franchises.

Sherman offered to sell his franchises to a number of MPC field service employees, whose response was to laugh at him. They told him "FireMaster doesn't want the franchise program any more. Sherman's expert witness testified that in his opinion, Sherman's franchises were not saleable because the franchise system was being phased out, because MPC was no longer selling franchises or repurchasing them, and because MPC was in fact competing with its own franchisees by supporting its employee system.

MPC's principal argument regarding damages is that the court erred in awarding damages representing the full value of the franchises because the franchises were not worthless and in fact continued to produce income for Sherman. Uncontroverted evidence, including Sherman's testimony, showed that the income produced by the two franchises had steadily increased over the years, in spite of MPC's phase-out plan. In 1999, the year upon which the court based its damages award, income from the two franchises was at a record high. Even if MPC's conduct in moving to an employee-based system may have rendered Sherman's franchises unmarketable, the franchises continued to have some value as income-producing assets. According to MPC, it was therefore error to award Sherman the full value of the assets while he retained the assets and the benefit of the income they continued to produce. Such an award, MPC argues, resulted in an impermissible double recovery.

The damages award was only a double recovery, however, if it represented the full fair market value of the franchises. The evidence showed that it did not. The amount awarded by the trial court was derived from the formula set forth in parties' franchise agreement-one times gross sales for the previous year. There was no evidence that this corresponded to fair market value.

The trial court, having found that the franchisor had wrongfully refused to buy back the franchise at this amount, and having found that the franchisor had essentially rendered the franchise unmarketable to others at any price, assessed damages based on the customary formula. Under the circumstances, the court's use of the formula in the franchise agreements was reasonably based in the evidence.

The judgment is affirmed.

SECTION 9.11
SECURITY REGULATIONS AND INVESTOR PROTECTION

The **Securities and Exchange Commission** (SEC) was created as the result of the Great Depression and stock market crash of 1929 to restore confidence in the stock market. The SEC was established as an independent regulatory agency with the authority to enforce the provisions of the 1933 and 1934 Securities Exchange Acts.

The SEC considers its mission to be one of protection of investors, maintaining fair, orderly, and efficient markets, and to facilitate capital formation. As the Commission notes on its website:

The laws and rules that govern the securities industry in the United States derive from a simple and straightforward concept: all investors, whether large institutions or private individuals, should have access to certain basic facts about an investment prior to buying it, and so long as they hold it. To achieve this, the SEC requires public companies to disclose meaningful financial and other information to the public. This provides a common pool of knowledge for all investors to use to judge for themselves whether to buy, sell, or hold a particular security. Only through the steady flow of timely, comprehensive, and accurate information can people make sound investment decisions.

With a staff of almost 4,000 employees scattered throughout the United States, the Commission is responsible for the interpretation of federal securities laws; to oversee the inspection of securities firms, brokers, investment advisers, and ratings agencies; to oversee private regulatory organizations in the securities, accounting, and auditing fields; and to coordinate U.S. securities regulation with federal, state, and foreign authorities.

For instance, these goals have led to a variety of remedial actions such as the required disclosure of facts concerning the offering of listed securities, the regulation of trading of listed securities, the investigation of securities fraud, the regulation of securities dealers, the supervision of mutual funds and to recommend administrative sanctions for violations of securities laws.

The following is an overview of some of the important legislation that is within the purview and enforcement of the SEC.

A. Securities Act of 1933

The **Securities Act of 1933** authorizes the SEC to regulate the trading of listed securities, investigate securities fraud, regulate securities dealers, supervise mutual funds and recommend administrative sanctions for violations of the various securities laws.

Additional authority has been given to the SEC over the years such as: expansion of authority over securities fraud cases, the power to sanction those who violate foreign securities laws and authority to exempt persons or securities from the requirements of securities laws.

After the collapse of the Enron Company and the revelation of massive accounting fraud and misleading corporate financial reports, Congress enacted the **Sarbanes-Oxley Act**. Described by President Bush as "the most far reaching reforms of American business practices since the time of Franklin Delano Roosevelt," the law seeks to enhance corporate responsibility, enhance financial disclosures and combat corporate and accounting fraud.

The Sarbanes-Oxley Act only applies to publicly traded companies and seeks to increase corporate accountability through a number of initiatives such as the requirement that the CEO and CFO of a firm must certify the validity of financial statements and there can be no personal loans to officers and directors. The law also provides more protection for corporate whistleblowers, and extends the Statute of Limitations for securities fraud to two years after discovery or five years after violation, whichever is earlier.

The Securities Act of 1933 also governs the initial sales of securities by a business and mandates that all information concerning the issuance of securities must be made available to the public.

A **security** is defined in the Act to include such investments as a note, stock, bond, and evidence of indebtedness, certificate of interest or participation in any profit sharing agreement. For our purposes, however, it is best to think of a security as stocks and bonds issued by a corporation.

If a corporation wants to "go public" or sell stock to the public, it must file a **Registration Statement** with the SEC. In turn, a prospective investor in the business is provided with a **prospectus** with information similar to the Registration Statement. The SEC does not recommend any security for purchase. Rather, its job is to make sure a prospective investor has all of the information needed to make an informed decision as to whether to buy the security.

The Registration Statement must provide information as to the significant provisions of the security, how the proceeds of the sale are to be used, the registrant's property, the management of the company and compensation arrangements, a certified financial statement and a listing of pending lawsuits. There is a twenty-day waiting period after registration before a sale can take place.

It is a violation of the Securities Act of 1933 to intentionally defraud investors by misrepresenting or omitting facts in a Registration Statement or prospectus. Liability is also imposed on anyone who is negligent in failing to discover the fraud, such as the accountants, lawyers, and underwriters hired by the firm.

Defenses to a violation of the Act include such things as the false statement or omission was not material, and the buyer knew of the misrepresentation but bought the stock anyway.

The SEC has broad powers and can impose both criminal and civil penalties. Criminal penalties consist of imprisonment, fines or both while civil remedies include damages and injunctions against any further sales of the securities. In addition, a person who purchases a security as a result of false or omitted statements in the prospectus can sue to recover those losses.

B. Securities Exchange Act of 1934

While the Securities Exchange Act of 1933 focuses on the original offerings of a security, the **Securities Exchange Act of 1934** regulates the subsequent sale of securities and requires the registration of security exchanges, brokers, and dealers of the markets in which securities are traded. This is known as the secondary market and would include the regulation of the New York and American Stock Exchanges.

As for the Act itself, it prohibits the use of any manipulative or deceptive device in violation of the SEC rules. In fact, **Rule 10b-5** prohibits the commission of fraud in connection with the purchase or sale of any security and provides:

It shall be unlawful for any person… by the use of any means or instrumentality of interstate commerce, or of the mails or of any facility of any national securities exchange:

1. To employ any device, scheme, or artifice to defraud,

2. To make any untrue statement of a material fact or to omit to state a material fact necessary in order to make the statements made, in the light of the circumstances under which they were made, not misleading, or

3. To engage in any act, practice, or course of business which operates or would operate as a fraud or deceit upon any person, in connection with the purchase or sale of any security.

The Securities and Exchange Commission is also concerned with **insider trading** and aggressively pursues these types of cases. The SEC defines illegal insider trading as the buying or selling of a security, in breach of a fiduciary duty or other relationship of trust and confidence, while in possession of non-public information about that security.

When officers and directors are privy to information others do not possess, they cannot take advantage of this information so material information about the company must be disclosed to the public before an insider can buy or sell that security.

The key to liability is whether the insider's information is material such as the fraudulent trading in the stock by a broker, a dividend change (up or down), sale of corporate assets, a newly discovered process or product, a significant change in financial position and potential litigation.

Insider trading also encompasses **tipping,** which refers to the practice of buying or selling of securities by a person who is "tipped," with non-public information in a stock or bond. The SEC has used several legal theories to establish liability for such insider trading.

The **Tipper/Tipee Theory** deals with someone who acquires inside information as the result of a corporate insider's breach of that person's fiduciary duty to the corporation.

On the other hand, the **Misappropriation Theory** deals with an individual who wrongfully obtains or misappropriates inside information and trades on it for that person's own benefit. In essence, the individual is considered to have stolen the information belonging to another.

In order to reduce the potential for insider trading, the SEC requires corporate insiders, who trade in their own securities, to report those trades to the Commission. A corporate insider includes a company's officers and directors, as well as any beneficial owners of more than ten percent of a class of the company's equity securities.

The SEC has also issued a regulation to prevent **short swing profits**. This rule requires company insiders, who buy and sell their firm's securities within a six-month period, to return any profits made from those transactions to the business.

Insider trading retards investor confidence in the integrity of the securities markets. Therefore, the SEC, by its own admission, considers the detection of insider trading as one of its top priorities. In fact, the Commission will issue a reward to any individual who provides information leading to the recovery of a civil penalty from an inside trader, from a person who "tipped" information to an inside trader, or from an individual who controlled an inside trader.

Penalties can include the Commission's filing of a civil enforcement action or the request of a fine not to exceed three times the amount of the profit gained or lost avoided as a result of a violation or in a criminal prosecution by the Department of Justice.

C. Private Securities Litigation Reform Act of 1995

In an effort to limit some types of securities litigation, especially those resulting in class action lawsuits, Congress enacted the **Private Securities Litigation Reform Act of 1995**. Prior to this legislation, there was a spate of securities litigation in which the plaintiffs claimed that the corporation provided information concerning its future prospects, such as the projection of revenues and earnings that turnout to be inaccurate. The Act now provides a "safe harbor" or lack of accountability for forward-looking company statements that are considered financial forecasts. The corporation, however, must accompany the forecast with meaningful cautionary statements that identify the various factors that could cause changes in the projections.

SECTION 9.12
REVIEW QUESTIONS

1. Jones, Jackson and Daly are lawyers. Each was a sole proprietor of his own law practice and shared an office suite. They each paid one-third of the rent, photocopier, fax and cost of a receptionist to answer their telephones. Each had his own telephone number and stationary, paid his own secretary, postage and all other expenses associated with the law practice. They each kept all fees earned individually and did not share fees with the others. When a client called the office, the receptionist would answer, "Law office of Jones, Jackson, or Daly" depending on whose line rang. One day, they were having lunch together and Jones said they might be able to make more money if potential clients believed they were partners. Jackson and Daly agreed so they changed their stationary to read "Jones, Jackson and Daly–Attorneys at Law." Each kept his own telephone number, but if someone called the receptionist, she would answer "Jones, Jackson and Daly–Attorneys at Law, how may I direct your call?" They each still

paid one-third of the rent, photocopier, fax and receptionist expenses and continued to keep the fees each earned. One day, Ellie Vator came into the law suite and asked to see a lawyer in regard to a recent motor vehicle accident in which she sustained serious injuries. The receptionist directed her to Mr. Jackson who handled negligence cases and he agreed to represent her. Unfortunately, Mr. Jackson did not file Ellie's lawsuit within the appropriate Statute of Limitations and her case was dismissed by the court. Ellie wants to bring a legal malpractice case to collect damages for her loss as the result of Jackson's negligence. Can Ellie successfully sue Jones and Daly as partners of Mr. Jackson? Can Ellie sue the law partnership of "Jones, Jackson and Daly–Attorneys at Law." Do Jones and Daly have any legal redress against Jackson?

2. Bob is the Deputy Assistant Associate Vice-President of Intergalactic Industries. One day his boss, Big Joe, called Bob into his office and told him that because Intergalactic lost a big government contract, he had to let Bob go. Big Joe was sorry but he had no alternative. However, Bob had back vacation pay and would be given a severance package of $100,000 to ease his transition to another job. About a week later, Bob saw an ad in the Business Journal for a new franchise seeking franchisees for a business venture known as "Roadkill Restaurants." Bob was interested. He always wanted to own a restaurant but he did not have the education or knowledge as to how to fulfill this dream. What questions should Bob ask Roadkill? Should Bob talk to anyone else other than Roadkill? What information is Roadkill required by FTC regulations to provide Bob? What advantages are there for Bob in obtaining a Roadkill franchise as opposed to staring his own restaurant?

3. Joe and Diane, a married couple, started a business selling left socks. At first, they sold the socks out of a cart they pushed down the street, but the business prospered and they opened a store. They then incorporated the business under the name Left Socks, Inc. As the years went by, they expanded and at their death, they operated six retail outlets selling left socks. They left the business to their two sons and daughter and the business grew into 25 stores. Eventually the three children died. Each son had two sons and the daughter had one daughter. These children inherited their parent's share. They all worked in the business and were members of the Board of Directors. They received a salary for the work they did and dividends for the shares they owned each year. One day, the four male cousins who owned two-thirds of the shares in the business decided to fire their female cousin who owned one-third of the shares. Then they removed her from the Board of Directors, decided not to declare any dividends and raised their own salaries to compensate for the lack of dividends. What action can their cousin take to get her position back? What can she do to get back on the Board of Directors? Can she compel her cousins to authorize the payment of a dividend? Will she be successful in her efforts?

4. Westside Sand, Inc. is a corporation and Gerald Webber is the president and stockholder of the business. An agent for Westside Sand Company purchased materials from P&L Construction Materials for use by Westside Sand Company. When the business defaulted on the payment of the bill, suit was instituted against Webber in his personal capacity. The evidence demonstrated that the agent never informed P&L that she was buying the materials for Westside Sand, Inc. Since the identity of Westside Sand, Inc. was not disclosed by the agent to P&L at the time of the purchase, does that make the president of Westside personally liable for the corporate debt? **Deroche v. P&L Construction Materials, Inc., 554 So.2d 717 (Ct. App. La., 1989).**

5. A&M Records sued M.V.C. Distributing Corporation and Donald Merry for the unauthorized duplication and distribution of musical recordings. Merry ran the business. These pirated or bootlegged tapes were reproductions of the original records marketed under a different record label. The record companies attempted to pierce the corporate veil of M.V.C. in order to hold Merry personally liable as a corporate officer for the music piracy. Is the officer of a business personally responsible for the improper or illegal actions of a corporation? **A&M Records, Inc. v. M.V.C. Distributing Corp., 574 F.2d 312 (6ᵗʰ Cir., 1978).**

SECTION 9.13
INTERNET REFERENCES

For more information about topics discussed in this chapter, see the following Internet sites:

A. Starting a Business

- **www.businesstown.com/gettingstarted/index.asp**
  This site provides a step by step process of starting a small business.

- **www.irs.ustreas.gov/bus_info/index.html**
  The IRS offers this site in order to provide tax information for businesses.

- **http://aol.toolkit.cch.com**
  This is a comprehensive site providing news updates, and information on planning, starting, and financing a business.

B. Starting an Internet Business

- **www.buildyourhomebiz.com**
  Those interested in starting an Internet business may find this address helpful since it offers articles, advice, and answers to frequently asked questions about the topic.

C. Limited Liability Companies

- **www.llc-usa.com**
  This site is dedicated to those interested in limited liability companies. Several links are provided to resources on the topic.

- **www.llcweb.com**
  General information about limited liability companies is contained at this site.

KEY TERMS

Agency
Agent
Alter-Ego Theory
Articles of Incorporation
Articles of Partnership
Business Judgment Rule
Buy and Sell Agreement
Certificate of Incorporation
Certificate of Limited
    Partnership
Chain Style Business
    Operation
Charter
Closely Held Corporations
Corporate Officers
Corporation
Derivative Suit
Directors
Dissolution
Distributorship
Domestic Corporation
Double Taxation
Family Limited Liability
    Partnership
Foreign Corporation
Fictitious Name Registration
Franchise
Incorporators
Information Return

Insider Trading
Limited Liability Company
Limited Liability Partnership
Limited Partnership
Misappropriation Theory
Officers
Organizational Forms
Partnership
Piercing the Corporate Veil
Principal
Private Securities Litigation
    Reform Act of 1995
Processing Plant Franchise
Prospectus
Proxies
Publicly Held Corporations
Registration Statement
Rule 10b-5
S Corporation
Sarbanes-Oxley Act
Securities Act of 1933
Securities and Exchange
    Commission
Securities Exchange Act of 1934
Shareholders
Short Swing Profits
Sole Proprietorship
Termination
Tipper/Tipee Theory

CHAPTER 10

EMPLOYMENT LAW*

SECTION 10.1
INTRODUCTION

Jamie Pierce, an employee of Tyler's Sport's Bar and Grill, was angry during a business meeting. He decided to leave the bar to "cool off." However, as he left, he shoved a half open door, fracturing his hand. Pierce was partially disabled for about two weeks. He requested workers' compensation benefits, but his request was denied on the grounds that the injury did not grow out of his work. Pierce then sued Tyler's and won—the court ruled that his injury was, in fact, job related.[1]

Managers have always had tough, demanding jobs, but in recent years, the law has added complicated, frustrating new expectations. The threat of lawsuits, like Pierce's, has become an important consideration in management decision-making. As union strength has declined, government rules and court decisions protecting employees have expanded. Those increased legal protections, a volatile economy, downsizing, decreased employer–employee loyalty, and other forces have led to unprecedented levels of employee litigation.

Rapidly changing technology is enhancing employee efficiency, but it too brings new litigation risks:

> Most of us have probably seen and maybe are also guilty of the daring and increasingly dangerous practice of "driving while dialing." This means cruising down the highway or zipping around city streets while chatting on a cell phone. Now, with the increasing popularity of PDAs (personal digital assistants), such as Palm Pilots and pocket PCs, some people are beginning to boldly master tapping the screens of the PDAs (as they sit in their laps) with one hand, and clutching the wheel with the other.

SECTION 10.2
SELECTION OF
AN EMPLOYEE

The nature of the selection (hiring) process and the laws governing it depend on the type of relationship the employer decides to build with the worker. The traditional, stable model of long-term direct employer–employee relationships now is often replaced with new, flexible, nontraditional staffing arrangements including outsourcing and employee leasing, along with the use of freelancers, temporary agencies, and professional employer organizations. (Firms save money and increase expertise by contracting with these PEOs to administer the firms' human resource services.) These new contingent workers, along with

---

* **This Chapter is reprinted from McAdams, Chapter 12, Employment Law 1: Employee Rights, Eighth Edition, Law, Business and Society, McGraw Hill Publishing Company.**

independent contractors, who are increasingly relied on to perform specific, shorter-term, nonrecurring jobs, permit employers to rapidly and inexpensively inflate or shrink their work forces as competitive and regulatory conditions change. The bad publicity and bad feelings associated with downsizing can be reduced with greater reliance on temps, and the cost savings can be large. Employers who choose to provide health and retirement benefits for their traditional employees need not do so for their contingent workers. Nor must they withhold income, Social Security, Medicare, and unemployment taxes. With fringe benefit costs reaching 40 percent of total compensation and averaging $15,000 (including payroll taxes) per employee, shrinking benefits has become an important consideration for many firms.[2]

The impact of many legal themes discussed in this chapter depends, initially, on whether the worker in question is considered, as a matter of law, an **employee** whether, long-term or contingent, or an independent contractor. That is, when an enterprise hires, for example, a trucker, programmer, or service technician, is that person an employee or an independent operator under contract to the organization but not, legally, a part of that organization?

The dominant test in settling the employee–independent contractor question is one of control. Where a worker's performance is controlled by an employer, or where the employer has the right or the ability to control that work, the worker is likely to be considered an employee. A business that hires an independent contractor generally is not required to comply with a wide range of employment and labor law standards that would apply were the worker an employee. Thus, a business must provide unemployment insurance, workers' compensation coverage, minimum wages, and so on to employees, but generally would not need to do so for independent contractors.

Microsoft agreed in 2000 to pay $97 million to settle federal lawsuits involving independent contractors and other contingent workers who won a long court battle to establish that they were entitled to employee benefits.[3] That coverage was especially important in the Microsoft case because it entitled many of the workers to very valuable Microsoft stock options. Basically, the Ninth Circuit Federal Court of Appeals found that the freelancers did the same work as Microsoft employees, and thus, had to be treated the same for benefit purposes despite the fact that the workers had signed contracts acknowledging their temp status and agreeing that they had no right to participate in the benefit plans.[4] The U.S. Supreme Court declined to review that ruling.[5] One of Microsoft's strategies to deal with the worker classification problems was to enact a new policy providing that temporary employees could not work for more than one year before taking a hiatus of at least 100 days.[6]

In conventional employer–employee relationships, contingent deals, and in some cases, independent contractor arrangements, a growing variety of potential legal problems have emerged.

- *Resume fraud:* HireRight, an Internet-based company, reviewed about 200,000 job applicants in one year and concluded that 80 percent of résumés are misleading, 20 percent list fraudulent degrees, and 40 percent have inflated salary histories.[7] Another study found that 13 percent of college students falsified their résumés even before beginning their careers.[8]

- *Background checks:* The 9/11/2001 attacks and the duty to provide a safe workplace have dramatically increased employers' attention to background and security checks. A recent survey found that about 80 percent of companies conducted criminal background checks in 2003, up from 51 percent in 1996, while credit checks increased to 35 percent from 19 percent in the earlier survey.[9]

- *Inappropriate questions:* About 21 percent of 1,000 workers in a national survey said they had been asked inappropriate questions in a job interview.[10] Often these questions, such as "How old are you?" and "Are you married?" raise discrimination concerns. The questions themselves are not technically unlawful, but discrimination based on the answers to those questions would be illegal. But what about the enormous array of awkward, intrusive, but nondiscriminatory interview questions that might leave the candidate feeling uncomfortable if not wronged? For example:

  > Following a job interview this year, Megan Johnson sent a handwritten thank-you note on fine stationery. But she didn't make the impression she intended. "You aren't a Republican, are you?" asked the hiring manager during a follow-up phone call. Ms. Johnson was stumped until she remembered the small blue elephant with an upturned trunk engraved along the upper margin of her note card.[11] The elephant was, in fact, supposed to represent good luck, but Johnson did not get the job. Furthermore, she cannot sue the company because questions about politics break no employment laws.[12]

- *Noncompete clauses:* In November 2002, Frank Cumbo and 10 colleagues left a New York temporary staffing agency to start a competing business. Two months later, their former employer sued all 11 for unfairly attempting to solicit business from its clients.[13]

Cumbo says he and the others built their new business from scratch and took no information with them. The lawsuit is pending at this writing. To address problems like these, employers sometimes require employees and new hires to sign agreements providing that they will neither pass trade secrets to others nor work for a competitor for a specified period. Cumbo and his colleagues had not signed such a pact, but a recent survey found that 30 percent of companies now require employees to sign non-compete agreements, and 51 percent require nondisclosure agreements.[14]

- *Arbitration:* New hires are sometimes expected to sign agreements specifying that disputes with the employer will be settled by arbitration rather than by litigation. Employers like arbitration because they view it as less adversarial than a trial—faster, cheaper, and more consistent. Often employees see arbitration as stacked in favor of corporate interests and as a denial of the fundamental right of access to the legal system. Sherri Warner is one of those:

> When Sherri Warner claimed a former employer sexually harassed her, the California secretary had to abide by a legal agreement requiring any claims to go to arbitration instead of court. Warner lost her arbitration case, but that was just the beginning of her problems. Warner's lawyer says she was then required to pay her former boss's legal fees. After three years of hearings, the total bill came to more than $200,000. . . .[15]

An important 2001 U.S. Supreme Court decision in the **Circuit City** case generally upholds the enforceability of legitimate, equitable employment arbitration agreements.[16] The federal government's anti-discrimination agency, the **Equal Employment Opportunity Commission**, however, retains authority to file lawsuits to secure damages for employees despite arbitration agreements that might prevent the employee herself from suing.[17]

Historically, a job applicant's previous performance record was an important ingredient in the hiring decision, but legal difficulties have significantly reduced the usefulness of the standard reference letter. Employers fear that providing references may lead to defamation claims (*slander* when spoken; *libel* when written) by former employees.

Many state courts, however, recognize what is labeled a **qualified privilege** as a defense in an employment-related defamation suit. The privilege applies where the one communicating the statement and the recipient share a legitimate, business-related interest in the information conveyed. Thus, references, internal employee evaluations, and the like are protected in most states from defamation claims in the absence of malice or extreme recklessness. Similarly, a number of states have passed statutes protecting legitimate reference communications from defamation claims. Nevertheless, some recent court decisions appear to have eroded the qualified privilege a bit, leading many employers to "play it safe" by limiting their references to strictly factual details such as the date of hire, date of departure, and job title.

Broadly, a successful **defamation** suit requires the following conditions:

1. A false statement.

2. The statement must be "published" to a third party.

3. The employer must be responsible for the publication.

4. The plaintiff's reputation must be harmed.

Truth is a complete defense in defamation cases, and firms that avoid second-hand information, personal issues, and potential discrimination themes such as age are likely not to have problems. A mistake, however, can be expensive.

<table>
<tr><td>

SECTION 10.3
LONDON V.
TYLER'S SPORTS
BAR AND GRILL

PROBLEM TEN—A

</td><td>

PARK, BROWN & SMITH, P.C.
ATTORNEYS AT LAW
MEMORANDUM

To: All Law Clerks

From: Peter Smith, Esquire

Re: The Mechanical Bull

</td></tr>
</table>

I know that you will find this hard to believe, but the owners of Tyler's Sports Bar and Grill have another legal dilemma. When the bar opened, Joe Roberts hired an outside security firm named Armed Services Security to maintain order at the premises. In this way, he did not have to find and train a security staff, a task that he knew nothing about. Joe turned to Armed Services Security, which was run by a former major in the army who only hired ex-military police officers and specialized in security for bars and nightclubs.

Tyler's entered into a contract with the outside firm for a two-year period. Armed Services Security agreed to supply at least four veteran security guards each night and the document specified that the agency "shall be considered an independent contractor at all times."

Tyler's caters to all tastes, so in its quest to be a success, it leased a mechanical bull in order to appeal to the country and western crowd. This machine operated ride simulated the bucking experience of a rodeo bull made so popular in the movie Urban Cowboy.

Because the machine was dangerous and required a lot of skill to use, Tyler's has a firm policy that no one who appears to be intoxicated could ride the bull.

One night, a group of Dallas Cowboy fans appeared at the bar and became obnoxiously drunk. The leader of the group, Willie London, was very loud and kept bad mouthing the Philadelphia sports fans as being losers. This bantering eventually led to a dare. The Cowboy fan taunted everyone in the bar that he could ride the mechanical bull longer than anyone else and offered $1,000 to any person who could beat his time riding the bull.

The bar patrons immediately lined up to ride the mechanical device. After 25 attempts by people to stay on the bull, one person was able to ride the mechanical bull for the required time. Not to be outdone, London staggered up to the bull and attempted to get on. Boastfully, he shouted to his friends to turn up the setting for difficulty to the highest speed. The bar manager overheard this order and realized that the customer was drunk so he signaled to the security guards to remove him from the bull. When London refused the requests to dismount, the manager told the security guards to forcible remove him. Four guards then violently grabbed the Cowboy fan and throw him to the floor. The customer landed awkwardly and broke his hip and wrist.

Mr. Roberts informed me this morning that Tyler's has been sued for the injuries sustained by the patron. The owner doesn't understand the claim and read me the language in the security guards' contract that says the security guards shall be considered "independent contractors." Joe looked up the law on the Internet and found a series of comments that an employer is not liable for the actions of an independent contractor. I went to the bar later in the day and took a statement from the bar manager. I am concerned about the fact that the manger was the one who told the guards to forcible remove the Cowboy fan from the mechanical bull.

Please read the following case and let me know whether you think that Tyler's will be liable for the actions of the security guards.

FIFTH CLUB, INC. V. RAMIREZ
196 S.W.3D 788 (TEX., 2006)

Fifth Club, Inc. operates a nightclub known as Club Rodeo. David West, a certified peace officer, was hired as an independent contractor by Fifth Club to provide security at the nightclub. Late one night, Roberto Ramirez arrived at Club Rodeo after several hours of drinking. Ramirez and his brother tried to enter the club but were denied admission by the doorman, allegedly because they were intoxicated. The doorman signaled to West and another parking lot security officer to escort Ramirez and his brother out of the club's entrance. West allegedly grabbed Ramirez, slammed Ramirez's head against a concrete wall, knocking him unconscious, and then struck him several times. The altercation resulted in multiple injuries to Ramirez, including a fractured skull.

Ramirez claims Fifth Club is vicariously liable for West's conduct in spite of his independent contractor status because it controlled West's security activities. Fifth Club contends there is legally insufficient evidence it retained sufficient control over West's security activities to make it vicariously liable for his conduct.

Generally, an employer has no duty to ensure that an independent contractor performs its work in a safe manner. However, an employer can be held vicariously liable for the actions of an independent contractor if the employer retains some control over the manner in which the contractor performs the work that causes the damage. One who entrusts work to an independent contractor, but who retains the control of any part of the work, is subject to liability for physical harm to others for whose safety the employer owes a duty to exercise reasonable care, which is caused by his failure to exercise his control with reasonable care.

A right of control requires more than a general right to order the work stopped or resumed, to inspect its progress or to receive reports, to make suggestions or recommendations, which need not necessarily be followed, or to prescribe alterations and deviations. Such a general right is usually reserved to employers, but it does not mean that the contractor is controlled as to his methods of work, or as to operative detail. There must be such a retention of a right of supervision that the contractor is not entirely free to do the work in his own way.

Employers can direct when and where an independent contractor does the work and can request information and reports about the work, but an employer may become liable for the independent contractor's tortious acts only if the employer controls the details or methods of the independent contractor's work to such an extent that the contractor cannot perform the work as it chooses.

In this case, there was no evidence that Fifth Club gave more than general directions to West or that it retained the right to control the manner in which West performed his job. Fifth Club's action in directing West to remove Ramirez from the premises did not rise to the level of directing how the work was to be performed or directing the safety of the performance because West retained the right to remove Ramirez by whatever method he chose. Fifth Club, therefore, cannot be held vicariously liable for West's conduct.

Because the character of West's work for Fifth Club alone does not impose employer liability, we conclude Fifth Club is not vicariously liable to Ramirez.

ANSWER SHEET
PROBLEM TEN—A

Name: **Please Print Clearly**

1. By ordering the security guards to remove the Cowboy fan from the bull, did the security guards become transformed from independent contractors to employees of the bar?

_____

_____

_____

_____

_____

_____

_____

_____

_____

2. Will the bar be liable for the injuries sustained by Mr. London?

_____

_____

_____

_____

_____

_____

_____

_____

SECTION **10.4**
LIABILITY

Once hired, what happens when employees make mistakes or engage in misconduct on the job that hurts others? Must the employer bear the loss in these situations? Job classification is an important first question in determining company liability for workers' job-related injuries, injuries to others, and crimes. An enterprise ordinarily will not be liable for the acts of its independent contractors. Employers, on the other hand, often bear legal responsibility for employees' accidents or wrongs. That liability often springs from the doctrine of respondeat superior), a form of **vicarious liability** (sometimes called *imputed liability*).

Employer liability for employee injuries, accidents, or wrongs is largely dependent on whether the employee was on the job at the time of the incident in question. As explained later in the chapter, employers are generally liable, under **workers' compensation** statutes, for injuries to employees regardless of the cause of those injuries if they occurred within the **scope of employment** (on the job). Likewise, employers will be held liable under vicarious liability/respondent superior reasoning for harm to third parties caused by the intentional or negligent acts of their employees when those acts occur within the scope of employment. A finding of employer liability, of course, does not excuse the employee from her liability, but the vicarious liability/respondent superior reasoning does have the potential effect of opening the employer's deeper pockets to the plaintiff. The central inquiry in assigning employer liability lies in the scope of employment question; that is, broadly, did the accident happen while the employee was on the job? The following questions ordinarily determine whether the harm occurred within the scope of employment:

1. Was the employee subject to the employer's supervision?

2. Was the employee motivated, at least in part, by a desire to serve the employer's business interests?

3. Did the problem arise substantially within normal working hours and in a work location?

4. Was the act in question of the general kind the employee had been hired to perform.

In a 1991 case, **Mary M. v. City of Los Angeles**,[18] the city was held liable under the doctrine of respondent superior for a sexual assault committed by a police officer. At 2:30 AM on October 3, 1981, Sergeant Leigh Schroyer was on duty, in uniform, carrying a gun, and patrolling in his marked police car. He stopped Mary M. for erratic driving. She pleaded not to be arrested. He ordered her to enter his patrol car and took her to her home. He entered her home and said that he expected "payment" for not arresting her. He raped her and was subsequently sentenced to a term in state prison. Mary M. sued the City of Los Angeles. The general inquiry was whether Schroyer was acting within the scope of his employment during the rape episode. The jury found for

Mary M. and awarded $150,000 in damages. The Court of Appeals reversed, saying that Schroyer was not acting within the scope of his employment. The case went to the California Supreme Court. The city argued that Schroyer was acting on behalf of his own interests rather than those of the city, and that the city had not authorized his conduct. Therefore, Schroyer could not have been acting within the scope of employment. However, the court said that the correct question was not whether the rape was authorized but whether it happened in the course of a series of acts that were authorized. The court reversed, saying that a jury could find the city vicariously liable (imputed to the principal from the agent) given the unique authority of police officers in our society. The City was therefore held liable for the sexual assault committed by a police officer.

QUESTIONS FOR DISCUSSION:

1. Gonzalez, working for Land Transport, was driving his employer's tractor-trailer behind Nichols, who was driving his pickup. Gonzalez followed at an unsafe distance and twice attempted to pass in no-passing zones. Nichols responded with "predictable obscene gestures." While both drivers were stopped at a red light, Gonzalez left the company truck and attacked Nichols with a rubber-coated metal cable and a knife.

    Gonzalez was convicted of assault. Nichols sued Land Transport.

    a. What is his claim?

    b. Decide the case. Explain. See **Nichols v. Land Transport, 233 F.3d 21 (1st Cir., 2000).**

2. Williams, Hemphill, Dixon, and Osborne, while driving in Chicago, noticed some pizza boxes on top of a car parked in front of the Italian Fiesta Pizzeria. Dixon and Hemphill jumped out, discovered the boxes were empty, dropped them, and reentered their Jeep. Hall, a driver for Italian Fiesta, observed Dixon and Hemphill, yelled at them to return the pizza boxes, and then followed them in his vehicle. Dixon turned the wrong way onto a one-way street and Hall followed. Dixon then collided with another vehicle. Williams died and Hemphill was injured. Italian Fiesta was subsequently sued on negligent hiring and vicarious liability claims. The negligent hiring claim was rejected by the judge, but the vicarious liability theme was allowed to proceed to trial. The defendants provided evidence showing the pizzeria specifically informed employees that they were not to attempt to recover stolen property or punish perpetrators. Rather, the pizzeria's policy was for supervisors to contact police. Further, drivers were not penalized if property was stolen.

    a. What was the central issue in this case?

    b. Decide the case. Explain. See **Williams v. Hall, 681 N.E. 2d 1037 (Ill. App., 1997).**

3. What policy justifications support the imposition of liability on an employer for the wrongs of an employee operating within the scope of employment?

In recent years, employers' potential liability for employee wrong has been significantly expanded by a line of cases finding employers liable for **negligence in hiring an employee** or retaining an employee who subsequently causes harm to a third party, or for careless training or supervision. Typically, the employer is liable on negligence grounds for hiring or retaining an employee whom the employer knew or should have known to be dangerous, incompetent, dishonest, or the like where that information was directly related to the injury suffered by the plaintiff. The case that follows examines the law of negligent hiring, supervision, and retention.

YUNKER v. HONEYWELL, INC.
496 N.W. 2D 419 (MINN. APP., 1993)

Honeywell employed Randy Landin from 1977 to 1979 and from 1984 to 1988. From 1979 to 1984 Landin was imprisoned for the strangulation death of Nancy Miller, a Honeywell co-employee. On his release from prison, Landin reapplied at Honeywell. Honeywell rehired Landin as a custodian in Honeywell's General Offices facility in South Minneapolis in August 1984. Because of workplace confrontations, Landin was twice transferred, first to the Golden Valley facility in August 1986, and then to the St. Louis Park facility in August 1987. Kathleen Nesser was assigned to Landin's maintenance crew in April 1988. Landin and Nesser became friends and spent time together away from work. When Landin expressed a romantic interest, Nesser stopped spending time with Landin. Landin began to harass and threaten Nesser both at work and at home. At the end of June, Landin's behavior prompted Nesser to seek help from her supervisor and to request a transfer out of the St. Louis Park facility. On July 1, 1988, Nesser found a death threat scratched on her locker door. Landin did not come to work on or after July 1, and Honeywell accepted his formal resignation on July 11, 1988. On July 19, approximately six hours after her Honeywell shift ended, Landin killed Nesser in her driveway with a close range shotgun blast. Landin was convicted of first-degree murder and sentenced to life imprisonment.

Jean Yunker, as trustee for the heirs and next-of-kin of Kathleen Nesser, brought this wrongful death action based on theories of negligent hiring, retention, and supervision of a dangerous employee. Honeywell moved for summary judgment and, for purposes of the motion, stipulated that it failed to exercise reasonable care in the hiring and supervision of Landin. The trial court concluded that Honeywell owed no legal duty to Nesser and granted summary judgment for Honeywell.

The issue is whether Honeywell had a duty to Kathleen Nesser to exercise reasonable care in hiring, retaining, or supervising Randy Landin? In determining that Honeywell did not have a legal duty to Kathleen Nesser arising from its employment of Randy Landin, the district court analyzed Honeywell's duty as limited by its ability to control and protect its employees while they are involved in the employer's business or at the employer's place of business.

Negligent hiring and negligent retention do not rely on the scope of employment but address risks created by exposing members of the public to a potentially dangerous individual. These theories of recovery impose liability for an employee's intentional tort, an action almost invariably outside the scope of employment, when the employer knew or should have known that the employee was violent or aggressive and might engage in injurious conduct.

Minnesota first explicitly recognized a cause of action based on negligent hiring in **Ponticas** in 1983. **Ponticas** involved the employment of an apartment manager who sexually assaulted a tenant. The Supreme Court upheld a jury verdict finding the apartment operators negligent in failing to make a reasonable investigation into the resident manager's background before providing him with a passkey. The court defined negligent hiring as predicated on the negligence of an employer in placing a person with known propensities, or propensities which should have been discovered by reasonable investigation, in an employment position in which, *because of the circumstances of the employment,* it should have been foreseeable that the hired individual posed a threat of injury to others.

Honeywell argues that under **Ponticas** it is not liable for negligent hiring because, unlike providing a dangerous resident manager with a passkey, Landin's employment did not enable him to commit the act of violence against Nesser. This argument has merit, and we note that a number of jurisdictions have expressly defined the scope of an employer's duty of reasonable care in hiring as largely dependent on the type of responsibilities associated with the particular job. **Ponticas** rejected the view that employers are required to investigate a prospective employee's criminal background in every job in which the individual has regular contact with the public. Instead, liability is determined by the totality of the circumstances surrounding the hiring and

whether the employer exercised reasonable care. The court instructed that [t]he scope of the investigation is directly related to the severity of the risk third parties are subjected to by an incompetent employee. Although only slight care might suffice in the hiring of a yardman, a worker on a production line, or other types of employment where the employee would not constitute a high risk of injury to third persons, when the prospective employee is to be furnished a passkey permitting admittance to living quarters of tenants, the employer has the duty to use reasonable care to investigate his competency and reliability prior to employment.

Applying these principles, we conclude that Honeywell did not owe a duty to Nesser at the time of Landin's hire. Landin was employed as a maintenance worker whose job responsibilities entailed no exposure to the general public and required only limited contact with co-employees. Unlike the caretaker in **Ponticas**, Landin's duties did not involve inherent dangers to others, and unlike the tenant in **Ponticas,** Nesser was not a reasonably foreseeable victim at the time Landin was hired.

Honeywell did not breach a legal duty to Nesser by hiring Landin because the specific nature of his employment did not create a foreseeable risk of harm, and public policy supports a limitation on this cause of action. The district court correctly determined that Honeywell is not liable to Nesser under a theory of negligent hiring.

In recognizing the tort of negligent hiring, **Ponticas** extended established Minnesota case law permitting recovery under theories of negligent retention.

The difference between negligent hiring and negligent retention focuses on when the employer was on notice that an employee posed a threat and failed to take steps to ensure the safety of third parties. The Florida appellate court has provided a useful definition:

Negligent hiring occurs when, prior to the time the employee is actually hired, the employer knew or should have known of the employee's unfitness, and the issue of liability primarily focuses upon the adequacy of the employer's pre-employment investigation into the employee's background. Negligent retention, on the other hand, occurs when, during the course of employment, the employer becomes aware or should have become aware of problems with an employee that indicated his unfitness, and the employer fails to take further action such as investigating, discharge, or reassignment.

The record contains evidence of a number of episodes in Landin's post imprisonment employment at Honeywell that demonstrate a propensity for abuse and violence toward co-employees.

While at the Golden Valley facility, Landin sexually harassed female employees and challenged a male coworker to fight. After his transfer to St. Louis Park, Landin threatened to kill a coworker during an angry confrontation following a minor car accident. In another employment incident, Landin was hostile and abusive toward a female coworker after problems developed in their friendship. Landin's specific focus on Nesser was demonstrated by several workplace outbursts occurring at the end of June, and on July 1 the words "one more day and you're dead" were scratched on her locker door. Landin's troubled work history and the escalation of abusive behavior during the summer of 1988 relate directly to the foreseeability prong of duty. The facts . . . show that it was foreseeable that Landin could act violently against a co-employee, and against Nesser in particular.

This foreseeability gives rise to a duty of care to Nesser that is not outweighed by policy considerations of employment opportunity. An ex-felon's "opportunity for gainful employment may spell the difference between recidivism and rehabilitation," but it cannot predominate over the need to maintain a safe workplace when specific actions point to future violence. Our holding is narrow and limited only to the recognition of a legal duty owed to Nesser arising out of Honeywell's continued employment of Landin. It is important to emphasize that in reversing the summary judgment on negligent retention, we do not reach the remaining significant questions of whether Honeywell breached that duty by failing to terminate or discipline Landin, or whether such a breach was a proximate cause of Nesser's death. These are issues generally decided by a jury after a full presentation of facts.

We affirm the entry of summary judgment on the theories of negligent hiring and supervision, but reverse the summary judgment on the issue of negligent retention.

QUESTIONS FOR DISCUSSION:

1. What did the court mean when it said that "negligent hiring and negligent retention are based on direct, not vicarious, liability"?

2. Why did the court reject the negligent supervision claim?

3. Why did the court reject the negligent hiring claim?

SECTION 10.6
MINIMUM WAGE

A note was passed to President Franklin D. Roosevelt in 1936 from a young girl:

> I wish you could do something to help us girls. We have been working in a sewing factory, getting our minimum pay of $11 a week. Today, 200 of us girls have been cut down to $4, $5 and $6 a week.[19]

Roosevelt reportedly remarked that something needed to be done about child labor. The Depression and its tragic suffering, even of those working hard, shattered many Americans' faith in the free market and led to government intervention including, in 1938, the **Fair Labor Standards Act** (FLSA), which is directed to these major objectives:

1. The establishment of a minimum wage that provides at least a modest standard of living for employees.

2. A flexible ceiling on hours worked weekly, the purpose of which is to increase the number of employed Americans.

3. Child labor protection.

4. Equal pay for equal work regardless of gender.

Pat Williams of Shreveport, Louisiana, lost her home gas service in April 2001 because, according to *The Wall Street Journal,* a $477 payment was overdue. She works for $5.55 per hour in her daytime nursing assistant job and $5.15 per hour in her evening cleaning job. She is a 46-year-old mother of three. She reports having been able to live comfortably and even indulge herself occasionally while working minimum wage jobs 20 years ago. Why is she unable to have a similarly comfortable life today with her current minimum wage jobs? *The Wall Street Journal* answered:

> There's little wonder why. As a longtime low-wage worker, Ms. Williams has felt the sting of one of the most profound shifts in American economic policy during the past 20 years: a mounting disdain for the minimum wage.

> This sea change began when Ronald Reagan swept into office. From 1950 through 1982, the minimum wage was allowed to fall below 45 percent of the average hourly wage in the U.S. in only four separate years. Since 1982, the minimum wage has never reached 45 percent, and it currently stands at 36 percent of that benchmark.[20]

Many politicians and economists, however, fear that a minimum wage increase from the current federal requirement would unfairly drive up the cost of doing business and reduce the number of entry-level jobs.

Some evidence supports that view, but other studies have found that a higher minimum wage does not harm job growth. For example, in the 17 states and the District of Columbia that have minimum wages above the federal required level, job growth appears to have been at least as strong as growth in the states with the federal minimum wage.[21]

The most interesting recent development in this area is the "living wage" movement. Since 1994, more than 100 communities have passed laws aimed at pushing wages high enough to lift families above the federal poverty line. The laws typically apply only to companies contracting to provide goods and services to the cities, although some cover city employees as well. Santa Fe, New Mexico, may have the most aggressive living wage plan. All Santa Fe businesses with more than 25 employees must pay $8.50 per hour, increasing to $10.50 by 2008.[22] Critics fear that businesses will lay off staff to fall below the 25 threshold, others will decline to expand, while others will simply leave. A 2002 study found, however, that the higher minimums have been effective in reducing poverty despite some increase in unemployment.[23]

Vickey Ramsey, a former Wal-Mart assistant manager, was working 48 hours per week, but most of that time was occupied by stocking shelves and doing other tasks normally performed by hourly workers. Ramsey was moved to an hourly role at her request, but she sued Wal-Mart for classifying her as a manager in order, she claimed, to avoid paying **overtime**.[24] At this writing in 2005, Wal-Mart is facing some 30 overtime lawsuits.[25] Wal-Mart is not alone. A New Jersey appeals court ruled that Pepsi improperly failed to pay overtime to delivery truck drivers and others whom the company had classified as "outside" salespeople.[26] Disneyland paid $1.7 million to settle claims that it unlawfully failed to pay workers for their time spent getting into and out of costumes and for time spent wearing costumes before reaching the work site.[27]

In general, workers are entitled to FLSA protections, including the minimum wage and overtime (normally time and one-half for hours over 40 per week), but certain occupational classes are exempt; that is, those workers are not entitled to FLSA protections. In response to corporate pleas for relief from lawsuits, the Bush administration approved a 2004 revision of overtime rules. While still complicated, the new rules attempt to clarify the murky distinction between exempt and nonexempt employees.

At the simplest level, nearly all workers making less than $23,660 per year will be nonexempt (entitled to time and one–half overtime pay), whereas very few of those making $100,000 or more will be entitled to that pay. The tens of millions in between may or may not receive overtime depending on some rather vague rules. Those who fall in one of the following classes may, after close analysis of their duties, prove to be exempt from the overtime protections: executives, administrators, professional/creative workers, computer professionals, and outside salespeople. Some workers such as police officers, firefighters, and better-paid blue-collar workers are expressly granted the right to overtime pay. Others, such as insurance adjusters, dental hygienists, pharmacists, and journalists, are expressly exempt and thus not entitled to overtime. Critics say millions of workers will be ineligible for overtime pay under the new rules, but at this writing, the impact is unclear.

QUESTION FOR DISCUSSION:

1. Answer this person's complaint: "I work at a business that offers overtime. There are two employees, myself and one other, who do the same job. The other person is always offered overtime, and I'm left working regular hours only. Is there a law that requires an employer to equally distribute overtime? Is there some place I can complain to?"[28]

SECTION 10.7
WORKPLACE HAZARDS

An illegal Mexican immigrant, Jose Alatorre, took a job for $8.75 an hour as a welder at a dairy farm in the California Central Valley. He was 22. On his first wedding anniversary, (February 22, 2001) his wife asked him to stay home, but he said he had to go to work for the morning to repair a machine. The farm's 1,700 cattle produced 200,000 gallons of waste per day. That day the waste pump clogged. Alatorre went down a 30-foot shaft, was overcome by hydrogen sulfide gas, plunged head first into standing manure, and drowned. Another worker died trying to rescue him.

At the time of their deaths, *The New York Times* reported that the two men's lungs were packed with cow manure, and they had eight pennies and one dime in their pockets. In telling Alatorre's story, the *Times* reported on his first encounter with his wife-to-be: It was not a promising pickup line. "I don't own a car, I'm not legally here, and I don't earn much money," he said, flashing a smile. "It's up to you." Angelica Acevedo Hernandez followed Jose Alatorre onto the dance floor.[29]

Perhaps we are not surprised to learn that the American workplace is particularly hazardous for Mexican workers. The Associated Press recently studied Mexican workplace deaths:

- The workplace death rate for Mexicans in a number of western and southwestern states is four times that of the average for United States–born workers in those states.

- Mexican death rates are rising while the U.S. workplace grows safer overall.

- "Though Mexicans often take the most hazardous jobs, they are more likely than others to be killed even when doing similarly risky work… These accidental deaths are almost always preventable and often gruesome: Workers are impaled, shredded in machinery, buried alive. Some are as young as 15."[30] Government officials note, however, that the most recent data show, for the first time, a decline in workplace deaths among foreign-born Hispanics.[31]

Although Mexicans working in America are significantly at risk, the total American workplace has gradually become safer because of tighter rules, improved workplace technology, and the shift to service industry jobs. Here is the data:

- Nationwide workplace deaths in 2003 totaled 5,559, up from 5,534 in 2002,[32] but the rate of fatalities remained at 4.0 per 100,000 workers, and the fatality rate fell some 11 percent from 1998 to 2003.[33]

- Injuries and illnesses continued their steady decline with a 2002 rate of 5.3 injuries and illnesses per 100 workers, down from 6.7 in 1998.[34]

- In fiscal year 2004, the federal government found nearly 87,000 workplace violations of its rules, a 9.5 percent increase over the previous five years, with serious violations up by 3 percent in one year and willful violations up by 14 percent during that year.[35] Of course, that increase might reflect more effective government oversight.

SECTION 10.8 OCCUPATIONAL SAFETY AND HEALTH ACT

The **Occupational Safety and Health Act** imposes a general duty on most employers to provide a workplace free of "recognized hazards causing or likely to cause death or serious physical harm to employees." Employers have an absolute duty to remove any serious and preventable workplace hazards that are generally recognized in the industry and are known to the employer or should be known to the employer. That general duty is then supplemented with numerous, detailed, and demanding specific standards. A federal agency, the **Occupational Safety and Health Administration** (OSHA), is responsible for ensuring safe workplaces.

OSHA, through the secretary of labor, promulgates and enforces health and safety standards that identify and seek to correct specific workplace hazards and problems. These can range from exposure to cancer-causing agents (such as the chemical benzene), to the surprisingly commonplace problem of one worker restarting a machine while another is servicing it, to mundane requirements for sanitary toilet facilities in agricultural jobs.

A battle is inevitable when OSHA considers new workplace safety measures. A pair of safety issues demonstrates some of the competing considerations in determining whether further government intervention is needed.

Repetitive motion and overexertion injure about 1.8 million workers annually.[36] These musculoskeletal injuries, such as carpal tunnel syndrome and back strains, total one-third of all workplace injuries and cost billions of dollars.[37] Employers often try to address those problems via ergonomics, "the science of fitting the job to the worker."[38] In response to the many injuries and their high costs and after 10 years of study commencing with the George Bush Senior administration, OSHA issued new ergonomics standards at the close of the Clinton administration in 2000 that were intended to provide strict rules for adapting workplaces to employee practices (for example, changing the height of a workstation or slowing down a production line). However, with the backing of the Bush administration, Congress repealed those rules in 2001 after the business community complained about the cost of compliance.

The government had estimated that the rules would cost about $4.5 billion annually[39] and save $9 billion,[40] but business groups said the costs could balloon to $125 billion.[41] A new plan was issued in 2002 to replace the mandatory rules with voluntary guidelines, but OSHA in 2003 asserted its general duty power to once again issue ergonomics citations in high-hazard workplaces such as nursing homes and grocery chains. OSHA has indicated that citations will be directed only to employers with high injury rates who do not make a good faith effort to address those problems.

"Going postal" has become, probably unfairly, a readily recognizable shorthand expression for **violence in the workplace**. Workplace homicides, the third leading cause of on-the-job deaths, increased to 631 in 2003 from 609 in 2002.[42]

With other workplace deaths declining steadily and national overall murder rates falling precipitously in recent years, we must wonder what accounts for rather steady or, in some years, increasing workplace homicides. Stress from job insecurity, deadlines, tight work spaces, overwork, and so on seem to be ongoing problems. In a recent survey, 42 percent of office workers said yelling and verbal abuse happened frequently in their offices.[43]

But should OSHA assert its authority? Do we need new rules to curb workplace violence? Would those rules prove effective? Can management take steps to reduce workplace tensions? OSHA, at least during the Bush years, is unlikely to take an activist stance except for situations like ergonomics, where some industries clearly can improve their safety measures. Indeed, in 2004 OSHA levied a $2,500 fine and cited a Dallas janitorial firm that allegedly failed to protect employees who worked at night in Dallas Area Rapid Transit stations.[44]

Employers may seek both permanent and temporary **variances** (exceptions) from OSHA standards. A permanent variance may be granted only if the workplace will be as safe as if the standard were enforced. A temporary variance permits additional time to put in place the necessary compliance measures. Employees have a right to a hearing to contest variances.

OSHA has adopted an **employee hazard communication standard** to protect employees from the dangers associated with chemicals and other toxins in the workplace. Chemical manufacturers and importers must develop material safety data sheets for all chemicals. Employers must then label all chemical containers so that employees will know about the chemical and its dangers, and employers must educate employees about chemical hazards and how to deal with them.

Businesses must maintain records listing and summarizing injuries, illnesses, and deaths on the job. A summary of those records must be posted at the job. Notice of any OSHA citations of imminent dangers on the job must also be posted at the job site. OSHA reformed and simplified the record-keeping process effective in 2002. Some smaller companies, especially in non-hazardous activities, do not need to meet the record-keeping requirements.

OSHA's most publicized **enforcement** mechanism is the unannounced on-site inspection. Inspections arise at the initiative of the agency itself or at the request of employees or their representatives. The inspections must be conducted in a reasonable manner during working hours or other reasonable times, and ordinarily they must not be announced in advance. Employers can demand a warrant prior to inspection. With proper justification, warrants can easily be secured from a federal magistrate. Employer and employee representatives may accompany the inspector.

To enhance efficiency, OSHA practices a targeted, site-specific inspection plan designed to identify the workplaces most likely to have safety and health problems. The targeted sites are those that reported at least 14 injuries or illnesses for every 100 full-time workers where lost workdays or restricted activity resulted. OSHA explains its enforcement policy at its Web site:

> OSHA seeks to assist the majority of employers who want to do the right thing while focusing its enforcement resources on sites in more hazardous industries, especially those with high injury and illness rates. Less than 1 percent of inspections, about 300, came under the agency's Enhanced Enforcement Program, designed to address employers who repeatedly and willfully violate the law. Outreach, education, and compliance assistance enable OSHA to play a vital role in preventing on-the-job injuries and illnesses.[45]

Citations may be issued if violations are discovered during the inspection process. Immediate, serious threats can be restrained with a court order. Following a citation, the employer may ask to meet with an area OSHA official to discuss the problem. Often a settlement emerges from these meetings. Failing a settlement, the employer can appeal to the independent OSHA Review Commission and thereafter to the federal court of appeals. Violations may lead to fines and/or imprisonment.

The business community criticizes OSHA for unfairly increasing the cost of production by imposing inflexible and overzealous expectations. Labor organizations and job safety advocates, on the other hand, see OSHA as a timid, faltering safety shield. The AFL–CIO estimates that OSHA can inspect each American workplace only once each century.

Concerns about workplace deaths led *The New York Times* to conduct an eight-month investigation of OSHA enforcement policy. The *Times* concluded that OSHA officials had not fulfilled their promises to aggressively pursue the worst of workplace safety wrongs:

> Over a span of two decades, from 1982 to 2002, OSHA investigated 1,242 of these horror stories—instances in which the agency itself concluded that workers had died because of their employer's "willful" safety violations. Yet, in 93 percent of those cases, OSHA declined to

seek prosecution. What is more, having avoided prosecution once, at least 70 employers willfully violated safety laws again, resulting in scores of additional deaths. Even these repeat violators were rarely prosecuted.[46]

When, if ever, should managerial misjudgments, carelessness, and indifference be treated as crimes with serious penalties including imprisonment? Or does the market, in most cases, provide an effective, just method of addressing workplace deaths? Consider the criminal prosecution that emerged from the aforementioned case of Jose Alatorre and a would-be rescuer who, while working, drowned in cow manure at the bottom of a 30-foot-deep sump hole. California officials decided to charge dairy manager Patrick Faria with involuntary manslaughter in the Alatorre episode. Faria was not on the site when the workplace deaths occurred, but officials reportedly had "indications that he knew the dangers of the shaft."[47] A newspaper account summarized the prosecution view:

As a volunteer county firefighter, he aced the test on safety in confined spaces. But he hadn't relayed that information to his workers, prosecutors say, and did not supply them with proper fans to ventilate the air or a harness to extract a stricken worker. Faria could have hired a professional crew to clean the pump for about $600, according to prosecutor Gale Filter, instead of sending down three low-wage dairy hands. "It's about money, M-O-N-E-Y," Filter told the grand jury that indicted Faria.[48]

SECTION 10.9 WORKERS' COMPENSATION

Korey Stringer, a 27-year-old Pro Bowl tackle, died of heatstroke complications on August 1, 2001, after going through a preseason Minnesota Vikings workout. Normally, when an employee is injured or dies on the job, the employee or the estate may not sue for damages. Rather, recovery is limited to the fixed sum provided for by the workers' compensation statute, regardless of fault. Stringer's family, however, filed a wrongful death suit trying to hold the Vikings and various individuals responsible for negligence, intentional infliction of emotional distress, and other wrongs in responding to Stringer's heatstroke. The Vikings argue that the Stringer suit is barred by the state workers' compensation law. Minnesota is one of a number of states, however, that recognizes an exception to **workers' compensation** exclusivity provisions in cases of gross negligence by the defendants. At this writing, the Minnesota Supreme Court has agreed to review the case after two lower court defeats for the Stringer family.[49]

Early in the twentieth century, the states began enacting workers' compensation laws to provide an administrative remedy for those, like Stringer, who are injured or killed on the job. Previously, employers' superior financial resources and various technical legal defenses meant that employees often could not successfully sue to recover damages for their on-the-job injuries. Thus, all states now provide some form of workers' compensation not requiring a lawsuit.

Workers or their families simply apply for compensation based on illness, injury, or death. Typically, the system is governed by a state board or commission. Most decisions are routine and are accomplished by completing the necessary forms. Often a claims examiner will verify the nature and severity of the injury. In return for the ease and predictability of the system, however, workers and families are, by law, denied the right to sue, barring unusual circumstances such as gross negligence (as alleged in the Stringer case).

In most states, employers are compelled to participate in workers' compensation, depending on state law, either by purchasing insurance privately, by contributing to a state-managed fund, or by being self-insured (paying claims directly from their own funds). Firms with good safety records are rewarded with lower premium payments. A benefits schedule specifies the sum to be awarded for the injury (or death) in question. The amount of the award is normally a percentage of the worker's salary either for a specified period or indefinitely, depending on the severity of the injury. Injury benefits normally amount to one-half to two-thirds of regular wages. Death benefits ordinarily are tied to the wages of the deceased.

Certain employment classifications such as agriculture may be excluded from workers' compensation, but about 90 percent of the labor force is covered. Most on-the-job injuries are covered, but those that are self-inflicted (including starting a fight) and others such as those springing from alcohol or drug use may not be.

In general, injuries, illnesses, and deaths are compensable where the harm (1) *arose out of the employment,* and (2) *arose in the course of employment.* Proof of employer negligence is not required, and the traditional defenses such as contributory negligence are not available to the employer. Thus, workers' compensation provides a form of no-fault protection in the workplace. Workers give up the right to sue, and employers participate in an insurance system that recognizes the inevitability of workplace harm.

Although workers' compensation recovery is the exclusive remedy for workplace injury, illness, or death, some jurisdictions allow litigation in cases of intentional torts and/or gross negligence.

Notwithstanding its no-fault character, workers' compensation has generated many lawsuits. For example, Manuel Guico had worked for two years in an Excel meat packing plant until he was fired after sustaining an injury on the job. Guico's knife slipped, cutting his thumb and a finger, and causing an 11 percent permanent partial disability. Guico had repeatedly been told to wear his steel-mesh gloves and mesh apron whenever he was using his knife, but he was not doing so when he was injured. Guico applied for and received workers' compensation benefits. Excel appealed to the courts but lost when the Nebraska Supreme Court ruled that Excel failed to show that Guico was willfully negligent.[50]

QUAKER OATES CO. V. CIHA
552 N.W.2D 143 (IOWA, 1996)

In May 1991, petitioner Bradley Ciha was employed by defendant Quaker Oats Company at its Cedar Rapids plant as an area maintenance supervisor. Ciha's normal workweek at Quaker Oats was Monday through Friday. On a typical weekend including Saturday and Sunday, Ciha was not on duty and was not expected to be on call to drive to the plant for emergency maintenance purposes.

While preparing dinner at his home on Sunday, May 26, Ciha was contacted through a company electronic paging device. He was informed that several large cooling fans at the plant were malfunctioning. Ciha responded to the breakdown by electing to drive his motorcycle to the plant to remedy the problem himself. To reach the plant, Ciha drove a direct route on Johnson Avenue. After reaching the plant without incident, he personally remedied the problem by cooling the fans with an air hose. At approximately 5:45 pm, Ciha telephoned his wife and informed her that she could resume dinner preparations because he was about to return home.

Ciha drove a different route from the plant to home than he drove earlier from his home to the plant. The return-home route was on Ellis Road and was admittedly not the most direct route from the plant to Ciha's home. The Ellis Road route was scenic and subject to less traffic and traffic signals than the direct route Ciha commonly drove from home to the plant.

On his return trip from the plant to home along Ellis Road, Ciha was involved in a serious motor vehicle accident in which he suffered a broken neck and was rendered a quadriplegic.

Following the accident, Ciha was admitted to St. Luke's Hospital in Cedar Rapids until he requested transfer to a specialized care facility, Craig Hospital, located in Englewood, Colorado.

In addition to the health care Ciha received while at Craig, the hospital also provided Kim specialized training in order for her to be able to care for Ciha upon his return home.

Ciha was discharged from Craig Hospital on September 14, 1991, to his home in Cedar Rapids. Since his discharge, Kim has performed necessary, extensive home nursing services. Ciha requires assistance in dressing, changing urine bags, and transferring between his wheelchair and his bed. At night, he must be repositioned in bed one to four times in order to prevent him from developing pressure sores.

Ciha first returned to work at Quaker Oats in January 1992 in a new position as materials supervisor. In this position, he works at a computer (with the aid of an adaptive device and telephone headset) in the company's purchasing department. In his position as materials supervisor, he receives the same base salary, not including raises, as that of an area maintenance supervisor. Ciha no longer has the same opportunity, however, to earn overtime as he had as an area maintenance supervisor.

In order to return to work, Ciha relied on the county's disabled persons transportation service to and from Quaker Oats. Based on the hours of the transportation service, however, Ciha was not able to return to work full-time.

Ciha was readmitted to Craig for one week in March 1992 for a comprehensive evaluation. A driving specialist from the hospital concluded Ciha would need to purchase a specially modified van in order to be able to drive independently. At some time thereafter, Ciha purchased the recommended van.

Many of Ciha's medical expenses from the accident were paid for through a group health and accident insurance plan available to Ciha through his employer

Quaker Oats. However, there were significant limitations in coverage under the group plan. For example, in addition to a lifetime cap on medical expenses, the group plan did not provide Ciha coverage for necessary home health care services, home modifications, or motor vehicle conversions.

In November 1991, Ciha filed a claim for permanent partial disability benefits with the Iowa Industrial Commissioner's Office against his employer, Quaker Oats.

In Iowa, every employer, not specifically excepted by the provisions of Iowa Code shall provide, secure, and pay compensation according to the provisions of this chapter for any and all personal injuries sustained by an employee arising out of and in the course of the employment.

To obtain such compensation, an injured employee has the burden of proving by a preponderance of the evidence that his injuries arose out of and in the course of his employment. An injury arises "out of" the employment when there is a causal relationship between the employment and the injury.

Quaker Oats contends Ciha did not sustain his injury in the course of his employment because the injury was sustained away from the employer's premises and while Ciha was on his way home from the plant. The employer relies on the well-established "going and coming" rule, which generally provides, "[A]bsent special circumstances, injuries occurring off the employer's premises while the employee is on the way to or from work are not compensable."

Under the "going and coming rule," Ciha admittedly did not sustain an injury in the course of his employment: He was injured while driving his motorcycle home from the Quaker Oats plant.

There are, however, several exceptions to the going and coming rule. The first exception to the going and coming is the "special errand" exception. Under the exception, if an employee is on a special errand or mission for his or her employer at the time of the injury, the injury is held to have arisen in the course of employment.

After considering all arguments raised by the parties, we believe substantial evidence supports the commissioner's conclusion that Ciha was on a special errand at the time of his injury.

In answer to the question "whose business was the employee pursuing at the time of the injury?" the answer must be Quaker Oats' business. The fact that Ciha was contacted on Sunday while he was on duty was truly "special." It was unusual, sudden, and unexpected.

Notwithstanding our conclusion that the special errand exception to the going and coming rule applies in the present case, Quaker Oats contends Ciha had "deviated" from his trip home from the plant to such an extent that he abandoned his employment at the time of the accident. The commissioner and district court rejected this argument, and we do the same.

In concluding Ciha did not deviate from his special errand, the commissioner stated, Ciha testified that he often took the Ellis Road route home because it was more scenic, it had less traffic, it had fewer stoplights, and the actual difference in miles between this route and the more direct route was minimal. Ciha's call to his wife from the plant to start the grill for their meal shows that his purpose was to return home, and that he had no other destination other than to return to his residence. The record does not show a deviation from the course of the employment.

Affirmed.

QUESTIONS FOR DISCUSSION:

1. The Iowa Supreme Court in *Quaker Oats* (and most courts in workers' compensation cases) required a two-part showing that the injury must "arise out of" and "in the course of" employment.

    a. Explain those two standards.

    b. Must an employee be engaged in a prescribed task in order to be "in the course of employment?" Explain.

    c. Why did the court conclude that Ciha was on a "special errand?"

2. Fernandez, a waitress at Tyler's Sports Bar and Grill, left her job drunk and was seriously injured in a crash while riding as a passenger in a car driven by another employee. The crash came within one hour of leaving work. Her intoxication led to her decision to ride with her intoxicated coworker. Fernandez sought workers' compensation. She claimed that Joe Roberts required her to socialize with male customers when not serving food or taking food orders and to generate at least two drinks per hour from customers. Weight staff were not required to drink, but most consumed six to eight drinks per night, if not more. Did Fernandez's injury arise out of and in the course of employment so that she can recover workers' compensation? Explain. See **2800 Corp. v. Fernandez, 528 N.W.2d 124 (Ia., 1995).**

3. Joseph Smyth, a college mathematics instructor, was killed while driving his personal auto home from work. At the time, Smyth had student papers with him, which he intended to grade that evening. He often worked at home. Many faculty members took work home in the evenings. However, the college did not require that practice. Indeed, the college neither encouraged nor discouraged working at home. The widely adopted "going and coming rule" provides that employees injured while commuting to and from work, in general, are not covered by workers' compensation.

    a. Should Smyth (and other teachers) be exempted from the going and coming rule, thus permitting recovery by Smyth's family? Explain. See **Santa Rosa Junior College v. Workers' Compensation Appeals Board and Joann Smyth, 708 P.2d 673 (Cal., 1985).**

    b. Would you reach a different conclusion had a student been accompanying Smyth? Explain.

4. Casimer Gacioch worked at a Stroh Brewery. The company provided free beer at work. When he began work in 1947 he drank only three to four beers on the weekend. He was fired in 1974, by which time he was drinking 12 bottles of beer daily. After Gacioch's death, his wife sought workers' compensation benefits. The evidence indicated that Gacioch had a predisposition to alcoholism but was not an alcoholic at the time he was hired. How would you rule on the widow's workers' compensation claim? Explain. See **Gacioch v. Stroh Brewery, 466 N.W. 2d 303 (Mich. Ct. of Appeals, 1991).**

SECTION 10.10
RIGHTS OF PRIVACY

Do we have a **"right to privacy"** on the job? Increasingly, employers are engaging in an array of testing and monitoring procedures both before and after hiring. Drug testing, integrity tests, personality tests, spying, television and computer monitoring of work performance, and so forth are routine personnel practices in many firms. Employers have an interest in these strategies not only to hire better employees and improve productivity but also to protect coworkers, reduce insurance claims, and shield consumers from poor products and service. On the other hand, job applicants and employees often feel "Big Brother" looking over their shoulders, as corporate critic Barbara Ehrenreich argues:

> Only a person of unblemished virtue can get a job at Wal-Mart—a low-level job, that is... A drug test eliminates the chemical miscreants; a detailed "personality test" probes the job applicant's horror of theft and willingness to turn in an erring coworker.

Extreme submissiveness to authority is another desirable trait. When I applied for a job at Wal-Mart, I was reprimanded for getting something wrong on this test: I had agreed only "strongly" to the proposition, "All rules have to be followed to the letter at all times." The correct answer was "totally agree."[51]

Do employers' financial goals justify policies that significantly reshape employee lives—especially their off-the-job lives? Should employers be able, for example, to require employees to lose weight or to quit smoking? One study of large employers finds 11.5 percent of the population accounting for 80 percent of health costs, with the chronically ill being particularly expensive.[52] Many employers offer wellness programs and various incentives to encourage employees to achieve more healthful lifestyles. Now some are going further by firing workers who refuse to take nicotine tests to prove they do not smoke. Others are beginning to charge higher insurance rates for those who fail to meet weight and health standards. The law offers only limited protection for employees. About half the states offer some form of "smoking discrimination" protection, and the federal **Health Insurance Portability and Accountability Act** (HIPAA) generally forbids discrimination based on health status or conditions.

And what about "office romance?" Changing cultural patterns have made the workplace a primary venue for romance and marriage. A 2003 poll found 47 percent of office workers had had an office romance and 19 percent more would like to do so.[53] Managers, however, are increasingly concerned about those relationships. More than one-third of 558 companies surveyed in 2001 said employees involved in office romances could be fired, up from 27 percent taking that position in 1998.[54] Managers are concerned about productivity and fairness, but perhaps the bigger fear is the possibility of sexual harassment charges.

SECTION 10.11 DRUG TESTING IN THE WORKPLACE

Drug testing in the corporate workplace is simply a fact of life, especially for blue-collar workers. Most *Fortune* 500 companies use some form of drug testing, although some companies, including Hewlett-Packard, have found so few job applicants testing positive that drug testing is not cost-effective for them. Regardless of the severity of the risk, many companies feel they must engage in drug testing to protect themselves against liability claims should an impaired employee cause harm and to comply with the federal **Drug-Free Workplace Act**.

The Drug-Free Workplace Act of 1988 applies to employers who have contracts of $100,000 or more with the federal government or who receive aid from the government. Those employers are required to develop an anti-drug policy for employees. They must provide drug-free awareness programs for employees, and they must acquaint employees with available assistance for those with drug problems, while also warning them of the penalties that accompany violation of the policy. The act requires employees to adhere to the company policy and to inform the company within five days if they are convicted of or plead no contest to a drug-related offense in the workplace.

Broadly, employment-based alcohol and drug testing occurs in six circumstances: (1) pre-employment screening, (2) routine physical examinations, (3) "reasonable suspicion" testing, (4) post accident testing, (5) random testing, and (6) follow-up testing.[55]

1. Ordinarily, private-sector, pre-employment testing is lawful although some state and local laws may impose restrictions. In general, public-sector employers have less drug testing latitude because of constitutional limitations, but when challenged in court, those programs have generally been approved.

2. Drug testing as a part of periodic physical examinations is generally lawful if properly conducted. To avoid legal problems, employers should notify job applicants and current employees of drug testing in association with physicals.

3. Reasonable suspicion is something less than probable cause and means that the employer has evidence, such as lapses in performance that would justify a drug test. Such tests, given a sound factual foundation and even-handed application, ordinarily are permissible.

4. Post accident testing involves employees who have been involved in a serious on-the-job accident. Such tests normally are permissible.

5. Selecting employees at random, without notice, for drug testing can be very effective in deterring drug use, but the practice raises significant legal questions. Some states explicitly forbid random testing, except for safety-sensitive jobs such as those in transportation. The Supreme Court has upheld such testing for public sector employees where public safety is involved and for those having access to particularly sensitive information.[56]

6. Follow-up testing is used for employees who are returning from drug or alcohol rehabilitation. The testing acts as an incentive for recovering drug users to remain "clean." All states permit follow-up testing, but employers should create contracts with rehabilitating employees to establish testing arrangements.

Drug use as a societal problem is undeniable, but critics are concerned that personal rights may be trampled in our zeal to attack substance abuse. Some of the doubts are that the tests (1) are often unreliable, (2) invade employee privacy, and (3) do not measure actual job impairment.

Challenges to drug testing ordinarily spring from the following claims and defenses:

1. **Federal constitution:** The Fourth Amendment to the United States Constitution forbids unreasonable searches and seizures. Thus government officials ordinarily cannot conduct a search without individualized suspicion—that is, without probable cause. Certain exceptions, however, have been recognized in cases involving safety, national security, athletic participation, and other special needs. Remember that the Constitution protects us from the government, not from private-sector employers (with limited exceptions).

2. **State constitutions:** Many state constitutions offer privacy protection, but court decisions, to date, have generally not extended those protections to private-sector employers. On the other hand, certain states, such as California and Massachusetts, explicitly offer constitutional protection to private-sector employees.

3. **Federal statutes:** Drug testing could violate Title VII of the Civil Rights Act of 1964 or the **Americans with Disabilities Act** if the testing fails to treat all individuals equally. The ADA protects *recovering* drug addicts and those erroneously believed to be drug users.

4. **State and local statutes:** Historically, most state and local drug testing legislation placed limits on that testing; but in recent years, fears about drug use in the workplace and often intense business community lobbying have, in some cases, relaxed those testing restraints.

5. **Common law claims:** Some of the more prominent judge-made (common law) claims that might provide a challenge to drug testing include invasion of privacy, defamation (dissemination of erroneous information about an employee), negligence (in testing or in selecting a test provider), intentional infliction of emotional distress, and wrongful discharge.

A McDonald's manager in Elmira, New York, began an affair with a McDonald's employee in another town. They exchanged "steamy" messages by voice mail. An Elmira coworker retrieved the messages and played them for the manager's wife and boss, whereupon the manager was fired. He filed suit claiming violations of a federal wiretapping law and a state eavesdropping statute.[57] The case was settled out of court.

Nearly 75 percent of major U.S. companies monitor their employees on the job,[58] and misconduct can result in severe sanctions. Dow Chemical, for example, fired 50 employees and disciplined over 200 more after discovering widespread use of its computers to receive pornography.[59] Employees are, of course, concerned about privacy, while employers' worries include reduced productivity and company liability for criminal or tortuous conduct (such as sexual harassment or defamation). Electronic oversight is gradually altering the workplace:

> At New York law firm Akin & Smith LLC, paralegals, receptionists, and clerks clock in by placing a finger on a sensor kept at a secretary's desk. "It keeps everyone honest," says Derek T. Smith, a managing partner at the firm.[60]

In general, employers can lawfully monitor workers' attendance, performance, e-mail, use of the Internet, and so on; but uncertainty remains. Certainly the prudent course of action is to expect employees to sign an agreement such as the following language from the Principal Financial Group employee handbook:

> The corporation's electronic mail system is business property and is to be used for business purposes. The corporation reserves the right to monitor all electronic mail messages.[61]

The primary federal legislation, the **Electronic Communications Privacy Act,** prohibits private individuals and organizations from intercepting wire, oral, or electronic communications. The act provides for two exceptions, however: (1) prior consent by one of the parties to the communication, and (2) employer monitoring in the "ordinary course of business" by telephone or other device furnished by a provider of wire or electronic communication service. Thus workplace monitoring of phone calls (except for purely private conversations), workplace computers, voice mail, e-mail, and Internet use are all likely to be considered lawful at this point if approached in a reasonable manner.

The case that follows is one of the few judicial examinations of privacy and monitoring. The plaintiff, Smyth, was an **at-will employee** meaning that he did not have an employment contract for a specified period. Under the law of Pennsylvania, where the case took place, at-will employees could be fired for any reason unless the discharge violated public policy. The **Smyth** case examines whether an e-mail interception amounts to an invasion of privacy and is thus a violation of public policy.

Smyth v. Pillsbury Co.
914 F. Supp. 97 (E. D. Pa., 1966)

Plaintiff claims he was wrongfully discharged from his position as a regional operations manager by the defendant. Presently before the court is the motion of the defendant to dismiss. Defendant maintained an electronic mail communication system ("e-mail") in order to promote internal corporate communications between its employees. Defendant repeatedly assured its employees, including plaintiff, that all e-mail communications would remain confidential and privileged. Defendant further assured its employees, including plaintiff that e-mail communications could not be intercepted and used by defendant against its employees as grounds for termination or reprimand.

In October 1994, plaintiff received certain e-mail communications from his supervisor over defendant's e-mail system on his computer at home. In reliance on defendant's assurances regarding defendant's e-mail system, plaintiff responded and exchanged e-mails with his supervisor. At some later date, contrary to the assurances of confidentiality defendant, acting through its agents, servants, and employees, intercepted plaintiff's private e-mail messages made in October 1994. On January 17, 1995, defendant notified plaintiff that it was terminating his employment effective February 1, 1995, for

transmitting what it deemed to be inappropriate and unprofessional comments over defendant's e-mail system in October 1994.

Plaintiff claims that his termination was in violation of "public policy, which precludes an employer from terminating an employee in violation of the employee's right to privacy as embodied in Pennsylvania common law." In support for this proposition, plaintiff directs our attention to a decision by our Court of Appeals in **Borse v. Piece Goods Shop, Inc., 963 F.2d 611 (3d Cir.,1992).** In **Borse**, the plaintiff sued her employer alleging wrongful discharge as a result of her refusal to submit to urinalysis screening and personal property searches at her workplace pursuant to the employer's drug and alcohol policy. After rejecting plaintiff's argument that the employer's drug and alcohol program violated public policy encompassed in the United States and Pennsylvania Constitutions, our Court of Appeals stated "our review of Pennsylvania law reveals other evidence of a public policy that may, under certain circumstances, give rise to a wrongful discharge action related to urinalysis or to personal property searches. Specifically, we refer to the Pennsylvania common law regarding tortious invasion of privacy."

In the case before us we find that plaintiff has failed to state a claim upon which relief can be granted. In the first instance, unlike urinalysis and personal property searches, we do not find a reasonable expectation of privacy in e-mail communications voluntarily made by an employee to his supervisor over the company e-mail system notwithstanding any assurances that such communications would not be intercepted by management. Once plaintiff communicated the alleged unprofessional comments to a second person (his supervisor) over an e-mail system, which was apparently utilized by the entire company, any reasonable expectation of privacy was lost. Significantly, the defendant did not require plaintiff, as in the case of a urinalysis or personal property search, to disclose any personal information about himself. Rather, plaintiff voluntarily communicated the alleged unprofessional comments over the company e-mail system. We find no privacy interests in such communications.

In the second instance, even if we found that an employee had a reasonable expectation of privacy in the contents of his e-mail communications over the company e-mail system, we do not find that a reasonable person would consider the defendant's interception of these communications to be a substantial and highly offensive invasion of his privacy. Again, we note that by intercepting such communications, the company is not, as in the case of urinalysis or personal property searches, requiring the employee to disclose any personal information about himself or invading the employee's person or personal effects. Moreover, the company's interest in preventing inappropriate and unprofessional comments or even illegal activity over its e-mail system outweighs any privacy interest the employee may have in those comments.

In sum, we find that the defendant's actions did not tortiously invade the plaintiff's privacy and, therefore, did not violate public policy. As a result, the motion to dismiss is granted.

QUESTIONS FOR DISCUSSION:

1. Why did the court reject Smyth's invasion of privacy claim?

2. Why did Pillsbury win even though it repeatedly promised employees that the e-mail system would be private and would not be used against employees?

3. In your opinion, should on-the-job e-mail messages be free from employer monitoring? Explain.

4. Does an employer have the right to search the office of an employee? Explain.

5. What if the employer provides a locker for the employee and allows the employee to provide a lock? Explain.

Have we reached that uncomfortable and perhaps socially destabilizing moment when the generous benefits (health insurance, life insurance, pensions) we have come to expect from our jobs are beginning a permanent decline? For decades employers used benefits to attract and retain the best employees, but the economic downturn in recent years forced employers to shift benefit burdens to employees by raising insurance deductibles and co-pays, for example. Indeed, from 2001 to 2003, nearly 9 million Americans lost their employer-provided health insurance, although most of those people subsequently moved to publicly subsidized plans such as Medicare.[62] At this writing, prosperity has returned to a considerable extent, but the benefit cuts have not been restored; and the future for improvements, especially in the prized but highly expensive health care area, does not look promising for employees. Benefits add 22 percent in value to the average employee's paycheck.[63] We prize the security of knowing that we will be shielded in the event of a health catastrophe. But can we sustain that comfort in this intense global market? A 2004 study found that a majority of surveyed companies are not raising benefits, and the small number who are increasing perks are doing so only slightly.[64] Further, *The Wall Street Journal* anticipates that any future growth in benefits will be in work/personal life balance, involving matters such as elder and child care rather than the stratospherically expensive health care costs.[65]

Even as benefits decline, American employees try harder. Almost 40 percent of us work more than 50 hours per week, and we have the stingiest vacation policies among industrialized nations with vacation allocations averaging about 10 days after three years on the job, as compared with Australia, for example, where four weeks are required by law.[66] Yet more, Expedia.com found that vacations for 2004 were expected to decline by 10 percent from 2003 as at least 20 percent of Americans report that they feel guilty about taking vacation.[67]

Meanwhile, the unmarried subset of the working population is increasingly aggressive in its pursuit of legal and economic benefits equal to those of families. Married employees have enhanced health care plans and unemployment benefits, for example, and differential treatment on the job allegedly is commonplace. The American Association for Single People receives complaints from singles:

> In the workplace, singles are expected to put off summer vacations so married colleagues can visit Disney World while their kids are out of school. Married people get family leave and special dispensations to work at home, while singles often feel chained to their desks.[68]

QUESTION FOR DISCUSSION:

1. Are single people wronged at work and in the American economy, generally?

Perhaps the most notable legally mandated insurance benefit is the **Consolidated Budget Reconciliation Act** (COBRA), which requires employers with 20 or more employees to permit departing employees to retain group health coverage at their own expense for up to 18 months as long as they are not terminated for gross misconduct.

The **Family and Medical Leave Act** (FMLA) requires up to 12 weeks of unpaid leave in any 12-month period for family needs such as the birth or adoption of a child, caring for a child or parent, or for the employee's own serious illness. Employees taking leave are entitled to reinstatement to the same or equivalent job. The law applies to all companies employing 50 or more workers and covers about 50 percent of the workforce. The business community has opposed the FMLA from the beginning, and experience with the law has not decreased that opposition, as *The Wall Street Journal* reported:

> While the act is helping employees, it's leaving many employers frustrated. They say the vague definition of what can trigger time off and the right of employees to take leave in increments—weeks, days, even hours—at different times make the law ripe for abuse. What's more, many human resource administrators believe employees sometimes use the law for bogus or questionable reasons. Among employers, this has earned the FMLA the nicknames "the Slacker's Protection Act" and the "Far More Leave Than Anyone Intended Act."[69]

But one FMLA advocate reminds us; FMLA has made an extraordinary difference in the lives of over 50 million Americans who haven't had to choose between their jobs and caring for a family member.[70]

In any case, only 16.5 percent of the workforce took leave under the FMLA in 2000,[71] and the FMLA has had no impact on males' propensity to take leave, while new mothers are taking leaves only slightly more frequently than before the FMLA.[72] Financial considerations often make FMLA leaves unattractive, but California has addressed that problem by becoming the first state to require private employers to provide *paid* time off. The program is paid for by employee payroll deductions and allows up to six weeks of leave at 55 percent of wages up to $728 per week.

SECTION 10.13 UNEMPLOYMENT COMPENSATION

The tragedy of the Depression, when up to 25 percent of the workforce was unemployed, led in 1935 to the passage of the Social Security Act, one portion of which provided for an unemployment insurance program. Today, all 50 states and the federal government are engaged in a cooperative system that helps protect the temporarily jobless. The system is financed through a payroll tax paid by employers.

The actual state tax rate for each employer varies, depending on the employer's *experience* ratings—the number of layoffs in its workforce. Thus employers have an incentive to retain employees.

Rules vary by state, but in general, employees qualify for **unemployment benefits** by reaching a specified total of annual wages. Those losing their jobs must apply to a state agency for unemployment compensation, which varies by state. Benefits may be collected up to a specified maximum period, usually 26 weeks. During that time, those collecting compensation must be ready to work and must make an effort to find suitable work. Workers who quit or who are fired for *misconduct* are ineligible for unemployment compensation. The episodes that follow illustrate the foolish and often funny cases where compensation has been denied:

- The Swiss Valley Farms dairy worker who led her coworkers in an after-hours swim in the cheese vat (filled with water at the time).[73]

- The bored production worker who removed her underwear, put the garment on the production line, and asked a supervisor if he "wanted to sniff them."[74]

- The sheriff's department dispatcher who was dismissed for refusing to remove her tongue stud. The dispatcher had initially been granted benefits, but she lost on appeal when the stud caused her to slur her words as she pleaded her case to the administrative law judge.[75]

The **Worker Adjustment and Retraining Notification Act** (WARN) requires firms with 100 or more employees to provide 60 days notice if they lay off one-third or more of their workers at any site employing at least 150 workers, drop 500 employees at any site, or close a plant employing at least 50 workers. A General Accounting Office study concluded, however, that the law had been ineffectual, with half of plant closings not covered by the law.

Some employers began to adopt pension plans for their employees by the late 1800s. Comprehensive protection for pension rights did not arrive until 1974, when Congress approved the **Employee Retirement Income Security Act** (ERISA), under which the government regulates pension funds to help ensure their long-term financial security by reducing fraud and mismanagement. ERISA requires that fund managers keep detailed records, engage in prudent investments, and provide an annual report that has been certified by qualified, impartial third parties.

ERISA also establishes strict *vesting* rights (the point at which the employee has a nonforfeitable right to the funds) to ensure that employees actually receive the pensions to which they are entitled. Employer contributions typically vest after three years or in a six-year, graduated system. Broadly, pensions take two forms: defined benefit plans and defined contribution plans. **Defined benefit** pensions are the traditional form of company-sponsored and company paid plans that provide specified monthly payments upon retirement. Defined benefit plans provide security for employees who remain with a firm for many years; but for those changing jobs, benefits will likely be smaller. **Defined contribution plans**, such as the popular 401(k), specify in advance the "match" the employer will provide to go with the employee's own contributions and allow the employee a menu of investment options in which to place that retirement money; but they make no promises about the amount that will be paid upon retirement. Defined contribution plans often are attractive to employees because the money vests quickly and follows the employee who changes jobs. ERISA requires that defined benefit fund managers diversify their investments for greater safety, putting no more than 10 percent of the plan's funds in the employer's stock. Defined contribution plans, in general, have no such limit under the law. Defined benefit plans were once the norm in the business community, but defined contribution plans are now much more common. The latter are less expensive to manage, they shift the risk from employer to employee, and they are free of some ERISA requirements.

ERISA established the **Pension Benefit Guaranty Corporation** (PBGC), which insures defined benefit plans to protect retirees in the event that their employer's pension fund fails. The PBGC, which is funded by company contributions, guarantees that vested persons will be paid up to a specified maximum if their plan cannot meet its obligations.

But even the PBGC-protected defined benefit pensions will eventually be at risk if company contributions to the PBGC fund are not significantly increased. As costs go up, however, can American companies compete successfully with lower-cost foreign competition? Can we afford the generous promises we have made to retirees? Will we see, in the decades to come, something of a generational battle between the young and the old about how big a slice of American wealth each will receive?

Unlike defined benefit plans, defined contribution arrangements are not covered by the PBGC. Thus the more relaxed and, in some ways, highly desirable 401(k) holds some big risks for employees, as we have learned in this era of corporate scandals.

Tens of thousands of employees at Enron, World-Com, and other financially devastated corporations lost most of their retirement savings in 2001–02 largely because their 401(k) plans were heavily invested in their employers' stock. Enron shares fell from a high of $90.56 in August 2000 to 36 cents in late November 2001, after the firm's alleged financial corruption became public.[76] Enron's 401(k) plan lost an estimated $850 million in two months. One employee explained his personal loss:

> "I feel like I've been betrayed," said Roy Rinard, 54, a veteran lineman at Enron subsidiary Portland General Electric in Oregon. "I have lost my savings, my plans for the future, everything." He lost the lion's share of his retirement account—once valued at more than $470,000—because he says he invested in Enron stock on the advice of plan administrators... His lawyer valued Rinard's 401(k) at about $40,000.[77]

That sense of betrayal, if not outrage, doubtless is exacerbated by the news that Enron executives cashed out more than $1 billion in company stock when it was near its peak value, and 600 key employees received $100 million in bonuses just before the energy giant collapsed.[78] Enron reached a $356 million settlement in 2005 with about 20,000 current and former employees, but Enron assets available after its bankruptcy suggest that claimants are likely to receive only 15–20 percent of the settlement.[79]

Congress and President Bush promised new laws to reduce the likelihood of future, huge employee retirement losses. At this writing, changes have been limited, but two prominent rules are in place: (1) Participants in **401(k)** and similar retirement plans must receive 30 days' notice of any "blackout" periods when they cannot buy, sell, or borrow from their plans, and (2) corporate executives are forbidden from selling their company stock during blackout periods when employees are locked out of transactions involving their 401(k) holdings. Reform zeal has now cooled, but perhaps it should be so because employees doubtless must bear part of the risk, and more rules are likely to reduce efficiency and competitiveness.

In some ways, a more tragic but less spectacular retirement threat than Enron and WorldCom has been visiting hundreds of thousands of retirees across America in recent years. Many companies under tremendous financial pressure have been forced, in most cases entirely legally, to reduce or withdraw health care benefits that had once been promised to workers. Health care costs have been, for many companies, their most rapidly increasing cost of doing business. Consider GM's rather astonishing health care burdens for both its retirees and its current employees:

> Health care is one of the single biggest costs GM faces each year—representing about $1,400 per vehicle produced. The company's health plans cover 1.21 million employees, retirees, and their dependents. For 2003, the company reported that it spent $4.8 billion, or about $3,966 per person, for health care benefits.[80]

Companies feel they have no choice but to expect retirees to pay more of their own health care costs, but the retirees must endure a humiliating and frightening struggle for survival when the money they expected is no longer there. Richard Bruce, a retired Sears manager, paid $95 a month nine years ago for health care coverage for himself and his wife. As Sears' subsidy has fallen from 75 percent to less than 50 percent of his medical insurance premium, Bruce must now pay over $450 per month to maintain his coverage.[81]

In a sense, only demographics and a changing economy are to blame. Many employers simply have too many retirees to support in this era of long life spans, huge medical costs, and a highly competitive world economy. Bethlehem Steel, for example, employs 13,000 people but has 74,000 retirees.[82]

SECTION 10.14
UNEMPLOYMENT CASE

PROBLEM TEN—B

PARK, BROWN & SMITH, P.C.
ATTORNEYS AT LAW
MEMORANDUM

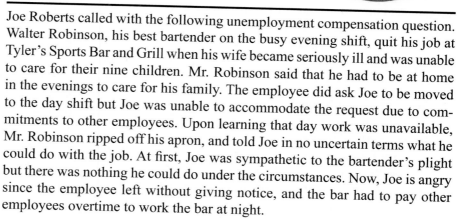

To: All Law Clerks

From: Peter Smith, Esquire

Re: The Unemployment Claim

Joe Roberts called with the following unemployment compensation question. Walter Robinson, his best bartender on the busy evening shift, quit his job at Tyler's Sports Bar and Grill when his wife became seriously ill and was unable to care for their nine children. Mr. Robinson said that he had to be at home in the evenings to care for his family. The employee did ask Joe to be moved to the day shift but Joe was unable to accommodate the request due to commitments to other employees. Upon learning that day work was unavailable, Mr. Robinson ripped off his apron, and told Joe in no uncertain terms what he could do with the job. At first, Joe was sympathetic to the bartender's plight but there was nothing he could do under the circumstances. Now, Joe is angry since the employee left without giving notice, and the bar had to pay other employees overtime to work the bar at night.

Mr. Roberts has just received notice from the Unemployment Compensation Board that the bartender has filed a claim for unemployment compensation benefits claiming that he had no recourse but to quit his job in order to take care of his family. Joe wants to fight the claim and desires to know who is right in this dispute.

Please read **Draper v. Unemployment Compensation Bd. of Review** and let me know who you think should win the case. Please write a memo explaining the law and your conclusions so that I can present it to Mr. Roberts.

DRAPER V. UNEMPLOYMENT COMPENSATION BD. OF REVIEW
718 A.2D 383 (PA. CMWLTH., 1998)

The issue presented is whether Joseph Draper (Claimant) terminated his employment with Frankel Chevy Buick, Inc. (Employer) for reasons of a necessitous and compelling nature, thus entitling him to benefits under the Unemployment Compensation Act. Because he did not, the decision of the Unemployment Compensation Board of Review (Board), which denied benefits, is affirmed.

The relevant facts are as follows. Claimant was employed as a department manager for Employer until August 22, 1997, at which time he resigned in order to move to Virginia. At that time, Claimant's ill 95-year-old mother lived in Virginia with his sister, but his sister was becoming increasingly unable to care for his mother. Claimant purchased a home in Virginia and moved his mother into his home where she is now cared for by Claimant and his wife. In addition to his sister, Claimant also has two brothers in Virginia, but Claimant testified that neither of them is capable of taking care of his mother.

Claimant subsequently filed for unemployment compensation benefits with the Interstate Claims Office on the grounds that, although he voluntarily quit his job with Employer, he did so for a necessitous and compelling reason, i.e., the necessity to move to Virginia to take care of his mother. The Interstate Claims Office denied the claim, and a hearing was held before a referee on March 10, 1998.

At the March 10 hearing, Claimant testified as follows in response to questions from the referee:

Q. All right. Now, Mr. Draper, tell me clearly when you realized your mother couldn't live with your sister down in Virginia any longer. Rather than quitting your job in Pennsylvania why didn't you bring your mother up here to live?

A. **Well, I had made plans to just go down there.**

Q. Why did you decide to go to Virginia rather than bringing your mother up to Pennsylvania?

A. **Well, Virginia is where I thought I was going to find myself a job, and because all my family is here also.**

Q. What I'm asking you, sir, is why didn't you bring your mother to Pennsylvania instead of you resigning your job to move to Virginia.

A. **Sir, here in Virginia I had purchased my property, and I wanted to be here with [my mother] and I felt this was where I was going to be located.**

By decision dated March 12, 1998, the referee denied benefits. Claimant appealed to the Board, which affirmed on May 6, 1998, adopting the opinion of the referee.

Claimant argues that caring for his ill mother constituted a necessitous and compelling reason for terminating his employment and moving to Virginia. The Board acknowledges that domestic circumstances can indeed rise to the level of necessitous and compelling reasons for terminating one's employment, but argues that the facts of this case do not support such a conclusion.

A claimant who voluntarily terminates his employment yet seeks to receive unemployment compensation benefits bears the burden of proving that he quit for cause of a necessitous and compelling nature. Cause of a necessitous and compelling nature is such cause as results from overpowering circumstances that produce both real and substantial pressure to terminate employment and that would compel a reasonable person to terminate employment. Cause of a necessitous and compelling nature may arise from purely domestic circumstances and need not be related to a claimant's employment situation. The question of whether quitting one's employment to care for an ill parent constitutes cause of a necessitous and compelling nature must be decided on the specific facts of each individual case. A claimant who terminates his employment to care for a chronically ill parent cannot be said to have done so for cause of a necessitous and compelling nature unless he has given the employer an opportunity to accommodate him, has explored alternative options for care of the parent, or has considered the possibility of relocating the parent so that he can continue his employment.

In this case, we find it likely that Claimant did in fact move to Virginia primarily because he wanted to take care of his ill mother, and such a commitment is certainly laudable. However, this does not entitle Claimant to unemployment compensation benefits absent evidence that Claimant explored other options less drastic than quitting his job, such as purchasing a home in Pennsylvania in which to care for his mother or asking Employer for a leave of absence or some other accommodation. Had Claimant presented evidence that he explored such options and found them to be fruitless, then his termination of employment and move to Virginia might have been found "necessitous and compelling." Not having done so, we conclude that the Board did not err in concluding that Claimant failed to sustain his burden of proving that he terminated his employment for cause of a necessitous and compelling nature.

Accordingly, the order of the Board is affirmed.

Name: _____   **Please Print Clearly**

1. Please tell me the law about quitting one's job because of a medical issue.

_____

_____

_____

_____

_____

_____

_____

_____

_____

2. What do you think the outcome of the unemployment compensation case will be? Please explain your answer.

_____

_____

_____

_____

_____

_____

_____

_____

_____

SECTION 10.15
AT-WILL EMPLOYEES

Catherine Wagenseller, an Arizona nurse, her boss, Kay Smith, and some co-workers joined a Colorado River rafting trip where Wagenseller declined to participate in a "Moon River" skit in which the group allegedly "mooned" the audience. Likewise, Wagenseller did not join Smith in the heavy drinking, "grouping up," public urination, and similar behaviors that allegedly marked the trip. Despite favorable job evaluations preceding the trip, Wagenseller's relationship with Smith deteriorated following the trip, and eventually she was terminated. Wagenseller, an at-will employee, sued claiming that she was wrongfully discharged. An **at-will employee**, by definition, is not under contract for a definite period of time, and as such can be fired at any time. Wagenseller, however, argued that Arizona should adopt the *public policy exception* to the at-will doctrine. She claimed that she was fired because she refused to engage in behaviors that might have violated the Arizona indecent exposure statute. The state Supreme Court agreed with Wagenseller by finding in the statute a public policy favoring privacy and decency. The case was returned to the trial level, giving Wagenseller the opportunity to prove that her refusal to violate state public policy by engaging in public indecency led to her dismissal.[83]

The **Wagenseller** decision is an exception to the long-standing American rule that at-will employees can be fired for good reasons, bad reasons, or no reason at all. Of course, the employee is likewise free to quit at any time. Furthermore, both employer and employee freely entered the bargain understanding its terms, and thus the court should, in general, enforce those terms, Critics, however, argue that the doctrine ignores the historic inequality of bargaining power between employers and employees. In recent decades the at-will rule has been softened in most states by legislative and judicially imposed limitations. Statutory exceptions to the at-will rule include our labor laws protecting union workers and the equal employment opportunity laws that forbid the dismissal of an employee for discriminatory reasons.

An increasing number of court decisions provide grounds for dismissed at-will employees to claim that they have been **wrongfully discharged**. Those judicial decisions were often provoked by transparently unjust dismissals including, for example, whistle-blowers who exposed their employers' misdeeds and employees who declined to commit perjury on behalf of their employers. Those judicial limitations to the at-will doctrine fall into three categories: (1) express or implied contracts, (2) an implied covenant of good faith and fair dealing, and (3) the tort of violating an established public policy, as in **Wagenseller**. Additional tort claims may substitute for or supplement wrongful discharge claims.

1. **Express or implied employment contracts:** A number of states have adopted a contract protection for at-will employees that arise, typically, either from the employee handbook or from employer conduct and oral representations. The notion here is that the courts will recognize a contract based either on language in the handbook or on such assurances of continued employment as routine promotions, no notice of poor performance, longevity, and oral communications.

2. **Implied covenant of good faith and fair dealing:** A few state courts have held that neither party to a contract may *act in bad faith* to deprive the other of the benefits of the contract. For example, Bruce Rubenstein gave up his job with Arbor Mortgage and took an at-will position with Huntington Mortgage with the understanding that he would be manager of a new branch office in central New Jersey. After a few weeks, however, Huntington decided on a downsizing strategy that included not opening the new branch. Rubenstein was offered a job as a loan originator, but he declined. He sued Huntington asserting, among other things, that Huntington had breached the covenant of good faith and fair dealing. Rubenstein believed that Huntington knew of the possibility of downsizing before hiring him. The court agreed that Rubenstein may have had a viable claim for breach of the implied covenant of good faith and fair dealing if the facts, at trial, proved to be as Rubenstein alleged.[84]

3. **Public policy:** Most states have now adopted some form of public policy (the general preference of the citizenry) exception providing that a dismissal is wrongful if it results from employee conduct that is consistent with the will of the people as expressed in statutes, constitutions, and the like. Those exceptions are established case by case, and they differ from state to state. In addition to the whistle-blowing and perjury situations noted, the exception often protects, for example, those fired for pursuing a lawful claim (like workers' compensation) and those fired for fulfilling a civic responsibility (like jury duty).

Dismissed employees are increasingly turning to a variety of tort actions (often labeled *tag-along torts*) to enhance potential financial recovery, including punitive damages. Those tort possibilities include, among others, defamation, intentional infliction of emotional distress, interference with contract, and invasion of privacy. The following case raises public policy and false imprisonment tort claims following an employment termination.

BARRERA V. CONAGRA, INC.
244 F.3D 663 (8TH CIR., 2001)

Manuel Barrera appeals from the district court's order granting summary judgment to ConAgra, Inc., and Swift & Co. (collectively, Swift), on Barrera's claims of retaliatory discharge in violation of public policy and false arrest and imprisonment.

On June 14, 1996, Barrera, a Mexican national who speaks very little English, was fired from his job on the cut floor of Swift's hog processing plant in Marshalltown, Iowa, after allegedly violating a company policy against eating in the employee locker room. Barrera was asked to report to human resources, where Swift alleges that he threatened the lives of several employees.

Barrera contends that he was fired in retaliation for filing a worker's compensation claim related to a slip-and-fall accident that occurred on or about March 22, 1996. He alleges that Swift staged the incident in the locker room as a pretext for his termination and that he was actually fired prior to the time he reported to human resources and before the alleged threats were made. Barrera also denies threatening to kill anyone at Swift, although he concedes that he may have threatened, depending on the translation, to "kick their asses" or "spank their buttocks."

In Iowa, an employer's ability to discharge an employee is limited when the discharge clearly violates the well recognized and defined public policy of the state. Discharge in retaliation for filing a worker's compensation claim clearly violates Iowa's public policy. To prevail on a retaliatory discharge claim, Barrera must establish (1) that he engaged in a protected activity; (2) that he suffered an adverse employment action; and (3) that there existed a causal connection between the protected activity and his termination.

We agree with the district court's conclusion that Barrera failed to produce evidence sufficient to raise a genuine issue of material fact regarding causation. As the court noted, other than the timing of the discharge, Barrera produced "almost no evidence" that his termination was in any way related to his worker's compensation claim. Under Iowa law, the fact that Barrera was fired after filing a worker's compensation claim is not alone sufficient to prove causation.

Iowa law demands, rather, that Barrera produce evidence demonstrating that his worker's compensation claim was the determinative factor in Swift's decision to terminate his employment. Barrera's version of the facts, however, suggests nothing more than rude and callous behavior on Swift's part. We conclude that the grant of summary judgment on Barrera's first claim was proper.

Affirmed.

QUESTIONS FOR DISCUSSION:

1. Why did Barrera lose this lawsuit?

2. The criminal harassment charges against Barrera were dropped, and the court noted that Barrera (according to his account) was the victim of "rude and callous" behavior by Swift.

3. Given this version of the facts, does it appear that Swift had legitimate grounds for dismissal?

4. If not, should Barrera have prevailed in this appeal? Explain.

5. Schuster worked, in an at-will relationship, for Derocili for 15 months, during which time she claims he touched her inappropriately and made numerous sexual comments despite her repeated rejections of those behaviors. Schuster received bonuses and good evaluations, but in a meeting between Schuster, Derocili, and Schuster's direct supervisor, Goff, she was fired for poor performance. Schuster's sexual harassment complaint with the Delaware Department of Labor was rejected as unsubstantiated. She sued Derocili for breach of contract, but the trial court dismissed that complaint. She appealed.

   a. Does Schuster have a legitimate wrongful discharge claim? Explain.

   b. Does she have any other plausible causes of action? Explain. See **Schuster v. Derocili, 775 A.2d 1029 (Del. S. Ct., 2000).**

6. Gilmartin took a job as station manager at a Texas television station. He was hired on a year-to-year basis under an oral agreement providing that his employment would continue as long as his work was satisfactory. Gilmartin was subsequently blamed for declining profits, and he was fired. Gilmartin sued. In his pleadings, Gilmartin said that he was informed of his annual salary, vacation time, and possible future raises, that his contract was to be renewed from year to year contingent on satisfactory performance, and that a commitment by KVTV for one to three years was "very doable." He was also told that a written agreement was not necessary. Was Gilmartin wrongfully discharged? Explain. See **Gilmartin v. KVTV-Channel 13, 985 S.W.2d 553 (Ct. App. Tex., 1998).**

7. IBP operates a large hog-processing plant in Storm Lake, Iowa. IBP prohibits possession of "look-alike drugs" on company property. An employee, Michael Huegerich, was randomly and lawfully inspected as he was entering the plant. The inspection revealed an asthma medication, Maxalert, which was identical in appearance to an illegal street drug, "speed." Maxalert contained the stimulant ephedrine. The pills actually belonged to his girlfriend and were in his possession by accident. Huegerich was terminated for possessing a look-alike drug in violation of company

policy. Huegerich admitted that he was generally aware of IBP drug policies, but since he was a transfer from another IBP division, he had not gone through the company orientation program where new employees are advised of the policy against look-alike drugs. About six months after his dismissal, two IBP employees told Huegerich that they had heard he was fired for possessing speed. Huegerich then sued IBP for, among other claims, wrongful discharge and defamation. At trial, Huegerich provided no evidence as to how, when, and from whom the IBP employees had heard that he was terminated for possession of speed. The district court found for Huegerich in the amount of $24,000 on the wrongful discharge claim and $20,000 on the defamation claim. The court said that IBP was guilty of negligent discharge in failing to inform Huegerich about its drug policy. IBP appealed to the Iowa Supreme Court. Iowa law recognizes the doctrine of at-will employment with "narrow" exceptions for public policy violations and where a contract is created by an employer's handbook. Decide. Explain. See **Huegerich v. IBP, 547 N. W. 2d 216 (Iowa S.Ct., 1996).**

8. Freeman, a television anchorperson employed by KSN, gave birth to her second child. On the day she returned from the hospital, she was notified that she had been dismissed. Six weeks later, she became unable to lactate. She sued KSN for wrongful discharge, tortious interference with contract, and negligent infliction of emotional distress. Decide. Explain. See **Freeman v. Medevac Mid-america of Kansas, Inc., 719 F. Supp. 995 (D. Kan., 1989).**

SECTION 10.16
IMMIGRATION

Immigration is vital fuel for America's economic and cultural growth, but immigration is also a source of deep divisions in national opinion—especially since September 11, 2001. Thirteen percent of the nation's workers are immigrants, both legal and illegal.[85] About 700,000 legal immigrants enter the United States each year, and another 300,000 arrive illegally or overstay their visas.[86] In total about 30 million immigrants live in the United States, and an estimated 8.0 million of those are here illegally.[87]

About one-half of the nation's farm workers and 9 percent of restaurant employees are illegal immigrants.[88] A recent federal study found that immigrants provide a $10 billion annual boost to the American economy, and immigrants, over a lifetime, are no greater drain on public money for welfare and the like than are native-born citizens.[89] Without heavy immigration in the 1990s, unemployment probably would have been so low that wages and prices would have spiraled upward, threatening inflation.[90] A steady influx of highly skilled workers has been vital in maintaining high-tech growth.

Foreign workers seeking permanent residence in the United States on the basis of employment must have an offer of a permanent, full-time job. If so, the employer and the foreign national employee apply to the appropriate state Department of Labor for *labor certification,* which affirms that no one is available for the job and the hiring will not harm wages and working conditions in similar jobs. Some exceptions are provided for people in occupations where shortages exist and for those with exceptional abilities.

In hiring those already in the United States, federal immigration law, including the 1986 Immigration Reform and Control Act, requires employers to verify that each new hire is a U.S. citizen, a permanent resident, or a foreign national with permission to work in this country. To meet this requirement, employers must complete an employment eligibility verification form (I–9) for each new employee. New employees must present documents establishing the employee's identity and eligibility to work in the United States. The employer must examine the documents and complete the I–9 if the documents appear legitimate. Of course, employers cannot knowingly hire illegal immigrants, but neither can they discriminate against legal immigrants because of national origin and similar factors.

SECTION 10.17 REVIEW QUESTIONS

1. In general, employers are forced to bear (or at least share) the legal burden for their employees' negligent conduct on the job. Why do we force employers to bear that responsibility? Should we do so? Explain.

2. Abplanalp, a five-year employee of Com-Co Insurance, signed an employment agreement including a restrictive covenant providing that, should he leave Com-Co, he would not use Com-Co customer lists or solicit business from Com-Co clients for three years. Abplanalp moved to Service Insurance, where he sold insurance to some friends and relatives. He did not sell to any other persons whom he came to know while working for Com-Co. Abplanalp was sued by Com-Co for violating the restrictive covenant. Decide. Explain. See **Com-Co Insurance Agency v. Service Insurance Agency, 748 N.E.2d 298 (Ill. App. Ct., 2001).**

3. Many companies refer to credit reports when investigating job applicants. The Fair Credit Reporting Act requires employers to notify applicants if they are rejected because of information in a credit report.

   a. In your judgment, does evidence of failure to pay debts constitute useful information in the job selection process? Explain.

   b. Is the use of that information an "invasion of privacy" as you understand it? Explain.

4. A group of Fargo, North Dakota, nurses were paid a sub-minimum wage for their "oncall" time. When on call, the nurses were required to be able to report to their hospital within 20 minutes, they were required to provide a

phone number where they could be reached, and they were not to consume alcohol or drugs. After being called, nurses returned to regular pay. In three years, 36 of the 135 nurses who sued had been called in more than once. The nurses sued the hospital for violating the Fair Labor Standards Act's minimum wage provision. Decide. Explain. See **Reimer v. Champion Healthcare Corp., 258 F.3d 720 (8th Cir., 2001).**

5. Simons, an engineer at the CIA, downloaded child pornography on his workplace computer. The computer was to be used only for work. The pornography was discovered by a search of employee computers. Simons was then convicted of receiving and possessing child pornography. Simons appealed on Fourth Amendment grounds. Decide. Explain. See **United States v. Simons, 206 F.3d 392 (4th Cir., 2000); cert. den. 122 S. Ct. 292 (2001).**

6. Guz, a longtime Bechtel employee, was dismissed during what Bechtel said was a business slump. Bechtel's personnel policy included a provision saying employees "may be terminated at the option of Bechtel." Guz sued for wrongful dismissal claiming, among other things, that Bechtel breached an implied contract to be terminated only for good cause, and that Bechtel breached the implied covenant of good faith and fair dealing. A lower court concluded that Guz's promotions, raises, favorable performance reviews, together with Bechtel's progressive discipline policy and Bechtel officials' statements of company practices supported Guz's position. Bechtel appealed. Decide. Explain. See **Guz v. Bechtel National Inc., 8 P.3d 1089 (Cal., 2000).**

7. Sharon Kay Riddle sought workers' compensation claiming she had been totally and temporarily disabled by mental stress caused by the implementation of a no-smoking ban in the electronics manufacturing plant of her employer, Ampex. Riddle had smoked one to two packs per day for 24 years. Following the plant-wide ban, Riddle took leave and was diagnosed as suffering from major depression, nicotine dependence, and posttraumatic stress disorder. The administrative law judge found that Riddle had established three of the statutory requirements for her workers' compensation claim, but that she had failed to establish the fourth, which provided that work-related stress disabilities are not compensable if they are based "in whole or in part, upon facts and circumstances that are common to all fields of employment" and that the "facts and circumstances" were "not unique to [claimant's] employment." Riddle appealed the unfavorable ruling to the Colorado Court of Appeals. Is she entitled to workers' compensation? Explain. See **Riddle v. Ampex Corporation, 839 P. 2d 489 (Colo. App. Ct., 1992).**

8. As discussed in this chapter, many recent judicial decisions have afforded at-will employees much-improved protection against unfair dismissals. A special area of concern is whether at-will employees can be dismissed for off-duty conduct. The decisions are split, but the trend seems to be toward greater respect and protection for employee privacy. Nonetheless, companies still retain broad latitude to dismiss. For example, an employee convicted of selling drugs would most likely not be protected by the courts from a company dismissal.

> Virginia Rulon-Miller, an IBM salesperson, had been dating another IBM employee, Matt Blum, for several years. Her supervisors were aware of the relationship. Blum left IBM to join a competitor, QYX, and he moved from San Francisco to Philadelphia. QYX transferred him back to San Francisco, and he and Rulon-Miller resumed dating. Again, her superiors were aware of the relationship, and one mentioned that he didn't "have any problem" with her romance. Rulon-Miller did well in her sales role and was promoted to a management position, where she continued to do well, as evidenced by a $4,000 raise. Nonetheless, one week after receiving notice of the raise, Rulon-Miller was either dismissed (her version) or "transferred" (the company's version). IBM felt her romance and her concern for the success of Blum created a conflict of interest. Despite being an at-will employee, Rulon-Miller argued that she was protected by IBM's written policies that detail those circumstances under which an employee's private life can become a company issue. She filed suit, claiming wrongful discharge. Decide. Explain. See **Rulon-Miller v. IBM, 1 BNA IER Cases 405, 162 Cal. App.3d 241 (1984).**

9. Terrell was employed by Red Giant Foods as a forklift driver. Terrell's supervisor, Rowsey, had received reports from employees that Terrell was drinking on the job. Rowsey later observed Terrell drinking in his car, parked on company property during the noon break. An hour later, Rowsey entered the unoccupied, unlocked car and found beer. Subsequently, Terrell was terminated for violating company policy against drinking on the job. Terrell filed suit.

    a. What claim(s) would Terrell raise?

    b. Decide. Explain. See **Terrell v. Rowsey and Red Giant Foods, 647 N. E.2d 662 (Ind. App. Ct., 1995).**

10. In most drug testing cases, courts have balanced the employee's privacy interests against the employer's need for information. What business justifications are likely to be most persuasive to a court reviewing the legality of employee drug testing?

11. Millions of workers can be regarded as telecommuters. As such, they bring new legal problems to the workplace. As a manager, what legal difficulties would you want to anticipate and protect against as more and more of your employees work off-premises and often from his or her own homes?

12. A reader sent the following story to a newspaper question and answer forum:

    > I was fired recently by my employer, an architecture firm, immediately after serving for one month on a federal grand jury. From the moment I informed my boss, I was harassed, and told I was not putting the company first. I was told to get out of my jury service, "or else." I was fired exactly one week after my service ended.[91] Was the dismissal of this at-will employee lawful? Explain.

13. Katherine Born and Rick Gillispie were employed by a Blockbuster Video store in Iowa. Blockbuster maintained a policy that forbade dating between supervisors and their subordinates. Born and Gillispie were dismissed for violating the policy. They denied that they were romantically involved and filed suit for wrongful dismissal. Under Iowa law, an at-will employee can be discharged at any time for any reason, but Iowa law does recognize the public policy exception. To prevail in this lawsuit, what must the plaintiffs show about Iowa law? See **Katherine Born and Rick Gillispie v. Blockbuster Videos, Inc., 941 F. Supp. 868 (S. D. Ia., 1996).**

14. A pregnant employee at a retail store was operating a buffing machine when propane gas that powered the machine led to a carbon monoxide buildup, causing the worker and others to be taken to a hospital. The worker's fetus sustained oxygen deprivation, resulting in injuries including abnormal motor functions, cerebral palsy, and a seizure disorder. The worker sued on negligence grounds for her child's injuries. The employer defended by arguing that workers' compensation provides the exclusive remedy in such situations. Does workers' compensation bar the child's suit? Explain. See **Snyder v. Michael's Stores, Inc., 945 P.2d 781 (Cal. S. Ct., 1997).**

15. Lang, a white male working in a factory, called a black coworker such names as "watermelon" and "buckwheat." The coworker told Lang to stop. Lang continued the racist name-calling and his coworker then called Lang a "cracker" and a "honkey." Later, while Lang was talking with his supervisor, the coworker twice struck Lang, who then filed a workers' compensation claim.

    a. Is Lang entitled to workers' compensation?

    b. What is the key issue? Explain. See **Redman Industries v. Lang, 326 Or. 32 (Sup. Ct. Or., 1997).**

16. LaTourette worked for a California college and was attending a conference for work purposes when he suffered a heart attack. He underwent various operations including bypass surgery, subsequent to which he died in the hospital from a bacterial infection. His estate sought workers' compensation, claiming that his heart attack was a response to job stress. Is his estate entitled to workers' compensation? Explain. See **LaTourette v. Workers' Compensation Appeals Board, 72 Cal. Rptr.2d 217 (Sup. Ct. Cal., 1998).**

SECTION 10.18
INTERNET REFERENCES

The following internet references offer more information on employment law:

- **http://dir.yahoo.com/Government/Law employment_Law Driving while Dialing**
  This site provides an extensive employment law database.

- **http://www.toolkit. cch.com/tools/indcon_m.asp**
  A sample of independent contractor agreements can be reviewed at this site.

- **www.employlaw.com**
  This site offers an overview on employment law.

- **www.dol.gov**
  The U.S. Department of Labor home page may be accessed at this site.

- **www.dol.gov/esa/minwage/america.htm**
  More information can be learned about the state minimum wage laws at this reference.

- **www.dol.gov/esa/regs/compliance/whd/fairpay/main.htm**
  Details about the new overtime rules are contained at this internet reference.

- **www.osha.gov**
  This is the internet address for the OSHA home page.

- **www.osha.gov/comp-links.html**
  OSHA standards may be accessed at this site.

- **http://ergo.human.cornell.edu**
  This site contains advice on measures to reduce repetitive stress problems for students.

- **www.wcrinet.org**
  The Workers' Compensation Research Institute may be accessed at this site.

- **www.questdiagnostic.com**
  More details on drug testing results is available at this reference.

- **www.hrlawindex.com/email/email.html**
  This reference offers more information on e-mail and privacy.

- **www.dol.gov/esa/whd/fmla**
  More information about the Family Medical Leave Act is contained at this site.

- **http://uscis.gov/graphics/formsfee/forms/i-9.htm**
  This site offers an introduction to the I–9 requirements.

KEY TERMS

At-Will Employee

Consolidated Budget Reconciliation Act

Defined Benefit

Defined Contributions Plan

Drug-Free Workplace Act

Electronic Communications Privacy Act

Employee

Employee Retirement Income Security Act

Equal Employment Opportunity Commission

Family and Medical Leave Act

Fair Labor Standards Act

Health Insurance Portability and Accountability Act

Immigration

Independent Contractor

Minimum Wage

Negligence in Hiring an Employee

Overtime

Pension Benefit Guaranty Corporation

Qualified Privilege

Right to Privacy

Scope of Employment

Unemployment Compensation

Vicarious Liability

Worker Adjustment and Retraining Notification Act

Workers' Compensation

Wrongfully Discharged

Footnotes:

1. Power, Kinder, & *Sweeney,* "Employee Strikes Door in Anger but Receives Workers' Comp," *Rhode Island Employment Law Letter, May 1999.*

2. Craig J. Cantoni, "The Case against Employee Benefits," *The Wall Street Journal,* August 18, 1997, p. A14.

3. "Microsoft Settles Federal Lawsuit," *Des Moines Register,* December 13, 2000, p. 8C.

4. **Donna Vizcaino v. Microsoft Corporation, 120 F.3d 1006 (9 Cir., 1997).**

5. **Microsoft Corporation v. Donna Vizcaino, 522 U.S. 1098 (1998).**

6. Staff Reporter, "Microsoft Says Temps Must Take a Hiatus after Working a Year," *The Wall Street Journal,* February 22, 2000, p. A32.

7. Sally Richards, "Résumé Fraud: Don't Lie to Get That Job!" *High Technology Careers Magazine* **[http://www.hightechcareers.com/doc699nextstep699.html].**

8. "Lying on Résumés: Why Some Can't Resist," *Dallas Morning News,* December 22, 2001, p. 8A.

9. Kris Maher, "The Jungle," *The Wall Street Journal,* January 20, 2004, p. B8.

10. Carlos Tejada, "They Asked What?" *The Wall Street Journal,* March 27, 2001, p. A1.

11. Kris Maher, "The Jungle," *The Wall Street Journal,* September 28, 2004, p. B10.

12. Maher, "The Jungle," p. B10.

13. Kris Maher, "The Jungle," *The Wall Street Journal,* June 8, 2004, p. B4.

14. Maher, "The Jungle," p. B4.

15. Stephanie Armour, "College Grads Confront Tough Job Market," *USA TODAY,* June 12, 2001, p. 1B.

16. **Circuit City Stores, Inc. v. Adams, 532 U.S. 105 (2001).**

17. See Sidney L. Gold and Hyman Lovitz, "Arbitration Agreements Don't Supersede Authority to Recover Damages," *The Legal Intelligencer,* June 6, 2002, p. 6.

18. 814 P.2d 1341 (Cal. S. Ct., 1991).

19. Jenny B. Davis, "Still Working after All These Years," *ABA Journal,* October 2001, p. 67.

20. Rick Wartzman, "As Officials Lost Faith in the Minimum Wage, Pat Williams Lived It," *The Wall Street Journal,* July 19, 2001, p. A1.

21. For a study involving 12 of the higher minimum wage states, see Gwendolyn Bounds, "Argument for Minimum-Wage Boost," *The Wall Street Journal,* July 27, 2004, p. B3.

22. Editorial, "Living in Santa Fe," *The Wall Street Journal,* July 9, 2004, p. A10.

23. Associated Press, "Study Shows 'Living Wage' Helping to Reduce Poverty," *Waterloo/ Cedar Falls Courier,* March 14, 2002, p. A2.

24. Ann Zimmerman, "Big Retailers Face Overtime Suits as Bosses Do More 'Hourly' Work," The Wall Street Journal, May 26, 2004, p. A1.

25. Zimmerman, "Big Retailers Face Overtime Suits," *Id.*

26. Michael Orey, "Lawsuits Abound from Workers Seeking Overtime Pay," *The Wall Street Journal,* May 30, 2002, p. B1.

27. Associated Press, "Disney Workers Win Pay Ruling," *Des Moines Register,* April 8, 2001, p. 2K.

28. "Call the *Courier,*" *Waterloo/Cedar Falls Courier,* February 4, 2001, p. C1.

29. David Barstow, "California Leads in Making Employer Pay for Job Deaths," *The New York Times,* December 23, 2003, p. A1.

30. Justin Pritchard, "Mexican Worker Deaths Rise in U.S. Even as Safety Improves," *Des Moines Register,* March 14, 2004, p. 1D.

31. "OSHA Enforcement Focuses on the Triple Bottom Line," *U.S. Newswire,* November 22, 2004.

32. Leigh Strope, "U.S. Workplace Deaths Up Slightly in 2003," *Des Moines Register,* September 23, 2004, p. 8C.

33. "OSHA Enforcement Focuses on the Triple Bottom Line," supra.

34. "OSHA Enforcement Focuses on the Triple Bottom Line," supra.

35. "OSHA Enforcement Focuses on the Triple Bottom Line," supra.

36. Robert J. Grossman, "Making Ergonomics," *HR Magazine,* April 2000, p. 36.

37. Grossman, "Making Ergonomics," *Id.*

38. Grossman, "Making Ergonomics," *Id.*

39. Bloomburg News, "Poultry, Grocery Firms Face Ergonomic Rules," *Los Angeles Times,* June 12, 2002, Part 3, p. 4.

40. "U.S. Repeated Trauma Rates Decline for Third Straight Year," *CTDNEWS Workplace Solutions* for Repetitive Stress Injuries 8, no. 1 (January 1999).

41. Diane E. Lewis, "Voluntary Ergonomic Proposal Released, Business Cheers Plan; Foes Say It Lacks Teeth," *The Boston Globe,* April 6, 2002, p. C1.

42. "OSHA Prepares to Turn the Spotlight on Workplace Homicides," *Security Director's Report,* January 2005.

43. Daniel Costello, "Incidents of 'Desk Rage' Disrupt America's Offices," *The Wall Street Journal,* January 16, 2001, p. B1.

44. "OSHA Prepares to Turn the Spotlight," supra.

45. "OSHA Facts, December 2004" [http://www.osha.gov/as/opa/oshafacts.html].

46. David Barstow, "U.S. Rarely Seeks Charges for Deaths in Workplace," *The New York Times,* December 22, 2003, p. Al.

47. Justin Pritchard, "Mexican Workers More Likely to Die on the Job," *Marin Independent Journal,* April 14, 2004 [**www.marinij.com**].

48. Pritchard, "Mexican Workers More Likely to Die on the Job," *Id.*

49. **Stringer v. Minnesota Vikings, 686 N. W.2d (Minn. Ct. App., 2004); Stringer v. Minnesota Vikings, 2004 Minn. LEXIS 752 (Minn. S. Ct.).**

50. **Guico v. Excel Corp., 619 N.W.2d 470 (Neb. S. Ct., 2000).**

51. Barbara Ehrenreich, "Two-Tiered Morality," *The New York Times,* June 30, 2002, sec. 4, p. 15.

52. Bernard Wysocki Jr., "Companies Get Tough with Smokers, Obese to Trim Costs," *The Wall Street Journal,* October 12, 2004, p. B1.

53. Sue Shellenbarger, "Getting Fired for Dating a Coworker: Office Romance Comes under Attack," *The Wall Street Journal,* February 19, 2004, p. D1.

54. Shellenbarger, "Getting Fired for Dating a Coworker," *Id.*

55. Littler and Mendelson, *The 1996 Employer* (San Francisco: Littler, Mendelson, Fastiff, Tichy & Mathiason, P.C., 1996), p. 860.

56. See, e.g., **National Treasury Employees Union v. Von Raab, 109 S.Ct. 1385 (1989).**

57. Frances A. McMorris, "Is Your Office Voice Mail Private? Don't Bet on It," *The Wall Street Journal,* February 28, 1995, p. B1.

58. "Does Your Boss Watch You Work?" *Des Moines Register,* June 18, 2000, p. 3D.

59. Associated Press, "Study: Employers Monitoring Internet Use of a Third of Online U.S. Work Force," Waterloo/Cedar Falls Courier, July 10, 2001, p. B5.

60. Kris Maher, "Big Employer Is Watching," *The Wall Street Journal,* November 4, 2004, p. B1.

61. Mark P. Couch, "Eyes Are on Your E-Mail," *Des Moines Register,* January 26, 1997, p. 1G.

62. *Hartford Courant,* "Study Finds Millions Lost Health Insurance at Work," *Waterloo/Cedar Falls Courier,* August 3, 2004, p. D6.

63. Kathy Chu, "Good Times Return, Not Benefits," *The Wall Street Journal,* June 30, 2004, p. D2.

64. Chu, "Good Times Return, Not Benefits," *Id.*

65. Chu, "Good Times Return, Not Benefits," *Id.*

66. Joe Robinson, "Vacation Deficit Disorder," *Des Moines Register,* August 1, 2003, p. 9A.

67. Robinson, "Vacation Deficit Disorder," *Id.*

68. Jeffrey Zaslow, "The Singles Lobby: Unmarried People Seek Economic Perks Enjoyed by Couples," *The Wall Street Journal,* June 24, 2004, p. D1.

69. Sara Munoz, "Leadership (A Special Report); A Good Idea, but...: Some Businesses Complain That the Family and Medical Leave Act Should Be More Aptly Named the Slackers Protection Act," *The Wall Street Journal,* January 24, 2005, p. R6.

70. Munoz, "Leadership (A Special Report)," *Id.*

71. Munoz, "Leadership (A Special Report)," *Id.*

72. Knight Ridder Newspapers, "Study: New Parents' Leave Is Unchanged," *Waterloo/Cedar Falls Courier,* February 21, 2003, p. A10.

73. Patt Johnson, "Getting the Boot," *Des Moines Register,* May 4, 2003, p. 1D.

74. Johnson, "Getting the Boot." *Id.*

75. Clark Kauffman, "Stud-Wearing Dispatcher Gets a Tongue-Lashing," *Des Moines Register,* March 20, 2004, p. 1A.

76. Liz Pulliam Weston, "Betting It All on Company Stock Is Risky Business," *Los Angeles Times,* November 30, 2001, p. 1.

77. James T. Madore, "Enron Employees See 401(k)s Wiped Out," *Newsday,* November 30, 2001, p. A75.

78. "Enron: Deconstructing the Energy Giant's Fall," *The Scotsman,* January 11, 2002, p. 5.

79. Ellen Schultz, "Enron Settles with Employees Who Lost Retirement Money," *The Wall Street Journal,* July 12, 2005, p. A8.

80. Lee Hawkins Jr., "GM's Liabilities for Retiree Health Top $60 Billion," *The Wall Street Journal,* March 11, 2004, p. A3.

81. Sandra Guy, "Coverage Causes Pain," *Chicago Sun-Times,* June 20, 2002, p. 47.

82. Kristine Henry, "Steel Workers' Benefits in Peril," *Baltimore Sun,* July 10, 2002, p. 1A.

83. **Wagenseller v. Scottsdale Memorial Hospital, 710 P.2d 1025 (Az. S. Ct., 1985).**

84. **Rubenstein v. Huntington Mortgage Company, N. J. Supp.Ct., App.Div., 1997.** For a journalistic account of the case, see Pitney, Hardin, Kipp, and Szuch, "Employers Must Be Cautious about Failing to Disclose Business Plans That Will Affect the Jobs of New Hires," *New Jersey Employment Law Letter, September 1997.*

85. Laura Parker, "USA Just Wouldn't Work without Immigrant Labor," *USA TODAY,* July 23, 2001, p. 1A.

86. Parker, "USA Just Wouldn't Work," *Id.*

87. Miriam Jordan, "Arizona Limits Illegal Immigrants' Access to Benefits," *The Wall Street Journal,* November 4, 2004, p. A4.

88. Deborah Kong, "Illegal Immigrants Abound in Some Jobs," *Des Moines Register,* March 22, 2002, p. 1A.

89. Mark Siebert, "Immigrants Aid Economy, Study Shows," *Des Moines Register,* February 18, 2001, p. 3B.

90. Adam Ninklewicz, "Keeping the Hive Humming," *BusinessWeek,* April 24, 2000, p. 50.

91. *Washington Post,* "The Boss Can't Fire You for Doing Your Civic Duty," Waterloo/Cedar Falls Courier, May 26, 1999, p. C8.

CHAPTER 11

INTERNATIONAL LAW

BY: MICHAEL VALENZA, ESQ.

"Insofar as international law is observed, it provides us with stability and order and with a means of predicting the behavior of those with whom we have reciprocal legal obligations."

–J. William Fulbright

SECTION 11.1
INTRODUCTION

The evolution of modern international law has progressed along two distinct, but sometimes overlapping, tracks. On the one hand, there are the political and organizational affairs of nation states. The second track involves the commercial activities of countries and private business entities. Many law texts distinguish these categories as being covered by either public international law or private international law.

Public international law deals with those relationships between and among nations, as evidenced through treaties, conventions, and adherence to the rules and policies of international organizations. For instance, a **treaty** is an agreement between two or more countries, and it may be further classified as bilateral or involving two states, or multilateral, meaning that more than two countries are parties to the arrangement. Since treaties are established by the particular nations involved, they only apply to those countries which are parties to the agreement. In the United States, the word treaty may only be properly applied when the agreement has been ratified by the Senate. On the other hand, a **convention** is an agreement negotiated usually by members of international organizations, which resulting document is then open to adoption by member states and other nations. Another form of international arrangement is the **protocol,** an agreement on a matter considered to be of less significant impact than the subject of a convention. There are literally thousands of such treaties, conventions, and protocols in effect and they serve to create a substantial body of international law applicable to those nations that have made them part of their system of jurisprudence. Membership in international organizations may also create legal obligations and responsibilities by virtue of the charters of such organizations. Human rights and equal rights for men and women are, for example, guaranteed by the UN Charter.

Private international law is generally used to refer to the laws applicable to private parties in their business affairs when those entities are citizens of different nations. Issues of jurisdiction (a court which has the power to exercise control over a dispute), conflicts of laws (which nation's laws will apply to a dispute), and enforcement (whether judgments and arbitration awards will be enforceable in jurisdictions other than where the judgments are rendered) will always, absent agreement of the parties, be implicated in these disputes. As a consequence of the potential for irreconcilable differences between the involved legal systems, trading nations sought the creation and acceptance of trade practices.

The international norms that were created by commercial entities became known as **lex mercatoria** or law merchant. These norms were applied and enforced by the merchants themselves to their transactions. The lex mercatoria eventually became a part of the English common law and was applied to international commercial transactions until partially replaced in the nineteenth century by various multilateral treaties. Nations in addition to England also incorporated elements of lex mercatoria into their domestic laws such that there continued to be a more or less common approach to international commercial affairs.

One of the earliest U.S. cases invoking recognition of international law arose out of the events of the Spanish-American War. The case, known as **The Paquete Habana,** involved the seizure of two Spanish fishing vessels by an American naval ship off the coast of Cuba. The Paquete Habana and The Lola, with civilian crews of three and six fishermen respectively, were seized while returning to Cuba, which was a Spanish territory at the time. The fishing vessels were unarmed and not participants in any of the on-going hostilities between the U.S. and Spain. The owners of the fishing vessels brought claims against the U.S. Government for the value of their seized vessels and cargoes. The U.S. Supreme Court in 1900 issued its ruling in favor of the ship owners and stated:

> By an ancient usage among civilized nations, beginning centuries ago, and gradually ripening into a rule of international law, coast fishing vessels, pursuing their vocation of catching and bringing in fresh fish, have been recognized as exempt, with their cargoes and crews, from capture as prize of war...

> The doctrine which exempts coast fishermen with their vessels and cargoes from capture as prize of war has been familiar to the United States from the time of the War of Independence.

> Since the English orders of council of 1806 and 1810... in favor of fishing vessels employed in catching and bringing to market fresh fish, no instance has been found in which the exemption from capture of private coast fishing vessels, honestly pursuing their peaceful industry, has been denied by England, or by any other nation...

> International law is part of our law, and must be ascertained and administered by the courts of justice of appropriate jurisdiction, as often as questions of right depending upon it are duly presented for

their determination. For this purpose, where there is no treaty, and no controlling executive or legislative act or judicial decision, resort must be had to the customs and usages of civilized nations; and, as evidence of these, to the works of jurists and commentators...

Upon the facts proved in either case... [those of both The Paquete Habana and of The Lola]...it is the duty of this court, sitting as the highest prize court of the United States, and administering the law of nations, to declare and adjudge that the capture was unlawful, and without probable cause; and it is therefore, in each case, Ordered, that the proceeds of any sale of her cargo, be restored to the claimant, with damages and costs.

The codification of the lex mercatoria has been supplemented by a more active participation of governments in recognition of international legal norms of not only commercial enterprises but also nation states. Numerous laws have been enacted by Congress and many treaties and multilateral conventions have been signed by the United States that incorporate general international legal principles into U.S. law. A full listing of such laws is not feasible, but several do deserve mention as they have had broad application to U.S. businesses and commerce.

For example, in 1892, Congress passed the Harter Act, which set forth the liability of ocean carriers for cargo losses (replaced by the Carriage of Goods by Sea Act, when the shipment is between a U.S. port and a foreign port, leaving the **Harter Act** in place as to shipments between two U.S. ports). The United States became a signatory nation to the **Warsaw Convention** that dealt with the liability of airlines in international travel and capped their exposure at a set dollar amount for injuries to passengers and luggage. This protection was needed in the 1920's to allow the fledgling airline industry to expand around the world. In 1999, the Warsaw Convention was amended by the **Montreal Convention** which expanded the liability of airlines to about $150,000 a person without the need to show fault and by giving more protection to air travelers for such things as lost baggage. The **Foreign Sovereign Immunities Act** codified the immunity of foreign governments in U.S. courts. The language of this Act, however, specifies that foreign governments are not immune when conducting commercial activities. In 1982, Congress passed the **Foreign Trade Antitrust Improvements Act.** This law made it illegal when anti-competitive conduct outside of the U.S. has a direct, substantial, and reasonably foreseeable impact on commerce within the U.S., or on the business of U.S. exporters outside the U.S. This country also enacted the **Foreign Corrupt Practices Act (FCPA),** which makes it illegal for U.S. companies and their agents to bribe foreign officials. The FCPA, as well as many other enactments, represent examples of the extraterritorial effect of certain U.S. laws, that is, those laws that apply to U.S. citizens and sometimes non-citizens outside of the U.S., even when the prohibited conduct is not illegal in the country where performed.

The passage of the Foreign Corrupt Practices Act was the result of a series of publicized efforts on the part of U.S. business interests to secure favored contracts in countries where bribery of public officials was done, even if the process was not legal. The FCPA was intended to reach such conduct through prosecution in the federal courts. No matter where the conduct of the U.S. party takes place, the person violating the Act is subject to the reach of the FCPA. Exactly what conduct is covered by the FCPA is addressed in **USA v. David Kay and Douglas Murphy.** The opinion of the federal district judge in dismissing charges of FCPA violations is also instructive on the importance of legislative history in the interpretation of statutes that are not ideally clear.

UNITED STATES OF AMERICA V. DAVID KAY AND DOUGLAS MURPHY
200 F. SUPP.2D 681 (S.D. TEX., 2002)

Defendants Douglas Murphy and David Kay are charged with violations of the Foreign Corrupt Practices Act of 1977 ("FCPA"). The indictment alleges that the Defendants, as president and vice president of American Rice, Inc. ("ARI"), made improper payments to officials in Haiti to reduce customs duties and sales taxes owed by ARI to the Haitian government.

The FCPA prohibits payments to a foreign official to "obtain or retain business"… The question before the Court, therefore, is whether payments to foreign government officials made for the purpose of reducing customs duties and taxes fall under the scope of "obtaining or retaining business" pursuant to the text of the FCPA. Defendants contend that the FCPA does not prohibit such payments. Rather, the FCPA only prohibits payments made to "obtain or retain business," which, according to Defendants, limits the scope of the FCPA to payments to secure new business or to renew existing business. Here, Defendants argue that they did not make the alleged payments to Haitian officials to obtain new business or to renew existing business, as ARI had already established its business in Haiti and made the payments to reduce customs duties and taxes on incoming goods. The Government responds that the FCPA applies, without any textual limit, to all bribes made for the purpose

of obtaining or retaining business. The Government further argues that Defendants' payments to reduce customs duties and sales taxes were essential to ARI to be able to conduct business in Haiti and, thus, the payments constituted prohibited payments made to retain business.

In applying criminal laws, federal courts must follow the plain and unambiguous language of the statute. Reviewing the "obtain or retain business" language, the Court determines that the FCPA is ambiguous under these circumstances. Therefore, the Court turns to an analysis of the legislative history of the FCPA. Congress enacted the FCPA to stop bribery of foreign officials by domestic corporations.

In the course of enacting the FCPA, Congress rejected two bills that would have broadened the scope of the FCPA's prohibited activities… Congress rejected these proposals in favor of the phrase "obtain or retain business" as found in the current version of the FCPA.

In response to business concerns that the FCPA placed American businesses at a competitive disadvantage in the foreign marketplace, Congress amended the FCPA. These amendments included exceptions for… "routine governmental action"… The House also sought to amend the FCPA to prohibit payments for "procurement of legislative, judicial, regulatory, or other actions in seeking more favorable treatment by a foreign government." Congress rejected this proposed amendment in favor of the original statutory language.

In response to the Organization for Economic Cooperation and Development Convention on Combating

Bribery of Foreign Officials in International Business Transactions ("the OECD Convention"), Congress again amended the FCPA… [but] …again declined to amend the "obtain or retain business" language in the FCPA.

Given the foregoing, counts one through twelve of the indictment are hereby dismissed.

SECTION 11.2 INTERNATIONAL ORGANIZATIONS AS SOURCES OF LAW

International organizations, in addition to domestic governments, non-governmental trade organizations and business entities, play a role in formulating international legal principles and rules that govern the community of nations. These organizations, whose charters typically encompass the development of friendly relations among states and the promotion of basic human rights, also facilitate the implementation of the international legal norms which they create. Membership in these organizations ordinarily means adherence to their charter principles.

A. United Nations

The United Nations is the most extensive international organization, both in its geographic and member nation coverage and in the number of multilateral agreements it has produced. Created in 1945 to replace the largely ineffective League of Nations, the goals of this body are to prevent war, to safeguard fundamental human rights, to maintain the obligations arising from treaties and other sources of international law, and to promote social progress and better standards of life.

The United Nations consists of six principal divisions: the General Assembly, the Security Council, the Economic and Social Council, the Trusteeship Council, the International Court of Justice and the Secretariat.

Each country that belongs to the United Nations is represented in the **General Assembly** which has been referred to as a "parliament of nations" since it meets regularly to discuss world issues. Article 10 of the UN Charter provides the General Assembly with the authority to adopt resolutions, which are recommendations on matters within the scope of the Charter. The UN General Assembly is also primarily responsible for analyzing legal matters of interest to the group and in formulating international conventions. These legal activities are delegated to the International Law Commission and the Sixth (Legal) Committee of the General Assembly. Subjects covered by these law committees have included matters such as trade relations, the exploitation of the seas, and genocide. The committees typically draft proposed conventions that are then submitted to the General Assembly for consideration.

The real power in the United Nations rests with the **Security Council,** an organization of 15 countries, whose purpose is to maintain international security and peace. There are five permanent members of this important Council: the United States, Russia, China, France and England. The remaining members are selected by the General Assembly and serve two-year terms. This group has the power to impose economic sanctions, order an arms embargo, or even to dispatch troops to an area.

The **International Court of Justice (ICJ),** also known as the World Court, is the main judicial arm of the United Nations. This court is located in The Hague, Netherlands, and its role is to apply international law to legal disputes in an attempt to settle controversies. It also gives advisory opinions on legal questions referred to it by authorized United Nations and other specialized agencies. The court consists of fifteen judges who are selected by the Assembly and the Security Council.

The court functions as a place where member nations may seek binding rulings on such issues as boundary disputes, offshore maritime claims, and claims to the continental shelf resources. For example, ICJ cases handled in 2007 pertained to territorial and maritime disputes involving mainly Central and South American nations. Not all disputes will be heard by the ICJ, however, because the court's jurisdiction is dependent upon its acceptance by the parties involved.

Only countries which have accepted the jurisdiction of the World Court may be parties to contentious cases. In this regard, the Court is competent to hear a dispute only if the countries concerned have accepted its jurisdiction in one of the following ways:

- by entering into a special agreement to submit the dispute to the Court;

- by virtue of a jurisdictional clause, i.e., typically, when they are parties to a treaty containing a provision whereby, in the event of a dispute of a given type or disagreement over the interpretation or application of the treaty, one of them may refer the dispute to the Court; or

- through the reciprocal effect of declarations made by them whereby each has accepted the jurisdiction of the Court as compulsory in the event of a dispute with another State having made a similar declaration.

Despite the good intentions of this judicial body, very few cases are brought before the World Court. From its inception in 1945 until 2008, only 137 cases have been entered on the Court's General List.

The United States enjoys an uneasy relationship with the World Court and has actually withdrawn as a member of that organization. This country will only submit to the court's jurisdiction on a case-by-case basis. For instance, the United States, to the chagrin of many countries, has withdrawn from an agreement signed by President Clinton to establish an International Criminal Court because it is concerned that the court can be used as a mechanism to bring charges against the United States for war crimes. The court has also criticized the United States justice system for its handling of Mexican defendants who have been accused of committing crimes in which the death penalty can be imposed. The United States was rebuked for not allowing these foreigners to talk to their consular officials following arrest in violation of the Vienna Convention.

The UN has also established specialized tribunals for the purpose of handling such matters as war crimes and genocides that occurred in Bosnia-Herzegovina and in Rwanda. These tribunals, empowered by the Security Council of the UN, prosecute crimes by individuals whereas the ICJ limits its jurisdiction to nation parties.

B. European Union

The **European Union,** consisting of twenty-seven nations, had its genesis in the European Coal and Steel Community formed in 1952, which under the 1957 Treaty of Rome, transformed it into the European Economic Community. Subsequent treaties strengthened the Community through the creation of common institutions, including a Parliament and a Court of Justice. The Treaty on European Union (Maastricht Treaty) was concluded in 1993 thereby formalizing the European Union (EU). Membership in the EU has expanded rapidly from the original six members, consisting of Belgium, France, West Germany, Italy, Luxembourg, and the Netherlands, to its current number. Today, the European Union is a powerful political and economic force that has torn down the geographic barriers of many European countries. Its goal is to promote a common market in which people, money, goods and services can move unimpeded among member countries. This organization represents almost one-half billion people, which makes it the third largest population behind China and India. Its citizens no longer need passports to travel between countries and a single currency, the Euro, has been established.

The **European Court of Justice** is the supreme judicial authority of the EU and retains jurisdiction over EU legal matters that cover not just the relationships among the EU member states but also those non-EU business enterprises that operate within the EU. Once the ICJ has issued a ruling, the authority to implement and enforce the ruling is then within the control of the judicial branches of the individual member states.

C. North American Free Trade Zone

The **North American Free Trade Zone** is the product of the North American Free Trade Agreement (NAFTA) that went into effect in 1994. This agreement provides for the reduction, and eventual elimination, of almost all trade tariffs on goods moving among the three members, the United

States, Canada, and Mexico. NAFTA also provides for the elimination of trade barriers, increased competition through market access, protection of intellectual property rights, and other aspects of trade liberalization. According to the United States government, trade among NAFTA counties rose between 1993 and 2006 a staggering 198% or from $297 billion to $883 billion. Exports from the United States to NAFTA partners grew more rapidly than our exports to the rest of the world, and Canada and Mexico are our largest export partners accounting for 35% of all United States exports.

D. Association of Southeast Asian Nations

The **Association of Southeast Asian Nations** or ASEAN was created by Indonesia, Malaysia, Philippines, Singapore, and Thailand in 1967 to stimulate economic growth, cultural development and social progress in Southeast Asia and to promote regional peace and stability. The organization was subsequently joined by Brunei, Darussalam, Vietnam, Lao PDR, Myanmar, and Cambodia. ASEAN represents almost 500 million people, and has trade of about $850 billion. It, too, has created a free trade area in order to provide a competitive edge by operating as a single unit. This is done through the elimination of tariff and non-tariff barriers among its member countries. According to the European Union, ASEAN is its second largest trading partner accounting for 11.7% of ASEAN trade.

E. World Trade Organization

The **World Trade Organization (WTO),** whose membership is in excess of one hundred and fifty nations, is the successor to the General Agreement on Tariffs and Trade (GATT) organization. GATT, established in 1947, was designed to reduce trade barriers and covered the international sale of goods among its then twenty-three members. Membership grew steadily until 1994 when the original agreement was replaced by a significantly revised "GATT 1994." The new agreement established broad rules for trade in goods and services that are intended to provide sweeping reductions in artificial trade barriers imposed by individual nations. GATT 1994 also established the World Trade Association, consisting of all prior GATT members and it is opened to new members if accepted by a vote of two-thirds of the existing membership.

Dispute resolution rests with the General Council of the WTO. This process includes opportunities for an informal "consultation," and a more formal panel review. Parties may appeal a panel's decision to an "Appellate Body" appointed by the "Dispute Settlement Body," which also functions as a reviewing entity. If a trade violation is found and the violation is not cured by the offending nation, the party bringing the action will be given authorization to institute retaliatory trade measures.

In the United States, the decisions rendered by the WTO dispute resolution bodies are not binding on the courts. The decisions however are not without some weight. The following is an example of the weight afforded to a WTO ruling.

HYUNDAI ELECTRONICS CO., LTD. ET AL. v. UNITED STATES OF AMERICA
53 F. SUPP.2D 1334 (CT. INT'L. TRADE, 1999)

The U.S. Department of Commerce had issued an antidumping order (an increased tariff to compensate for the sale of the product in the U.S. at below fair market value) against Korean manufacturers of DRAM semiconductors. Federal Regulations allow the Commerce Department to lift the anti-dumping order if it is determined that the offending party has not sold the product at less than foreign market value for at least three consecutive years and that it is "not likely" that the offending party will make a below foreign market sale in the future (the only two of the regulations at issue). The court found that plaintiff LG Semicon had failed to meet the first test. As to plaintiff Hyundai, the Department of Commerce was not assured regarding the future of that party's conduct and refused to lift the anti-dumping order.

Hyundai argued that the satisfaction of the "not likely" standard is an unreasonable requirement given the circumstances of the chip marketplace, which is subject to periodic downturns during which dumping of chips is commonplace. Plaintiff LG Semicon argued that the "not likely" standard espoused by Commerce also violates the international law obligations of the U.S., as those obligations are expressed by the WTO. In a semiconductor dumping case filed with the WTO, a panel ruled that the "not likely" standard promulgated by Commerce violates WTO rules.

On this latter question of whether a WTO report constitutes precedent, Judge Goldberg of the U.S. Court of International Trade wrote:

> As an initial matter, the WTO report itself has no binding effect on the court. In **Footwear Distributors and Retailers of America v. United States, 852 F. Supp.1078 (1994)**, the court was confronted with a claim that an adopted GATT panel decision should govern the outcome of the case. Upon thorough review, the Footwear Distributors court reasoned that the response to a panel report is the prerogative of the executive branch, not the judiciary, because it implicates political decisions.

> The WTO panel report does not constitute binding precedential authority for the court. Of course, this is not to imply that a panel report serves no purpose in litigation before the court. To the contrary, a panel's reasoning, if sound, may be used to inform the court's decision.

SECTION **11.3**
SCOPE OF
INTERNATIONAL
TRANSACTIONS

One would be hard-pressed to find any nation that does not conduct some level of international political and commercial relations; even countries as isolated as North Korea and Myanmar (Burma) engage in international trade. Then, there are those nations that, as a result of the absence of natural resources and manufacturing capacity, have commerce restricted to the receipt of foreign assistance. Yet, even these nations participate in multinational agreements. Trade, whether conducted directly by governments, or by commercial businesses, has expanded exponentially in recent times. And, while international business was long the arena of large corporations and trading companies, advances in transportation and the internet have brought together participants from distant nations to conduct business activities that previously could never be accomplished.

The catch-word of the new millennium is **"globalization,"** and the pioneers of this process are global businesses supported by governments to deregulate and liberalize world markets and re-define the legal rules that govern commercial relationships. An emerging aspect of globalization is the changed perception of national boundaries and domestic laws. Global competition has led to mergers and acquisitions on an international scale. Technology transfers have expanded the reach of businesses beyond domestic markets and in a manner that could hardly have been envisioned twenty years ago. Countries have re-defined their roles as members of regional or common markets.

For instance, the European Common Market has been transformed into the European Union with an integration of currency, banking and other legal aspects. The United States and Canada formalized a free trade zone which has been expanded to include Mexico and now has more than five hundred million regional customers as part of the North American Free Trade area. India and the People's Republic of China have liberalized their laws regarding foreign investment and have added two trillion more individuals to the global marketplace. This process has engaged an ever-increasing movement of goods, services, and information across national boundaries. Some nations have, to an extent, kept pace with these economic developments by establishing elements of a world legal order and incorporating these elements into their domestic legal systems. Other nations have, however, been slow to adhere to international legal principles, thus requiring international businesses to remain vigilant regarding where and how they should conduct their businesses. Many global business activities remain subject to multiple risks. While the international legal environment has become the focus of multinational conventions and agreements intended to manage some aspects of this risk, the global business community itself has developed mechanisms intended to encourage commerce and at the same time reduce, if not eliminate, the risks entailed in moving the goods, services, and information across boundaries.

**SECTION 11.4
RISKS OF
INTERNATIONAL
COMMERCE**

A. Political Risks

Governments may require foreign enterprises to follow procedures or they may impose trade quotas or restrictions on the quantity of goods that can be imported, enact embargoes, or otherwise restrict trade with certain nations or in certain goods or services in their entirety. For example, the **Trading with the Enemy Act,** passed by Congress to restrict trade with nations at war with the United States, was repealed in 1977, but replaced with a prohibition against trading with Cuba and North Korea. Also, Congress passed the **International Emergency Economic Powers Act (IEEPA)** that grants authority to the President to place restrictions on trade and international financial transactions during peacetime as well as wartime. For example, trade and travel to Libya had been banned until a 2007 loosening of those restrictions, and sales of computer equipment and other sensitive products to numerous countries have been prohibited. As a direct response to the terrorist attacks of September 11, 2001, Congress passed the **Patriot Act** which, while granting extensive authority to the U.S. Government to freeze foreign assets held in the U.S. pending IEEPA investigations, also requires U.S. financial institutions to maintain detailed records and to report transactions made by certain individuals and groups.

Expropriation or nationalization is the taking of property by a foreign government without adequate compensation. This is a serious risk that businesses and individuals face when investing in foreign lands. For example, Fidel Castro and his government confiscated the property of a number of U.S. business enterprises in Cuba following the 1959 Revolution which, in fact, is partially responsible for the longstanding animosity between the two countries.

Unlike the Due Process Clauses of the Fifth and Fourteenth Amendments to the United States Constitution, which prohibit governmental takings of property without payment of fair compensation, seizures of property by local governments may be considered a legitimate exercise of sovereignty. Whether or not compensation is paid to the former property owners will generally be determined by whether the seizing power adheres to a traditional theory of legitimizing seizures upon payment of compensation, or whether the seizure is made in defiance of the international norm that takings are linked to some degree of compensation. In the latter instance, the question arises as to what, if any, recourse may be had in response to seizures without compensation. For instance, there have been a series of decisions involving nationalization of business interests by Iran that illustrate the distinction made between the two theories. The more prevalent view is that sovereign nations have an absolute right to take private holdings within the country but must pay reasonable compensation for that taking. The less prevalent view is that full compensation is not required. While most of the arbitration panels of the Iran-United States Claims Tribunal have followed the more prevalent view, other panels have provided for lesser amounts of compensation.

B. Economic/Currency Risks

Commercial transactions involve the movement of capital from one country to another. This often requires the transfers of funds, whether physically or electronically, between financial institutions. These types of transfers experience a variety of problems. Exchange rates may fluctuate, and restrictions may be imposed by governments upon the movement of funds from one country to another. Also, some currencies do not have convertible value in the international marketplace and are unacceptable as a medium for exchange. Regardless of currency risks, the income tax implications of foreign operations are always a part of the profit calculus.

Of particular interest to the Internal Revenue Service are pricing issues related to the movement of goods, services, and capital across international borders. Moreover, the examination of transfer pricing arrangements has also been given greater attention by many non-U.S. tax jurisdictions. Transfer pricing arrangements entail income allocation between entities in different tax jurisdictions. This could result in an unjustified allocation by a multinational company of greater levels of income to a low tax jurisdiction. Each country in which profits are earned will be interested in taxing the full value of those profits and, when the full value of profits that should have been created domestically has instead been understated, the taxpayer company should be prepared to explain and defend how and why its pricing and profit methodology has been applied.

C. Transaction Risks

The sale of goods moving across national boundaries is subject to the risks of non-payment to a seller and non-delivery to a buyer. Parties may not wish to do business on cash or open account terms because of the risks of non-payment and non-delivery. Goods moving long distances may be subject to harsh transportation conditions and to loss or theft of goods. Most trade in goods still involves ocean transport, and the risks inherent in such transport have, in most nations, been subject to the limitations of carrier liability set forth in the laws governing ocean transportation. The **Carriage of Goods by Sea Act,** for example, provides significant protection to ocean carriers against claims made by the owners of cargoes arising from loss or damage to their goods. The carrier, absent failure to ship goods on seaworthy vessels or absent mis-delivery or non-delivery of goods, will ordinarily be held harmless for claims made by shippers and consignees. This very effective degree of carrier protection makes it imperative for those parties that would otherwise bear the risk of loss to secure pertinent marine insurance.

D. Legal Risks

Those business entities engaging in foreign commerce will encounter a variety of legal systems in the global marketplace. Whether these legal systems are based upon the English common law, French civil law, religious codes, or some combination of these, one can be assured that inherent differences, however subtle, will provide numerous opportunities for legal disputes.

In the United States alone there is a separate body of law for each of the 50 states and territories. In addition, there is a separate body of federal law, some of which is enforceable only within the United States, but other portions of which have been given extraterritorial effect; that is, some federal laws apply to U.S. citizens and business entities outside of the U.S.

Substantive differences in domestic and foreign law, in areas as presumably straight forward as contract law and as complex as antitrust law, require careful attention when engaging in trans-national business activities. One example of how businesses may find themselves in uncharted legal territory is created by the principle of **pre-contractual liability**. This principle is rarely studied in American schools because it is not generally recognized as part of our system of jurisprudence. Pre-contractual liability encompasses a duty to negotiate in good faith and a duty to proceed with negotiations in accordance with prior representations and promises. Since most nations other than the U.S. have some form of pre-contractual obligations and liability as part of their legal systems, legal consequences may arise even in the absence of a final written contract.

Another example of potential contractual risk involves the question of whether a contract may be enforceable even if not reduced to writing. The study of contract law will include a discussion of the statute of frauds, a doctrine that has been incorporated in the laws of every state. Application of this doctrine requires that some contracts, including those for sales of goods worth more than $500.00 will be unenforceable if not in writing. Yet, the contract laws of many nations, as well as the **Convention on the International Sale of Goods (CISG),** provide that there will be many international contracts that are clearly enforceable, even if not reduced to writing, because the statute of frauds is not widely followed outside the U.S. For example, Article 11 of the CISG states: "A contract of sale... need not be concluded in or evidenced by writing and is not subject to any other requirement as to form. It may be proved by any means, including witnesses."

**SECTION 11.5
PROTECTING
AGAINST THE RISKS
OF INTERNATIONAL
TRANSACTIONS**

Recognition of the risks connected to international business transactions is only the first step in the process of risk avoidance, if not risk prevention. While opportunities to do business exist around the world, the risks attendant to doing business in different locations will differ significantly from country to country. What may work in one country might not always work in another jurisdiction, and what might work with respect to one business opportunity might not be subject to duplication elsewhere.

It is, therefore, important for the business entrepreneur to select how to do business from the several available models: sales/direct exporting, agency sales/indirect exporting, licensing, joint ventures/subsidiary, direct investment/ subsidiary, and direct investment/branch facility.

Regardless of the choice of business model, all such international transactions will be subject to contract law principles. Consequently, an understanding of international contract law is critically important.

**SECTION 11.6
PRINCIPLES OF FOREIGN
CONTRACT LAW**

Consider the following facts: a Pennsylvania company negotiates a contract to sell machine parts to a firm in Helsinki, Finland. The Pennsylvania firm manufactures the parts at its Chicago factory, and ships the items from Chicago to Germany where the parts are assembled into printing presses. The presses are then sold by the Finnish company to a publishing house in Australia, where the presses are found to be defective because the parts manufactured in Chicago were not made to specifications. The Australian publishing company makes claim against the Finnish company and the Finnish company claims against the Pennsylvania company. Which country's laws will apply to these transactions? What happens if more than one body of law could apply? What happens when the laws differ from one country to another? One of the legal risks inherent in such a geographically complex transaction is known as **conflicts of law** or whose laws should apply to a transaction, and the applicable rules used to address these conflicts are themselves complex and sometimes irreconcilable.

In the U.S., these contracts prior to 1988 were subject to Article Two of the Uniform Commercial Code. In Finland, Germany, and Australia, there would also be differing versions of commercial law. In order to impose uniformity and a level of certainty involving international disputes involving the sale of goods, some fifty-five nations, including the United States, conducting a significant percentage of international trade, have signed the **United Nations Convention on Contracts for the International Sale of Goods**, thereby replacing their own contract laws with the provisions of the CISG when the transactions are between companies located in nations that have signed the convention. As noted by the United Nations, the Convention creates a set of rules governing the formation of contracts between merchants for the international sale of goods, the obligations of the buyer and seller, remedies for breach of contract and other aspects of the contract. These rules, however, do not apply to consumer transactions. This Convention also allows the parties to avoid the uncertainty of whose conflicts of law principles should apply to a transaction. The foregoing hypothetical contracts (Pennsylvania firm and Finnish company in the first one, and Finnish company and Australian business in the second) would only involve application of the CISG if the particular parties to the contracts have places of business in those countries that have signed the CISG, or if the contracts themselves specified that the CISG would apply.

Not to be outdone by the Uniform Commercial Code which has been adopted in the various states in the United States, the European Union in 1997 created its own union-wide body of contract law principles embodied in the European Contract Law. Contracting parties located in EU member countries may choose to have their contracts governed by the **European Contract Law** as a replacement of their domestic contract laws and even in place of the CISG.

UNIDROIT stands for the Governing Council of the International Institute for the Unification of Private Law and this group is responsible for the creation of the **Principles of International Commercial Contracts.** While these principles do not carry the weight of law, they may be referenced by foreign courts and arbitration panels to interpret ambiguous contract provisions when contract rules do not provide adequate guidance.

In order to resolve the uncertainty of which body of law will apply in international transactions, the parties may include dispute resolution provisions in their agreements. Such provisions would include choices of the country in which the matter will be heard and how legal disputes would be decided, what body of law would be applied to those disputes, and how court judgments or arbitration awards would be enforced.

While the full faith and credit clause of the United States Constitution provides that the judgments rendered in any of the states in this country must be honored in every other state, this constitutional requirement is not extended to the decisions of the courts of other nations, nor would U.S. judgments necessarily be enforced outside of this country. **Comity** is the concept that represents the international equivalent of full faith and credit. This international principle allows a country to recognize the laws and judgments of another jurisdiction as a matter of courtesy but not as a right. Generally, as long as the laws of another country are not contrary to public policy or prejudicial to the interests of the forum jurisdictions, the laws will be upheld.

There is no guarantee, however, when conducting international business transactions and in seeking to enforce U.S. court judgments in other lands, that those judgments will be enforced. Any expectation that the results of court proceedings in one nation will be honored in another must be based upon existing treaties or the incorporation of the comity principle in national law by either statutory enactment or judicial construction. For example, in 1895, the

Supreme Court in **Hilton v. Guyot, 16 S. Ct. 139,** was faced with deciding whether a judgment secured in France by a French citizen in an action against a U.S. defendant would be enforceable in a U.S. court without the case being retried. The Supreme Court stated:

> No law has any effect, of its own force, beyond the limits of the sovereignty from which its authority is derived. The extent to which the law of one nation, as put in force within its territory, whether by executive order, by legislative act, or by judicial decree, shall be allowed to operate within the dominion of another nation, depends upon what our greatest jurists have been content to call "the comity of nations." Although the phrase has been often criticized, no satisfactory substitute has been suggested.

> Comity, in the legal sense, is neither a matter of absolute obligation, on the one hand, nor of mere courtesy and good will, upon the other. But it is the recognition which one nation allows within its territory to the legislative, executive or judicial acts of another nation, having due regard both to international duty and convenience, and to the rights of its own citizens or of other persons who are under the protection of its laws.

The consideration of the rights of its own citizens was the focus of a much more recent decision reached by a federal district court in California. Unlike the Hilton case which involved a purely commercial matter without U.S. constitutional implications, the **Yahoo! Inc. v. La Ligue Contre le Racisme et l'Antisemitisme** litigation questioned the enforceability of a foreign judgment when that judgment results in an alleged impermissible restriction on the First Amendment freedom of speech. In 2000, a French court held Yahoo! Inc. criminally liable for the offering of Nazi memorabilia on Yahoo's auction site in France. Sales of Third Reich materials were violations of the French Criminal Code. The French trial court, after ruling that it had jurisdiction over Yahoo because the auction website could be accessed by French citizens, issued orders imposing financial penalties. More significantly, however, the court also ordered Yahoo to restrict access to the site and to warn French users to leave the site whenever it contains prohibited items for sale.

Yahoo! filed a declaratory judgment action in a federal district court in California seeking to challenge the legality and enforceability of the French judgment. The district court ruled that it had personal jurisdiction over the French citizens and that the French interim orders would be an impermissible restriction on Yahoo's First Amendment rights. On appeal, the Ninth Circuit Court of Appeals, while upholding the jurisdictional rulings, held that the Yahoo's declaratory judgment action was not ripe because there had been no effort made by the French parties to enforce the French orders. And, on the question of Yahoo's First Amendment rights, the Ninth Circuit was clear that such a right could not be enforced in France as to French citizens but was to be limited to the U.S. The decision of the federal district court and the French tribunal demonstrate the unpredictability of comity.

There is one other convention worthy of mention. In 1970, the United States ratified the **New York Convention on Recognition and Enforcement of International Arbitral Awards,** thus embracing a policy encouraging the arbitration of international disputes. Currently, more than 130 nations have adopted this Convention which requires all signatory nations to recognize arbitration agreements made by contracting parties and to enforce the results of these proceedings unless procured by fraud, misconduct, or clear error, or are decisions that exceed the panel's authority.

SECTION 11.7 DOCUMENTARY TRANSACTIONS

Another method utilized to protect a seller's expectation of payment and a buyer's expectations of delivery is the **documentary sale**. This process involves the operations of a transit carrier and the separate contractual promise of payment made by a bank. Upon receipt of goods by a carrier, e.g., air transport or ocean transport, the carrier generates an irrevocable **bill of lading** that operates as a receipt for the goods, title to the goods, and a contract for transporting the goods. Whichever party possesses the bill of lading owns and controls the goods. The buyer will, as a stated requirement in the underlying sales agreement, already have secured a letter of credit issued by its bank. The letter of credit contains a promise by the bank to make payment to the seller upon receipt by the bank of the bill of lading. When the bill of lading is forwarded to the buyer's bank, title to the goods has been transferred to the bank. The bank will then issue a payment to the seller in accordance with the terms of the underlying transaction.

The process of moving goods from one country to another will sometimes result in loss or damage to the goods being shipped. Fungible goods may deteriorate if arrival at the destination is delayed. Heavy seas may cause damage to goods in the holds of cargo vessels. Operators of loading equipment or ocean and air transports may, by their negligence, cause cargo losses. When goods are handed over to a domestic transport carrier, issues of liability are ordinarily subject to the law of bailment. A **bailment** is the physical transfer of goods by the owner (bailor) into the hands of another party (bailee), for safekeeping or for some other purpose consistent with the terms of the bailment. Typically, the carrier in possession of the goods is responsible for the return of the goods to the bailor or delivery of those goods without damage to the designated recipient.

The customary domestic bailment rules do not, however, apply in trans-national shipments. In order to make international commerce financially feasible, it was necessary, in the past, to provide some manner of protection to the carriers against claims made by the owners of their cargos. Without some measure of protection, the carriers could simply not have afforded to operate without charging substantially higher fees, thus making commerce that much more difficult. And, as these transactions always involved transportation between the ports of different countries, these trading nations recognized the need to create uniformity in the rules applied to their commerce. What emerged were the **Hague Rules,** which have now been codified in many nations, and in the United States as the Carriage of Goods by Sea Act. While this law imposes upon the ocean carrier a duty to exercise due diligence in shipping goods on a seaworthy vessel and in delivering the goods to the named consignee, the law also limits the liability of ocean carriers when loss or damage occurs based both upon the cause of the loss and in the amount of loss. While such limitations result in reduced shipping costs, they also make it incumbent upon sellers and buyers to purchase the pertinent type and amount of marine insurance to protect against in-transit losses.

When the parties to a sales contract negotiate the terms, the resulting agreement will place the risk of loss on either the buyer ("shipment" contract) or seller ("destination" contract) while the goods are in transit. If the carrier is deemed not liable for the loss, the parties will be responsible for the loss based upon their contractual allocation of risk.

SECTION 11.8 INCO TERMS

As a further element of contract uniformity and in the interest of eliminating variations in contract interpretation, the **International Chamber of Commerce** has published the International Rules for the Interpretation of Trade Terms, a set of trade term definitions that have been generally accepted in the global business marketplace. When contract parties incorporate the **Incoterms,** or international commercial terms, as part of their agreements, they add a measure of uniformity to those agreements and the expectation that courts will adhere to these usual and customary trade term definitions.

The following is an example of how the Incoterms have been accorded general acceptance. Shared Imaging, a U.S. company, purchased MRI equipment from Neuromed, a German company. The sales contract specified that the sale was "CIF" but there was no explanation in the contract regarding the meaning of the CIF term. The MRI machine was damaged while in transit, and Shared Imaging received an insurance payment from St. Paul Guardian Insurance Company. St. Paul then filed a subrogation action against Neuromed in federal district court.

ST. PAUL GUARDIAN INS. CO. V. NEUROMED MEDICAL SYSTEMS & SUPPORT, GMBH
2002 U.S. DIST. LEXIS (S.D. N.Y., 2002)

The parties concede that pursuant to German law, the U.N. Convention on Contracts for the International Sale of Goods ("CISG") governs this transaction because (1) both the U.S. and Germany are Contracting States to that Convention, and (2) neither party chose, by express provision in the contract, to opt out of the application of the CISG...

"CIF," which stands for "cost, insurance and freight," is a commercial trade term that is defined in *Incoterms 1990,* published by the International Chamber of Commerce, ("ICC"). The aim of INCOTERMS, which stands for international commercial terms, is "to provide a set of international rules for the interpretation of the most commonly used trade terms in foreign trade..." INCOTERMS are incorporated into the CISG through Article 9(2) which provides that, "The parties are considered, unless otherwise agreed, to have impliedly made applicable to their contract or its formation a usage of which the parties knew or ought to have known and which in international trade is widely known to, and regularly observed by, parties to contracts of the type involved in the particular trade concerned." INCOTERMS defines "CIF" (named port of destination) to mean the seller delivers when the goods pass "the ship's rail at the port of shipment." The seller is responsible for paying the cost, freight and insurance coverage necessary to bring the goods to the named port of destination, but the risk of loss or damage to the goods passes from seller to buyer upon delivery to the port of shipment... Thus, because (1) Neuromed's risk of loss of, or damage to, the MRI machine under the contract passed to plaintiff upon delivery of the machine to the carrier at the port of shipment and (2) it is undisputed that the MRI machine was delivered to the carrier undamaged and in good working order, Neuromed's motion to dismiss for failure to state a claim is hereby granted.

SECTION 11.9 INTELLECTUAL PROPERTY IN THE GLOBAL ENVIRONMENT

Physical goods are by no means the only products that form the substance of international contracts. Intellectual property has become an increasingly larger and more problematic component of global commerce. Patent rights, trademarks, copyrighted material, and trade secrets, the sum total of intellectual property, have become the substance of legitimate international licensing agreements and, sometimes, the stuff of illegal pirating and gray market transactions.

Recognition of intellectual property rights (IPRs) in the global marketplace is by no means a recent phenomenon. The **Paris Convention for the Protection of Industrial Property,** providing basic rights of protection of patents and trademarks, dates back to 1883, and has been adopted by the United States and some 170 other nations. The rights granted by the Paris Convention are in addition to those granted by signatory nations' domestic patent and trademark laws, and signatory nations must give the same protections to foreign parties as they give to their domestic patent and trademark applicants. In 1978, the

Patent Cooperation Treaty went into effect and it created uniform procedures that allow patent applications to be filed initially as an international application, then to be followed by individual country applications.

The **Berne Convention for the Protection of Literary and Artistic Works** originated in 1886. It has been amended many times, but always aims at protecting rights of authorship. Works first published in the United States are given protection virtually world-wide through this international convention. A second international agreement, the **Universal Copyright Convention,** to which the United States is a signatory, provides recognized protection for not only literary and scientific writings but also sculpture, visual arts, music, and cinematographic works.

The business model that has been developed to govern the legitimate transfer of IPRs is the license agreement. The owner of the IPR (the licensor) grants to a licensee the right to use the licensor's patent, trademark, copyright or other know-how in return ordinarily for a fee or royalty. The cost of operation in the geographic area subject to the license is borne by the licensee. Licensing arrangements permit the owner of the IPR to do business in multiple locations without incurring any additional production/distribution costs.

Inherent in the transfer of IPRs are risks associated with violations by the licensee of the standard confidentiality obligations and non-competition agreements. Additional problems may be caused to IPR owners should the governments where the licensees operate not enforce the legal and contractual rights of the licensors.

**SECTION 11.10
TRIPS**

Lax enforcement of IPRs in many countries led to the **Agreement on Trade-Related Aspects of Intellectual Property Rights (TRIPS),** which became effective on January 1, 2000. TRIPS require all signatory nations, including all members of the World Trade Organization, to enforce the Paris and Berne Conventions and to create minimum standards for protection of IPRs.

IPR protection and enforcement had already existed in the industrialized nations, so TRIPS was aimed essentially at attempting to secure protective IPR action in the developing nations and the newer industrializing economies. While TRIPS provides a mechanism for signatory countries to avoid compliance where, for example, health issues are concerned, the goal of securing protection of IPRs has had at least some support where in the past there was minimal enforcement.

SECTION 11.11
THE FUTURE OF
INTERNATIONAL LAW

The end of the Cold War in the closing decades of the twentieth century may have generated a sense of security and personal well-being that is noticeably absent in the opening years of the twenty-first century. The ethnic and religious conflicts of the 1990's have multiplied in the first decade of the 2000's. Rwanda, Bosnia, and other less extensive conflicts, have been joined by the Congo, Afghanistan, Iraq, Darfur, Sri Lanka, and many others. And, after years of public debate over whether global warming is or is not real, there is finally a consensus that action must be taken to curtail fossil fuel emissions, as well as to preserve what continental forests remain uncut, and somehow end the degradation of the world's oceans through pollution and over-harvesting. Recognition that the plight of refugees, the spread of AIDS/HIV, depletion of the ozone layer, international terrorism, and air and water pollution are matters of international proportion and require international solutions, may also lead to appreciation of the need for global legal remedies.

SECTION 11.12
TYLER'S SPOILED WINE

PROBLEM ELEVEN

PARK, BROWN & SMITH
ATTORNEYS AT LAW
M E M O R A N D U M

To: All Law Clerks

From: Peter Smith, Esquire

Re: The Spoiled Shipment of Wine

Tyler's Sport's Bar and Grill ordered twenty cases of vintage wine from a winery in Southern France. The contract called for the wine to be shipped "CIF" aboard a vessel leaving Nice and arriving at the Port of Philadelphia on the Delaware River two weeks later. When Joe Roberts uncorked the first bottle soon after the shipment arrived, he discovered that all of the wine had spoiled. A sample bottle had been tested prior to shipment and no problem was detected. Roberts is now wondering what, if any, legal action he may take to recover the cost of the wine.

Please answer the following questions for Tyler's Sports Bar and Grill.

1. In what court and against what parties may Tyler's bring the action for the spoiled wine?

2. Based upon what laws will this matter proceed?

3. Who do you believe will win the lawsuit?

**ANSWER SHEET
PROBLEM ELEVEN**

Name: _____   **Please Print Clearly**

1. In what court and against what parties may Tyler's bring the action for the spoiled wine?

_____

_____

_____

_____

_____

_____

_____

_____

2. Based upon what laws will this matter proceed?

_____

_____

_____

_____

_____

_____

_____

_____

3.   Who do you think will win? Please explain.

SECTION 11.13
REVIEW CASES

1. In 1967 a Houston-based U.S. manufacturer of drilling equipment contracted with a German ocean towing company to have the German company tow a barge carrying drilling equipment from the Gulf Coast to Italy. A storm in the Gulf of Mexico caused damage to the drilling equipment when the German towboat captain failed to secure the equipment properly. The contract contained a forum selection clause (London Court of Justice), a choice of law clause (English law), and a hold harmless clause protecting the German company against negligence claims (enforceable in England but not in Florida). The U.S. company filed suit against the German company and the towboat in the federal district court in Tampa, Florida. Does the federal court have subject matter jurisdiction? Does the court have personal jurisdiction over the German company? Should the forum selection, choice of law, and hold harmless provisions of the contract be enforced? Why was the towboat made a party defendant? **M/S Bremen v. Zapata Off-Shore Company, 407 U.S. 1 (1972).**

2. A Canadian manufacturer of wood shingles entered into an oral agreement to sell eighty-eight truckloads of cedar shakes to a U.S. company. After accepting only thirteen truckloads, the U.S. company refused further deliveries of shakes. The Canadian company filed a lawsuit against the U.S. company, claiming the profit lost on the rejected seventy-five truckloads. The U.S. company raised the statute of frauds as a defense to the claims presented by the Canadian company. Which party should prevail on the statute of frauds issue? What international convention should apply in this case? **GPL Treatment, Ltd. v. Louisiana-Pacific Corp., 894 P. 2d 470 (Or. Ct. App. 1995), aff'd. 914 P. 2d 682 (Or., 1996).**

3. A Pennsylvania manufacturer of farm tractors has received a purchase order from a buyer in Japan. The standard wait period before all of the import approvals are secured by the Japanese buyer is longer than the Pennsylvania seller wishes to incur. The Japanese buyer offers to make the pertinent inquiries in Japan in order to reduce the wait time. This process will cost the seller $50,000 for the necessary political influence to move the approval and paperwork on an expedited basis through the proper trade ministry channels. The buyer has however agreed to share the cost. Will the proposed $25,000 share payment violate the Foreign Corrupt Practices Act?

4. A Hong Kong exporter (C-ART) has contracted to sell and ship goods to a New York Merchandising Company (NYMCO). C-ART hands the goods over to Hong Kong Islands Line (HKIL), an ocean carrier, for shipment to California. HKIL issues to C-ART a bill of lading stating that the goods are to be delivered only to the party holding the original bill of lading. The original bill of lading was retained by C-ART pending payment by NYMCO. Upon arrival in California, HKIL delivered the goods to a

NYMCO agent upon the agent's presentation of a corporate guaranty but not the original bill of lading. When C-ART could not recover the contract price from NYMCO due to NYMCO's bankruptcy, C-ART files suit against HKIL. Will C-ART be successful? **C-ART, Ltd. v. Hong Kong Islands Line America, S.A., 940 F.2d 530; 1991 U.S. App. LEXIS 17414.**

SECTION 11.14
INTERNET REFERENCES

For more information about international law, see the following internet sites:

A. International Court of Justice

- **www.icj-cij.org**
  The International Court of Justice provides decisions, recent cases, and general information at this site.

B. United Nations

- **www.un.org**
  This is the United Nations' official site and offers general information, materials on international law, humanitarian affairs, peace and security, human rights, economic and social development, as well as conferences and events, about the UN's work around the world.

C. Other International Organizations

- **www.usitc.gov**
  The International Trade Commission's web site is located at this address and provides news releases, tariffs, and trade resources.

- **www.wto.org**
  This is the World Trade Organization's official site which discusses intellectual property and environmental issues, trade policy, and dispute settlement.

- **www.ita.doc.gov**
  The International Trade Administration maintains this address and provides information about trade rights, tariffs, exports, and answers to frequently asked questions.

- **www.nato.int**
  The North Atlantic Treaty Organization's (NATO) official site is maintained at this location.

- **www.europa.eu.int/index-en.htm**
  This is the European Union's site, giving news, basic information about the European Union, its policies, and its institutions.

- **www.dfait-maeci.gc.ca/nafta-alena/menu-e.asp**
  To learn background information about NAFTA, the text of that agreement, as well as information on dispute settlement, trade agreements, and answers to frequently asked questions, visit this address.

D. **Foreign Corrupt Practices Act**

- **www.tannedfeet.com/Business/Importing_and_ Exporting/Foreign_Corrupt_Practices_Act/foreign_ corrupt_practices_act.html**
  This site offers an explanation of the Foreign Corrupt Practices Act.

- **www.abanet.org/cle/articles/turza.html**
  An article about the Foreign Corrupt Practices Act, is maintained at this address including information about the elements of a violation and an introduction to due diligence.

E. **Miscellaneous**

- **http://august1.com/pubs/dict/**
  This site provides an international law dictionary.

- **http://www.state.gov**
  The United States government maintains a site that discusses doing business abroad.

- **http://www.unidroit.org**
  UNIDROIT maintains a site that explains its functions and role in international transactions.

- **http://www.jus.uio.no/lm/eu.contract.principles.1998**
  Principles of European Contract Law may be accessed at this location.

- **http://www.lexmercatoria.com**
  This is the address for the Lex Mercatoria website.

- **http://cisgw3.law.pace.edu**
  More information about the Convention on Contracts for the International Sale of Goods is located at this reference.

- **http://www.unzco.com/basicguide**
  Information on documentary transactions may be accessed at this site.

KEY TERMS

Agreement on Trade-Related
   Aspects of Intellectual
   Property Rights
Association of Southeast
   Asian Nations
Berne Convention for the
   Protection of Literary
   and Artistic Works
Bill of Lading
Carriage of Goods by Sea Act
Charter
Comity
Conflicts of Law
Convention
Convention on the International
   Sale of Goods
Documentary Sale
Documentary Transactions
European Contract Law
European Court of Justice
European Union
Expropriation
Foreign Corrupt Practices Act
Foreign Sovereign
   Immunities Act
Foreign Trade Antitrust
   Improvements Act
General Assembly
Globalization
Hague Rules

Harter Act
International Chamber of
   Commerce
International Court of Justice
International Emergency
   Economic Act
Lex Mercatoria
Montreal Convention
New York Convention on
   Recognition and Enforcement of
   International Arbitral Awards
North American Free Trade Zone
Paris Convention for the
   Protection of Industrial Property
Patent Cooperation Treaty
Patriot Act
Pre-contractual Liability
Principles of International
   Commercial Contracts
Private International Law
Protocol
Public International Law
Security Council
Trading with the Enemy Act
Treaty
United Nations
Universal Copyright Convention
Warsaw Convention
World Trade Association
World Trade Organization

CHAPTER 12

THE JUDICIAL SYSTEM

SECTION 12.1
THE FEDERAL
COURT SYSTEM

"A Court is only as sound as its jury, and a jury is only as sound as the men who make it up."
—**Harper Lee**
To Kill a Mockingbird, 1960

Today's legal environment makes it a very real risk that a business will become involved in the litigation process during its existence. In fact, a number of states have established specialized courts to hear business cases such as the Commerce Court which has been created in Philadelphia. This chapter will present an overview of the court system in the United States so that the business entrepreneur or executive may gain a better understanding of the different types of courts, their rules and their specializations.

Article III of the Constitution provides that "the judicial power of the United States shall be vested in one Supreme Court, and in such other inferior courts as Congress may from time to time establish."

The court is the last branch of the government to be addressed by the Constitution and very little direction is provided by the framers in that historic document. Article III merely creates the **Supreme Court** of the United States and it glaringly fails to set forth the Court's powers, composition or jurisdiction. In what one may call a lack of respect, the framers also gave Congress the power to create the remaining courts thereby making the court system seem subservient to the legislature.

The First Congress of the United States accepted this grant of power when it enacted the Judiciary Act of 1787. Through the efforts of Senator Oliver Ellsworth of Connecticut, the legislature created thirteen judicial districts and three circuit courts throughout the country. Initially, the Supreme Court consisted of one chief justice and five other jurists who met twice a year in the Nation's Capital, the initial session commencing on the first Monday of February, and the other on the first Monday in August.

The Supreme Court has exclusive jurisdiction over all controversies of a civil nature in which a state is a party and exclusive jurisdiction over proceedings against ambassadors or other public ministers consistent with the law of nation. The Supreme Court also has appellate jurisdiction or the ability to hear cases on appeal from the federal circuit courts and courts of the states.

During its first few years, the Supreme Court heard very few cases and was viewed as the weakest branch of the government. This perception changed dramatically in 1801 when John Marshall became the Chief Justice and issued the landmark ruling in **Marbury v. Madison**. This case established the fundamental principle that the Supreme Court uniquely has the power to declare a law of Congress unconstitutional. It is also the final arbiter of the meaning of the Constitution. With these powers, the Supreme Court became an equal partner in the government, and it has enjoyed that status ever since.[1]

The **federal courts** are frequently described as the guardians of the United States Constitution because their decisions protect the rights and liberties guaranteed by this historic document. While Congress makes the laws that govern the nation as a whole, the federal courts interpret and apply those edicts to resolve disputes.[2]

Presently, the court of **original jurisdiction** or trial court in the federal system is the District Court, and appeals are entertained by the Circuit Court of Appeals. On rare occasion, the Supreme Court of the United States will review a lower court's decision if it presents a compelling national question that needs to be answered.

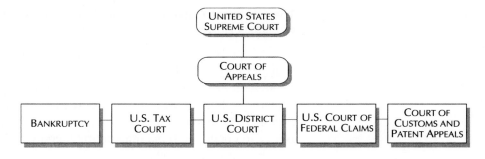

The **United States District Court**, or trial court, is in direct contact with the parties, hears the evidence, and applies the appropriate law to the facts of a case. There are ninety-four district courts in the United States and its territories. A state may have one or more district courts within its boundaries depending on its population. For example, the state of New York has four district courts within its boundaries, whereas Maine only has one.

The type of cases the federal court may hear are limited to questions involving federal law, the United States Constitution, and disputes between citizens of different states where the amount in controversy exceeds $75,000. Congress has also created several specialized courts that hear cases involving very narrow issues, such as tax matters and customs or patent appeals.

The **Court of Appeals** is the intermediate appellate court within the federal court system. There are thirteen circuit courts throughout the United States. Eleven of the circuit courts hear cases on appeal from the district courts. The twelfth circuit is devoted to hearing cases from the District of Columbia. Congress has also created one specialized court called the United States Court of Appeals for the Federal Circuit. This Federal Circuit hears appeals involving tort claims against the United States government, patent cases, and appeals from the United States Court of Federal Claims and the Court of International Trade. Parties may appeal to the Circuit Courts of Appeal as a matter of right.

Because the Supreme Court's decision to hear a case is discretionary, the Courts of Appeal are usually the last place that a party will appeal a federal case. When a Court of Appeals decides a case, that decision is binding over all of the district courts within that circuit.

The **Supreme Court of the United States** is the final arbiter of all legal disputes. It handles a very limited number of cases each year and those disputes may start in the federal or state courts, and they usually involve important issues about the Constitution or federal law.[3] As a result, it often decides very controversial issues that affect our daily lives. Supreme Court decisions establish precedent and bind all other courts. Commentators and constitutional scholars analyze each word of an opinion and predict how a particular holding will impact society.

The Court has undergone significant changes over the past forty years and established legal doctrines have changed drastically. For example, the death penalty was unconstitutional but is now considered appropriate punishment under certain circumstances.

What has caused this change in judicial philosophy? Shifting attitudes of the public certainly has an influence in court interpretation. The modification of the law, however, is more a reflection of the personalities of the members of the Supreme Court. There has been a dramatic turnover of Supreme Court justices during the past four decades, which has altered the judicial philosophy of the Court. Today, a conservative majority rules this country's highest court.

The court itself consists of a Chief Justice and eight Associate Justices who are appointed by the President of the United Sates subject to the confirmation of the Senate.

The composition of the Supreme Court at the start of the twenty-first century was divided into three groups. Justices Sandra Day O'Connor and Anthony Kennedy, President Reagan appointees, joined Justice Souter and Stephen Breyer to form a moderate voting block. Rehnquist, Thomas, and Antonin Scalia collectively practiced judicial restraint. John Paul Stevens, a Ford appointee, usually maintained the liberal or Activist position.

Justices Ruth Bader Ginsberg and Stephen Breyer were appointed by President Clinton and their votes helped shift the Court's voting record to a more middle-of-the road position. This "do not rock the boat" philosophy continued until the death of Chief Justice Rehnquist in 2005 and the retirement of Sandra

Day O'Connor in 2006. These vacancies provided President George W. Bush with the opportunity to appoint their replacements. John Roberts, Jr. was appointed and selected as the new Chief Justice and Samuel Alito, Jr. became the newest Associate Justice. Both individuals were judges on the Circuit Court of Appeals and were conservative in their judicial thinking. During their early tenures, these individuals have maintained their conservative judicial philosophies, and have joined Clarence Thomas, and Antonin Scalia to form a solid conservative voting block.

President Obama has had the opportunity of appointed two justices to the Supreme Court. Sonya Sotomayor, the first Hispanic justice, was appointed in 2009 to replace David Souter. One year later, or in August of 2010, the commander-in-chief replaced Justice John Paul Stevens with Elena Kagan, his Solicitor General. Therefore, the current composition of this important court is as follows:

- Chief Justice John Roberts
- Samuel Alito, Jr.
- Stephen Breyer
- Ruth Bader Ginsburg
- Clarence Thomas

- Anthony Kennedy
- Antonin Scalia
- Sonia Sotomayor
- Elena Kagan

At the current time, Justice Kennedy appears to wield the true power on the court. His vote tends to tip the scales in favor of the majority ruling, and the Huffington Post predicts that his influence will become even more important with the retirement of Justice Stevens.

It was predicted at the time of the nomination of John Roberts to the Supreme Court that he would be a boom to big business because he handled a number of matters for large corporations during his years in private practice. While it is too early to gauge how he will vote on key issues involving business interests, it is known that the court under his leadership has heard a large number of business related cases. For instance, in 2005, the court featured twenty business cases from a total of seventy-two matters in which it issued signed opinions. During the 2006 term, the Court granted certiorari in twenty-five business related cases out of the sixty seven appeals that it heard. Cases have ranged from issues involving Title VII of the Civil Rights Act to the Commerce Clause.[4]

It is not technically accurate to use the labels "liberal" and "conservative" when speaking about members of the Court. The proper terms for current judicial philosophies are activist v. judicial restraint oriented. An **activist** is one who views his or her role as bringing about social change. If there is something wrong with the system, a justice will take an active stance in imposing remedial measures to correct a problem. A justice that is **judicial restraint-oriented** tends to believe that his or her role is merely to make sure that a rule is constitutional. If there is something wrong with the system, it is up to the legislature to bring about the necessary change.

The operational aspects of the Supreme Court reveal that its term starts on the first Monday in October and ends when the list of scheduled cases is reached during the summer. Before World War II, the Supreme Court had 1,300 docketed cases. Today, about 10,000 cases are appealed each year and an additional 1,200 applications are filed that can be acted upon by a single Justice.[5] The Supreme Court is also a court of both original and appellate jurisdiction. Cases involving Ambassadors, Consuls, litigation between the federal government and a state as well as suits between states may be heard directly by the Supreme Court. There are no appeals of these decisions. Most cases, however, reach the Supreme Court on appeal of a lower court's decision. These appeals are originated by the filing of a **writ of certiorari** which is Latin for "we wish to be informed."[6]

History demonstrates that few appeals are actually heard by the court. In 2008, the Justices decided only 83 cases even though it takes a mere four of nine jurists to agree to hear the appeal. This has become known as the "Rule of Four." The Justices meet on Wednesdays and Fridays to review recent appeals and the junior most Justice acts as the "doorkeeper" when it is necessary to retrieve materials. Their deliberations are secret and what is said among the justices is not available for public consumption.[7]

Supreme Court Rule 10 governs these petitions and provides that the acceptance of a case on a Writ of Certiorari is not a matter of right but within the sound discretion of the court and the appeal will only be entertained for compelling reasons. Some of the factors the court considers in determining whether to grant an appeal include:

A. A conflict in United States Court of Appeal decisions on the same issue;

B. A state's highest court has issued a ruling on an issue that conflicts with a decision of another state's highest court or with a United States Court of Appeal; or

C. A state court or a United States Court of Appeal has decided an important question of federal law that has not been, but should be, settled by the Supreme Court.

A Petition for a Writ of Certiorari is rarely granted when the alleged error merely consists of factual mistakes or the misapplication of a properly stated rule of law.

For additional reading about the workings of the United States Supreme Court, see *Gideon's Trumpet* by Anthony Lewis and *The Brethren* by Bob Woodward and Scott Armstrong.

The official web address for the United States Supreme Court is:

- **www.supremecourtus.gov**
  This site provides information about the high court, including biographies of the current Court members, an overview of how the court works, Supreme Court Rules, and Supreme Court decisions.

SECTION 12.2 THE 10 WORST SUPREME COURT DECISIONS*

On April 9, 2010, just 11 days before his 90th birthday, U.S. Supreme Court Justice John Paul Stevens gave notice of his retirement which allowed President Obama to appoint a second Supreme Court Justice less than two years into his first term. Elena Kagan, was nominated and confirmed after lengthy and probing examination in Senate confirmation hearings. Since nominees are often asked about past Supreme Court decisions and, if confirmed, will be asked to wrestle with monumental legal issues, perhaps an examination of how previous Supreme Court justices sometimes got it so wrong and did so much damage might be valuable for all.

Only 111 human beings have served on the nation's highest court since its creation on Sept. 24, 1789 by the first Judiciary Act. One-hundred nine (98 percent) of those unelected jurists have been white, only two African-American. All men (97 percent), except three women. All were Christian (93.6 percent), except seven Jews.

From its first case, the uneventful and purely procedural **West v. Barnes, 2 U.S. 401 (1791),** to a more recent one providing First Amendment protection for "crush videos" (if you have to ask, you do not want to know), **United States v. Stevens, 08-769 (4/2/2010),** the court has issued almost 25,000 opinions. Of those, some are very brief, others quite lengthy, some are erudite, others are crude, some are mundane and others are awe-inspiring. And, some are really, really bad. Not just in style or language, but in principle, holding and, most importantly, in the effect on millions of lives.

While there is disagreement based mostly on extremes in ideology and/or religious belief, there appears to be legal and historical scholarly consensus on a number of opinions that are the "worst." Since there are more than 10, honing the list down to the "Top 10" is not easy or simple, but I have tried, acknowledging that others may disagree with one or more being included or feel I have omitted one or more of their "favorites."

I have tried to include those cases that (a) dealt with fundamental issues important to society as a whole, (b) had a profound effect on a large number of people for a long time and (c) were ultimately overruled and/or rendered a nullity by subsequent decision, legislation, constitutional amendment and/

---

*   This article was written by M. Kelly Tillery, Esquire. Mr. Tillery is a partner in the Intellectual Property Group of Pepper Hamilton LLP. Copyright 2010, Philadelphia Bar Association. This article has been reprinted with permission.

or common consensus. Thus, the list cannot include decisions that were just dumb, like **FCC. v. Pacifica Foundation, 438 U.S. 726 (1978)** [upholding a ban on the broadcast of George Carlin's famous "seven words you can't say on radio"], or highly controversial ones like **Bush v. Gore, 531 U.S. 98 (2000)** [2000 presidential election], **Roe v. Wade, 410 U.S. 113 (1973)** [legalization of abortion] or **Kelo v. City of New London, 545 U.S. 469 (2005)** [eminent domain taking for private developers]. After selection based upon these criteria of my own design, I discovered, somewhat to my surprise, an interesting and disturbing common theme. Each one, as shall be seen, involved the shameful, disdainful treatment by the powerful of minorities and their rights. And in each, the court sided with the powerful, consigning the minority often to generations of abuse and/or denial of fundamental rights. In each, unbiased observers agree that the decisions adversely impacted millions for several and sometimes many generations.

Only one was a 5-4 decision. Four were unanimous. Seven deal with laws of the states of the Deep South. All, but one, were decided by all white men over 50 years of age. Some majority opinions were by legendary justices, such as Oliver Wendell Holmes Jr., some by racist ideologues such as Roger B. Taney, and some by rightfully unheralded journeymen such as George Sutherland. Size did not seem to matter. **Dred Scott** produced the longest opinions at 234 pages and **Pace** the shortest at two.

While the majorities in each case seemed tone deaf to the fundamental wrongheadedness of their decisions, at the time of each, there was always a small, but often vocal, minority of individuals, lawyers, academics and organizations who recognized that the court had done the wrong thing and would inevitably end up on the wrong side of history. Sometimes vindication took as little as a few years, sometimes almost a century.

A review of this list may also inform and enlighten as to where the court is going and/or should go on such timely and difficult issues as same-sex marriage, **Perry v. Schwarzenegger,** N.D.CA., cv-09-2292, or Arizona's "Papers, Please," immigration law, which are likely to land on the court's docket in the not-so-distant future.

And the "winners," in chronological order, are:

1. **Dred Scott v. Sandford, 60 U.S. 393 (1857)** [actually, "Sanford," but a clerk's error altered this infamous slave owner's name].

   Majority Opinion: Chief Justice Roger B. Taney

   Vote: 7 to 2 (Justices John McLean and Benjamin R. Curtis Dissenting)

   Overruled By: 14th Amendment, Section 1 (1868)

This is, of course, the "Mother of All Bad Supreme Court Decisions." Even the most rabid "strict constructionist" and the most bleeding heart liberal will readily agree that this one merits inclusion.

The court, per octogenarian Chief Justice Taney (pronounced Tawney), the original "originalist," held that Mr. Dred Scott was a slave and not a citizen of the United States as that word is used in the Constitution, and thus had no standing to sue his owner in a federal court for his freedom and/or for the freedom of his wife, Harriet, and their children, Eliza (14) and Lizzie (7). In 20,000 words of tortured logic and faulty legal history, Taney condemned an entire family to servitude because the court found it had no jurisdiction.

I have read a great deal about slavery in America, from Harriet Beecher Stowe's iconic *Uncle Tom's Cabin* (1852) to Kenneth M. Stampp's classic *The Peculiar Institution* (1956), but I have never felt the chill of governmental indifference to the then 4 million-plus human beings in bondage until I read this opinion of our highest court as it so blithely turned the freedom of a man and his family into a matter of civil procedure.

2. **United States v. Cruikshank, 92 U.S. 542 (1875).**
    Majority Opinion: Chief Justice Morrison R. Waite
    Vote: 8 to 1 (Justice Nathan Clifford Dissenting)
    The Civil Rights Cases, 109 U.S. 3 (1883)
    Majority Opinion: Justice Joseph P. Bradley
    Vote: 8 to 1 (Justice John M. Harlan Dissenting)
    Overruled By: Civil Rights Act of 1964 - Upheld in **Heart of Atlanta Motel, Inc. v. U.S., 379 U.S. 241 (1964)**

Although separated by seven years, these two related cases share a spot since they concern, respectively, the criminal and civil abandonment by the court of Negro citizens in the South to Jim Crow and the KKK for almost a century. In **Cruikshank,** a case arising from the Colfax Massacre of 1873 when almost 100 negro men were murdered by an organized group of white men in Louisiana, the court held that the U.S. could not charge the accused with violations of the Civil Rights' Enforcement Act of 1870 ("The Ku Klux Klan Act"). In one fell swoop, the court effectively emasculated all efforts of the U.S. to use federal criminal law to restrain the abuses of the KKK and similar groups throughout the South. One hundred years of lynchings, murder, abuse and mayhem would follow.

Likewise, in The Civil Rights Cases, the court via Justice Bradley (former railroad lawyer, already infamous for being the deciding vote that made Rutherford B. Hayes president in the "Stolen Election of 1876" - yes, there was one before 2000), struck down as unconstitutional the Civil Rights Act of 1875, which was enacted to ensure equal access for all, no matter what their race or color, to "inns, public conveyances on land or water, theatres and other places of public amusement." In dissent, Justice John Marshall Harlan opined that the Acts were well within the power of Congress, including under the Commerce Clause.

Almost a century later, the court would uphold a similar Civil Rights Act in Heart of Atlanta Motel, utilizing much of the reasoning of "The Great Dissenter."

3.   **Pace v. Alabama, 106 U.S. 583 (1883).**

Majority Opinion: Justice Stephen Field

Vote: Unanimous

Overruled By: **Loving v. Virginia, 388 U.S. 1 (1967)**

The heartless court, in a barren two-page decision, upheld the convictions of Tony Pace, a negro man and Mary T. Cox, a white woman, who had been found guilty of violation of an Alabama law that prohibited marriage, adultery or fornication between "any negro" and "any white person." Each had been sentenced to two years in the state penitentiary. Justice Field, in a clever feat of legal legerdemain, held that the statute did not violate the 14th Amendment Equal Protection Clause because it, in fact, treated whites and Negroes equally – both races were prohibited from marrying, cheating with, and fornicating with the other.

Eighty years later, the Warren Court would disagree in the aptly named **Loving v. Virginia,** establishing not only those laws against interracial marriage are unconstitutional, but that Virginia really is for lovers.

4.   **Plessy v. Ferguson, 163 U.S. 537 (1896).**

Majority Opinion: Justice Henry B. Brown

Vote: 7 to 1 (Justice John M. Harlan Dissenting)

Overruled By: **Brown v. Board of Education, 347 U.S. 483 (1954)**

Though known for little else, former Detroit corporate lawyer Justice Henry Billings Brown bequeathed to generations of Americans the insidious "legal" concept of "separate but equal." The court held that enforcement of a Louisiana statute that required railway companies to provide and police "equal, but separate accommodations for the white and colored races" did not violate either the 13th or 14th Amendment. Homer Plessy had challenged racial separation in public transportation 63 years before Rosa Parks. Justice Harlan, in a brilliant and bitter dissent, stated presciently, "In my opinion the judgment this day rendered will, in time, prove to be quite as pernicious as the decision made by this tribunal in the **Dred Scott** case." It would take 58 years, the eloquence of NAACP Counsel Thurgood Marshall and the political skills of Chief Justice Earl Warren for the court to overrule this vile concept unanimously.

5. **Cumming v. Richmond County Board of Education, 175 U.S. 528 (1899).**

    Majority Opinion: Justice John M. Harlan

    Vote: Unanimous

    Lum v. Rice, 275 U.S. 78 (1927)

    Majority Opinion: Chief Justice William H. Taft

    Vote: Unanimous

Though separated by 28 years, these two gems deserve joint scorn as they both evidence the court's insensitivity to race and equality in public education. In **Cumming,** Justice Harlan, surprisingly, opined for the court that Georgia's failure to provide a high school for "colored" children as it did for white children did not violate the 14th Amendment, while in **Lum** the court held that Mississippi's refusal to permit a child of Chinese descent to attend the "white" school in her district, rather than a "colored" school in a neighboring district, because she was not "white" was constitutionally permissible. The court did everything but sanction a Pantone® chart test for entitlement to educational benefits.

While no case specifically overruled either, **Brown v. Board of Education** effectively negated each.

6. **Lone Wolf v. Hitchcock, 187 U.S. 553 (1903).**

    Majority Opinion: Justice Edward D. White

    Vote: Unanimous

    Overruled By: **Delaware Tribal Business Comm. v. Weeks, 430 U.S. 73 (1977)**

Justice White, in fewer than six pages, cavalierly dismissed the entire history of the indigenous peoples of America and, more particularly, all of the agreements made with them by the United States, holding that they exist in a "relation of dependency" "toward the government," that is, "wards of the nation," and thus the Congress has "paramount power" over Indian lands. The court held that the Fifth Amendment did not protect interest in Indian lands and the federal government could pretty much do what it wanted with them. And, of course, it did, abrogating treaties, ignoring promises and agreements for generations, treating the Indian as badly as, if not worse than, Jim Crow treated the Negro.

7. **Buck v. Bell, 274 U.S. 200 (1927).**

    Majority Opinion: Justice Oliver Wendell Holmes Jr.

    Vote: 8 to 1 (Justice Pierce Butler Dissenting)

In 1927, the "eugenics" movement was gaining ground, and not just in Germany. When the State of Virginia engaged the mighty force of the U.S. Supreme Court to prevent Carrie Buck, 18, from ever bearing children again, the venerable Civil War veteran Oliver Wendell Holmes Jr. obliged. The court ruled that it was not unconstitutional for a state to determine that it, the unwilling adult victim and presumably her yet-to-be-born children, would be better off if she were forcibly sterilized.

Holmes observed that Buck was "feeble minded," as was her mother and her daughter. Though later investigation proved that not to be entirely true, Holmes relied on the trumped-up record to pontificate that, in his infamous observation, "Three generations of imbeciles are enough."

After reading these cases, one might come to agree with Holmes if it applied to certain Supreme Court justices.

Like some others, **Buck** was never officially overturned, though no one seriously believes it is still good law.

8. **Ozawa v. United States, 260 U.S. 178 (1922).**

   Majority Opinion: Justice George Sutherland

   Vote: Unanimous

   United States v. Thind, 261 U.S. 204 (1923)

   Majority Opinion: Justice George Sutherland

   Vote: Unanimous

Some of the court's opinions on race are so absurd as to be laughable if they were not so sad and serious in effect. **Ozawa** and **Thind** rank together as such. In Ozawa, the court held that "a person of the Japanese race" is not a "white person" and therefore cannot become a naturalized citizen. In **Thind**, the court held similarly for a "high caste Hindu of full Indian blood." More Pantone® testing, courtesy of Justice Sutherland, one of the conservative "Four Horsemen" who held back the progress of the New Deal for years.

9. **Korematsu v. United States, 323 U.S. 214 (1944).**

   Majority Opinion: Justice Hugo L. Black

   Vote: 6 - 3 (Justices Owen J. Roberts, Francis W. Murphy and Robert H. Jackson Dissenting) "Overruled" By: **Korematsu v. United States, U.S. D.Ct., N.D. Cal. (1983)** Writ of Coram Nobis granted-conviction overturned

It is said that "hard cases make bad law." If our current experiences post-9/11 are too close in time and too personal to bring that home, nothing can do it better than **Korematsu**. Therein, the court upheld the conviction of an American citizen of Japanese descent (Nisei) for failure to obey an executive/military order to leave his home and evacuate the West Coast solely because he was of Japanese descent. Although the court was asked to pass "…upon the whole subsequent detention program in both assembly and relocation centers ...," in obtuse and cowardly fashion, it refused to do so. However, the court made its feelings clear that it would give ultimate deference on such matters to the military and the executive branch. That had always worked out so well for protecting rights of minorities in the past.

10. **Bowers v. Hardwick, 478 U.S. 186 (1986).**

   Majority Opinion: Justice Byron R. White

   Vote: 5 to 4 (Justice Harry A. Blackmun for the Dissenters)

   Overruled By: **Lawrence v. Texas, 539 U.S. 553 (2003)**

Only 24 years ago, the court upheld as constitutional a Georgia statute that criminalized private, non-commercial, adult, consensual sexual activity. Despite the fact that the law applied equally to heterosexual as well as homosexual activity, Justice White focused oddly and only on homosexual activity, apparently fearing, in homophobic paranoia, that any contrary ruling might establish a society-destroying "fundamental right to engage in homosexual sodomy."

Justice Powell cast the deciding vote, although his concurring opinion evidences reluctance to join the majority. Indeed, some years later, he expressed regret about his vote, saying he "just had not known any gay people." In fact, unbeknownst to him, he had, very well. One of his law clerks from only five years before **Bowers** was gay.

Seventeen years later the Court overruled **Bowers,** though even then by only a 6 to 3 vote.

If nothing else, this Top 10 evidence that the court does sometimes make grievous errors and that it can, at least in time, correct them. As (if) we continue to become a more enlightened society, I predict that we will in the foreseeable future see at least two fundamental societal changes brought on by Supreme Court decisions: (1) the legalization of same-sex marriage and (2) the elimination of the death penalty. Stay tuned.

SECTION 12.3
THE STATE
COURT SYSTEM

We are a nation of states, each state maintaining its own independent court system. While the configuration of the court system will vary from state to state, each will have a trial court and at least one appellate court. The National Center for States Courts is an organization created to improve the administration of justice through leadership and service to state courts and courts around the world. They maintain a website that provides links to each state court in the country. That site may be accessed at **http://www.ncsconline.org/D_KIS/ info_court_web_sites.html.** The state court system in Pennsylvania is provided as an illustration.

The court of original jurisdiction in Pennsylvania is known as the **Court of Common Pleas** and it was established as part of the Pennsylvania Constitution in 1776 and it is subdivided into the following three divisions: the Trial Court; the Family Court; and Orphan's Court.

The Trial Division hears both civil and criminal cases. Orphan's Court is concerned with matters involving estates, such as will contests, trusts, and incompetence hearings. Family Court decides juvenile cases and matters involving the family unit such as divorce, custody, support, paternity, and domestic violence.

To reduce the backlog of cases, a specialized court has been created to handle small disputes. In Philadelphia, this court is called the Municipal Court and is divided into civil and criminal divisions. It handles all landlord/tenant problems, civil disputes of $10,000 or less, criminal cases where the penalty involves five years or less imprisonment, and code violations. In the surrounding counties, magisterial district justices who have offices in the various townships throughout the Commonwealth handle these matters. Parties appearing in Municipal Court do not enjoy the right to a jury trial, so most cases can be appealed directly to the Court of Common Pleas at which time the person will receive a new trial equipped with a jury if so desired.

Because of the frequency and complexity of business related matters, an increasing number of state courts have established specialized forums to hear business related matters such as antitrust lawsuits, intellectual property issues, and complex mass torts. This type of system will allow judges to better understand the issues and to develop expertise in the area of business disputes. As the Ninth Judicial Circuit Court of Florida noted in establishing a business court, "The goal is to handle business litigation matters in an effective and efficient manner. Benefits of a business litigation section include the following: 1) implementation of standardized procedures; 2) higher degree of consistency of rulings on recurring issues; and 3) economic stimulus to the community."

PENNSYLVANIA STATE JUDICIAL SYSTEM

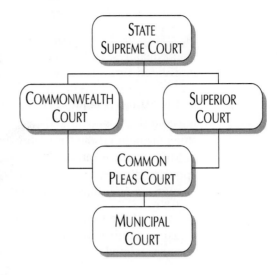

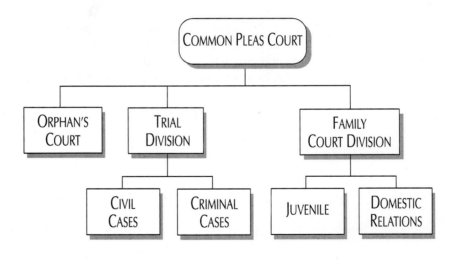

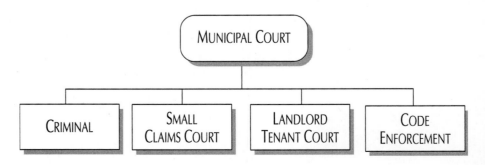

SECTION 12.4
THE JURY SYSTEM

The right to a trial by one's peers is a basic building block of American democracy guaranteed by the United States Constitution. In fact, it has been estimated that this country accounts for 95% of all jury trials in the world.[8] As the Supreme Court noted, "The guarantees of a jury trial reflect a profound judgment about the way in which the law should be enforced and justice administered. Providing an accused with the right to be tried by a jury of his peers gives him an inestimable safeguard against the corrupt or overzealous prosecutor and against the compliant, biased, or eccentric judge."[9]

While the right to a jury trial is firmly engrained in our system of jurisprudence, it was not conceived by the founders of this country. Jury trials have been in existence in England for centuries and some scholars contend that the concept originated in thirteenth-century England as an outgrowth of the *Magna Carta*.

During the founding days of this country, the right to a jury trial was brought to America by the English colonists. In fact, it was adopted by the First Congress of the American Colonists in 1765 with the declaration that "trial by jury is the inherent and invaluable right of every British subject in these colonies."

The founding fathers considered the concept to be so fundamental that it is contained in two different Amendments to the United States Constitution. The Sixth Amendment guarantees the defendant in a criminal case the right to a speedy and public trial by an impartial jury. The Seventh Amendment entitles citizens to a jury trial in civil cases involving a dispute of more than twenty dollars.

In application, a judge presides over the trial and decides questions-of-law. The jury, on the other hand, is the ultimate arbiter of the facts. They decide which party should win a controversy based upon the evidence presented at trial.

To better understand the distinction between a question of law and a question of fact, consider the following hypothetical situation:

> Joe Roberts is driving his car south on Broad Street and enters the intersection on what he maintains is a green light. Bill Smith is proceeding east on Montgomery Avenue and enters the same intersection on what he too alleges is a green light. The vehicles collide on Broad Street, and Roberts maintains that he is injured. Joe institutes suit against Smith for personal injuries.

The judge will inform the jury that a party who enters an intersection against a red light is negligent and responsible for the injuries caused by that negligence. This is a statement of law. On the other hand, it is up to the jury to decide which party entered the intersection after the light turned red. This is a determination of fact.

A jury in a criminal trial generally consists of twelve people whose decisions must be unanimous. The origin of this number is not clear. Some say it represents the number of apostles from the bible, Solomon's officers which numbered twelve, or twelve was a favorite number in medieval times. The Supreme Court, however, has noted that the number is a historical accident that became fixed in the fourteenth century. The essential feature of a jury rests in the collective judgment of a group of people, and in the community participation that results from that group's determination of innocence or guilt. The performance of this role is not dependent on a specific number of citizens that make up the jury.[10] Jury requirements, therefore, vary by state and type of proceeding. For instance, Pennsylvania requires that a defendant in a criminal trial be provided with twelve jurors and all must agree on the verdict. In a civil case, however, the verdict need not be unanimous, and the jury will consist of eight members unless a litigant specifically demands a trial by twelve.

More than 120,000 jury trials a year are conducted in the United States. In contrast, only about one-percent of trials in England are conducted with the help of a jury. France utilizes juries for only the most serious crimes, and Italy uses panels of three judges. Germany, Finland and Sweden have mixed tribunals of a professional judge and several laymen.[11] Russia has only recently reinstituted the use of jury trials in serious criminal matters, and Japan will utilize six-person juries starting in 2009.

Mark Twain stated in a 1873 speech that: "We have a criminal jury system which is superior to any in the world; and its efficiency is only marred by the difficulty of finding twelve men every day who don't know anything and can't read."

Is the jury system the best way of having a matter decided in a court of law? The verdict in the O.J. Simpson case left many people questioning the validity of the jury system, and who can forget the two-million dollar award against McDonald's for the coffee that spilled on a woman's leg as she rode in a car. Fortunately, these examples are not representative of jury verdicts. Most legal experts agree that it is the best system available despite certain recognized short comings and occasional erroneous verdicts. After all, it is better to be tried by the collective judgment of one's peers than by the wisdom of a single individual. This is the backbone of a democracy.

The jury system does have inherent weaknesses. The law is very complicated, and a trial is an intimidating proceeding. Jurors are thrust into the role of deciding complex cases without the proper legal training or experience. As a generalization, they tend to be plaintiff oriented and are more apt to award money than to find for the defense. Verdicts also tend to be higher in metropolitan cities than those in rural counties.

An analysis of civil jury verdicts by the United States Department of Justice determined that in 53% of the cases, the jury found in favor of plaintiffs and awarded a total of 3.9 billion dollars in compensatory and punitive damages during the one-year period under review. The average finding was $37,000 and juries awarded punitive damages in 6% of the cases with a median punitive damage award of $50,000.[12]

On the other hand, some scholars have found the very weaknesses of the jury system to be its strength. In a speech given by Oliver Wendell Holmes on January 17, 1899, he stated:

> *"I confess that in my experience I have not found juries especially inspired for the discovery of truth...they will introduce into their verdict a...large amount...of popular prejudice, and thus keep the administration of the law in a court with the wishes and feelings of the community."*[13]

SECTION 12.5
JURISDICTION

Jurisdiction refers to the power of a court to determine the merits of a dispute and to grant an aggrieved party relief. In order for a court to properly entertain an action, it must have jurisdiction over the subject matter in dispute and jurisdiction over the parties involved.

Subject matter jurisdiction is quite simple. The particular court where the dispute is heard must have the power to hear the kind of case that is in controversy. The courts are very specialized, and the plaintiff must institute suit before the proper court. For instance, a divorce proceeding may not be instituted in tax court. The court's power to hear these specific types of cases is usually granted by the legislature.

Jurisdiction over the person requires the court to have power to exercise its authority over the defendant. Traditionally, suit was instituted where the defendant could be found. This was either in the state where he resided or where he worked. Now, a court is considered to have jurisdiction over the parties when the defendant has "minimum contacts" with the state where the court is located (the **forum state**). **Minimum contacts** are generally deemed to exist when the defendant takes actions that are purposefully directed toward the forum state.

The rule of serving a defendant where the defendant can be found was expanded over time by the passage of long arm statutes that allow a jurisdiction to reach beyond the state boundaries to serve a defendant with the lawsuit. The most common **long arm statutes** deal with a non-resident who commits a tort within a state, a party who owns property in a state, and one doing business in a state.

In order to satisfy the requirements of due process, the Supreme Court has ruled that a state court may exercise personal jurisdiction over a non-resident defendant as long as there are *minimum contacts* between the defendant and the state in which the suit has been filed. The concept of minimum contacts protects defendants against the burdens of litigating in a distant or inconvenient court. Usually, a defendant will have some kind of presence in the forum. In the case of transacting business within a state, however, it is not necessary to have an office in that jurisdiction. Soliciting business through sales representatives or by placing an advertisement in a local newspaper have been held to constitute minimum contacts.

SEVERINSEN V. WIDENER UNIVERSITY
768 A.2D 200 (N. J. SUPER., 2001)

The question presented is whether New Jersey courts may exercise personal jurisdiction over an out-of-state university based upon the university's recruitment activities in this state. Plaintiff, a law student at Widener University, brought suit in New Jersey for injuries sustained at the University's campus in Delaware. The Law Division found that Widener's contacts with New Jersey were insufficient to support plaintiff's claim of jurisdiction. We agree.

Plaintiff was struck in the face by a bathroom door while a resident at Shipley Hall, a University dormitory. The dormitory was part of the on-campus housing supplied to students by Widener. Plaintiff asserted in his complaint that the door hinge was defective.

Widener moved to dismiss plaintiff's complaint for lack of personal jurisdiction. In response, plaintiff contended that Widener maintained a substantial presence in New Jersey by virtue of its recruitment activities. These activities included sending agents to New Jersey college and law school fairs, advertising in local newspapers, mailing unsolicited letters to potential students, conducting sports activities with New Jersey colleges and universities, recruiting athletes, and sponsoring alumni events.

A New Jersey court may exercise personal jurisdiction over a non-resident defendant to the "outermost limits permitted by the United States Constitution." Minimum contacts with the forum state provide the predicate for exercising personal jurisdiction over

a non-resident defendant. The nexus between the forum state and the non-resident defendant must be such that the maintenance of the suit does not offend traditional notions of fair play and substantial justice.

To assess the reasonableness of subjecting the defendant to jurisdiction, the court must undertake a "minimum contacts" analysis. This analysis ensures that the jurisdictional requirement of due process is met. The minimum contacts analysis consists of two prongs. First, the court must determine whether or not minimum contacts exist at all. Second, the court must decide "whether those minimum contacts establish jurisdiction consistent with considerations of fair play and substantial justice." Essentially it must be determined whether the defendant has purposely availed itself of jurisdiction in the forum state.

Plaintiff asserts that Widener's targeted solicitation of New Jersey high school and college students through advertisement and other recruitment activities supports the exercise of general jurisdiction. In a series of decisions, we have said that a non-resident defendant's advertising and soliciting activities in New Jersey, if sufficiently systematic and continuous, may render that entity subject to general jurisdiction.

The common thread throughout these decisions upholding general jurisdiction was the non-resident defendant's purposeful availment of the forum state's laws for the pursuit of profit. In each of these cases, the defendant was a business entity seeking economic entry into New Jersey's marketplace. In contrast, the defendant in this case is an institution of higher education. It is arguable that in determining whether jurisdiction exists the spreading of education and the selling of widgets are not equivalent.

In **Gehling v. St. George's School of Medicine, Ltd., 773 F.2d 539 (3rd Cir., 1985),** the plaintiffs brought a wrongful death action against St. George's University School of Medicine, a Grenada educational institution, after their son died in the course of a school sponsored road race. They asserted jurisdiction on the basis of St. George's "continuous and substantial" recruitment efforts in Pennsylvania. These recruitment activities included placing advertisements in the New York Times and the Wall Street Journal, two newspapers that are circulated throughout Pennsylvania. St. George's also established a joint international program with a Pennsylvania university to serve as a "feeder" for the recruitment of international students. The Third Circuit held that these activities were not sufficient to permit the exercise of jurisdiction over the non-resident defendant. The Court emphasized that advanced educational institutions typically draw their student body from numerous states, and the plaintiffs' theory would subject them to suit on non-forum related claims in every state where a member of the student body resides. The fact that residents of the state apply and are accepted for admission to St. George's was found to be of no moment.

While perhaps some of Widener's recruitment efforts were targeted to New Jersey students, we believe that the noncommercial educational mission of the University is a salient factor weighing against the exercise of personal jurisdiction. It is arguable that institutions of higher education should be permitted to advertise and solicit students on a regional basis without being burdened by having to defend against lawsuits involving wholly unrelated transactions. It is natural that these universities and colleges will have an increased profile in the states in close proximity to their campuses. Accordingly, traditional notions of fair play and substantial justice strongly militate against holding that a non-profit educational institution renders itself subject to service of process in every state of the union from which it may seek or attract outstanding athletes or scholars. Such a decision would as well place an unreasonably onerous burden on small educational institutions throughout the nation. We thus conclude that the Law Division was correct in dismissing plaintiff's suit.

With the advent of websites and their ability to convey information to people around the world, additional jurisdictional issues arise. For instance, is a business that places information about itself on the internet subject to lawsuits in any place where an individual can access the site even if the business has no presence in that state and has not solicited business in that state?

A series of cases have established the law concerning when jurisdiction in a particular location is proper based upon the type of Internet transaction and website involved. The courts use a sliding scale for ascertaining whether a nonresident has submitted to a state's jurisdiction by establishing the requisite contacts through Internet-based activity. At one end of the scale are cases where a defendant clearly does business over the Internet. If that person enters into contracts with citizens of another state that involve the repeated transmission of information over the Internet, jurisdiction is proper. At the opposite end of the spectrum are those cases where a defendant has simply posted information on a website which is accessible to users in another jurisdiction. This is called a passive website and does little more than to make information available to those who are interested in the information. This type of Internet transaction does not give rise to the exercise of personal jurisdiction. The middle ground is occupied by interactive websites where a person can exchange information with the host computer. In these situations, the exercise of jurisdiction is ascertained by looking at the level of interactivity and commercial nature of the exchange of information that occurs on the web site. See: **Zippo Mfg. v. Zippo Dot Com., 952 F. Supp. 1119 (W. D. Pa., 1997).**

It is now possible to buy large ticket items such as automobiles through the Internet and to participate in auctions conducted by organizations such as e-Bay. Suppose the product, which is the subject of the Internet transaction, is not what was promised? Where can the aggrieved party bring suit? That is the issue in the following case.

AERO TOY STORE, LLC v. GRIEVES
631 S. E.2D 734 (GA. APP., 2006)

Gordon Grieves, a Georgia resident, sued Aero Toy Store, a Florida company for breach of contract arising from Grieves' purchase of an automobile from Aero over the Internet. Aero moved to dismiss for lack of personal jurisdiction.

While conducting an Internet search of the eBay Motors auction website, Grieves identified a 2001 BMW car being offered for sale. The website contained a description of the BMW and its features. And it provided an "Ask seller a question" button that, when activated, identified Juan Almeida as the seller's agent. On or about April 13, 2004, Grieves began making e-mail inquiries to Almeida concerning the car. Almeida responded to Grieves with various e-mails.

Grieves asserts that, in reliance on Almeida's representations, he calculated his winning bid and that, after Almeida faxed copies of the purchase agreement to him, he signed the agreement, faxed it back to Almeida, and mailed a check to Aero in payment of the $31,926 purchase price.

In support of its motion to dismiss, Aero tendered an affidavit of its automotive manager, to show that it does not have any agents, representatives, officers, or employees in Georgia; that it is not licensed to do business in Georgia; that it does not own or rent property in Georgia; that it does not maintain an office in Georgia; and that it has no subsidiaries or business affiliates in Georgia. Aero maintained that, since its formation in 2002, it had made only two Internet sales to persons in Georgia totaling $193,199, amounting to less than one-half of one percent of its gross revenues.

Resolution requires us to review the traditional three-part test used in determining whether long arm jurisdiction exists based on the transaction of business, and then review a test developed in other jurisdictions for determining the existence of minimum contacts in cases involving the Internet.

In considering whether a Georgia court may exercise jurisdiction over a nonresident based on the transaction of business, we apply a three-part test:

Jurisdiction exists on the basis of transacting business in this state if (1) the nonresident defendant has purposefully done some act or consummated some transaction in this state, (2) if the cause of action arises from or is connected with such act or transaction, and (3) if the exercise of jurisdiction by the courts of this state does not offend traditional fairness and substantial justice.

Regularly doing or soliciting business in the state, deriving substantial revenue from goods or services in the state, having agents or representatives or officers or employees in the state, maintaining an office in the state, and having subsidiaries or business affiliates in the state are factors most directly relevant to the existence of general jurisdiction. Factors such as regularly doing or soliciting business, or deriving substantial revenue from goods or services, in this state may also be relevant in determining whether sufficient minimum contacts exist for the purpose of supporting specific jurisdiction, where such activities relate to the suit at hand.

In other jurisdictions, a line of decisions has developed recognizing the technological revolution ushered in by the Internet and utilizing a sliding scale for determining whether a nonresident has submitted to a state's long arm jurisdiction by establishing the requisite minimum contacts through Internet-based activity. This sliding scale was initially articulated in **Zippo Mfg. Co. v. Zippo Dot Com.** As recognized in that case, [a]t one end of the spectrum are situations where a defendant clearly does business over the Internet. If the defendant enters into contracts with residents of a foreign jurisdiction that involve the knowing and repeated transmission of computer files over the Internet, personal jurisdiction is proper. At the opposite end are situations where a defendant has simply posted information on an Internet website which is accessible to users in foreign jurisdictions. A passive website that does little more than make information available to those who are interested in it is not grounds for the exercise [of] personal jurisdiction. The middle ground is occupied by interactive websites where a user can exchange information with the host computer. In these cases, the exercise of

jurisdiction is determined by examining the level of interactivity and commercial nature of the exchange of information that occurs on the website.

In **Butler v. Beer Across America,** a minor left alone at his Alabama home ordered 12 beers from corporate sellers in Illinois through the sellers' Internet website. Under the applicable provisions of the UCC, the beer was delivered to the carrier acting as the purchaser's agent in Illinois and then shipped by the carrier to the purchaser in Alabama. The purchaser's mother brought an action for damages against the sellers in federal district court in Alabama.

The court in **Butler** recognized that Alabama courts had found sufficient minimum contacts to support in personam jurisdiction over nonresident defendants in other actions related to out-of-state sale of goods to Alabama residents for use in Alabama, as in cases such as **Atlanta Auto Auction v. G & G Auto Sales.** The Butler court concluded, however, that the contacts in those cases differed in both kind and extent from the de minimis connections in the **Butler** case. Cases such as **Atlanta Auto Auction** involved sales of automobiles, with transactions presumably worth thousands of dollars each, as opposed to the less than $25 purchase in **Butler**. And applying **Zippo** principles, the **Butler** court found that **Beer Across America's** website did not anticipate the regular exchange of information across the Internet or provide for such interaction. The court concluded that, instead, it was more like an electronic bulletin board for the posting of information.

Similarly, in **Barton Southern Co. v. Manhole Barrier Systems,** the federal district court in Georgia found that the nonresident defendant's Internet website failed to furnish a Georgia contact adequate to support personal jurisdiction where there was nothing on the website showing an intent to reach out to persons living in Georgia and no evidence that any Georgia residents had done business with the defendant either through the Internet or otherwise.

In this case, unlike in **Barton Southern Co.,** the defendant operated an interactive website through which it has reached out to, and done business with, persons in Georgia. This case, like **Atlanta Auto Auction,** involves the sale of an automobile with the transaction worth thousands of dollars and involving shipment of an automobile to be operated in Georgia. The car was shipped into Georgia by the nonresident seller and not by a carrier acting as the resident buyer's agent. Although Aero does not have officers, employees, offices, or business affiliates in Georgia, and although the revenue it derives from goods sold here may not be substantial in relation to its overall revenue, it does regularly solicit business in Georgia through the Internet, and the revenue it has derived from shipping cars to Grieves and other persons in Georgia is substantial enough to establish sufficient minimum contacts with the state of Georgia in a case involving the exercise of specific jurisdiction. Applying the expansive interpretation of the "transacting any business" provision of our Long Arm Statute, the state court did not err in determining that Aero has established sufficient minimum contacts with this state to warrant exercise of personal jurisdiction over it in this case.

Judgment affirmed.

SECTION 12.6
VENUE

Venue is the place where a case should be heard. The plaintiff decides where to institute suit. This decision will rarely be disturbed unless the defendant can demonstrate a compelling reason to remove the matter to another jurisdiction. This will occur if the defendant cannot obtain a fair trial in the location where the lawsuit was filed because of prejudice or bias. For instance, one may remember the D.C. sniper who terrorized the nation's capital and surrounding area in October of 2002 with the random killing of ten people and the wounding of several others. Eventually, a man and a boy were captured for these heinous crimes. The young man was John Lee Malvo and he was 17 at the time of his arrest. Subsequently, murder charges were filed against him in Fairfax County, Virginia and his attorney requested that the trial be moved to a location where the members of the jury pool would not have been residents of the area of where the killings took place. The court agreed and moved the trial to Chesapeake, Virginia.

The second reason for requesting a change of venue derives from the concept of **forum non-conveniens**. This Latin term means that the place of the trial is inconvenient for the parties and the witnesses involved in the litigation. A court may refuse to exercise jurisdiction over the parties if it would be more convenient for a court in another jurisdiction to hear the case.

Gonzalez v. State is an example of a case in which the defendant maintains that he was denied a fair trial because of the pretrial publicity surrounding the crime he was charged with committing. The court noted that three issues need to be considered in entertaining a change of venue motion based upon pretrial publicity: **1)** the nature of the publicity, **2)** any evidence presented at a change of venue hearing, and **3)** testimony received from prospective jury members at voir dire.

GONZALEZ v. STATE
222 S. W.3D 446 (TEX. CRIM. APP., 2007)

On October 29, 2002, appellant and Adam entered a Good Times Store in El Paso County. Adam carried a .22 rifle. The store was equipped with surveillance cameras, which recorded appellant and Adam entering the store, threatening the victim with the rifle, and demanding that he turn over "everything." After appellant took the cash, Adam shot the victim once in the chest, killing him. In an attempt to identify and locate the suspects, local newscasts aired the surveillance tape depicting the murder of the convenience store clerk. Numerous newspaper articles also covered the murder and the search for the culprits. Appellant was recognized and reported to the police.

Appellant was arrested for capital murder. At a pretrial hearing on a defense motion for change of venue, appellant called two witnesses. The first testified that he did not believe that appellant could receive a fair trial in El Paso County. He based this conclusion upon his conversations with individual citizens, both in the courthouse and throughout the community.

The second witness was private investigator Arnold Davis. Davis testified that he had become familiar with the case from seeing footage from the surveillance video on the news, which he described as "playing the video repeatedly." He was unable to remember specifically how often it was played, other than saying that it was "at least every time the news was on." Finally, he testified that he believed that appellant would not be able to receive a fair trial in El Paso County.

After hearing this testimony, the court stated, "Although appellant's witnesses testified that the pretrial publicity has touched certain people, I have no evidence before me as to what extent it has permeated into the community." At voir dire, roughly two-thirds (121 out of 180) of the jury panel members informed the trial court that they had heard of

the case, and roughly one-third (58 out of 180) of the panel members stated that they had formed an opinion about the case that they could not set aside. Appellant was subsequently convicted and sentenced to life in prison.

Section 31.03(a) of the Code of Criminal Procedure provides that a change of venue may be granted if the defendant establishes that "there exists in the county where the prosecution is commenced so great a prejudice against him that he cannot obtain a fair and impartial trial." To justify a change of venue based upon media attention, a defendant must show that the publicity was pervasive, prejudicial, and inflammatory. The mere existence of media attention or publicity is not enough, by itself, to merit a change of venue.

At the hearing, appellant introduced into evidence three newspaper articles, all written at the time of the offense. Appellant also presented the opinions of two witnesses on the amount of publicity that the case had generated, the surveillance video that was included in newscasts, and the effect of that publicity on the community at large. However, there was no evidence of how many times the video was shown nor of how many people actually saw the broadcast. Similarly, no evidence was presented as to how many people saw the newspaper coverage of the case. The only evidence of how widespread the publicity's audience was, or the effect of the publicity on that audience, came from appellant's two witnesses at the venue hearing, as laid out above, which the trial court had discretion to consider or discount as it saw fit.

In examining whether the pretrial publicity is prejudicial and inflammatory, a trial court may take three matters into consideration: 1) the nature of the publicity, 2) any evidence presented at a change of venue hearing, and 3) testimony received from prospective jury members at voir dire. News stories, be it from print, radio, or television, that are accurate and objective in their coverage, are generally considered by this Court not to be prejudicial or inflammatory. Appellant points to the publication of the surveillance video as a distinguishing feature of this case. He describes the video as "gruesome and disturbing," and "the most prejudicial piece of evidence" presented by the State in its prosecution. Appellant argues, in light of the testimony presented at the hearing and the answers given by the jury panel at voir dire, that the inclusion of the surveillance video, along with the other coverage of the crime, makes the pretrial publicity inflammatory and prejudicial.

Over the last forty years, this Court has been reluctant to hold that pretrial publicity in a case was so prejudicial and inflammatory that the trial court's decision to deny a change of venue was outside the zone of reasonable disagreement. Jack Rubenstein, also known as Jack Ruby, was arrested and indicted for the murder of Lee Harvey Oswald. Rubenstein shot and killed Oswald as he was being moved from the Dallas city jail to the county jail. The jail transfer was being covered by both national and local press. In the local coverage, news stories stated "directly, indirectly, by hints and innuendoes that a Communist conspiracy existed between Oswald and Ruby." Rubenstein was referred to as a "tough guy" or "Chicago mobster" in the press, and Rubenstein's shooting of Oswald was seen on television by "countless thousands" of Dallas County residents. Rubenstein filed a pretrial motion for change of venue, which was denied. His conviction was overturned on appeal on other grounds, but this Court also held that the trial court erred in denying the change of venue. In a concurring opinion, Judge McDonald described the publicity surrounding Rubenstein's case as "a background of unusual and extraordinary invasions of the expected neutral mental processes of a citizenry," which contributed to the Court's reasoning that the trial court abused its discretion in denying a change of venue.

We find the present case to be distinguishable from Rubenstein. The coverage by the local media in this case was accurate and objective. Although a large number of panelists were disqualified for cause because they were unable to set aside their opinion of appellant's guilt, those circumstances do not require a conclusion that the publicity was inflammatory or prejudicial. Moreover, the surveillance video that appellant labels as prejudicial and inflammatory was evidence of the crime that in fact was later admitted in its entirety at trial. Because the jurors were going to be exposed to this evidence anyway, we cannot hold that the publication of a surveillance video, absent other facts, was by itself prejudicial and inflammatory.

The trial court received the documentary evidence and heard the testimony of the witnesses during the pretrial hearing, and it heard the responses of the jurors at voir dire. This court affords great deference to trial courts because a trial court is in a better position to resolve issues involving testimony and other questions of fact as a result of its ability to observe the demeanor of witnesses and scrutinize their veracity face to face. We see nothing in this record other than the video to distinguish this case from numerous others in which we have upheld a trial court's denial of a motion to change venue. That sole distinguishing characteristic is not sufficient to place beyond the zone of reasonable disagreement the trial court's decision to deny appellant's motion.

SECTION 12.7
STANDING

In accordance with the United States Constitution, courts are only permitted to hear actual cases or controversies. That is, courts cannot offer advisory opinions to people who are not actually involved in a dispute. The plaintiff in a lawsuit must have a direct and substantial interest in the outcome of the case that he or she intends to bring. This concept is referred to as **standing**. To meet this requirement, the plaintiff must show that he or she has actually been injured by the action that is the subject of the lawsuit. The injury can be physical, economic, environmental, or aesthetic, but must injure the plaintiff in fact. To have standing to have a case heard, it is also necessary that the relief sought by the plaintiff either correct or compensate for the harm alleged in the lawsuit.

Consider this example: Estelle Roberts was in the process of researching the environmentally fragile nature of the Nevada mountains when she discovered that someone planned to build an amusement park in that area. The park would have a detrimental effect on the environment in the mountain region. If Estelle makes no allegation of the way in which the building of the park would cause an actual injury to her personally, she will be denied standing to bring that case.

Elton John authored the composition *Can You Feel the Love Tonight* as the featured song in the Disney film, *The Lion King.* Subsequently, two publishing companies instituted suit over the composition, claiming it infringed on their copyright to a previous work, *Listen to Your Heart.* Since only one company may be the proper owner of the song, the court had to ascertain which publisher had standing to maintain the action for copyright infringement.

HALWILL MUSIC, INC. V. ELTON JOHN
2000 U.S. DIST. LEXIS 7067 (S.D. N.Y., 2000)

Two different companies seek to assert the same copyright against the same purported infringers; but only one has the right to do so, and the other must be dismissed.

The first suit was brought by plaintiff Gold-Rhyme Music Company ("GoldRhyme") against The Walt Disney Company and other defendants, alleging that the Elton John composition *Can You Feel the Love Tonight,* featured in connection with the film *The Lion King,* infringed the copyright on a previous work, *Listen To Your Heart,* composed by Glenn Medeiros. Subsequently, however, Halwill Music, Inc. ("Halwill") filed suit, making essentially the same claim against essentially the same defendants and further alleging that Medeiros had conveyed to Halwill the sole and exclusive right to sue for copyright infringement with respect to *Listen To Your Heart.*

The Court hereby grants Halwill's motion and dismisses the action brought by GoldRhyme for lack of standing.

Under the **Copyright Act of 1976,** "the legal or beneficial owner of an exclusive right under a copyright is entitled… to institute an action for any infringement of that particular right committed while he or she is the owner of it."

It is undisputed that in 1988, as part of an agreement conveying to Halwill an undisputed half-interest in certain of Medeiros' musical compositions (including *Listen to Your Heart),* Medeiros agreed that Halwill shall have the sole and exclusive right to administer and protect the Musical Compositions on behalf of both parties throughout the world. Pursuant to that 1988 agreement, Halwill registered a claim for copyright in *Listen To Your Heart* in 1993.

In 1996, Medeiros entered into a separate agreement with GoldRhyme that gave GoldRhyme the exclusive right to initiate all actions for infringements of any Medeiros compositions covered by that agreement. This 1996 agreement, however, was limited to compositions "that have not been assigned in writing to any third party as of the date hereof." Therefore, the 1996 agreement does not in any way pertain to *Listen To Your Heart* which was covered by the 1988 agreement.

Although GoldRhyme attempts to attack the validity of the 1988 agreement between Halwill and Medeiros, its arguments in this regard are without merit. For example, GoldRhyme contends that the 1988 agreement is not signed and is therefore invalid. In fact, however, the signed amended agreement between Halwill and Medeiros specifically refers to and incorporates prior agreements.

Accordingly, the Court hereby grants plaintiff Halwill's motion and dismisses with prejudice GoldRhyme's action against defendants for lack of standing.

SECTION 12.8
FULL FAITH AND CREDIT

Full Faith and Credit is a constitutional mandate that requires each state to uphold the laws and decrees of every other state. As the Supreme Court noted in **Sherrer v. Sherrer, 334 U.S. 343,** the Full, Faith and Credit Clause "is one of the provisions incorporated into the Constitution by its framers for the purpose of transforming an aggregation of independent sovereign states into a nation." This guarantee is contained in **Article Four** of the United States Constitution which provides that full, faith and credit shall be given in each state to the public acts, records, and judicial proceedings of every other state. Essentially, this means that a judgment in one state will be enforced in another state as long as the first state has jurisdiction. Without this provision, the legal system would become uncertain and chaotic. People would never know if a different state would enforce a validly obtained judgment in another jurisdiction. How does this concept work in reality?

Assume that John Smith, a New Jersey resident and college student, goes to Florida for spring break. Upon his arrival in Florida, he rents a car, but unfortunately Smith runs over the clerk as he is pulling away from the rental agency. He is so distraught by the incident that he takes the next plane back to Newark International Airport in New Jersey. The clerk files suit in Florida for her injuries. John ignores the lawsuit since he has no plans of ever returning to Florida, and a judgment is rendered against him in the amount of $100,000. Is Smith correct in assuming that nothing can be done to him as long as he stays out of Florida? Pursuant to the "Full Faith and Credit Clause" of the Constitution, the Florida judgment can be transferred to New Jersey and be enforced in that jurisdiction. Florida had jurisdiction over the New Jersey resident since he committed a tort in that state.

There is a *public policy exception* to the Full, Faith and Credit Clause which allows a state to disregard the laws of another jurisdiction if the enforcement of those rules and acts would be inconsistent with the public policy of its own state. However, will a court disregard an adoption of a child from a same sex relationship which is valid in the state where the adoption took place after the parties moved to a state in which a same sex couple can not adopt a child? That is the issue in the next case.

EMBRY V. RYAN
11 SO.3D 408 (FLA. APP. 2 DIST., 2009)

Lara Embry appeals an order dismissing with prejudice her petition to determine parental responsibility, contact and support as to her adopted daughter.

In 2000, Embry and Kimberly Ryan, the child's biological mother, were engaged in a romantic relationship while living in the state of Washington. Ryan gave birth to the child on February 12, 2000, and Embry adopted her on May 10, 2000. After moving to Florida, the parties ended their relationship in 2004. During that same year, the parties entered into a child custody, visitation and property settlement agreement. Apparently, the relationship between the parties further deteriorated, and in October 2007, Ryan refused to allow Embry to have any visitation with the child. Embry thereafter filed the petition to determine parental responsibility, contact and support. Ryan moved to dismiss Embry's petitions, arguing that Florida was not required to give full faith and credit to the Washington adoption because, Ryan alleges, it is contrary to the public policy of Florida prohibiting same-sex couple adoptions. We reverse because the trial court was required to give the Washington adoption judgment full faith and credit.

The United States Constitution's Full Faith and Credit Clause provides as follows: "Full Faith and Credit shall be given in each State to the public Acts, Records, and judicial Proceedings of every other State. And the Congress may by general Laws pre-

scribe the Manner in which such Acts, Records and Proceedings shall be proved, and the Effect thereof." U.S. Const. Art. IV, § 1. In interpreting the Full Faith and Credit Clause, the United States Supreme Court has held that "[a] final judgment in one State, if rendered by a court with adjudicatory authority over the subject matter and persons governed by the judgment, qualifies for recognition throughout the land." Further, there are no public policy exceptions to the full faith and credit which is due to judgments entered in another state.

We note that Florida law specifically provides that adoption decrees from other states must be recognized in this state: A judgment ... establishing the relationship of parent and child by adoption issued pursuant to due process of law by a court of any other jurisdiction within or without the United States shall be recognized in this state, and the rights and obligations of the parties on matters within the jurisdiction of this state shall be determined as though the judgment were issued by a court of this state.

Embry therefore must be given the same rights as any other adoptive parent in Florida. Regardless of whether the trial court believed that the Washington adoption violated a clearly established public policy in Florida, it was improper for the trial court to refuse to give the Washington judgment full faith and credit.

SECTION 12.9
COMITY

Comity is derived from the Latin word "comitas" which means courteous. In the arena of international law, this principle allows for the courteous recognition of the rules and laws of a foreign jurisdiction. States are simply not mandated to enforce the laws and judgments of another country. Rather, each determines on its own the extent to which it will provide courtesy and respect to a foreign sovereign taking into consideration the state's international obligations and rights of its own citizens.[14] Generally, as long as the laws of another country are not contrary to public policy or prejudicial to the interests of the forum jurisdiction, the law will be upheld.

The death penalty is not uniformly supported around the world. This issue of philosophical differences can strain relations between countries–even those sovereignties with which we otherwise maintain good relations. This fact is evident in two recent cases in which the United States has sought the return of a person from a foreign country in order to face murder charges in which the death penalty could be imposed.

A new generation has learned the name of Ira Einhorn, a man dubbed the "Unicorn Killer." This 1960's activist was charged with the Philadelphia murder of Holly Maddux, whose mummified body was found in a steamer trunk in Einhorn's closet. Shortly before his criminal trial, the defendant disappeared. Nevertheless, the trial went on in his absence, and Einhorn was found guilty of first-degree murder and was sentenced to death. After twenty years on the run, Einhorn was located in France in 1997. That country, however, refused to return him to the United States because of its opposition to the death penalty. It was only after the Pennsylvania legislature agreed that Einhorn would not face the death penalty and that he would be granted a new trial that the French court ordered the fugitive's return to Philadelphia. That new trial was granted and Mr. Einhorn was convicted by a Philadelphia jury in 2002 of first degree murder despite his claim that Ms. Maddux was killed by the CIA.

Comity was the focal point of a New Jersey case dealing with whether a valid same-sex marriage in Canada between two New Jersey residents should be recognized in New Jersey. The court refused to validate the Canadian marriage because New Jersey had considered legalizing same-sex marriages but opted instead to limit their recognition to civil unions.

HENNEDELD V. TOWNSHIP OF MONTCLAIR
22 N.J. TAX 166 (2005)

This matter is on appeal from the Judgment of the Essex County Board of Taxation denying the application of Plaintiffs Louis Paul Hennefeld and Blair William O'Dell for a 100% disabled veteran's property tax exemption. Plaintiffs are the owners of real property located at 512 Park Street, in the Township of Montclair, County of Essex.

The facts are not in dispute. After approximately 15 years of service in the military, Mr. Hennefeld received an honorable discharge. Thereafter, the Veterans Administration determined that Mr. Hennefeld's "wartime service-connected disability was totally disabling."

The Plaintiffs are a same-sex couple who have lived together since September 1975. They purchased the subject property as their home on September 9, 1985, taking title as joint tenants with right of survivorship. Since 1985, the Plaintiffs have received a 50% disabled veteran's exemption on the subject property.

On October 22, 2003, the Plaintiffs were legally married under Canadian law in the city of Niagara Falls, Ontario, Canada.

The Plaintiffs filed an application with Mont-clair Tax Assessor on January 17, 2004, claiming that they qualified for a 100% disabled veteran's exemption. On March 1, 2004, the Tax Assessor issued the Plaintiffs a Notice of Disallowance of Claim for Veteran's Exemption/Deduction.

The Township's counsel indicated that pursuant to the Township's long-standing interpretation, the full disabled veteran's exemption is customarily approved when the qualified disabled veteran is married under a traditional marriage (i.e. male and female).

While it is undisputed that Plaintiffs were legally married under Canadian law, the court finds no basis under New Jersey law that would allow recognition of that marriage.

In urging this court to recognize their same-sex marriage in Canada, the Plaintiffs cite **Hilton v. Guyot, 159 U.S. 113 (1895)** arguing that "comity of nations" is an obligation that depends on considerations of international duty and convenience, and a preference for comity exists when the laws of the foreign nation are consistent with those of the sovereign. However, "[a]s a general matter, the laws of one nation do not have force or effect beyond its borders."

Furthermore, Comity, in the legal sense, is neither a matter of absolute obligation, on the one hand, nor of mere courtesy and good will, upon the other. But it is the recognition which one nation allows within its territory to the legislative, executive, or judicial acts of another nation, having due regard both to international duty and convenience....Comity is voluntary.

The Plaintiffs contend that since New Jersey has no law specifically declaring that same-sex marriage is against the State's public policy, their Canadian marriage should therefore be recognized in New Jersey. The court rejects this argument.

The Federal Government weighed in on the debate in 1996, when Congress enacted the Defense of Marriage Act ("DOMA"). DOMA provides that: No State, territory, or possession of the United States, shall be required to give effect to any public act, record, or judicial proceeding of any other State, territory, possession, or tribe respecting a relationship between persons of the same sex that is treated as a marriage under the laws of such other State, territory, possession, or tribe, or a right or claim arising from such relationship. DOMA states that, for federal purposes, marriage is solely the union between one man and one woman.

The debate over same-sex marriage has not eluded New Jersey. In the recent decision of **Lewis v. Harris, 2003 WL 23191114 (Law Div. 2003),** the court concluded that marriage statutes in New Jersey do not permit same-sex marriages, and the right to marry does not include a fundamental right to same-sex marriage.

After the decision in **Lewis v. Harris,** the New Jersey Legislature adopted the DPA recognizing domestic partnerships and providing domestic partners with certain "rights and benefits that are accorded to married couples." The legislative findings and declarations set forth in the DPA, as well as the Assembly Appropriations Committee Statement attached to that legislation, are nevertheless pertinent and instructive to ascertain legislative intent and public policy at the time of the DPA's adoption, concerning same-sex marriage.

In setting forth "a clear and rational basis" for making available certain health and pension benefits to same-sex domestic partners and not to opposite sex domestic partners, the Legislature found with regard to same-sex marriage that, domestic partnerships in which both persons are of the same sex, are unable to enter into a marriage with each other that

is recognized by New Jersey law, unlike persons of the opposite sex who are in a domestic partnership but have the right to enter into a marriage that is recognized by State law.

In the aftermath of the court's ruling in **Lewis v. Harris,** the Legislature had the opportunity to enact law permitting same-sex marriage in New Jersey. Instead, the Legislature provided certain rights and recognition to domestic partners through the enactment of the DPA, while also making it clear in that same legislation, that same-sex marriage is not recognized by New Jersey law.

This court finds that the marriage laws of Canada which recognize same-sex marriage are not consistent with those of New Jersey which do not recognize same-sex marriage. Moreover, the explicit legislative declarations of the DPA, along with the Committee Statement, set forth the public policy of this state against same-sex marriage. Accordingly, the Plaintiffs' Canadian marriage cannot be afforded comity in New Jersey.

SECTION 12.10
ALTERNATIVE
DISPUTE RESOLUTION

Controversies may be resolved in ways other than by using the state and federal court systems, which may be too time-consuming or expensive. Parties may agree to submit to any of a number of alternative methods for resolving their disputes. In considering an **alternative dispute resolution** mechanism, the parties will focus on factors such as cost, who will represent them, who will arbitrate the dispute, and whether the alternative method will lead to a more helpful or fair resolution.

Arbitration is often used in a commercial setting where both parties agree to have a third party or arbitrator resolve the controversy. When the parties agree to abide by the arbitrator's decision, they are involved in a binding arbitration, and the court will automatically enforce the arbitrator's award. Both parties must agree on who the impartial arbitrator will be. Arbitration proceedings are usually informal, and the parties are not bound by the rules of evidence that control court cases.

Because of the binding nature of arbitration, courts will rarely overturn an arbitrator's decision unless there is clear evidence of fraud or gross misconduct.

Mediation is used primarily in disputes between labor and management, but also is suited for disputes between neighbors and family members. Mediation is different from arbitration because it is advisory in nature. A mediator makes recommendations to the parties in order to aid them in solving their differences. Successful mediation will keep the parties out of court. Mediation is gaining popularity in divorce cases by helping the parties work out their differences.

Private judging is used when both sides are constrained by time and can afford to hire a private judge, usually a retired judge. Private judging proceeds as a normal trial would be conducted.

Non-binding or **mini-trials** are another form of private dispute resolution in which the parties may or may not be represented by a lawyer. The parties usually submit their case to a panel of experts and a neutral advisor, who aids both sides. The panel and advisor suggest the likely outcome if the case were to go to court. This method is helpful for business disputes involving long processes of fact-finding.

Neighborhood Justice Centers derive from a program initiated in the 1970s. The centers receive their cases from local police or magistrates' offices. The cases usually involve neighborhood or family disputes, in which the two sides represent themselves before a panel of local residents. The aim is to avoid having the disputes escalate to the point where the criminal court system takes over.

SECTION 12.11 PROBLEM CASES

1. Francis Thomas received an envelope at his New Jersey home with a return address from the Philadelphia Chamber of Commerce. Upon opening the letter, he discovered two tickets to a Philadelphia 76ers game. Mr. Thomas could not believe his good fortune and took his son to the contest at the First Union Center. During the second period, the Sheriff tapped Thomas on the shoulder and served him with a lawsuit concerning a motor vehicle accident that had happened one year earlier in New Jersey. Does the Philadelphia Court have jurisdiction over this New Jersey resident because Thomas was served with the lawsuit within its boundaries? See: **M. H. Eastburn v. Saul Turnoff, 147 A.2d 353 (Pa., 1959).**

2. Robert DeLuca had a long history of being involved in violent crimes. During his criminal trial for extortion, the trial judge empaneled an anonymous jury in order to safeguard the panel members' identity and to prevent jury tampering. Spectators were also screened and had to produce identification before being allowed into the courtroom. DeLuca claimed that his Sixth Amendment right to a public trial was violated by the judge's unusual actions. Do you agree? **United States v. Robert DeLuca, 96-1173, (1st Cir. Ct., 1998).**

3. A franchise agreement between Charles Jones and General Nutrition Companies, Inc., required that all disputes concerning the agreement be litigated in a Pennsylvania venue. Jones operated a GNC store in California. Following a dispute with General Nutrition, he sued GNC in California where his store was located, the contracts were entered into and the majority of witnesses resided. GNC requested a change of venue so that the case could be removed to Pennsylvania based upon the forum selection clause in the contract even though California does not favor this type of clause. Where should the case be heard? **Charles Jones v. GNC Franchising, Inc., CV-98-10611-DMT (9th Cir. Ct., 2000).**

4. Beer Across America sold beer to a minor via the Internet. The liquor was shipped from the store's location in Illinois to the child's home in Alabama. After the parents returned home from vacation, they discovered the beer in the refrigerator. This prompted the parents to file a suit in Alabama against the Illinois company for the unlawful sale of liquor to a minor. Beer Across America was not registered to do business in Alabama, and it owned no property within the state. Is a passive Internet site that can be accessed from anywhere in the world sufficient to confer jurisdiction over a non-resident defendant for doing business in Alabama? **Lynda Butler v. Beer Across America, 83 F. Supp. 2d 1261 (2000).**

SECTION 12.12
INTERNET REFERENCES

To learn more information about the court system and the jury selection process, see the following sites:

A. **The Jury Process**

- **www.fija.org**
  This is the official website for the Fully Informed Jury Association, a non-profit educational association devoted to providing information about jury duty, including a citizen's guide to this citizen function, and frequently asked questions.

- **www.edwright.com/voir_dire_intro.html**
  Tips on the voir dire process are offered on this site, which is maintained by an attorney.

- **www.geocities.com/heartland/7394/lysander.html**
  A historical justification for trial by jury is presented in this article.

B. **The Court**

- **www.law.emory.edu/caselaw**
  This site features federal court decisions from 1995 through the present.

- **http://law.about.com/newsissues/law/library/courts b1899_toc.htm**
  This site provides a general discussion on the federal court system.

- **www.uscourts.gov/faq.html**
  This Federal Judiciary homepage provides answers to frequently asked questions about the federal court system.

- **www.supremecourtus.gov**
  The Supreme Court's official site is contained at this address and contain copies of the Court's opinions, Court rules, and other general information.

- **http://vis.law.villanova.edu/locator/federalcourt.html**
  Villanova University School of Law maintains this website which provides access to federal court decisions from the district court to the United States Supreme Court. The law school's website also maintains a variety of links to legal magazines and search engines for law related subjects. You may access this site through:
  http://vls.law.villanova.edu/library/express/

- **www.aopc.org/index/ujs/courtswork.htm**
  An overview of the Pennsylvania's court system can be found at this address.

- **http://oyez.nwu.edu**
  Northwestern University maintains this multimedia data base and virtual tour of the United States Supreme Court.

Footnotes:

1. **Marbury v. Madison** http://usinfo.state.gov/usa/infousa/facts/democrac/9.htm.
2. "About U.S. Federal Courts," U.S. Courts, www.uscourts.gov/about.html.
3. "United States Supreme Court," U.S. Courts, www.uscourts.gov/supreme-court.html.
4. Greve, "Does the Court Mean Business?," Federalist Outlook, September 20, 2007, www.aei.org/publications/pubID.926834/pub_detail.asp.
5. Supreme Court of the United States, Supreme Court Historical Society, http://www.supremecourthistory.org/.
6. *How the Court Works,* The Supreme Court Historical Society, www.suprmecourthistory.org.
7. *Id.*
8. **Williams v. Florida, 399 U.S. 78 (1970).**
9. **Duncan v. Louisiana, 88 S. Ct. 1444 (1968).**
10. *American Bar Association Points: Trial by Jury,* www.abanet.org.
11. See: *Criminal Justice Across Europe,* www.crimeinfo.org.uk.
12. Civil Justice Statistics, U.S. Department of Justice, Bureau of Justice Statistics, http://www.ojp.usdoj.gov/bjs/civil.htm.
13. Shrager and Frost, "The Quotable Lawyer," Facts on File, at 152.
14. New York Times, February 3, 1969 as cited in the "Quotable Lawyer" at 154.
15. American Bar Association Journal, November 1995, page 72.
16. *Id.*
17. See: *Lesson 7-9: Voir Dire,* American Bar Association.
18. *Judgment of the Court of Foreign Countries as Entitled to Enforcement of Extraterritorial Effect in State Court,* 13 A. L R. 4th 1109.

KEY TERMS

Activist
Alternative Dispute Resolution
American Arbitration
   Association
Appellate Court
Arbitration
Article III
Article IV
Certiorari
Circuit Court of Appeals
Comity
Commonwealth Court
Court of Common Pleas
Court of Federal Claims
District Court
Driver's License Compact
Federal Court
Federal Mediation and
   Conciliation Service
Forum Non-Conveniens
Full, Faith and Credit
Judicial Restraint Oriented
Jurisdiction
Jurisdiction over the Person
Jury

Long Arm Statute
Magna Carta
Mediation
Minimum Contacts
Municipal Court
Neighborhood Justice Centers
One-Day or One-Trial
Original Jurisdiction
Private Judging
Questions-of-Facts
Questions-of-Law
Rule of Hour
Service
Seventh Amendment
Sixth Amendment
Standing
State Court
State Supreme Court
Subject Matter Jurisdiction
Superior Court
Supreme Court Rule 10
United States Supreme Court
Venue
Voir Dire

CHAPTER 13

ETHICS AND THE LAW
BY: TERRY ANN HALBERT, ESQ.

SECTION 13.1 AN OVERVIEW OF ETHICS

Peter Christopher is walking through a park and is attracted to the sight of a pond where children are swimming. He notices that some of the children's cries sound more like desperation than enjoyment, and he realizes that a child is drowning. Christopher is a trained lifeguard. Since he is on the way to a concert, and not in the mood to get his clothes wet, Christopher turns and walks away from the pond. Would he be violating the law by failing to help the child in distress?

Surprisingly, the answer is no. Our legal system, which was greatly influenced by the notions of individual freedom, will not force a person to help a stranger in an emergency unless that person has somehow caused the problem in the first place or there is a special relationship between the parties, such as a parent and child. If, as in this example, an individual just happens to discover a stranger in grave danger, that person is legally allowed to continue walking without stopping to help.

This principle is probably understandable in terms of the basic principles of our legal system, which generally finds a person liable for some wrong or careless action, not for inaction, not for something they failed to do. There are also practical reasons why the law backs away from demanding a rescue in these kinds of situations: Where is the line to be drawn? Who should rescue? Is everyone who hears the child screaming responsible for jumping in the pond to help? And how much help is enough? Suppose a person cannot swim, or suppose the pond is polluted?

But beyond the law is the concept of what is right, what is **ethical**. One might believe that there are ethical reasons for trying to help the drowning child, regardless of what the law expects. In fact, this is the major difference between law and ethics: the law is about what one must do to avoid liability, while ethics is about what one should do; about "doing the right thing."

Legal and ethical responsibilities do not necessarily overlap. The "No Duty To Rescue Rule" or "American Bystander Rule" demonstrates this point. Often the ethically right decision goes beyond the expectations of the law, sometimes far beyond. The gap between law and ethics is demonstrated in the following case involving the duty owed by a victim to her assailant when she injures or kills him in self-defense. The case also provides an overview of the law involving the duty to rescue.

STATE OF MONTANA V. MONTANA THIRTEENTH JUDICIAL DISTRICT COURT
298 MONT. 146 (MONT., 2000)

Yellowstone County Sheriff's deputies were dispatched on April 19, 1998, to the home of Bonnie Kuntz and Warren Becker to investigate a reported stabbing. When the deputies arrived at the trailer house, Becker was dead from a single stab wound to the chest.

Kuntz told the deputies that she and Becker had argued the morning of April 18, 1998. At some point during the day, both parties left the trailer home. After Kuntz returned that evening, a physical altercation ensued. The alleged facts indicate that Kuntz and Becker, who had never married but had lived together for approximately six years, were in the process of ending a stormy relationship. When Kuntz arrived at the mobile home that night, she discovered that many of her personal belongings had been destroyed and the phone ripped from the wall. Kuntz told the deputies that she then went into the kitchen and Becker physically attacked her, and at one point grabbed her by the hair, shook her, and slammed her into the stove.

Kuntz told the deputies that she could not clearly remember what happened; only that she had pushed Becker away and had then gone outside by the kitchen door to "cool off." When she thought it was safe to go back inside, she returned to the kitchen. She discovered a trail of blood leading from the kitchen through the living room and out onto the front porch where she found Becker collapsed face-down on the porch. Kuntz does not allege that she personally contacted medical or law enforcement personnel; rather, authorities were summoned by Kuntz's sister-in-law.

Kuntz was charged with negligent homicide for causing the death of Becker by stabbing him in the chest. Kuntz entered a plea of not guilty based on the defense of justifiable use of force. Shortly before

trial, the State filed amended information alleging that Kuntz caused the death of Becker by stabbing him once in the chest with a knife *and* by failing to call for medical assistance.

For criminal liability to be based upon a failure to act, there must be a duty imposed by the law to act, and the person must be physically capable of performing the act. As a starting point in our analysis, the parties have identified what is referred to as *"the American bystander rule."* This rule imposes no legal duty on a person to rescue or summon aid for another person who is at risk or in danger, even though society recognizes that a moral obligation might exist. This is true even "when that aid can be rendered without danger or inconvenience to" the potential rescuer, **Pope v. State, 284 Md. 309.** Thus, an Olympic swimmer may be deemed by the community as a shameful coward, or worse, for not rescuing a drowning child in the neighbor's pool, but she is not a criminal.

But this rule is far from absolute. Professors La Fave and Scott have identified several common-law exceptions to the American bystander rule: 1) a duty based on a personal relationship, such as parent-child or husband-wife; 2) a duty based on statute; 3) a duty based upon voluntary assumption of care; and 4) a duty based on creation of the peril. Our review of the issues presented here can accordingly be narrowed to a duty based upon a personal relationship and a duty based on creation of the peril.

One of the lead authorities on the personal relationship duty arose in **State v. Mally, 139 Mont. 599 (1961).** This Court held that a husband has a duty to summon medical aid for his wife and a breach of that duty could render him criminally liable. The facts of the case described how Kay Mally, who was suffering from terminal kidney disease, fell and fractured her arms on a Tuesday evening. Her husband, Michael Mally, put her to bed and did not summon a doctor until Thursday morning. "During this period of time, she received but one glass of water." Although his wife ultimately died of kidney failure, Mally was found guilty of involuntary manslaughter.

As for a personal relationship other than husband and wife, a duty cannot be extended to a temporary, non-family relationship. For instance, a married defendant has no duty to summon medical help for his mistress, who was staying in his house for the weekend, after she took morphine following a bout of heavy drinking and fell into a "stupor."

When a person places another in a position of danger, and then fails to safeguard or rescue that person, and the person subsequently dies as a result of this omission, such an omission may be sufficient to support criminal liability. The legal duty based on creation of the peril has been extended in other jurisdictions to cases involving self-defense.

The legal duty imposed on personal relationships and those who create peril are not absolute; i.e., there are exceptions to these exceptions. The personal relationship legal duty, for example, does not require a person to jeopardize his own life. See **State v. Walden, 306 N.C. 466** (stating that although a parent has a legal duty to prevent harm to his or her child, this is not to say that parents have the legal duty to place themselves in danger of death or great bodily harm in coming to the aid of their children).

Similarly, the law does not require that a person, who places another person in a position of peril, risk bodily injury or death in the performance of the legally imposed duty to render assistance. Therefore, where self-preservation is at stake, the law does not require a person to save the other's life by sacrificing his own.

Does one who justifiably uses deadly force in defense of her person nevertheless have a legal duty to summon aid for the mortally wounded attacker? We hold that when a person justifiably uses force to fend off an aggressor, that person has no duty to assist her aggressor in any manner that may conceivably create a risk of bodily injury or death to herself, or other persons. This absence of a duty necessarily includes any conduct that would require the person to remain in, or return to, the zone of risk created by the original aggressor. We find no authority that suggests that the law should require a person, who is justified in her use of force, to subsequently check the pulse of her attacker, or immediately dial 911, before retreating to safety.

We conclude that the victim has but one duty after fending off an attack, and that is the duty owed to one's self-as a matter of self-preservation-to seek and secure safety away from the place the attack occurred. Thus, the person who justifiably acts in self-defense is temporarily afforded the same status as the innocent bystander.

QUESTIONS FOR DISCUSSION:

1. Could there have been any circumstance in this case that would have resulted in liability against Bonnie Kuntz?

2. Should the duty of rescue when a special relationship exists between the parties be limited to those of spouses and parents and children?

3. Can you think of an example of a duty created by statute to help another?

4. France requires people to go to the aid of another. What country's law do you think is better?

The Hippocratic Oath, one of the oldest documents applicable to heath care professionals, requires physicians to use their best efforts to treat and cure patients. In fact, one of the tenets provides that a doctor shall remember that he or she is a member of society, with special obligations to fellow human beings, including those of sound mind and body as well as the infirm. Does this tenet change the "No Duty to Rescue Rule" and impose a legal obligation upon a physician to help another in need of medical care? Consider the following case:

WILSON V. ATHENS-LIMESTONE HOSPITAL
894 SO.2D 630 (ALA., 2004)

Ms. Wilson, as mother of Starsha L. Wilson, deceased, brought a medical-malpractice action against the hospital and Dr. Bibi Teng, who was a pediatrician, employed by the hospital, alleging that Dr. Teng wrongfully caused the death of her four-year-old daughter, Starsha Wilson, by not providing proper care while Starsha was a patient in the emergency room of the hospital.

The record reveals that Starsha was diagnosed with sickle-cell anemia and Dr. Teng became Starsha's regular pediatrician. Dr. Teng had instructed Wilson to take Starsha to the emergency room and to telephone Dr. Teng whenever Starsha had a fever of 101 degrees or higher.

On the morning of May 19, 1994, Starsha's temperature was 105 degrees, so Wilson rushed Starsha to the emergency room. The emergency room nurses checked Starsha's vital signs, and Dr. Patrick Tucker, an emergency room doctor, ordered medication for pain and fever, blood work, a renal profile, and a chest X-ray.

Dr. Teng testified that as she was leaving the hospital, she was informed that Starsha was in the emergency room, and she decided to stop by on the way out of the hospital. When Dr. Teng arrived at the emergency room, she briefly talked to both Wilson and Starsha and told Wilson that she would talk to Dr. Osborn, an emergency room physician, before she left the hospital.

After briefly discussing Starsha's case with Dr. Osborn, Dr. Teng returned and told Wilson that "everything looked good" and that Dr. Osborn would take good care of Starsha. Dr. Teng also told Wilson that Starsha had a mild infection.

Dr. Osborn discharged Starsha from the hospital but Starsha returned to the emergency room in cardiac arrest. Dr. Teng returned to the emergency room and attempted to resuscitate Starsha, but was unsuccessful, and Starsha died. The cause of death was an infection, a complication of sickle-cell anemia.

Dr. Teng testified that on Starsha's first visit to the emergency room, Dr. Teng did not have a physician-patient relationship with Starsha. Dr. Teng further testified that it would have been improper for her to take over Starsha's care because Starsha was an emergency room patient and Dr. Osborn was the emergency room physician when Starsha was admitted. Dr. Osborn testified that she was Starsha's doctor on that morning and that all decisions concerning Starsha's care, including the decision to discharge Starsha, were made by her.

Liability for medical malpractice depends, first, on the existence of a duty to the patient, which, in turn depends on the existence of a physician-patient relationship creating the duty. The following is the general rule concerning the creation of a physician-patient relationship:

> A physician is under no obligation to engage in practice or to accept professional employment, but when the professional services of a physician are accepted by another person for the purposes of medical or surgical treatment, the relation of physician and patient is created. The relationship between a physician and patient may result from an express or implied contract, and the rights and liabilities of the parties thereto are governed by the general law of contract, although the existence of the relation does not need to rest on any express contract between the physician and the person treated.

Wilson argues that Dr. Teng owed Starsha a duty to intervene in Dr. Osborn's treatment of Starsha.

In **Dodd-Anderson v. Stevens, 905 F. Supp. 937 (D. Kan., 1995),** the court, under similar circumstances, held that a duty did not exist. We find the following rationale from **Dodd-Anderson** persuasive:

> This court is not persuaded by the expert's opinion that defendant had a duty to assume control of the patient's care and order her immediate transfer. The court finds that no reasonable person, applying contemporary standards, would recognize and agree that a physician has, or should have, a legal duty to unilaterally and perhaps forcibly override the medical judgment of another physician, particularly a treating physician. The list of adverse consequences to the medical community and to patients is obvious and endless and need not be elaborated upon. The result would be medical, and ultimately legal, chaos.

While there are possible factual scenarios where such a duty may exist, the specific facts of this case do not create such a duty. The undisputed facts show that Dr. Teng did not treat or diagnose Starsha during Starsha's first visit to the emergency room on the day Starsha died and did not prescribe any medication or give any medical advice on that first visit. The emergency-room doctors, Dr. Osborn and Dr. Tucker, retained control over Starsha's course of treatment at all times during that first visit. There is no evidence showing that their medical treatment of Starsha was such that Dr. Teng had a duty to override their independent medical judgment. Under these facts, we hold that as a matter of law Dr. Teng did not have a duty to intervene in Starsha's treatment by Dr. Osborn.

QUESTIONS FOR DISCUSSION:

1. Should people who are trained to rescue or assist others in emergency situations be held to a higher standard of care?

2. The Hippocratic Oath, which outlines the ethical goals of doctors, contains the following promise: "According to my power and judgment to use the medical knowledge for the benefit of those who suffer, as judged by myself to be fair, and to avoid from doing any harm or injustice." Did Dr. Teng violate the Hippocratic Oath?

All states contain Good Samaritan statutes that protect people who are medically trained from being held liable in an emergency rescue should they decide to help. These laws, however, do not demand that the medically-trained offer assistance in these situations. Today a doctor may decide to "walk on by," unless she or he is already treating the patient, or is on duty in a medical facility offering treatment.

Over the years, a few exceptions to the "No Duty to Rescue Rule" have developed. There is the "Special Relationship" exception: between members of a family, between employers and employees, between providers of public transportation and passengers, or between owners of business and their customers, for instance, the law insists on a reasonable attempt at assistance in an emergency. So, if the person in the park was a father who was hearing his own drowning daughter's screams, he would have a duty to take reasonable steps to help her.

SECTION 13.2
ETHICAL THEORIES

If ethics is about choosing the right behavior, the moral way to live one's life, how does society achieve this goal? There are many different ethical beliefs individuals can hold. Abortion is just one example of an issue that separates people who have very strong but completely opposite ethical beliefs. And in a multicultural society, doesn't it become even more difficult to decide on one single ethically correct position? Who is to say which personal or cultural ethical standard is correct or is there a universal ethic?

For centuries, human beings have struggled to determine the answers to these types of questions. Within Western civilization, two major philosophical theories about ethics have evolved:

1. **Utilitarian Theory:** Focuses on the consequences—both short and long term—of any particular action for all individuals affected. Benefits and harms are balanced against one another, to determine which action produces the most happiness for the greatest number of people.

2. **Rights Theory:** Concerned with the reasons for action, not just the results. People have certain basic rights—the right to life, freedom of expression, privacy, for instance—that are of value in themselves and must be pro-

tected. This theory also includes the notion of "Universality:" Whatever we choose to do must be behavior we would be willing to have done to everyone, including to ourselves—a version of the Golden Rule.

Sometimes these two theories serve the same purpose. For example, a student who sees another student cheating on an exam employs her freedom of expression to alert the professor. Not only has she acted for ethical reasons — the Rights Theory — but she has come to the aid of the rest of the class, who benefit by having their grades accurately measured. Thus, she has also acted in accordance with the Utilitarian Theory, the greatest good (better grades) for the greatest number (the rest of the class).

Occasionally, however, the two theories are diametrically opposed to each other. The classic example is slavery, where a minority of the population is enslaved, but the rest of society benefited economically. Before the Civil War, the economy of the Southern states prospered, providing the greatest good to the greatest number and satisfying the Utilitarian Theory. But the Rights Theory suffered, since human beings were enslaved, prevented from enjoying the same rights as the other members of society.

Can you think of other examples where the two philosophies go hand-in-hand? How about situations where they diverge? Consider these examples when you work on the following problem.

Park, Brown & Smith, P.C.
Attorneys at Law
Memorandum

To:	All Law Clerks
From:	Peter Smith, Esquire
Re:	Kathy Roberts and Eastcoast Airlines

Kathy Roberts decided to obtain a job in order to prove to her parents that she has finally grown up. To her credit, she landed a position in the real estate department of Eastcoast Airlines.

Eastcoast has tried to diversify by acquiring a number of properties in Florida. Eastcoast Airlines, like so many of its competitors, has been suffering substantial losses in the years since airline deregulation, and has a negative cash flow. Unless the company can control its high labor costs and increase its popularity with the flying public, bankruptcy is a possibility. Kathy's boss, Robert Stingle sees selling off the Florida properties, as an important way of alleviating the company's financial crisis.

Kathy contacted Silvertooth, Inc., a developer of nursing homes, about the sale of the Florida properties and found an interested buyer. The corporation thought that one of the parcels would be perfect for a retirement villa and would feature elaborate walking trails and outdoor recreational facilities.

Eastcoast had conducted a full environmental audit of the property six months earlier, and no problems were revealed. A copy of the report was given to a Silvertooth representative who also examined the property and discovered no problems.

As negotiations progressed with Silvertooth, Kathy was approached by one of her friends at Eastcoast, Steve Flame. He told Kathy that there is highly toxic waste on the property that she is attempting to transfer to Silvertooth, Inc. The person who told Steve about the situation was recently in Florida at the site, and had found several buried metal containers marked "Danger! Biohazard. Radioactive medical waste." The containers were cracked and liquid was seeping out onto the ground. Steve said he wanted Kathy to know about the dangerous condition because he was concerned that innocent people would be harmed if the sale went through.

Kathy contacted her boss, but before she could mention the containers, Stingle told her it was vital that the sale be closed quickly, and that their jobs at the airline depended on it. Kathy consulted with a lawyer who explained that Florida law does not require disclosure of hazardous substances on commercial property so long as there hasn't been a fraudulent misstatement about the condition of the property.

Kathy is very upset. She knows that Silvertooth is considering other similar properties, and if she mentions the toxic spill problem to the potential buyer, they will back out of the sale. Kathy also realizes that she will never deal with Silvertooth again since Eastcoast didn't own any other property that is suitable for a retirement community.

Although there may be no legal consequences if Kathy says nothing, and allows the sale to go through, from an ethical perspective the situation might be different. Write an advisory memo to Kathy on the ethics of the choice she must make, "To Disclose or Not To Disclose?"

1. First apply the Utilitarian Theory. Who are the people affected by Kathy's decision? What choice would result in "the greatest good for the greatest number?"

2. Now do the analysis from the Rights Theory perspective. What rights do the various affected individuals and groups have in this situation? How do they weigh against one another? What would be the result if Kathy thinks about the Golden Rule?

3. Finally, summarize your own ethical opinion: If you were in Kathy's shoes, what would you do, and why?

ANSWER SHEET
PROBLEM THIRTEEN—A

Name _____   **Please Print Clearly**

1. First apply the Utilitarian Theory. Who are the people affected by Kathy's decision? What choice would probably result in "the greatest good for the greatest number?"

_____

_____

_____

_____

_____

_____

_____

_____

2. Now do the analysis from the Rights Theory perspective. What rights do the various affected individuals and groups have in this situation? How do they weigh against one another? What would be the result if Kathy thinks about the Golden Rule?

_____

_____

_____

_____

_____

_____

_____

_____

3. Finally, summarize your own ethical opinion: If you were in Kathy's shoes, what would you do, and why?

_____

_____

_____

_____

_____

_____

_____

_____

_____

_____

_____

_____

_____

_____

_____

_____

_____

_____

SECTION 13.4
THE WHISTLEBLOWER

Suppose Kathy decides to warn Silvertooth about the hazardous waste and the deal falls through. Kathy feels good about this outcome, but not so good when she discovers that she has been fired. Since all her other work for Eastcoast has been highly commended, Ms. Roberts believes she was fired in retaliation for letting the toxic cat out of the bag. (Under the federal "Superfund" law, Eastcoast as owner of the property will be responsible for paying for the clean up of the site.)

Kathy is a **whistleblower,** a person who feels compelled to get certain information into the hands of the people who can act to correct a problem, when it seems that the problem won't be corrected otherwise. When employees "blow the whistle," they might tell a superior, or they might go outside their company and tell government authorities, or even the media.

There is no one exact definition of a whistleblower. As the court noted in **Winters v. Houston Chronicle Pub. Co., 795 S.W.2d 723 (Tex., 1990),** a whistleblower is the person who sounds the alarm "when wrongdoing occurs on his or her beat, which is usually within a large organization." Another definition is set forth in a report co-edited by Ralph Nader in which it was said that whistleblowing is "the act of a man or woman who, believing that the public interest overrides the interest of the organization he serves, publicly blows the whistle if the organization is involved in corrupt, illegal, fraudulent, or harmful activity." *Whistle Blowing: The Report of the Conference on Professional Responsibility*, R. Nader, P. Petkas & K. Blackwell, eds. 1972.

What are Kathy's legal rights in this situation? She may have none. Unless she has an employment contract with Eastcoast for a certain stated period, she is an **employee at will**. (Most employees fall into this category.) Generally speaking, an employer can fire at-will employees at any time for any reason, or for no reason at all, unless the reason violates a statute, such as a law against discrimination on the basis of race, gender, age, or handicap. Kathy might also be protected if she was part of the 14 percent of American workers who belong to a union. She could then argue she was fired in violation of a collective bargaining agreement between her union and her employer. (A union contract generally provides that workers cannot be fired unless for "just cause.)" Finally, some state and federal laws protect whistleblowers who report violations of those laws to the government. For instance, Congress passed the **Whistleblower Protection Act of 1989** in order to strengthen and improve the protections of federal employees who report fraud, waste, abuse and unnecessary expenditures within the government. The Act, however, does not allow an employee to file a lawsuit for retaliation by a supervisor. Instead, the worker must pursue an administrative remedy that is usually administered by the U. S. Department of Labor. A number of states have also passed laws protecting the whistleblower. For instance, Pennsylvania has enacted the **Whistleblower's Law** which provides that no employer may discharge, or otherwise retaliate against an employee because the employee makes a good faith report or is about to report to the employer or appropriate authority, an instance of wrongdoing or waste. A person who alleges a violation of this Act may bring a civil action within 180 days after the occurrence of the alleged violation. **43 P. S. §1421.** The Superfund law, for example, would protect Kathy if she had gone straight to the Environmental Protection Agency with news about the spill. Since she told Silvertooth, she may not be protected.

Why does the law give so much freedom to employers to hire and fire workers as they see fit? Is "employment at will" a fair rule? How should society strike a balance between an employer's right to control and an employee's right to bring ethical concerns forward without fear of retaliation? Consider these issues as you read **Geary v. United States Steel Corporation.** In it, the Pennsylvania Supreme Court deals with the tort of "wrongful discharge," which would hold an employer responsible for firing an employee in a way that violates public policy. The case is one of first impression.

GEORGE GEARY V. UNITED STATES STEEL CORPORATION
319 A.2D 174 (PA. SUPER., 1974)

The complaint avers that appellant, George Geary, was continuously employed by appellee, United States Steel Corporation from 1953 until July 13, 1967, when he was dismissed from his position. Geary's duties involved the sale of tubular products to the oil and gas industry. His employment was at will. The dismissal is said to have stemmed from a disagreement concerning one of the company's new products, a tubular casing designed for use under high pressure. Geary alleges that he believed the product had not been adequately tested and constituted a serious danger to anyone who used it; that he voiced his misgivings to his superiors and was ordered to "follow directions," which he agreed to do; that he nevertheless continued to express his reservations, taking his case to a vice-president in charge of sale of the product; that as a result of his efforts the product was reevaluated and withdrawn from the market; that he at all times performed his duties to the best of his ability and always acted with the best interests of the company and the general

public in mind; and that because of these events he was summarily discharged without notice. Geary asserts that the company's conduct in so acting was "wrongful, malicious and abusive."

[Geary] candidly admits that he is beckoning us into uncharted territory. No court in this Commonwealth has ever recognized a non-statutory cause of action for an employer's termination of an at-will employment relationship. Pennsylvania law is in accordance with the weight of authority elsewhere. Absent a statutory or contractual provision to the contrary, the law has taken for granted the power of either party to terminate an employment relationship for any or no reason.

We recognize that economic conditions have changed radically since [the turn of the century, when employment at will was first established.] The huge corporate enterprises which have emerged in this century wield an awesome power over their employees.

Against the background of these changes, the broad question to which [Geary] invites our attention is whether the time has come to impose judicial restrictions on an employer's power of discharge. [His] argument is an appeal to considerations of public policy. Geary asserts in his complaint that he was acting in the best interests of the general public as well as of his employer in opposing the marketing of a product which he believed to be defective. Certainly, the potential for abuse of an employer's power of dismissal is particularly serious where an employee must exercise independent, expert judgment in matters of product safety, but Geary does not hold himself out as this sort of employee. So far as the complaint shows, he was involved only in the sale of company products. There is no suggestion that he possessed any expert qualifications, or that his duties extended to making judgments in matters of product safety. In essence, Geary argues that his conduct should be protected because his intentions were good. No doubt most employees who are dismissed from their posts can make the same claim. We doubt that establishing a right to litigate every such case as it arises would operate either in the best interest of the parties or of the public.

Given the rapidity of change in corporate personnel in the areas of employment not covered by labor agreements, suits like the one at bar could well be expected to place a heavy burden on our judicial system in terms of both an increased case load. Of greater concern is the possible impact of such suits on the legitimate interest of employers in hiring and retaining the best personnel available. The ever-present threat of suit might well inhibit the making of critical judgments by employers concerning employee qualifications.

The problem extends beyond the question of individual competence, for even an unusually gifted person may be of no use to his employer if he cannot work effectively with fellow employees. Here, for example, Geary's complaint shows that he by-passed his immediate superiors and pressed his views on higher officers, utilizing his close contacts with a company vice president. The praiseworthiness of Geary's motives does not detract from the company's legitimate interest in preserving its normal operational procedures from disruption. In sum, while we agree that employees should be encouraged to express their educated views on the quality of their employer's products, we are not persuaded that creating a new non-statutory cause of action of the sort proposed by appellant is the best way to achieve this result. On balance, whatever public policy imperatives can be discerning here seem to militate against such a course.

It may be granted that there are areas of an employee's life in which his employer has no legitimate interest. An intrusion into one of these areas by virtue of the employer's power of discharge might plausibly give rise to a cause of action, particularly where some recognized facet of public policy is threatened. But this case does not require us to define in comprehensive fashion the perimeters of this privilege, and we decline to do so. We hold only that where the complaint itself discloses a plausible and legitimate reason for terminating an at-will employment relationship and no clear mandate of public policy is violated thereby, an employee at will has no right of action against his employer for wrongful discharge.

QUESTIONS FOR DISCUSSION:

1. What are the reasons for the court's decision?

2. Would the case have turned out differently if the tubular casings Geary was worried about were being manufactured in violation of federal safety regulations?

3. Do you agree with the court's decision?

Partly in response to this case, the Pennsylvania legislature passed the following law on whistle-blowing:

> No employer may discharge, threaten or otherwise discriminate or retaliate against an employee regarding the employee's compensation, terms, conditions, location of privileges of employment because the employee...makes a good faith report or is about to report, verbally or in writing, to the employer or appropriate authority an instance of wrongdoing or waste.

> It shall be a defense to an action under this section if the defendant proves...that the action taken by the employer occurred for separate and legitimate reasons, which are not merely pretextual.

Here are some of the definitions of terms used in Pennsylvania's whistleblower law:

Appropriate authority: A federal, state or local government body, agency or organization.

Employee: A person who performs a service for wages or other remuneration under a contract of hire, written or oral, for a public body.

Good faith report: A report of conduct defined in this act as wrongdoing or waste which is made without malice or consideration of personal benefit and which the person making the report has reasonable cause to believe is true.

Waste: An employer's conduct or omissions which result in substantial abuse, misuse, destruction or loss of funds or resources belonging to or derived from Commonwealth or political subdivision sources.

Wrongdoing: A violation that is not of a merely technical or minimal nature of a federal or state statute or regulation or of a code of conduct or ethics designed to protect the interest of the public or the employer.

QUESTIONS FOR DISCUSSION:

1. Considering the definitions as well as the body of law, would Kathy Roberts be protected for telling Silvertooth about the toxic spill? Why or why not? Would George Geary be protected?

2. Write your own version of a whistleblower law.

SECTION 13.5
ETHICS, LAW
AND PRIVACY

It may be granted that there are areas of an employee's life in which his employer has no legitimate interest. An intrusion into one of these areas by virtue of the employer's power of discharge might plausibly give rise to a cause of action, particularly where some recognized facet of public policy is threatened.

—Pennsylvania Supreme Court
Geary v. U.S. Steel

As the Court in **Geary** suggests, there are times when an employer's power to control its employees is in danger of stretching too far. For instance, should an employer have the right to insist that none of its employees smoke cigarettes? Consider the following statistics. The Centers for Disease Control and Prevention estimates that 44.5 million people in this country smoke cigarettes even though this habit will result in the death or disability of half of all continuing smokers. In fact, the economic burden of tobacco use is staggering with more than $75 billion per year being spent in medical care and another $92 billion per year resulting from lost productivity. As for secondhand smoke exposure, it causes heart disease and lung cancer in non-smoking adults and non-smokers who are exposed to smoke at work or at home increase their risk of heart disease by at least 25%. Research also shows that smokers have a 50 percent greater absentee rate and produce 50 percent higher medical costs. But does this mean that an employer should be able to screen out and refuse to hire smokers, or fire them if they refuse to stop? And if these practices are allowed, what is to stop employers from insisting that employees change other expensive, unhealthy personal habits? What if a worker has a high cholesterol count, or is obese? Assuming that people who get regular exercise and eat sensibly are healthy and will produce fewer medical expenses, should an employer be able to insist that its workers eat salads for lunch and use a gym three times a week?

These are some of the questions raised by the conflict between employee privacy rights and an employer's interest in controlling its operations. There is also the question of testing. Workers with AIDS will end up with horrendous medical and insurance expenses: Therefore should employers be allowed to test their workers for the AIDS virus? (This is illegal under the Americans with Disabilities Act of 1990.) These types of issues were put to the test when Weyco, Inc, a

Michigan firm specializing in employee benefit plans, informed their workers that as of January 1, 2005 anyone testing positive on nicotine testing would be fired. Not only would an employee be discharged if he or she was caught smoking at work, but the no-smoking policy also applied to employees who smoked while off of the job. While it is true that an employer may pay higher insurance costs because of the adverse consequences of smoking, should an employer be allowed to regulate what a worker does while home? According to the American Civil Liberties Union of Michigan, this practice is lawful since the state has no law barring employers from regulating employee practices outside of the office. As reported by *The Detroit News,* state and federal civil rights laws prohibit job action based upon color, age, gender, national origin and religion. Smoking, however, does not fall within one of these protected classes so an employer can enforce what it considers to be desirable traits and skills in the work place.

At the current time, a small group of states, including Florida, California, Massachusetts, Delaware and New York have enacted legislation banning smoking in the work place.

SECTION 13.6 DRUG TESTING

Illegal drug use is tremendously expensive. In 1988, the government estimated it to be a $100 billion drain on our economy, and employers can expect that drug use cost them plenty in terms of absenteeism, lower productivity, injuries and theft. Yet does this mean employers should be allowed to force their workers to undergo urinalysis testing for illegal drugs?

Drug testing in the workplace had its inception in 1986 when President Regan initiated such a program among federal employees. The President stated that the Federal government, as the largest employer in the Nation, is concerned with the well-being of its employees, the successful accomplishment of agency missions, and the need to maintain employee productivity. The Executive Order also required that federal employees refrain from the use of illegal drugs whether on or off duty and provided that the head of each Executive agency shall establish a program to test for the use of illegal drugs by employees in sensitive positions. Since this initiative, drug testing has become firmly embedded in the work place both inside and outside of the government and three types of programs have emerged: pre-employment screening, random drug testing and post-incident drug testing. The following materials highlight some of the issues with drug testing in the work place.

PAUL LUEDTKE V. NABORS ALASKA DRILLING, INC.
834 P.2D 1220 (ALASKA, 1992)

This case addresses one aspect of drug testing by employers. A private employer, Nabors Alaska Drilling, Inc. [Nabors], established a drug testing program for its employees. Paul Luedtke worked on drilling rigs on the North Slope [and] refused to submit to urinalysis screening for drug use as required by Nabors. As a result [he was] fired.

Luedtke began working for Nabors, which operates drilling rigs on Alaska's North Slope, in February 1978. [He] began as a "floorman" and was eventually promoted to "driller." A driller oversees the work of an entire drilling crew. Luedtke started work with Nabors as a union member, initially being hired from the union hall. During his tenure, however, Nabors "broke" the union. Luedtke continued to work without a union contract. He had no written contract with Nabors at the time of his discharge.

During his employment with Nabors, Luedtke was accused twice of violating the company's drug and alcohol policies. Once he was suspended for 90 days for taking alcohol to the North Slope. The other incident involved a search of the rig on which Luedtke worked. Aided by dogs trained to sniff out marijuana, the searchers found traces of marijuana on Luedtke's suitcase. Luedtke was allowed to continue working on the rig only after assuring his supervisors he did not use marijuana.

In October 1982, Luedtke scheduled a two-week vacation. Because his normal work schedule was two weeks of work on the North Slope followed by a week off, a two-week vacation amounted to 28 consecutive days away from work. Just prior to his vacation, he was instructed to arrange for a physical examination in Anchorage. He arranged for it to take place on October 19, during his vacation. It was at this examination that Nabors first tested Paul's urine for signs of drug use. The purpose of the physical, as understood by Luedtke, was to enable him to work on offshore rigs should Nabors receive such contracts. Although Luedtke was told it would be a comprehensive physical he had no idea that a urinalysis screening test for drug use would be performed. He did voluntarily give a urine sample but assumed it would be tested only for "blood sugar, any kind of kidney failure [and] problems with bleeding." Nabors' policy of testing for drug use was not announced until November 1, 1982, almost two weeks after Luedtke's examination.

[On] November 16, Luedtke received a letter informing him that his urine had tested positive for cannabinoids. The letter informed him that he would be required to pass two subsequent urinalysis tests, one on November 30 and the other on December 30, before he would be allowed to return to work. In response Luedtke hand delivered a letter drafted by his attorney to the Manager of Employee Relations for Nabors, explaining why he felt the testing and suspension were unfair. Luedtke did not take the urinalysis test on November 30 as requested by Nabors. On December 14, Nabors sent Luedtke a letter informing him that he was discharged for refusing to take the test on November 30.

The right to privacy is a recent creation of American law. The inception of this right is generally credited to a law review article published in 1890 by Louis Brandeis and his law partner, Samuel Warren. They wrote:

> Recent inventions...call attention to the next step which must be taken for the protection of the person, and for securing to the individual ...the right "to be let alone." Instantaneous photographs and newspaper enterprise have

invaded the sacred precincts of private and domestic life; and numerous mechanical devices threaten to make good the prediction that "what is whispered in the closet shall be proclaimed from the housetops."

While the legal grounds of this right were somewhat tenuous in the 1890's, American jurists found the logic of Brandeis and Warren's arguments compelling. By 1960, Professor Prosser could write that "the right of privacy, in one form or another, is declared to exist by the overwhelming majority of the American courts." He cited cases in which private parties had been held liable in tort for eavesdropping on private conversations by means of wiretapping and microphones, or for peering into the windows of homes. Eventually the right to privacy attained sufficient recognition to be incorporated in several state constitutions.

Interpreting the Constitution of the United States, the United States Supreme Court in 1965 held that a Connecticut statute banning the use of birth control devices by married couples was "repulsive to the notions of privacy surrounding the marriage relationship." **Griswold v. Connecticut, 381 U.S. 479, 486 (1965).** The Supreme Court wrote that "specific guarantees in the Bill of Rights have penumbras, formed by emanations from those guarantees that help give them life and substance. Various guarantees create zones of privacy..." Since Griswold the Supreme Court has found the federal constitutional right of privacy to apply a number of other situations. **Roe v. Wade, 410 U.S. 113 (1973)** (right of privacy broad enough to encompass a woman's decision whether or not to terminate her pregnancy); **Eisenstadt v. Baird, 405 U.S. 438 (1972)** (regulation which made contraceptives less available to unmarried than married couples invalidated). But see **Bowers v. Hardwick, 478 U.S. 186 (1986)** (due process clause of Fourteenth Amendment does not confer any fundamental right on homosexuals to engage in acts of consensual sodomy).

Thus, the concept of privacy has become pervasive in modern legal thought. But a clear definition of this right...has eluded both courts and legal scholars. It is the fundamental nature of the concept that leads to such great difficulty in application.

The next question we address is whether a public policy exists protecting an employee's right to withhold certain "private" information from his employer.

We believe such a policy does exist, and is evidenced in the common law, statutes and constitution of this state. Alaska law clearly evidences strong support for the public interest in employee privacy. First, state statutes support the policy that there are private sectors of employee's lives not subject to direct scrutiny by their employers. For example, employers may not require employees to take polygraph tests as a condition of employment. In addition, Alaska Statute 18.80.200(a) provides:

> It is determined and declared as a matter of legislative finding that discrimination against an inhabitant of the state because of race, religion, color, national origin, age, sex, marital status, changes in marital status, pregnancy, or parenthood is a matter of public concern and that this discrimination not only threatens the rights and privileges of the inhabitants of the state but also menaces the institutions of the state and threatens peace, order, health, safety and general welfare of the state and its inhabitants. [It is] unlawful for employers to inquire into such topics in connection with prospective employment. Second, as previously noted, Alaska's constitution contains a right to privacy clause. Third, there exists a common law right to privacy.

[T]here is a sphere of activity in every person's life that is closed to scrutiny by others. The boundaries of that sphere are determined by balancing a person's right to privacy against other public policies, such as "the health, safety, rights and privileges of others."

Luedtke claim[s] that whether or not [he] use[s] marijuana is information within that protected sphere into which his employer, Nabors, may not intrude. We disagree. As we have previously observed, marijuana can impair a person's ability to function normally.

We also observe that work on an oil rig can be very dangerous. We have determined numerous cases involving serious injury or death resulting from accidents on oil drilling rigs. In addition, the trial court expressly considered the dangers of work on oil rigs.

Where the public policy supporting Luedtke's privacy in off-duty activities conflicts with the public policy supporting the protection of the health and safety of other workers, and even Luedtke himself, the health and safety concerns are paramount. As a result, Nabors is justified in determining whether Luedtke is possibly impaired on the job by drug usage off the job.

We observe, however, that the employer's prerogative does have limitations. First, the drug test must be conducted at a time reasonably contemporaneous with the employee's work time. The employer's interest is in monitoring drug use that may directly affect employee performance. The employer's interest is not in the broader police function of discovering and controlling the use of illicit drugs in general society. In the context of this case, Nabors could have tested Luedtke immediately prior to [his] departure for the North Slope, or immediately upon his return from the North Slope when the test could be reasonably certain of detecting drugs consumed there. Further, given Nabors' need to control the oil rig community, Nabors could have tested him at any time he was on the North Slope.

Second, an employee must receive notice of the adoption of a drug testing program. By requiring a test, an employer introduces an additional term of employment. An employee should have notice of the additional term so that he may contest it, refuse to accept it and quit, seek to negotiate its conditions, or prepare for the test so that he will not fail it and thereby suffer sanctions.

These considerations do not apply with regard to the tests Luedtke refused to take. Luedtke was given notice of the future tests. He did not take the test on November 30. As a result, Nabors was justified in discharging him.

THE PROBLEM OF THE FALSE POSITIVE

Both employers and employees share at least one concern: whether or not urinalysis is a reliable means of uncovering drug use. Employees are concerned over the accuracy of drug testing since they may be hired or fired on the basis of results. Employers are interested because they don't want to waste time and money ferreting out innocent workers, only to spend more time and money replacing them.

There are many serious reliability problems. Certain over-the-counter drugs may register as illegal ones. Test results on people using the familiar cold remedies Contac or Sudafed have (wrongly) indicated that they were on amphetamines. The pain relievers Datril and Advil have shown up as marijuana, and cough syrups containing dextromethorphan may register as opiate traces. False positives can be produced in the oddest ways: A person with the disease lupus (in remission) might appear to be taking amphetamines. A person who had ingested poppy seeds just before urinalysis might seem to have opium in his system. Research indicates that "passive inhalation" can also cause positive results. In other words, a person could test as a marijuana user, not because of actually smoking the drug, but because of being at a concert, a party, or on a bus where it was smoked.

How often are these mistakes made? The testing laboratories assert that the most commonly used procedures are 95-99 percent accurate. At best, then, the industry itself claims an inaccuracy rate of 1 percent. But since 4 to 5 million people are tested annually, 40,000 to 50,000 people must be falsely accused each year.

Perhaps most telling are the results of a 1987 study performed by the National Institute on Drug Abuse, which found that 20 percent of the 50 laboratories tested reported the presence of drugs in urine specimens when no drugs were present. These mistakes were made even though each laboratory had been warned in advance that its competence was about to be evaluated by the federal government.[1]

TEST REVELATIONS

Urinalysis picks up traces of certain substances in the blood. Although drug testing cannot tell an employer whether an employee was "high" while at work (it measures the presence of a substance, not the time it was ingested), it can reveal that the employee had used marijuana sometime during the past few weeks. Some substances linger in the body longer than others: drug tests can reveal that the subject smoked one marijuana cigarette as many as 81 days earlier, while cocaine traces will be undetectable after 2-3 days, and evidence of alcohol will be flushed from the body within a half day.

Urine tests can also reveal extraneous information—whether a worker is pregnant, or is taking medication for a heart condition, asthma, epilepsy, diabetes, or manic depression, for example.

CONTROL OF PERSONAL INFORMATION

Privacy is not just a matter of minimizing the amount of information known about a person. It also involves control over that information. Employees worry that the confidentiality of test results is not guaranteed. Will they become part of a permanent, computerized file, accessible to any number of people? Will a worker be blacklisted because of a false positive, and never know why his or her career was stagnating?

SECTION 13.7
THE DRUG TESTING
OF TONY ROBERTS

PROBLEM THIRTEEN—B

PARK, BROWN & SMITH, P.C.
ATTORNEYS AT LAW
MEMORANDUM

TO: All Law Clerks

FROM: Peter Smith, Esquire

RE: Tony's Drug Testing Problem

In the middle of the season with the Stallions, Tony Roberts took a short vacation during the team's off week and returned to Philadelphia. He spent Saturday night with an old girlfriend. They had dinner and went dancing at the Aztec Club on the waterfront. One thing led to another, and he spent the night at her apartment. The next day, it all seemed like a dream. Tony had spent much of the previous night high on something that she had given him to smoke. But it was Sunday, and he had to return to the Stallions.

The player arrived at practice on Monday, and the coach greeted the team with a stack of small, plastic specimen cups. "I hate to surprise you guys," said the coach, "But life can be surprising." Tony realized that he and his teammates were expected to produce a urine sample while the team's trainer looked on. Tony felt embarrassed—but he also felt scared because of the consequences if he tested positive. Therefore, he refused the test and the team suspended him. Read **"Luedtke v. Nabors Alaska Drilling Company"** and the materials about drug testing and answer the following questions:

1. What are the chances that Tony will show "positive" results from the urinalysis test?

2. If Tony does test positive and is fired from the team, would he win a lawsuit for wrongful discharge?

3. What ethical issues are raised here and what do you think is fair in this situation?

ANSWER SHEET
PROBLEM THIRTEEN—B

Name   **Please Print Clearly**

1. What are the chances that Tony will show "positive" results from the urinalysis test?

_____

_____

_____

_____

_____

_____

_____

_____

_____

2. If Tony does test positive and is fired from the team, would he win a lawsuit for wrongful discharge?

_____

_____

_____

_____

_____

_____

_____

_____

_____

3. What ethical issues are raised here and what do you think is fair in this situation?

SECTION 13.8
SEXUAL HARASSMENT

In 1964 Congress passed comprehensive Civil Rights legislation including this excerpt, known as **Title VII**:

a. It shall be an unlawful employment practice for an employer:

   1. to fail or refuse to hire or to discharge any individual, or otherwise to discriminate against any individual with respect to his compensation, terms, conditions, or privileges of employment because of such individual's race, color, religion, sex, or national origin.

The statute itself outlaws discrimination in broad, general language. The job of clarifying the statute by providing detailed examples of illegal discrimination is left to an administrative agency. In the case of Title VII, that government agency is the **Equal Employment Opportunity Commission** (EEOC), created by Congress to interpret and enforce the employment provisions of the Civil Rights Law.

In 1980, the EEOC adopted the following guidelines:

a. Harassment on the basis of sex consists of unwelcome sexual advances, requests for sexual favors, and other verbal or physical conduct of a sexual nature and will constitute sexual harassment when:

   1. submission to such conduct is made either explicitly or implicitly a term or condition of an individual's employment,

   2. submission to or rejection of such conduct by an individual is used as the basis for employment decisions affecting such individual, or

   3. such conduct has the purpose or effect of unreasonably interfering with an individual's work performance or creating an intimidating, hostile, or offensive working environment.

b. In determining whether alleged conduct constitutes sexual harassment, the Commission will look at the record as a whole and at the totality of the circumstances, such as the nature of the sexual advances and the context in which the alleged incidents occurred. The determination of the legality of a particular action will be made from the facts, on a case by case basis.

c. An employer is responsible for its acts and those of its agents and supervisory employees with respect to sexual harassment regardless of whether the specific acts complained of were authorized or even forbidden by the employer and regardless of whether the employer knew or should have known of their occurrence. (In its first sexual harassment case, the Supreme Court in 1986 made it clear that in cases of "hostile environment" sexual harassment an employer would only be held responsible if he knew or should have known about the harassment.)

d. With respect to conduct between fellow employees, an employer is responsible for acts of sexual harassment in the workplace where the employer (or its agents or supervisory employees) knows or should have known of the conduct, unless it can show that it took immediate and appropriate corrective action.

e. Prevention is the best tool for the elimination of sexual harassment. An employer should take all steps necessary to prevent sexual harassment from occurring, such as affirmatively raising the subject, expressing strong disapproval, developing appropriate sanctions informing employees of their right to raise and how to raise the issue of harassment under Title VII, and developing methods to sensitize all concerned.

TYPES OF SEXUAL HARASSMENT

Courts have identified two kinds of sexual harassment. The first, called **quid pro quo** (or "tangible benefit loss") happens when an employee is expected to give into sexual demands or suffer the loss of some specific job benefit: a raise, a promotion, or even the job itself. Quid pro quo harassment would exist where a woman is fired for refusing to go on a date with her supervisor, for example.

The other kind of harassment, labelled **hostile environment**, involves less specific consequences. It could occur when a woman is constantly subjected to sexual harangues and obscenities in her workplace, or when she must repeatedly refuse unwanted sexual advances from her supervisor. Although she suffers no economic loss, she is a victim of discrimination because she must put up with a down-graded work atmosphere, pervaded with unpleasantness.

This second type of harassment has proved to be complicated: How offensive must the environment be to justify a complaint of sexual harassment? What factors should a court take into account in considering whether or not a particular workplace is so hostile to women that it discriminates against them? The next case provides contrasting views on hostile environment sexual harassment.

Vivienne Rabidue v. Osceola Refining Co.
805 F.2d 611 (6th Cir., 1986)

The plaintiff was a capable, independent, ambitious, aggressive, intractable, and opinionated individual. The plaintiff's supervisors and co-employees with whom plaintiff interacted almost uniformly found her to be an abrasive, rude, antagonistic, extremely willful, uncooperative, and irascible personality. She consistently argued with co-workers and company customers in defiance of supervisory direction and jeopardized Osceola's business relationships with major oil companies. She disregarded supervisory instruction and company policy whenever such direction conflicted with her personal reasoning and conclusions. In sum, the plaintiff was a troublesome employee.

The plaintiff's charged sexual harassment arose primarily as a result of her unfortunate acrimonious working relationship with Douglas Henry. Henry was a supervisor of the company's key punch and computer section. Occasionally, the plaintiff's duties required coordination with Henry's department and personnel, although Henry exercised no supervisory authority over the plaintiff nor the plaintiff over him. Henry was an extremely vulgar and crude individual who customarily made obscene comments about women generally, and on occasion, directed such obscenities to the plaintiff. Management was aware of Henry's vulgarity but had been unsuccessful in curbing his offensive personality traits during the time encompassed by this controversy. The plaintiff and Henry, on the occasions when their duties exposed them to each other, were constantly in a confrontational posture. The plaintiff, as well as other female employees, were annoyed by Henry's vulgarity. In addition to Henry's obscenities, other male employees from time to time displayed pictures of nude or scantily clad women in their offices and/or work areas, to which the plaintiff and other women employees were exposed.

[T]o prove a claim of abusive work environment premised upon sexual harassment, a plaintiff must demonstrate that she would not have been the object of harassment but for her sex. It is of significance to note that instances of complained sexual conduct that prove equally offensive to male and female workers would not support a Title VII sexual harassment charge because both men and women were accorded like treatment.

[S]exually hostile or intimidating environments are characterized by multiple and varied combinations and frequencies of offensive exposures which require the plaintiff to demonstrate that injury resulted not from a single or isolated offensive incident, comment, or conduct, but from incidents, comments or conduct which occurred with some frequency. To accord appropriate protection to both plaintiffs and defendants in a hostile and/or abusive work environment sexual harassment case, the trier of fact, when judging the totality of the circumstances impacting upon the asserted abusive and hostile environment must adopt the perspective of a reasonable person's reaction to a similar environment under essentially like or similar circumstances. Thus, in the absence of conduct which would interfere with that hypothetical reasonable individual's work performance and affect seriously the psychological well-being of that reasonable person under like circumstances, a plaintiff may not prevail. The plaintiff must also demonstrate that she was actually offended by the defendant's conduct and that she suffered some degree of injury as a result of the abusive and hostile work environment.

The trier of fact should also consider such objective and subjective factors as the nature of the alleged harassment, the background and experience of the plaintiff, her co-workers and supervisors, the totality of the physical environment of the workplace both before and after the plaintiff's introduction into its environs, coupled with the reasonable expectation of the plaintiff upon voluntarily entering that environment. As Judge Newblatt aptly stated in his opinion in the district court:

> Indeed, it cannot seriously be disputed that in some work environments, humor and language are rough hewn and vulgar. Sexual jokes, sexual conversation and girlie magazines may abound. Title VII was not meant to– or can– change this. It must never be forgotten that Title VII is the federal court mainstay in the struggle for equal employment opportunity for the female workers of America. But it is quite different to claim that Title VII was designed to bring about a magical transformation in the social mores of American workers.

In the case at bar, Henry's obscenities, although annoying, were not so startling as to have affected seriously the psyches of the plaintiff or other female employees. The evidence did not demonstrate that this single employee's vulgarity substantially affected the totality of the workplace. The sexually oriented poster displays had a de minimis effect on the plaintiff's work environment when considered in the context of a society that condones and publicly features and commercially exploits open displays of written and pictorial erotica at the newsstands, on prime-time television, at the cinema, and in other public places. In sum, Henry's vulgar language, coupled with the sexually oriented posters, did not result in a working environment that could be considered intimidating, hostile or offensive. It necessarily follows that the plaintiff failed to sustain her burden of proof that she was the victim of a Title VII sexual harassment violation.

KEITH, Circuit Judge, dissenting in part:

For seven years plaintiff worked at Osceola as the sole woman in a salaried management position. In common work areas plaintiff and other female employees were exposed daily to displays of nude or partially clad women belonging to a number of male employees at Osceola. One poster, which remained on the wall for eight years, showed a prone woman who had a golf ball on her breasts with a man standing over her, golf club in hand, yelling "Fore." And one desk plaque declared, "Even male chauvinist pigs need love..."

In addition, Computer Division Supervisor Doug Henry regularly spewed anti-female obscenity. Of plaintiff, Henry specifically remarked "All that bitch needs is a good lay" and called her "fat ass." Plaintiff arranged at least one meeting of female employees to discuss Henry and repeatedly filed written complaints on behalf of her herself and other female employees who feared losing their jobs if they complained directly. Osceola Vice President Charles Muetzel stated he knew that employees were "greatly disturbed" by Henry's language. However, because Osceola needed Henry's computer expertise, Muetzel did not reprimand or fire Henry. In response to subsequent complaints about Henry, a later supervisor, Charles Shoemaker, testified that he gave Henry "a little fatherly advice" about Henry's prospects if he learned to become "an executive type person."

In my view, Title VII's precise purpose is to prevent such behavior and attitudes from poisoning the work environment of classes protected under the Act. To condone the majority's notion of the "prevailing workplace" I would also have to agree that if an employer maintains an anti-Sematic workforce and tolerates a workplace in which "kike" jokes, displays of Nazi literature and anti-Jewish conversation "may abound," a Jewish employee assumes the risk of working there, and a court must consider such a work environment as "prevailing." I cannot. As I see it, job relatedness is the only additional factor which legitimately bears on the inquiry of plaintiff's reasonableness in finding her work environment offensive. In other words, the only additional question I would find relevant is whether the behavior complained of is required to perform the work.

QUESTIONS FOR DISCUSSION:

1. According to one survey, when people were asked how they would feel about having a co-worker express romantic interest in them when they didn't want to respond, two-thirds of the women said they would feel insulted, and two-thirds of the men said they would be flattered. This is one of many indicators that men and women view the same behavior in very different ways. What are the implications of this?

2. Remember the two ethical theories: Utilitarian, focusing on consequences for all concerned, and Rights-based, focusing on the competing rights of all concerned. How does each theory guide us in looking at sexual harassment?

3. What do you think should be done about sexual harassment?

SECTION 13.9
SHARON ROCK
v. JOSEPH ROBERTS

PROBLEM THIRTEEN—C

PARK, BROWN & SMITH, P.C.
ATTORNEYS AT LAW
M E M O R A N D U M

TO: All Law Clerks

FROM: Peter Smith, Esquire

RE: Sexual Harassment

Joe Roberts owned a construction company a few years ago. However, it seems like a distant memory now that Joe owns a bar, but a case from his past has come back to haunt him. Joe's construction firm was mostly made up of male employees. Over the years, the only women in the company were those who worked in the office: the receptionist, secretaries, and the bookkeeper. But Joe decided to hire a woman, Rhonda Rock, for one of his crews. She was a certified electrician. Joe also liked her looks, especially since she was shapely, even in work clothes.

Things seemed to be going well with Ms. Rock. After about a month though, Joe saw something that made him wonder. On one of the stalls in the bathroom, he noticed lewd comments about Rhonda. On a job site about a week later, he overheard some of his men laughing together about something. As he walked over to listen, he noticed Rhonda pushing through the knot of men. She seemed upset. Joe asked what was going on. "It's Mizz Sensitive," said the foreman. "What's that about?" asked Joe. "Nothing. It's about nothing, but she wants it to be something." Joe changed the subject, and began talking about the job at hand.

Several weeks later, Rhonda told Joe that she had to talk to him. He was busy, but she seemed upset. Rhonda explained that she felt she was being picked on by her co-workers. "Maybe they're jealous of me because I am a really good electrician, but I think they just hate me because I'm a woman. They think it's their kingdom or something." When Joe asked who was doing what, she was unsure. "Someone's been taking my equipment. I'll be missing a tool, or my hard-hat, things like that. And when I don't have the hat, the foreman sends me home." Joe asked her if she'd talked to the foreman. "I went to Bill right away, but he just said I was paranoid."

Joe spoke to Bill after his interview with Rhonda, and got nowhere. It seemed that she was imagining things, and she couldn't take a joke. "It's rough out here," said the foreman. "Maybe she can't take it."

The next time Joe saw Rhonda they were both in the parking area. It was early in the morning and no one else was around. Joe thought Rhonda seemed a little depressed. He said, "Ron, what about having dinner tonight?"

She looked up at him, squinted, paused and said, "Okay." But there was no chance to find out why the employee seemed depressed. Later that day, Joe's secretary told him that Rhonda had quit and gone home. Supposedly, the crane operator had dropped a stack of pallets from a height of about two stories onto the ground in front of Rhonda. She had left the site in tears, telling the foreman she would never be back.

Last week, Joe received papers for a sexual harassment lawsuit that Rhonda brought against him and his former company. She alleged that the atmosphere at work had been filled with tension from the minute she arrived, that she was belittled by sexual jokes and graffiti, constant teasing, and other harassing behavior—all of which, she alleged was due to the fact that she was a woman. She even accused Joe of sexual harassment for asking her out. The implication was that Joe would use his power over her as the boss if she refused to go out with him.

Joe was shocked, and nervous about the probable reaction to the news by his wife. Based upon the materials in this section on Sexual Harassment, and **Rabidue v. Osceola Refining Company**, answer the following questions:

1. What are the types of sexual harassment, and which one(s) might apply to whom in this situation?

2. What is the likely outcome if a judge follows the reasoning of the majority in the **Rabidue** case?

3. What is the likely outcome if a judge follows the reasoning of Judge Keith in **Rabidue**?

4. Assume Joe is not liable for merely asking Rhonda out on a date. Is he still liable for the behavior of his former employees?

ANSWER SHEET
PROBLEM THIRTEEN—C

Name _____

Please Print Clearly

1. What are the two types of sexual harassment, and which one(s) might apply to whom in this situation?

_____

_____

_____

_____

_____

_____

_____

_____

_____

_____

2. What is the likely outcome if a judge follows the reasoning of the majority in the **Rabidue** case?

_____

_____

_____

_____

_____

_____

_____

_____

_____

3. What is the likely outcome if a judge follows the reasoning of Judge Keith in **Rabidue**?

_____

_____

_____

_____

_____

_____

_____

_____

4. Assume Joe is not liable for merely asking Rhonda out on a date. Is he still liable for the behavior of his former employees?

_____

_____

_____

_____

_____

_____

_____

_____

_____

**SECTION 13.10
PROBLEM CASES**

1. Butler was shopping at a supermarket when she walked towards her car in the parking lot. Suddenly, she was assaulted and her pocketbook was stolen. An investigation showed that over a period of one year, there had been seven attacks on the Acme market premises. Five of these attacks, occurred in the parking lot during the four month period immediately preceding the assault on Butler. The supermarket had hired off-duty police officers to act as security guards during the evening hours. However, there was only one security guard on duty at the time of the attack. Does the supermarket owe a duty of care to safeguard its patrons when they are in the parking lot of their store? **Helen Butler v. Acme Markets, Inc., 426 A.2d 522 (N.J. App., 1981).**

2. The car being driven by Wagner collided with a bicycle ridden by a ten year old boy. The child's father, thinking that his son was dying, ran from the house, jumped from the porch, over the steps and onto the ground thereby fracturing his leg. The father sued the driver of the automobile on the basis that the father owed a duty to rescue his son and his injury was a natural consequence of the car driver's negligence. Wagner argued that the father rashly and unnecessarily exposed himself to danger and should be barred from recovery. Should the driver of the automobile be responsible for the father's broken leg? **Mark v. Wagner, 307 N.E. 2d 480 (Oh. App., 1977).**

3. Saltsman went to an entertainment complex in order to use the batting cage. The manager noticed a patron carrying alcoholic beverages and asked that individual to leave. In response, the patron slammed the cup of beer into the manager's face. Saltsman followed the assailant to the parking lot in order to obtain a license plate number from the assailant's vehicle. This led to a physical encounter in which Saltsman was attacked by the assailant with a golf club. Saltsman sued the entertainment complex for his injuries. An investigation showed that there had been no similar criminal activity on the premises in the past. Is the sporting complex responsible for the injuries to Saltsman? **Doug Saltsman v. Michael Corazo, 721 A.2d 1000 (N.J. Super., 1998).**

4. Estella brought a sexual harassment suit against her employer, Garage Management Corporation, for sexual harassment by a person of the same sex. The employer argued that same sex harassment does not rise to the level of a hostile work environment because the aggrieved party cannot prove that the harassment complained of was based upon her sex. Does sexual harassment of an individual by a person of the same sex, give rise to a viable cause of action? **Estella v. Garage Management Corporation, 2000 W.L. 1228968 (S.D. N.Y., 2000).**

5. A high school student was engaged in a sexual relationship with one of her teachers. She did not report that relationship to school officials. After the couple was discovered having sex, the teacher was arrested and terminated from his employment. The school district had not distributed any type of official grievance policy for lodging sexual harassment complaints as required by Federal regulations. The high school student then filed suit against the school district claiming a violation of Title IX which provides inpertinent part, "that a person cannot be subjected to discrimination under any educational program or activity which receives Federal financial assistance." An investigation into the incident revealed that no one in a supervisory power over the high school teacher knew of the affair with the student. Can the student recover damages for teacher-student sexual harassment because they failed to have a sexual harassment policy in place even though the school district officials were unaware of the teacher's misconduct? **Alida Gebser v. Lago Vista, Independent School District, 524 U.S. 274 (1998).**

SECTION 13.11
INTERNET REFERENCES

For a discussion of some of the topics contained in this chapter, see the following Internet sites:

A. **Drug Testing**

- **www.mrinc.com/**
  A drug testing company maintains this site and provides news on drug testing, and provides answers to frequently asked questions about drug testing in the workplace.

B. **Sexual Harassment**

- **www.capstn.com/quiz.html**
  This site offers a quiz about sexual harassment.

- **www.EEOC.gov/facts/fs-sex.html**
  The Equal Employment Opportunity Commission may be found at this address and Internet users may obtain information about sexual harassment, as well as the text of Title VII of the Civil Rights Act of 1964.

- **www.feminist.org/911/harass.html**
  This site lists various national hotlines for sexual harassment, including information on what to do if you or someone you know is sexually harassed.

C. Ethics

- **www.legalethics.com/ethics.law**
  This site provides ethics information in each state involving, lawyer ethics, confidentiality, and advertising.

- **www.usoge.gov/**
  The United States Office of Government Ethics Home Page is maintained at this location.

Footnote: 1. "Labs Err on Drug Test, Study Finds," *The Philadelphia Inquirer*, April 8, 1987, at A3, col. 1.

KEY TERMS

Drug Testing
EEOC
Employee at Will
Ethics
Ethical Theories
Good Faith Report
Hippocratic Oath
Hostile Work Environment
No Duty to Rescue Rule
Quid Pro Quo

Rights Theory
Sexual Harassment
Special Relationship
Title VII
Utilitarian Theory
Waste
Whistleblower
Whistleblower Protection
   Act of 1989

APPENDIX

Abandon Property – that property which has been discarded and the owner has no intention of reclaiming.

Acceptance – the unconditional promise by a party to be bound by the terms of an offer.

Activist – a judge who views his/her role as bringing about social change.

Administrative Agency – a governmental body charged with administering and implementing particular legislation; administrative agencies have legislative, executive, and judicial powers.

Adverse Possession – a means of acquiring title by possessing and using property for a required statutory period of time in a way that is adverse, actual, open, and exclusive.

Affirm – when a decision is affirmed, the appellate court determines that the lower court reached the correct decision.

Agreement of Sale – a document entered into between a buyer and seller to reflect the future transfer of an asset such as land.

Agreement on Trade Related Aspects of Intellectual Property Rights – requires all signatory nations to enforce the Paris and Berne Conventions to create minimum standards of protection for intellectual property.

Alimony – the obligation of a person to provide periodic payments of support to a spouse or former spouse.

Alter-ego Theory – piercing of the corporate veil in order to impose personal liability upon corporate officers, directors and stockholders.

Alternative Dispute Resolution – an alternative way of resolving a legal dispute without going through the court system.

Annulment – occurs when there is a legal impediment to a marriage so that the union is null and void from its inception.

Anti-cybersquatting Consumer Protection Act – Federal Legislation which protects businesses and consumers against the improper registration of a domain name.

Apparent Authority – involves those situations where the master's conduct or words would lead another to conclude that the agent is clothed with the authority to act on the master's behalf.

Appellant – person who appeals the lower court's decision.

Appellee – party against whom the appeal is filed.

Arbitration – a form of alternate disputed resolution often used in a commercial setting where both parties agree to have a third party or arbitrator resolve a controversy.

Arraignment – that process in which a defendant is charged with a crime, given the bills of indictment and a date is set for the trial.

Articles of Incorporation – the formal application for a corporate charter which articles must contain the proposed name of the business, the term, purpose, number of shares, and information about the initial corporate officials.

Association of Southeast Asian Nations – an organization of nations that stimulates economic growth, cultural development and social progress in Southeast Asia.

Assumption of the Risk – a defense to a negligence action asserting that when the plaintiff knows of the danger but voluntarily exposes himself to the harm, the plaintiff will be barred from recovery.

Attractive Nuisance – that doctrine which affords protection to young children who trespass upon the land of another whose land contains an inviting, but dangerous condition.

At-Will Employee – refers to an employment situation in which the employee is not under contract to work for a definite period of time and can be discharged at anytime.

Auction With Reserve – an auction that is merely inviting people to make an offer and no contract is formed until the gavel is struck.

Auction Without Reserve – the highest bidder will obtain the item regardless of the bid.

Bailee – the person in possession of personal property in a bailment.

Bailee's Lien – a bailee may retain possession of an item until a bailor pays the bailee's compensation.

Bailment – the delivery of personal property by the owner to another person usually for a particular purpose.

Bailor – the owner of personal property in a bailment.

Bankruptcy – those protections given to a debtor by offering a fresh start or the ability to repay the obligations over a period of time.

Bankruptcy Fraud – a scheme to defraud a creditor through the filing of a bankruptcy petition or the making of a fraudulent representation concerning a bankruptcy.

Bench Trial – a trial with no jury where the judge decides both factual and legal questions.

Berne Convention for the Protection of Literary and Artistic Works – deals with the protection of authorship.

Bilateral Contract – the exchange of mutual promises that give rise to a contract.

Bill – the form used for the introduction of proposed legislation.

Bill of Lading – a document evidencing the receipt of goods for shipment issued by an entity engaged in the business of transporting or forwarding goods.

Bribery – offering something of value to another with the intent of influencing that person's opinion or to have something done in return by that entity.

Burglary – the entering of a building or occupied structure not open to the public at the time with the intent to commit a crime.

Business Judgment Rule – requires that directors of a business use their best judgment in making decisions for the corporation.

Business Visitor – one who enters the premises for a business purpose.

Buy and Sell Agreement – provides for manner of compensation for the interests of the deceased or withdrawing owner.

Buyer in the Ordinary Course of Business – a person that buys goods in good faith, without knowledge that the sale violates the rights of another person in the goods, from a person in the business of selling goods of that kind.

Capacity – a requirement of a valid contract in which the party is of proper age or sound mind.

Caption – that part of a case that identifies the parties to the lawsuit.

Carriage of Goods by Sea Act – provides protection to ocean carriers against claims made by the owners of cargo arising from loss or damage to their goods.

Certificate of Incorporation – a document issued by a state once a corporation has been formed.

Chain Style Business Operation – a franchisee operates the business under the name of the frachisor and must follow standard methods of operations.

Chapter 11 Bankruptcy – a reorganization that allows the debtor to regain solvency by seeking an adjustment of its obligations, either by reducing the debt or by extending the time for repayment.

Chapter 13 Bankruptcy – a wage earner's plan that allows an individual with regular income to develop a plan to repay all or part of the debts over time.

Chapter 7 Bankruptcy – a straight bankruptcy that extinguishes the debts and allows the person to start over.

Chattel – all forms of personal property: animate (living), inanimate, tangible (physical) or intangible.

Child Support – that sum of money awarded to the custodial parent or caregiver for the support of a child for such things as food, shelter and medical expenses.

Circuit Court of Appeals – the intermediate appellate court in the federal court system.

Classical Theory – this ethical theory refers to the liability imposed on corporate insiders who trade on the basis of confidential information obtained by reason of their position within the business.

Clickwrap License – an agreement that is provided by the distributor or manufacturer of software which is contained in the packaging of the product and contains non-negotiable terms and conditions imposed by the seller.

Closely Held Organization – a business owned by only a few people.

Comity – the principle that allows for the recognition of the rules and laws of a foreign jurisdiction in this country.

Commerce Clause – that part of the Constitution that gives Congress the power to regulate commerce and trade between states.

Common Law Marriage – a marriage in which the parties have the capacity to marry, agree to be married, and hold themselves out to the world as being married. This concept is no longer recognized in Pennsylvania.

Communication Decency Act – legislation to protect interactive computer services from the growing number of lawsuits being filed against internet providers as a result of the improper conduct of its customers.

Comparative Negligence – a defense to a negligence action which holds that as long as the plaintiff's negligence is not greater than the defendant's, the plaintiff may recover damages, but the verdict will be reduced by the percentage of the plaintiff's negligence.

Compensatory Damages – a sum of money that will return an aggrieved party to the status quo as though nothing ever happened.

Compurgation – one of the three English pre-jury methods of trial that was necessary when a person's oath was questioned; compurgation required the accused person to bring forward 11 supporters, called compurgators, making 12 people in all who would be willing to take an oath on behalf of the accused.

Concurrent Ownership – a term used when ownership to property is shared and title is held by two or more people (see also "joint ownership").

Concurring Opinion – an opinion written by a judge who agrees with the outcome of the case but wants to note a difference in logic for reaching the decision.

Conditional Fee – a form of ownership which conveys all the rights of ownership so long as the owner complies with a certain condition (see also "fee simple defeasible" or "qualified fee").

Condominium – a multi-unit structure where a resident owns the unit together with an interest in the common areas.

Conflicts of Law – rules to determine whose laws should apply to a transaction when there are multiple jurisdictions involved.

Consolidate Budget Reconciliation Act – requires employers with twenty (20) or more employees to permit departing employees the right to retain group health coverage at their own expense for up to eighteen (18) months as long as they are not terminated for gross misconduct.

Conspiracy – an agreement between two or more people to commit an unlawful act or to do a lawful act in an unlawful manner.

Constitutional Relativity – the concept that the constitution was intentionally written in broad and vague terms to ensure that the constitution could adapt to changing times.

Consumer – refers to an individual who enters into a transaction primarily for personal, family, or household purposes.

Contract Implied-in-Law – a contract that arises by implication to prevent unjust enrichment.

Contract – the exchange of promises voluntarily made by those whose agreement is enforceable in court; the five essential elements of a contract are: offer, acceptance, consideration, capacity, and legality.

Contributory Negligence – the failure of the plaintiff to act as a reasonable person under the circumstance. This is a complete bar to recovery.

Convention – an agreement negotiated by members of an international organization in which the resulting document is open to adoption by member states and other nations.

Convention on the International Sale of Goods – provides that many international contracts dealing with the sale of goods will be enforceable even if not reduced to a writing because the Statute of Frauds is not widely followed outside of the United States.

Conveyancing – the processing and transferring of title between the owner of real estate and the buyer.

Copyright – the granting of property rights, including the exclusive ability to reproduce and distribute copyrighted materials, to display the work publicly or to create a derivative product, such as the development of a screen play from a novel.

Copyright Infringement – the unauthorized distribution of a copyrighted work.

Corporation – an artificial entity created under the authority of a state's law whose ownership is not necessarily tied with the management of the corporate organization.

Counter-Offer – a change in the terms of the offer by the offeree.

Court of Common Pleas – the trial court in the state court system.

Crime – a violation of those duties which an individual owes to the community and for breach of which the law requires that the offender make satisfaction to the public; an offense against society or the state that violates a penal law and carries a possible punishment of imprisonment.

Criminal Complaint – a statement of facts about a crime which later becomes the basis for formal charges against the accused.

Criminal Trespass – the unlawful entry into real estate without permission or the legal right to be there.

Damages – money awarded to an injured person as the result of the wrongful or improper conduct of another or by a breach of contract.

Defamation – a statement that is false and tends to harm the reputation of another or to lower her in the estimation of the community.

Defendant – the party who is being sued.

Defined Benefit – refers to a pension sponsored by a company that provides specified monthly payments upon retirement.

Defined Contribution Plan – refers to a plan in which the employer will match a contribution made by an employee and that sum will be placed into the employee's investment plan.

Derivative Suit – litigation brought by a minority shareholder on behalf of the corporation to contest the illegal or improper acts of the majority.

Descriptive Mark – a mark that cannot identify the source of goods. Rather, it describes some feature or characteristic of the product.

Destination Contract – the seller is required to deliver the goods to a specific destination and the risk of loss does not pass until the items have been properly delivered to that destination.

Directors – individuals who set the objectives or goals of the corporation, and appoint the officers.

Dissenting Opinion – a judge writes a dissent when he or she disagrees with the result reached by the majority; the dissent has no value as precedent.

Dissolution – a change in the ownership of an organization that changes the legal existence of that organization.

Distributorship – a manufacturing concern that licenses a dealer to sell its products such as an automobile dealership.

Divorce – the legal dissolution of a marriage.

Documents of Title – documents used to prove ownership, e.g. a title to a car, a deed to a house, or a bill of sale for merchandise.

Domestic Partnership – a relationship in which an unwed couple, including those of the same sex, can acquire legal rights and protections by contract to the other's assets.

Double Jeopardy – the protection afforded by the Fifth Amendment which provides that no person shall be tried twice for the same crime.

Drug Free Work Place Act – applies to employers who have contracts of a $100,000.00 or more with the federal government or receive aid from the federal government. These employers are required to develop an anti-drug policy for their employees.

Duty of Care – establishes the type of behavior a person must exhibit in a given situation; the basic rule is that a person must conform to the standard of care of a "reasonable person under the circumstances."

Easement – the granting of the right by the owner to use a part of the land by another entity.

e-Contract – a voluntary exchange of promises between two or more people that constitutes a legal obligation which contract is created through an internet transmission.

e-Defamation – a defamatory message transmitted through the internet.

Eighth Amendment – the Constitutional protection that prohibits cruel and unusual punishment.

Electronic Communications Privacy Act – provides the primary statutory protection against the interception of electronic communications, including e-mail transmissions.

Electronic Fencing – the use of the Internet to sell property gained through unlawful means.

Electronic Signatures in Global and National Commerce Act – legislation that will make online transactions the equivalent of a signed paper contract.

Embezzlement – occurs when someone takes ownership to property that has been entrusted to him/her with a fraudulent intent to deprive the owner of that property.

Eminent Domain – the power of the government to take private property for public use.

Employee Hazard Communication Standard – the rules adopted by the Occupational Safety and Health Act (OSHA) to protect employees from the dangers associated with chemicals and other toxins in the work place.

Employee Retirement Income Security Act (ERISA) – is a federal law in which the government regulates pension funds to help insure the long term financial security of those funds by reducing fraud and mismanagement.

Encumbrance – any right or interest that someone has in another's property.

Entrustment – the giving of possession of goods to a merchant who deals in goods of that kind.

Equal Employment Opportunity Commission (EEOC) – an agency of the United States Government that enforces the federal employment discrimination laws which state that discrimination is prohibited on the basis of age, race, sex or creed.

Equity – the power of the court to fashion an equitable remedy when a remedy at law is not available.

Escheat – the doctrine under which property will revert to the state if there are no legal heirs.

Estate – refers to a person's interest or rights to land.

Estate at Sufferance – the lowest interest in land and refers to a person who retains possession of the land with no title.

European Community – an organization comprised of European countries whose purpose is to achieve economic unity and whose objectives include the free movement of goods, services, labor, transportation and capital among member states.

European Contract Law – created by the European Union, this law provides for a uniform law on contracts.

European Court of Justice – is the supreme judicial authority of the European Union and retains jurisdiction over European Union legal matters that cover not just the relationship among member states but also regulates non-member business enterprises that operate within the European Union.

European Union – a membership of countries in Europe to foster economic growth.

Express Authority – occurs when an agent has received written or spoken words that signify the principal has delegated authority to the agent and the agent has accepted the grant of power to act of behalf of the master.

Express Contract – the parties spell out the specifics of the agreement in direct terms.

Expropriation – the taking of property by a foreign government without adequate compensation.

Fair Labor Standards Act – refers to legislation that establishes a minimum wage, a ceiling on the number of hours an employee can work weekly, child labor protection and equal pay for equal work regardless of gender.

Fair Use – an exception to the Copyright Act which permits the utilization of copyrighted work for the restricted purpose of criticism, comment, news reporting, teaching, scholarship or research.

Family Court – the court that decides juvenile cases and matters involving the family unit.

Family Law – those rights, duties and obligations involving marriage, the family, a civil union, domestic partnership, divorce and other family related issues.

Family Limited Liability Partnership – is a business entity in which the partners are related to each other and it is used as an estate planning tool.

Fanciful Mark – consists of made up words which serve as a product's brand name.

Family Medical Leave Act – requires an employer to provide up to twelve (12) weeks of unpaid leave in any twelve (12) month period for family needs, such as the birth or adoption of a child, caring for a child or parent, or for the employee's own serious illness.

Federal Register – is the official publication of the United States Government and provides access to Presidential Orders and federal laws.

Federal Trademark Dilution Act – legislation to protect the owner of a famous mark from dilution regardless of the likelihood of confusion between the products.

Fee Simple Absolute – the most complete form of ownership in real property and includes the right to possess, use and exclude others in the property.

Fee Simple Absolute Estate – the most complete form of ownership of real property which includes the right to possess, use, exclude others, encumber and alienate the property.

Fee Simple Defeasible Estate – a form of ownership which conveys all the rights of ownership so long as the owner complies with a certain condition (see also "conditional fee" or "qualified fee").

Foreign Corruption Practices Act – this law makes it illegal for United States companies and their agents to bribe foreign officials.

Foreign Sovereign Immunities Act – the law that deals with the immunity of foreign governments in the United States. Those entities, however, are not immune when conducting commercial activities.

Foreign Trade Anti-Trust Improvements Act – makes it illegal when anti-competitive conduct outside of the United States has a direct, substantial, reasonable and foreseeable impact on commerce within the United States.

Forum non-conveniens – means that the place of the trial is inconvenient for the parties or the witnesses involved in the trial.

Fourth Amendment – the Constitutional provision that prohibits an unlawful search and seizure by the police.

Franchise – is an agreement in which the owner of a trademark, trade name or copyright allows another to offer its products for sale or use in a geographic area.

Franchisee – the owner of the store offering the item to the public.

Franchisor – refers to the owner of the business idea.

General Agreement on Tariffs and Trade – an international treaty that requires member countries to abide by certain rules of trade, prohibits discrimination in national regulations covering imports and prevents the establishment of import quotas. Its abbreviation is GATT.

Generic Mark – merely describes a type of product regardless of its source.

Gift – a transfer of title to property without payment or compensation.

Gift Causa Mortis – the transfer of personal property made in contemplation of one's approaching death.

Globalization – the process of global businesses supported by governments to deregulate and liberalize world markets and redefine the legal rules that govern commercial relationships.

Good – personal property that is both tangible and movable.

Good Samaritan Statute – a law which provides immunity to certain classes of health care providers in the event that he/she renders emergency help to a person in danger.

Grand Jury Indictment – that process in which 23 people determine whether probable cause exists to warrant a person standing trial for a crime.

Hague Rules – limits the liability of carriers when loss or damage occurs. Liability is based upon the cause and amount of the loss.

Harter Act – sets forth the liability of ocean carriers for cargo loss.

Health Insurance Portability and Accountability Act (HIPAA) – legislation that forbids discrimination based on health or medical conditions. It also protects the records of a patient from disclosure.

Hostile Environment – a type of sexual harassment that does not involve specific consequences like economic loss, but under which a victim suffers a down-graded work atmosphere, pervaded with unpleasantness.

Housing Code – the rules established by a township, city or state to establish minimum standards for an apartment.

Housing Cooperative – a form of entity that owns the real estate but allows a person to use the premises.

Identity Theft – the use of a victim's personal information to obtain a financial advantage, such as the misappropriation of a credit card or money from a bank account.

Identity Theft and Assumption Deterrence Act – a Federal law that makes it a crime to misuse the identifying information of another.

Illusory Promise – the act or performance of a contract that is left solely to the discretion of one party.

Implied Warranty of Habitability – the right of a residential tenant to insist that the premises are fit for human habitation.

Imputed Negligence – the concept that because of a special relationship that exists between the parties, one person can be held liable for the negligence of the other; also called vicarious liability.

Incorporators – individuals who apply for a charter to start a corporation.

Independent Contractor – one who undertakes to perform the act requested on his own and is not subject to the control of an employer.

Infliction of Emotional Distress – this tort arises when a person uses extreme or outrageous conduct causing severe emotional distress to another.

Injunction – an equitable order issued by a court that directs a person to do something (mandatory injunction) or not to do something (prohibitory injunction).

Insider Trading – occurs when corporate insiders, such as officers, directors and employees, buy or sell stock in their own company based upon information that has not yet been released to the public.

Intangible Property – property that is not a physical object, e.g. a patent or trademark.

Intentional Tort – when a wrongdoer purposely sets out to harm another.

Inter Vivos – a gift made while the donor is alive.

Interference with a Contract – occurs when a party wrongfully interferes with an existing contract or a future business opportunity.

International Chamber of Commerce – sets forth trade term definitions that have been generally accepted in the global business market place.

International Court of Justice – the judicial branch of the United Nations which consists of fifteen judges representing all of the world's major legal systems.

International Emergency Economics Powers Act – a law that grants authority to the President to place restrictions on trade and international financial transactions.

International Monetary Fund – encourages international trade by maintaining stable foreign exchange rates and works closely with commercial banks to promote orderly exchange policies with members.

Internet Corporation for Assigned Names and Numbers – a non-profit corporation recognized by the United States Government as the business which coordinates the management of the internet domain name system and IP address numbers.

Intoxication – this act is not a defense to a crime unless it negates a specific mental state.

Invasion of Privacy – the intentional tort consisting of an unwarranted intrusion upon a person's right to be left alone.

Joint Ownership – a term used when ownership to property is shared and title is held by two or more people (see also "concurrent ownership").

Joint Tenancy with the Right of Survivorship – a form of concurrent or joint ownership in which the co-owners have essentially equal rights to the property; if one co-owner dies, her share will pass to the surviving co-owner.

Judge – the person who presides over the trial and decides questions of law.

Judicial Remedies – refers to the remedies that the court can fashion to compensate an aggrieved party who has been injured by the conduct of another or to grant equitable remedies such as an injunction or declaratory judgment.

Judicial Restraint Oriented – a judge who believes his/her role is merely to make sure a rule is constitutional. The term generally refers to a judge that is conservative.

Jurisdiction – refers to the power of a court to determine the merits of a dispute and to grant an aggrieved party relief.

Jurisdiction Over the Person – the power of the court to hear a dispute involving the parties of a case.

Lanham Act – federal legislation that regulates trademark law.

Larceny – the taking and carrying away of property of another without consent and with the intention of depriving the other of the goods permanently.

Lease – an encumbrance upon property where a landlord holds property as a fee simple absolute but has given a tenant the rights to possess and use the property exclusively.

Legal Capacity – the capacity of the organization to sue and be sued in its own name.

Legality – the requirement of a valid contract in which the purpose and subject matter of the agreement must be legal.

Lessee – a tenant who is given the rights to possess and use the property exclusively by a landlord who holds property as a fee simple absolute.

Lessor – a landlord who holds property as a fee simple absolute but has given a tenant the rights to possess and use the property exclusively.

Lex Mercatoria – refers to the international norms that are created by commercial entities.

Libel – the publication of defamatory matter by written or printed words.

Licensee – a person who comes on the property of another with the owner's consent or with a legal right to be on the land. It generally refers to a social guest.

Life Estate – an ownership interest which is limited to the life of the person holding it.

Limited Liability Company (LLC) – a business entity that offers limited liability to its owners who are also known as members. It is less formal then a corporation in that the business does not have to maintain minutes and hold formal meetings of its owners.

Limited Liability Partnership (LLP) – this is a hybrid between a partnership and corporation in which the limited liability partners manage the business on a routine basis.

Limited Partnership – a hybrid between a general partnership and a corporation which has the attributes of a partnership except that the limited partners are not permitted to be involved in the control or operation of the business.

Liquidated Damages – a sum of money agreed upon by contracting parties in advance that will be paid in the event of a default or breach of contract.

Long Arm Statute – provides the court with jurisdiction over non-resident defendants who commit a tort within a state, own property within a state or do business within a state.

Lost Property – this is property in which the owner has involuntarily and accidently parted with the asset and does not know where to find it.

Majority Opinion – a decision reached by more than half of the judges of an appellate court panel; a decision rendered by the majority of the court which is the law.

Making a False Statement to a Bank – this crime occurs when someone knowingly makes a false statement of a material fact or overvalues property for the purposes of inducing a bank to take action.

Manufacturing Plant Franchise – the frachisor provides the franchisee with the essential ingredients or formula to make a particular product such as between Coca-Cola and a Coca-Cola Bottling plant.

Marriage – in most states, this is a contract between a man and a woman to marry for life.

Mediation – a form of alternate dispute resolution used primarily in disputes between labor and management; mediation is advisory in nature.

Mens Rea – the necessary state of mind that a perpetrator must have to be found guilty of committing a particular crime; criminal intent.

Merchant – a person that deals in goods of a particular kind or otherwise holds itself out by occupation as having knowledge or skills peculiar to the practices or goods involved in the transaction.

Minimum Contact – the court can hear a case when a defendant has taken actions that are purposely directed towards the forum state.

Mini-trial – a form or alternate dispute resolution where the parties submit their case to a panel of experts or neutral advisor who suggest the likely outcome if the case were to go to court.

Miranda Warnings – those rights guaranteed by the Fifth Amendment. These warnings are designed to notify the person that he/she does not have to speak to the police.

Misappropriation Theory – imposes liability on outsiders who trade on the basis of confidential information obtained by reason of their relationship with a person possessing insider information.

Mislaid Property – that property which has been voluntarily and intentionally placed somewhere by the owner but forgotten.

Mistake – allows a contract to be rescinded if the enforcement of the agreement would be unconscionable or if the other party had reason to know of the mistake or he/she caused the mistake.

Money Laundering – a crime involving the concealment of the real source of illegally obtained money by having a third party claim ownership to the currency.

Montreal Convention – expanded the liability of airlines to one hundred and fifty thousand dollars a person without the need to show fault and by giving more protection to air travelers for such things as lost baggage.

Moral Obligation – this type of promise does not constitute a valid contract since it lacks the necessary elements to form an enforceable agreement.

Mortgage – a lien that a bank or lender may record against real property to secure that person's interest in the asset until the loan has been repaid.

Municipal Court – the lowest court in the state court system, which handles such matters as small claims cases, landlord/tenant problems and minor criminal offenses.

Negligence – the failure to do what a reasonable person would do under the circumstances; the three elements of negligence are 1) a duty, 2) breach of duty, 3) the negligence must be the proximate cause of the harm, and 4) the person sustains damages.

Negligence in Hiring an Employee – refers to the potential liability of an employer for the actions of an employee. Typically, the employer is liable on negligence grounds for the hiring and retaining of an employee whom the employer knew or should have known to be dangerous, incompetent, dishonest or the like.

Neighborhood Justice Centers – programs where local cases, usually neighborhood or family disputes, are decided by a panel of local residents.

No Duty to Rescue Rule – the rule under which the law does not force a person to help a stranger in an emergency unless that person has somehow caused the problem or has a special relationship to the party.

Nominal Damages – provide a remedy where a technical wrong has been committed but no actual harm has resulted.

Non-binding Trial – see "mini-trial."

Non-Conforming Use – the use of property that is inconsistent with the current zoning code but which allows the user to maintain the current use.

North American Free Trade Zone (NAFTA) – provides for the reduction and elimination of almost all trade tariffs and goods moving among United States, Canada and Mexico.

Occupational Safety and Health Act (OSHA) – imposes a general duty on most employers to provide a work place free of recognized hazards, causing or likely to cause, death or serious harm to employees.

Offer – a proposal by one party to the other showing a willingness to enter into a valid contract.

Officers – individuals who manage the daily operations of the corporation.

Original Jurisdiction – refers to the trial court

Orphans Court – the court that hears matters involving estates such as will contests.

Ownership – those rights that a person has with respect to property that he/she may exercise to prevent others from using that property.

Pain and Suffering – an amount of money to compensate an individual for the anguish and discomfort he/she has endured because of the carelessness of another.

Palimony – is the support and provisions given to assets of non-married parties assets based upon a contract entered into by the parties before separation to share their assets.

Paris Cooperation Treaty – creates uniform procedures that allow patent applications to be filed initially as an international application which is then to be followed by individual country applications.

Partnership – an agreement between two or more people to share a common interest in a commercial enterprise and to share profits and losses.

Past Consideration – an agreement to base future performance on a prior obligation.

Patents Convention for the Protection of Industrial Property – provides basic rights of protection in trademarks.

Patriot Act – grants authority to the United States government to freeze foreign assets held in the United States.

Pension Benefit Guarantee Corporation – this law insures that defined benefit plans will protect retirees in the event that their employer's pension fund fails.

Permanent Injunction – a final resolution of a dispute issued after a full hearing of all relevant factors.

Personal Property – consists of all property that is not land or attached to land; the two kinds of personal property are tangible and intangible; includes such things as a car, book, clothes, and furniture as well as bank accounts, stocks, bonds, patents and copyrights.

Piercing the Corporate Veil – when the corporation is being misused so that the shareholders are treated like partners and have unlimited liability for the organization's debts.

Plaintiff – the party who initiates the case.

Possession – a means of acquiring personal property.

Postal Reorganization Act – a federal law that makes it an unfair trade practice to send unsolicited products to a consumer in the mail.

Precedent – the process whereby judges apply the decision and rules or prior cases to the present case over which they are presiding; see also "stare decisis."

Preliminary Arraignment – a court proceeding that occurs within hours of a person's arrest at which time the person is informed of the charges, bail is set and the date for the preliminary hearing is scheduled.

Preliminary Hearing – the first hearing at which a victim or witness is called to testify in order to establish that there is a basic case to hold the defendant for trial.

Preliminary Injunction – an order granted as an emergency measure before a full hearing on the merits can be held.

Pre-Nuptial Agreement – a contract entered into before a marriage or civil union that spells out the financial consequences in the event the union fails.

Principles of International Commercial Contract – those principles that do not carry the weight of law but may be referenced by a foreign court or arbitration panel to interpret ambiguous contract provisions when the contract rules do not provide adequate guidance.

Private International Law – exams relationships created by commercial transactions and utilizes treaties, agreements, and the individual laws of nations to resolve business disputes.

Private Judging – a form of alternate dispute resolution used when parties are constrained by time and can afford to hire a private judge; private judging proceeds as a normal trial would be conducted.

Private Law – involves matters between individuals; most common forms are contract, tort, marriage, and property law.

Private Securities Litigation Reform Act of 1995 – provides a safe harbor or lack of accountability by a company who issues statements that are considered financial forecasts of the business.

Procedural Law – the way that substantive law is made, enforced, and administered.

Production – refers to the process of when a person takes scraps of material and creates another item through his/her labor.

Products Liability – the concept of holding sellers of defective products liable for harm caused to the user, consumer, or his property even though the seller has exercised all possible care in the preparation and sale of the product; also called strict liability. The law is contained in Section 402A of the Restatement (Second) of Torts.

Property – everything that may be owned, either as real property or personal property.

Property Law – deals with the rights and duties that arise out of the ownership or possession of real or personal property; defines and enforces the rights and responsibilities that accompany ownership.

Protocol – an agreement on a matter considered to be of a less significant impact than the subject of a convention.

Proximate Cause – requires that there be a reasonable connection between the negligence of the defendant and the harm suffered by the plaintiff.

Proxy – an agent appointed by a shareholder for the purposes of voting the shares.

Public International Law – exams the relationships between nations and uses rules that are binding on all countries in the international community.

Public Law – involves the rights of society as a whole, and those interests are usually handle by a government agency; most common forms are criminal, constitutional, and administrative law.

Publicly Held Organization – a business owned by many people and includes those whose stock is traded on a public exchange.

Punitive Damages – a sum of money awarded to punish the tort-feasor for his or her misconduct so that the type of incident in question will never occur again.

Purchase – the transfer of title from one owner to another for payment or compensation.

Qualified Fee – a form of ownership which conveys all the rights of ownership so long as the owner complies with a certain condition (see also "fee simple defeasible" or "conditional fee").

Quid Pro Quo – a type of sexual harassment where an employee is expected to give in to sexual demands or suffer the loss of some specific job or benefit.

Quiet Title Action – with respect to real property, a suit in which the court is asked to determine who among several contenders has ownership rights to a given piece of property.

Real Property – land and everything attached to the land.

Receiving Stolen Property – intentionally obtaining property of another that has been stolen, or believed to be stolen.

Reformation – a remedy that allows modification of a contract that does not reflect the true intention of the parties.

Registration Statement – this is a document filed with the SEC by a corporation to let the governmental agency know that the business is going to sell its stock to the public.

Remainder – a future interest in real property.

Remand – the appellate court remands—or sends back—a case to the trial court when the appellate court finds that the trial judge committed an error in deciding the case or additional evidence must be obtained.

Res Judicata – "the thing has been decided."

Rescission – the voiding of a contract for some reason such as misrepresentation, fraud, duress, undue influence or impossibility, under which each party must return the property they received from the other.

Respondeat Superior – refers to the agent or employee of a company who has the authority to bind the business when he/she acts within the scope of the authority.

Restitution – a remedy to prevent one party from unfairly benefiting at the expense of another.

Retail Theft – a crime involving the theft of property that occurs at a commercial establishment open to the public.

Reverse – the appellate court reverses a decision when it finds that the lower court's decision was incorrect.

Reversionary Interest – when property reverts back to the original owner or the owner's legal heirs if that person is no longer living.

Rights Theory – the ethical theory that focuses on the reasons for actions.

Risk of Law – determines which party bears the responsibility if the goods are lost or damaged.

Robbery – larceny plus the additional requirement that the taking be accomplished by force or threat of force.

Sale – is the passing of title from the seller to the buyer for a price.

Sarbanes-Oxley Act – this federal law only applies to publicly traded companies and seeks to increase corporate accountability, enhance financial disclosures and combat corporate and accounting fraud.

Sealed Bid – used in construction, municipal and service contracts in which a party requests bids that only constitute an invitation to negotiate.

Search Warrant – a court order allowing the police to search a person or premise.

Securities and Exchange Commission (SEC) – an agency created following the stock market crash of 1929 to enforce the provisions of the Securities Exchange Act. Its primary mission is to protect investors, maintain fair and efficient markets and to facilitate capital formation.

Security – refers to an investment such as a note, stock, bond and evidence of indebtedness, certificate of interest or participation in any profit sharing agreement.

Security Council – consists of fifteen countries, has the power to authorize military action and to sever diplomatic relations with other nations.

Security Exchange Act of 1933 – allows the SEC to regulate the trading of securities, investigate securities fraud, regulate securities dealers, supervise mutual funds and recommend administrative sanctions for violation of the security laws.

Security Exchange Act of 1934 – regulates the subsequent sale of securities and requires the registration of security exchanges, brokers and dealers of markets in which securities are traded.

Seller – a person that sells or contracts to sell goods.

Shipment Contract – occurs when the seller is required to ship the goods and the risk of loss passes to the buyer when conforming goods are delivered to the carrier.

Short Swing Profits – refers to a rule in which company insiders, who buy and sell their firm security within a six (6) month period, must return any profits made from those transactions to the business.

Slander – a defamatory statement that is verbal or oral in nature.

Social Host Liability – liability imposed upon a person who furnishes alcohol beverages to a guest. The term does not include bars and other establishments who serve liquor on a commercial basis.

Sole Ownership – when only one person enjoys the bundle of rights and liabilities of a property.

Sole Proprietorship – a business owned by only one person.

Sovereign Immunity – the concept that prohibits suits against any level of the government unless the sovereign gives its expressed consent to the litigation.

Special Damages – those losses in a breach of contract that are foreseeable, reasonably certain and unavoidable.

Specific Performance – an equitable remedy for breach of contract that is used when money damages are inadequate to make the aggrieved party whole.

Standing – the concept that a plaintiff in a lawsuit must have a direct and substantial interest in the outcome of the case that he or she intends to bring.

Stare Decisis – the process whereby judges apply the decision and rules of prior cases to the present case over which they are presiding; (see also "precedent").

Statute of Frauds – the requirement that certain agreements be in writing in order to be enforceable by the court.

Statute of Limitations – the time period within which an aggrieved party must institute suit or the claim will be forever barred.

Strict Liability – see "products liability."

Subchapter S Corporation – has all the characteristics of a corporation except that its shareholders must report profit and losses on their individual tax returns.

Subject Matter Jurisdiction – the type of case a court can hear.

Substantive Due Process – the requirement that the law be fundamentally fair; legislation must be capable of serving a legitimate public interest, and the law cannot be vague.

Substantive Evidence – the standard used in administrative hearings. The term merely requires that a finding by a referee be supported by relevant evidence that a reasonable mind would accept as adequate to support a conclusion.

Substantive Law – this is the "actual law" which defines the duties and rights of members of society.

Suggestive Mark – requires imagination in order to figure out the nature of the product which the mark represents.

Supreme Court – the highest court in the state or country.

Tangible Property – a physical object.

Temporary Restraining Order (TRO) – an injunction granted without notice to the other side.

Tenancy by the Entirety – a special form of co-ownership for married couples which carries the right of survivorship; however, neither spouse can convey his or her interest in the property since each spouse owns a 100 percent interest in the property.

Tenancy in Common – a form of concurrent or joint ownership in which the co-owners have essentially equal rights to the property; if one co-owner dies, his share will pass to his heirs.

Testamentary Gift – property given by will.

Tipper/Tippee Theory – this deals with someone who acquires insider information as a result of a corporate insider's breach of that person's fiduciary duty to the corporation.

Tipping – the supplying of insider information to another who does the trading of the stock of a company from which the confidential information has been learned.

Title – the right of ownership.

Tort – a private civil wrong against an individual or business for which the court will award money damages; torts are classified into the categories of negligence or intentional torts.

Tort Damages – a sum of money that should place the injured party in as substantially a good position as she had occupied before the injury.

Trademark – is a word, name, symbol or slogan which identifies the origins of a product or services from those of a competitor.

Trademark Infringement – occurs when there is a likelihood of confusion as to the source, origin, or sponsorship of a product in a commercial environment.

Trading with the Enemy Act – this law was passed by Congress to restrict trade with nations at war with the United States.

Treasure Trove – property that has been hidden or concealed for so long as to indicate that the owner is probably dead or unknown.

Treaty – an agreement between two or more countries.

Trespasser – one who comes upon the premises of another without consent and with no legal right to be on the property.

Trial by Ordeal – an old fashioned method of determining justice where the accused was subject to some sort of physical test, the results of which were supposed to indicate guilt or innocence; e.g. trial by hot water, trial by cold water, trial by fire.

TRO – (temporary restraining order) an injunction granted without notice to the defendant.

U.S. – Canada Free Trade Agreement – a pact to phase out all tariffs and quotas between the two countries and guarantees equal treatment for those that invest across the border.

Unenforceable Contract – the agreement has the technical requirements of a contract but won't be enforced by the court.

Uniform Commercial Code – a uniform act that regulates the sale of goods and certain other commercial transactions.

Unilateral Contract – a promise for an act that gives rise to a contract.

United Nations – its primary goal is to "save succeeding generations from the scourge of war" and authorizes "collective measures for the prevention and removal of threats to peace, and for the suppression of acts of aggression or other breaches of the peace."

United Nations Commission on International Trade Law – develops standardized commercial practices and agreements.

United States Constitution – the legal document which establishes the fundamental rights of United States citizens and protects them from unlawful governmental interference.

United States District Court – is the trial court in the federal court system.

Utilitarian Theory – the theory of ethics that focuses on the consequences of actions.

Valid Contract – a contract that satisfies all of the requirements of a binding agreement.

Variance – permits a use of property that is not designated in the zoning code for the property.

Venue – the place where a case should be heard.

Vicarious Liability – see "imputed negligence."

Void Contract – refers to an agreement that lacks one or more of the essential elements of a valid contract.

Voir Dire – process for selecting a jury by which members of the jury are questioned by the judge or attorneys to ascertain whether they are suitable to serve at trial; issue of prejudice, conflicts of interest, and philosophies of life are explored.

Wager of Law – one of the three Ancient English methods of trial that simply required the accused person to take an oath, swearing to a fact.

Warranty of Habitability – the obligations imposed upon the landlord to maintain a leased premise in a condition fit for human habitation.

Warsaw Convention – limits compensatory damages in a personal injury action against an airline in international travel.

Whistleblower – a person who feels compelled to get certain information into the hands of people who can act to correct a problem when it seems that the problem cannot be corrected otherwise.

White Collar Crime – those illegal acts perpetrated in a business setting.

Winding Up – that process in which partners move to terminate a partnership by collecting the business assets, paying the debts and providing the partners with the remaining value of the business.

Worker Adjustment and Retraining Notification Act – requires firms with one hundred (100) or more employees to provide sixty (60) days notice if they lay off one-third or more of their workers at any location employing at least one hundred and fifty workers, drop five hundred employees at any location, or close a plant employing at least fifty workers.

Worker's Compensation – refers to the liability of an employer for the injuries sustained by an employee during the course of the employment.

World Bank – promotes economic development in poor countries by making loans to finance necessary development projects and programs.

World Intellectual Property Organization – the leading dispute resolution service for disagreements arising out of the registration or use of internet domain names.

World Trade Organization (WTO) – was designed to reduce trade barriers and cover the international sale of goods among its members.

Writ of Certiorari – an appeal to the United States Supreme Court.

Zoning – rules created by local governments to regulate the development and use of property.

STUDENT NOTES